Karl Mannheim.

The development of his thought

Karl Mannheim.

Karl Mannheim.

The Development of his Thought:

Philosophy, Sociology and Social Ethics,
With a Detailed Biography

Henk E.S. Woldring

St. Martin's Press
New York

© 1986, Van Gorcum, P.O. Box 43, 9400 AA Assen, The Netherlands

All rights reserved. For information, write:
Scholarly & Reference Division,
St. Martin's Press, Inc., 175 Fifth Avenue, New York, NY 10010

First published in the United States of America in 1987

Printed in The Netherlands by Van Gorcum, Assen

ISBN 0-312-00555-5

Library of Congress Cataloging-in-Publication Data

Woldring, H.E.S.
  Karl Mannheim: the development of his thought.

  Translated from the Dutch by Stanley M. Wiersma.
  Bibliography: p.
  Includes index.
  1. Mannheim, Karl, 1893-1947. 2. Sociologists-Germany-Biography. 3. Sociology-Germany-History. 4. Social ethics. I. Title.
HM22.G3M36 1987   301.092'4   87-4738
ISBN 0-312-00555-5

The publication of this book was made possible through a grant from the Netherlands Organization
for the Advancement of Pure Research (Z.W.O.)

For my wife
Ans C. van der Weele Woldring

Table of Contents

Foreword

Not yet a century ago, on 27 March 1893, Karl Mannheim was born. He died prematurely, at the age of 53. The important publications to his credit already at that age insure him a definite place in the history of philosophy and sociology. Even now he continues to be read, quoted, and regarded as a pathfinder in the study of several problem areas in sociology. In the words of Tacitus (*Agricola*, fragment 44), we can say of Mannheim:

> Although wrenched away in the midst of his life,
> he lived a very long time measured in fame.

The study of Mannheim's work has given me great satisfaction. This satisfaction arises not only from a scientific concern for his work, but also from being gripped by the social and political relevance and specificity of that work. Mannheim particularly continues to fascinate me because he demonstrates the passion of the true sociologist, who continually teaches us to "see" society and sociological problems.

For Mannheim the practise of sociology is not only the elaboration of specialized methods and techniques and the application of this knowledge within the discipline. In such practise of scientific scholarship, which can analyze society meticulously, society will become "a valley of dry bones" in which the breath and spirit of living people is lacking. With a variant of a quotation from Goethe about history (1949, IX: 563), we can say what such scientific practise forgets:

> The best thing we get from society
> is the enthusiasm which it arouses.

My concentration on Mannheim's work dit not simply show me for the first time who he was historically. Rather this study has revealed an enduring meaning in his sociological view and in his spirit, a spirit sociologically alive and able to quicken that sociological life in many readers. Perhaps that quatrain form Gerrit Achterberg's "Word" ("Woord") is the most accurate way to express my attitude with regard to Mannheim:

I can meet only words, but no more you.
Yet once the greeting starts, it grows so strong
I actually believe that you must listen
as though, reversed, your stillness speaks in me.

I am conscious that I could not have completed this work without the help of many others.

Assistants from the Royal Library in The Hague, from the library of the British Museum in London, from the Calvin College Library in Grand Rapids, Michigan, and from the libraries of the following universities: Amsterdam, Chicago, Frankfurt, Freiburg, Groningen, Heidelberg, Keele, Lancaster, London and Utrecht – colleagues from all of these libraries have been most helpful. At the conclusion of this book I mention all the facilities from which I have received help. I also mention there the names of the individuals who have provided me with information about Mannheim's life and work.

Those publications of Mannheim which were written in Hungarian have been translated for me by Mr. K. Dekany and by Professor S.A. Varga form the Free University in Amsterdam.

A scholarship from Calvin College in Grand Rapids and a research-fellowship from the University of Chicago during the academic year 1981-1982 put me in a position to complete this book. I mention only dr. Mary VanderGoot, Professor of Psychology at Calvin College and coordinator of the research team at Calvin College of which I formed a part. In thanking her, I thank all my colleagues who have been helpful in my research.

Professor David Kettler (Trent University, Peterborough, Ontario) and Professor Edward A. Shils (University of Chicago) read the entire manuscript and gave me their critical comments, which I have used gratefully in the rewriting of various portions of this manuscript. I extend a special word of thanks to Professor Shils. I have conducted extensive interviews with him about Mannheim's work.

I am greatly indebted to Professor Stanley M. Wiersma (Calvin College), who prepared the English version of my manuscript, originally written in Dutch. I have respect and admiration for his insight into the material, for his literary sensitivity, and for his energetic way of working. I deeply regret his unexpected death on 22 June 1986, during his sabbatical leave in the Netherlands, which means that he did not live to see the publication of this book.

I sincerely thank the Netherlands Organization for the Advancement of Pure Research (ZWO) in The Hague for its financial support which makes the publication of this book possible.

Various versions of the manuscript have been typed by the following secretaries, all connected with the Subfaculty of Social and Cultural Sciences and with the Central Interfaculty of Philosophy of the Free University: Mesdames M.A. de Vries, M.G. Lambert, F. Mager, J. Mevius, P. Wigman Schenk and Mr. J. Roelfsema.

To my wife I dedicate this book. She has experienced intensely how much work the collected works of Mannheim provide and how much energy they require.

Henk E.S. Woldring
Free University, Amsterdam

Introduction

"Establishing again the relationship between humanity and culture" is the theme of the symphony of Mannheim's work. Struggle and suffering, passion and sacrifice are the opening chords which define the composition. These issues also point out the relevance of Mannheim's work to-day. Mannheim's work contributes in an important way to the understanding of the modern crisis of Western culture. His philosophical and sociological analysis of problems of technology, bureaucracies, large-scale organizations, planning, freedom in tension with human responsibility, and his criticism of mainstream philosophical and sociological theories are illuminating and helpful for our understanding of the modern world situation, particularly of Western welfare states. We may consider Mannheim as one of the most influential architects of an "ideology" or political philosophy of the welfare state. In his political philosophy he stresses the calling of the state to intervene into social, economic, and cultural processes on the one hand, and the limits of state intervention and the necessity of a new moral solidarity in society on the other.

A great gulf, according to Mannheim, has developed between the human subject and objective culture, between the human being on the one hand and religion, philosophy, ethics, society, and science on the other. This objective culture surrounds and overwhelms a person as would a Leviathan. This objective culture can, however, only develop itself further through the cooperation of individuals. On the other hand, individuals can only be fulfilled if each one can give meaningful form to the objective culture and thus inherit it for one's own. How shall a person give form to culture? In his answering this question all of the following strongly influenced Mannheim: Dilthey, Husserl, Lukács, Simmel, Troeltsch, Alfred and Max Weber. In addition to this intellectual context, the social and political situation in which he lived is also important for understanding his work. The Dutch sociologist P.J. Bouman (1974: 174) says correctly that for Mannheim, who insisted on pressing through to the existential and social backgrounds of thought, biographical givens were not minor appendages. L.A. Coser (1971) and D. Kettler (1967) agree with this opinion in their publications on Mannheim. For that reason in Part I of this study, Mannheim's life's story is set down in some detail. This biographical portion is based on a study of the archives and contains facts never before published. This part

1

contains three chapters: his life in Hungary, in Germany and in England. In Parts II, III and IV, which discuss his scholarly work, the same division – Hungary, Germany and England – is used, not only for biographical reasons, but because of the phases which I distinguish in his work. My interest in his work is theoretical and systematic as well as historical. My historical concern can be expressed in this question: How shall we understand the development of this sociologist's thought in relation to the flow of philosophical and sociological thought generally, and to the socio-political events of his time? But my concern is also theoretical and systematic: How do the various subdivisions of his work relate to each other? What changes of approach to central issues appear in his thought? To what extent are the topics as treated by Mannheim relevant for social philosophy and sociology now, and of practical concern for society and politics today? In other words: What is living and what is dead in Mannheim?

Different from the recently published book by Collin Loader, *The Intellectual Development of Karl Mannheim* (1985), written from the perspective of the history of ideas, my study is a philosophical-sociological one.

Answering the questions above, I devote attention to the 'motifs and contours' of his philosophy in Part II of this study. By *motifs* I mean the starting point, the purposes, and the themes of his philosophy. Although *contour* is a vague term in connection with his philosophy, it intends to provide a view of the general territory which he explored during the early years of his philosophical journey.

Mannheim is most widely known as a sociologist. Specifically, he pursued studies in cultural sociology, the sociology of knowledge, systematic sociology, political sociology, and educational sociology. These various sub-categories of sociology are discussed in Parts III and IV.

The sub-title of this book includes "Social Ethics." That subject is treated in Part IV. Although Mannheim published a very few studies in ethics, this field requires particular attention, because his philosophy and sociology are nowhere more acutely distinctive than in their application in social ethics.

PART I: Biography

Chapter I

Mannheim in Hungary

- *The Youth and the Student*
- *Hungary at the Turn of the Century*
- *The Political and Social Situation*
- *The Intellectual Milieu*
- *The Lukács Group*
- *Departure from Hungary*

The Youth and the Student

Karl Mannheim was born on 27 March 1893 in Budapest (on Sas Street 19, in the inner city) and received the Hungarian first name Károly. Although the family name was originally spelled with only one *n* (Károly's grandfather was named David Manheim), his father is listed in the Budapest directory (1910) as Gusztáv Mannheim. In the municipal archives of Budapest earlier issues of the directory are not available. It seems impossible now to find out who changed the name or when. In any case, Károly was duly inscribed in the register of the Jewish community in Budapest in 1893 with two *n*'s in his family name. Also in the municipal register his name is spelled in this way.

Károly was the eldest child of his Hungarian-Jewish father, Gusztáv Mannheim, a textile merchant, and of his German-Jewish mother, Rosa Eylenburg. His cousin Ernest Manheim (Kansas City, Missouri) told me in 1982 that a brother named György, seven years younger than Károly, died at 13 from a heart problem. The valves of Károly's own heart were defective from birth, and because of it, he was sickly during his youth; his parents worried very much about his health. Already at twenty he suffered a light heart attack. Throughout his life he fought ill health.

His mother was an intelligent woman with broad interests. She took pains with the cultural and intellectual development of her child. Károly attended the gymnasium and on 9 June 1911 successfully passed his comprehensive examinations. As student in the gymnasium he had already acquired an interest in philosophy, specifically of the thought of Hegel. Stimulated by Georg Lukács, he translated two Hegelian texts from German into Hungarian: *Concerning the Existence of the Philosophical Critique in General and its Relationship to the Current Situation in Philosophy in Particular* (1802) and *Who Thinks Abstractly?* (apparently dating from Hegel's Berlin period). Already in 1911 these translations were published in the periodical *Szellem (Spirit)*.*

---

* While this book was in process I discovered the article of Mátyás Sárközi, "The Influence of Georg Lukács on the Young Karl Mannheim in the Light of a Newly Discovered Diary." *The Slavonic and East European Review* LXIV, 3 (July 1986), pp. 432-439. Sárközi has published parts of Mannheim's recently discovered diary notes (1911-'14). Regretably I have not been able to incorporate this material in this chapter.

After the examinations at the gymnasium he matriculated at the university as a special student. The University of Budapest had a fixed enrollment at the time: a number of students who applied could not be admitted. From 1912 until 1915 he was registered as a regular student with the faculty of philosophy. During this time, Bernát Alexander, Akas Pauler, and Géza Révész were his most important teachers. During the academic year 1912-1913 he entered a contest administered by the faculty of philosophy at his university and for his entry, *The Theory of Judgment in the Literature of Logic During the Last Half of the Nineteenth Century*, he received the first prize.

Because Mannheim was a very gifted student and because his parents were comfortably established in the middle class of Budapest, he was able to pursue his studies elsewhere. From 1913 to 1915 he studied at the University of Berlin. He lodged here with Karl Balod, Professor of law, in the lovely district of Berlin called Grünwald. Specifically, he attended the lectures of Georg Simmel, who as extraordinary professor in social philosophy, attracted many students. At the time Simmel was one of the most gifted and many-sided philosophers in Germany. Mannheim also attended the lectures of Ernst Cassirer, Alois Riehl, and Ernst Troeltsch. Because of his interest in French literature and because he wanted to visit his Budapest friend Arnold Hauser while studying in Paris, Mannheim went to the French capital in the spring of 1914. Together with Hauser he attended the lectures of Henri Bergson for two months.

During the academic year 1915-1916 he remained in Budapest. The relationship between the meditatively inclined Károly and his business-oriented father was such that he chose not to live with his parents. He rented a room in the city. Because of his fragile health, he was rejected for military service. Toward the end of World War I, however, he was required to fulfill his obligation; he was assigned to the service of General Say as tutor for his family.

In 1918 he took extensive notes for an essay on the topic *Leibniz as the Fountain of Inspiration*. He did this on the occasion of a collection which had appeared in Budapest on the bicentenial of the death of Leibniz (1916). He had particular interest in an article by Akas Pauler about the metaphysics of Leibniz, and in another by Paul Dienes about Leibniz as logician and mathemetician. In this collection and in the work of Leibniz himself Mannheim found important ideas which inspired him in the writing of his dissertation, in which he dealt with logical and structural problems of epistemology.

On 9 November 1918 Mannheim, 25, became a doctor of philosophy, *summa cum laude* (see Appendix 1). His dissertation, *Az Ismeretelmét Szerkezetá Elemzése,* appeared in the philosophical journal *Athenaeum* (1918), and was published in 1922 in German under the title *Strukturanalyse der Erkennt nistheorie* (Structural Analysis of Epistemology). The examination which was part of the doctorate program covered his major field, philosophy, and his minor fields, education and the history of German literature. Before his doctorate, in May 1918, he discharged the examinations administered by the state, in the German and French languages and literatures. For these examinations he

2. Arnold Hauser and Karl Mannheim (right) in August 1916.

wrote two composition: 1. "Wilhelm von Humboldt as Critic" and 2. "Louise Labé and the French Renaissance." Just as his prize-winning essay mentioned before, these two compositions were not published. After his death these pieces were not found in his archives. As far as we know, no copies exist. The biographical givens above are borrowed from a *curriculum vitae* which Mannheim himself composed in 1926 for the purpose of securing German citizenship; it is preserved in the "Badische Generallandesarchiv" in Karlsruhe. About his activities in Budapest, Mannheim adds this: "I discharged the usual teachers' training at a state secondary school and on the basis of my diploma for teaching at a secondary level was assigned to the College of Business in the Eight Ward in Budapest. Later I lectured in philosophy at the College of Education in Budapest."

During his student days Mannheim published seceral reviews of books: Arthur Liebert, *The Problem of Validity*; Ernst Cassirer, *Freedom and Formal Studies in the History of German Thought*; Ernst Bloch, *Spirit and Utopia*; Georg Lukács, *The Theory of the Novel*; and Georg Simmel, *The War and Religious Divisions*. He also wrote an article, "Georg Simmel as Philosopher" and a speech, "Soul and Culture."

Hungary at the Turn of the Century

Already before his journey to Berlin, Mannheim had taken an active part in the discussions of a small but growing group of intellectuals in the Hungarian capital. L.A. Coser (1971: 441, 442) mentions that these Hungarian intellectuals are, in a number of respects, like the critical intelligentsia in Russia in the previous century. To speak of similarities in "a number of respects" is imprecise. These Russian intellectuals stood in a critical adversary relationship to the politics of the czars, and they argued for social and political renewal. When we distinguish the various views of life and the philosophical and political directions among the Russian intellectuals – the Western-oriented, the nihilistis, the conservative, and the more modern Slavic partisans – then the comparison with Hungary is not particulary accurate. Similar comparisons, for instance, can be found between the Hungarian intellectuals and the "Fabian Society" in England and with "The Society for Social Politics" in Germany (Coser, 1971: 443; Kettler, 1967:9). In the first place, the political, social, and intellectual traditions of the countries mentioned are all different from each other. In the second place, we shall see that in Hungary – as in other lands – critical intellectuals cannot be lumped together under one label, but that various currents and cross-currents are to be distinguished among them.

To study the ethos of the criticism of the Hungarian intellectuals, one must first focus attention on their place in the social and political situation in Hungary between the turn of the century and World War I, and then on the intellectual milieu.

The Political and Social Situation

For centuries already (since 1520) the ranking monarch of the Hapsburg house had been king of a great part of Hungary. Another portion of it was occupied by the Turks as late as 1686. Though the Hungarian nobility vigorously asserted, in spite of their suffering, that their country was an independent and sovereign state, the Hapsburgs regarded it as only a minor part of their empire. Consequently, the Hungarian nobles were always at swords'points with the Habsburg emperors.

The government in Vienna wished to curtail the power of the Hungarian nobility and at the same time wished to abandon the feudal system. In the first decade of the nineteenth century a political and social conflict in Hungary resulted in the abolition of serfdom, universal taxation (even for the nobility), and the introduction of the Hungarian language in place of Latin in state documents.

The conflict between Hungary, striving for independence, and Austria became more and more acute, until it escalated into a military battle for freedom in 1848. Austria, assisted by the czar's troops from Russia, squelched the uprising. For a time Hungary was ruled by a dictatorship from Vienna. In 1867 an agreement at last was reached between the two states: the Austrian-

Hungarian monarchy was established with the understanding that both parts of the realm would be independent of the other.

The tensions between them remained, however. In Hungary the striving for total self-determination lived on, but complicated by the question of nationalities within Hungary. Among the Hungarians who formed the numerical majority, there were also some hardly insignificant minorities: Germans, Russians, Slavs, Roumanians, and Serbians. These minorities were standing up for their rights and identities (Z. Horváth, 1966:54; O. Jászi, 1924;1-17).

In spite of the various reforms mentioned above, the spirit of feudal tradition lived on in Hungary (Horváth, 1963: 18-21; 1966; 19, 36). During the second half of the nineteenth century and into the beginning of the twentieth, the country was ruled by mighty nobles, who lived from the produce of their vast estates; this nobility was oriented toward Vienna. The lower nobility discharged the administrative functions of the country. Together with the church, which owned just as much land as the nobility, a narrow-minded, conservative nobility dominated a poor, uneducated, and rural populace. The government had virtually no contact with the rural population nor with the various minorities. Social and political life in Budapest was isolated from the farm land round about and from its rural people.

In Budapest a rather prosperous middle class had developed, mostly Jewish, but strongly assimilated into the culture; this middle class had a powerful political consciousness. From this class came Mannheim and other intellectuals. The greater part of the population of Budapest consisted of an underpaid and unorganized working class. As in all European cities of the time, the protests of workers in the Hungarian capital against unjust social and political situations became stronger and more clearly defined; they demanded especially an eight-hour rather than a ten-hour work day and universal suffrage. Since the nineties, strikes had been a regular occurrence. Socialism spread by means of publications among farmers and laborers. Now and then the government would summon troops to preserve civil peace. The workers' movement gained more and more influence around the turn of the century, but feudal traditions were strong. If approximately 4.5% of the population had the right to vote in 1900, even after the reforms of election procedures in 1913 fewer than a third of the male population had the franchise (Z. Horváth, 1966: 19; L.A. Coser, 1971: 442; D. Kettler, 1967: 7).

The Intellectual Milieu

Budapest University and the Academy of Sciences together formed the center of intellectual life in Budapest. In the field of philosophy Hungary had not yet produced any great creative spirits. This is the opinion of Horváth (1966: 91), who, nevertheless, mentions with admiration the names of Károly Böhms, Bernát Alexander, Akas Pauler, and Gyula Kornis – not the foundation builders of independent philosophies – but eclectics. Alexander was the first

Hungarian translator of works by Descartes, Diderot, Hume, and Kant. Others translated the classical texts of Comte, Spencer, and neo-Kantian and French rationalists. As mentioned, Mannheim translated two publications of Hegel.

Bernát Alexander complained that philosophical thought in Hungary after 1867 had a one-sided German influence. In intellectual circles more and more protests were heard, not only against feudal traditions, but against the overriding influence of Austria and Germany in the field of culture. Expressions of this protest were *Huszadik Század (Twentieth Century)*, a periodical which first appeared in 1900, and The Society for Social Sciences, organized in 1901. The leaders in the society were also leaders in the periodical. It is noteworthy that the leadership for the Hungarian Philosophical Association, organized in 1901, and for the philosophical journal *Athenaeum* came principally from the university (Bernát Alexander, already mentioned, as chairman of the association and editor of the periodical). Together with the rising socialism and the workers' movement, *Huszadik Század* and the Society for Social Sciences, coming out of the rising intelligentsia of Budapest's wealthy middle class, were of great importance for the development of Hungarian social and political awareness around World War I. In addition to conducting theoretical studies, the members of the Society for Social Sciences were active in various aspects of political life; they propagandized and fought for universal suffrage, agricultural reform, and minority rights (Jászi, 1924: 25).

The Society for Social Sciences was not on the radical-left politically. In addition to studies of Marxism and socialism, they also published translations of H. Spencer, L. Ward, B. Kidd, K. Kautsky, and G. Ratzenhofer. True, it is clear that "The Society" was not open to reactionary ideas. Both "The Society" and *Huszadik Század* were financially independent. They were not supported by political parties, churches, or corporations; they made no concessions to pressure groups (Horváth, 1966: 129, 130, 240; Kettler, 1971: 41-42).

Both in "The Society" and in the periodical *Huszadik Század*, attention was drawn to specific problems, and the meaning of socialism was placed at the center of these discussions. In 1904 leaders from "The Society" and the periodical organized courses of study for factory workers. As a result of these activities "The Free School for Social Studies" appeared. This project was a great success; more than two thousand people attended courses. "The Society" numbered more than three thousand members at that time (Horváth, 1966: 133-134).

Oszkar Jászi, who was the principal of the new school, said at its opening that a new ethic was necessary, an ethic that would go beyond religion and metaphysics and would be founded on science and human solidarity. He pleaded for a fruitful use of "the basis principles and methods of the universal scientific objectivity" applied to all disciplines (Horváth, 1966: 135-136).

One discerns the influence in these words of the positivism of De Saint-Simon and Comte. They, too, desired a science that would be based only on positive facts, and that would abandon religion and methaphysics. Just as their spiritual

3. Karl Mannheim (ca. 1918)

kin in England, John Stuart Mill and Herbert Spencer, they believed strongly in the progress of humanity. They strove for a worldview founded on science and erected in utility. A late phase of positivism can be seen taking shape in Austria at the end of the nineteenth century, particularly around the figures of Mach and Avenarius. They were for a precise description of the scientific and economic "givens"; nevertheless, their ideas were closely related to pragmatism and to various forms of neo-Kantianism (Vaihinger). In "The Society," in *Huszadik Század*, and in the "Free School," all of these cross-currents were studied. Horváth is right in judging that in all of these institutions a materialistic and naturalistic ethos prevailed (1966: 120, 287).

11

"The Society" argued for a scientifically based politics. In its view the ideal state of Plato pointed in the right direction; philosophers, people with a perfect theoretical knowledge and moral purity, ought to be in control of the government. The leadership of the Social-Democratic Party, however, suspected the intellectuals who, after all, were strongly bound to the wealthy middle class. Party members saw them as elitist and proud. Only a few of the intellectuals were members of the Social-Democratic Party. Actual contact between critical intellectuals and the vast majority of the population was hardly possible.

Concurring with the ideas of "The Society," and supported by free masons, progressive students in Budapest – among them Oskar Jászi, Karl and Michael Polanyi, and few members of the Social-Democratic Party – organized "The Galileo Group." This organization was to study the pragmatism of William James and the neo-positivism of Mach and Avenarius. Before his departure for Berlin, Mannheim participated in this group (Coser, 1971: 443-444; Horváth, 1966: 352-353; Kettler, 1967: 10-11). Although among the members critical, intellectual Marxists could be found, their discussions and courses were in no sense radical or socialistic. Their concern for extending the influence of positivism, pragmatism, and German idealism was far too great.

This "Galileo Group" also waged campaigns against religious fanaticism and against alcoholism. Jewish students were the leaders. Everyone knew that the group was strongly influenced by anti-military and anti-corporation ideas, so that a few weeks before the October Revolution of 1918, they were forbidden to meet, and several members were arrested (Jászi, 1924: 25).

The Lukács Group

Another group of intellectuals that had great importance for political life in Hungary, particularly at the time of the Revolution in 1918, had gathered around the figure of the philosopher Georg Lukács after 1915. Mannheim also participated in this group. Born in 1885 in Budapest, Lukács had studied philosophy in the Hungarian capital. He made academic journeys to various cities, including Berlin, where he attended lectures by Simmel, and Heidelberg, where he made contact with the discussion group forming around Max Weber. In 1915 and 1916 he returned to Budapest for a stay of several months, and in 1917 he returned to stay.

Lukács had an enormous influence on Mannheim during his student days. From their correspondence, part of which has been preserved and translated into English by Eva Gábor (KL), it would seem that Mannheim was open and trusting in his relationship with Lukács. In his letter of 3 January 1912 he wrote Lukács that he found philosophizing about the existence of God as Prime Mover an unfruitful enterprise. Then he wrote:

> I do not wish to abandon God, certainly not, only I find it unworthy to the feeling which drives us to seek and to know him, to turn to him in this way. God – or however I might call him – is in me *a priori*, all one can do is "to get from Him to Him."

4. A meeting of the followers of Georg Lukács, who was himself not present. Left to right: Karl Mannheim, Béla Fogarasi, Ernö Lorsy, József Nemes Lampérth, Elza Stephani, Anna Schlamadinger, Edith Hajós, Béla Balázs.

Citing Cusanus, he explains further that his belief in God is a question of knowing himself. We can only get to know ourselves in interaction with things, and we can only learn to know this Other in interaction with ourselves: "This is the path of the soul from itself to itself." These philosophical questions (to which I shall return later in this study, especially in handling "Soul and Culture") were, according to Mannheim, searchingly thought through and answered in the novels of Dostoevsky.

> I wish to write on Dostoevsky. Not only that I feel I should be able to pose my problems and my questions through a study of his work, but because I feel that a knowledge of his life promises solutions.

Mannheim also mentions his interest in the eastern philosophies and his investigation of Kant. In later letters Mannheim wrote Lukács of his plans to visit him in Heidelberg.

From 1915 until 1918 the Lukács group assembled at the dwelling of Béla Balázs almost every Sunday. The group discussion would go on from 3.00 PM until 3.00 AM with Lukács holding the floor for ten or twelve hours. For further information regarding the Lukács group, I refer to Kettler (1967; 1971), who reproduces interviews with contemporaries of Mannheim and Lukács.

In 1917 the group began to organize lectures and seminars under the name of "Free School for Studies of the Human Spirit." In sharp contrast to the positivistic orientation of "The Society for Social Sciences" and to "The Free School for Social Studies," this "Free School" was founded on the basis of German idealism (F.J. Raddatz, 1976: 17-37). Yet, one must be careful not to overestimate the difference, according to Coser (1971: 445). Mannheim, for

13

instance, attended gatherings of "The Society for Social Sciences," while at this same time being a visible member of the Lukács group. In the autumn of 1917 he delivered a lecture entitled "Soul and Culture" at the opening of the second semester of "The Free School for Studies of the Human Spirit." He set out to clarify the social background for the lectures of the second semester. B. Fogarasi would speak about methods in cultural studies, Lukács about aesthetic problems, A. Hauser about aesthetic dilletantism, E. Szabó about the foundations of Marxism, and Z. Kodály and B. Bartók about the Hungarian folksong. In addition Mannheim announced lectures by Zalai, Antal, Varjas, and others. And, building on the lectures he had delivered during the first semester on "Epistemological and Logical Problems," Mannheim himself would lecture on a structural analysis of systems of epistemology, the subject of his doctoral dissertation accepted the next year. An average of seventy listeners attended the lectures at "The Free School for Studies of the Human Spirit" (E. Fekete, E. Karádi, 1981: 71).

Belá Balázs noted in his dairy (28-05-1917) several short evaluative comments about lectures and lecturers in the "Free School for Studies of the Human Spirit." Among other comments, he records this:

> Mannheim's [lectures] on the logic of epistemology were excellent, exciting, and rich; the first appearance of an important philosopher of the future. (L. Congdon, 1973: 70)

The Lukács group can not justly be called political-revolutionary. The talk was mostly about philosophy and literature (Kierkegaard, Dostoevsky) and about religion and mysticism (Meister Eckhart). Although political lectures were seldom heard, it was known that Lukács took a position to the far left, combined with a somewhat personal interpretation of Marxism. With Szabó, he was one of the founders of the club called "Revolutionary Socialist Students of Budapest." Already at the time he was a student at the university, he was studying Marx. His version of Marx continued to be strongly influenced by Simmel. During World War I he read Marx again: "This time it was indeed Marx, no longer through the glasses of Simmel, but still, nevertheless, through the Hegelian glasses. No longer a Marx raging forward as the lonely philosopher, as economist and sociologist. The comprehensive thinker, the great dialectician dawned on me" (Lukács, 1933: 326). At the end of the war, during the revolutionary period in Russia, he read Rosa Luxemburg and Lenin's *State and Revolution*. He himself wrote of this period: "I was in an ideological atmosphere like this when the Revolution of 1917 and 1918 struck. After a short deliberation I joined the Communist Party in December of 1918, and since that time have remained in the ranks of the revolutionary workers' movement" (1933: 33; cf. G. Lichtheim, 1970: 16-54). Lukács and his followers became political revolutionaries only after they became members of the Communist Party at the time of the Revolution in 1918 (D. Kettler, 1967: 6).

In 1918 World War I came to an end; with Germany and Austria, Hungary

5. Cartoon (1918) drawn by Gergely Tibor, who, with Mannheim, belonged to the discussion group around Georg Lukács and Béla Balázs. The cartoon allows a psychoanalytic interpretation: The ego is Mannheim reading his dissertation. The id is Mannheim's sexual inclination, shown in the form of a naked lady sitting on his knee. The superego, in mist and smoke coming from his pipe, is Mannheim shown as a child of great promise for all humanity, in the arms of a madonna.

belonged to the defeated side. Demonstrations in the streets of Budapest were expressions of great dissatisfaction with the agreements of 1867. The government in Budapest lost respect and credibility. A national council was formed in which both Social Democrats and representatives of groups of the radical left had their places. In this way members of "The Society for Social Sciences" and other critical intellectuals came into the government. Troublesome times in Budapest: soldiers returning from the frontlines and officers, workers, students, and anxious citizens filling the streets with demonstrations to make the revolution a reality.

15

Departure from Hungary

The October Revolution of 1918 reformed the government under the leading of the moderate socialist Károlyi. Given the social, economic, and political situation in the country, the new government strove realistically for what it could achieve: independence from the federal government, universal suffrage, friendly relations with the people of neighboring countries, and redistribution of the land. According to Kettler (1967: 16-17), the greater part of the population agreed with these plans. There was a general turning aside from Lenin's plans for Russia. There was no absolute state authority, no dictator to represent avant-garde party politics, but rather cooperation between farmers, workers, and critical intellectuals. What the Károlyi government lacked, however, was organizing ability to formulate a practical program of reform and efficiency in carrying it out.

In December 1918 Lukács joined the newly organized Communist Party. Many of his group – Béla Bálazs, Belá Fogarasi, and others – followed him. Mannheim and Hauser did not. The Communist Party instituted a fierce opposition to the government of Károlyi, which they renounced as betraying the Revolution. They organized rallies and demonstrations; and by the beginning of 1919 they had control of the streets of Budapest (Kettler, 1967: 29). The government of Károlyi fell in the spring of 1919 and the Social Democrats formed a coalition with the Communists for the purpose of establishing a parliamentary republic under the Communist Béla Kun. Lukács became Commissioner of Education in the summer of 1919 in this government, having already served as substitute commissioner for several months.

The Lukács group, with its idealistic ethical and mystical ideas, formed a unique current in the Communist Party. They were certainly at swords' points with Béla Kun, who was oriented toward Lenin. His very joining of the Communist Party, Lukács felt to be a necessity and a self-sacrifice. He did not regard it as a permit to justify each and every arbitrary move the Party made; he joined because he looked for what he called "the renewal of culture," a process which requires sacrifices from everyone (Lukács, 1919: 3-11; Kettler, 1967: 34-35; Raddatz, 1976: 43).

With the reorganization of the university in Budapest, Lukács appointed Mannheim as lecturer in philosophy in the College of Education. From the point of view of his vision of a renewed culture, Lukács trusted him, even though Mannheim was not a member of the Communist Party.

At the beginning of August 1919 the government of Belá Kun fell. His regime did not have sufficient contact with the agricultural population, while in Budapest the government lost respect because it had failed to bring its plans for reorganizations into reality within a short time. An alliance of power was steadfastly determined to bring about the fall of the Communist government. Helped by Roumanian and Polish armies, the "White Army" of Admiral Von Horthy overthrew the government in August 1919. Reactionaries occupied the governmental castle in Budapest; Von Horthy assumed leadership of the coun-

16

try in 1920 and carried out an actual reign of terror: 5.000 revolutionaries were killed, 75.000 were taken prisoner, and more than 100.000 were exiled (G. Lichtheim, 1970: 47f.; O. Jászi, 1924: 160). Lukács fled to Vienna. Although Mannheim was a leftist in his political orientation, he was not known for being an extremist. He was moderate in his position and violently opposed to the politicizing of scholarship. He could maintain himself under the moderate Socialist government of Károlyi and the Communist regime of Béla Kun.

Yet the counter-revolutionary regime of Von Horthy was openly anti-Semitic. For a young, promising intellectual like Mannheim it was not at all attractive to remain in Hungary. He questioned the legitimacy of the Von Horthy government and detested its policies. Moreover, the new government was hostile not only toward outright communists, but toward their sympathizers. Its influence in the governance of the university began to be noticeable immediately. Even after Mannheim's departure from Hungary, "a disciplinary procedure" was undertaken against him on the basis of "his unlawful actions in favour of the Hungarian Soviet Republic." He was accused because of his "accepting a professorship from the proletarian system" (Gábor, 1983: 8, 13).

In December 1919 he departed by boat for Vienna, where for several weeks he lived in a camp for Hungarian refugees. In the barracks of this camp the members of the Lukács group living there held regular meeting. Their departure from Hungary and their stay in the camp is described by Anna Seghers in the novel *The Travellers (Die Gefährten*, 1968: 79-265). Mannheim appears in this novel as Steiner.

On invitation of Vilmos Szilasi, who later became a renowned philosopher of Hungarian origin (he succeeded Heidegger as professor at Freiburg), Mannheim went to Freiburg. Although he did not allow himself to be enrolled at the Albert Ludwig University in Freiburg, he attended lectures for two semesters with Husserl, who was a regular professor there, and with Heidegger, who at the time was functioning as a private tutor. In the *City Directory of the Capital City of Freiburg in Breisgau* (1919-1921), Mannheim's name does not appear. From the archives of the city of Freiburg we know that on 4-5-1920 he checked in at the Hotel Hohenzollern and after four weeks (28-4-1920) checked out again. Given the status of the Hotel Hohenzollern at that time (since then, Hotel Roseneck, Lorettostrasse), we may conclude that Mannheim's financial situation was comfortable. Apparently after 28-5-1920, he enjoyed the hospitality of the Szilasi family, because he was good friends with them. In the hotel he gave his occupation as "university lecturer," and – no doubt because anti-semitism existed in Germany as well as in Hungary – his religion as "Catholic." Before Mannheim arrived in Freiburg, he had lodged in Saig (near Lenzkirch), in the Black Forest.

After Freiburg his way led to Berlin, where he allowed himself to be enrolled in the university for the winter semester. Afterwards he moved to Heidelberg, one of the most famous centers in the world of German universities. Brinkmann, Jaspers, Lederer, Rickert, and Alfred Weber are a few of the lecturers who taught there.

As will appear from this study, I share the opinion of Gabel (1966) and Gábor (1983) that the Hungarian intellectual milieu influenced Mannheim substantially. His contacts with Alexander, Jászi, Zalai, and others determined the direction of his intellectual course of development. As Mannheim himself says (SEG: 298):

> Early impressions tend to coalesce into a natural view of the world. All later experiences then stand to receive their meaning from this original set, whether they appear as that set's verification and fulfillment or as the negation and antithesis. (...) This much, however, is certain, that even if the rest of one's life consisted in one long process of negation and destruction of the natural worldview acquired in youth, the determining influence of these early impressions would still be predominant.

That Mannheim's works from the start must be placed in a tradition of liberalism (Locke, A. Smith, and J.S. Mill), as Kettler, Meja, and Stehr argue (1984: Chapter I), does not seem convincing to me. They cite Cumming (1970, 1:16), who "identifies two central features of liberal ventures in political philosophy: first, the liberal-political thinker defines his own intellectual situation as a period of 'transition' or 'crisis,' requiring a major reinterpretation of the 'tradition' made up of certain ethical ideals and political ideas; second, the modern liberal believes that in politicial thought as in politics conflicts are not 'insurmountable,' that they represent 'differences of opinion'... resolvable by some kind of translation and adjustment."

In my opinion, Cumming sketches a *formal* framework into which we can place Mannheim, but his own working out of these points is fundamentally different in many respects from the "tradition of liberalism." Kettler and the others point out that Mannheim criticized liberalism from the perspective of a philosopher. Consequently, it is correct that they describe Mannheim as someone who participated in "liberal" groups in the Hungary of his time. They characterize him as a "Central-European liberal"; it would be better to call him "a Hungarian liberal," that is, a liberal in the social, cultural, and political context of Hungary. As Gabel has demonstrated, Mannheim's being a liberal must be modified by that context. Precisely that context is what does not justify placing Mannheim simply in the tradition of liberalism. When Mannheim speaks about liberalism, he means, as I see it, a liberalism within a socio-cultural context of a particular time and place.

Chapter II

Emigrant in the Weimar Republic

The Weimar Republic

After her defeat in World War I, Germany was disabled. Mutiny broke out among the sailors in Kiel and spread to other cities; Keizer Wilhelm fled to the Netherlands; in the grove of Compiegne the German delegation agreed to an armistice; on 9 November 1918 Karl Liebknecht declared a Soviet Republic in Berlin. When communist and far-left socialists tried here and there to establish a dictator of the proletariat, the provisional socialist government of Friedrich Ebert assembled the officers of the old army with its various detachments, for the purpose of bringing the communistic uprising to a standstill. Berlin and other cities became battle grounds where independent socialists and communists fought against the troops of the Ebert government. The Ebert government prevailed; Karl Liebknecht, Rosa Luxemburg, and others were shot. The strong alliances between the ruling socialist groups and the armies of the old Germany paralyzed all striving for social renewal. Redistributing the land and nationzalizing the major industries came to a standstill.

In Weimar on 11 February 1919 a National Congress formulated a constitution. Ebert was chosen as President of "Das Reich," known as "The Weimar Republic." Politically and economically Germany appeared to be desintegrating. Only with the greatest difficulty were coalitions made possible. During Mannheim's time in Germany (1920-1933) there were twenty successive prime ministers and seven dissolutions of government.

The reparations which Germany was forced to pay after the war and its loss of various territories undermined the German economy. In 1923, when Germany was still handicapped by reparation payments, France occupied the Ruhr Valley. The weakness of the ruling party, the exaggerated demands of the allies, and the vengeful attitude of France, together constituted an ominous situation for the young Weimar Republic. The political and economic desintegration caused the populace to be demoralized; the murder of the Minister of Foreign

Affairs, Walter Ratenau, in 1922, was a symbol for everything that was wrong (Bouman, 1955: 117-197).

The crisis in the world economy in the twenties and thirties did even more to torment the country; it aggravated unemployment and accelerated the demoralization. Who could lead this country out of darkness? Both the Communists and the National Socialists attracted growing constituencies. Although Adolf Hitler had planned a coup in Munich in 1923 (it miscarried), ten years later, operating along democratic lines, he became the Chief of State and moved the seat of government from Weimar to Berlin.

The Weber Group

Such was the context in which Mannheim settled in Heidelberg in March 1921. He remained sympathetic to leftist causes and approved of the workers' movement, but refrained from political activities. "He himself was never throughout his life unequivocally identified with any political party," says Stewart (1967: 10). Mannheim was a political refugee, but no activist. Not being an activist is understandable; he did not yet have German citizenship, and so his position was vulnerable. On the other hand, the political situation in every respect gave the occasion for political activities, especially because in Heidelberg he was in contact with the Weber group. He had heard of it already through Lukács, who during his stay in Heidelberg has been in contact with this circle. At the time of World War I the discussions were held on Sunday afternoons. Lask, Bloch and Jaspers were among the regular visitors to the great house at 17 Siegelhäuser Landstrasse: the windows at the back looked out over the Philosophenweg; the windows in front looked out over the Neckar River, and over the city center of Heidelberg.

The house in Ziegelhäuser Landstrasse was built in 1847 by George Friedrich Fallenstein, Max Weber's grandfather on his mother's side. Frequent callers knew it as "Home on the Old Bridge," and it was the home of many important Heidelberg professors: G.G. Gervinus (1805-1871), A. Hausrath (1837-1909), Ernst Troeltsch (1865-1923), who for several years lived on the second floor while the Webers lived on the first floor. Marianne Weber remained living in this house until her death in 1954. During the National Socialist period of Germany, the house was a refuge for many outcasts from public life who could not forsake the spirit of opposition and who stimulated and sustained each other's subversions. Other inhabitants were Professors W. Benecke, E. Levy, R. Thoma, G. Wobbermin, and Goldschmitt.

In addition to discussions about religion, mysticism, and writers such as Dostoevsky and Tolstoy, the chief subject discussed in the Weber group was the politics of the Keizer (Honigsheim, 1926: 284; Mitzman, 1970: 256-276). Weber had criticized government policy all the while, and during the war he became more and more active politically, writing political articles for the *Frankfurter Zeitung*. After the war the government asked him to take part in the delegation to the peace talks in Versailles. He took part in the committee which framed the new Weimar constitution (Mommsen, 1959; Marianne Weber, 1950: 603, 604, 681-692).

20

About possible contacts between Mannheim and Max Weber before his death in 1920, we know nothing. We know that Mannheim had a good relationship with Marianne Weber. After the death of her husband, she continued to organize Sunday gatherings. Norbert Elias told me (16-11-1977) that she was an intelligent woman with a forceful personality. Whoever wanted to write a book under the supervision of Alfred Weber needed first to gain permission from Marianne Weber, especially if the book were to be the basis for an academic appointment. Mannheim was a regular caller at the gatherings which she organized. He introduced his friend Elias in her house, where he read a paper which was discussed. During Mannheim's stay in Heidelberg he also participated in another discussion group which was regularly attended by Martin Buber, H. Ehrenberg, E. Ludwig, and Ernst Bloch, the latter being an especially good friend (cf. N. Elias, 1984: 23-25).

In 1920 he gave a private seminar under the title "What is Sociology?" Some of the regular members were Alfred Weber, Marianne Weber, Heinrich Rickert, Karl Jaspers, Martin Buber, Emile Lederer, and his wife Emmy Seidler Lederer. That Mannheim was so cordially received in the university circles of Heidelberg was certainly due in large part to his being known as a student and a friend of Lukács. At the time of his stay in Heidelberg, Lukács had been very much respected as a scholar in the university world (Gábor, 1983: 9, 13).

During his years in Germany, Mannheim concentrated on solid scholarship. He examined the work of those who followed the neo-Kantian position of the schools of Baden and Marburg. He became thoroughly familiar with the conflict concerning methods in the natural and human sciences. He understood thoroughly the conflict between evaluatively-neutral as opposed to value-oriented judgment. Specifically, he studied the work of Dilthey, Husserl, Lask, Rickert, Troeltsch, and the Weber brothers. In the twenties he published extensive articles about interpretations of worldviews, historicism, and the sociology of knowledge. In this time he also wrote a manuscript entitled *The Distinctive Character of Cultural Sociological Knowledge* and the incomplete manuscript *A Sociological Theory of Culture and its Knowability (Conjunctive and Communicative Thinking)*. On the title page of the first manuscript Mannheim wrote "Sulz at the Neckar. Begun September 1922." The second manuscript is not dated. Both manuscripts were found in the Mannheim archives after his death and not published until 1980 (ST).

Marriage

On 22 March 1921 Karl married Juliska Lang (born 23 September 1893 in Budapest). Her father, Josef Lang was an industrialist in Budapest; her mother owned and operated a studio for silver art work. Jewish people of means, they were not happy with their daughter's choice; they had fancied someone socially

6.   Juliska Lang (ca. 1918)

and economically secure. The somewhat strained relations with Juliska's parents was reason that the marriage was held, not in Budapest, but in Heidelberg. More important, under the fascist regime in Hungary the situation for returning emigrants was too dangerous.

Juliska has studied psychology in Budapest. There she had received her doctorate in 1918 under Professor G. Révész, who after the coup of Von Horthy also forsook Hungary and later was named Professor at the University of

Amsterdam. Her dissertation was entitled *A Psychological Investigation of the Musical Factor*. With her sister Elisabeth (who became the wife of the sociologist Paul Kecskemeti, one of the editors of Mannheim's posthumous published works), she had left Hungary in 1919, just as Mannheim had. In fact, their romance had begun in the refugee camp in Vienna.

The marriage between Karl and Juliska Mannheim remained childless. According to the description of Elias, Juliska was a slender, charming, and very intelligent woman, a characterization confirmed without exception by all who knew her.

Although Mannheim had chosen education as his minor at the time of his study in Budapest, his growing fascination with this subject in Germany was probably stimulated by her interests. It is known and documented that at the time of his lectures and seminars in Heidelberg he gave much thought to social-psychological and educational problems (Kluke, 1972: 545). As with Marianne Weber and Gertrud Simmel, we can see Juliska helping to shape the intellectual development of her husband.

Not Immigrant, but Emigrant

Mannheim regarded and experienced his stay in Germany as the life of an exile, having strong feelings of homesickness for the life in Budapest and for the contacts with friends from that former time. In 1921 he requested the Lukács group, which had relocated in Vienna, whether he might take part in their Sunday gatherings. This group, which had become strongly politicized, denied this request because it regarded Mannheim as an apostate (Kettler, Meja, Stehr, 1984: Chapter II).

In one of his letters written in Heidelberg and translated under the title "Letters from Exile," he made very clear the distinction between Hungarians who left out of protest against the Von Horthy government, and those who left especially to further career possibilities (Gábor, 1983: 8-9). He saw himself not as an immigrant to Germany, but as an emigrant from Hungary. "Who then is the real emigrant?" he asked, and answered thus:

> It is he who thinks that a bridge between his own viewpoint and that of the government is impossible. Among these there are some who could have stayed at home. They were not harassed, but they simply could not stay at home due to the differences between their viewpoint and that of the regime. (...)These emigrants will go home only if the regime is abolished.(...) So exile should not be abolished. It has an important "national goal." It saves and keeps alive the free spirit of the Hungarian mind and awakes the conscience of the Hungarian people. (LE)

This "emigrant" consciousness was apparently the reason why Mannheim did not take steps to become a citizen during his first years in Germany. That occurred later, under the pressure of circumstances.

23

Appointment to Academia

On 12 June 1926 Mannheim became an extraordinary lecturer *(Privatdozent)* in sociology at the University of Heidelberg, where he worked closely with Alfred Weber. His parents remained responsible for part of his support. As academic project to support his candidacy, Mannheim submitted *The Old Conservatism: A Contribution to the Sociology of Knowledge*, which in 1927 was published in a shortened form under the title "Conservative Thought," and which recently was published completely as *Conservatism*.

In the archieves of the Rupert Karl University in Heidelberg the records of Mannheim's appointment are preserved. On 14-12-1925 he submitted the required original to the Department of Philosophy, in order to get certification as an extraordinary lecturer in sociology. On 16-12-1925 he received the preliminary candidate status; he was to be evaluated by Professor Lederer with Professors Weber and Brinkmann as references. At the faculty meeting of 8-2-1926 the appointment was to be made final. The written opinions by the professors were very favorable. Lederer wrote an elaborate opinion to the faculty, in which he cited Mannheim's study as a concrete and substantial model for research in cultural sociology and called it a work of great importance. He wrote in part:

> This work about the *Sociology of the Old Conservatism* in Germany sets forth in the most fruitful and most inspiring manner the direction of a series of investigations, which together comprise one part of the academic work of Dr. Karl Mannheim, concerning which I shall give a more comprehensive oral report to the faculty.

In addition, he wrote that in Mannheim's work the rights of both philosophy and the history of ideas to stake out their proper field of problems had not been contested. Both philosophy and the history of ideas proceed from crucial assumptions, however: that a conclusion in thought is separable from its prior genesis and occasion, and that the implications of ideas could be examined in isolation from the social and cultural constellation in which they appear. According to Lederer, Mannheim would never deny the immanent development of the human sciences, but intended only to open the discussion of dependence of the human sciences on social structures.

Perhaps Lederer intended only to take the wind out of the sails of the opposition within the faculty. Yet, with his distinction between the immanent approach and that of the sociology of knowledge, he struck a fundamental problem in Mannheim's thought.

In the document submitted to support his application, Mannheim distinguished between traditionalism and conservatism. Lederer's commentary to the faculty includes the following:

> Conservative thought is every bit as modern as bourgeois thought, since it grew up as a contrast to it. In the same way as bourgeois thought, conservative thought is a new phenomenon. ... Conservatism is not synonymous with "traditionalism," as the author

[Mannheim] describes them, for all the elements of earlier thought and experience are reflected in conservative thought. Even traditionalism is an organic holding fast to the remembered past, and can accomodate itself to any direction of thought and any life style. Even progressive people can and will continue to act traditionally. Conservative thought, in contrast to these, is in thought and action more complicated, and is a result of an objective, ready-made structure, in which the interdependent elements all interlock.

Conservative thought, according to Lederer, proceeds from the totality to the specific; it has a dynamic concept of reason, in contrast to the static, universally valid, and a-historical thought. Accordingly, even reason is caught up in the historical process. The knowing subject stands in a stream of events, of becoming, Lederer goes on:

At this point the concept of a stream of life beclouds what we once thought of as The Pure Dynamic. The line of thought from here also leads, by the way, to Bergson, whose philosophy becomes very important for the directions of the eruptive and volitile social currents, but at the same time relativizes the reasonable and the systematic out of the irrational mainstream of life.

Lederer fixes his attention here on the point that Mannheim himself had made in his study. Mannheim had caught the influence of Bergson in Paris and saw many diverging streams of German cultural study draw together in the thought of this philosopher. This Bergsonian impulse unites on the one hand with those currents which tended toward phenomenology, and on the other with historical philosophies (KD: 161-163; H: 107, 108).

Lederer concludes his commentary thus:

A great, significant assignment, which the author has set for the history of old-conservative thought, which can only be comprehended through a full mastery of the philosophical thoughts of our time, through a thorough understanding of the System as an immanent model of thoughts on the one hand, and on the other through a thorough understanding of the concrete circumstances surrounding the system. That system is here grasped for the first time with truly academic materials and with a method free from subjectivity – far beyond all aphorisms about the relationship between foundation and superstructure.

In sum, the document Mannheim submitted to support his candidacy for academia was a significant achievement. Alfred Weber also thought so:

This work I hold as an important entry in the bibliography. The problem which the author treats is one which is very familiar to me, namely, that of the anchoring of sociological thought and, closely associated with it, the meaning of the progression of worldviews. This work is the first concrete and definitive study after numberless methodological and critical preliminary studies. It is important not only because of the author's perfect mastery of a large field of scholarship, and not only because of his convincing analysis of the meaning of his stated thesis, but important because of the statement of the thesis itself and this very attempt to prove it.

Weber concludes: "And so I heartily believe that the work ought to be accepted as a valid document to support his academic appointment."

Mannheim had suggested that for the special faculty meeting on 8-2-1926 he would deliver a lecture on one of three topics: 1. Concerning Max Weber's Sociology, 2. The Sociological Problem of the Generations, and 3. The Sociological Problem of Intelligence. Several professors preferred the first topic. Although the formal minutes record nothing about it, apparently Mannheim did deliver a lecture on Max Weber's sociology. In a letter of the same date the dean of the Department of Philosophy wrote to the "Inner Senate" of the University of Heidelberg (i.e., the *Senatus Contractus*, the Rector Magnificus, with the deans of the various faculties): "The Department of Philosophy in its session on 6 February has declared Dr. Karl Mannheim suitable for a position in the field of sociology." The *Senatus Contractus* immediately forwarded the resolution to the Ministry of Culture and Education at Karlsruhe for endorsement. Thus it is noteworthy that at its meeting of 15-2-1926 the *Senatus Contractus* again discussed this appointment. According to notes that have been preserved, several professors were of the opinion that Mannheim "first must demonstrate German citizenship. The appointment shall proceed no higher than the *Senatus Contractus* until the name of Dr. Mannheim is inscribed among the German cirizenry." The Department of Philosophy took up Mannheim's case and informed the *Senatus Contractus* (8.4.1926) that it had discussed his naturalization already at the time of the discussions preliminary to Mannheim's appointment (25-7-1925). It had decided then, on advice of the dean, Prof. E.R. Curtius, not to make naturalization a condition for appointment. Rather the candidate would be urged, immediately after his appointment, to take the necessary steps to secure German citizenship. The Philosophy Department gave the following grounds for this step:

1) Dr. Mannheim's numerous and comprehensive academic studies have until now exclusively appeared in the German language, so that throughout the world of academia he is known as a German scholar. Dr. Mannheim's mother is – or was before her marriage – a German citizen; more of his relatives on the maternal side are Germans, and work in Germany as officials, judges, and officers.

2) Dr. Mannheim already has lived in Heidelberg more than five years. He is well known to his colleagues in the Department of Philosophy (and not at all only to the official examiners in his field) as well as to many colleagues throughout the whole faculty. The examiners in particular have given the faculty a satisfactory step-by-step account throughout their investigations of the personality of Dr. Mannheim, who neither earlier took political stands, nor, considering his whole orientation and inclination can be construed as political at present. The Messrs. Weber and Lederer have already made explanations of this point to satisfy the official demands.

3) Meanwhile, the Department of Philosophy, for the purpose of answering the opinion of the Senate, has taken the opportunity to get opinions from the Minister of the Interior and his deputies concerned with citizenship. And so, the necessary assurance

has been given in this case: Dr. Mannheim's citizenship is in process, the forms are all in order, and the ministry will support his citizenship.

4) The Department believes that it has put aside the qualifications which could possibly arise in the Senate against the academic appointment of Dr. Mannheim. On all counts, the Department suggests that the Senate, following the *Act of Appointment* (no 7, in our order of appointment), contact the Ministry to purpose this matter further.

Mannheim must have made a determined effort in his defense before Lederer and Weber, who had felt before that he had not been sufficiently engaged in politics. In his "Letters from Exile" he demonstrates clearly that he was a political refugee who knew what it was to take a political position (cf. Kettler, Meja, Stehr, 1983b: 4, 5).

On 9-4-1926 the Rector wrote to the members of the *Senatus Contractus* that the letter from the Department of Philosophy had convinced him. Alfred Weber shared this view. Not all members of the Senate agreed. Some wanted to discuss the matter again in the assembly. This occured on 3-5-1926. "The appointment of Dr. Mannheim was discussed at length," the minutes read, and making Mannheim's full citizenship a condition for appointment was unanimously defeated. Afterwards the request of the Department of Philosophy that Mannheim be appointed was accepted, six votes against four, Lederer and Alfred Weber being among the six. The *Senatus Contractus* informed the Ministry of Education in Karlsruhe (8-5-1926) that it supported the appointment of Mannheim, and it referred to its letter of 8-2-1926. The ministry confirmed the appointment on 14-5-1926, and on 6 Juni 1926 Mannheim delivered his inaugural address on "The Present Situation of Sociology in Germany."

Did some of the professors fix on Mannheim's Jewishness to impede his appointment, or maybe even to prevent it? There is no overt evidence for thinking so. Apparently the strongest reason for the delay in the appointment was that Mannheim was a foreigner, and the university wished to avoid setting a precedent. Nevertheless, his Jewishness seems to have been a factor in the private convictions of some.

Professor Lederer seems to have taken particular pains to further Mannheim's entry into the university as an extraordinary lecturer. Lederer, married to a Hungarian woman, was a personal friend of Mannheim's. (It is noteworthy that in 1926 they were neighbors; Karl and Julia Mannheim kept house at 6 Landfriedstrasse; the Lederers lived at 8. That the Mannheims could afford this house indicates their financial prosperity). Lederer wrote to the dean of the Department of Philosophy (5-3-1926) that he had conferred with the Minister of the Interior in Baden about Mannheim's naturalization. Two times he mentions in the letter that in the minister's opinion political and religious matters had no bearing on naturalization. He also mentions that the minister had no objections to Mannheim's naturalization. The minister's opinion certainly enhanced the possibility for the appointment. This letter also clarifies, why the Department of Philosophy delayed seven weeks in answering, the reservations raised by the

Senatus Contractus. Apparently the Department of Philosophy wished to enlist the help of the minister, and Professor Lederer was prepared to discuss the matter with him. In any case, in Heidelberg Mannheim made no secret of his Jewishness. In the "Act of Appointment" his religion is listed as "Mosaic"; in other documents he is referred to as "Israelitish."

After his appointment to academia, Mannheim applied for German citizenship. Yet, even this dit not proceed smoothly. In response to the post-World War I flood of refugees from Eastern Europe to the West, the Regional Government of Baden apparently followed a somewhat different naturalization process from Württemberg. The latter contested Mannheim's naturalization, and even though he was living in Heidelberg, under the jurisdiction of Baden. The periodical *German Future (Deutsche Zukunft)* of 5-6-1929 reported on a conflict between the two Ministries of Internal Affairs. Württemberg maintained that anyone living in Germany from only 1920 could not be ready for citizenship. Taking in foreigners on a large scale would mean that "a certain kind of people with a strange culture" would from "foreign sub-cultures" among the German people, and these subcultures would increasingly threaten the German way of life. Baden was of the opinion that, although Mannheim was a Jew, he came from Budapest, was a loyal subject of the Austrian-Hungarian crown, and thus inherited a predominantly German cultural ethos. Mannheim's application statement made the same point: he belonged to the general domain of German culture.

Additional materials about Mannheim's naturalization are to be found in the District Archives for Baden in Karlsruhe. From the archives it seems that Bavaria as well as Württemberg had objections to the naturalization. The Bavarian government wrote that Mannheim was to be counted among "eastern foreigners of dubious origin who had not fulfilled the requirement of a probationary period of at least twenty years." The Baden government replied in a note, lacking both date and inside address, that Mannheim's mother as a born German citizen; after her marriage she had acquired Hungarian citizenship: "The applicant Mannheim was educated by her in the German language." Baden also wrote: "We have to do in the case of Dr. Mannheim with an intellectual of entirely special capabilities, whose academic work deserves the most careful critical attention." To this high praise Baden added further: "He enjoys a significant respect in university circles, and a great number of students register for his classes." Given his "extraordinary intellectual powers and his significant achievements," the government of Baden was of the opinion that the usual twenty-year probationary period could be waived in Mannheim's case. He would be an exeption. After a short time, Württemberg and later Bavaria as well seem to have agreed with the decision of Baden.

After his appointment to the university, Mannheim was naturalized. A short time afterwards he was appointed to the editorial committee of the "Archive for Social Science and Political Science" (*Archives für Sozialwissenschaft und Sozial politik*). From 1928 until 1930 Hans H. Gerth was his assistent. Also

28

worthy of mention is Mannheim's statement in his *curriculum vitae*, drawn up by himself, that before 1926 he had been giving lectures at the "People's College" in Darmstadt; the precise dates are not supplied.

With the citizenship issue behind him, Mannheim's scholarship again came to the fore. In 1928 he spoke on "Competition as a Cultural Phenomenon" for the Sixth Conference of German Sociologists. Alfred Weber and Werner Sombart engaged in discussion with him, and expressed great respect for his report. (An interesting view of Mannheim's relationship to Alfred Weber at this time is provided by Norbert Elias, 1984: 36-48). In the same year Mannheim wrote to Siebeck Publishers in Tübingen to suggest that they publish a book which would include his article "Historicism" (1924), "The Problem of a Sociology of Knowledge" (1925), and a new article as well, "Mind and Community" (about Max Weber). He suggested as title: *A Sociology-of-Knowledge Analysis of the Contemporary Basis for Thought: Three Essays about M. Weber, Troeltsch, and Scheler.* From the exchange of letters with the publisher, it seems that the article about Weber became considerably expanded, and he finally offered it as a book on its own. He judged it would contain some 300 to 350 pages, and would still take several months to complete. After a vacation in Switzerland, Mannheim wrote (27-9-1929) to the Department of Philosophy in Heidelberg, asking to be relieved of teaching responsibilities during the winter semester of 1929-1930, in order to complete the Weber manuscript by the tenth anniversery (1930) of Max Weber's death. The Department's response was positive, as was that of the *Senatus Contractus*, which referred the matter to the Ministry of Culture and Education in Karlsruhe. The Ministry, however, had objections, believing Mannheim to be obliged to give some of the regular instructions. And so Mannheim assumed his teaching position as usual during the winter semester. For whatever reason the Weber book did not appear, nor has the manuscript ever surfaced.

According to the *Personnel and Academic Catalogue* of the university (1926-1927 until 1930-1931), the lectures which Mannheim delivered in Heidelberg were concerned with the following themes: sociology and history, economic and political sociology, the sociology of Max Weber, the sociology of the press and public opinion, the sociology of knowledge, and sociology and phenomenology. In addition, in the winter semester 1928-1929, Mannheim and Alfred Weber organized a seminar about Lukács' *History and Class Consciousness*, the syllabus of which still survives.

Professor in Frankfurt

Early in December 1929, Mannheim received an invitation from the Goethe University in Frankfurt to be the successor to Professor Oppenheimer, who had retired. The *Frankfurter Zeitung* (11-12-1929) knew and reported that Professor Lederer had been the first invited to fill the position, but that he had declined. In a letter to the curators of the university (6-9-1929) the faculty nominated

Hans Kelsen, a philosopher of law, for the position. It seems that discussion about the matter, orally or in writing, must have gone on with the ministry in Berlin, because in a letter dated 4-10-1929, the minister extended the following invitation to the faculty:

> Since Professor Dr. Lederer in Heidelberg has declined the call to the University of Frankfurt, I invite the Faculty of Economics and Social Sciences to appoint as soon as possible the extraordinary lecturer Dr. Mannheim from Heidelberg, to assume the chair lately occupied by Professor Oppenheimer.

It is not clear why the ministry should write this letter. The curators of the university sent back a noteworthy reply:

> The curators have decided, after prolonged debate, to request permission to procure Mr. Kelsen for Frankfurt, if possible, thus making a contrary appointment to Dr. Mannheim impossible.

Like Lederer, Kelsen seems not to have been attracted to the appointment in Frankfurt. And so at last the faculty came back to Mannheim and wrote (27-12-1929) to the ministry in Berlin that the extraordinary lecturer from Heidelberg would indeed be the best qualified successor for Oppenheimer. The letter went on to say that the faculty teaching sociology would have preferred to appoint a sociologist with an orientation toward economics or jurisprudence. According to the faculty, Mannheim was too philosophically inclined – all of which explains its inclination toward Lederer and Kelsen. The faculty also had discussed Th. W. Adorno, but according to the correspondence, he never became a serious candidate. To friends Adorno confided that he was offended at having been passed by.

And so Mannheim was appointed. He wrote a letter (17-12-1929) to the President of the Curators of the Goethe University, Professor Dr. Kurt Riezler, in which he listed a few requests. He very much wanted an independent sociological institute, separate from the Institute of Economics; he also requested a position for an assistant (to be filled by Norbert Elias) and a budget for library. Riezler agreed with these conditions; the ministry concurred and wrote (27-1-1930) that Mannheim would be expected to assume his duties in Frankfurt with the summer semester in 1930.

Soon after the offer from Frankfurt became known in Heidelberg, the dean of the Philosophy Faculty wrote to the Minister of Education in Karlsruhe (10-12-1929), asking whether Mannheim's position in Heidelberg could be improved, so that, in spite of the invitation from Frankfurt, he could give serious consideration to staying in Heidelberg. It seems Mannheim was esteemed. His book *Ideologie und Utopie* had recently appeared. Meanwhile, he had also received teaching assignments in the Institute for Journalism at the University of Heidelberg. In 1929 he became Max Scheler's successor as editor of the series of books entitled *Schriften zur Philosophie und Soziologie* (Publications in

7.　Karl Mannheim (ca. 1930)

Philosophy and Sociology). Although Heidelberg wished to keep him, the minister answered (30-12-1929) that he could not comply with the dean's requests.

His students prepared Mannheim a splendid farewell. They produced a play: *The Clouds* or *Politics as Science*. Löwenthal was one of the writers. The title page mentions only: "Freely adapted from Aristophanes by 'Collective Sociology 1930' " (Appendix 2).

On 1 April 1930 Mannheim became Professor of Sociology in Frankfurt. He invited his good friend Elias to go with him to Frankfurt as his assistant. At the same time Mannheim was named Director of the newly established College of Sociology at the university. In a letter (12-4-1930) the university curators informed the Director of the Institute of Economics:

> On the occasion of the appointment of Professor Mannheim the Honorable Minister decrees that an autonomous College of Sociology shall be established beside the Institute of Economics, to which college Professor Doctor Mannheim is appointed Director. At the same time the Honorable Minister demands that out of the budget of the Institute of Economics a yearly amount of 1000 Marks shall be deposited as a yearly obligation to the College of Sociology.

The College of Sociology was established at the Victoria Alley 17 (the present Senckenberganlage); the College, just as Mannheim's dwelling at West-endstrasse 103, were destroyed in World War II. Both were a stone's throw from the university.

A few more biographical peculiarities. Mannheim wrote (20-5-1930) to the curators:

> Since I have been found unfit for military service by several concurring examiners, I do not possess any of the usual military papers.

Considering his weak health, his rejection for military service is no wonder.

On 22 June 1930 Mannheim, in presence of the rector of university and following the standard procedure, took the oath to support "the Constitution of the German Reich of 11-8-1919 and the Prussian Constitution of 30-11-1920." The oath was confirmed by a handshake from the rector. The oath to the Prussian Constitution was also required because the University of Frankfurt on the Main lies in the district of Hesse, which, at the time, formed a subdivision of the Prussian state.

Colleague and lecturer
Mannheim had little contact with the "Institute for Social Research," which had been founded in 1923 and of which Max Horkheimer became director in 1930. The contacts that obtained were distant but friendly. In his history of the University of Frankfurt, Paul Kluke (1972: 508) writes about a "certain rivalry" between Horkheimer and "the workgroup which has been established around Karl Mannheim, Chairman of Sociology." On opposition to National Socialism they were agreed. Mannheim, however, did not share the strongly Marxist theories of the learned scholars of the Institute: Theodor Adorno, Walter Benjamin, Erich Fromm, Max Horkheimer, Leo Löwenthal, Herbert Marcuse, Franz Neumann, and Karl Wittfogel. Although Mannheim was not attached to a political party, he was sympathetic to the Social Democrats, whereas Horkheimer took a much more critical stand towards this party. Still many of Mannheim's students also called themselves Marxists or Communists.

Mannheim maintained friendly contacts with Löwe and Riezler. He was a very good friend of Paul Tillich (Hannah Tillich, 1973: 143, 147-152), who in 1928 had succeeded Max Scheler upon his death. Though in some ways their relationship was strained, it did not prevent Horkheimer and Mannheim from seeing each other regularly. With Löwenthal, Pollock, Riezler, Löwe, Mennicke, and Tillich, Mannheim and Horkheimer formed a group for discussing societal, political, and academic problems. Mannheim also participated in a discussion group consisting of sociologists, philosophers, theologians who followed dialectical theology, and theologians who advocated Christian socialism: Emil Blum, Emil Brunner, Martin Dibelius, Heinrich Frick, Max Horkheimer, Carl Mennicke, Friedrich Pollock, Kurt Riezler, and Theodor Adorno. At one gathering (27-6-1931) the subject was "Secular Culture and the Missionary Task of Christendom." In this discussion, Mannheim made the following observations, among others:

> I should like to speak for a person, as an example, whom you want to convert when you speak of missions, and specifically he is a person who simply does not know what this conversion can do for him.(...) The word which has taken hold of me and through which I until now have found the connection to positive action is this: In all districts in all parts of the world, to squelch religion as a basic motivating force. (...)
>
> The question is ... why shall I not reformulate these broken-off basic religious principles for my own situation? The answer should be this: The spiritual and religious content can only be expressed in traditional language. The positive counterpart is your response to me: "You can never be finished with those basically religious principles, without selling yourself out to propositions which arose in earlier times, and thus we can offer you a secularized religion, very far removed from the Church and independent from it." But then what becomes of those basically religious principles and what exactly does tradition mean?(...)
>
> With the new discovery of the worn-out elements, the guiding star has not at all passed into oblivion, but has developed into a new one, one within us – and I call this the utopian element in us. (...) Because that which can be preserved out of the past is not the past as such, but rather that which is already present in us, speaking to our contemporary needs and prodding us forward. If I should wish to stop speaking about what is involved in basically religious ideas, the danger would be that I would still be using these basically religious principles by using concepts which had been shaped by earlier religious experience. (...) And so, when I ask what the religious person can give me, who one way or another is bound in his tradition,... or should I ask, what can Protestant theology give me? I should be so afraid in my suspicion and my refusal, that what it can give me is the very dangerous thing: those words which originated in an entirely different situation and which contemporary people would prefer to mock. When these words fairly ring with their erroneous elements, they are more valuable than when the earlier thought forms are accidentally borrowed in. (Albrecht, Trautmann, 1983: 323-325)

These thoughts of Mannheim are important. It will serve us well to keep them in mind in order to understand the concepts in his later work.

Mannheim, according to the description of Kluke (1972: 545), was the first professor at Goethe University to undertake and encourage cross-disciplinary teaching on behalf of his students:

> Since 1931 Mannheim, Adolf Löwe, Ludwig Bergsträsser, and Ulrich Noack established an interdisciplinary group on the subject "The History of Society and Ideas," which could

continue through an indefinite numer of semesters. For example, they held lectures and worked assignments on political problems of the commonwealth, various subjects of social psychology and new educational methods were discussed point by point, and there was an open discussion on early liberalism in Germany. The Nazi regime abruptly ended this much discussed attempt at a new method of working academically.

Tillich also participated in this interdisciplinary seminar on liberalism, which was attended by more than eighty students (Greffrath, 1979: 63).

From the *Catalogue for Lectures and Personnel* (1930-1931 through 1932-1933), it seems that Mannheim lectured on the same subjects as in Heidelberg but supplemented these with cultural sociology, the sociology of social mobility among the intelligentsia, and the origin of modern society and of the typical modern person. In the archives of the library of the University of Keele two sets of extensive lecture notes are preserved. The Subjects: *The Theory and History of Social Classes: Problems and Steps and the History of Culture* and *The Nature of Contemporary Society and the Typically Modern Person* (the first probably from 1931 and the latter from 1932).

Bouman (1974: 178) writes that Horkheimer and Adorno regarded Mannheim's position as too contemplative. He does seem to have a retiring figure. Bouman told me (Spring 1976) that he had received the impression from Horkheimer that Mannheim had been "from one point of view, a shy man." A contrary opinion comes from Salomon (1947: 350): "Karl Mannheim was not a contemplative character." And in another place, Horkheimer said that Mannheim could be a humourous man and was a born teacher, who attracted enthusiastic students to his lectures (Remmling, 1975: 66).

Kettler wrote me (19-7-1979) that Mannheim distanced himself in social settings, was inhibited emotionally, and behaved with formal correctness. In discussions Mannheim's presence was self-confident and dominating. The impression, according to Kettler, was partially caused by Mannheim's view of his own work as a moral, social, and political mission. As advocate for humanitarianism in society, he wanted to provide accurate diagnoses and recommend sound therapies (cf. Kettler, 1967a: 406; 1975: 69; Salomon, 1947: 350).

Finally, a few comments from students. Gisèle Freund says this (1977: 12):

Mannheim always let the distance be felt between him and students. His lectures and seminars were not always easy for me, a beginning student, to follow. He loved, as so many German professors, to clothe his ideas in a terminology that was understandable to his students, a kind of secret language. Norbert Elias was the connecting link between Mannheim and his students.

Ilse Seglow (1977: 17) also contrasts Mannheim to Elias,

Mannheim was probably fundamentally more relativistic, more haunted by the memory of the short-lived Bela Kun revolt in Hungary and the right-wing reaction against it. ... Mannheim was concerned with the main lectures, with large audiences, not only of students but also of visitors from the town's intelligentsia, and with all the varied aspects of university politics (which he did very well). He and his wife, Julia, came from Budapest and always spoke Hungarian when alone. Consequently, as German was not his mother tongue, he was haunted by the fear that he might make mistakes when lecturing in German and Elias often went to his lectures simply to reassure him that he did not make any mistakes (which he didn't). On the other hand, Elias himself was mainly concerned with the problems of students, for which Mannheim had not the time.

Elias could not substantiate all of these memories. He does not remember Mannheim as introverted person; he was easy in social contacts, friendly and out-going. Although he was very busy, he found time for regular conferences with students. According to Elias, it was actually customary that an assistant would maintain almost all of the contact with students. This opinion is shared by Mannheim's assistant in Heidelberg, Hans Gerth (Greffrath, 1979: 60, 61). Elias also remembered that Mannheim regularly received German and foreign colleagues, among whom were Raymond Aron, the French sociologist and philosopher, and the American sociologist Louis Wirth (Chicago), with whom Mannheim discussed the English translation of *Ideologie und Utopie* (interview with Elias, 16-11-1977).

Elias' view is confirmed by S. Baracs, who was born in Budapest and lives in the Netherlands. During the twenties he studied in Frankfurt and had family members and friends who studied in Heidelberg. According to him, in Heidelberg University circles, Mannheim was spoken of with admiration as a learned man, and his upright modesty and his delightful, sometimes comical, company was much praised; "He was somebody who had something that he could be genuinely modest about," said Baracs. His brother living in London, Dr. J. Baracs, told me (27-11-1979) that he would have to contest the opinion of Gesèle Freund and Ilse Seglow. He attended the first seminar given by Mannheim in 1926-1927, on the subject of Lukács' *History and Class Consciousness*. J Baracs called Mannheim a person who was always friendly and modest; he sought contact with students, invited them into his home, and spontaneously lent them books. His lectures were clear, inpiring, and lively (cf. K.H. Wolff, 1981: 324-328).

As to his first important colleague Mannheim knew that Lukács regarded him as a decadent, bourgeois thinker on the basis of Mannheim's publications during the twenties. Still Mannheim respected Lukács very much. In his teaching he devoted a great deal of time to Lukács' works, but criticized the worldview which lay at the basis of his philosophy. The estrangement between the two scholars resulted in their seeing each other very rarely, even in Germany: they had little to say to each other. The last time they met was at a conference in Frankfurt in early 1933, organized by the *Kant Gesellschaft*; Lukács gave two seminars – about the young Hegel and about the dialectical method – and for the last time Mannheim was part of his firend's audience (Gábor, 1983: 10).

Departure from Germany

Although Mannheim had filled out the religion blanks "without religion" on all the forms connected with his appointment at Goethe University, it was widely known that he was of Jewish descent. A pointed linking of his work to that descent came from Professor Dr. E.R. Curtius, who at the time of Mannheim's appointment to academia had been Dean of the Faculty of Philosophy at Heidelberg, and since 1 October 1929 had been Professor of Romance Studies at Bonn. In his *Deutscher Geist in Gefahr* (*German Mind in Danger*, 1932) he warned German intellectuals about Mannheim, who he thought was getting closer and closer to a dangerous sociological approach to a theory of knowledge. Although Curtius denied anti-Semitism, he did acknowledge that he believed that a special relationship existed between sociology and Jewry. (During that time sociology was often regarded as a Jewish discipline, a conception which was strenthened by the fact that many Jews were active in the socialist cause.) Because Jews wanted to preserve their own identity, they did not become full-fledged citizens of the state; moreover, according to Curtius (1932: 79-102), they were not interested in the state at all, but rather in society and in social problems like integration and assimilation. Earlier (1929) Curtius had written an article in the *Neue Schweitzer Rundschau (New Swiss Outlook)*, which attacked Mannheim's *Ideology and Utopia* and denounced Mannheim for following fads, for encouraging nihilism, and for opposing idealism. Mannheim defended himself in a later issue of the *Outlook*, and that essay will concern us again in discussing his theory of knowledge.

Particulary for political reasons Mannheim found the situation too hot. On 30 January 1933 Hitler had become chancellor of the realm and in the elections of 5-3-1933 his National Socialists received 44% of the vote. Soon after January 1933, legislation was in place which restricted freedom and challenged property rights. The Communist Party was deposed first, and in June 1933 the Socialist Party followed. On 7-3-1933 a new law was established "for the restoration of civil servants to their offices"; that is, on the basis of this law, officials who were of non-Caucasian descent or who were opposed to Hitler's National Socialists could be dismissed. Shortly after this law went into effect, Mannheim received a letter (13-4-1933) from the Prussian Minister for Scholarship, Art, and Folk Culture (UI Nr. 753.1):

> On the basis of the "law for the restoration of civil servants to their offices" of 7 April 1933 (RGBL. S. 175ff), I find myself obliged to give you leave of absence from your position with the receipt of this letter, the leave to continue until a final decision is reached. This leave of absence also holds for every kind of activity connected with your discipline or dependent on your position in the university. Your compensation will continue to be paid in the manner it has been until some time in the future.

A copy of this letter went to the curators of the university. The following professors also received a copy: H. Heller, M. Horkheimer, P. Tillich, and A. Löwe.

In a letter to Louis Wirth in Chicago (18-4-1933) Mannheim wrote about his so-called "leave of absence," and asked about getting a position at an American university; he invited Wirth to send his answer to the address of Professor G. Révész, Overtoom 47, Amsterdam. He sent a letter like it to Oscar Jászi, Oberlin College, who again wrote about the matter to Wirth (6-5-1933).

On 1-9-1933 Mannheim was put on "the retired list"; that is, he was retired with a pension. Mannheim had not waited for this decision; immediately after receiving the letter of 13-4-1933, the Mannheims had decided to leave Germany and to go to Révész in Amsterdam. Elias could not remember that they ever talked to others about a possible move. Thus Mannheim joined – with Horkheimer, Tillich, Adorno, Marcuse, Buber, Geiger, Freud, Einstein, Popper, Plessner, and many other intellectuals – the great intellectual flight from Germany (Bleuel, 1968: 220; Bouman, 1969). Between Januari 1933 and January 1939 at least twelve-hundred intellectuals left Germany. From the Goethe University in Frankfurt alone, 108 out of 334 academics (not counting assistants) left the country. According to Bentwich (1953: 1, 4, 10), this was the greatest migration of intellectuals since the Greek intellectuals fled Constantinople in the fifteenth century.

That Mannheim's departure from Germany was undertaken in chaotic haste can be seen from a letter (3-6-1933) from Dr. Kirchner, Director of the Rothschild Library, referring to an earlier letter of 12-5-1933. Mannheim had borrowed a number of books from the library and also some on interlibrary loan, some from foreign libraries. Mannheim had not returned them, and Kirchner invited him to do so before Thursday, 8-6-1933. If he did not, Kirchner would be obliged to "give the matter to the municipal court, which would further conduct an equitable disposition of the case." The rector of the university received a copy of the letter, which is how it has come to my attention. Apparently Mannheim never received it.

His very hasty move may also be inferred from another event. Although he was pensioned off from the university by the government, no pension in fact was paid because he had not yet served in academia for ten years. Counting his years as an extraordinary lecturer, he had accumulated only seven years of service (1926-1933). In a letter (29-9-1933) the curators informed Mannheim that he would continue to receive his salary until 31 December of that year, and that on grounds of duly named reasons he was not able to appeal the matter of pension payments. This letter was returned to the curators, undelivered. It was sent again. In the archives of the Goethe University the following address is to be found: "Londen, Madway 17, with Löwenstein." Apparently, the word had gotten out that Mannheim had fled to London.

Chapter III

Refugee in England

Via Amsterdam and Paris to London

Their precipitous departure from Frankfurt made it impossible for the Mannheims to take all their possessions along with them. The furniture and most of the books were put into storage and finally transported to Londen in 1939. They travelled (apparently in April) to Amsterdam and lodged for a few weeks with Révész, who had become Professor of Psychology at the University of Amsterdam. Afterwards in May they departed for Paris where they visited, among others, Raymond Aron. Although Aron (1935: 75-96) was critical of Mannheim's sociology of knowledge, they had kept in contact. Even in later years they still visited each other.

By letter (11 May 1933) the London School of Economics and Political Science, part of the University of London, invited Mannheim to deliver a commemorative lecture in 1934, dedicated to L.T. Hobhouse, the first professor of sociology at the London School of Economics (from 1907 to 1929), on the fifth anniversary of his death. Mannheim was generally regarded as one of Germany's most eminent sociologists.

The famous economist William Beveridge, Director of the London School, invited Mannheim on 16-5-1933 for postgraduate teaching. Morris Ginsberg, Hobhouse's successor, had taken the initiative. Mannheim answered from Paris (19-5-1933) that he accepted the invitation for the Hobhouse commemoration, and that he would be willing to discuss possibilities for teaching at the London School of Economics.

The Department of Sociology at the University of Chicago discussed inviting Mannheim. From the Hotel Florida in Paris Mannheim (20-5-1933) wrote to Louis Wirth in Chicago that an offer would be attractive. A short time later (29-

5-1933) he sent a telegram to Wirth: "Having offer from New School New York – Please give your advice STOP What about possibilities of Chicago." Wirth telegraphed back: "Advise you to accept New School offer – This will not prejudice Chicago possibilities – University in touch with New School." The "New School" was the New School for Social Research. Mannheim's friend and teacher from Heidelberg, Lederer, who, just as Mannheim, had left Germany in the spring of 1933, had become a professor there and hoped that Mannheim would join him. A month later (21-6-1933) Louis Wirth wrote Mannheim about the possibility of a temporary appointment at the University of Wisconsin.

Meanwhile, the Mannheims had already decided to settle in London, where they arrived on 24 May 1933. They were heartily welcomed, particularly by Ginsberg and Harold Laski. Mannheim wrote to Wirth (26-7-1933) that the reception had been so heartwarming that they had decided to remain in London for the immediate future. He continued to seek a position in the United States, however, and asked Wirth to investigate the possibilities that might occur. He called the London School of Economics "a springboard for something permanent." In a later letter (13-10-1933) he wrote enthusiastically about his contacts with English colleagues.

In the first days after their arrival in London, the Mannheims had lodged with Ginsberg. After that they settled in at the Red Court Hotel at Bedford Place near Russel Square, the location of the Senate House of London University. In 1939 they bought a house at 5 The Park, in a good neighborhood in the northwest of London.

It is noteworhty that in his letter to Wirth (26-7-1933) Mannheim wrote that he was working on a new book which would be entitled *The Sociology of the Spirit*. The publisher J.C.B. Mohr (Paul Siebeck) in Tübingen had requested it. One chapter would be called "Concerning the Generations" and another "Homogeneous Grouping on the Basis of Intelligence and its Meaning for Politics and Culture." Already during his last years in Heidelberg he had proposed a number of articles to the publisher Paul Siebeck, all on the general subject of "The Sociology of Mind." He wrote Wirth how surprised he was that a German publisher dared to bring out a book of his at this time. Mannheim had, evidently, assessed the situation in Nazi Germany correctly. Apparently the publisher also reconsidered because the book never appeared.

It is also noteworthy that Mannheim never makes mention of the possible publication of his essays "The Distinctive Character of Cultural Sociological Knowledge" and "A Sociological Theory of Culture and its Knowability," which were published posthumously under the title, *Structures of Thinking*. Nor does he mention the other essays which he wrote at the beginning of the thirties: "Towards the Sociology of Mind: An Introduction" and "The Democratization of Culture," which together with the essay "The Problem of the Intelligentsia," were published under the title *Essays on the Sociology of Culture* (SC). He makes no mention of another article, "The Emergence of Intellectual Groups from the Changing Structure of Society" ("Die Entstehung der intellektuellen Gruppen aus der sich wandelnden Gesellschaftsstruktur: Teil II." Perhaps Part I is published in SC. The original German texts of these essays have not been preserved in SC (Wolff, 1978: 551, 552; Kettler, Meja, Stehr, 1984).

In May 1933 the faculty of the London School of Economics decided unanimously to accept the proposal of Beveridge and Laski, to deduct two percent of their gross salaries for a fund that "was spent in providing for displaced German teachers" (Beveridge, 1960: 49). In October 1933 Mannheim was temporarily appointed as lecturer in sociology on the postgraduate side for the academic year 1933-1934. The appointment was made possible by the faculty fund and mainly by the financial support of the Rockefeller Foundation.

On 15 December 1933 Mannheim wrote an application for financial support to the Rockefeller Foundation; he asked for a grant for his research project "The Sociological Causes of the Cultural Crisis in the Area of Mass Democracies and Autarchies." He wanted to carry out this research with a team consisting of the following persons: E.K. Bramstedt, N. Elias, W. Falk, H.H. Gerth, E. Manheim, A. van Martin, F. Neumann, S. Neumann, O. Reik, S. Riemer, and A. Salomon. Mannheim had the intention to help these young German scholars to find a job in England. However, the Rockefeller Foundation answered Mannheim that the special fund for aid of German scholars was practically exhausted. His grandly conceived and ambitious plan was rejected because of its staffing cost. The Rockefeller Foundation acknowledged that Mannheim had submitted a proposal of very considerable importance. Therefore, it was willing to revise its judgment another time. If a British institution were to become interested in the program and were to present it as a part of a general project for development of research in the social sciences, some financial support from the Rockefeller Foundation might later be envisaged. Considering the outline of Mannheim's research project we may conclude that part of it was published in articles, in *Man and Society*, and in *Freedom, Power and Democratic Planning*.

On 7 March 1934 Mannheim delivered his memorial address in honor of Hobhouse: "Rational and Irrational Elements in Contemporary Society." A year earlier he had spoken on this topic for the International School of Philosophy in Amersfoort, The Netherlands. In 1934 the London School of Economics extended the temporary appointment for one year. In the following year the appointment was extended to 1938, not only for postgraduate work but also for some undergraduate teaching. During the last mentioned period, the Rockefeller Foundation paid half of Mannheim's salary. All grants of the Rockefeller Foundation made to institutions employing German refugee scholars were conditional on the possibility of permanent absorption of these individuals in to the staffs of these institutions. However, the Rockefeller Foundation, of course, realized that no absolute guarantee could be provided by any institution. Although the London School of Economics had serious financial problems, in 1938 and following years Mannheim received a new appointment.

During World War II the London School moved to Cambridge. Part of the archives of the school was moved to Cambridge and was mislaid; another part remained in London and was either demolished in the violence of the war or are not preserved because of improper precautions. In either case, because the archives are gone, very little is known about Mannheim's stay at the London School of Economics.

In The Netherlands

After Karl and Julia had settled in England, they made a trip every year (concluding with the trip in 1938) to Budapest, to see Julia's mother and others. Often they travelled by way of the Netherlands. Mrs. Judith Révész Laqueur (29-10-1979) told me she remembered that the Mannheims and her parents regularly visited each other during the thirties. In view of the occupation of Czekoslovakia by Nazi Germany (March 1939), the German invasion of Poland, and the declaration of war by France and England on Germany (3-9-1939), a trip to Budapest seemed undesirable that year or thereafter.

When the Mannheims had lived in London for a few years and were in Amsterdam again for a visit, Mrs. Révész also remembered (according to a transcript of an interview of 6-3-1970) that the Mannheims said: "... in London everything bad is considered all right. If you are cold, that is all right. If your front is roasted before a fireplace and you are getting pneumonia from the cold at your back, that is all right. When the food is bad, that is all right." In spite of these critical remarks, which certainly are not evidence of enthusiasm, Mrs. Révész also remembered that the Mannheims generally liked London.

Besides his friendship with Révész, his contacts in university circles also brought Mannheim to the Netherlands in the thirties. Already on 25 October 1932 he had given a quest lecture at the University of Amsterdam on "The Social and Political Meaning of Intelligence" (SPI). At a conference on "The Contemporary Period of Culture," held from 12 to 27 September 1933 and organized by the International School of Philosophy in Amersfoort, Mannheim, according to the program, was to present two position papers: the first on "Structure and Mental Development" and the second on "Laying the Foundation for Social Analysis." From the proceedings of the conference, it seems that the first paper was not delivered. The proceedings do mention that Professor Dessauer from Frankfurt could not deliver his lecture on the subject: "The Nature of Technique, Technique and Society, and Technique and the Economic Crisis." Mannheim served as his substitute on the subject: "Rational and Irrational Elements in Society." Paul Tillich, Carl Mennicke, Buytendijk, Katz and Cassirer were also present as speakers (ANTW).

One year later, from 15 September to 1 October 1934, the International School of Philosophy organized a conference on "Philosophy, World, and Life." Mannheim was one of the speakers along with Martin Buber, Helmuth Plessner, Harold Laski, Georg Gurvitch, Carl Mennicke, and the Amsterdam lawyer Paul Scholten. He spoke on the subject: "The Reconstruction of People." During these years he also gave guest lectures at the universities of Groningen, Leiden, Utrecht, the College of Economics at Antwerp, and at the University of Budapest.

At the time of his visit to Budapest in the thirties he also gave some public lectures. Under the auspices of the Hungarian Cobden Federation he gave a lecture in 1934 on "The Role of Understanding and Passion in Contemporary Society," and in 1936 he lectured on "The Middle Class and the Emerging

8.   Karl and Julia Mannheim (ca. 1935)

Worlds." He also published articles in 1937 in the Hungarian periodical *Szép Szó (True World)* (Gábor, 1983: 11, 13, 14).

England: Democracy at the Boundary Between Two Worlds
At the time of Mannheim's arrival in Great Britain, that country was the center of an empire which included almost one quarter of the world's population: some 500 million people. Of these, 70 million lived in England and Scotland but there unemployment was 23%.

World War I had greatly enhanced the British position in the world market, but England had not grown stronger in the process. British industry had dominated the world market for decades, but England's economic power weakened because it did not keep its technology up to date. Many factories, merchant ships, and coal mines became obsolete; no proper analysis of the situation, and hence no modernization, came about. In addition, scientific and technical research, in which the English had done important pioneer work, was not producing obvious results. Already during the 1930's England was gradually falling behind Germany. The competition with Japan and the United States was disturbing; England lost markets to these countries.

During the period between the world wars, Great Britain, with a few exceptions, was governed by conservatives. The government position was based first of all on maintaining profits and on a protectionist policy of taxing imports. The economic conference of Ottawa (1932) was important in this regard. It strengthened the bonds between the member nations of the British empire. The systems of "imperial preferences" was formulated: marketing advantages between countries in the Empire and import taxes on products from other lands. Many conservative members of Parliament supported this policy, because they themselves were engaged in business and industry, and found these policies advantageous. In the 1930's approximately 79% of the means of production was in possession of 5% of the population. Most workers earned no more than subsistance-level wages; a significant minority fell below that level.

The labor-union movement, so powerful elsewhere, could achieve little, and politicians were proud of the fact that there was no class struggle in England. Under the calm surface of the society, however, the tendencies toward rioting were alive and well, resulting in severe conflicts between workers and the ruling party. On 15 September 1932, 12.000 sailors from the Navy went on strike at Invergordon over a lowering of wages, crippling a substantial part of the Atlantic fleet. At the same time, local hunger marches were dispersed by the police. In August 1932 in Lancashire a strike of 150.000 weavers broke out, also because of a lowering of wages. This strike was followed by another by coal miners. Many more strikes and demonstrations against government policy could be mentioned here.

In 1934 England's trade and shipping picked up considerably, but lasting improvements did not come for mining and industry. After 1936 unemployment began to decrease, because the military advances of Germany led to an arms race and stimulated great industrial activity. The enormous economic problems were never really solved structurally; rather, they came to stand in the shadow of the approaching horror of World War II.

The economic crisis, which first led to social and political unrest and then to demoralization, shattered the confidence that many English people had in free enterprise. No alternative proposals could be expected from the *laissez-faire* philosophy to help the conservative policy of the government. The opposition pleaded for socialistic measures. In the second half of the thirties, students also chose their political parties with a view toward social activism. They made propaganda for the class struggle and at the same time demonstrated against the conservative policy of the government, against British imperialism, and against fascism as the outgrowth of a decadent capitalism. During World War II, these voices did not fall silent, but they were overshadowed by the events of war. At every level of society, discussions took place about pursuing a social and political policy immediately after the war. Thus, already during the war the "Beveridge plan" was formulated – named for the man who was Director of the London School of Economics at the time of Mannheim's arrival in London. The plan revised and expanded social legislation and was implemented after the war. In 1944 the "Education act" of Minister Butler was instituted, which made a start at democratizing education at all levels. By means of publications, lectures, and conversations with leading educators, Mannheim exerted an indirect influence on the realization of this Act. Contrary to the expectations of some, he was actually in favor of preserving the elite traditions of education in England. He was enthusiastic about the "public school" and "grammar school" as the training grounds for "gentlemen." In these respects he seemed a moderate enough reformer.

Soon after the surrender of Nazi Germany, in May 1945, parliamentary elections were held. Led by England's leader during the war, Churchill, the conservative pary nevertheless suffered severe losses; from 358 seats to 198. The new labor government of Atlee and Bevin prepared for decolonization and carried out that policy, bit by bit. But it was not possible for them to realize a more socialistic society, and their economic policies failed in several important respects (Remmling, 1975: 85, 87, 126, 127; R.R. Palmer, 1956: 791-795).

Mannheim observed that an ideological struggle was now breaking out in Great Britain, the same which had worked so violently in the Weimar Republic. Although England still had a functional democracy, he observed problems comparable to Germany's, which could lead to results no less devastating. English democracy balanced on the border between "two worlds": on the one hand England was constrained by strong, living traditions; on the other, by the problems of the economic and political crisis of the thirties, by the problems of the war, and by postwar problems, all of which required solutions other than traditional ones. A democracy of the *laissez-faire*, constrained by tradition, would lead to chaos and, just as in Germany and Italy, would bring about a dictatorship. Mannheim regarded himself called to place his philosophical capacities at the service of English society, and thus at the service of European culture in general. In articles, position papers, and radio lectures he pleaded tirelessly for his "third alternative": planning for freedom and renewing morale. Although he was not actively involved in practical politics, he participated much more strongly in social processes than he had done in Germany. His concern for psychology and pedagogy moved him to deliver lectures for teachers, headmasters, youth leaders, and officials. He delivered addresses on the BBC and published philosophical essays aimed at a popular audience. In these popular essays, he gave more and more attention to religious and

44

theological problems. Dogmatic and rigid religious attitudes, according to him, were barriers not to be underestimated in bringing up children; education should, therefore, be established on the basis of a new social order, which should and could be achieved after World War II. An example of religious and ideological rigidity came to expression in the problem of Northern Ireland. The Irish problem, which had dragged on for centuries already, seemed to be approaching a solution in the thirties. The Irish Free State was established in 1922, but maintained a tense relationship with the government in London. De Valera, chosen in 1932 as President of the Irish Free State, went to London in 1938 to reach an agreement with the English government. These attempts failed, due to the violent opposition from predominantly Protestant Ulster, which did not want to join with Catholic Ireland. Already in the thirties this ideological conflict led to terrorism by Irish in England and Northern Ireland.

Not Immigrant, but Refugee

Although Mannheim never lost the sense of himself as an emigrant from Hungary, it is noteworthy that he now began to speak of himself as a refugee. He asked the question how people who had assimilated two or more cultures could best serve the country where they finally came to live. The first possibility is to be regarded as dangerous monsters; it was how the National Socialists in Germany regarded foreigners. Another possibility is to attempt to be assimilated as much as possible as quickly as possible: Mannheim chose a third possibility:

> ...they try to discover the constructive element which may be present in the very peculiarity of their own position in the world. (...) The peculiar virtue of the emigre is that he has the ability to think more easily of alternative solutions.

Without giving up his own cultural background, the stranger, because of his experience, can make a constructive contribution to all kinds of solutions:

> In this connection, surely, a new constructive task awaits the refugee or any person who has absorbed the mental climate and the scientific thought of different countries – to serve as a living interpreter between different cultures and to create living communication between different worlds which so far have been kept apart. This, of course, is impossible without a very farreaching assimilation of the traditions of the adopting country and a fundamental identification with her aims and existence. But once this can be taken for granted, the constructive task does not consist in being a yes-man to everything but rather... in being a pointer to such developments as have been by-passed by the prevailing tradition and might become relevant in the next phase of development. (FR)

Repeatedly Mannheim warned against the danger of emigrants thinking they held a monopoly on the truth; in the end the English would decide on the direction of events in their land. But particularly in an age of reconstruction, when unusually far-reaching decisions needed to be taken, Mannheim saw a

45

significant task laid out for refugees. He attempted to carry out this task for himself by writing articles and books, speaking in public and on the radio, and participating in discussion groups.

Translation of "Ideology and Utopia" and "Man and Society"
Already at the time of his visit to Mannheim in Frankfurt in 1930, Louis Wirth had discussed with him the possibility of translating *Ideologie und Utopie* into the English *Ideology and Utopia*. Subsequently an elaborate correspondence developed between the two. Although Mannheim's brother-in-law, Paul Kecskemeti, had already begun with a translation of the first two chapters, Edward Shils, in cooperation with Wirth and in consultation with Mannheim, undertook the whole translation as his own responsibility. Wirth provided a draft of a Preface for the English version which was rewritten and completed by Shils.

Two topics out of Mannheim's correspondence with Wirth and Shils deserve notice. First, Mannheim wrote Shils (25-3-1936) that he had suggested several changes in translations, while reading the English manuscript. The very accurate translation by Wirth had been changed by Mannheim at a number of crucial points. For instance, the concepts of *Geist* and *Falsches Bewusstsein* were sometimes rendered by Mannheim respectively as "mind" (rather than "spirit") and "invalid ethical attitude" (rather than "false consciousness"). Although these changes were not rigorously carried out through the whole text, it is clear that Mannheim translated a number of typically German philosophical terms with a psychological and pragmatic twist. In the discussion of *Ideology and Utopia* I shall discuss this matter more carefully. The second point is that the English edition was expanded with a new first chapter and with an already published article, "Sociology of Knowledge," from Alfred Vierkandt's *Dictionary of Sociology* (1931). Mannheim took pains to make the English version as accessible as possible to English readers, who generally do not know the German philosophical tradition. For this reason he preferred a totally new format for the English edition. On this subject he wrote (15-2-1936) a lengthy clarifying letter to Wirth (see Appendix 3).

In 1935 Mannheim's *Mensch und Gesellschaft im Zeitalter des Umbaus (Man and Society in an Age of Reconstruction* appeared in German from the Dutch publisher A.W. Sijthoff in Leiden. Part I of this book contained the commemorative address in honor of Hobhouse, which also had been published as an independent book at Oxford University Press. Much of the material from other sections of the book had also already been published in the form of learned articles (for further information see the bibliography). This book caught the attention of Western Europe. In spite of criticism leveled against it, which will be discussed in Part IV of this book, it was generally received as a sensationally good book.

Apparantly Mannheim, immediately after the appearance of the German *Man and Society*, had already considered the possibility and the desirability of having it appear in English. In the archives of the London publisher Routledge and Kegan Paul (at that time Routledge and Sons) a letter from Mannheim (23-3-1938) is to be found, in which he spoke about a publication which he called *Man and Society in an Age of Re-organisation*. According to the letter, he seemed to expect the book in the fall of 1938. The publisher had given *Man and Society* to Lewis Mumford for evaluation, and according to a note in the publisher's archive, Mumford thought the book important philosophically and relevant politically. In addition Mumford called Mannheim "one of the foremost of modern sociologists, the first to develop to this point the new sociology which had many followers already in this country and abroad." Also, Mumford found that as a whole this new book was more readable than *Ideology and Utopia*, which had appeared in English translation in 1936.

Although Edward Shils took the responsibility for the translation of *Man and Society*, Mannheim himself took care of preparing the final draft. He wished to include some new chapters in the English version. To prepare the final draft of the manuscript was a far greater task than he had anticipated; because of his many duties at the London School of Economics he had too little time to work at it. He wrote this to the publisher, and in a letter of 3-5-1939 he let the publisher know that he could not finish the manuscript until September 1939. The publisher responded by return mail (4-5-1939) and wrote that they were very much disappointed with this information; they had already announced the book. Especially the expanded bibliography, which would appear at the end of the book, seemed to cost much time and worry. He wrote the publisher (23-10-1939) that he had already been working on this bibliography for years.

In the summer of 1939 Routledge heard the rumor that the publishing house of Harcourt and Brace in New York was eager to prepare an American edition of Mannheim's new book and had offered him a sizable honorarium. There is no way of finding out exactly what transpired between Mannheim and the two publishers. Apparently the publishers found a way fo cooperating together, which led to *Man and Society*'s coming out in England and in the United States, and to Mannheim's receiving an honorarium from Harcourt-Brace as early as 1939. He wrote this to Routledge (29-10-1939) and added that he now had enough money to give him time to prepare the manuscript for another book which could appear in English. This book would consist in part of an essay which had already been published in German. In the letter of 29-10-1939 he gave the title of this publication as *Sociological Approaches to the Study of History*, a topic that had occupied him for a long time. He had previously published articles on the topic, but increasingly felt need for a systematic presentation of the matter. In a letter to Routledge (17-5-1937) he named the plan. A section of this study would be entitled "The Social Structure of Romantic and Feudalistic Conservatism"; that part of the manuscript went to the publisher for approval. But the book never appeared. Fragments of it are to be found among the works which were published posthumously.

Meanwhile, he had completed the manuscript of *Man and Society*. In October 1939 he corrected the galley-proofs – quite heavily, the publisher complained (28-10-1939). The same happened with page-proofs; with layout completed, the publisher wrote (20-12-1939): "... on looking them over we find they are heavily corrected and it is advisable to revise as we think many of the additions may overrun the pages and upset your index." We may conclude that Mannheim did not restrict himself to correcting typing mistakes but added editorial comments and amplified the thought. In the early spring of 1940 *Man and Society in an Age of Reconstruction* appeared.

Intended Travel to the United States

During the summer and fall of 1939, Mannheim corresponded with Wirth about the visit he planned to make to the United States in 1940. Mannheim planned to arrive there at the end of March. Wirth arranged his appointments with colleagues and universities. The Rockefeller Foundation gave a grant to the New School for Social Research in New York to enable it to invite Mannheim to come to the United States. He would also give guest lectures at Columbia University in New York; at the University of Chicago; at the School of Religion at Berkeley, California; at Swarthmore College in Pennsylvania; at the University of Wisconsin at Madison; at the University of Mexico City; and possibly at Harvard and Yale. He would give lectures on the following subjects: 1. Social-psychological Problems of Planning; 2. Conservative, Liberal, and Radical Thought; 3. The Middle Class; 4. The Intellectual; 5. The Problem of Social Selection in Planned Society; 6. Freedom and Planning; 7. The Striving for Success: Its Psychological and Economic Significance; 8. The Sociology of Knowledge; and 9. Conflicting Ideologies in Contemporary Society.

The Director of the London School of Economics, Professor A.M. Carr-Saunders, inquired whether the Rockefeller Foundation would be in a position to help Mannheim to spend a whole year in the United States. Carr-Saunders felt committed to maintain Mannheim's readership in sociology at the London School as long as he had not received the offer of an equivalent position elsewhere. He was convinced of the very great intellectual capacity of Mannheim and his undoubted brilliance. In a letter of 19 September 1939 Carr-Saunders wrote to Mr. Tracy B. Kittredge of the Rockefeller Foundation that it was most unlikely that the School would be able to use Mannheim's teaching services in war since his particular subject was one which only a few students took. Although the Rockefeller Foundation rejected Carr-Saunder's request, Mr. Kittredge wrote a letter (16 November 1913) to Herbert Blumer, a sociologist at the University of Chicago, and also to other sociologists in the United States, and asked whether some American Department of Sociology would be interested in hiring Mannheim. Blumer answered (9 January 1940) that he

9. Karl and Julia Mannheim (ca. 1940)

discussed this question with some colleagues and that he was very sceptical about Mannheim's possibilities in the United States.

In the spring of 1940 Mannheim cancelled the trip and wrote Wirth that he hoped to come in the summer of 1941. He gave as his reason "a few complications" regarding his application for citizenship in England (6-7-1938). They were not serious complications, but his naturalization took longer than planned. With the outbreak of the war, the bureaucratic wheels turned even more slowly than usual. At the beginning of Juli 1940 he was finally naturalized. But Mannheim never made the projected trip to America; his work at the University of London was expanding considerably.

To the Institute of Education

From the catalogues of the London School of Economics (1933-1934 through 1939-1940) it seems that Mannheim lectured on the general theme of "Social Structure" and in connection with it these various topics: the group and the individual, social powers, social integration, institutions, sociology and history, modern society, and political sociology. Each year he expanded his handling of these topics, particularly in a psychological direction. Two of the courses he gave in 1935 were "Historical Sociology" and "Woman's Place in Society." Judging from his expanded notes (preserved in the archives of the University of Keele) he treated, along with other topics, the sociological and psychological

49

consequences of male domination and the psychological aspects of sexuality. Interested in the problems connected with the reconstruction of society, he realized more and more that he needed to incorporate social psychology for his sociological analysis. He held public lectures and published articles on problems concerned with social psychology and the sociology of child rearing. In 1941 he had joined the International New Education Fellowship (today, the World Education Fellowship), at that time under the chairmanship of J.A. Lauwerys. Mannheim presented position papers for this society and took active part in the discussions.

In his study *Man and Society in an Age of Reconstruction*, he not only deepened the psychological side of his sociological studies, but also placed psychological study in a sociological and historical perspective. Mannheim's publications on these subjects attracted attention and were esteemed by many. Professor F. Clarke, Professor at the Institute of Education at the University of London, admired Mannheim's insights and invited him (in a letter of 21-10-1941) to become a part-time member of his staff; Mannheim would be responsible for giving instruction in the sociological aspects of child rearing. He was to have three tasks: 1. from eight to twelve lectures for "diploma-course students" with the possibility of additional group discussions; 2. seminars with student papers, the students to be MA candidates who met on Saturdays; 3. the supervision of MA students who were engaged in research projects in sociology. Mannheim answered by return mail (23-10-1941) that he was happy with the offer, because "I feel that your Institute is bound to develop into a center of intellectual reconstruction."

Although the matter was swiftly concluded between Clarke and Mannheim, the Director of the London School of Economics, Professer A.M. Carr-Saunders, had some objections. He was of the opinion that he must disapprove of Mannheim's salaried part-time position because Mannheim was employed at the London School of Economics on a full-time basis. Opposite to his earlier expectations he feared that Mannheim's work at the London School of Economics would be crowded out. Moreover, the London School of Economics moved to Cambridge during the war, but the Institute of Education moved to Nottingham. Because both institutes were parts of the University of London, Carr-Saunders did not want to refuse to cooperate, and the London School of Economics gave Mannheim permission to work part-time at the Institute of Education, but only during the summer semester of 1942. After that the matter would be judged anew. Above all, Clarke was not to get the impression that the terms of employment would gradually be increased, because Carr-Saunders was of the opinion that it was a highly irregular situation.

The theme Mannheim treated during the summer semester of 1942 was "Education and Present-day Society." Professor W.A.C. Stewart (Keele University) and Dr. H.G. Schenk, whose wife attended Mannheim's lectures, told me that Mannheim was very popular among the students. Clarke worte (1947c):

It is not easy to describe the marked effect that his teachings had, particularly on the keener and abler students. The cliche that he opened a new world to them would be false and insufficient. He did something of more immediate importance; he illuminated for them the world in which they actually were. So keen was the interest that his teaching aroused that I even had complaints from colleagues to the effect that students were neglecting other work in the pursuit of the new interest that Mannheim had aroused. Advanced students who came under his guidance in their more socialized studies can testify to the value of what they derived form his scholarly judgement and his vast store of knowledge.

But is was not only the matter of his teaching that proved so effective, the manner of it was even more so. The gentle, whimsical smile with which he met the eager questioner or objector, and the quiet humor which so often spiced his answers can fairly be described as all-conquering. I have seen many teachers of many kinds, but I cannot recall one who had to the same extent Mannheim's happy gift of making every pupil feel at once that he was genuinely interested in him . I suspect that the secret lay somewhere in that combination of a rich natural sweetness with inexhaustible patience.

Professor J.A. Lauwerys, Professor at the Institute of Education, confirmed the opinion of Clarke; he wrote me (17-9-1980): "Karl Mannheim was one of the most 'charismatic' lecturers I've ever met or heard… our students hung on his words, fascinated and hypnotised." The observations of E. Shils also deserve attention. He wrote me (25-3-1981): "Mannheim seems to have been, from what I was told by those who studied under him in the early 1930's, an extremely popular lecturer. He was eager to be liked and tried to please the students. He selected those students who were favourably inclined toward him, encouraged them, paid personal attention to them, perhaps flattered them."

Professor W.A.C. Stewart, who at the time was one of Mannheim's students at the Institute of Education, confirmed Clarke's view without reservation. Mannheim seemed always to be carefully prepared for his lectures. The students were of the opinion that he had written out every word. Whoever inspects his lecture notes (to the extent that they are preserved, they are in the archives of the University of Keele) sees that he usually had summarized his lecture material in a number of catchwords; only a few of his sentences were written out entirely. The most important points were underlined in red pencil. Very much bibliographical material is carefully listed in the lecture notes. (A noteworthy peculiarity is that Mannheim drew pictures in the margins of his lecture notes: little dolls and human faces.) Although Mannheim mastered the grammar of English exceptionally well, he had a strong German accent and was sometimes hard to follow. Still, he engaged students by means of the urgency and moral intensity with which he presented his material.

Clarke had plans to attach Mannheim to his Institute of Education permanently. He wanted Mannheim to acquire the chair for "Sociology of Education." After Mannheim's death Clarke wrote (1947c): "Mannheim had something to say that was of urgent importance for the future of English education." Nevertheless, Mannheim's work at this institute continued to be limited. The

London School of Economics gave him permission to work at Clarke's Institute of Education only during the summer semesters of 1943 and 1944. The theme of his lectures remained constant, even though he continued to make them more elaborate.

Not only colleagues and students, but others also esteemed his work. In 1936 he had sent a copy of his *Ideology and Utopia* to Lord A.D. Lindsay, form 1935-1938 Vice-chancellor of Oxford University and after that Chairman of the Oxford Joint Recruiting Board. Lindsay invited him for a visit, which he described later in his biography:

> He came; I had a free week-end and we talked to our hearts' content, ranging over our whole social theories. I, while welcoming and interested in all he said, thought him too systematic, too much of a planner. He thought me too empirical, too intuitive; but each was interested in the other's view. That was the beginning of a warm friendship between us. He sent me his writings and I sent him mine and we continually exchanged ideas. (D. Scott, 1971: 266)

The principal difference of insight between Lindsay and Mannheim was that Lindsay had an organic view of society; he wanted to attack the most urgent social problems and for the rest trusted in the essential health of society as a whole. Mannheim, on the other hand, was of the opinion that social problems cannot be isolated and localized; as an "interdependent thinker," he sought attention for the structural problems of society, which in his opinion, was very seriously ill. In spite of the difference of approach, Lindsay was of the opinion that Mannheim possessed a valuable combination of knowledge and wisdom, and that his sociology was of great importance for England (D. Scott, 1971: 266).

Mannheim and Ginsberg

Although Clarke and others esteemed Mannheim's work, the criticism of others did not lag far behind. Indeed these can be seen in the failure of the London School of Economics to hold on to Mannheim and to secure a professorship for him. While the financial situation of the school did not allow it, the truth is that the London School of Economics did not fight to get Mannheim a professorship. Sociology was not free from attack there. Already Hobhouse and after him, Ginsberg, were criticized by Beveridge, who promulgated a positivistic approach to philosophy and pleaded for empirical and quantifiable research (Collini, 1979: 248). In the 1930's the School was more interested in developing empirical sociology, and Mannheim had not the particular qualifications necessary for this empirical orientation. Moreover, although he was a popular lecturer at the Institute of Education, he had a very few students at the London School of Economics. From the correspondence between the London School of Economics and the Rockefeller Foundation we know that Carr-Saunders had the opinion that Mannheim would possibly be able to find a chair of sociology elsewhere before 1940 which could enable him to develop his own particular type of work.

Moreover, the relationship between Mannheim and Ginsberg had cooled over the years. During the thirties Ginsberg had exerted himself on behalf of Jewish intellectuals from Germany and other European countries. He secured English academic positions for them; he had helped Mannheim, too. The distance that grew between them was partially due to the difficulty Ginsberg had accepting Mannheim's great prestige among colleagues and students and popularity outside of academia. Ginsberg was at the time the only Professor of Sociology in England. As sociologist and social philosopher he had an international reputation. Nevertheless, he came to stand in Mannheim's shadow. Ginsberg was also disappointed in Mannheim. The London School of Economics had expected that Mannheim would lecture on the sociology of Western Europe, especially Germany. Instead, Mannheim worked especially at a broadening and deepening of his own sociology and social philosophy, and he did not distinguish between these two. According to the strict theoretician Ginsberg, Mannheim was too casual about drawing social-philosophical conclusions from sociological argumentation. In addition, Ginsberg was of the opinion that Mannheim's publications in England were too superficial and often had the style of popular philosophy. The fundamentally scholarly investigations which Mannheim had demonstrated in his German publications – and Ginsberg (1948: Chapter V) was among the first to be impressed by this early scholarship – was lacking in his English publications. In the twenties Mannheim had published articles in the most prestigious scholarly journals in Germany and in 1932 had published an article in *The American Journal of Sociology*. He no longer wrote articles on this level in England, and he never published anything in the English sociological journals: *Sociological Review* and *British Journal of Sociology*. He delivered many popular lectures on scholarly topics for audiences not educated at the universities. These activities did not fit in at all with Ginsberg's style of pursuing his discipline, for not only did he have little concern for the problems that engaged Mannheim, but neither did he share Mannheim's intense moral involvement with problems. Also, for Ginsberg, the agnostic, Mannheim's participation in discussion groups with religious people, Anglicans and Presbyterians, was incomprehensible.

The characterizations of Shils (letter of 25-3-1981) help to clarify the problem:

> Ginsberg was a shy person, lacking in self-confidence, and very sceptical in his attitude toward contemporary sociology. (...) Mannheim was a very different sort of person. He constructed generalizations easily and not always with precision or logical coherence. He expressed his views in dramatic terms and with the appearance of self-assurance.
>
> He [Ginsberg] was not a flatterer and he could not become friendly with students as easily as Mannheim could. (...) Ginsberg might have felt that Mannheim was winning away his students, and perhaps even winning them away by what he regarded as "cheap" and "demagogic" methods.

At the same time, according to his critics, Mannheim never totally adjusted to the English way of doing scholarship and specifically not with English sociology. Although he tried his best to orient himself to the English and American literature in the field of the social sciences, he remained essentially a German academician who sought to incorporate elements of English and American sociological scholarship into his work. Typical of Mannheim's faulty perception of the English social sciences was his estimate of these as predominantly descriptive disciplines, devoid of all theoretical traditions. This judgment brought him into direct conflict with Ginsberg (Kettler, Meja, Stehr, 1984: Chapter III). Although during his life in England Mannheim became more and more seriously interested in problems of anthropology, psychology, child rearing, and morale, we must recall that he was first and foremost a sociologist, oriented toward philosophy and history. This is clearly expressed in a letter from him to Clarke (17-1-1943), in which he acknowledges his debt to Max Weber, expecially because Weber had taught him to combine sociology and history. The study of contemporary society is greatly advanced when it takes whatever it can from history, provided history is also studied with the help of sociological concepts and with sociological statements of problems. Not only does history need sociology, but sociology needs history every bit as much, according to Mannheim; if sociology goes its own way, "there will be only ad-hoc sociologies."

It is important to pay some attention to Mannheim's performance at the time of British conferences of social scientists in 1935 and 1936. The first conference took place in September 1935. The theme was "The Social Sciences: Their Relations in Theory and Teaching." One of the lecturers was T.H. Marshall, Mannheim's colleague at the London School of Economics, who clearly voiced his suspicions regarding interdisciplinary academic work. Mannheim lectured on "The Place of Sociology" (PS), defending the thesis that sociology is a basic discipline for all the social sciences. Ginsberg complimented Mannheim on his lecture, but his own lecture was totally different and, as such, was critical of Mannheim's position. It criticized idealistic theses and a priori theoretical systems in sociology, and defended an empirical responsibility on the part of a sociologist for his work. Without mentioning Mannheim's name, Ginsberg asserted that a systematic sociology does not deserve support as a basic science for all other social sciences, at least not until the results in the fields of physiology and psychology are more familiar.

At the time of the conference of sociologists in 1936, Ginsberg spoke about "Rational and Irrational Elements in Human Behaviour." The similarity of this title to that of Mannheim's Hobhouse lecture (1933) and his lecture in the Netherlands (1933), "Rational and Irrational Elements in Contemporary Society," is remarkable. Ginsberg states that the word *rationality* and *irrationality* are used with a bewildering pluriformity of meanings. This pluriformity apparently is the result of the lack of a generally accepted theory about the meanings of these words and about the value judgments which play a role in social philosophy. Ginsberg juxtaposed his opinion sharply against Mann-heim's, and declared that "rational action" is ultimately the same as "right action," that is, purposeful activity which is directed toward satisfying human needs. Mannheim had critically contrasted this purpose-oriented or functional rationality with a substantial rationality in all social processes, to the detriment of human insight.

Mannheim also gave a lecture at this conference, but it is remarkable that he did not go into the distinction, so important for Ginsberg, between social philosophy and sociological knowledge. Because he could have known that Ginsberg ascribed great value to the formation of theories in sociology, it was rather defiant and not very sensitive on Mannheim's part to speak about the tendency in English sociology to describe, to gather statistical data, and to prevent the society from practising historical and theoretical analysis. It was defiant and provocative, because Mannheim himself did not examine the con-tent of Ginsberg's critical comments, and he made no effort to do so. All of this must have been painful for Ginsberg, and must have furthered the estrange-ment between both of them (cf. Kettler, Meja, Stehr, 1984: Chapter III; cf. Elias, 1984).

In spite of Mannheim's efforts to be integrated into the intellectual climate of England, it is understandable that Kettler and others see Mannheim's position as resembling that of many other scholars who have left their native lands: "They found themselves forced to choose between accepting a role as alien and esoteric prophets, praised for the 'heuristic' value of their work for the ongoing scholarly enterprise but not as contributors to the going concern, or recasting their thought into modes whose capacities for subtlety they could not easily master" (Kettler, Meja, Stehr, 1984: 158).

Some colleagues, however, simply dismissed this criticism about Mannheim. In an undated article about Mannheim, preserved in the University of Chicago Library, Clarke wrote that in a short time Mannheim learned how to operate in the English culture and with the English mind; he was an Englishman among Englishmen. Révész wrote (1947:3): "It is characteristic of his personality that he understood the English mentality as thoroughly as probably no other foreigner."

Another point of criticism was that he took a less active part in administrative and organizational activities at the London School of Economics than his colleagues expected of him. Some colleagues were particularly disappointed in him during World War II, when the School of Economics moved to Cambridge temporarily, requiring instructional and administrative planning. They were irritated by his self-confident attempts to exert his influence on the policy of the London School of Economics.

For these reasons it is not strange that the London School of Economics had reservations about Mannheim's relation with the Institute of Education and made no attempt at all to secure a professorship for him. That they gave their approval to Mannheim's involvement there was in large measure due to the friendship between Clarke and Carr-Saunders. According to Lauwerys, Ginsberg was embittered in the case of Mannheim and seems to have worked against Mannheim's appointment to the Institute of Education. This distancing was a painful experience for Ginsberg as well as for Mannheim. They did not speak to third parties about each other; that is, they preferred not to talk about each other, but if such talk came about, their attitude and choice of words were cool and objective.

Difficult Years

In 1940 Mannheim was invited to become the editor of a series of books under the general title: *The International Library of Sociology and Social Reconstruction*, brought out by the London publishing house of Routledge and Kegan Paul. In this capacity he wrote to various colleagues, inviting their contributions; among these was Professor H.R. Hamley from the Institute of Education, whom he invited to write a book about bringing up children. Mannheim considered such a study of the utmost urgency in a changing society. In the *curriculum vitae* which he kept up-to-date for the Institute of Education, Mannheim wrote that in this series of books "I try to develop the Education Section as fully as possible, and correlate it with philosophical, psychological, and historical research." Elsewhere he wrote:

> The Library is meant as a platform for the exchange of ideas and experiences between English, American and continental scholarchip. Its contributors are English, American, Swedish, German, Czech, Hungarian and Chinese and, as the series is also being published in the U.S.A. and preparations are being made for publication on the continent, it equally well serves the purpose of bringing the thoughts of other countries to this country and of disseminating British ideas in other parts of the world. (FR)

The publisher put similar sentiments into his announcements of the series. Mannheim also planned to publish a book about Dilthey, an edition of the works of Lukács, and other pieces. From a correspondence between Lord Lindsay, one of the members of the Library's Advisory Board, and Mr. T. Murray Ragg, the responsible publisher from Routledge, it appears that Mannheim's plans did not always receive their support. Lindsay wrote that the quality of the books in the series was rather uneven, and that Mannheim never sought counsel from anyone in judging the manuscripts. Murray Ragg stated in a letter that he as publisher had rejected at least a dozen of the suggestions made by Mannheim (Archives of Routledge and Kegan Paul). However, Mannheim assumed his task as editor with the utmost seriousness. On 9-4-1943 he wrote to Louis Wirth about finding an American publisher to bring out the "International library" for an American audience: "When I planned the series, one of my main aims was to make it an organ of exchange of ideas where the American contribution would play a considerable role." Later these books were brought on the American market by the New York branch of Oxford University Press.

Although Mannheim's work was admired by many, the first half of the 1940's were difficult for him and in many ways uncomfortable. His precarious health and frequent illnesses made travel between London, Cambridge, and Nottingham difficult; now and then he was also required to travel to Oxford for lectures. In addition there were the loss of the professorship he so much desired and the strained relationship with Ginsberg. He was also disappointed in the policy of The Royal Institute of International Affairs (Chatham House, London). This institution formulated the plan to publish a series of books about democracy, beginning in 1941. Provisionally, a subcommittee of the Publications Committe had decided to invite Mannheim to write one of the books. He was informed about this decision soon after it had been made and was to receive a generous honorarium. Lack of clarity and a misunderstanding delayed the final decision for more than a half year. The question was whether the plans of the committee for the contents of the book corresponded with Mannheim's intentions. Lord Lindsay, the good friend of Mannheim already mentioned, played a conspicuous role in the decision-making process. He took Mannheim's side. In a letter on 11-6-1941 he wrote to Miss M. Cleeve, secretary of The Royal Institute, that the Institute was too slow in this matter. He continued that the more he saw Mannheim, the more he was impressed by Mannheim's capacity to adapt himself to the English atmosphere and understand it better. In the same letter Lindsay mentioned a conversation in which Mannheim had confessed to being worried about his future in England and to be considering a move to the United States.

In October 1941 the subcommittee decided that Mannheim would write a short book on the following subject: "The Essentials of Democratic Planning." Because Mannheim had set up a research project at the London School of Economics on the subject of "Social Planning," he agreed to have the book finished by the end of 1942. Nevertheless, illness and the press of duties interfered. According to the plan which he formulated and the notes which he took for this book in 1941, we may conclude that his first posthumously published work, *Freedom, Power, and Democratic Planning*, is the execution and elaboration of what was first conceived as his little book for this series.

Concern for the Christian Religion
On New Year's Day 1945 Mannheim was officially placed in the service of the Institute of Education on a half-time basis. On 1 October 1945, he became a fulltime Professor of Eduction at the University of London, with special responsibility for the sociology of education. With this promotion he became the successor to Professor Clarke. In connection with his preparation for the latter appointment, Mannheim wrote a *curriculum vitae*, already mentioned, with a list of his publications and of three works in progress: 1. *Planned Society and the Problem of Human Personality* (an elaboration of a critical report), 2. *History of the Concept of the State as an Organism* (an elaboration of a lecture

10.   Mannheim's study at home: 5 The Park, London

delivered in Cambridge), 3. *Essentials of Democratic Planning* (on the invitation of The Royal Institute of International Affairs).

None of these projected works appeared under such titles. Apparently they were incorporated into works that came out posthumously under other titles. This also holds for various critical reports and speeches which he delivered. The *curriculum vitae* mentions the following institutes and societies for which he spoke: London School of Economics, Manchester College (Oxford), Cambridge University, Institute of Education (London), International Gathering of Friends' Social Service Council (Woodbrook), Ethical Society (London), Masaryk Society (Oxford), British Psychological Society, Association of Psychiatric Social Workers (London), Institute for the Scientific Treatment of Delinquency, Royal Institute of International Affairs, Research Unit (BBC), Conference of Allied Ministers of Education, Conference of Federal Union (Oxford), New Education Fellowship Conference (Oxford), Youth Leaders' Conference (Oxford), and the University of Newcastle. The topics on which he lectured at these events all pertained to the crisis in Western Civilization, social change, planning, democracy and to related problems of a psychological, sociological, and ethical nature.

Mannheim gave also radio lectures about ethics on the BBC between 24 September and 19 November 1943; between 19 January and 23 March 1945 he

58

gave ten radio lectures about "What is Sociology?" Again Mannheim was looking for opportunities to bring sociology into the reach of the common man. More publications in sociology should be available for the growing number of people interested in sociology (P:xi). He wanted to demolish the ivory tower of academia and to narrow the gap between academia and society.

A few of his speeches appeared in 1943 under the title *Diagnosis of Our time.* The last chapter of this book was originally written as a position paper for a discussion group called "The Moot," made up of a few colleagues, theologians, clergymen, high officials in the Ministry of Foreign Affairs, and writers (DT: 100). The group was formed in 1938; among those who were active in its formation were J.H. Oldham, editor of the *Christian Newsletter*, and William Temple, at first Archbishop of York (1929-1942) and later of Canterbury (1942-1944). The group met four times per year, during weekends. Members concentrated their discussions on the crisis of Western culture, politics, the nature of social change, and the meaning of Christianity in society. The papers read at the group had a confidential character and often led to further correspondence between the members. That these discussions and letters were fruitful and stimulating can be seen from the fact the Mannheim expanded his first essay called "Planning for Freedom" into part V of *Man and Society*, and that he published his position paper "Toward a New Social Philosophy," together with a few other critical reports and articles, under the title *Diagnosis of Our Time*. A position paper by Clarke, *Education and Social Change*, was published in book form in 1940 with the same title. Mannheim had become a member of "The Moot" already in 1938. That he was invited to join was in part due to the fact that he was generally active in attending conferences, in delivering public lectures, and in sending copies of his books to people who occupied key positions in the society – sending them, moreover, at his own expense and initiative. Among others, Temple received copies. Mannheim attended all meetings of "The Moot" and at discussions feel naturally into a position of leadership (Clarke, 1947c; Kojecky, 1972: 237-239; Hodges, 1970: 106,107). Other leaders of the group were Lord Lindsay, member of the Presbyterian Church and oriented politically toward the left wing of the Labor Party; Oldham, also a Presbyterian and on the political left; and the writer J. Middleton Murry, a Christian pacifist. None of the participants can be considered far left. The majority would have considered themselves moderate leftists. To the more orthodox flank of the organizations belonged the poet and literary critic T.S. Eliot, who in 1948 received the Nobel Prize for literature; in the discussions he directed the attention of the group to discovering the meaning of the Christian tradition. Also participating were C. Dawson, C. Fenn, H.A. Hodges, G.B. Shaw, W. Oakeshott, and A.R Vidler. Sometimes the members of "The Moot" welcomed a guest to join their discussion, for instance on 11 May 1939, Jacques Maritain, the Roman Catholic philosopher. Until 1940 Adolph Löwe also was a member of the group. In 1944 Michael Polanyi joined; in Budapest, he along with Mannheim, had been a member of the Galileo group. In July 1947, a half year after Mannheim's death, "The Moot" assembled for the last time.

It is worthy of note that at the February meeting in 1940 tensions arose among the members concerning the relationship between thinking and doing. Particularly Mannheim argued that the exchange of ideas in "The Moot" ought to be translated into actions: "... a revolution from above must be initiated." In the next meeting (April 1944) he explained his position more precisely:

> The Germans, Russians, and Italians are more advanced than we are in the techniques of managing modern society, but their purposes are wrong and even atavistic. We may look to elite groups in our society, e.g., the Moot, or enlightened Civil Servants, to use these techniques for different ends.

He continued:

> We want to mobilize the intelligent people of good will in this country who are waiting for a lead. At the same time there must be a popular movement to back what the elites are doing. You cannot build up a great movement without the dynamism of social leadership. I am amazed by our lethargy. (Kojecky, 1972: 174, 175)

Although Clarke, Hodges, and Löwe sympathized with this position, Middleton Murry, Vidler, and others entertained second thoughts. At the meetings which followed, the members of "The Moot" remained divided on this issue (Kojecky, 1972: 163-197; cf. Kettler, Meja, Stehr, 1984: Chapter IV).

Various friends and colleagues criticized Mannheim for participating in this group of religiously oriented thinkers. His friends the Hajnal family, who also were of Hungarian extraction and lived in the Park near the Mannheims, warned him that in their opinion this Christian group was after something quite different from Mannheim and were activated by motives far different from his. Therefore, he should not allow himself to be identified with this group. Yet Mannheim remained a member because, in his opinion, the Christian tradition was one of the great supporting pillars of Western civilization and would remain so indefinitely. He found the discussions between sociologists and theologians to be of genuine importance, because he wanted to interrogate Christians about the essential values of their faith and about the utility of these values in the process of social change. On the other hand, he was willing to learn from theologians, because he acknowledged as sociologist that no society can function without norms and values; he found he needed to look at religion to find the essence of these norms and values. Also, his own position in this group was not threatening for him. Precisely by inviting him and other non-Christians, the group displayed the broad-mindedness which improved the quality of the discussions. In December 1942 he reported for this society on the following subject: "Cultural Reconstruction in Central Europe: Planning for the Eradication of the Fascist Mentality in Europe." For other introductions to various topics presented to "The Moot," consult the bibliography.

Death

On 28 December 1946 Mannheim wrote to Professor G.B. Jeffery, Director of the Institute of Education, that he had received invitations from Columbia University in New York and from an unnamed university in Australia. Révész (1947: 3) specifies that this invitation came from the University of Canberra. In 1946 the Hungarian government invited Mannheim and other fugitive intellectuals (among them G. Révész from Amsterdam) to return to their fatherland; Mannheim would return as Professor of Sociology at the University of Budapest. Mannheim expressed thanks for the confidence placed in him, but declined the offer; he felt himself to be morally indebted to the University of London and had made promises which he intended to keep. In the above-mentioned letter to Jeffery he did not mention the nature of the teaching assignments which Colombia and Canberra had offered him, only that he was not accepting the invitations.

Although he gave no reasons for his decision, we can mention four considerations. First, since 1940 he had been an English citizen and he gave everyone the impression that he felt very much at home in England. Second, his newly acquired professorship gave him satisfaction. His correspondence indicates that he treasured his friendly contacts with colleagues and students. He also was on friendly terms with the German and Hungarian communities in London. Third, the invitations from the other universities all implied full-time appointments; this was too much for Mannheim. A part-time appointment for a few months each year would have been manageable, perhaps; at any rate, he was eager to hang on to his appointment at the University of London – not only because this university continued to attract him, but because he was an European and intended to remain one. He felt responsibility for the task – he regarded it as a calling – to work at the cure for the cultural crisis in Western civilization. Fourth, his health, which had always been precarious, became much worse during the war years and particularly in 1946. His heart was weak, his lungs were regularly affected so that breathing was difficult, and he was chronically tired.

Already in 1942 (letter to Clarke, 9-3-1942) Mannheim mentioned that his physician allowed him to travel no more than necessary and insisted that he avoid all physical strain. The travel between London, Cambridge, and Nottingham apparently fatigued him to such an extent that he requested Clarke to provide him with a room in one of the university buildings, furnished with a sofa or a bed, during the times when he lectured in Nottingham. His physician had advised him to leave the precincts of the university as little as possible.

Because he was in precarious health and in overweight, he avoided physical exertion as much as possible. At home he often spent most of his day in bed. He assembled books around him to read and to examine for notations taken earlier. During the last year of his life he needed to rest at least twice while climbing the stairs from ground level to the second floor.

During the summer of 1945 Dr. H.G. Schenk, the historian from Oxford, visited Mannheim. Schenk, who originally came from Prague, was planning to write a book about romanticism and knew that Mannheim was very much interested in this topic. The conversation lasted a whole afternoon, during which Mannheim told Schenk that he had wanted to write a sociological study about romanticism. (I mentioned this plan above, including Mannheim's 1937 correspondence about it with the publisher Routledge). He now complained to Schenk about his health and in the course of the conversation confessed that he would not be able to do the study. He gave Schenk some books to borrow and wished him strength for the task with a smile and these words: "I give you my kingdom." Schenk told me (27-4-1978) that the talk with Mannheim had been a stimulating experience. Schenk noticed that between them Karl and Julia still spoke Hungarian. When Schenk expressed amazement at this, Mannheim replied that such had been the case in Germany as well as in England: "A person does, after all, need a home away from home."

In spite of his intellectual alertness, Mannheim did not seem physically healthy to Schenk, but rather fatigued and almost depressed. This impression was confirmed by Professor Dr. M.J. Langeveld from Utrecht, who visited Mannheim in 1946 and conferred with him about methodology and other more theoretical problems in psychology.

The Mannheims received many callers in their home. Before and during World War II it was chiefly a meeting place for displaced Hungarians. Mannheim was a gracious and lively host; speaking about politics of the war, he showed himself to be very realistic, sometimes almost cynical. One evening before the war, a number of Hungarian students were visiting at the Mannheim home. One of them said she had heard that her parents were finding themselves in an extremely difficult situation back home. She felt like going back to Budapest and asked Mannheim for advice. Mannheim's only answer: "Choose the place you would most like to die."

In the fall of 1946 he was appointed chairman of the European division of UNESCO (United Nations' Educational, Scientific, and Cultural Organization). On 27-12-1946 he asked the administration of the Institute of Education for increased heating in his office. His chronically precarious health and his current sickness were well known in the Institute. At the beginning of Januari 1947 the extra heat was provided. In December 1946 his heart trouble came back again; breathing was particularly difficult. He spent almost all of a typical day in bed. At the beginning of January he contracted pneumonia. His physician prescribed total rest, but Mannheim did not observe the prescription. As was his custom, he took books from his study and read them in his bed. On the last day of his life, according to Shils (1947):

> ...he arose from his sick bed to receive an Education officer from the British Control Group in Germany who wished to discuss the problems of German re-education with him.

In the afternoon of Thursday, 9 January 1947, he suffered a heart attack. At evening, he died.

11. In the crematorium at Golders Green, London.

Several hundred concerned people, colleagues, students, and friends were present at the funeral in the crematorium at Golders Green, not far from his home. In connection with his death, commemorative articles appeared in many newspapers. *The New Zürich Newspaper (Die Neue Züricher Zeitung*, 15-1-1947) stated two reasons why Mannheim's work cannot be overlooked:

> ...first because of his meaningful, pertinent content and his powers to stimulate the thought and second, because of his personal and philosophical attitude, which makes Mannheim an example of a particular psychological type of intellectual at the time of World War I. Mannheim articulated a program for sociology which reaches far beyond its original intention. Through this program sociological study in the narrower sense (that is, the academic statement of the forms and principles of societal life) is totally redefined. Sociology meant more for him; sociology was a diagnosis of an age, best expressed something like this: the philosophy of culture.

The German *Currier (Kurrier*, 15-1-1947) wrote:

Another gaping hole has been ripped into the fabric of academic life; someone whose return from emigration would have provided a bitterly needed healing and help fot the German academic world. At 53 years of age, Karl Mannheim died in London, "one of the leading sociologists of the world," as the foreign press praises him, and not only on the occasion of his obituary.

The Times (11-1-1947) wrote about Mannheim's stay in England and his influence on that country:

> In this country he soon became known to a great company of students and readers, who found in him a wise and far-seeing guide amid the social and cultural upheavals of our age. Profound humility and a wide-embracing humanity, purged and tempered by suffering, were at the roots of his power. In a remarkably short time he penetrated to the essence of the English spirit, and became in some ways more English than the English themselves. He entered with complete sympathy into our way of life and yet could stand apart from it, pointing out those elements of strength and weakness of which an insular and unanalytic people is apt to be insufficiently aware. Of his standing as a sociologist there is abundant evidence. He was no fact-finding statistician for his approach was mainly historical, and in it he was strengthened and steered by a rich equipment in philosophy and psychology. A voracious reader, he seemed to have absorbed everything that had significance for his task. *Ideology and Utopia* will probably be regarded as his greatest work – a book which might almost be compared with Freud's writings in its dissection of the subtleties of human functioning. *Man and Society in an Age of Reconstruction*, a fullscale attempt at a diagnosis of the concerned with the problems and possibilities of education. The comptability of planning and democracy had perhaps not hitherto been argued so cogently as in *Man and Society*.

His cousin Ernest Manheim (1947: 471) found these words to comment on the poignancy of this untimely death:

> ... the end came at the beginning of what was in the nature of a new period of his life, entered with the accustomed burst of mental energy which characterized his career as a sociologist.

Julia Lang Mannheim
One week after his death, Julia Mannheim wrote to Jeffery (17-1-1947):

> There was no greater course for him than education. You may know that his job was to teach philosophy at a Training College and I am lucky enough to sit in all those lectures.

Julia was ambitious to get the early writings, many of which had appeared first in German, translated into English, and also to get her husband's hitherto unpublished or partially written manuscripts into print. For this purpose she called on the friends Adolph Löwe and Paul Kecskemeti (married to her older sister) for help, and also on former students like Mrs. J. Floud and Professor W.A.C. Stewart. She limited herself to initiating and stimulating this work; she

12.   Julia Mannheim (ca. 1945)

never made it her concern to work with the actual manuscripts.

Although she did not feel herself competent to that task, in September 1947 she went to New York for consultations with Adolph Löwe, a staff member of the New School for Social Research and the editor of Mannheim's posthumous works, and with the American publisher of these works, Oxford University Press. The Rockefeller Foundation gave a grant (October 1947) to the New School for the use of the Institute of World Affairs in preparing the Mannheim manuscripts for publication by Löwe. Professor Robert Merton of Columbia

University and Professor Hans Speier of the New School agreed to act as advisors. Mannheim's posthumous books were published by Oxford University Press and in the series he himself had started at Routledge and Kegan Paul in London. Till now eight posthumous books were published. Both during his lifetime and later various books appeared in translations: German, French, Spanish, Italian, Chinese, and Japanese. K.H. Wolff prepared the publication of twee volumes of selected essays (1964; 1971). In this connection we must take account of the editors' sometimes flexible understanding of their task. In this study I shall sometimes need to compare the original German text with the English translation, a procedure recommended for any careful study of Mannheim's work.

In the archives of the library of the University of Keele lie three typed manuscripts ready for the press (going by incidental marginal corrections), on the following subject: "The Future of Education for Maturity" (6pp), "The Problem of Modern Education" (8pp), and "How is Modern Education Possible?" (10pp). Althought these essays are not published under these titles, the content in its broad contours is to be found in Karl Mannheim and W.A.C. Stewart's *Essays on the Sociology of Education*.

In connection with the 'restitution' by the Republic of West Germany to Germans who had fled the country before the Hitler regime took over, Julia gave notice (via her lawyer, 14-12-1949) to the Interior Ministry of the German province of Hesse that she was claiming the back salary and the pension of her husband. An extensive correspondence followed among the ministry, the Goethe University in Frankfurt, and Julia Mannheim; it lasted until 1954. On 27 August 1954 the decision was made that for the period lasting form 01-01-1934 until 31-3-1950, when the pension money was not paid in by the Mannheims, Julia would receive a cash settlement and that beginning with 1-4-1950 Julia would regularly receive a widow's pension. The correspondence concerning this subject is preserved in the archives of the Goethe University. The size of the sums is mentioned in the correspondence, but the university regards these sums as inappropriate for publication.

After settling in London, Julia Mannheim had become increasingly more interested in psychoanalysis. She kept up a good relationship with Anna Freud and her clinic, where she was on the staff. She also had a small practice in her home. In addition, she gave lectures regularly and cooperated in providing courses for the students of the Hampstead Child-therapy Course.

Although Julia generally enjoyed good health, early in the autumn of 1954 she contracted an acute attack of rheumatoid arthritis, according to what she wrote to her friends, the Révész family in Amsterdam (16-6-1955). It seems from her letters of the spring of 1955 that she had been in hospital for several months; from her description of the disease and the prescribed medicines, we may conclude that she had a severe case of rheumatoid arthritis. She died on 16

December 1955, and like her husband, was cremated at the crematorium at Golders Green. One day before her death she signed over her house, furniture, and library to her friend and housekeeper, Julia Molnear. In 1939 Molnear had come along as housekeeper with Julia Mannheim's mother from Hungary; Julia's mother decided to settle in London and until her death in 1941 made her home with the Mannheims. Julia Molnear stayed on as housekeeper for the Mannheims, married a Polish immigrant, and changed her name to Mrs. Piliszanska. In accordance with the decision of Julia Mannheim, Mrs. Piliszanska donated the library of 6.000 volumes to the Hebrew University of Jerusalem; many of Mannheim's students were Jews and had immigrated to Israel.

PART II: Motifs and Contours of the Philosophy

Chapter IV

Critique of Culture

Philosophical Milieu of the German Intelligentsia
As a philosopher, Mannheim is typical of the first decades of the twentieth century. Philosophy in the German milieu around the turn of the century was preoccupied with the analysis of the times. This was not only regarded as an analysis of social, political, and economic attitudes, but rather "as a criticism of contemporary culture, understood as the essence of self-consciousness." The philosophy of central Europe was predominantly anti-rationalistic; a central concern was the concept of *life* (Lieber, 1974: vii). The title of Lieber's work analyzing these strains, *Kulturkritik und Lebensphilosophie (Cultural Criticism and a Philosophy of Life)*, was also characteristic of Mannheim's philosophical thought.

The intellectual milieu in Hungary and Germany, in which Mannheim was trained and shaped philosophically, could be likened to a delta; various philosophical and cultural streams left their deposits in him. In his philosophical publications one finds influences from the systems of Hegel, Marx, Comte, Kant, Dilthey, Rickert, Lukács, Simmel, Husserl and still more. His development philosophically was turbulent.

Soul and Culture
In the lecture mentioned before, "Soul and Culture," Mannheim appeared on the scene as a spokesman for a critical generation, and he provided an overview of the various lectures that would be delivered in the Free School for Studies of the Human Spirit during the spring of 1918. (Earlier lectures of this sort, to which he alludes in this lecture, have not been preserved.) He wished to identify and clarify the common background which united the various lecturers (sk: 66,78).

71

I see this unity, often discussed already, in the common point-of-view which we take toward isolated cultural phenomena such as religion, philosophy, ethics, art, society, and history; in our common attempt to focus on these phenomena from the same perspective; and in that we attempt to explain the structure and meaning of these phenomena in our own distincitve way. (SK: 68)

He saw the commonality in the influence of Dostoevsky's worldview and intuitions about life, in Kierkegaard's ethics, in the German idea of *logos*, in the Hungarian spirit, and in the new French poetry in the *Nouvelle Revue Fran- caise*. In addition, the Free School owed much to naturalism, to impressionism, and, in sociology, to Marxism. He refers to these influences on himself as the conditions for development, which he does not intend to deny, but which he has, nevertheless, outgrown. For the Free School, commonality existed because:

... for our ethical and aesthetic comprehension a certain normativity was defined. (...) Further, for our worldview, a metaphysical idealism gives substance, which is totally and definitely unrelated to a certain compulsory idealism found in the established religions. (SK: 68)

As spokesman for a certain "unity of the younger generation," Mannheim set down these words as his starting point; he reached the heart of his lecture-essay when he came to the subject of the Free School's right to exist:

What gives a school a right to exist in the present condition of culture is systematic fertilizing of the requirements of the culture around us. Since the greatest danger of contemporary culture is this: that culture washes over us, and allows our relationship to culture to become more and more precarious. (SK: 66)

Soul in the title of the lecture, Mannheim does not intend a religious meaning, but the "subject," the individual person. Mannheim's theme is the relationship between the subject as individual person and the objective culture, "since the distance between these two polarities has become uncommonly great" (SK: 69).

This objective culture, which Mannheim regards as an "objectivizing of spirit" and as humanity's inheritance, is formed through religion, science, art, the state, and other social forms. He speaks of "subjective culture" when the soul finds its fulfillment by means of obtaining the objective manifestations of the culture. By means of this detour Mannheim wishes to arrive at the concept of "the fulfillment of the soul." This detour brings him at the same time to still another possible route for achieving fulfillment of the soul. This second way emphasizes the inner life that is followed by oriental ascetics and Christian mystics. What was granted to them we still sometimes experience, even in our times, as experiences of grace. Thus, the importance Mannheim places on Meister Eckhardt, Dostoevsky, and Kierkegaard.

> Our highest moments can still bring us the same experience of grace as was granted to them, but not redemption, since our apostasy has made us unfit for a thoroughgoing confrontation with ourselves. (SK: 69)

According to Mannheim, Western humanity has lost a religious self-awareness; this is what he means by "apostasy." Therefore, no course remains open for us to choose than to seek the "fulfillment of the soul" by means of the detour of cultural objectives.

Do the historical forms of objective culture have meaning for the human subject today? According to Mannheim (SK:70), the meaning is restricted by the relationship between a person and his work. Our work, which originally was an expression of the soul, becomes a cultural concern when it acquires an histori-cal-social dimension. For Mannheim , this is the meaning of work: every deed or thought, yes, every self-expression by a person, who is attempting to come to himself, to realize himself, to come to fulfillment by means of the foreign (that is, not himself) materials around him. In this connection it is important that Mannheim provides a justification for "the most fundamental quest involved in mankind's journey: that we can establish contact with others and with ourselves only by placing a foreign material, work, between ourselves and others, and between our selves" (SK: 70). Work has a primary function of bonding the soul to objective culture, in which culture the soul can both express itself and in which it can reach fulfillment. Our work has a secondary function in that it can serve as an interpersonal bridge; it "achieves its worth in establishing the social connection" (SK: 72; cf. ST: 231, 232).

In its historical-social context, work acquires another particular law of its own. Literature is not simply the accumulation of all that has been written, art is not simply accumulated art works, religion is not the sum of all cultic rituals, and culture is more than a sum of its objective manifestations. Not only the creative artist is establishing conformity to aesthetic law by his production of cultural artifacts, "but also the effect of the few individuals ready to welcome the new artifacts; these also maintain the continuing life of culture and they exert an enormous influence" (SK: 72).

The objective culture becomes an independent reality which cannot simply be reduced to a cooperative venture by separate people. The independent development of culture causes a growing distance between culture and the public. This development is always accompanied by a loss of content; that which was originally meaningful will eventually lose its meaning. Culture then has the appearance of a *Leviathan*; Mannheim also uses the Hebrew word *golem*, a massive entity without soul. The objects of culture can assume significance totally foreign to their original meaning (Kettler, 1967: 408-412).

Mannheim's Idea of Work
Mannheim's perception of *work* demonstrates a relationship to Hegel's and Marx' interpretation of *labor*. Hegel saw labor as a typically human

phenomenon and as the self-realization of a person as a self-conscious being; labor defines the being of a person (Hegel, 1821: 124, 187). Hegel spoke chiefly about labor which mediates between needs and satisfying those needs. Labor has a significant place in Hegel's work entitled "The System of Needs" (Hegel, 1821: par. 189-208). In this system labor takes on the characteristics of "an abstract universal"; that is, a person works not only for the purpose of satisfying his own specific, physical needs, but also toward the possibility of a universal satisfying of human needs.

Marx was to designate labor for the production of means to satisfy needs as "the basic condition for all history"; in doing so, Marx agrees with an idea that Hegel had already seen as essential. Just as Hegel, Marx sees labor as the self-actualizing of a person; the actual person is to be perceived as a result of his work. On the other hand, he states that the actual person can only be realized in the "realm of freedom." Although labor in a bourgeois society can only be a means "for increasing the accumulated labor to be done" and has degenerated to a commodity; yet, in Marx's view and in the communistic society which he envisioned, labor defines what it is to be a person. "The accumulated labor is but a means to widen, to enrich, to promote the existence of the laborer" (Marx, 1848: 233).

Like Hegel, Marx conceived of labor as a dialectical process of objectifying and deobjectifying, concretely expressing and abstracting. In the bourgeois society this process has come to a halt in alienation; this alienation, according to Marx, can be removed only by revolutionary means (see Beerling, 1964b: 69, 70).

In Mannheim's thought as well as in Marx's, the subject is alienated from objective culture. This alienation must be undone by means of work; it must be worked away. As labor for Hegel and Marx, work for Mannheim defines the existence of a person. In this connection Mannheim does not use the word *labor*. Although he nowhere argues the distinctive meanings of the words *work* and *labor*, it is clear that he speaks of *labor* with a restricted economic meaning. Regardless how seldom the word *labor* occurs in his early publications, it often occurs in an economic-sociological treatise from 1930 (WE). *Work* has a broader definition for Mannheim: every act and thought, every expression of the soul (SK: 70). This interpretation of *work* diverges from that of Hegel and Marx, who regard *labor* as the mediating actions between needs and satisfying those needs. Just as Hegel and Marx, Mannheim sees the individual achieving self-actualization by means of a detour. But unlike Marx, Mannheim does not speak of a detour through nature by means of labor; rather, he speaks of a detour through objective culture by means of work. Just as labor for Hegel and Marx, work for Mannheim has a dialectical dimension. The subject expresses itself by means of work in the objective culture, which in our time has grown independent and as a monstruous Leviathan has posited itself against the human being. The subject grows alienated from the objective culture. In work, these two polarities are reconciled; a synthesis must be achieved in a subjective culture. Yet, the following problems remain: How is it possible that objective culture comes to stand opposite humanity and alienated from it? And, to the extent that alienation is worked away, to that extent does work lose its dialectical character? Mannheim does not take up these problems. He is still at the very beginning of his intellectual development and is oriented more toward diagnosis than toward therapy.

Spirit as Totality

By *objective culture* Mannheim means "the collective objectifications of the spirit" (SK: 69). In a discussion of Lukács' *Die Theorie des Romans (The Theory of the Novel)*, Mannheim discusses the multiplicity of art forms, all of which must be understood as manifestations of one spirit:

> Their variety can by no means be imputed to an arbitrary play impulse, which, to amuse itself, takes on now this form, now that. Instead, in the actualization of each of these forms, there is always an element of necessity, which becomes fully explicable only by reference to that spirit of which alone it can be adequately interpreted. (BL: 6)

The meaning of an art form "can be adequately explained only by the spiritual content which avails itself of the form" (BL: 6). Cultural objectifications are not to be understood simply in terms of the activities of the creating individuals. To understand the normative "law of cultural phenomena," "the cooperation of those few who are ready to welcome (the new phenomenon) is also of considerable influence" (SK: 72, 73). The objective culture *can only be understood adequately* "in the actual origin of each creative tendency, which we locate in the spirit, which we can describe only metaphysically; and we derive differences among the forms form the differences among the ultimate, historically changing points-of-orientation of this spirit" (BL: 6).

What does Mannheim mean by *spirit*? According to him, this question is difficult to answer. He says of spirit "that it never explicates itself in its creations, but only manifests itself through them" (BL: 6). One must try to grasp the distinctive-philosophic-actual out of the forms which the spirit has taken, and all of this in the context of the "historically changing point-of-orientation of the spirit in its most contemporary form." Concerning the way this must happen, Mannheim says no more than this in his early publications: it happens through "a particular ability, which in a rudimentary form is possessed by everybody" (BL: 7).

He wants to make plain that, while a psychological interpretation of a work of art, proceeding form the psychic life of the individual artist, can come to interesting insights, "it can, nevertheless, yield nothing as far as the intrinsic meaning of the corresponding aesthetic object is concerned. The reason is that its logical object is only the work of art as experience, not the complex of meanings that is valid in and of itself. (...)The psychological, experiental context yields explanations only of psychological phenomena and explains the work of art only insofar as it contains or suggests psychological phenomena. The aesthetic object, on the other hand, is something essential to the spirit. (...) It is just these spiritual aspects (such as composition, etc.) that can be adequately explained only in an appropriate teleological frame of reference" (BL: 4).

He is of the opinion that our interpretations ought not to go "from bottom to top." Sociological and psychological studies cannot explain "the intellectual phenomenon in all its uniqueness" (BL: 5). It is entirely different when one interprets an aesthetic object, for instance, a painting, form a metaphysical, historical, and philosophical context. A work of art is an objectification of spirit. An art form is an abstract component "of the full spiritual content of the work of art and can be adequately abstract only from an aesthetic perspective. It follows that an interpretation of the abstract part is justified and possible only by proceeding form the whole" (BL: 5).

From the previous quotations we see that Mannheim speaks about *spirit* as "the whole." Spirit is that totality wherein the meaning the adequate comprehension of cultural phenomena, must take place. Without taking over Hegel's philosophy, Mannheim puts one in mind of the famous word from the "Preface" to Hegel's *Phenomenology*:

> The True is the whole. But the whole is nothing other than the essence consummating itself through its development. Of the Absolute it must be said that it is essentially a *result*, that only in the *end* is it what it truly is. (1807: 11)

For Hegel "the whole" is the truth which completes itself in its development. In its individual outward manifestations spirit never reveals itself in the fullness and truth of its being. Not the system of Hegel's philosophy, but spirit in its external manifestations, "the multiplicity of the historically changing, contemporary orientation-points of the spirit": this is Mannheim's framework for interpretation. That is why one cannot interpret art works adequately "from bottom to top" (by medium, by psychology, by sociology, but "from top to bottom": that is, proceeding from the totality of the spirit, as this has been expressed in a given period. Nevertheless, it never becomes clear exactly what Mannheim means by *totality*. We may not simply identify it with Hegel's interpretation. Apparently a metaphysical-idealistic tradition, in which Hegelian ideas often appeared without a precise rationale, shows itself, too, in Mannheim's thought, just as it showed itself everywhere in German culture in the previous century.

Metaphysical Idealism as Starting Point
Mannheim spoke about objective culture as a *Leviathan*. People are turned off by their culture. The subjective significance of the maker is no longer part of the stuff of culture; it is a process which he calls the "deactualization of the conceptual content" (SK: 75); later he works out this process in sociological

terms as alienation (Wolff, 1964: 15) – a process which already began at the end of the Middle Ages.

He calls the dialectical relationship between soul and culture *tragic*, but it is not hopeless. He does not come to a pessimistic "negative dialectic" as did Adorno later (1966: 146, and elsewhere); Mannheim strives for the renewal of culture on the basis of structural analysis of the various cultural phenomena, analysis which will be undertaken in other lectures. By structural analysis he means this process:

> To raise into consciousness the specific primal conditions for separate cultural images and to trace the regularity of their development. These investigations convinced us that cultural objects are distinguished from each other in their very being, and without the danger of distorting them, neither the objects nor their essential being can be reduced to the other. (SK: 77)

> Givens such as the intellectual and the experiential have nothing in common with the physical world. (...) Instead of denying these undoubted givens, we enlarge them to a narrowly prescribed concept of reality, and we maintain that these givens appear to us in various and hidden forms. (SK: 77)

He rejects every monistic approach to the problem, because monism brings a narrowing of philosophical orientation with it. He declares himself committed to a methodological pluralism which had brought him to idealism, because especially the idealist Kant had recognized the peculiar nature of three important forms of culture: theory, ethical action, and aesthetic contemplation (SK: 77, 78).

In one of the quotations above, Mannheim speaks about the "specific primal conditions" of cultural phenomena, which are "distinguished from each other in their very being." He intends to trace out the regular norms. The norms for a marble statue lie in the nature of the marble medium; for a poem "they are grounded in the laws of rhythm" (SK: 71). He attempts to expose the forms which have no content. He wishes to place the "domain of deactualized phenomena of culture" in a clear light of cultural philosophy, and to study and have in his consciousness the truth of that cultural domain, as it exists in its diversity. He rejects the conception that variety is appearance and that unity, spirit, is the only reality. There is a "movement of interpretation" from variety to unity, to the end of understanding variety from the point of view of unity. This movement is brought about by thought. Idealistic influences on his thought can be easily demonstrated. The influence which he was subject to from other philosophies will become clear in the course of this study. In his first publication, however, he rightly identifies the starting point of his thought as metaphysical idealism.

It is interesting that Juliska Lang, who was to become Mannheim's wife, gave a brief review of his lecture "Soul and Culture" in the *Athenaeum*. This review is not critical. She seems to agree with Mannheim's ideals and program, as presented in the lecture. She mentions particularly Simmel's influence on Mannheim's thought, structural analysis, and methodological pluralism, all of which she finds evident in his approach (1918: 159, 160), subjects which I shall discuss either in this chapter and in the chapters following.

Mannheim and Simmel

We meet a noteworthy concurrence of ideas between Mannheim and his Berlin teacher Georg Simmel. Mannheim regarded Simmel highly – as can be seen by the two articles he devoted to him – and characterized him as superior to all his contemporaries in the Socratic method and intellectual power (GS: 194; LAB: 416-418). The essential ideas of "Soul and Culture" had already been expressed in words by Simmel in the essay *Der Begriff und die Tragödie der Kultur (The Idea and Tragedy of Culture.*

The tension between subjective and objective culture, which we are always being alerted to in Mannheim, appears as often and as clearly in Simmel. Simmel makes a distinction between the form and content of cultural phenomena, and asserts that the established forms of culture stand in opposition to the person who would live meaningfully. The cultural phenomena have received a form which is foreign and hostile to human life; they are forms which degenerate, and thus kill human life. He speaks about the paradox of the culture as the subjective life that strives for an inner meaning and fulfillment "by means of the forms that have become entirely foreign to it, leading to a crystal-clear form of self-satisfied alienation" (Simmel, 1911: 240). A tragic situation arises when the dualism of subject and object develops in such a way that neither one finds meaning in the other, "and the inner logic strives for that which each of the two develops by itself, and then the two collapse with each other in total incomprehensibility" (1911: 254).

Mannheim also speaks of the tragedy of culture and means that the formal aspects of cultural phenomena and their intended meaning do not share a parallel development. According to Mannheim, in certain respects Simmel never rose above his time, because he shared the scepticism of his generation. In one way Simmel's writings contain fragments of a new metaphysics, but in another way these fragments remained undeveloped because he himself lacked confidence in them (LAB).

With Simmel and Mannheim the aesthetic-dramatic category *tragic* has become a philosophical category for interpreting reality. Reality has become fragmented, antinomian, and paradoxical. Paradox is not the last word for Mannheim, however. Paradox only forces us to deeper analysis and a more careful searching for answers. The tragic philosophy need not be closed or predetermined. Dualism and tragedy can be conquered, if reciprocal communication exists between subject and object, each anticipating the needs of the other (LAB: 416-418; cf. EC: 410). Mannheim does not mention that Simmel speaks of a "sociological tragedy," also when social processes become repressive, with the result that social interaction becomes minimal, and individuals become socially isolated. In later work Mannheim was to elaborate on these ideas (Simmel, 1950, 31, 32).

Just as we can call Simmel both a philosopher of culture and a philosopher of life, so we can call Mannheim both. A significant moment in the philosophy of life is the stand of protest taken by the personal-subjective power against impersonal-objective powers, freedom against restriction, interpretive understanding of the cultural disciplines against the explanations of the natural sciences. At the same time a heavy accent is laid on becoming and changing, called "Heraclitian moment" by philosophers of life. In all these moments of change a continuing appeal is placed before the individual: to philosphize is not only a rational matter; it is an existential occupation, which addresses itself primarily to the life of the person who calls models and structures into life; and these forms and structures must please him in order to become objectivized, and later he must free these forms and structures from superficiality, which means finding new forms again (cf. Loader, 1985: 30-38, 62, 63).

Mannheim and Young Lukács

Another influence on Mannheim was the young Lukács. In the first place we can establish this from frequent contact they had in Budapest (KL, 1975: 93-94). In the second place there is evidence of the influence in Mannheim's already mentioned review in 1920 of Lukács'book *The Theory of the Novel*.

Already earlier another book by Lukács had appeared, *Die Seele und die Formen (The Soul and the Forms*, 1911) a translation of the Hungarian version. These two works belong to his pre-Marxist period, which ends in 1918. At the time he was still strongly influenced by Dilthey, Simmel and Max Weber; he was also preoccupied with Hegel and Kant (Lukács, 1920: 8, 9).

While Mannheim in "Soul and Culture" writes about the relationship of the subject to objective culture, Lukács writes in *The Soul and the Forms* that one must construe a literary work as a striving to express the total feeling of life – that is, the "soul" – in a literary form. This striving is inevitable, but at the same time, every form limits the content. The societal life outside of the person is characterized by chaos and meaninglessness, by unconceivable powers in irreconcilable conflicts which explode chaotically. The artist brings order to chaos; he gives form to it and creates meaning from the raw material of experience. The forms are various modalities of the relationship between the human soul and the world. The forms are the aesthetic expression of certain coherent human attitudes, and the forms correlate to the attitudes. The epic expresses the ability to conceive of the individual and society as a totality. On the contrary, the novel is the dialectical form of the epic; it is a form which expresses the loneliness and homelessness of man in the midst of society. Moreover, tragedy represents modern society, in which it is no longer possible even to posit an immediate totality of the individual and society; a seperation exists between these two. Alienation is total and thoroughgoing; alienation from nature is the result of man's being alienated form the society he has created (cf. Lukács, 1920: Chapters 1-4: Frisby, 1983: 79). The tragic view is, according to Lukács, a true view of reality as far as it represents human alienation from society. However, in opposition to Mannheim, he dismisses this view as meaningless because it does not posit an immediate totality of the individual and society as the epic does, and because it is fragmentary and thus a deception of life. Unlike Mannheim, he does not use the concept of tragic as a means to think the social and cultural problems through in order to overcome them.

Mannheim actually never discusses Lukács' *The Theory of the Novel*. After the appearance of the book, he wrote an independent essay on the multiplicity of forms which aesthetics investigates. According to him, it is in the nature of the products of the spirit that they can be investigated from various perspectives: psychological, sociological, metaphysical, technological, and historical-philosophical, to name a few. These various methods of approach answer to various dimensions of any work being studied. As was shown earlier, in his opinion, the metaphysical and historical-philosophical methods are best for *adequately* understanding a work of art, for interpretation. Lukács acquitted himself well in his *Theory*; he gave historical-philosophical interpretation of the literary forms as expressions of continually changing socio-historical totalities, which by means of artistic creativity strive for self-definiton. Art forms are objectifications of the *Zeitgeist* of these totalities (BL: 5).

The agreement between the ideas of young Lukács and young Mannheim requires no commentary. Both found themselves unmistakably in the Hegelian tradition and were expecially influenced by Dilthey and Simmel. Both were deeply troubled by the development of Western civilization. Both rejected positivism, as wel as physical monism. Both tended toward a metaphysical idealism of a total view of society which Lukács elaborated after 1918 in his Marxist manner, and Mannheim is his sociological historicism (see Chapter IX and X).

Conclusions

In this part the topic is the motifs and contours of Mannheim's philosophy. The influence of Kant and Hegel can be discerned in his early publications. Also, by way of his contact with the pre-Marxist Lukács, who also had studied in Berlin, the influence of Simmel's cultural philosophy is prevalent.

When one examines this chapter, it seems that the deepest motive that drove Mannheim was a troubled concern for the tragedy of the development of Western civilization since the Middle Ages. This tragedy shows itself in the rending apart of the experiencing subject and the objective culture. Mannheim looks for a restoration of the relationship between soul and culture. To bring about this restoration, the initiative lies with the subject, who with pain and aversion observes the cultural phenomena which have come from him and which are being alienated from him – and this subject wishes to realize himself by means of these very cultural phenomena. The starting-point for Mannheim's thought seems to be metaphysical-idealistic: the spirit as a whole and as the frame work for interpretation, for by the spirit everything that exists can be interpreted ("from top to bottom"). It is not a totally clear category, but one must attempt to grasp the essence of the forms of the spirit in the objective culture. And it is possible to grasp this essence because of a "particular ability, which in a rudimentary form is possessed by everybody."

The contours of his philosophy are of the cultural-philosophical sort: restoration of the relation between soul and culture as the renewal of culture. This process must proceed form individuals, in whom the understanding of the spirit in its historical-social context has a pivotal function. A new ethic is necessary for a society of such individuals (Kettler, 1967: 21). Moreover, the contours of Mannheim's philosophy will be sharpened when we examine his epistemology; that is very important for understanding his later publications on sociology.

Chapter V

A Structural Analysis of Epistemology

Mannheim's Dissertation

Mannheim's dissertation, written in the Hungarian language (1918), appeared in 1922 in a German edition under the title *Strukturanalyse der Erkenntnistheorie (A Structural Analysis of Epistemology)*. In this work he develops his theme of "Soul and Culture" in an epistemological direction. He intends to develop a *"logic* of philosophy," rather, a method for doing philosophy. Everyone acknowledges that mathematics, natural science, history, and poetry each has its own methods. There is, however, great disagreement about any unity of method in philosophy (SE: 15, 16). In Mannheim's opinion, each area of culture has its own (ontic) structure, and in a structural analysis (as already noted, SK: 77) the uniqueness of the particular area of culture and its building up are worked out. In this structural analysis, systemizing has top priority. This does not simply mean rubrics formulated according to classified ideas, but the cautious analysis of, and the subsequent relating to each other, of phenomena in reality (outside of the subject), which, in their uniqueness, form the presuppositions for the systemizing:

> It is not an antecedent line of thought which the individual must have gone through before he can understand or form a concept; it is a set of implications he needs to accept, acknowledge, take for granted, whenever he uses a theoretical concept significantly or turns his attention to it. (SE: 20)

Mannheim construed his task as working out the "systematic presuppositions" which exist in reality; these sytematic presuppositions are involved in any theoretical concept whatsoever (SE: 20). This systemization is one of the activities which constitute the transcendental-logical subject's reacting to any given, to any fact of experience; all the elements which belong together and which restrict each other reciprocally must be worked into a totality (SE: 25).

By structural analysis of knowledge Mannheim means, a logical reflexive investigation which concentrates on the systemizing of a given cultural field, and intends to understand the forms of thought which lie behind that field.

All epistemologies have in common that they restate the question concerning the essence of knowledge into a question about presuppositions. But not in every epistemology are presuppositions regarded as logical. Not only to seek for the most basic presuppositions, but also to be the purposeful ego without presuppositions: that is what epistemologies all have in common. That striving toward presuppositionlessness, a position of "without presuppositions," is to be explained from the paradoxical situation in which epistemology acquires its distinctive task. Because it attempts to investigate and evaluate the presuppositions for *all* possible knowledge, epistemology is also knowledge in its turn; as such, epistemology uses presuppositions, the knowledge and value of which are the actual objects of its study. From this paradoxical situation, Mannheim concludes:

> It is typical of all theories of knowledge that their search for ultimate pre-conditions is inseparably linked up with a pretension to be without presuppositions – a fact which engenders a peculiar dialectical movement in the history of epistemology, often resulting in an infinite regress and a stalemate. (SE: 45)

Looking for the final presupposition is intimately connected with that peculiar capacity of consciousness which we call the "choice of references." The presuppositions of knowledge can always become the object of knowledge: this principle stands as the sign which characterizes the participant in "choice of references" theory.

Mannheim claims a structural analysis of epistemology which will clearly reveal the forms, constituent elements, and characteristics of every epistemology. Not *what* knowledge, but *how* knowledge is possible at all is his central question. He characterizes Kant's standpoint as one-sided transcendental-logical (47). When he considers the history of epistemology, he also discovers transcendental presuppositions of a psychological and ontological kind. According to him, an autonomous epistemology is non-existent. Every epistemology needs a concrete analysis of logic, psychology, and ontology. These three "fundamental sciences" or "ancillary disciplines," in Mannheim's view, have at their disposal a certain universality. That is,

> ... they are capable of encompassing "anything that exists" by creating a certain abstract framework. Under the aspect of psychology everything is "experience," in the light of logic all is "meaning," and for ontology everything appears as "being" in the same fashion. (In how far this specific homogeneity of reference is justified in the respective universal systematizations must here be deliberately left open.)

> That, of course, is the precise point where the critique of a particular theory of knowledge would have to enter, if the object in view is absolute truth-value. We, on the other hand, have to limit ourselves to a discussion of the "possibility" of these view-points, and of its

grounds. They cannot all be true at a time, but nevertheless all three may be "possible" as significant points of view. The grounds of these possibilities are to be found in the universal scope of every one of these systematizations. (SE: 48)

To summarize: Mannheim's epistemology seeks first of all for the presuppositions which make knowledge possible; and secondly, it aims at making definite the value of the ultimate presuppositions. Thus, epistemology has an *anlytical* and an *evaluative* function.

In its question about presuppositions of every possible kind of knowledge, his epistemology needs help from its basic sciences: psychology, ontology, and logic. It is a typically epistemological problem to determine which of these three basic disciplines has the priority in studying the nature of the ultimate presuppositions. Psychological epistemology posits the primacy of psychology; everything which the disciplines discuss is to be traced to the kind of experiences in which they originate; advocates of the priority of logic, while accepting that psychology is the science of experience, declare that one can arrive at the ultimate presuppositional givens only by logical means, in order to achieve genuine insight into those givens. This insight into the ultimate presuppositions at an irrational level, can, thus, only be achieved through rarional, logical means. The primacy of the ontological is based on the thesis that everything that happens belongs to Being, construed in its broadest form. Also the experience and knowing of a person belong to Being. The most general laws of Being encompass and ground the specific laws of knowledge; even logical relations are regarded as ontic phenomena.

Mannheim interprets the working of the above-mentioned presuppositions of epistemology in three levels of thought, with a growing commonality of validity. Although he does not name representatives of the psychological, logical, and ontological orientations, we can think here of Dilthey, the neo-Kantians, and the phenomenologists, respectively. The role which the basic disciplines play in epistemology is only to be made definite when the specific epistemological concepts are elaborated.

A specific epistemological concept, for Mannheim, is the subject-object relationship. Epistemology labels the facts of the disciplines as *knowledge* and places this knowledge between the two "elements" of the subject-object correlation. Something becomes knowledge when that something exists, outside the subject, as knowable object and when that object is known by a subject.

In psychology, logic, aesthetics, ethics, and ontology, the concepts of subject and object have a multiplicity of meanings. Which idea of subject epistemology uses is dependent on the priority among the basic sciences in the particular epistemology. Nevertheless, something in epistemology remains constant: the logical tension which always exists between subjects and objects (53ff).

For Mannheim there are just as many criteria for truth as there are epistemologies. The epistemologies do not measure the final presuppositions (characterized by the basic disciplines) without the particular standards of the basic

84

disciplines; they declare these basic disciplines as standards, their own presuppositions, analyzed and identified by epistemology. In other words, the choice of a criterion for truth is already decided in the choice of what gets the priority in epistemology. It is now possible to put into words the paradox of epistemology: Epistemology has set as its task to solve, by means of its own activity, by means of and through factual evidence, the problem of knowledge and of all knowing, and to judge the value of that knowing; epistemology, in the course of its development of a line of thought, has shoved back this problem of evaluation to the level of the ultimate presupposition for each knowable fact; epistemology is now forced simply to declare as valuable the presuppositions which have been made public by its analysis. The task of epistemology becomes the following: a system must be constructed in which we can discover how we can acquire knowledge, because this knowledge we start with is shown to be trustworthy on the basis of its presuppositions. Epistemological criticism had thus undergone a change. Instead of providing a critique of knowledge, a regrouping of the components of the problem arises, and a new systemization is the result. Epistemology solves a problem other than the one it had set itself. Instead of providing a critique for value, epistemology becomes a theory for the acquisition of value and how to bring it to realization.

Mannheim regarded his task not so much in judging the comparative value or in the possibility of an epistemology, but rather in the explication of its logical structure. In his interpretation it is not a purely logical systemization, but a mixture, which is dependent on the help of its basic sciences. In his dissertation Mannheim does not judge the adequacy of the basic sciences (psychology, logic, and ontology). Implicitly he attaches great value to ontology, because his analysis of the structure of epistemology is a theory founded on an ontology, which claims that reality in all of its multiformity is knowable. From that point he proceeds to his argument that the systemization of the "original givens" of reality, which givens ground the various academic disciplines, give direction to the practitioners of those disciplines. Various epistemologies function in these disciplines, and in each, one of the three mentioned basis sciences has the priority. Elsewhere he rejects the ontological epistemology as static, uncritical, and not directed toward the various basic disciplines which study the various fields of reality. Moreover, he is of the opinion that people lose perspective on the highly differentiated nature of reality if they reduce reality to a logical form or to a psychological interpretation (SE: 71; AL: 492-493; cf. EC: 410). The context of the psychological, the logical, and the ontological becomes worthy and reliable in the framework of a specific method of systemization and in a particular discipline.

Critique of Kant
Although in Chapter I it looked as though Mannheim was inspired in his thought about epistemology by Leibniz and in a more general way by Hegel and

Marx, in his dissertation he mentions Hegel only obliquely and never mentions Marx at all. He clearly orients himself on Kant and Rickert, but goes his own way. Mannheim is of the opinion that every cultural field has its own structure, and that in the structural analysis the distinctiveness, development, and regulation of these cultural fields can be elaborated.

We spoke about the methodological pluralism of Mannheim, which placed him in the footsteps of Kant. He says this already in his lecture "Soul and Culture":

> ... since in him we see the champion for the critical attitude. We saw his meaning in this fact: that he first fully acknowledged the autonomy and individual structure of the three most weighty forms of culture: of the theory, of ethical practise, and of aesthetic contemplation. (SK: 78)

Mannheim's term for the knowing person is the same as Kant's "the transcendental-logical subject." Also for Mannheim *transcendental* means the same; it refers to the ultimate presuppositions which make knowledge possible. Nevertheless, he regards Kant as one-sided: first, because Kant looked for these presuppositions only in the knowing subject, and next because Kant regarded these ultimate presuppositions as of narrowly logical import, and not as appearing *along with* the surface phenomena and coming out of the same reality on which a given discipline rests. The transcendant-idealistic epistemology of Kant – in which the person constitutes knowledge and delivers the laws to nature and regards reality as the result of the process of knowledge – this Kantian epistemology is rejected by Mannheim. His systemization does not mean the ordering of chaotic empirical perceptions through the categories of reason. The world outside of the knowing subject has order, which puts him in a position to distinguish various fields of reality according to their own nature and structure. In my opinion, this contribution makes it possible to avoid epistemological onesidedness.

The order or structure of a given field of reality forms presuppositions which the transcendental subject interprets. To think academically is, therefore, *no more and no less*, than qualifying phenomena in a logical-analytical direction. It is indeed logical in orientation, but *not exclusively logical*, because it posits other areas of reality over against itself and undertakes a synthesis with the field of reality, a special scientific field comes into being. From this point Mannheim goes on to speak of an ontic pluralism, and based on it, a methodological-pluralist concept of *logical* with a special meaning. He distinguishes it from formal logic (as an academic discipline) and from the logical aspect of methodology. The action of the investigator is of a logical nature, because it implies opposition and isolation: it places a given area of reality over against itself, and in this opposition it abstracts this area from others. At this point Mannheim makes use of the rules of formal logic and the methods of investigation which are appropriate for the study of particular areas of reality. (For a more detailed study concerning the epistemologies of Kant and Mannheim, see Glaeser, 1972 and the more broadly conceived study by Remmling, 1967; cf. Woldring, 1980: 233-235.)

Given his recognition of the peculiar nature of every area of reality and of the previously discussed one-sidedness in Kant's epistemology, I draw this provisional and cautious conclusion: that Mannheim gives evidence of a predisposition to philosophical realism. This is contradictory to Wolff (1971: xxvii), who says: "It is clear that of the two major components of his thought, 'idealism' and 'Marxism,' the former still dominates his analysis of epistemology." In my opinion this opposition in Mannheim's structural analysis of epistemology is beside the point (see the beginning of this section). Mannheim rejects a realism in which reality is reflected or imaged in consciousness; this *naive realism* does not modify itself to the conditions of possibilities or for extending the boundaries of knowledge. Judging from his epistemological study, I should like to call Mannheim a *transcendental realist. This characterization refers to the epistemological-realistic presupposition, that a reality exists independent from human thought, which is a knowable reality because of an order which is present in it everywhere. In addition, this characterization refers to the human subject as a constituent factor in the process of knowing, according to the basic disciplines.*

Without Presuppositions

All epistemologies have this in common, according ot Mannheim, that they seek the ultimate presuppositions of knowledge and, nevertheless, wish itself to be free from presuppositions. He speaks about a paradoxical situation. The quest for the ultimate presuppositions is closely connected with the "choice of references" of the consciousness, which is characterized by Mannheim as transcendental. By his interpretation of this characterization, Mannheim separates himself from Kant's transcendental method. Kant looks for the validation of the knowledge of facts in the transcendental-logical presuppositions of knowing. According to Mannheim, knowledge comes into being on the basis of factors which are present in the object as well as in the subject.

Traces of this problem, as Mannheim worked it out, can be found in Simmel (1910: 8), who also speaks of freedom from presuppositions:

> Just as it is not granted to people generally to start entirely at the beginning. ... so too our acknowledgment of anyting that occurs to us is restricted by realities or by inner laws; the thought process is very dependent on such factors, which themselves cannot produce the thought process, and the thought process is reduced in a multiplicity of ways: in control, in content, and in direction – if only in such matters as the rules of logic and method or the facts of a real world.

When thought "actually tries in this way to separate itself from presuppositions, thought turns into philosophy" (Simmel, 1910: 8). Mannheim began to philosophize in this sense of the word. In his *Structural Analysis* he strives to set to work without presuppositions, and he gives a logical analysis of epistemologies which all share the above-mentioned paradox. In the previous chapter we have already mentioned the paradox of subjective and objective culture. The paradox of "without presuppositions" is another kind of paradox. It is an epistemological problem, and a result of the logical analysis of epistemology.

Mannheim's academic systemization came about on the basis of "systematic presuppositions," which actually occur in reality; constraints are placed on these presuppositions by the structure of every area of reality. These structural differences appear in the different kinds of objectivizations in the various disciplines; the degree to which objectivization can take place is dependent on the nature of the metalogical "original givens." In Mannheim's epistemology, the debate concerning objectivity (universal validity) is of central importance. The point at issue: In the coming about of objectivity, what part does the knowing subject play and what part does the reality to be known play? A relationship exists between "without presuppositions" and objectivity (cf. Simmel 1910: 86-95; Dilthey 1931: 78, 79). It is a problem which Mannheim works out in greater detail in his sociology of knowledge.

Autonomous Truth

Looking for objectivity is closely related to looking for truth. In theoretical expressions, truth is never ours in its genuine, inevitable, and final form; theoretical expressions contain much that is provisional. "Nevertheless, we need to take it for granted that an ultimate, true, and complete form of any systemization exists objectiviely, independent of our own contributions" (SE: 26). This is not a moral or aesthetic demand, but a logical postulate, says Mannheim. He continues, that every statement and every concept has meaning only if people presuppose that, in spite of the fact that all of our solutions are mixed with error,

> nevertheless, there is a valid truth (no matter whether it has the form of many closed circles or of one), and that this does not originate with our thinking but is, on the contrary, sought by it, intended, and, if we are lucky, attained. (SE: 27)

The Hegelian concept "The true is the whole" was introduced in Chapter IV; this whole is in its development a completing truth, toward which all thought is directed; this truth is completing itself progressively.

In reference to the idea of truth, Mannheim posits the concept of truth as a logical postulate. Truth can receive froms in one or more "mutually exclusive spheres." That is, in the variety of historically changing "ultimate orientation points of the human spirit," truth (no matter how incompletely) receives forms in the "systematic presuppositions" which exist in the real world. By means of a structural analysis of these "systematic presuppositions" in a "closed sphere," relative validity and cultural manifestations can be studied. People make a fundamental mistake when they do not regard phenomena from the perspective of an historical argument of causality. That is, too often the mistake is made of trying to explain the meaning itself with reference to the temporal features of the work in question – with reference to empirical, real factors. If we seek to validate or invalidate meanings by such factors we shall inescapably fall into relativism. (SE: 37)

The structural study of an historical period must protect him from relativism. We see that this structural conception of truth is important for Mannheim's *transcendental realistic* interpretation of epistemology.

Priority of Disciplines

Concerning the ultimate presuppositions, epistemology calls in the basic sciences for help: psychology, ontology, and logic, in Mannheim's view. In the historical development of epistemology these disciplines seem to have played an important role in getting back to the presuppositions.

Mannheim's starting point for philosophizing is experience, a starting point he shares with Dilthey (1911a: 7). Dilthey (1883: 64, 66) assigned a fundamental place to psychology – especially in his early works – that is, to the knowing processes in the social sciences. Mannheim does not accord the primacy to psychology. He names only three basic sciences, because these three have played an important role in the history of epistemology. I have already noted that Mannheim criticizes the presuppositions behind these basic disciplines because their realizations are all one-sided, and, therefore, limited. In the framework of Mannheim's argument about the basis for scientific theory, is it not justifiable to name more disciplines as basic for epistemology? This question we cannot answer on the basis of his dissertation, at least not without doubt, but on the basis of his later works the answer is clear. Such elaboration would be more extensive than Mannheim's projected structural analysis of epistemology. Although at the end of his study he says he cannot go into these problems any further, because it lies outside of his investigation, nevertheless, the meaning of his argument is that there can be additional sciences which can serve as the basis of epistemology. Later he will count sociology among them.

Paradox

Mannheim asserts that to explain the striving for doing philosophy "without presuppositions" can only be done from the perspective of the paradoxical situation in which epistemology operates, with its unique task. Epistemology aspires to study the presuppositions of all possible knowledge; but epistemology itself is also knowledge and, thus, has its own presuppositions. Still, it strives to be without presuppositions: a paradoxical situation "form which that peculiar dialectic arises."

Epistemology has taken as its first task the study of the nature of the criteria by which to evaluate the presuppositions for knowledge, while in the developmental process of its line of thought in history, it has shoved this problem back into the value of the ultimate presuppositions; epistemology is forced simply to declare as reliable the presuppositions which have been exposed.

In every epistemology the subject-object correlation is central. This correlation is of a dialectical kind, says Mannheim (SE: 58); it seems it arises from the paradoxical situation: a paradox brought about by the philosopher in his striving for thought "without presuppositions" which cannot be achieved. Mention is made here, therefore, of a theoretical dialectic, for which historical importance is claimed and which is elaborated in Mannheim's later publications. His logical analysis of epistemology results in a *dialectical, transcendental realism.*

"Concerning the Problem of Classifying Sciences"

A confirmation of our characterization of Mannheim's philosophy as transcendental-realistic is to be found in his "Zum Problem einer Klassifikation der Wissenschaften" ("Concerning the Problem of Classifying Sciences"). In this article he discusses the book of Erich Becher entitled *Geisteswissenschaften und Naturwissenschaften (Social Sciences and Natural Sciences, 1921).*

Becher (1882-1929), philosopher of nature and a critical realist, was a professor in Munich. In his book he wanted to strive toward "a comparative theory of the sciences, and in particular, the real sciences" (1921, Foreword). He counted among the ideal sciences mathematics and geometry, and among the real sciences the natural and social sciences as well as metaphysics. Classification of the disciplines is hardly necessary, according to Becher, when one possesses insight into the inner structure of things themselves. He aims at a division of given disciplines according to a principle, a preconceived and consistently applied point of view (KW: 155, 156). It all comes down to how the perspective is to be chosen: whether it agrees more or less with the actuality of the variety of objects to be classified. The classificiation cannot be carried out on the basis of formal logic. An ontological anchoring is indispensable. When one tries to make an adequate division on the basis of an "objective" criterion like this one, then one must also hold the opinion that the field to be classified is constituted by a spiritual act (even before a methodological handling of it), with its own intrinsic meaning, and with one or another method of division implied in the material itself as a controlling factor.

According to Mannheim, classification, however, is a theoretical activity. We can never comprehend being in all of its implied ontic directness and totality. Mannheim brings up here the problems of circular argument; a classification can only proceed on the basis of a definite perspective; which perspective is the most adequate is dependent on ontology; but the ontic dimension can only be achieved from a chosen perspective. In order to escape from this circular argument, Mannheim uses as the most adequate "perspective" or methodology, the "particularity of systemization," and the "plurality of systemization" already discussed. Becher lacks this anchoring in his classification of disciplines.

With Becher, Mannheim opposes Rickert, who does not attempt to ground

90

his division of sciences in the ontic dimension, but on the "methodological form of what is comprehended by controlled perception" (KW: 158). Rickert attempted in his philosophy to *think* reality as a cosmos. Philosophy must bring order to the chaos of subject matter which it investigates; order is the product of thought (1921: 6-13). According to Becher, the "objective givens" provide the most adequate division. Subsequently, Becher demonstrates that with his division, the differences in methods and in basic epistemologies run parallel, and he proceeds to demonstrate, with the help of the discrepancies between method and basic principles, the correctness of his division.

Mannheim objects that neither methods create reality nor can we comprehend being in all of its implied ontic-directness. According to him, systemization is the methodologically adequate approach. This means that there is always a distance between the interpeting subject and the ontic fields of reality, the *interpretandum*; there is a continuous "cross-process" in which the classification of disciplines *follows* the ontic structure of reality. Mannheim, however, does not make totally clear what he means by that.

This difference makes clear the distinction between the *critical realism* of Becher and *transcendental realism* of Mannheim. Becher stands between naive realism and the transcendental realism of Kant. Contrary to naive realism, he is convinced that what is given to us in our consciousness, exists only in our consciousness and is not to be identified with reality. Contrary to Kant, he does not maintain that the structure of reality is essentially unknowable. The methods of investigation become Becher's key for studying reality. Mannheim tries to find the boundaries for epistemology and for the various disciplines: these boundaries are provided by an interaction between the structural analysis by the investigator on the one hand and the ontic givens on the other.

Conclusions

In the beginning of this chapter, we noted that Mannheim's structural analysis is an epistemological elaboration of the theme "Soul and Culture." Although in "Soul and Culture," a cultural-philosophical work, Mannheim speaks often about the paradox of culture, in his epistemology he speaks of the paradox of "without presuppositions," a logical paradox.

Mannheim's intention in his study of epistemology was to provide a *logical analysis* of the development of this discipline, at last to break through the ultimate ontic *presuppositions*; he speaks about the structure of reality. This leads me to characterize the starting point of his thought as *transcendental-realistic*. The contours of his philosophy become apparent where the epistemological problems are restated as problems in the theory of science. His structural analysis, which operates in his analysis both of the presuppositions of epistemology and of the relationship between knowledge and reality, arrives at the problems surrounding the theory of science, affecting the construction and method of science, the variety of sciences, the inter-relationships of the sciences, and, finally, their meaning. In connection with this, we do well to remember the conclusions of Chapter IV: the renewal of culture and ethics. Although in the background, these problems also play a role in his dissertation. A change in Mannheim's thought is to be noted: from *metaphysical idealism* to *transcendental realism*. This change will be more illuminated in the discussion of Mannheim's analysis of worldviews.

Chapter VI

On the interpretation of Worldviews

- *Worldview(s)*
- *From Spirit to Worldview*
- *Mannheim's Interpretation*
- *Positivism Well-understood*
- *Phenomenology*
- *Interpretive Understanding in Context*
- *Conclusions*

Worldview(s)

From the formulation of the title of his article "Beiträge zur Theorie der Weltanschauungs-Interpretation" (Contributions Towards a Theory of Interpreting Worldview(s)) it is apparent how carefully and cautiously Mannheim approaches the problem. He does not intend to analyse *Weltanschauung* (worldview) itself, but rather to interpret the concepts which *Weltanschauung* uses.

The whole problem and paradox of these worldviews arises from the fact that they are a-theoretical and not "products of thinking" (WI: 38; Dilthey, 1911a: 15). Although a *Weltanschauung* in a rationalist model would express itself exclusively in philosophical-theoretical statements, the irrational element within the humanities demonstrates that theoretical propositions from within a worldview are not adequate representations, but are only one of several components which make up an a-theoretical totality. A *Weltanschauung* defines the spiritual identity of a group or a culture. A *Weltanschauung* defines the manner of thinking and speaking, of observing and feeling, as well as the whole field of norms and values. When Mannheim calls *Weltanschauung* "a philosophy of life" in an English publication (ESSP: 221), then he simplifies this concept, borrowed form the history of German culture in order to clarify it somewhat for English readers. In doing this he is not totally consistent with his earlier interpretation; that is, that a *Weltanschauung* is an a-theoretical totality, is to be rationalized only in part, and, therefore, can also only partially be thought through philosophically.

From Spirit to Worldview

In his article about the interpretation of *Weltanschauung*, Mannheim to a great extent orients his thought according to Dilthey's. If in the previous chapters, spirit is spoken of as an a-theoretical totality, which forms the basis and unity of the fields of culture, the totality of the *Weltanschauung* now occupies this position. With the help of his interpretation of *Weltanschauung*, Mannheim proposes to provide a contribution to the interpretation of culture. Mannheim does not provide a precise definition for *Weltanschauung*. This is hardly surprising for *Weltanschauung* has both an a-theoretical nature, and it is not "immediately given." *Weltanschauung* is, rather, "mediately given." Thus we are referred to "something mediate," proxies, for the study of it (WI: 43). *Weltanschauung* reveals itself in cultural phenomena, without ever being totally revealed.

Yet, just as spirit, *Weltanschauung* must be understood in terms of itself. On the one hand Mannheim wishes to study how the totality of the *Weltanschauung* is built up out of cultural objectivizationns, and on the other hand how the objectivizations are to be understood in terms of the totality. Mannheim calls this a paradoxical situation; according to Wolff (1964: 19), he never worked out the problem, but as will become clear in what follows, I think that, with help from a "positivism well-understood," phenomenology, and interpetative understanding in context, he attempted to find a solution.

Why does Mannheim sometimes speak of *Weltanschauung* and sometimes refer to the same concept as spirit? Does he, after all mean to convey a difference in meaning by the two terms? I there a difference in emphasis? In his earliest handlings of the philosophy of culture (SK and BL) he spoke in a metaphysical-idealistic manner about spirit, by which the totality of the cultural objectivizations is to be understood:

> The meaning of a form can be adequately explained only by the spiritual content that avails itself of it. (BL: 6)

In his article about *Weltanschauung* the emphasis is different: from the cultural objectivizations he wishes to make a contribution for interpreting spirit as *Weltanschauung*. From the variety of ontic fields of culture, he intends to build this concept of totality and to be academically responsible in doing so:

> The crucial question is how the totality we call spirit, *Weltanschauung*, of an epoch, can be distilled from the various "objectifications" of that epoch – and how we can give a theoretical account of it. (WI: 73)

Can we here already read an inclination toward realism? I have characterized his epistemology as (transcendental-)realistic, and we shall see that influences of realism are demonstrable in his later theories.

Mannheim's Interpretation
Mannheim's intention is to demonstrate that each cultural form can be included in the concept of *Weltanschauung*, only under the following conditions: first, one must apprehend the cultural form phenomenologically in its objective meaning, that is as a thing by itself (*Es selbst*); second, after that one must widen the view to include the being of a thing in relationship to the "totality" of beings

of the mediate kind. In connection with this second point, two levels of meaning are distinguished for every cultural form:

a) the intentional *expressive meaning* – the expressive meaning, for instance which an actor gives to the playing of his part, and
b) the *documentary meaning* which arises from the more inclusive social-cultural context in which a production or cultural phenomenon is situated (WI: 43, 44).

A cultural form never becomes only phenomenological in its objective meaning, as a self, but also is seen as expression and as document.

Mannheim (WT:44 ff) gives the following example in which the characteristic moments of meaning become apparent. I walk with a friend and he gives an alms to a beggar. I do not see the motion of his hand as physiological, but as the bearer of meaning, namely, help. In the process of understanding, the happening itself becomes the bearer of a phenomenological *objective meaning*, which, according to Mannheim, lies in the sociological sphere. In the social context the "one" becomes a beggar; the "other" the giver of help; the money becomes alms. The cultural form is here a concept which must be localized sociologically as a meaningful form: help. This meaningful concept assumes no knowledge about my friend's psychic life, nor that of the beggar, but only about the objective social context.

The example becomes more elaborate: the friend shows sympathy. Through the gesture of granting, the bearer of the objective meaning (help) now acquires a second moment of meaning: *expressive meaning*. With his deed the friend desired to bring something to expression. This moment of meaning cannot detach itself from the world of experience of the subject. Only from within the inner experience does this moment of meaning acquire its significance.

As a third possibility of interpretation Mannheim names the *documentary meaning*. The gift may be interpreted as hypocrisy. Not what he has done objectively, not even what he intended, but what an observer documents about him and his deed. Here the emphasis is on the interpretation by the observer. This interpretation of meaning can be very far removed from the second meaning which comes forth from the actor himself; he can remember the meaning. What the action means in a documentary way depends on a new interpretation. The relevant action is "evidence for his substantial being." "Every behavioral datum will serve to illustrate my synoptical appraisal of his personality as a whole; and this appraisal need not be limited to his moral character – it may take his global orientation as a whole into its purview." In the documentary meaning a unity is granted which we call spirit. In Mannheim's examples, this spirit refers to the "total" *Weltanschauung* of a person; moreover, he wishes to investigate the worldview-meaning or documentary meaning of a whole era (WI: 47).

Mannheim's argument reaches its climax in his scholarly analysis of the documentary meaning or the *Weltanschauung* meaning. In other words, how can the totality of spirit or of worldview of a particular time be built up out of particular objectivizations? If it is demonstrated that the documentary meaning is one of the givens in cultural forms, then its knowability is guaranteed by means of a mature positivsm or a "positivism well-understood," phenomenology, and interpretive understanding in context.

Positivism Well-understood

In his interpretation of *Weltanschauung*, Mannheim expresses a paradox: on the one hand the spirit or the*Weltanschauung* is built up out of the cultural objectivizations, and on the other hand these objectivizations receive their significance from that same totality mentioned before. At the basis of this paradox of interpretation, according to Mannheim, lies a principal paradox: the *Weltanschauung* is in its very nature a-theoretical and not a product of thought. That is, the *Weltanschauung* is, according to theoretical principles, impossible to state conclusively. Although he understands this, he nonetheless desires to make a contribution to the interpretation of the *Weltanschauung*. He attempts to solve the paradox of interpretations and in doing so at the time wrestles with the solution to the principal paradox. This struggle with the paradoxes, as we shall see in the following paragraphs, gives a tremendous tension to the elaboration of his view. Contrary to the insoluble logical paradoxes discussed in the previous chapter, Mannheim intends to solve the paradox of interpretation with help from "positivism well-understood," phenomenology, and interpretive undersstanding.

Just as Dilthey, Mannheim assumes a polemic stance against positivism and empiricism, in order to emerge above both of these adversary positions. According to Dilthey, positivism handles the approach of the natural sciences too dogmatically; in its study of society, this approach violates what it is to be human. With respect to empiricism, Dilthey demarcates his standpoint against what he thought was an inaccurate use of the word *experience* by Kant, for whom experience is grounded on induction and the possibility for the truth of experience is based on a necessary and valid agreement by everyone. According to Dilthey, empiricism is often interpreted unjustly as positivism. Unlike conventional positivists, he wants to look away from established ideas about things and from a priori approaches. He wants to get the *object itself* into focus *without labeling beforehand*. Experiences, for Dilthey, have a fuller and more comprehensive meaning than do the arbitrary and atomistic ideas of experience for the empiricists. *He wants to regard experiences without mutilating them, in their underlying relationships and in historical context.*

In this context, Dilthey values positivism and empiricism, because "they allow something to start in relation to themselves" (1911: 3, 77). Dilthey wanted to study life as it is. The *Weltanschauung* is part of life; an analysis of life implies an analysis of the *Weltanschauung*. The analysis of the *Weltanschauung* "will certainly serve to look more deeply into history, and certainly more deeply from within life" (1911a: 30).

96

Dilthey combined his interpretation of positivism and empiricism with Husserl's phenomenology (Dilthey, 1911b: lxxvif; Bollnow, 1936: 21) Mannheim finds himself totally in the tradition of Dilthey, when he rejects positivism based on the natural sciences alone and when he becomes a champion for a "positivism well-understood." He also makes use of phenomenological insights in obtaining from reality knowledge which is true to reality.

Phenomenology

In the German edition of his dissertation Mannheim already refers to Husserl's *Ideen zu einer Phaenomenologie und Phaenomenologischen Philosophie (Ideas Toward Phenomenology anda Phenomenological Philosophy, 1913)*. In his interpretation of *Weltanschauung*, he cites only the *Logische Untersuchungen (Logical Investigations, 1900/1901)* by Husserl. Mannheim uses the phenomenological method and remarks in passing in a footnote:

> It will be obvious to anyone familiar Husserl's work to what extent this phenomenological analysis is indebted to him, and in how far his procedure has been modified for our purposes. (WI: 43)

This means, certainly, that Mannheim counted himself among the initiates. Just as with other philosophers, Mannheim seems to feel neither the need for particular quotations nor argumentation to announce at which points exactly he differs from Husserl. Mannheim has taken account of Husserl's phenomenology, and only uses that approach to the extent that it advances his argument.

Mannheim must not have agreed with Husserl's method for universal mathematics. If Mannheim was characterized in the preceding chapter as a transcendental realist, the word *transcendental* may not be interpreted in the sense that Husserl (1913: 72) gives to the transcendental or pure consciousness – or what is left after the phenomenological reduction. Mannheim speaks of an *historical consciousness*, which guarantees the possibility that "some approximate understanding of the intended meaning may be possible even in respect of works remote in time" (WI: 55). Also on this point we see the influence of Dilthey, to whom he refers, and who saw historical reason as a basis for a critical reflection of the self, a reflection which expresses itself in the guarantee for universal validity and for obtaining knowledge. The concept "approximate understanding" allows Mannheim the opening to approach and to clarify, with interpretive understanding, the *Weltanschauung*, which, theoretically can not be expressed completely.

Mannheim agrees with Husserl, that the disciplines in their specialized approaches to reality must endeavor to keep in mind whatever evidence from reality gives meaning and value to their discipline. For studying the objective meaning of cultural forms, Mannheim takes over an eidetic reduction. He renounces the expressive and the documentary meaning and looks for the *eidos*. He wants to direct himself according to the essence, the being of cultural forms.

97

If Husserl speaks about "essential intuition" (*Wesensschau*), Mannheim (40) speaks of the "a-theoretical attitude of form perception":

> The evocative passages (of the best criticism) merely serve to make the structure of the various cultural products visible. The object of pure aesthetic intuition as such precedes theoretical analysis. (WI: 72)

Mannheim also speaks about a cultural phenomenon which he wishes to study as "a thing in itself," and afterwards comes to understand it as "expression" and "document" (WI: 72).

As mentioned above, Mannheim's use of the concept *transcendental* is not the same as Husserl's. Mannheim is concerned with the historical consciousness. Does this imply that the rejects the transcendental consciousness of Husserl as a supra-temporal consciousness, as he explicitly does later (H: 90; IU: 59)? Although in this connection Mannheim does not write about the transcendental consciousness, could it be interpreted as a component part of his philosophy, specifically to the extent that it relates to his study of the objective level of meaning? The phenomenology of Husserl, after all, intends to be pre-theoretical and a preparation for philosophical and disciplinary research. This place is actually secured for pre-theoretical study in Mannheim's system: after a phenomenological study follows a study of expressive and documentary meanings. But how do the historical and transcendental consciousness relate to each other in Mannheim's philosophy? Because the claims of the historical and transcendental consciousness are mutually exclusive, it is a problem to see the transcendental consciousness as a part of the historical consciousness. As was written above, Mannheim never justifies his use of Husserl's phenomenology. It is a neglect that gets its revenge, because it leads to philosophical inconsistencies.

Interpretive Understanding in Context
Mannheim proceeds from his "positivism well-understood" and his phenomenological insights, that, indeed various fields are to be distinguished and that each field "possesses its own manner of being given," such as its own possibilities, demands, limits, and mode of theory. We encounter anew his ontic plurality and the methodological plurality based on it.

With great sensitivity Mannheim goes to work when he states that there are fields which are extremely difficult to theorize about. We get no farther with such fields than a circumscription and a "lightening" of phenomena in a given context.

For the adequate understanding of the meaning of cultural forms, he uses the method of "interpretive understanding" (*verstehen*). Without discussing all the various interpretations of understanding, Mannheim briefly states that his interpretation differs from that of Husserl, Rickert, and Spranger (WI: 41). Although the concept "interpretive understanding" is reminiscent of the method of "interpetive understanding" in Max Weber's sociology, Mannheim does not mention Weber in this connection. This is understandable because Weber elaborates "interpretive understanding" in a rational meaning which can be further subdivided into logical and mathematical (1921: 90). Mannheim discusses historical studies by Weber with esteem; however, he differs from Weber's methodological-sociological elaboration of the "interpretive understanding" of social action "in order thereby to arrive at a causal explanation of its course and effects" (1921: 88).

Although Weber argues that we should interpret social actions in a rational or a mathematical-calculable manner, he is aware that this interpretation of causality is related to natural phenomena, and that in sociology we can transcend the pure calculation of "laws." In sociology we can understand behavior in a way that is impossible in the natural sciences. It seems that we can understand human behavior with an interpretive method that transcends mathematical calculation (1921: 103-104). He acknowledges the influences of passions, emotions, and beliefs. Therefore, he does not speak of the *exact* calculation of the development of social actions, but of the *chance* to calculate these actions. In other words, sociology as a science calculates what a person *can* do and *how* he can do it, but never what he *should* do or *will* do. But does Weber clarify how we can understand in an interpretive way that transcends causal explanation?

Answering this question, we need to combine the causal method of the social science with his concept "value relatedness" *(Wertbeziehung)*. According to Weber, sociologists, psychologists, historians, and other social scientists can never be "objective" in the same way as physicists. In opposition to physicists, they consider reality from the perspective of their subjective worldview and values. A purely "objective" scientific analysis of social phenomena does not exist. The basis for this opinion is the particular perspective and goal of knowledge that every social scientist has, to transcend every "formal" consideration of social phenomena (1904: 72).

The following step is that, within his perspective, the sociologist tries to understand interpretatively the context of meaning of a chosen phenomenon. Moreover, this interpretative understanding is controlled by the causal explanation. In other words: the causal explanation takes place within the framework of the interpretative understanding, and it is an elaboration of this interpretation.

Although Mannheim in this connection has no relationship to the causal explanation of interpretive understanding, on the subject of interpretive understanding that transcends mathematical calculation and of interpretive understanding in Weber's historical studies there is such a relationship. With the help of this interpretive understanding Mannheim attempts to solve the paradox of the *Weltanschauung* analysis: that the *Weltanschauung* is a-theoretical and hence is principally impossible to comprehend theoretically, and at the same time we seek to interpret it theoretically. (Compare the philosophic-historical interpretive understanding in social-historical context by Dilthey, 1927: 84-87; Simmel; 1905: 36ff).

In the foreword to this *Gesammelte Aufsätze zur Religionsoziologie (Collected Essays on the Sociology of Religion*, also included in *Protestant Ethics*, 1904/05), Weber writes about a chain of circumstances which contributed to the dynamic development of Western culture. He is not concerned with analysis of simplistic causal relations, for instance, between rationality and the development of Western culture, or between the Calvinist ethic and the rise of capitalism. Weber emphasizes repeatedly that many more factors have led to the origin of any phenomenon and that the scholar looks at only one of these. To this abstracted factor he attributes a special power of illumination or "causal imputation," a concept cited by Mannheim. Weber does not aim with this concept to establish general laws after the model of the causality of the natural sciences, but to understand the individual phenomenon in a functional relationship with other components in an historical constellation. In other words, causality has its place in seeing through the functional relationships within historical constellations; there is a richly varied and many-sided causality in functional relationships, in which one abstracts all kinds of factors and harnesses other powers which bring into existence a given phenomenon. The scholar gives an imputation to these established factors within the functional constellation of richly varied causality. In such a way Weber desires to understand "interpretive understanding" in his historical studies.

This conception of interpretive understanding appeals to Mannheim. He desires to illuminate the particular cultural form in its objective meaning and in tis expressive meaning, in order to understand, in the plural context of the *Weltanschauung*, the documentary meaning. Or, to get it from Mannheim himself:

> Meaning in its proper essence can only be understood or interpreted. Understanding is the adequate grasping of an intended meaning or of the validity of a proposition (this, then, includes the objective as well as the expressive stratum of meaning); interpretation means bringing the abstractively distinguished strata of meaning in correlation to each other and especially to the documentary stratum. (WI: 81)

Moreover, each documentary interpretation does not have the same claim of validity or adequacy. Various interpretations of the *Weltanschauung* of a particular period are possible, and we can ask which is the most adequate. That is, "which one shows the greatest richness, the greatest substantial affinity with the object" (WI: 62). Our task is to translate less adequate into more adequate interpretations. "Neither objective nor expressive interpretations show this dynamic character" (WI: 62; cf. J.B. Harms, 1982).

Remmling's interpretation (1975: 25) of the objective meaning in a sociological manner instead of a phenomenological one is inaccurate. Probably this interpretation is based upon Mannheim's example of the imaginary walk with a friend who gives an alms. Then he says this event "belongs to the sociological field" (WI: 45). This means that after the phenomenological analysis, a sociological investigation is possible. Moreover, Mannheim is not quite clear in his relationship to phenomenology. Remmling detracts from Mannheim's intention to comprehend the "thing itself" in terms of phenomenology, which precedes disciplinary study. A sociological innterpretation is possible in studying the expressive meaning; this has reference not alone to the conscious subjective significance, but also to the intentional expression of classes, groups, and communities. Concerning the relationship between the individual and the collective group, Mannheim says the following in connection with the expressive meaning:

> Since we can assign expressive meaning only to a real subject or to his stream of consciousness, we can construe the "expressive meaning" entertained by a group only in a strictly nominalist fashion as the meaning entertained *on the average* by the individual members of that group. The characterization of a group in the light of a documentary approach, however, is a different matter; for the purposes of such characterization, we may well make use of collective subjects which are pure constructs, and whose cognitive value consists merely in the fact that they serve as the subjective counterpart of the characterological units suggested by the documentary interpretation. (WI: 61)

We see that a study can be made of the socially-differentiated documentary meaning. We also see, that, with reference to the expressive meaning of the community, there is the possibility for a "general cross-sectional meaning," which comes to expression through individuals. Although the expressive meaning, or meaning as realized indirect experience,according to Mannheim (WI: 46, 47), can be acknowledged as historical fact, it would seem from the above that he also regards it as a social phenomenon.

Above, the subject was the interpretation of the mediately given *Weltanschauung* with the help of an analysis of the immediately given cultural manifestations. As we already discussed, something becomes a cultural matter only when it acquires an historical-social character (SK: 70). The fulfillment of the soul never comes about by means of introspection, but by way of the detour of cultural objects. In answer to the question as to which aspect of a person most nearly approaches Being, Mannheim answers that through the medium of work a person must actualize himself or herself. To answer the question about Mannheim's interpretive understanding of cultural objectivizations, we can answer that their being, the things themselves, must be related to the *Weltanschauung*, as this comes to expression in its social differentiation; or to put it briefly: we know cultural products on the basis of a differentiatied and various social-historical context.

Conclusions
Just as in "Soul and Culture," so Mannheim, in his essay on *"Weltanschauung,"* was motivated by his concern about the lack of vision of the unity of culture and, consequently, the various fields of culture which grow apart from each other.

On grounds of the arguments presented in the previous chapter, he is also still to be regarded as a *transcendental realist* in his essay on "Weltanschauung." Interpreting his philosophy we need, however, to consider that the influence of Dilthey and Husserl is powerful.

The contours of his philosophy are cultural-philosophical in kind. This philosophy of culture does not refer to a philosophy of the World Spirit (Hegel), but rather to the *Weltanschauung* for a given historical period, which needs to be studied in a differentiated-sociological manner. In addition, it is important that Mannheim wrote about the paradox of the interpretation of *Weltanschauung*; that he attempted to overcome the paradox with help from his "positivism well-understood," phenomenology, and with his interpretive understanding. Interpretive understanding is also the way to solve the principal paradox, mentioned earlier. This paradox cannot be explained rationally, but with help from his "interpretive understanding in context," he attempts to solve it in principle. Still, his use of phenomenology is problematic.

Chapter VII
Historicism

Historicism as Worldview

Mannheim's article about historicism appeared in 1924. We can regard it as the conclusion of his first phase of development, which is Remmling's opinion as well (1975: 13, 36). His essay on historicism is also the transition to the second phase: the sociology of culture and the sociology of knowledge.

Mannheim saw historicism in his time as "an intellectual force." For him it was an unavoidable "moral obligation to seek a solution to the problem of hisotricism." To name it an intellectual force means that for him it carries within it a *new worldview*. Just as Meinecke (1936: 1), Mannheim regards historicism as one of the greatest intellectual evolutions which has happened in Western civilization. He also calls historicism his own worldview; it not alone gives direction to intellectual and scientific life, but also to everyday life. In daily parlance, in words like *capitalism, social mobility*, and *cultural process*, a conception of history is implied; we apprehend these concepts as "potentialities, constantly in flux," as coming from somewhere in time and as striving for something (cf. ST: 171, 172). Mannheim does not provide a narrow definition of historicism. It is a worldview:

> Historicism, therefore, is a *Weltanschauung*, and at the present stage of development of consciousness it is characteristic of *Weltanschauung* that it should not only dominate our inner reactions and our external responses, but also determine our forms of thought. Thus, at the present stage, science and scientific methodology, logic, epistemology, and ontology are all molded by the historicist approach. Historicism exists only since the problems involved in the new ways of facing life – problems which found their most tangible expression in historiography – reached this level of self-consciousness. (H: 85, 86)

Already now I point out the following: if Mannheim in a previous publication had substituted the word *Weltanschauung* for spirit, in the article now being discussed, the word *Weltanschauung* is replaced by historicism. If in Chapter V the concept of "without presuppositions" was discussed as the beginning of all philosophizing, now he no longer discusses that. He proceeds with his philosophizing along the route of historicism, which also affects epistemology.

The Matrices of Historicism

Although the word *historicism* was coined at the end of the nineteenth century (K. Werner first used it in 1879, Carl Menger in 1884, Troeltsch in 1896; cf. J. Klapwijk, 1970: 45, 46), Mannheim just as Troeltsch and Meinecke, sees this pattern of thought originially in the end of the eighteenth century as a reaction against the Enlightenment.

The first reaction against the Enlightenment was expressed in the *Sturm-und-Drang* (Storm and Stress). In Romanticism the reaction against the strain of natural science in Enlightenment philosophy came to life. Not reason but passion, not accountability but feeling were regarded as the essential kernel of culture in Romanticism. The subjectivism of *Sturm-und-Drang* was also present in Romanticism, as were the reaction against conventions and laws, and the new honor accorded poetic genius. In romantic thought the person and society, the individual and the universal, are not related as part to whole (as was often the case in the thought of Enlightenment rationalism), but were linked together mysteriously. Social relationships were construed as organisms with a dynamic spirit held in common (cf. O. Walzel, 1912: 7-13; H.G. Schenk, 1966: 3-45). *Mysterious* is the right word: Romanticism lays a heavy accent on the individual and personal dimension among people and emphasizes self-expression as a protest against being shaped by customs; it seeks the infinite and universal. It seeks for the ends of the earth, then becomes insecure about its own identity, then turns to the personal consciousness again, and then returns to find a way back to the universal all over again. The life of a romantic is the opposite of a streamlined life; it is continually living in tension and release, in integration and disintegration, in objectifying and in deobjectifying. From the point of view of its metaphysical-organic communal thought, Romanticism is typically historical. All aspects of life and society are founded on a specific bonding together of culture, in an historical community. The forms of society are not rational associations, but typically historical communities, which arise out of the past. Everything is to be understood historically, as Mannheim describes it, as "potentialities, constantly in flux" or "a dynamic process of development" (H: 84, 85; cf. Vallas, 1979: 464).

Next to Romanticism, the idealism of Fichte must also be seen as the matrix for historicism. The romantic historiography referred to "the processes of growth" of the countless cultural fellowships. Fichte saw history as a universal history of mankind, individually and collectively. As the various cultures become one, the absolute Idea (Hegel's "World Spirit") will be revealed. The particular and distinguishable historical communities are only specializations of universal humanity which differentiates itself in countless riches of communities (cf. Klapwijk, 1970: 39, 40).

As the third matrix for historicism the discipline of modern history must be mentioned. This method of doing historical scholarship differs from the traditional practice of history, in Klapwijk's words (1970: 42), "particularly in the demand that the testing of the historical sources and the interpretation of historical events must observe the stated rules of academic criticism. Each bit of historical evidence tried to legitimatize itself before the judgment seat of reason, and not one interpretation handed down was accepted on the basis of authority." Although the interpretation of factual material was still strongly influenced by romantic and idealistic historicism, particularly Hegelian influence, historians of the nineteenth century seemed increasingly to be gripped by new methodological insights (cf. H.J. Störig, 1967: 18ff, 22).

In Mannheim's article on historicism, he distinguishes two lines of thought. The first line refers to the conception of history as a continuing stream, a flow, a continuous becoming, in which the idea of development is central. The second line of thought refers to the unique value of cultural periods and of cultural communities. All aspects of life are established in specific cultural relationships. This line wants to break through the relativism of the view that history is continuous development. A problem is whether the relativism can be broken down in the way or whether it simply gets reformulated. Between these two lines a great tension exists. What is unique about a particular period of culture in the stream of historical events? Is the uniqueness of a cultural period only a part of the continuous development? What is the continuity in the discontinuity, and what restricts the discontinuous in the continuous? Mannheim does not handle these questions. The first mentioned line of thought, continuity, gives him access to historicism, while the second, according to him, refers to the central kernel of historicism. He gives some attention to the first line of thought and elaborates on the second. He does not specifically treat tension between the two lines of historicism, although the tension is present in his work.

In later publications Mannheim speaks about the conservative origin of historicism; thus, historicism is construed as a continuing stream:

> Historicism... is an exceedingly complex and many-sided phenomenon, both in its internal structure and in its sociological foundation. But in its chief points it is of conservative origin. It arose everywhere as a political argument against the revolutionary breach with the past. A mere interest in history becomes historicism when historical facts are not merely lovingly contrasted with the facts of the present, but where "growth" as such becomes a real experience. This is the common meaning of Burke's "continuity," French traditionalism, and German historicism. (KD: 137)

Elsewhere he says that

> ...there was the historicism of the Conservatives who, for their part denied precisely the possibility of deducing by pure reasoning a system of solutions right in themselves. (...) They were extremely sceptical with regard to Reason, and doubted whether the deductive-constructive method could ever produce anything either true or applicable. For them, there existed only the object gradually developing through time, and the meaning contained in this process of becoming – in the last resort nothing but individual, completely self-contained epochs. Truth could only be formulated as relative to this historical reality,

but never in any absolute way. Ranke provides the classical expression of this approach with his remark: "Every epoch is God's own" *(Jedes Zeitalter is unmittelbar zu Gott)* (BK: 222,223).

It is necessary to perceive that Mannheim in rejecting conservative historicism meant only the first-named strain of historicism. His judgment does not affect the second line. He hangs on to that second line and proceeds on its basis (contrary to Lay, 1973: 66).

Historicism versus Enlightenment: The Idea of Development

Mannheim regarded the development of the Middle Ages until the nineteenth and twentieth centuries as occurring in three phases. After the religious worldview of the Middle Ages was undermined and after the secular worldview of the Enlightment had arisen, the worldview of historicism arose (H: 84, 85; cf. Vallas 1979: 461). He describes the *idea of development* as the pivot of this new worldview, which thoroughly experiences and thoroughly thinks through reality, and then presses on to unfold the totality of life and the system of thought which belongs to this new worldview (H: 86). A person does not acquire access to historicism until he/she studies the development of institutions, customs, religions, psychic phenomena, and other matters.

The stream of the Enlightenment thought which patterned itself on the classical form of the natural sciences has already been mentioned. In this stream, the faulty results of previous philosophies were replaced and mistakes removed. Ideas and results of today are the standards for the past. Actually the results of earlier philosophers were negated in a manner which Mannheim calls *unhistorical* (H: 117, 118, 90). This judgment implies that he rejected the idea of the development of the natural sciences, because it always judges that development, not according ot its historic significance, but according to the time-bound standards of the most recently obtained results.

Mannheim is of the opinion that philosophies and results in various disciplines constantly must be incorporated into new and more inclusive systems, through which a new meaning is given to each element. What has come before is not demolished nor completed, but reorganized from the perspective of a new center (H: 90, 118). This historical idea of development forms the philosophical fulcrum of Mannheim's historicism. Enlightenment philosophy, particularly Kant's, which proceeds on the basis of the supra-temporality of reason, rejects historicism out of hand as relativism. It confronts historicism directly with the formal a priori categories of reason. Mannheim disputes this criticism of Enlightenment philosophy, because its so-called a priori categories can, and in fact do, undergo changes in the course of history.

Others – Mannheim mentions no names, but for examples we can consider the Marburgers – alleged against historicism that logic and epistemology have a priority above the particular disciplines. As he had already demonstrated in his dissertation, Mannheim posits instead that epistemology reveals the ultimate presuppositions of the structure of thought which is dominant for a particular time. According to him, epistemology and logic orient themselves to the structure of various fields of life-experience and to particular academic disciplines. The ideal of an eternally identical reason is nothing other than a proposition which gives direction to the reconstruction of an epistemological system based on that proposition. The basis of such an epistemological system comes, according to Mannheim, from the analysis of the thought structure of the natural sciences. Finally to put the natural sciences on a sound basis, philosophers needed to construct a static Reason, which made eternal laws possible. Other epistemologies would have appeared, Mannheim holds, if other starting points had been chosen.

In all considerations of historicism the issue is a confrontation between the most recent positions of a static philosophy of reason on the one hand and a dynamic-historic philosophy of life on the other. For the study of the philosophy of historicism in the first decades of this century he concentrates his attention on Troeltsch's *Der Historismus und seine Probleme (Historicism and its Problems*, 1922).

Historicism without Relativism

From his assessment of Troeltsch it appears how much Mannheim was fascinated by this scholar. In the first place he saw in Troeltsch's historicism a dispute against relativism (many scholars identify historicism with relativism). In the second place, Troeltsch, as philosopher of religion and of history, was one of those scholars who had introduced sociology as part of the curriculum of the German universities. Thirdly, Mannheim must have been struck by Troeltsch's method of doing philosophy. He calls him "the journalist of academia" with no stigma attached to the term, because Troeltsch was not only a scholar in his study who accomplished detailed studies within a narrow discipline with the help of carefully formulated statements of the problems at hand; Troeltsch wished to stand in the midst of life and

> to combine his theoretic interests with the suffering of a deeply disturbed world. This sometimes leads to a fondness for uttering the latest conclusions without taking time for reflection, and for searching after unprecedented novelties.

Mannheim continues with a statement concerning the sociology of knowledge:

> He desires, it would appear, to unite in his person the two antagonistic types into which present-day German thought is divided as a result of sociological causes: that of the original and often profound non-academic scholar and connoisseur, who, however, often dissipates his energies as a result of his psychological and professional freedom, on the one hand, and that of the academic teacher who is master of his subject but is remote from the living centre of present-day life, on the other. Such a synthesis would seem te be highly desirable in itself. (H: 98)

Elsewhere he writes about Troeltsch:

> His philosophical works are characterized by minute attention to every aspect of a problem, but they never developed into a well-rounded and complete system. This may be explained partly by the fact that Troeltsch was the dynamic type of thinker who sought always to reflect the spiritual and social forces operating around him. (T: 106)

Mannheim wants to learn to know the contours of the philosophy and epistemology of Troeltsch, because these are not based on the natural sciences but on history. Speaking about the history-knowing subject, there is a contradiction between the philosophical starting points of Kant and Troeltsch. Kant and his followers make a sharp distinction between contemplation and practise, the knowing subject and the total person. In Kantianism the knowing subject is set free from the "concrete voluntary impulses" and form the "historically determined conditions of psychic life in general" (H: 101). As such it is a theoretical construction. This abstract epistemological subject is permitted according to the exact natural sciences; if one asks for the judgments of historians, one gets other answers. A positivist, an historicist, a Hegelian, and a Marxist each possesses his/her own chosen principle, which is tied in with other positions in the philosophy of history. So Troeltsch comes to his central thesis:

> that historical knowledge is only possible from an ascertainable intellectual location (*Standort*), that it presupposes a subject harbouring definite aspirations regarding the future and actively striving to achieve them. Only out of the interest which the subject at present acting has in the pattern of the future, does the observation of the past become possible. The trend of historical selection, the form of objectification and representation only becomes understandable in terms of the orientation of present activity. That is the ultimate meaning and these are the implications of that which Troeltsch designates by the expression "cultural synthesis within the present" (*gegenwärtige Kultursynthese*). (H: 102; cf. Troeltsch, 1922: 116, 164-179, 692)

The historical subject, who wishes for the cultural synthesis (that is, the productive binding together of the tendencies of the contemporary time, which to active people seems desirable and creative), may not be identified with the subjective-empirical 'I' of the historian. That 'I' of the historian stands midway between the historical subject and the Kantian abstraction, so that finally, it may break down the barriers of historic relativism and the supra-temporal idea of reason. The historically-philosophically relevant subject is the "kernel of the human personality whose being and dynamism is consubstantial with the dominant active forces of history" (H: 104).

Does a doctrine of the relativity of all historical knowledge necessarily follow from this position? In the work of Troeltsch, Mannheim sees a tendency that takes historicism away from relativism. In the first place, the values which serve as standards have grown and developed out of the very same historical process which they help us to understand. From this follows the limitation of applicability of standards to their *own* sphere of culture in a given period. Also, an evaluation and reproduction of those periods is only possible on the basis of their *own* values and standards. Mannheim calls this approach the *immanent critique and reproduction of the past* (H: 104f; cf. Troeltsch, 1922: 117, 171, 177, 183). The possibility for this critique and reproduction comes from interpretive understanding (*Verstehen*)

> as an intuitive faculty of the historian, which enables him to penetrate into his subject-matter, into the concrete valuations of the epochs in question, to a degree which is denied us when we are dealing with nature. (H: 105; cf.Troeltsch, 1922: 172)

From the above it is clear that Mannheim presents a global overview in his essay on historicism. He traces several lines and puts his special mark on historicism in opposition to the tradition of Enlightenment thought. He does place Troeltsch over against Kant, but he does not mention the influence of Rickert on the thought of Troeltsch. It would seem from his earlier publications that he was well-informed concerning the world of ideas of the neo-Kantians in Germany. The differences of interpretation concerning the distinction between natural sciences and humanities were well known to him. Still, the names of Rickert and Windelband never appear in his essay on historicism and the name of Dilthey appears only by the bye. Mannheim has crept through the problematical aspect of neo-Kantianism. In his view of historicism, it is clear that he is occupied in leaving the debates behind him. Also in later studies he hardly more than names Rickert and Dilthey and their followers. Troeltsch stands for a moment longer in the intense light from the spotlights of Mannheim's concentrated attention. But Troeltsch's historicism must be exploited and must be built upon. This building happens in a direction which will get more and more of Mannheim's attention: the sociological. Among the ways that this appears is his working out of Troeltsch's concept of the cultural synthesis within the present.

Contemporary Cultural Synthesis

Troeltsch understands by the *cultural synthesis* the necessity of binding together the past with the contemporary scene. Each social-cultural situation is more than an isolated totality; it not only goes through its own development; it also is caught up in a broader development of totality, a "universally historical" stream of development. Troeltsch sees the *cultural synthesis* directed toward this "universal history." In his own words:

> There is then a resulting universal history, which is organized on the basis of a contemporary cultural synthesis, and there is a contemporary cultural synthesis which is derived out of the developmental force of our historical context of life (1922: 692)

The concept of a universal-historical development, already acknowledged as a problem in idealist philosophy, is not conceived as a process of progress to a specific goal nor a realization of that goal. (The idea of a universal-historical development appears in the work of Hegel, Comte, Marx, Spengler, and others, and it is very different in each, but all agree in this respect, that there is a predetermined goal.) The new cultural synthesis is perceived as an "end point" of history, while history is seen as a course of development from which the synthesis can be explained. After 1920 Troeltsch raised some objections to the theory of an universal-historical development. He does not deny this theory, but he considers the histories of different peoples, a kind of comparative sociology of culture. The idea of a continuous cultural development is central, but only after the process of building up of the increasingly differentiated cultural components. This idea of building up proceeds, not on the basis of continuity, but on the basis of discontinuity, which can be distinguished sociologically. The past is seen as layered. The most richly influential intellectual motifs from a particular period in the past must be bound in the new cultural synthesis or cultural ideal, or model of society (cf. Troeltsch, 1922: 703-730).

Mannheim also strives for a new synthesis of culture. He wants to do justice to the various cultural spheres and cultural periods which can be distinguished from each other, and at the same time he wants to judge these by their own proper standards. He connects this idea with his first line of historicism. In spite of his great regard for Troeltsch, he finds Troeltsch's historicism unsatisfactory because it is not able to demonstrate exactly how historical tendencies (first line), and the theory of building up history (second line) could be brought together. Mannheim wants to make this binding together happen. By showing how this can be achieved, Mannheim desires to make a contribution to a new cultural synsthesis, a problem with which he has been struggling since his first publication. For him the intellectual dislocation of the Western world, expressed in the rupture between "soul" and "culture," was a tragedy. He wants to help promote the unity of these two elements. Working for the preservation and renewal of the cultural inheritance in these twilight lands would increasingly become a struggle for him.

Mannheim looks for the possibilities of a form for the idea of history which can be derived from the tendencies of history itself. He acknowledges two fundamentally different attempts: the Hegelian dialectic and the method of the historical school. According to Mannheim, Troeltsch looked for a connection between both ways; he establishes that Troeltsch did not work out a concrete, dialectical bonding between these two (H: 106ff). He wants to go farther than Troeltsch. If one regards the *dialectical philosophy of history* in the manner of Hegel on the one hand and on the other *the visible-organic reconstruction of forms from various cultural and experiential entities* in the manner of the historical school, then one notices that both methods are hardly adequate for certain aspects of culture and life.

He borrows from Alfred Weber the distinction between "cultural movement" and "the process of civilization":

110

> The psychic-emotional phenomena...can be adequately grasped only by methods of concrete intuition and representation, stressing the *Gestalt*, and by a specific type of concept evolved for this purpose. "Civilization," in Weber's sense on the other hand, can be described by the rationalizing method of the philosophy of the Enlightenment, which conceived of it as a continuous progress. (H: 114)

Mannheim goes on:

> We believe, however, that there is a third field, which stands midway between "culture"'and "civilization" in this sense, namely, philosophy and some related disciplines; and also that this intermediate field exhibits a strongly marked dialectical character in the structure of its development. (H: 115)

What he means by *dialectic*, in this context, in distinction from the "rationally progressive" Enlightenment thought, he formulates as follows:

> A development sequence is dialectical when the successive structures replace one another in such a way that the following structure preserves the earlier in the form of a new system with a new centre of systemization. A sequence, on the other hand, has the character of limited progress when the entire development is encompassed within *one and the same system* which merely becomes more complete as time passes and, so to speak, adds new chapters to a system which may still grow but is always coherent in itself. (H: 115)

In the process of the "civilization" model, faulty conclusions are replaced and mistakes are eliminated. One behaves principially in such a system. Ideas and conclusions of today are the standards for the past. The situation is entirely different for the spheres which move forward dialectically. What came before is neither demolished nor completed, but reorganized on the principle of a new center:

> These new centres are, however, supra-philosophically, or rather, supra-theoretically based; they are dependent on the new life situation, which, *in scientific epochs, includes the prevailing type of* scientific system. *It is these centres of organization, then, which, in this sense express the truth of the epoch concerned.* (H: 117; italics, W.)

These systems are not equally valuable nor progressive; they are dialectical because from inside of a comprehensive system they organize a world picture in which earlier insights are preserved.

Earlier I wrote that the idea of historical development gives access to historicism. This idea actually does not yet touch the essence of historicism. A second strain of historicism was also mentioned in which the uniqueness of various periods and fields of culture was emphasized. Between the two strains the tension, also mentioned before, exists. According to Mannheim, historicism ripens and its essence is apprehended when people see that the changing appearances of one time period are comparable to those of another, and when they perceive a principle of order at the base of the change, in other words, when people see that an *inner structure* is present in the changes. According to Mannheim, this principle of order can be worked out in two complementary directions. In terms of linguists such as De Saussure and structuralists such as Lévi-Strauss, one can summarize these two directions as the diachronic and the synchronic. In the first case one takes one or more motifs from socio-cultural life, follows these back, and attempts to explain how phenomena have come forth out of earlier continuously organic phases which follow after each other. In the second case the subject for study is how the particular motifs of a given phase of contemporaneity display an organic context mutually with the social-cultural life in general; the particular motifs are parts and functions of the whole, which is the actual subject of the total change. The purpose of historicism is to get the structure of this totality in focus by means of the study of particular moments (H: 86, 87). Not only the direct question "Why?" concerning a phenomenon is of interest to us, but even more the question "What does it mean?" Because we insert the element to be understood into a dynamic totality in order to understand its meaning within this context of the whole, we are active in philosophy. In particular phenomena lies much more than the things themselves; the totality permeates them; the systemizing principle is present in the particular phenomenon and forms the presuppositions for our knowing it, seeing it, thinking about it, and acting with regard to it.

If one proposes to think through entirely the philosophy of hsitoricism, then one must also be willing to look at philosophy itself historically and must be willing to assign to the history of philosophy a systematic meaning. One must be willing to answer the questions of how the philosophies of various time periods relate to each other. Do they complement each other? Do they negate each other? Do they constitute portions of a system which is still incomplete?

Mannheim is of the opinion that philosophies are always caught up in the framework of newer and more comprehensive systems, through which process a new meaning is given to each element. The negation of the conclusions of earlier philosophers would be unhistorical. He also declares it impossible to negate a new philosophy, which contains its own foundation as a basis for analysis and reflection, on the basis of the premisses of an earlier system – for this reason: that the earlier premises are necessarily in conflict with the later ones.

Sociological Differentiation within Historical Periods
Mannheim brings the previous ideas up for discussion only to this end: that they will provide possible solutions to the problems which had been raised by the historicism of Troeltsch. He wants to demonstrate "the sociological determination of methodological forms" (H: 124), and with reference to this "positional determination of knowledge," he discusses "a coordination and affinity between styles of thought and life on the one hand and certain social groups and their particular dynamics on the other" (H: 125).

Mannheim goes one step beyond Troeltsch. Both see the two lines of historicism: the historical continuity and the cultural phases which can be distinguished. Although Troeltsch had not been able, according to Mannheim, to bring about a synthesis between the historical continuum and the cultural-sociological progress of the epochs through history, Mannheim intends to reduce the tension between these two by means of a study of the internal structuring principle or the ordering principle of society. Here lies his transition form philosophy: he studies these internal structures primarily synchronically. That is, he goes about systemizing society as a whole by means of its "systematic presuppositions" (cf. his *Structural Analysis*). This systemization is continually elevated into a new systemization.

Inasmuch as he has insight into the sociological determination of these methodological forms, he deems it very likely that the activist-progressive directions taken in this time would elaborate the rational dialectic and absolutize it. The dialectic offers people a calculable standard for orientation for political activity; it is a totally different formulation from that which belongs to thought construed as organic (which in turn was a product of the post-revolutionary, contemplative period) – this organic thought being proper now for stabilizing conservative tendencies in society.

A philosophy of history which thinks in terms of historical periods and which is inclined to ignore the internal differentiations of these periods, must be completed by "a view of the social differentiations in the societal enterprise." No single societal stratum or class, moreover, carries the totality of the dynamic society. Therefore, in order to study this "societal enterprise," one may not orient himself or herself on only one social level or class, even if that one class turns out to bear the dominant theme for a particular period. He calls the problem of social differentiation and of the social relatedness of knowledge an enriching of the vision of the philosophy of history.

For sociology the problem of the dynamics of knowledge arrived at through historicism represented an enrichment (HC: 125ff). Kecskemeti (1952: 13, 14) asserts that the sociological approach in Mannheim's formulation of historicism acquires a determinative significance. This assertion is not unjustified; Mannheim writes at the outset of his essay (H: 84) that his historical view of life "has become through and through sociological." Of course, we must point out that in his *Interpretation of Weltanschauung* he already pointed the way toward social differentiation (especially important for his later sociology of knowledge) and states that in the course of historical development, the styles of art which appear "are expressions of certain voluntary tendencies of the levels and classes of the group which bears those tendencies" (WI: 174).

Historicism is not a combination of historical conclusions and conclusions from the various academic disciplines, but a principial philosophy which goes back to the epistemological starting point on which it is founded. Epistemology occupies the position that metaphysics formerly occupied, and is, thus, a kind of metaphysics!

According to Mannheim, historicism is the only solution for the communal striving to find a dynamic worldview with *substantive norms contained within it*. These norms are not based on static and supra-temporal rationality, nor on "Christian-Catholic" tendencies. Historicism aims "only to be able to point out the substantively expressed advancements of the philosophy of history, both for the parts and for the whole." The strenght of historicism is that it does not regard the dynamic as a unanalyzable remainder waiting to be relativized, but makes the dynamic a positive Archimedian principle (cf. Schoeck, 1949/1950: 381; Wagner, 1952: 303).

The question of truth in Mannheim's theory of historicism stands midway between a rational and religious absolutism on the one hand, and on the other, a total relativism. Criteria for the answering of the truth question are derived from the structural analysis for specific historical periods. He discusses imma-nent criteria thus: they "express the truth of the epoch concerned" (H: 117). Not that there are no truths, but every age has its own truths. An important change in his view of truth is noteworthy. In his dissertation he wrote about "a truth independent from us": "We need to take it for granted that an ultimate, true, and complete form of any systemization exists objectively, independently of our own contribution" (SE: 26). In his historicism essay he denies that there are static, supra-temporal, and eternal truths.

In this sense the formulation of Kecskemeti (1952: 15) is correct, that the truth which interests Mannheim is a *truth made flesh in a real process* and not the truth of rational discourse. At the root of the matter, it is a religious conception of truth; he *believes* in the truth of history. As it already seemed, he saw historicism as the legitimate successor to religion. That is why Kecskemeti does not call him an agnostic, but a relativizing *gnostic*: "history, for him, was a royal road to truth rather than a procession of errors" (1975: 16).

In this context I return to interpretive understanding. In Chapter VI Man-nheim brought interpretive understanding into relation with the *historical dialectic*. In what precedes, interpretive understanding is spoken of as a capacity of the historian, who, with help from a structural analysis of a time period, must bring the concrete values to light. Interpretive understanding of cultural manifestations can be illuminated methodically, as, in Chapter VI, the three levels of meaning in a particular context are said to do: objective, expressive, and documentary.

According to Mannheim, it is clear that a new vision of the world is necessarily implied in and belongs to his new starting point, discovered through experience. That is, the dialectical dynamic, the starting point for historicism, should go along with a sociologically differentiated view of society (cf. Loader, 1985: 53-61).

In the beginning of this chapter we saw that the matrix for historicism was formed by Romanticism, idealism (Fichte), and the discipline of history. An historicism patterned on these ideas resulted in a cultural-sociological elaboration by Troeltsch. Already in the nineteenth century this combination of historicistic and sociological modes of thought appeared, particularly in the work of Comte and Marx.

Previous to going into Comte and Marx, I ask attention for Mannheim's view of the sociological components in Hegel's philosophy of history. History, according to Mannheim, becomes more and more identified with a comprehensive and dynamic world vision. It touches not only what has happened in the past, nor a chronological descirption of specific events. "History will be considered for the present purpose an *explicit* account of change narrated *comprehensively* as a *continuous* process" (sc: 36). To this definition he adds the following explanation. Changes can only be made explicit when in a satisfactory way an account is taken of the effective powers which achieve the course and the results of these processes. This means the unraveling of a network of factors which constitute the historical situation. Phenomena to be studied must be comprehended in the context of historical reality; that is, "in an exclusive framework of interrelated activities." "The historian may, however, view his subject in any particular perspective he chooses. (...) He will then select for presentation those facts which bear on his specialized interest, but he will place them in the comprehensive functions which give life duration" (sc: 37).

History is a distinguishing mark of an evolving social collectivity. When one observes history without this social medium, it is no more than a motion without the very element which moves. From this point Dilthey wrote about "social-historial actuality" and Hegel about "spirit of the people" (*Volksgeist*). However vague the concept "spirit of the people" may be, it offers, according to Mannheim, a framework for understanding other ideas of Hegel. Alas, this socially-related philosophy of history never became common property in the German literature because of its vagueness. The a-social conception of history, articulate and definite, has also challenged the dialectic in the post-Hegelian philosophy of history. In Hegel's conception the dialectic is the development in which Spirit in its various phases creates contradictions out of self-realization and solves them. Because Hegel identifies thought with reality and the evolution of Spirit with the historical process, the dialectic leads thought, not only, but also the course of universal history. Although in post-Hegelian thought it has become customary to speak of "the dialectics of history *per se*," Mannheim posits the following:

"Actually what is dialectical is not history but gives social situations which reveal inconsistencies of contradictions in the social structure. (...) The seat of contradictions is not the mind, nor the foreordained rhythm of history, but concrete social situations which give rise to conflicting aspirations and, hence, to antagonistic interpretations of reality."

The task of sociology is this: how to interpret the objectivizations in a structured framework which transcends individual experience. In this regard Mannheim cites Hegel's *Encyclopädie der Philosophischen Wissenschaften (Encyclopedia of the Philosophical Sciences)*, paragraph 62: "... to understand an object is ... to grasp it in its determinate or mediate character...." Sociology is a scientific investigation for the complex structure which lies at the very basis of the everyday activity of people and which "is grasped in a series of interrelated acts" (sc: 40). The influence of Simmel on Mannheim's conception of sociology, to be perceived even in these few citations, is discussed in Chapters VIII and, particularly, XIV.

Now already I wish to indicate that Mannheim in his sociology of knowledge explicitly announced his relationship to Hegel when he quotes with agreement from his *Vorlesungen über die Geschichte der Philosophie (Lectures on the History of Philosophy*, 1908: 1080): "Where several philosophies merge simultaneously, we have to do with distinct aspects which together constitute the totality underlying all, and it is only because of their one-sideness that we can see in the one the refutation of the other" (sw: 179). Of the distinguishing difference between Hegel's position and his own, Mannheim says that Hegel "proclaimed his own standpoint to be the final phase of the entire dynamics." Contrary to this, Mannheim asserts concerning his own position: "... the point of dynamism is not to recognize that history is changing, but to acknowledge that one's own standpoint is no less dynamic than all others" (se: 178; cf. bk: 222-225).

With Comte (1844: Part I) we encounter a revival of the mode of thought of the classical natural sciences, typical of the Enlightenment. He sought for general laws for society. Social actuality was construed in his view as an organism and at the same time as a product of the historical dynamic. He combined the formulation of laws for the historical development of society (social dynamics) with the formulation of laws for the social order in society (social statics). Even before him De Saint-Simon had noted that from 1789 to 1815 in France ten constitutions had been called into being, but according to De Saint-Simon and Comte, society did not change in any radical way. This assertion brought them to the discovery of the impossibility that the regulation of the state should be the essence of societal life. Not the laws in the constitutions, but the *laws which establish the rights to private property* form the basis for society. The regulation of private property and the methods of production determine the formation of classes within society, which, according to De Saint-Simon and Comte, dominate the development of the society (cf. Dooyeweerd, 1957: 452-455; 1979: 201, 202).

Also in the dialectical materialism of Marx a combination of historical and sociological thought appears. Society is an historical phenomenon, which is determined through property relationships (also noted by De Saint-Simon and Comte), economic processes, and the formation of classes arising from the other two factors. The history of society is determined by the striving for emancipation on the part of the proletariat class, which is on its way to "a realm of freedom" in which oppositions will cease to exist.

As far as the historicism of Mannheim is concerned, we see that he does not refer to Romanticism nor to the historical-sociological thought of Comte, nor to the idealism of Fichte. He sees the central motifs of the life-philosophy of Dilthey and Simmel appearing in clear and organic conceptions of the forms of various units of culture and life. At the same time, he sees the idealistic-dialectical thought of Hegel working its way through Marx's realistic-dialectical view of history and society. From its very origin, there is an opposition between Hegelianism and historicism, because the Hegelian dialectic wants to remake the irrational aspect of a life philosophy into a logical problem. The followers of the "historical school" develop a division of all history into periods, without "being conscious of any need to combine these isolated portraits in the dynamic unity of one evolutionary process" (H: 107). Mannheim wants to unite both streams together, the life philosphy and the dialectical view of society, and to elaborate them in sociologically differentiated terms. In this elaboration he does not, as does Marx, give the priority to one particular social class. On the contrary, he warns against the one-sidedness.

It deserves careful consideration, that Mannheim with reference to his insight into historicism and the social differentiation of society, also acknowledges his great debt to Lukács; that is, to the Lukács who was a Marxist after 1918 and particularly to his book *Geschichte und Klassenbewusstsein (History and Class Consciousness*, 1923). However, it is necessary to mention here again that

Mannheim differed widely from Lukács and his followers with reference to the place of the consciousness of the proletariat in the process of human knowledge. Lukács writes this:

> The self-understanding of the proletariat is therefore simultaneously the objective under- standing of the nature of society. When the proletariat furthers its own class aims, it simultaneously achieves the conscious realization of the – objective – aims of society. (1923: 149)

What precedes testifies that Mannheim denies this opinion. With this glance at the problem we stand on the threshold of Part III: the sociology of knowledge.

Conclusions

In his essay on historicism Mannheim provides an academic defense for his view of the world. Historicism assumes for him, the place of religion, metaphysics, and the rationalistic philosophy of the Enlightenment. His concern for the development of the culture of a twilight civilization still colors the background of this thought. Hence, his plea for a new synthesis of culture. The contours of his historicistic view of the world became visible in his sociological study of historical periods.

One would be able to characterize the development of the younger Mann- heim very succinctly as follows: *form idealism to realism.* One can more precisely characterize it with these words: *his neo-Hegelian mode of thought was colored by the life philosophy of Dilthey and Simmel and by the artistic idealism of the younger Lukács. This neo-Hegelian thought developed into transcendental realism via the struggle about methods between neo-Kantians, positivists, and phenomenologists. This transcendental realism, thanks to his orientation to the philosophy of history of Dilthey, Troeltsch, and others, resulted in a sociologically worked out historicism, strongly influenced by the Marxist Lukács.* One can scrutinize the development of Mannheim's thought even more sharply.

In "Soul and Culture" he speaks of Spirit and later about *Weltanschauung.* Actually, his concern is not as the title suggests, with an interpretation of *Weltanschauung.* His concern is with an interpretation of the genuine form of culture, with help from the *Weltanschauung.* True, he advocates a method of interpretation form "top to bottom," but it must be directed toward under- standing concrete objectivizations. In this he differs from Dilthey, who wished to analyze *Weltanschauung* itself.

Later he speaks about historicism as his *Weltanschauung.* It is not an idealistic *Weltanschauung,* but the tendencies toward realism are worked out in sociologi- cal terms; the concept of truth is also interpreted sociologically. The sociologi- cal interpretation determines the essence of the historicism. In his judgment the relativism in historicism can be avoided in this manner. Referring to the hand- ling of his studies in the sociology of knowledge, the question remains whether

117

he has avoided relativism. It is a fascinating problem, because epistemology itself seems to be determined historically, that is, sociologically. About a knowledge independent from ourselves he never speaks again. "Without presuppositions" has given place to the "positional determination" of knowledge. In the before-mentioned sociological framework, also interpretive understanding acquires its own place. Unlike Dilthey, Mannheim's concern is not with mental processes. He perceives a relationship with interpretive understanding as Max Weber uses the concept in his *historical* studies. For Mannheim, interpretive understanding is the comprehension of a fixed, individual phenomenon in its objective sense, which is studied phenomenologically, and also an expressive meaning within a functional constellation to be studied from the perspective of the sociologically differentiated totality of society.

What keeps coming up in Mannheim's views is the problem of the paradox. This is typical of his thought as a philosopher of life. Philosophizing is an existential enterprise; it is more than a rational matter. Wherever human life is objectivized, also in academic knowledge, a paradox must arise. In "Soul and Culture" the paradox arises between the subject and the cultural objectivizations which stand opposite to him, and from which he is alienated, and through which alone he can come to self-actualization. In his *Structural Analysis* the paradox arises from the striving for "without presuppositions." Epistemology desires the study of the presuppositions of all possible knowledge, but, because epistemology itself is knowledge, it itself has presuppositions. Philosophizing in epistemology seems to have certain fixations; it seeks to overcome these, but seems not to be able to function without them, and continues, nevertheless, to function with. In the "Interpretation of Weltanschauung" a paradox seems to arise out of the striving for a theoretical grasp of an a-theoretical matter. Also in the formulation of historicism a paradox seems to exist between the line of continuity (to be understood in flux) and the line of discontinuity (to be understood in the various phases of culture). He intends to work out sociologically this second line, which, according to him, forms the essence of historicism.

The paradox has various significances for Mannheim. The literal etymological meaning of *paradox* (Greek: *para-doxa*) is "opposing an expectation." In everyday use it means that two judgments of a situation are inseparably intertwined, and the two judgments seem to be mutually exclusive logically. The paradox presents a problem in such a way that at first glance it seems insoluble; the problem demands the search for a solution, and, if that is impossible, it demands a fundamental reconsideration of the framing of the paradox itself.

In which way does Mannheim think about paradox? This happens for him along lines of the dialectic. Although in "Soul and Culture" he never writes explicitly about paradox, his thought is dialectical. By means of dialectics a paradox itself can be worked through. In his *Structural Analysis*, paradox is a matter of principial epistemology; likewise, the dialectical process itself is principial. By means of the dialectic the paradox can be raised to a higher level

118

and be formulated differently; it cannot, however, be thought away. He attempts to solve the "principial paradox" and the "paradox of interpretation" in the "Interpretation of Weltanschauung," with help from "positivism well-understood," phenomenological insights, and his specific meaning of interpretive understanding. Also in this connection, "the problem of the historical dialectic moves into our field of vision again." Concerning the *manner in which* the dialectic again comes into view and *how* it must be interpreted, Mannheim is silent. In his essay on historicism the dialectical course of thought assumes a central position. At the same time he forms an adequate explanation of the dialectic, which in earlier-mentioned essays was only mentioned. He wishes to take distance from the clear and organic representation of the cultural entities and units of life; he also takes distance from the rationalistic, progressive philosophy of the Enlightenment. His philosophy finds itself between these two directions, life and culture, and has a dialectical character; that is, it is a dynamic philosophy and the dynamic is determined by the dialectical development; "a development is dialectical when the successive structures replace one another in such a way that the following structure preserves the earlier in the form of a new system with a new centre of systematization" (H: 115). The new systemizing center he mentions is determined by the supra-theoretical,systematic presuppositions, which exist in reality; these presuppositions are incorporated into the development of his doing philosophy. In *this sense* these new centers proclaim the truth of a particular time. He works out this dialectical train of thought in a sociologtical direction – still only a limited way; he also says that the dialectic is in its rightful place in ethics, in metaphysics, and in epistemology (H: 114, 115). We already saw that in his *Structural Analysis* and in his "Interpretation of Weltanschauung" he accomplished a systematic investigation which brought to light an ontological pluralism in his philosophy. In his "Soul and Culture" and his essay "Historicism" this pluralism also is present, but actually his main approach is another. Although ideas from the earlier mentioned essays also appear in the last mentioned works, he here assumes the position that all of reality must be studied from the point of view of the philosophy of history. The question as to whether these two approaches signify a dualism in this thought, I shall discuss in the following section.

In this part I have discussed the motifs and contours of Mannheim's philosophy. In the introduction it was already remarked that the word *contours*, referring to someone's academic work, is vague. Still, the use of this term is justified for the purpose of clarifying Mannheim's concern for various philosophical themes and for the course of the development of his own philosophical thought. His thought becomes more clearly profiled during the course of the twenties; sociology takes on more and more significance in his thought during those years. First came the sociology of culture, and out of it the sociology of knowledge is developed. Hence the title for the next portion of this study: From the Sociology of Culture to the Sociology of Knowledge.

PART III: From the Sociology of Culture to the Sociology of Knowledge

Chapter VIII

The Sociology of Culture

Introduction

Already in Mannheim's philosophical publications his interest in sociology was evident, although it was still on the periphery. During the course of the twenties, his interest in this discipline grew and came to occupy the central position of his tought. His competence in this field was acknowledged early, as is evident in the commentary on his inaugural essay by his professors, Lederer and Alfred Weber. Moreover, in 1926 he already became a private lecturer in sociology at the University of Heidelberg, and in 1928 he gave a special lecture on the occasion of the Sixth Conference of German Sociologists.

We can best characterize the development of his second phase as follows: from the sociology of culture to the sociology of knowledge. Already in the beginning of the twenties Mannheim devoted himself to the study of sociology of culture and wrote two manuscripts: *Über die Eigenart kultursoziologischer Erkenntnis (Concerning the Distinctive Character of Cultural-sociological Knowledge* (1922), and *Eine soziologische Theorie der Kultur und ihrer Erkennbarkeit: Konjunctives und kommunikatives Denken (A Sociological Theory of Culture and its Knowability: Conjunctive and Communicative Thought)*, the latter incomplete and undated, but judging from references to other scholarly works, apparently written in 1924. His brother-in-law, Paul Kecskemeti, had these manuscripts in his possession after Mannheim's death. David Kettler managed to get photocopies of these pieces, and in 1980 they were published under the title: *Strukturen des Denken (Structures of Thinking*, 1982).

We can only surmise why Mannheim himself dit not release these manuscripts for publication. At the time of my visit in London with Julia Molnear Piliszanska, who shared the Mannheim's house, she gave me a later version of this manuscript. It seemed to me that *Soziologische Theorie* had been corrected by Mannheim; it was not completely corrected, but he had changed the earlier version which Kettler and the others had published in the German edition on several points; he had clarified certain matters but had not completed the process of clarification. In the English edition of this work these corrections have all been incorporated. A complication is that he advocates positions in the first essay that he opposes in the second and in later publications. Hence, my conclusion is that Mannheim, who had no fear of writing or publishing, but who reworked his manuscripts painstakingly and slowly, considered these manuscripts unready for publication and found no time to get them ready. In addition, during his time in England he became more interested in other subjects. His interest in the sociology of culture remained, as witnessed by his later publications about such matters as the sociology of knowledge, democracy, planning for democracy, and education, all illuminated from the perspective of the sociology of culture, but to this particular branch of socio-logy, the sociology of culture, he never returned again in order to work it out systematically. Hence we can only consider the two essays on the sociology of culture from the twenties, which were published later, but were written prior to his mature work. They bear the marks of exploratory studies, or, as Kettler and his associates said of them: "He experiments with the discipline while practising the discipline" (1982: 11). In order to get Mannheim's sociology of culture in focus, I shall not discuss the afore-mentioned essays separately. In the course of the treatment of these ideas, the contradictions between the two essays will become clear.

Toward a Sociological Concept of Culture

The sociology of culture is, according to Mannheim (ST: 37), not a full-fledged discipline; it is a science in the nascent state. There have always been disciplines such as philosophy, history, philology which study cultural phenomena, but none of them study these phenomena as cultural phenomena per se. This task is reserved for the sociology of culture. Speaking of the modern idea of culture, Mannheim lists six distinguishing characteristics:

1. The *relativizing* of the various spheres of culture in relationship to each other, in which the emphasis is on context. This means that no single sphere of culture, such as the religious or the economic, receives an a priori position in the socio-cultural context or totality.
2. Consciousness of the *relativity* and *brevity* of every historical formulation, which leads to the following characteristics.
3. Consciousness of the essentially *process-controlled* nature of culture. No cultural phenomenon exists by itself, or for itself, but has its meaning in the framework of what has preceded it and what is to follow.
   These three distinguishing characteristics of the idea of culture imply in turn the following three:
4. The "experience of culture as such, in a cultivated way, the ideal of cultiva-tion" (*Bildungsideal*), i.e., the meaning of cultural phenomena, is not to be understood outside of the cooperation and creativity of the subject. This

124

meaning must be experienced by the creative subject in the terms which describe it, and this description is necessary for its understanding.

5. The *antithetical relationship of the concepts of culture and nature.* Cultural phenomena are not simply facts and nothing but facts. They are creations, expressions of people, and they must be judged as such. Distinctions between being and meaning, between factuality and value, between "is" and "ought," should, according to Mannheim, establish the difference between nature and culture. According to him, nature is free of meaning, free of values, and free from "the spiritually incomprehensible." Culture, on the other hand, is not free of meaning, but possesses both meaning and value. Based on this primary distinction, he describes the difference between natural science and cultural science as a secondary one, "compared to the experiental contrast between nature and culture" (ST: 46).

6. Consciousness of the *societal character* of cultural phenomena. The societal character of cultural phenomena brings us to the sociology of culture. (However, in my opinion, this characteristic implies – in opposition to point 1 – that the social sphere of culture receives an a priori position). This characteristic of cultural phenomena was not discovered until the previous century.

When society or the social dimension of life was acknowledged as the object of an independent discipline, viz., sociology, then the sociology of culture also could demand recognition. In the Middle Ages social reality was totally overgrown, with religion and the church providing all meaning, which hampered the recognition of the uniqueness of the social dimension. Later, society was included in a political-juridical concept of the state. Especially De Saint-Simon wanted to acknowledge society according to its own distinctive nature, but at the same time he was strongly oriented toward an economic view in his studies. With Marx we encounter an even stronger inclination to interpret society economically. The study of society on its own terms – free of religious-ecclesiastical, juridical, political, and economic bias and with help from its own apparatus for managing concepts – is a recent development. Mannheim names the following as leaders in this regard: Georg Simmel, Theodor Kistiakowski, and Max Weber (ST: 42-49).

The sociology of culture investigates in which respects and to what degree society is a culturally formative factor and at the same time to what extent cultural manifestations are socializing factors (ST: 55-56). Mannheim thus distinguishes cultural phenomena (religion, ethics, science, technology, etc.) as *functions* of social life and as *socializing factors.* In the first instance they are object of the sociology of culture, and in the second instance they are the object of sociology as the study of social science. Sociology conceived in this sense he calls the basic discipline; the sociology of culture, according to him, is characterized by a special method of approach for interpreting the phenomena which lie outside of the actual field of sociology. For the development of the field of the sociology of culture, it is important that it acquires its own methods and concepts. Mannheim is convinced that in order to acquire access to the original phenomenon behind the cultural objectivizations, a pre-theoretical or intuitive "feeling into" and personal experience are indispensable; at the same time he is convinced that a system of concepts is indispensable. He distances himself from logic inasmuch as this posits that one can adequately grasp cultural phenomena in logical concepts and judgments. He posits over against logic that one can only grasp these phenomena if they can be comprehended adequately in terms of their *own* concepts. This does not mean that these concepts are representations of reality. These concepts must comprehend cultural phenomena adequately; however, at the same time, the significance of these understood phenomena is determined by the system of concepts of the discipline which applies to the phenomena. For example, concepts such as *interest* and *capital* acquire their significance in the systematics of the discipline of economics. For the sociology of culture, Mannheim defends a methodology poised midway between intuition and logic. That is, he deliberately intends to use concepts which make a pre-theoretical access possible to the original cultural phenomena. However, these concepts are hardly to be phenomenologically described, but depend rather on the closest possible context with the system of concepts in a discipline. That is why he considers a purely phenomenological description of a phenomenon to be inadequate. For instance, in the phenomenology of art, one can only understand the phenomenon to the extent that the phenomenlogical theory is free to permit it (st: 58-60).

The foregoing implies that the sociology of culture must particulary develop a sociological concept of culture; that is, it must establish which changes and which cultural phenomena present themselves for consideration and which concepts are proper to these phenomena, all to the end that phenomena may become the objects of a sociological approach of study. The sociology of culture does not aim to study such phenomena immanently, for phenomenology already does its research in this manner; sociology studies phenomena in their functionality in regards to society. To be focused on this functionality is not a theoretical but a pre-theoretical question. The subject of this social knowledge of culture is not the theoretical subject, but "the whole person, or the social person" (st: 65; cf. st: 50-52).

Because I return to this problem later in this chapter, it will be helpful to understand clearly Mannheim's own distinction: a *pre-theoretical focus* by the whole person as a social person on the social functionality of cultural phenomena; and the *phenomenological description* of these same phenomena, which actually is not adequate for culture because it must be supplemented by a *cultural-sociological system* of concepts.

Differentiations in Sociology
It is clear that sociology studies the dimension of life we call "social." The many

126

sidedness of this phenomenon makes possible both the generalizing and the individualizing approaches. Mannheim stipulates that the social dimension is not an independent object of study. Just as color is never independent of the material which bears color, so the social dimension is never to be seen as free from the presupposition that it has reference to a *multipersonality*. At the same time we must consider that a color is a specific aspect of the material involved and that we can distinguish the two. So, too, we can distinguish the social dimension in its multiple content from a specific number of people among whom social phenomena exist. In other word: the totality of a social phenomenon takes shape (st: 100). Accordingly, Mannheim regards the social dimension as "a dependent object," which "can be described from several sides" (st: 101).

To study the social dimension, he distinguishes three forms of sociology: pure sociology, general sociology, and the sociology which teaches the dynamics of history.

1. *Pure sociology*, regarded from an historical point of view, is the last of the three to emerge, but when sociology is considered systematically it must be named first because it asks the principial question regarding what the social dimension is. Mannheim names these representatives of pure sociology: Simmel, Tönnies, Vierkandt, Von Wiese, and those who represent the phenomenological approach. Often one calls "pure sociology," "formal sociology" or "general sociology." Mannheim chooses "pure sociology" because it is determined to discover the proper essence of social relationships in the multiplicity of variations of forms taken by these relationships. This quest is undertaken from various angles and perspectives. The most important of these, in Mannheim's opinion, are mechanistic naturalism (in Von Wiese's sociology), Kantianism (in Simmel's sociology), and phenomenology.

Mannheim himself, influenced by phenomenology, sees the task of pure sociology as the study of what is characteristic-essential, or objective-factual in social relationships. This essence is not knowable by a priori principles from a constructed academic system. One can never come to know it without the concrete forms of society. This also holds for the conscious actions which constitute society. If someone wants to understand an act of love, the act must be stripped of all non-essential elements; then attention can be directed to the essence of the act of love. However provisional and problematic the results of phenomenology may be in this regard, Mannheim sees a "close relationship" between its approach and that of pure sociology (st: 101-110). With the term *close relationship (Verschwisterung)* he wishes to indicate the relation of his research to phenomenology, on the one hand, while at the same time he is aware of a certain distance between the two although he does not seek to demonstrate the extent of the distance. He makes a point of not mentioning that the phenomenological approach and his own are the same.

2. *General sociology* is concerned with the factuality of social relationships. It is an inductive discipline which examines the concrete forms of society, not only

for the purpose of learning to know the historical uniqueness of these phenomena, but also to establish the regulation of social forms. This does not mean that this regulating has an inevitable or necessary character. This regulating refers, for instance, to the contexts which Max Weber describes in *Wirtschaft und Gesellschaft (Economy and Society)* and in *Die Protestantische Ethik und der Geist des Kapitalismus (The Protestant Ethic and the Spirit of Capitalism)*. It is not to be denied, according to Mannheim, that the method of ideal type and the thought of the natural sciences strongly influences general sociology, but this does not mean that research for historical regulation has no legitimate place in general sociology. Two disciplines are to be distinguished in general sociology: 1. the study of the types of actual forms of society and their relations and 2. an applied general sociology which serves as ancillary discipline for the study of history (ST: 110-113).

3. Sociology as a study of the *dynamics of history*, or *historical-dynamic* sociology, does not study the contexts and regulations between various social fields, but rather the empirically-perceived types of social forms in various philosophical and sociological phases of history.

It seems plausible that Mannheim uses the distinction made by him in connection with the *Interpretation of Weltanschauung* for the distinctions within sociology, i.e., that the objective, expressive, and documentary meanings are parallel to the pure, general, and historic-dynamic types of sociology. These directions in sociology are no more than differentiations with a clear connection and classification. Mannheim's concern for the sociology of culture inclines him most toward the historic-dynamic sociology. But we also see that all three types of sociology appear in the sociology of culture: the pure, general, and historic-dynamic sociology of culture (ST: 113-118).

Differentiations in the Sociology of Culture
1. *The pure sociology of culture* studies "pure culture formations in a state prior to historical concretization of any kind, in order to determine what it is by virtue of which they are able to become social factors at all, and to what extent they are constituted by the social" (ST: 120). A philosophy of culture generally sets out to study phenomena as such, free from the socio-historical context, in their own identity and uniqueness, and it does this in the immanent manner already discussed. Cultural phenomena, however, exist not only in isolation, but are always functional within a society. That is why these phenomena cannot be understood only by an immanent philosophy, but also require socio-genetic interpretation. Before one can cross from the sociology of culture to concrete historical analysis, in which one investigates how the phenomena arise in a socio-historical context, Mannheim poses a principial question: How is it possible that a person with an individual consciousness can produce cultural phenomena, which, however, do not remain closed within the isolation of an indivisible unit within that individual consciousness, but become common

property of a community of which the members form a unity with each other and also with the generations which came before and will follow after? Hidden behind this question is the desire for a methodology to find out to what extent our being human is determined by the world around us. As a result of historicism, the stable worldview in which all things and living beings had their fixed place in a divine plan for the world, was shaken. The historicist perception of life brought the following awareness along with it: everything in this world could have been different. From the perspective of historicism our feelings, experiences, and even our formal convictions are also all adrift. A pure sociology of culture desires neither the stable view of humanity and society, nor the view of historicism. It wants to take a third way

> of abandoning oneself, of separating the social and historical self from the substantial one, and of experiencing our humanity as such, purely in itself. (...) ...so does the most rigorous structural analysis of social consciousness transcend itself in the direction of new substantive insights, until finally we reach the ultimate point at which it is still possible to stand, a sociological *cogito ergo sum*, something which can no longer be doubted. (ST: 122)

Thus a *pure sociology of culture* will ask among other questions the following: How do groups relate generally to ideas? How do the fundamentally different structures within a group relate to the formal cultural shaping that is proper to that group?

2. A *general sociology of culture* attempts inductively to know and to order the most common relationships between the existing social and cultural structures. A general sociology of culture, which can utilize positivistic methods, investigates relationships on two levels, viz., the general-sociological structures and the general-cultural structures. The *Weltanschauung* arbitrates between the two.

3. The *dynamic-historic sociology of culture* refers to the functioning of cultural phenomena in relation to the "context of lived experience" *(Erlebniszusammenhang)* in society. We must point out in this regard that a cultural phenomenon, both in its uniqueness and in its functioning, stands in relation ot a "context of lived experience." Both this functioning and the *Weltanschauung* are subject to changes. Add to this that in the totality of culture in a specific period, one can speak of various fields of culture within the totality (art, literature, philosophy, etc.); they are expressions of the *Weltanschauung* within a given social-cultural totality. This approach (from top to bottom) complements the approach of those who wish to construct a social-cultural context for a period of culture based on cultural phenomena (from bottom to top). Mannheim emphasizes that one cannot work in a sociology of culture with a concept of time borrowed from the history of philosophy, for that would imply that in one particular period only one *Weltanschauung* can exist; one should be able to discern several *Weltanschauungen* in one period of culture, related to various social levels. A dynamic-historic sociology of culture investigates which actual changes arise in one particular period as well as the forms which the various

mutations of the *Weltanschauung* take. These are not judged to be real changes observed from the vantage-point of the changing processes within the totality of a period of culture.

Elsewhere Mannheim speaks of the following division of the sociology of culture: 1. the axiomatic view, 2. the comparative typology, and 3. the sociology of individuation (SC: 82-89). Although he places different emphases here and there, the division does not differ substantially from the preceding.

Weltanschauung Further Explained

For a sociology of culture to study cultural phenomena, an analysis of *Weltanschauung* is necessary. While in his "Interpretation of Weltanschauung" Mannheim writes about the objective, the expressive, and the documentary levels of meaning for cultural phenomena, in his essays concerned with the sociology of culture he writes only about the objective level, with two meanings: an immanent, purely objective meaning, and a functional meaning, which consists "in our attempting to show that every formation subject to objective understanding may also been as function of a pattern of experience...." This means that objective meaning depends on the experiental context of an individual and likewise on "the social-experiental context" (ST: 72; cf. SC: 54). So, Mannheim distinguishes a pre-theoretical focus to grasp the immanent meaning of a cultural phenomenon from a pre-theoretical focus in regard to the functional meaning.

In a footnote (ST: 136, note 43) Mannheim observes that in regard to the social-experiential context the functional meaning has a close "inner relationship with the documentary level of knowledge." Immediately he observes that in this connection he is not able to give a systematic description of the differences. It is important that the documentary meaning or the *Weltanschauung* meaning should relate to *Weltanschauung* as an a-theoretical totality, while the social-functional meaning, now being discussed, relates to society and to groups within it. Actually, it is important to see that Mannheim speaks here about an *inner relationship* between both. In the analysis of Mannheim's study of the theory of the "Interpretation of Weltanschauung," I already came to the conclusion that he actually desired to demonstrate that *Weltanschauung* needed to be conceived of as a functional constellation of a differentiated social totality which must be studied sociologically.

A sociology of culture studies this functionality, and it can do so because its object is not only focussed on this functionality, but especially because its subject, according ot Mannheim, it the total or social person who is characterized by the "social structure of consciousness" (ST: 73-75). According to him, this characteristic of the subject of the sociology of culture, implies a sociogenetic approach to cultural phenomena as an extension of the everyday life-experiences of the whole or social person. Access to cultural phenomena by means of general experience is particulary blocked and brought into discredit by those who wish to use the methods of the natural sciences in the social sciences. As we saw earlier, Mannheim rejects these methods of natural science in the social sciences because they do not reach the original well-spring of social reality and because they themselves block insight. He believes that the pre-theoretical presuppositions of the total or social person concerning socio-genetic knowledge do not imply a lack of exactness. Just as musicology presupposes a musical gift in the practitioner without relativizing the validity of the theories of musicology, so sociology presupposes the practioner's social focus on the already-mentioned functionality as a pre-theoretical condition for sociological theories (ST: 76, 77).

Although Mannheim writes of the intuitive or pre-theoretical experience of the total person as a condition *sine qua non* for achieving scientific understanding of cultural phenomena, pre-theoretical activities do not constitute scientific knowledge. True, the kernel of scientific interpretation, awaiting development, is hidden in these pre-theoretical activities.

Is it possible to give the characteristics of a complete context of experience? According to Mannheim, we do not possess adequate concepts for doing so. One can only characterize experiences by means of the cultural phenomena concerned which appear as results from that complete context. Speaking of "the context of lived experience" *(Lebenszusammenhang)*, we must constantly fix our attention on appropriate phenomena. We can establish the functional moment by means of the objective meaning; this is guaranteed by the fact that cultural phenomena not only have a phenomenologically objective significance, but they are also the result of a total context of related experience which stands behind all the phenomena. That is why experiences, according to Mannheim, are proper checkpoints; they are coupled with the object concerned, which at the same time is a result of the experiencing from which it came forth. One must, therefore, reach back to that "context of lived experience" behind any phenomenon in order to understand it in its functionality. When the "context of lived experience" is experienced along with others, when it is related to a particular phenomenon as its product, and the creator(s) live(s) in a particular time, then the "experiential contexts" are social in kind (ST: 87). This also holds for special groups and categories; when someone speaks about the bourgeoisie, that person does not mean only the role of a social class in a production process, but a "context of lived experience" which lets itself be restricted more narrowly into an economic, or social, or historical situation. With other groups as well the issue is the "context of lived experience" which then lets itself be more narrowly defined (ST: 91).

It is clear that with reference to his discussion of "experiential contextures" Mannheim is caught in a circular argument concerning social functionality and the objective sense of cultural phenomena. He distinguishes the phenomenological consideration inadequate, but he considers it necessary for the understanding of the functional meaning. Even so, the functional meaning

131

is guaranteed by the objective meaning. Thus, these two types of meaning presuppose each other.

For the purpose of uniting the spiritual *(geistlich)* and the sociological, Mannheim uses *Weltanschauung* as

> a structurally linked set of experiential contextures which makes up the common footing upon which a multiplicity of individuals together learn from life and enter into it. A world view is then neither the totality of spiritual formations present in an age nor the sum of individuals then present, but the totality of the structurally interconnected experiential sets which can be derived from either side, from the spiritual creations or from the social group formations. (ST: 91)

In Chapter VI Mannheim's "Interpretation of Weltanschauung" was already discussed. In his sociology of culture he adds a few sociological refinements:

1. Experiences which belong to the level of the life of individuals are never isolated cases, but people who belong to these same groups have these same experiences.

2. Separate directions or tendencies of experiences are not juxtaposed in isolation, but form an inward context among themselves and constitue a "system of life."

3. *Weltanschauung* is never a vast generalization for a period. It consists of various layers of meaning which refer to various problems. Only in such a model can a *Weltanschauung* be analyzed (ST: 92).

The task of a sociology of culture is not only to analyze cultural phenomena or social formations, but also to analyze the structure of *Weltanschauung*. That is, it studies cultural phenomena in relationship to the "contexts of lived experience" of social groups.

The Central Methodological Problem

The central problem in Mannheim's sociology of culture is this: that the methodological problems concerned with thought cannot be solved without a sociological orientation. Many scholars prefer to work out their methodological problems in a totally immanent way. They aim to acquire methodological insight from the structural problems in the thought within a specialized field; they preclude a social-historical statement of the problem. They make the enormous mistake, however, of thinking that thought is not time-bound. Methodological multiformity is interwoven through various lines of thought. We observe this interweaving particularly with reference to the methods of understanding in the social sciences. Both the thought of the social sciences as well as interpretive understanding are living functions of social communities (ST: 147-149). This means that the theory of methods also possesses philosophical-worldview presuppositions and that the far-reaching character and the fruitfulness of methods are restricted by the appropriateness of the field of study for the method. In particular the natural sciences, which arose after the Renaissance as a universally scientific method, strove to banish qualitative and anthropomorphic elements. In this attempt to think without anthropomorphisms another motif also played a part, viz. the elimination of the socialization of knowledge. That is, it wanted to eliminate from the conclusions of learning all personal elements and whatever was deemed important by a particular community (ST: 153-155).

In other words, one aspired to transcend the knowing subject, bound to a group and bound to a particular time and place in history, and to transform this subject into a general and abstract subject. That is why correlation developed between subject and object: the more abstract the objects studied, the more abstract the knowledge that is acquired, that is the more knowledge which counts as actual knowledge for more subject – a view criticized by Mannheim. Abstract or general knowledge is, therefore, generalized in two senses: it is valid for many objects and for many kinds of subjects. By means of this one-sidedness, it was overlooked that this mode of thought abstracts all thought processes out of existence. Mannheim formulates the challenge on behalf of cultural sciences and social sciences as follows: "In time the call must arise for a methodological doctrine, a theory of knowing the qualitative" (ST: 160).

Just as the phrase "thought in the natural sciences," so too the phrase "qualitative thought" is a characteristic expression for a particular style of thought which must still be more narrowly defined. In what follows Mannheim observes that he, in his pleading for a study of the great differentiation between possible modes of thought, which goes much farther than the simple dualism of natural sciences and social sciences – does not mean to dispute the "ultimate unity of consciousness or even of thought" (ST: 160).

The question remains, however, as to what is meant by this "unity of consciousness and thought." Why does he deny that he doubts this unity when at the same time he declares that no general consciousness, no general human thought, and no universal thought exist. Earlier I quoted what he himself speaks of a "sociological *cogito ergo sum* – something which can no longer be doubted" (ST: 120). Although I will return to this problem, here I would like to suggest that in the twenties Mannheim was still developing his position and that is why he does not argue consistenly. Does he waver between two opinions? The argument about method between the natural and the social sciences was in full swing at the turn of the century, particularly the discussions surrounding the views of Rickert, Weber, and Windelband. Mannheim wished to make clear that all thought could be understood in relation to the social position of the thinker. Mannheim distinguishes this sociological approach from the immanent. The relationship between the two approaches, however, remains unclear. Choosing his words carfully, he comes to the following observation:

> That while every instance of knowing is simply knowledge when viewed from the "inside," it simultaneously refers, when viewed from the "outside," to a specific knowing relationship between the knowing subject and the object known. (ST: 163)

Only if one has grasped this inner bonding between thought and social existence can that person gain access to the "formulations of the problem of the sociology of thought." The existential relationship between people and between people and things opens up new knowledge and is the foundation of that knowledge. As he observes in the following:

> Our essay in the sociological theory of thinking emerges from this tendency, taken to its logical conclusion in that one proceeds from a social existence which is dynamically changing and not from the existence of the individual (ST: 281).

Several years later he elaborated on this sociology of thought and of knowledge.

From the preceding it seems rather as though he is making a casual application of what was in effect a fissure in the terrain. He speaks of a knowledge which can be studied from within or by an immanent method, on the one hand, whereas he speaks of an existential relation of knowledge to the life-situation of the knowing subject, on the other. He defends this apparent dichotomy in the first essay in *Structures of Thinking*, although he abandons the idea in his second essay. In the second essay he defends the view that a dynamic-historical philosophy of life is the basis for the interpretation of all thought. In the first essay the socio-genetic interpretation seems to have boundaries. Here he declares that some philosophers consistently interpret thought and knowledge, both their internal structure and their content, in a socio-genetic context. Both forms of thought (abstraction, analysis, synthesizing, etc.) and the content of thought (ideas of freedom, universalism, etc.) are then perceived as conclusions form non-theoretical constellations. As an example he gives a quotation from *Das Elend der Philosophie (The Poverty of Philosophy)* by Karl Marx (1847: 166):

> The same men who establish their social relations in conformity with their material productivity, produce also principles, ideas, and categories, in conformity with their social relations. Thus these ideas, these categories are as little eternal as the relations they express. They are historical and transitory products. (ST: 81)

Mannheim sees a contradiction in this pronouncement, specifically between the content of the pronouncement and the pronouncement itself. This thesis proclaims the relativity of all knowledge, because all knowledge can only be the result of changing social relationships. At the same time Marx posits a thesis which makes claims to truth.

Mannheim corrected this Marxist interpretation in his later work. There he writes (IU: 112-118) that a dialectical relationship exists between the basis and the superstructure. The conception of the relative autonomy of scientific theories is one he can accept immediately, to the extent that this autonomy, based on the internal coherence, is not diminished on the basis of the relatedness of theories to the social dimension. For the rest, like Marx he justifies the social independence of mathematics and natural science.

Mannheim is of the opinion that every sociologist of knowledge finds himself in a dualistic position: as *sociologist* he directs his thought in a non-immanent direction toward the functionality of knowledge, and as *thinker/theoretician* he directs his thought immanently toward his theory. But Mannheim does not see this dualism as a contradiction. According to him, it means that an internal, theoretical argument can never be criticized sociologically and that "it will never be possible to construct a sociological critique of knowledge or, as recently has been asserted, *a sociological critique of human reason*" (ST: 82). This position explains at the same time how elsewhere he can defend an evaluative neutrality in sociology. There he says that in his scientific description of phenomena, a sociologist may neither praise nor criticize and must avoid every kind of value judgment. True judgment lies much deeper and is unavoidable; it comes from the perspective acquired from the *Weltanschauung* (ST: 248, 249).

This duality arises from the fact that the issue here concerns two different fields of study. The one concerns the result, arising from an non-theoretical origin, the other concerns the immanent content. This last-mentioned approach also makes possible an immanent interpretation of the sociology of culture. Every philosopher and every scholar who constructs his own theories in regard to the theoretical aspect of his work desires to judge this work on its own terms. The sociologist who is bent on considering the functionality of thought will subject his thought to a non-immanent scrutiny. Just as the sociology of religion and the sociology of art study their respective objects for research, not immanently, but in their functionality, so the sociology of knowledge studies its object of study in relation to non-theoretical fields. In this connection Mannheim warns against interpreting thought and knowledge only in their functionality. In that case one would only ride along on the streams of experience common to the whole community, without a relationship to an objective meaning – a course which would necessarily imply the relativism of knowledge (ST: 83, 84).

The question must now be asked: Is the dualism which Mannheim defends between the sociologist and the thinker/theoretician a tenable dualism? According to Mannheim, this dualism must not be construed as a contradiction, for in the sociologist of knowledge a personal unity must prevail between both. In a certain sense is the philosopher of knowledge then not turned into a schizophrenic? And what does the "logos" of the sociologist still contain if the thinker/theoretician is detached from it? In his description of general sociology Mannheim asserts that positivism has a place in it. No matter how much he rejected positivism, it still seems to have a legitimate place in the internal scientific enterprise. In addition, Mannheim is guilty of a seeming inconsistency, for why should this dualism be valid only for the sociology of knowledge and not for the sociology of religion and the sociology of art, both of which must be judged on the basis of non-theoretical phenomena? What remains of the consistency of the "logos" in these disciplines? And when he warns against relativism, he seems not only to defend methodologically the nature of internal-science but also to direct us by mediation *(Vermittlung)* toward the objective meaning of the phenomena. What then still remains of his socio-genetic approach? It is no wonder that David Kettler and the others in their introduction to Mannheim's *Structures of Thinking* note that in the first part of this book there is evidence of a good bit of indecision *(Unentschlossenheit)* (1982: 15). This word is well chosen, because Mannheim in the second essay and in some of his later publications intends to abandon this dualism. In the second essay "he seems to resolve the indecision" (Kettler, 1982; 1967). Still, in other of his later works this dualism recurs. In the second essay, however, he states that no immanent or pure-philosophical manner of knowing or of method exists. He abandons his above-mentioned critique of Marx when he writes:

> At work on the problems of a methodology for the humanistic sciences, we became convinced, after much reflection, that not even purely methodological problems of thinking can be solved without sociological orientation. (ST: 147)

In this connection it is interesting to see how in his essay "Toward the Sociology of Mind" (written at the beginning of the thirties and published in SC), Mannheim provides a sociological interpretation of Hegel's thought, an interpretation which follows the same line as the second essay in *Structures of Thinking*. He interprets Hegel's *Phenomenology* relative to the socio-historical situation in which this work was written. According to him, the book must be interpreted not only as a product of the thought of the philosopher Hegel, but also as a synthetic interpretation of the problems of his time concerning revolution, restoration, Enlightenment, and Romanticism. Hegel's influence in his own time and after is due to this interpretation. "Hegel simply voices in his own grammar the conscience and available knowledge of his period" (SC: 17).

The thesis that Mannheim defends with vigor and which is also used in interpreting Hegel and others is "that mental processes have a social dimension and hence the sociology of mind is but a systematic attempt to articulate the social character of mental processes" (SC: 51). His discussion of the social dimension of mental processes does not imply that this dimension is one of the many aspects of mental processes, but that the social dimension is the deciding qualification. According to Mannheim, one may not make a distincion in the thought of a philosopher between the social and meta-social spheres (SC: 51, 52, 55). According to him, the power of Hegel's concept of spirit lies in its grasping the social qualification of the meaning of reality. This fact makes the distinction between the subjective act and its objective counterpart, i.e., its socially relevant meaning, possible. Hegel's conception of spirit implies the collective framework of history which makes its continuity possible. The problems and possibilities of the individual person are presented to him in the social components of an objective spirit. This framework provides structures for the various roles a person needs to play; it transcends the individual's intentions. This structuring of the social framework brings us to the level of the objective assignment of meaning. We attempt then to derive the objective meaning form the subjective. Mannheim refers correctly in this context to a parallel with

Durkheim's "collective consciousness," without going into his sociology of knowledge (sc: 64, 65). The relationship discussed earlier about subjective and objective meanings poses an important problem for the sociology of knowledge.

Interpretive Understanding as Pre-theoretical Activity
One cannot work out an analysis of the idea of *Weltanschauung* without having an image of the totality of the reality and thereby arriving at a metaphysics of history. For Mannheim this metaphysics is historicism, which is not only caused by individual persons, but is also accomplished over the generations by histori-cal-sociological research. It incorporates all isolated researches, various analyses of the *Weltanschauung*, various structural analyses of cultural phenomena, phenomenological analyses of relationships between people, and unites them

> into planful work, in which they mutually complement one another and finally metamorphose, within this consolidated casing, into a content-rich philosophy of history. That is to say that they become the means for a genuine philosophical penetration of the world. (st: 172)

According to Mannheim, Dilthey accomplished pioneering work in this regard. For in his work Dilthey makes clear that interpretive understanding is the central problem in the methodology of the social sciences. Later, in a rationalis-tic mode, this problem is also elaborated by Rickert. Mannheim regards Rickert's elaboration, however, as unsuccessful, because ultimately he was oriented toward the thought of the natural sciences and toward the premises which are the basis of those sciences. Nevertheless, Dilthey himself demon-strated the fruitfulness of interpretive undertstanding because he founded a methodology *not only on an epistemological subject but on a whole person.* Although Dilthey in later years oriented himself to phenomenology, according to Mannheim, one must recognize that he agrees with Kantianism on this point: he then agrees a *supra-temporal consciousness.* In tracing the thought of the earlier Dilthey and Troeltsch, Mannheim speaks about an *historical conscious-ness*, which he makes more precise as the *social consciousness.*

Even before he worked out the presuppositions and the methodology for interpretive understanding Mannheim observed that interpretive understand-ing does not have reference to all fields of knowing. He is determined to treat only that field which can be grasped by the interpretive understanding, and only to the extent that it can be grasped. True, he is convinced that the most essential elements from history can only be mediated through interpretive understanding.

He distinguishes two modes of interpretive understanding: 1. "contagion-like relating to an alien psyche" and 2. "the penetration of a life context." In the first instance what he means by the "contagion-like relating to an alien psyche" or, as he elsewhere calls it, "psychic contagion," is an intuitive and unmediated "existential reception of something out there into consciousness," in other words, "a total process of taking up the object into the subject." Mannheim gives the following illustration: if someone I have never seen before enters my room , in one moment I absorb his whole being into myself, based on his attitude and bearing. "We taste the other human being, we taste him in our soul in his inimitable psychic uniqueness" (ST: 189). According to Mannheim, this "contagion" is an elementary form of subjective knowledge.

If the first mode of interpretive understanding is possible through psychic contagion, the second mode of interpretive understanding is possible by means of social-psychological ability; this is a conditioned reaction arising out of the life context of the group to which the subject belongs, This always happens by the means which are at the service of the group, e.g., language, values, symbols, etc.

Taken them all together, and the difference comes down to this: the distinction between interpretive understanding as a subjective conjunction, and interpretive understanding as an inter-subjective grasp of the significance of cultural phenomena. In discussing the premises of mathematics and geometry, Mannheim does not speak of interpretive understanding *(Verstehen)*, but of apprehending *(Begreifen)*. Afterwards he makes a distinction between interpretive understanding and interpretation. He describes *interpretive understanding* as an "elementary understanding" or grasping in a pre-reflexive manner, and *interpretation* as founded on the "elementary understandings" and at the same time as the theoretical-reflexive explication of them. Theoretical interpretation can never adequately grasp the pure essence of the phenomena. It is always limited by the theoretical insights held at the present time and by the historical-sociological context of the investigator, and hence is "essentially perspectival" or bound to a position (ST: 244).

According to Mannheim, the perspectival nature of interpretation does not arise out of theoretical-reflexive knowing, but out of the pre-reflexive interpretive understanding which lies at its base. The perspectival nature of thought is not the same, nor as biased, as selfish thought, which, indeed, can be present in subjective interpretive understanding; but it is intersubjective and is determined by the kind of group to which the observer belongs. From this perspective the dynamic nature of interpretive understanding and thus also of interpretation comes to expression. As such, they are expressions of a world-striving *(Weltwollung)*, a direction of will, and of the ideals caught up in this striving.

It is striking that Mannheim's view of interpretive understanding is much more nuanced than in his "Interpretation of *Weltanschauung*." In Chapter VI I spoke about the relationship between interpretive understanding in Max Weber's historical studies and Mannheim's concept of interpretive understanding. Although Weber in his historical studies conceives interpretive understanding as a *theoretical grasp* by an individual in a functional relationship to other components in an historical constellation, Mannheim distinguishes interpretive understanding as a pre-theoretical activity and interpretation as a theoretical activity. Also the pre-theoretical understanding and the inter-subjective grasp of meaning from a group context signify the grasping of the meaning of a phenomenon in a functional relationship with other components in a socio-historical constellation. This grasping is not done by a logical subject but by a total or social person.

"Community Culture" and "Cultivated Culture"

A common impediment to the apprehension of cultural phenomena is the prejudice that one wants to grasp cultural matters as though they were ordinary things. Any physical object, however, has something impenetrable about it for people, although we have the feeling that we can understand cultural phenomena from the inside out.

A person can know theoretically a piece of music or a painting, without adequately taking up into one's inner self the creativity of these cultural phenomena. This latter adequate interpretive understanding of the evidence is only granted to a restricted company of initiates. Still, according to Mannheim, it is unfair to conclude that the adequate knowing of cultural phenomena cannot be examined and that in regard to this knowledge we must be careful only about making mistakes. Also, for the more general study of cultural phenomena, we need to follow stringent rules in descriptions, source studies, and criticisms; for example, in descriptions all definitions must be clear and contradictions must be eliminated. The evidence of a cultural phenomenon, however, is never adequately known simply by virtue of the methods used but rather through grasping the qualitative essence of this phenomenon. In other words, the knowing of a cultural phenomenon is not the result of the methods used, but of their presuppositions and can only be known by the distinctive character of the phenomenon. Because all knowledge is position-bound, and because the mode of knowing always occurs from a particular social position, one can, as a result, arrive at a significant conclusion about a given work, and that conclusion is knowledge. The problem, however, is this: what is sound and true and what in this knowledge is distorted and hence not true? This means, for Mannheim, that one must conform to the evidence from, and the truth about, the object.

In this context Mannheim speaks of two levels of knowing and truth. On the one hand, there is the conjunctive, existential, and individual knowing of the meaning of cultural phenomena, and a mode of communicating this knowing appropiate to that knowing and appropiate to the specific phase in the historical process of society, for culture is made by communities and culture forms communities. On the other hand, there is a supra-conjunctive knowledge and a mode of communication appropriate to it which makes possible academic knowledge, technology, rationality in business and traffic, etc. Both kinds of knowing influence each other. Nevertheless, we must distinguish them, because the criteria for truth in the one sphere are not adequate for the other (ST: 237f., 241f., 263f.; cf LH). In general, we have to do here with a distinction between interpretive understanding (*verstehen*) and explanation (*erklären*), between social sciences and natural sciences (cf. Kettler, 1967: 421, 422).

This distinction has as its background the difference between "*community culture*" the immediate, existential bonding between individuals and their own territory, and the "*cultivated culture*" which arises out of the other through an elaboration and mixing together of traditional social groups. This cultivated culture crystallized during the time of the emergence of the Western nations where various social strata came into contact with each other and increasingly mixed with each other in a relatively independent culture. The experiences within the context of cultivated culture have as strong a perspectival character as does community culture. Still, here it refers to a relative detachment from the experiences of the concrete background of small communities. In a cultivated culture various communities meet each other. It is not the immediate result of the encounters, but it progressively develops itself from the tendencies, from the "germ ideas" and aspirations in these communities. Creative people seize these tendencies and exploit them. Hence the fact that in the conjunctive, immediate community culture an artist often remains anonymous, while in a cultivated culture he is a representative of the community and, as such, usually is known by name. Because the perspectival nature of perceiving and knowing remains in a cultivated culture due to the influence on it of community culture, and because a cultivated culture bears a polyphonic nature as a result of manifold influences – because of this complex of influences, the communication which is characteristic of cultivated culture bears within it every kind of current and cross-current. In cultivated culture, both supra-community or rational communication and conjunctive, immediate communication are present. One consequence is that rational-communicative thought in a cultivated culture or civilization is to be passed along to all the differentiated groups which constitute it, while conjunctive, immediate thought cannot be conveyed outside of its small community. As such, it is also understandable that we in the social sciences know various directions; the progress of these discipline is bonded to the very groups which define these disciplines (ST: 267f.). The distinction between supra-conjunctive and conjunctive thought brings along with it, not only a distinction between the consciousnesses in individuals, but it also brings about differentiation at the level of a cultivated culture. One grows up and lives in a particular social group or class, and one comes out of this milieu into a cultivated culture. Often this is accompanied by changes, tensions, and even conflicts. Although the evidence is abundant and it happens all the time that anyone who enters into a cultivated culture gives his contributions to it from the worldview and the aspirations which he inherits from his own community, still there is a certain freedom for people to choose their own views and aspirations. This is the basis for Mannheim's sociology of knowledge. Personal life-experiences and worldviews, of course, can play a part in this process. Particularly "socially free-floating" persons can contribute to it (ST: 268; EGG). It is in this connection that Mannheim first speaks about the "socially free floating intelligentsia" in relationship to culture.

Conclusion: Comparison with Alfred Weber

In his essays on the sociology of culture Mannheim regularly refers back to his philosophical publications. More precisely, out of the philosophical structure of his thought he develops a blueprint for the methodology of his sociology of culture. This blueprint is characterized by thoroughness because of his profound knowledge of the political-economic, historical, and sociological literature of his time. One of the people whom he acknowledges is Alfred Weber, though not so frequently as to be noteworthy on that account. This acknowledgement is not surprising because Weber not only enjoyed popularity as a political economist and as an historian at that time, but also because he was active in the field of the sociology of culture.

Mannheim's relationship to Alfred Weber is particularly interesting because his two essays on the sociology of culture were stimulated by Weber's seminars in the sociology of culture in Heidelberg (Frisby, 1983: 115, 116; Wolff, 1978: 290). Alfred Weber had also published certain essays on the sociology of culture. At the Second Conference of German Sociologists in 1912, Weber had given a lecture on "Der soziologische Kulturbegriff" ("The Concept of the Sociology of Culture"), and a few years later he had published his essays "Prinzipielles zur Kultursoziologie" ("Principles Toward a Sociology of Culture," 1920) and "Kultursoziologie" ("Sociology of Culture," 1923). Mannheim knew Weber as professor in Heidelberg and quotes him several times with approval (ST: 128, 282). The comparison between Mannheim and Alfred Weber which I now undertake only deals with a few aspects of their thought, especially as discussed thus far in this chapter.

1. Mannheim was deeply shocked by the spiritual crisis in Western culture which, in his characterization, had made a division between "culture" and "the human soul" (SK). This spiritual crisis found its correlatives in political and economic catastrophes. In social life this crisis found expression sometimes in dogmatism and sometimes in scepticism and relativism. This crisis forms the basic idea of Mannheim's sociology, both of culture and of knowledge – disciplines in which Mannheim systematizes the doubt, insecurity, and danger which had become manifest in the Western world (IU: 45, 214; cf. Krüger, 1968: 30, 31). Political and economic crises never have the last word. They are challenges to be met and wellsprings of new orientations and of utopian thoughts about renewing culture and society. In this renewal process in culture and society the sociologies of culture and of knowledge have important functions (Heiss, 1929: 242; Schoeck, 1948: 2).

In Alfred Weber's thought about the sociology of culture the shock of World War I functions only as a catalyst. Before this war he was already occupied with problems in the sociology of culture, but – as he writes in the introduction to "Prinzipielles zur Kultursoziologie" – the statement of the problem by sociology strikes him as important and justified, especially for his consciousness which has been conditioned by the experiences of war. He wants to practise the sociology of culture in such a way that its result can be applied to the situation of Western culture in his own time (1920: 1-2).

2. In the sketchy elaboration of his dynamic sociology of culture, Mannheim does consider it important enough to mention openly that he had written it under the influence of Alfred Weber. Without commenting on them he mentions in this connection Weber's three divisions: "the process of society" (*Gesellschaftsprozess*), "the civilization process" (*Zivilisationsprozess*), and "the cultural movement" (*Kulturbewegung*) (ST: 128, 138). One difference between these scholars, however, is that Weber regards "the socialization process" as a totality which arises from human urges and powers of the will under various geographical, climatological, and other natural conditions. Mannheim, on the other hand, sees social forms and processes arising out of various conscious acts which bring things into being, performed by conjunctive, existential people.

Weber's rationalistic process of civilization expresses itself in the rationalizing and generalizing sciences (general sociology, experimental psychology, and the natural sciences), which are relatively independent of group experiences by people, which have a supra-conjunctive and supra-personal character, and, thus, can convey their ideas to other groups: these are the Weberian qualities which Mannheim includes under *civilization* (ST: 259, 263 ff).

If Weber discusses the cultural movement which arises from the feeling of a psychical bonding with the meaning of things, Mannheim discusses "the experience of cultural phenomena." That is, that the meaning of cultural phenomena is only to be understood on the basis of the creativity and spontaneity of the subject. These two characteristics, however, are not the same as what Weber calls "feeling" (1920: 25; 1923b: 49). But elsewhere Mannheim also discusses the existential, pre-theoretical "feeling into" (*Einfühlen*) and experiencing (*Erleben*) which are necessary to achieve access to cultural phenomena, these phenomena are the result of a "context of lived experience" which is shared with others and, therefore, is primarily of a social kind. This also involves the nature of the communicability of culture (ST: 59, 87). Moreover, we must distinguish the access to cultural phenomena from the knowledge of these phenomena, because Mannheim at the same time pleads for a system of concepts and other methodological principles which, according to both him and Weber, belong to civilization.

3. Although this may be superfluous, it seems useful to me to point out that Mannheim's distinction between "community culture" and "cultivated culture" runs parallel to Weber's distinction between "the cultural movement" and "the socialization process." The "community culture" exists on the basis of immediate existential and conjunctive knowledge of people and has a primarily

social character. It is formed by communities and forms these communities. Although, according to Weber, culture is very difficult to pass on, it is not impossible but if it does occur, our existence, that is, our spiritual being, confronts the objective world and thus also confronts other people and other groups. When all of these confrontations take place, a synthesis is brought about (Weber, 1912: 42). For Mannheim the forms and processes of society also belong to "community culture," while for Weber, next to culture and civilization, they form a separate group, the process of society. Mannheim cites Weber's three-fold division as a useful distinction in his otherwise totally different sociology of culture, both in organization and in elaboration. Although Weber denies progress in culture and Mannheim recognizes it, from the point of view of the development of the "cultivated culture" which began with the development of the modern state, it is striking that both understand the word *culture* in a similar way. Not only the higher and the better qualities, not only the finest representatives of music, painting, literature, and the sciences are worthy of their attention. To the extent that they discuss scientific rationality, technology, and the like, they subsume it under the rubric of civilization. Culture is in principle accessible to all people and is to be created by all people in spite of enormous differences in the degree of their attitude and talent in all fields. Not only the high points, but also the "level flats of culture" (Bouman, 1960: 276, 286) are included in their view.

4. In their discussions of the idea of a sociology of culture, both scholars reject every reductionist interpretation of culture. According to Weber, the task of a sociology of culture is to study the essential unity of all cultural phenomena in relation to the "process of civilization" and "the process of society" (1920: 27, 34-38). He also studies the rhythm of cultural movements which he first characterizes and then attempts to relate these characteristics again to the "process of society" and the "process of civilization." In the framework of these studies, he can penetratingly ask about the "psychical germ" of a cultural movement for the purpose of making a contribution to the "psychical renaissance" which he hopes will occur (1920: 49). This renaissance points in the direction of renewing a culture which had been terribly damaged by World War I.

Mannheim goes about his task in quite another way. Even so, he hardly criticizes Weber. He only says that, to the extent that dualism – between the base (the process of society) and the superstructure (civilization) – has become the foundation of a modern sociology of culture, to that extent that dualism should be overthrown. In what follows he mentions Alfred Weber among others who have worked out the scheme of correlation in civilization and culture and who, therefore, remain dependent on that dualistic scheme (ST: 177f, 282). The basis of Mannheim's study of cultural phenomena lies in his analysis of the *Weltanschauung*. Coinciding with the distinctions he made in the analysis of the *Weltanschauung*, he comes to several differentiations in the sociology of culture: the pure, the general, and the dynamic sociology of culture. The formulation of the problem in a sociology of culture is this: In which respects and to what degree is society a culture-forming factor? It studies the cultural phenomena within the functional constellation of a differentiated society.

Finally, there is a clear distinction between Mannheim and Weber, in that Mannheim regards the sociology of knowledge as a part of the sociology of culture. For Weber, a sociology of knowledge played a minor role, but in Mannheim's sociology of culture it has an important place. Because Mannheim has sketched a framework for a sociology of knowledge in his writings on the sociology of culture, I have begun Part III of this study with a discussion of his *Structures of Thinking*.

Chapter IX

Roots of Mannheim's Sociology of Knowledge

- *Introduction*
- *The Relationship between Mannheim and Heidegger*
- *The Origin of the Sociology of Knowledge*

Introduction

In the title of the third part of this study I characterize the second period of Mannheim's thought (1925-1933) thus: from the sociology of culture to the sociology of knowledge. Also in his publications about this last-mentioned task of scholarship one can discern a development, particularly from the philosophical sociology of knowledge to the empirical knowledge-sociology. In other words: a development in which sociology first functions as a scientific thinking-through of the philosophical problems of epistemology (with the central questions: how does knowledge come to be? and what is its purpose?) and then moves to an empirical investigation concerning the mutual influence of various kinds of thinking and knowing, on the one hand, and societal structures, on the other. There is discussion, therefore, of a displacement in the statement of the question: from a philosophical question to a sociological one. Although the terms *sociology of knowledge (Soziologie des Wissens)* and *knowledge-sociology (Wissenssoziologie)* are used interchangeably in Mannheim's writing, it is worthwhile to distinguish them.

Although Mannheim makes the distinction between the philosophical sociology of knowledge and the empirical knowledge-sociology, and although he does refer to the area of study as a sociological discipline (IU: 237), we must remember that in his studies he is preeminently occupied philosophically (as established also by Heiss, 1929: 243 and by Hamilton, 1974: 12, 122). In other literature about this subject the distinction is seldom made. Usually both terms refer to a division or a special aspect of sociology (e.g., Merton, 1968: 510; Bouman, 1958: 189-191; 1966; Gadourek, 1955: 13, 14; Zijderveld, 1974: 9-11). The distinction between a philosophical sociology of knowledge and a more empirical knowledge-sociology is sometimes interpreted in precisely the opposite ways. Especially Wolff (1968: 148 ff) distinguishes between Mannheim's sociology of knowledge and the sociology-of-knowledge development in the United States, particularly as this last-named sociology is formulated by Merton (1968: 511) and Wirth (1936: xxiii). This last-named American approach is directed toward an empirical-scientific investigation of relationships between ideas, thoughts, knowledge, and social structures. Mannheim, however, in his knowledge-sociology, was not only interested in this empirical investigation, but ultimately in solving the problem of the crisis in culture, which we discussed earlier. He was interested not only in the question of truth and validity to the extent that this question is classified in the structures of empirical investigation, but he had his eye also on "existential truth" (Wolff) which could be described as a social-cultural truth. The social-psychological orientation of many American investigations did not interest him so much as did the direction of cultural development, which he wanted to describe in academic terms.

In connection with the distinction made by Wolff, we must consider that Mannheim in his knowledge-sociology (as Wolff defines this term) was not only concerned with truth as a cultural-philosophical problem, but was also concerned about epistemological questions concerning the nature of the objectives of sociology and the nature of sociological methods and of sociological knowledge. Therefore, I feel it necessary, to make a distinction between the *philosophical sociology of knowledge*, where the problem of knowledge is central, as a preeminently philosophical study, on the one hand, and on the other, *knowledge-sociology*, as a preeminently discipline-oriented study. It may be helpful to comment on the word *distinction* and on the twice-used word *preeminently*; clearly no break is implied in the distinction. To be specific, philosophical investigation is always directed toward interpreting the results of empirical investigations, and empirical disciplines never escape entirely the questions of epistemology.

The distinction made above between the philosophical sociology of knowledge and the empirical discipline of knowledge-sociology seems to get support from the Dutch sociologist Hofstra (1937: 38), who uses the designation of knowing-sociology for the study which is particularly occupied with the impact of social factors on the content of knowledge. This special discipline he distinguishes from the "more general sociology of knowledge" without giving this latter expression a more precise description or definition.

The distinction pointed out between the philosophical sociology of knowledge and knowledge-sociology is more clearly expressed in this, that the English idea of knowledge is more comprehensive than the German *Wissen*. *Wissen* means "scholarship" while *knowledge* refers to the presentation of an object to a mind, the idea of that object, and the full understanding of that object, thus Maquet (1973: 3); but Wolff disagrees and argues that *Wissen* is broader than *knowledge* inasmuch as the former does not only refer to scientific, but also to philosophical, artistic, mystical, and religious concepts. I do not go into the validity or error of these various ideas about *Wissen* as opposed to *knowledge*. What is clear is the difference beteeen knowledge in the broad sense – that is, the philosophical sense – and knowledge in the narrow sense of academic disciplines.

Does not this distinction imply that the philosophical sociology of knowledge already consists of two parts: 1. the academic discipline of sociology, which studies the social determiners of thought, and 2. philosophy, which studies epistemology? Recall that Mannheim subscribed to no general epistemology.

Rather we pointed out what an important place the basic disciplines occupy in the various theories of epistemology. Thus the epistemology which is directed at social reality has sociology as its basic discipline. We must also remember that Mannheim's worldview was historicism, worked out in sociological terms. This sociologically differentiated historicism provides him with the "systematic presuppositions" of his academic work in general, as well as of his philosophy and epistemology. Hence, he does not grant psychology the most important place in the process of knowing the social sciences (as Dilthey does), but rather gives that place to sociology. That is why we must not regard his reflections about the sociology of knowing as a narrowly disciplinary, sociological study, but as a philosophical study in which sociological knowledge occupies a foundational place (cf. Simonds, 1978: 24; Woldring, 1980: 227-229). In the following paragraph it will be shown that we must distinguish this social philosophy from general philosophy, for instance, from that of Heidegger.

The Relationship Between Mannheim and Heidegger

Mannheim makes a distinction between the philosophical and sociological concept of reality and states: "The nature of 'reality' or 'existence as such' is a problem which belongs to philosophy and is of no concern here" (IU: 174). He takes seriously the *historical and philosophical view* of reality. The existence of the person in society, according to Mannheim, is never a "dry existence" but is always a specific, historical form of social existence. For a sociologist, says Mannheim, being and existing are always concrete, social entities. On the one hand, Mannheim speaks about being, reality, and dry existence as a problem proper to the field of philosophy, but from another point of view he discusses being as a "concrete effective," that is, as "a functioning social order." In addition, he discusses being as an historical and social *view of reality*.

In Chapter VIII we already saw that he wanted to make clear the relationship between the immanent or from-inside-out "dry" grasping of cultural phenomena on the one hand and their socio-cultural interpretation on the other, with help from phenomenology (Heidegger). He also made the distinction between the thinker/theoretician who studies the "self" of cultural phenomena, and the sociologist who is occupied with socio-genetic interpretation. Elsewhere he notes that a person does not stand "in a world in general, but in a world of meanings, interpreted in a particular way" (BK: 197). In this connection he refers to Heidegger, who calls this subject the "they," who in one way or another interpret the world for us. Mannheim continues:

> We step at birth into a ready-interpreted world, a world which has already been made understandable, every part of which has been given meaning, so that no gaps are left. What Life means, what Birth and Death mean, and what one's attitude toward certain feelings and thoughts should be – all that is already more or less definitely laid down for us; something – this "they" – has gone before us, apparently determined that nothing should be left for us to do in this respect. (BK: 197, 198)

The philosopher Martin Heidegger focusses his attention on this "they" but has no interest, according to Mannheim, in how this "they" came about. In other words: "It is just at this point, where the philosopher stops, that the sociologist begins" (BK: 198; cf. Heidegger, 1962: 183 ff, §31).

Mannheim accepts this "they" to be sure, but then wants to explicate it sociologically. He states with emphasis that he does not want to replace philosophy with sociology:

> Philosophy in itself constitutes a particular problem level. Furthermore, I am not only not against, but expressly *for* metaphysics and ontology, and even teach their indispensability for an existence-related empiricism. (PSD: 269, 270)

He has some reservations only about a metaphysics which is used to absolutize specific values.

In 1929 Curtius had written an attack on *Ideologie und Utopie (Ideology and Utopia)* in the *Neue Schweizer (The New Swiss Outlook)*. Curtius critisizes him for "a trendy sociology," nihilism, and for an hostile attitude toward idealism. Mannheim answered him in later issue of the same periodical (PSD) and said that in his sociology of knowledge he was not practising a "trendy" sociology. Using empirical investigations into all directions of thought in the social sciences and in politics, his sociology of knowledge has as its purpose the pointing out of irrational elements and prejudices; in the use of certain ideas, these irrational elements and prejudices may even show patterned connection, and the end result might even be a solid academic self-criticism of the social sciences. He wants to relate all thought to social positions of people, and, thus, to demonstrate the limitation of all thought. For that reason he intends to apply his criticism to the absolutizing of certain one-sided views, without himself coming to nihilism. He also acknowledges ontology and metaphysics, but he intends to take "knowledge-sociology" out of the sphere of abstraction and make it more precisely nuanced.

In the framework of "philosophical ontology," knowledge-sociology brings about a reconsideration of particular entities which have until now always been construed as absolute, and it takes the ground from under the feet of the pseudo-metaphysicians, who burden our political-sociological thought with absolute values. Mannheim continues thus:

> In this context, the struggle for an ontology, such as Heidegger, for instance, represents, is actually one of the most decisive achievements of contemporary philosophy. (PSD: 270)

To understand Mannheim's position toward Heidegger, whom Mannheim quotes with approval, it is important that this philosopher of "the meaning of the Being of the entity," which he calls *Dasein*, sees this *Dasein* lying within the field of temporality (1962: 38,§5). Time is the horizon "for all understanding of Being and for any way of interpreting it" (39, §5). Temporality is the precondition which makes possible "historicality as a temporal kind of being which *Dasein* itself possesses" (1962: 41, §6). In regard to Mannheim, we see that, just as with Heidegger, he speaks of philosophy as ontology and phenomenology. According to Heidegger, temporality is the meaning of the Being of a person's *Dasein*, and it is the precondition for the possibility of historicality. *Dasein* is characterized further as *Mitdasein*, on which everyday life is founded (1962:

78ff, 149, 150, § 12, 25). Mannheim, on the contrary, speaks about *reality as such*, about *reality as a functioning social order*, and about the *historical and sociological view of reality*.

Heidegger speaks about the person's transcending his situation, about the quest for possibilities, and about the communicative aspect of language. Mannheim distinguishes between a pre-theoretical interpretive understanding as *subjective conjunction*, language for the clarification of things in their relation to the individual and to the conjunctive community, and a *rational interpretation*. In this connection he refers to Heidegger, and there is indeed a similarity to Heidegger in Mannheim's view. He has picked up some elements from Heidegger's thought regarding such matters as *Dasein*, *Mitdasein*, discourse, and language, but has worked these out totally in his own way. Such thoughts of Heidegger's philosophy regarding being thrown into the world, existence, looking for possibilities, and anxiety, (1962, 233, 294-296ff, §§ 32, 50, 51) are not entirely absent from Mannheim's thought. Mannheim also sees much crisis, doubt, and danger in the Western world. Nevertheless, his particular elaboration and the way he builds on Heidegger's thought are so different from this philosopher that I must conclude that he only uses a limited number of concepts in common with Heidegger.

When Mannheim discusses the fact that thought is bound to being, he does not mean the same *Sein* of Heidegger, but rather the being-there *(Dasein)* or the being-there-with *(Mitdasein)*. Mannheim gives the impression of wanting to advance his sociological studies in the framework of Heidegger's philosophical system, while he only picks up isolated elements from that philosophy and afterwards gives them a totally unique interpretation. In this sense we can concur with Lukács' claim that in his sociology of knowledge, Mannheim "flirts with existentialism" (1962: 149).

Neusüss is correct (1968a: 60, 61) when he remarks that Mannheim's distinction between being or reality-as-such and concrete social existence, together with all the distinctions which arise from this, is a distinction which rests on pseudo-definitions. In his *Ideology and Utopia, Being* is construed as whatever is empirically perceivable, describable, and measureable in the world of people, i.e. entities. It is totally unclear which philosophical idea of Being he is distinguishing from or how he wishes to make such distinctions. Neusüss continues:

> The philosophical concept of Being is not at all distinguished here from it (from the sociological idea of being); rather, it is redirected to another learned discipline as a problem. Again, where the "being-boundedness" is to be construed as "boundness to what is," in the analysis of the sociology of knowledge, there it happens for the benefit of "Being itself," which damages the ontology of the case made by the sociology of knowledge, for it is to be understood at the same time as temporal and historical. (1968a: 61)

Still, Mannheim refers to reality as such, to the *self* of cultural phenomena, to the historical-sociological vision of reality, and afterwards to the task of the sociologist. In Chapter VIII I discussed the dualism in his thought. Recall that

Mannheim changed from being a philosopher to a sociologist. The sociology of knowledge he calls a sociological discipline. As noted before, he wants to think through the epistemological problem of philosophy in sociological terms. This leads me to discuss his philosophical sociology of knowledge. During the twenties he claimed that he did not want to eliminate the philosophical in his sociological approach to epistemology, while, in fact, he does this very thing. This regularly brings him to the point where he must declare his position with respect to philosophy, a situation which causes all kinds of obscurities and inconsistencies in his work. These inadequacies are aggravated by this "essay-istic-experimental" method of writing (IU: 47). Almost all of Mannheim's publi-cations have a weak organization and are fragmentary in kind. In the discussion of his publications about the sociology of knowledge we shall see that his philosophical approach and ideas, particularly phenomenology, and his socio-logical approach and ideas are not clearly distinguished from each other and are accordingly open to question. Again and again it seems that his sociological approach absorbs the phenomenological.

Mannheim's lack of clarity regarding this problem is so great that Speier says that it is difficult to follow what is socially relevant in the thought of philoso-phers who participate in their own way in a certain socio-economic situation and its discussion. For the sociology of knowledge everything depends upon the evaluation by thinkers who themselves are ambivalent about their political and socio-economic situation; will they or will they not criticize the situation of their own time? Everything depends on the boundaries of the sociological interpreta-tion as they define it. Speier holds, and he is right if one wishes to avoid sociologism, that no thought can be interpreted with total adequacy by the sociological method. That Mannheim, nevertheless, attempts to relate all thought to the social dimension is seen by Speier, "as an indication that philosophical insight is incorporated into the antiphilosophical structure of his [Mannheim's] sociology" (Speier, 1937: 161). The claim of Mannheim's socio-logy of knowledge, resulting in his unclear demarcations of philosophy on the one hand, and the passionate critique of the adequacy of his interpretation by philosophers on the other, provides a certain tension which will become evident in his sociology of knowledge.

The Origin of the Sociology of Knowledge
At the dawn of the modern period the epistemological problem was sharply formulated, especially by Descartes. He chose as his starting point the reason of a free person, grounded in itself. This thought found over against it the world of physical substance which Descartes called extension. The material and physical could be grasped by thought with help from the universal laws of mechanics. In a person, thought (*res cogitans*) and extension (*res extensa*) come together. He is not only a body, but has a soul; he can think reasonably and morally. Since for Descartes thought and extension meet in a person, questions arise about the

150

nature of this meeting. Thought and extension are two substances, so different in kind that they cannot be compared; still, there is discussion of reciprocal activity between the two. What is the nature of this reciprocity? How can the laws of mechanics be an adequate application of this reciprocity?

In this restricted treatment no overview of the history of Western epistemologies will appear. We can say, however, that Descartes posited an epistemological problem which is typical for the practise of Western philosophy. Already in Part II we saw that Mannheim posed the question concerning the validity of the thought of the Western world. Is this thought directed at understanding reality as well as is possible, or is it unfair to reality? Mannheim asnwers the last part of this question affirmatively. According to him, all Western epistemologies have been oriented to the abstract polarities of subject and object. Whether a person chooses a starting point in the world of objects (an ontology of world order) or in the subject, whether it be in the rationalism of Descartes by way of Leibniz to Kant, or whether it be the more psychologically oriented epistemology (Hobbes, Locke, Berkeley, Hume), Mannheim is of the opinion that these epistemologies, which never take into account the social basis of all knowledge, can never lead to a valid knowledge of reality. The sociology of knowledge can close this gap, because it asks the transcendental question – How is knowledge possible? – on a supra-individual level – namely, at the social level, so that the transcendental question comes into view in a way that can be answered (Schoeck, 1948: 22).

It is noteworthy that Mannheim pays little or no attention to the precursors of the sociology of knowledge and of theories of ideologies such as Bacon, De Montesquieu, Destutt de Tracy, and Vico. Although the term *sociology of knowledge* was apparently used for the first time by the Viennese philosopher Wilhelm Jerusalem (1909: 140-153) and Durkheim also occupied himself with this branch of scholarship, I shall not discuss their theories. They exerted no influence at all on Mannheim's sociology of knowledge – at any rate, he himself pays scant attention to them but a great deal to others, particularly Marx, Lukács, and Scheler.

Mannheim regarded Marx as the father of the sociology of knowledge and was particularly grateful for the fact that he undermined the universality of thought, the universality which his opponents treasured (IU: 132, 133, 249). Marx pointed out that the "lordship of thought" were typical expressions of a *bourgeois thought* (1848: 46, 160). This thought, to which a general validity was attributed, in fact enhanced the concerns of only certain groups; it formed an *ideology* of the bourgeoisie and needed to be acknowledged as such and exposed as a false way of thinking. Opponents of Marxism, however, used the same argument against the proletarian thought. They pointed out ideological elements in Marxism, and so what had been called "pure thought" was underminded and the awareness grew that various social positions could lead to various ways of thinking and doing.

According to Marx, German philosophy, even that which called itself critical, had never stepped over the boundaries of philosophy; it had never examined its general philosophical presuppositions (1848: 46, 164). He attacked the German "critical" philosophy from Strauss to Stirner, which restricted itself to a critique of religious presuppositions and which brought the so-called metaphysical, political, juridical, and moral presuppositions all under the category of theological or religious presuppositions. It proceeded from the idea of the dominance of religion in society; thus, political, juridical, and moral consciousness were designated as religious consciousness. Marx directed his criticism against the younger Hegelians and against all German philosophers when he said that it had not occurred to any of these philosophers to ask about the relationship of German philosphy to German reality, or about its relationship to their own material environment (cf. 1845/46: 165ff).

What had been presented as eternal truth in the dominant thought in Germany was, according to Marx, either directly or indirectly a single unit of components of needs relating to class. He wanted to explain ideas sympathetically as functions of the thought of individuals who belonged to particular classes. Ideas of so-called general importance must be interpreted as a mode of thought typical of the ruling classes. Revolutionary ideas could only come from a revolutionary class. The participants of a particular class share in the material characteristics of that class and in its theoretical characteristics such as politics, morality, justice, philosophy, and theology. Marx, in his theory, accorded the primacy to being, in this case "economic reality," which is the foundation for the superstructure. Without a doubt, Mannheim is strongly influenced by Lukács' *Geschichte und Klassenbewusstsein (History and Class Consciousness*, 1923!). In his essay "Über die Eigenart Kultursoziologischer Erkenntnis" ("The Distinctive Character of Cultural Sociological Knowledge") Mannheim rejects the soundness of human thought as Lukács interpreted it in relationship to social factors. In his essay written in 1924 (!) "Eine soziologische Theorie der Kultur und ihrer Erkennbarkeit" ("A Sociological Theory of Culture and Its Knowability"), he defends what he rejected before, and, this is more like Lukács (cf. E. Gábor, 1983: 9, 10; Jay, 1974a: 74, 77; Kettler, 1967).

Lukács' philosophy follows closely the *Frühschriften (Early Writings)* of Marx. In the first decade of this century he represented a form of Hungarian Marxism which cannot be called dogmatic. It is strongly Hegelian, historical in orientation, and not all deterministic-materialistic. It is a philosophical and sociological movement in which primary attention is given to the problem of alienation, dialectics, and to quest for adequate solutions for political problems (J. Gabel, 1975: 185-191); 1983: 15; Frisby, 1983: 68-106).

According to Lukács, the germinating seed of Marxism is the *dialectical method*, a particular manner of thought about the social world, a particular way of participating in it, and of changing it. This conception of the dialectical method demands that the social world be construed as a totality. Society cannot be reconstructed by means of particular facts; the facts get their significance by being brought into relationship with the social totality, which has a logical primacy over specific facts. This means, in Marx's terms, the priority of the abstract over the concrete; the concrete can only be grasped as a "moment" of the totality. The "concrete totality" of society is a dynamic reality, which the Marxist – and also Mannheim – takes on as a challenge, in order to understand the direction of development of that concrete totality, that implies that the totality includes past and present as well as the future. And one can foretell the future development of society by helping to shape it. In the same context as the concept *totality* is the concept of *mediation*: the understanding of the menaing of facts within the framework of totality, within the comprehensive historical process of social totality, which also includes the future.

These conceptions make clear that Lukács is opposed to empiricistic or positivistic interpretations of Marxism, which do not acknowledge the logical primacy of the totality. Lukács' ideas also imply an opposition to Lenin's "theory of reflection," in which the economic infrastructure causally determines the forms of consciousness. If Marx says that being determines consciousness, then, according to Lukács, he could not have meant that only the economic structures of society are involved in "being," but also that the totality of society is involved; the totality is primary with respect to its parts and it has various influences, upon those parts.

Again, in contrast to Marx, Lukács is of the opinion that studying the basic structures of economic technical factors cannot be used for understanding *all* societies. It can only be used for capitalistic societies. The application of the Marxist dialectic must take into account that it is conditioned by historical and social factors. This use of the dialectic means that scholars must abandon the criteria of *absolute* truth and *absolute* untruth. True, Lukács believes that truth exists, but it exists only in relationship to the future, to the coming of the truly socialistic society (Lukács, 1923: 229, 238).

Lukács holds that the dialectical method contains a particular mode of thought about the social world and a particular mode of thought about the social world and a particular mode of participating in and changing this world. It is not applicable to nature (although Engels does not agree here), but only to social reality. Not everyone can appropriate this method as one's own or apply it by whim to every object under investigation. Only a social subject who is himself a totality, that is, one who belongs to a universal class, that is, in our time to the proletariat – only such a subject can recognize the social totality in the particular facts. The truth of the historical process of totality can only reveal itself in the perspective of the class called upon to take the initiative for revolutionary changes in a given epoch. Because the concerns of the proletariat are universal or total and they coincide with the concerns of society, the unity of subject and object is realized historically. When the proletariat is aware of its situation, and when it recognizes its own appointed task, which is its very essence, and when it sees through the falseness in other forms and classes in society, then the proletariat confronts its appointed task in conflict with itself. That is how the dialectical method is always necessarily a revolutionary dialectic. According to Lukács, it is the only method, which can combine theory and practice.

Although the thought of Marx and Lukács is characterized by a program to change drastically the relationships within society, according to Mannheim, Scheler's thought is characterized by a conservatism which brings tensions along with it into the structure of Scheler's philosophy (sw: 154 ff).

In his first essay about the sociology of knowledge Mannheim devotes extensive attention to Scheler's conceptions about this branch of learning. In other publications as well he regularly cites Scheler. It is not quite accurate to say that Scheler set Mannheim on the track of the sociology of knowledge, for that is precisely the question, vis-a-vis whether Scheler had an important influence on Mannheim's social and philosophical thought. In the beginning of the twenties Mannheim was intensively occupied with the sociology of culture and historicism. His concern for sociology, and particularly for the sociology of knowledge, had already been awakened by Lukács, and it grew, particularly under the influence of Dilthey, Troeltsch, and the Weber brothers, who themselves had experienced the transformation "from historicism to sociology" (Antoni). During the same period before 1925 the following works by Scheler appeared: *Schriften zur Soziologie und Weltanschauungslehre (Writings on Sociology and the Theory of Weltanschauung, 1923); Probleme einer Soziologie des Wissens (Problems of a Sociology of Knowledge, 1924)* published as a book entitled *Versuch zu einer Soziologie des Wissens (Investigations Toward a Sociology of Knowledge)*, published by Scheler himself and in 1926 included in a somewhat expanded form in his *Die Wissensformen und die Gesellschaft (The Forms of Knowing and the Society)*. These publications about the sociology of knowledge certainly attracted Mannheim's attention. From footnotes in earlier publications we gather that he had been reading Scheler. Mannheim described him as a living contemporary philosopher who had the drive to break through structures that time had rusted shut. But when we read his critique of Scheler's sociology of knowledge, then we see that their approaches are very different. For example, Scheler's philosophy and sociology of knowledge have important metaphysical elements, and Mannheim intends to eliminate such elements.

At the basis of Scheler's philosophy and sociological thought lies the principle that the individual and the society occupy a field of tension between two opposite poles. The one polarity is restricted to the so-called "real factors," the territory of passions and life forces, sometimes called the "substructure." The other polarity is the field of the "ideal factors," the territory of the free "spirit." The great question is how two fields relate to each and influence each other. Thus he distinguishes a *real sociology*, which has as its presupposition the "drive theory of human beings," which occupies itself with the state (of which the drive for power is the real basis), marriage and family (where the drive for propagation is the basis), and the economic system (where the drive for food is the basis). At the other polarity is a *sociology of culture*, which studies "the theory of the human spirit" including science, art, literature, music, and law; the sociology of knowledge belongs to this field (1926: 19, 44, 45).

"Spirit" for Scheler incudes all the possible ideas and actions of a person, all the activities that a person could possibly achieve. The actual reality is then also a possible reality, in which certain ideal factors come to realization. The real factors, which constitute the basic drives of life and which find expression in the institutions which are realized, for instance, in relationships of political power, relationships of economic productivity, and in other qualitative and quantitative relationships between people/groups – all of these real factors and institutions restrict what could be realized from the potentiality (possibility and freedom) of the spirit. When spirit aims at a reformation of the institutions of the real factors and does not enter into the "playroom" allowed by the real factors *own* "context of causality" for such reformation – when spirit does not synchronize itself with the real factors, "it bites on granite, and its utopia is scattered into nothing" (1926: 22). In Scheler's sociology of knowledge the real factors are specifically political and economic relationships and other relationships between people and groups. These factors either encourage or inhibit the actualizing of ideal factors as moral-religious values or as academic insights. That various groups and various phases of culture have their own forms of knowledge means, for Scheler, that values acquire forms in a variety of ways.

In his sociology of knowledge Scheler's first premise is the priority of society; from there he proceeds to the social character of all knowledge. The second premise is that the perspective of social concerns is about the choice of objects that can be known (the *what* is known, not the content, nor the validity). The third premise, is that the structure of the society partially determines the form of the mental processes through which knowledge is formed (cf. Becker, Dahlke, 1973: 212). In his opinion Scheler does not arrive at the relativity of all knowledge. The question of truth in human knowing can only be answered partially. The result is that we only know truth partially, specifically the portion of the spirit which becomes realized. Truth remains spirit, as a metaphysical reality. Scheler then discusses the "absolute kingdom of ideas and values," which is much higher in the factual hierarchy of values than are ethics, religion, or law. These last are socially and historically determined. Spirit is an a-historical, metaphysical "idea of the eternal, objective Logos" (1926: 26-28; cf. Frisby, 1983: 26-67).

Chapter X

Mannheim's Sociology of Knowledge

- *Introduction*
- *The First Approach to the Sociology of Knowledge*
- *The Second Approach to the Sociology of Knowledge*
- *The Third Approach to the Sociology of Knowledge*
- *Mannheim and Criticism by Adorno, Popper, Merton, Wright Mills, and Dooyeweerd*
- *Conclusions*

Introduction

In the course of the twenties Mannheim had already earned a good reputation in German university circles. His publications had appeared in the most prominent learned journals. In broader contexts, also outside of Germany, his name became known after the appearance of his book *Ideologie und Utopie (Ideology and Utopia,* 1929). The book appeared as Part III of a series begun by Max Scheler called *Schriften zur Philosophie und Soziologie (Writings on Philosophy and Sociology)*, and in 1930 already, this third volume received an unrevised reprinting. In 1936 this book appeared in English, the author adding two chapters to this edition. He opened with a new first chapter, which served as an introduction to the problem of the sociology of knowledge, and he concluded the book with the essay "Wissenssoziologie" ("Knowledge-sociology," 1931). After World War II the German edition and other translations of the complete English version appeared. In this chapter I shall discuss Mannheim's article "Das Problem einer Soziologie des Wissens" ("The Problem of a Sociology of Knowledge," 1925); then follows a discussion of his lecture at the Sixth Conference of German Sociologists, "Competition as a Cultural Phenomenon" (BK, 1928) and of the last chapter of *Ideology and Utopia* (1931); in conclusion I discuss the first chapter of *Ideology and Utopia.* My topic, "Three Approaches to the Sociology of Knowledge," is to be regarded as a description of three different methodological models of approach to the same problem.

Although regarded historically, the study of ideology formed the impetus for Mannheim's sociology of knowledge, in a systematic sense the study of ideology is actually a division of the sociology of knowledge. That is why I treat Mannheim's conceptions about ideology and utopia after an analysis of his sociology of knowledge.

The First Approach to the Sociology of Knowledge

According to Mannheim, the prevailing conception in the social sciences is that

156

a given problem cannot be brought up for discussion in every historical situation, and cannot often be solved if left alone. In a given period problems emerge that from a logical-rational viewpoint "out of the immanence of thought," would not be expected. (sw: 135). Naturally, theoretical problems can always arise, but Mannheim emphasizes that most often something becomes an academic problem in *social life*. Hence he asks,

> what intellectual and vital factors made the appearance of a given problem in the cultural sciences possible, and to what extent do they guarantee the solubility of the problem? (sw: 136)

For Mannheim the sociology of knowledge, the study of the constellation of various social factors from which the problems arise, emerges as a response to this stating of the question. In his own words:

> ... a maximally radical *structural analysis of the problems which may be raised in a given epoch*, an analysis which not only informs outsiders about what is going on in research, but points out the *ultimate choices* faced by the cultural scientist in the course of his work, the tensions in which he lives, and which influence his thinking consciously or unconsciously. (sw: 136)

The study of the constellation of various social factors as a *structural analysis* of these factors awakens memories of Mannheim's dissertation, *Structural Analysis of Epistemology*. In his analysis of epistemology there are systematic presuppositions. The nature of these systematic presuppositions is determined by the structure of the particular field of reality. In its question about the ultimate presuppositions epistemology calls for help on the academic disciplines as its basic sciences. In his dissertation he called psychology, ontology, and logic epistemology's basic sciences. In chapter V, I already pointed out that other disciplines could have been named as well. In Mannheim's second phase we see that sociology can serve as a basic discipline which studies the constellation of social factors within a given time.

In his essays "Interpretation of Weltanschauung" and "Historicism," Mannheim had brought attention to the study of time periods as totalities. Such study would need to occur with the help of a structural analysis of the historical period concerned. He spoke of the internal structure, immanent criteria, and the organizational principles within a given society in a particular historical phase; the study of this historically and socially differentiated constellation would ultimately need to be undertaken in a synchronic manner. In the sociological study of the particular constellation, four factors play a role.

1. The most important factor, which a sociological posing of the question makes possible, is the "transcending of the self" and the "relativizing of the self" (sw: 137). That is, no primacy is given to thought and the *Weltanschauung* of a particular period, but are seen as expressions of something else. By the "relativizing of the self" epistemological relativism is not meant, an accusation

often levelled against historicists in his time. Already in his early essays Mannheim argued against the accusation of relativism. Now he undertakes this again, and declares that, with his relativizing of the self, he will both combat the charge of relativism and the supposed autonomy thought. Thought is *related* to the situation; it is dependent on the situation (sw: 137; cf.bk: 193, 194 ff).

This relatedness of thought is not new. In mysticism and religion we have always construed thought as related to mystical ecstasy or to revelation. The new element in Mannheim's approach is his *sociological* relating of thought, which occupies the position that religion did in earlier times (h: 84, 85; sw: 139).

2. The second factor which can be made understandable by means of sociology, is that sociology is an oppositional discipline; that is, as a discipline it rejects both medieval religious convictions as well as those of the autonymous rationalism of the Enlightenment. This rationalism always had been strongly anti-theological and anti-metaphysical and took a strong position against the clergy, which before had been in control of all scholarship. Mannheim not only opposes the supremacy of the clergy, but also opposes the self-aggrandizement of the rationality of the Enlightenment. His sociology of knowledge as an oppositional discipline which carries within it the so-called "demystifying consciousness," consists in this, that it

> does not seek to refute, negate, or call in doubt certain ideas, but rather to *disintegrate* them, and that in such a way that the whole world outlook of a social stratum becomes disintegrated at the same time. (sw: 140)

3. Two matters which determine the mode of relatedness of thought to the situation deserve attention: a. Thought's relatedness to the situation had reference originally only to *occasional* matters of content; it was fragmentary. b. Also, we have not yet established toward *which points* this relatedness is directed.

It is possible to escape the theoretical immanence of thought by placing it more comprehensively with regard to social reality, of which thought is an expression or function. What is the proper point of social reality to which one can attach thought? This cannot be established by a whim; it lies in that sphere of social reality where consciousness is most intense. Formerly this was established by mystical ecstasy and belief in revelation, then by a social-historical constellation which was chiefly conceived as being established by economic relationships. In this sphere of being, thought receives a new place in the ontology, from where a person can transcend his immanence (sw: 142). Although Mannheim sees economic processes as important for understanding social processes, he certainly insists that these economic processes be distinguished from the social so that the social reality can be understood in its own terms (bk: 195).

4. According to Mannheim, the whole ideological superstructure, the total system of *Weltanschauung* must be regarded in relationship to the social dimen-

sion. Already historicism had taught him that ideas and images must not be regarded in isolation, but as parts of a whole. Not individual and isolated ideas, orientations, and evaluations bear relationships to the social stratum to which people belong, but their entire world of proposing, the whole superstructure, and also how problems are formulated, the method of approaching ideas, and the use of ideas. This relating of ideas is not at all concerned with denying any idea, nor with doubting, nor yet with unmasking a lie, nor is it reflective of any particular interests, but we must see:

> that they are part of a system, more radically, of *Weltanschauung*, which as a whole is bound to, and determined by, one stage of the developing social reality. From this point on, worlds confront worlds – it is no longer individual propositions pitted against individual propositions. (sw: 144)

In contradiction to Marx, Mannheim says that the exposure of ideology is not the privilege of a rising working class. It can be used just as well by the bourgeoisie.

In connection with this, he discusses the following problem: Is the social reality to which thought is related an eternal constant or a dynamic becoming? A characteristic of his time, which he interprets by historicism, is to see it as a dynamic becoming. To the extent that one is conscious of this, one must not look at the ideas of one class other than one's own and see those ideas as dependent on that social position; but one must be just as careful not to regard only one's own ideas as determined by a social position. Rather, we must construe all ideas and dynamic social reality as portions of "a comprehensive evolutionary process," "a total becoming," as the *ultimate*, but at the same time, a continually developing "absolute" (sw: 146)

For this concept of the "ultimate and developing absolute" we must remember Lukács' idea of the social totality and its influence in Mannheim's essay about historicism, in which he speaks about "the truth of the epoch concerned" (H: 117); that is, in every period a systemizing principle of organization or inner structure lies at the basis of the continually changing cultural phenomena. Mannheim speaks, thus, of all the phenomena together as a dynamic totality or the absolute in process of becoming, and about the inner structure and truth of that absolute. We must understand these matters as follows: all kinds of phenomena together form a particular period, that is, the dynamic totality, the absolute in process of becoming, or the totality of the *Weltanschauung*. By means of sociological research, the structure of an epoch is expressed, and in this structure an epoch expresses its truth. The meaning of particular phenomena is to be understood by means of this structure.

Although Mannheim criticizes Marx, he does not want to deny the reality of classes; still they are not presented for us in clear terms. Knowing classes is dependent on the way in which they are understood from within a systemizing center. He does not want simply to follow, coloring within the lines, the social-historical process of the becoming of phenomena, but to cut straight across the current situation and to establish the points of view in their *contemporaneity*. This synchronic mode of approach provides the sytemizing principles for a new statement of the problem. To do this, he requires the already mentioned inner structure or systemizing principles of order for a particular epoch. In this connection it must be studied socially and historically. It is not a unified stream; it is a broken unity; the multi-colored streams of mind represent the variety of the social strata.

Although posing the question on the part of the sociology of knowledge lies in a direct plane with the Marxist philosophy of history, Mannheim shuns every materialism and formulates the sociology of knowledge as purely as possible. This means that he never identifies a particular position of thought with any specific stratum of society. Then both proletariat and bourgeoisie would have its *own* science, *separated* from each other. This, according to Mannheim, is gross simplification and arises from a propagandistic perspective.

In his epistemology Mannheim wants to choose neither for a materialistic nor for a spiritual approach. This, according ot him, is not evidence of a weak character – as he writes in the conclusion he prepared for the Sixth Conference of German Sociologists. He calls the polarity a forced either – or. He wants to trace the causes leading to this polarity for the purpose of abolishing the opposition between the two. He continues thus:

> I want to know ... why then the person of today in his thinking necessarily stands in these widely-diverging polarities, neither of which can be correct. This question drives me to the sociology of knowledge. (s: 121; cf. sz and kls)

According to Mannheim, only by means of the detour of the *sociology of culture*, that is, by means of the analysis of *Weltanschauung*, can an attempt be made at a sociology of *knowledge*. One cannot place a style of thought, nor for that matter, an art work or other evidence of thought, into a *direct* relationship with the concerns of any particular class of group. A particular style of art, a style of thought, and a starting point for thought are all anchored in the *fundamental outlook or worldview (Weltanschauung)* of a period. This non-theoretical totality is a functional constellation of the differentiated connections of human experiences. As instances of this, Mannheim cites the worldview of the Enlightenment and that of Romanticism.

Further, Mannheim analyzes the structure of the worldview of a given period that contains *particular worldviews*, for instance, Roman Catholic, Calvinistic, humanistic, Marxist, and other certain *general intentions*, aspirations or world-strivings *(Weltwollungen)* embodied in worldviews, for instance the intention to Christianize, to secularize, or to humanize the society. Mannhiem subdivides them into *special strivings*: economic strivings, strivings of art, thought-strivings, etc. (sw: 185 ff). Thought-strivings are, for instance, rationalism, irrationalism, idealism, or holistic ways of thinking. Within a thought-striving Mannheim further distinguishes *styles of thought* such as traditionalist, conservative, ideological, utopian, reformist, and revolutionary. Those groups of people which combine their world-strivings or world postulates and a given style of thought he mentions as *intellectual strata (geistige Schichten)* (sw: 186).

In summary, sociology of knowledge puts the following questions: (1) what characterizes the general worldview of a period in which a person lives? (2) What are the characteristics of a person's particular worldview? (3) What characterizes that individual's intentions, aspirations, and thought-strivings? (4) What is that individual's style of thought? It is in this manner that Mannheim identifies the intellectual strata so as to achieve a nuanced approach to the sociology of knowledge.Studying the direct relationship between thought and societal classes and groups is too superficial, a simplification of the problems of the sociology of knowledge. Then it is important to study which social strata belong to which intellectual movements. The opposite also always deserves attention: the proletariat, which is a unity as a social stratum, is split with reference to the strivings and styles of thought. That is why Mannheim defines the task of the sociology of knowledge as follows:

> the main task consists in specifying, for each temporal crosssection of the historical process, the various systematic intellectual standpoints on which the thinking of creative individuals and groups was based. (sw: 189)

Then he asks:

> which of the "world postulates" coexisting in a given epoch are the correlates of a given style of thought. When these correspondences are established, we already have identified the intellectual strata combating each other. The sociological task proper, however, begins only after this "immanent" analysis is done – it consists in finding the social strata making up the intellectual strata in question. (sw: 189)

He defines the sociology of knowledge:

> ... as a discipline which explores the functional dependence of each intellectual standpoint on the differentiated social group reality standing behind it, and which sets itself the task of retracing the evolution of the various standpoints. (se: 190)

We can summarize what stands above under the following rubrics:
1. The cultural-sociological analysis of *Weltanschauung* is the preparatory work for the sociology of knowledge.
2. Various systems of thought exist in every socio-historical phase.
3. Systems of thought are divisions of the *Weltanschauung*, especially of world strivings or world postulates.
4. Groups and social strata with a particular postulate or striving and with a particular style of thought form an *intellectual stratum*.

Provisional Conclusions

Mannheim wants to relate thought to social reality, which must be understood sociologically. Moreover, one may not reason by means of simplified causes from social positions to thought. Between social situations on the one hand and human proposals, ideas, and concepts on the other, he places "the intellectual strata with their own postulates, strivings, and styles of thought" (see Appendix 4).

In this approach to the sociology of knowledge the idea of *Weltanschauung* occupies an important place. Originally Mannheim interpreted the meaning of the *Weltanschauung* as the documentary meaning of an a-theoretical totality (WI). Later he saw the *Weltanschauung* as a functional constellation of differentiated contexts of experience, which together form a functional constellation of a differentiated social totality (ST: 72). In his first approach to the sociology of knowledge he distinguishes *Weltanschauung*, strivings or aspirations (*Weltwollungen*), and particular strivings, a distinction to bring the investigator into recognition of the intellectual strata, that is, strata and/or groups which have a particular style of thought in a historical-social constellation. A problem in Mannhiem's view is that he does not provide precisely which characteristics belong to a "style of thought" and which to an "intellectual stratum." He remains unclear about the operational function of these ideas.

We must now pause at the following matter. In Part II it seemed that Mannheim at first attempted to understand cultural objectivizations on the basis of a metaphysical-idealistic concept of spirit. Later we discerned a change; in his "Interpretation of Weltanschauung" he aimed at being able to grasp the *Weltanschauung* of a particular period theoretically on the basis of the cultural objectivizations. In his first approach to the sociology of knowledge he declares on the one hand that no primacy is given to the *Weltanschauung*, but that it is an expression of social reality; on the other hand he uses a sociology-of-culture analysis of the *Weltanschauung* for the purpose of studying the various modes of thought in relation to differentiated social strata. Does the *Weltanschauung* have primacy or does it not?

In his "Interpretation of Weltanschauung" we saw that Mannheim spoke of a paradoxical situation, a paradox of interpretation. On the one hand the *Weltanschauung* seemed to be formulated from cultural objectivizations and to be understood as such; on the other hand it was a totality on the basis of which the objectivizations receive their meaning. He sought the solution to this paradox by means of the dialectical progress of thought: each new system in the succession of rational systems of a particular historical phase, with a new central principle of organization, takes up the earlier system into itself. We also encounter this paradox in the sociology of knowledge: on the one hand no primacy to the *Weltanschauung* (see the opening of this chapter, point 1); on the other hand, the meaning of all kinds of phenomena can only be known with help from the analysis of the *Weltanschauung*.

Maquet (1973: 29) points out that the concept *historical* does not only refer to the situation of a group in a particular period for Mannheim; it especially has significance for Mannheim, according to Maquet, as a metaphysical reality. It has normative value. Mannheim would acknowledge these indications of a metaphysics, but he marks his approach to the sociology of knowledge to Scheler's metaphysics. Unlike Scheler, he does not aim at a metaphysics which could comprehend essential verities which were pre-existent and separated from the historical-social constellation. He wants to combat a duality between temporal objects of culture and eternal ideas, but – as we saw – he himself seems not to escape a duality between being and meaning. This duality in Mannheim is of an entirely different sort from Scheler's. Mannheim concedes the duality at the start, but works it out inconsistently and obscurely. So, he says in the German version of "The Problem of a Sociology of Knowledge" (p. 363; a part that is missing in the English version), that the duality between being and meaning is a phenomenological one and not an ultimate one. In finding a solution to this problem, he is of the opinion that the connection between being and meaning is to be penetrated best by the analysis of the worldview of a socio-historical totality. Every phenomenon is always perceived from a particular perspective and with a particular context of meanings. From various perspectives people consider the same phenomenon. The possible pictures have that phenomenon as a "real" counterpart; those pictures refer to the same data and essences. So, one's perspective determines the meaning of the phenomenon, and in that manner one has access to its essence. As Mannheim writes: "Man has an access to entities [in the German edition 'Wesenheiten,' that is 'essences'] creating history and dominating the various epochs because, living in history, he is existentially linked to it" (sw: 167; German edition: 351). Therefore, he writes (sw: 175) that factual, historical knowledge and essential knowledge, knowledge of the philosophy of history, represent two different forms of knowledge, but that he does not admit a sharp seperation between the two. Moreover, the "essential knowledge merely goes farther and deeper in the same direction in which factual knowledge sets out" (sw: 175). In sum, the essences are not pre-existing, but they occur in the process of history. Although for this reason he claims not to maintain a sharp dualism mentioned before, he does not entirely escape from the duality (as I discussed in Chapter VIII and IX).

From the above it may seem clear that regardless of how highly Mannheim regards Scheler as thinker, also in the field of the sociology of knowledge, the differences between him and Scheler get his attention more than the similarities. Especially his ontology and metaphysics are far removed from Scheler. He speaks of Scheler's "grandiose systematic sketch, full of profound intuitions, but lacking in a clear, practicable method of investigation suited to a sociologically oriented, cultural science" (iu: 279).

The comment by Stark (1958: 122), that Mannheim and Scheler differ from each other more in details than in basic principles is, then, also false. Mannheim strives for particular values, as does Scheler and demonstrates other points of agreement with Scheler (for instance, their critique of positivism and Marxism, and particularly their criticism of Marxism for finding the claim of truth in the proletariat). In spite of these substantial points of agreement, their modes of thought are widely divergent.

Mannheim also marks his position with regard to Marx's and Lukács' philosophy. Briefly, we can say that Mannheim is strongly influenced by Marx. Especially his ideas about the bondedness of thought to social factors have a Marxist origin. As mentioned before, Mannheim does not accept the materialistic basis of Marx's philosophy. Neither does he share Marx's view that the proletariat would have the correct insights into reality, nor Marx's interpretation of the nature of social interrelationships from economic factors.

In his polemic writings Marx analyzed the relationship of specific ideas (for instance, the idea of God, the idea of metaphysics) to the social position of people, as a means of unmasking his opponents. Accurately, Mannheim declares (sw: 143), and later Coser (1971: 54), that Marx's meaning is more far-reaching. Not just isolated ideas, but all thought must be related to the social position of people. According to Mannheim, in studying this relationship, the sociology of knowledge should be thoroughly developed. It is unfair to interpret Marx's sociology of knowledge deterministically (as Mannheim did at first; st: 81), specifically in that the economic structures of the base determine the superstructure in a mechanical-causal way. This interpretation can only be defended insofar as individuals identify themselves with, and are the personifications of the classes and of the concerns of the classes, as Marx himself wrote in the first preface to *Das Kapital (Capital*, 1867). The superstructure is, however, not only a reflection of the economic infrastructure, but it reacts dialectically against that structure. The economic structures of the base are only determining factors *in the last instance*:

> According to the materialist conception of history, the ultimately determining element in history is the production and reproduction of real life. More than this neither Marx nor I have ever asserted. Hence, if somebody twists this into saying that the economic element is the *only* determining one, he transforms that presupposition into a meaningless, abstract, senseless phrase. The economic situation is the basis, but the various elements of the superstructure: political forms of the class struggle and its results, to wit: constitutions established by the victorious battle, etc., juridical forms, and then even the reflexes of all these actual struggles in the brains of the participants, political, juristic, philosophical theories, religious views and their further development into systems of dogmas, also exercise their influence upon the course of the historical struggles and in many cases preponderate in determining their forms. (Engels, 1890: 488)

Marx and Engels acknowledge that a relative autonomy exists for juridical, political, religious, literary, and scientific theories. Engels writes thus (1890: 493): "... law must not only correspond to the general economic condition and be its expression, but must also be an *internally coherent* expression. (...) And in order to achieve this, the faithful reflection of economic conditions suffers

164

increasingly." If this holds for law, it can also be said about scientific theories. Thought in the natural sciences, according to Marx, actually is totally independent from economic factors (1859: 12). According to Barth (1974: 159) one must conclude from this that for Marx the natural sciences include no ideological elements and that the knowing consciousness has a constant structure when it is directed to natue and its laws. The dependence of consciousness on the social dimension would only appear *to the extent* that consciousness concentrates on the production process.

In this context we need to acknowledge that while Mannheim says that thought is totally non-autonomous, but bound to being, and as such "ideological," Marx sees thought which is bound to being as ideological only *insofar* as it is presented as autonomous and *insofar* as it inhibits insight into the *true* nature of society (cf. Neusüss, 1968a: 40). Moreover, Marx distinguished ideology from progressive and fruitful ideas which arose from non-proletarian classes. With reference to the problem "idea vs ideology," is the question justified whether Mannheim satisfactorily examined Marx? Marx attributed a positive and progressive significance to certain ideas, for instance, the ideas of the French Revolution. On the opposite side he listed ideas which hampered ideologically the true insight into social reality (1845/46: 147, 153 ff). In conclusion, Mannheim continually confronts us with philosophical questions concerning the relationship between being and consciousness, the self which is to be studied phenomenologically and the sociological interpretation of it. The problem of duality comes up again – though in another form – when he declares like Marx:

> Whereas in mathematics and natural science, progress seems to be determined to a large extent by immanent factors, one question leading up to another with a purely logical necessity with interruptions due only to difficulties not yet solved, the history of cultural sciences shows such an "immanent" progress only for limited stretches. (sw: 135)

Why does he keep the natural sciences outside of the social determiners of consciousness? Indeed, there are certain differences between the determining in the social and the natural sciences, but Mannheim makes that distinction absolute and comes to a division of human consciousness into two parts (cf. BK: 193, 194). According to Larrain (1979: 103), this dualism leads to an epistemological idealism in the field of the natural sciences.

Although Marx gave an important impetus to the sociology of knowledge, his significance for the field remains limited. It would have been obvious, if Marxism had occupied itself with the elaboration of this branch of knowledge. It never came to this point, however. Mannheim gives two reasons for this development: Marx's theory is characterized by a paucity of abstraction and of specificity. The lack of abstraction is to be gathered from the fact that the relation between thought and being are matters for study only by his opponents. The lack of a critical reflection of its own social position prevented Marxism from undertaking a study of the relationship between thought and being in general. This not only increased abstraction, but an increased specificity seemed impossible for Marxism. A greater specificity could have expressed itself in a study of differentiations within classes and between classes, but this did not come about (cf. IU: 248, 249; cf. Merton, 1968: 516-542).

As for the rest, Mannheim gives Marx more than enough honor when he says that the sociology of knowledge sprouted forth from Marx's philosophy. It is certain that Marx struck the heart of the sociology of knowledge, but as was said before, Mannheim pays little or no attention to the other precursors, such as Bacon, De Montesquieu, Vico and others who also provided valuable insights for this field.

Although Troeltsch seemed to have an important influence on Mannheim's dynamic conception of reality, Mannheim also mentions Lukács's work as important for his thought in this regard (H: 124). Lukács' conception of the long view of history as a total complex, in which not causal interpretations, but dialectical interpretations account for a particular historical period, is also to be found in Mannheim, but worked out in another way (cf. Jay, 1974a: 77, 78; 1974b: 106-117; J. Schmidt, 1974: 168-180). Also for the understanding of the relationship between history and sociology, Mannheim refers to Lukács (H: 124, 125). The same can be said about the origin of Mannheim's concern for the sociology of knowledge (sw: 150), and about his conception of the sociological interpretation of scientific methodologies (H: 124, 125; KD; German edition: 420).

In addition, it is noteworthy that Mannheim in his sociology of knowledge gives a sterotypical Marxist interpretation of Lukács. There he writes that Lukács is not at all better than Marx, because he makes no distinction between unmasking ideologies and the sociology of knowledge, and also, naturally, because he grants to the knowing done by the proletariat the principal claim of truth (IU: 279; cf. E. Gábor, 1983: 9, 10).

It is a typically Leninist-Communist characteristic of Lukács' philosophy that he says (1923: 41) of the Communist Party that it is "the bearer of the consciousness of the proletariat and the conscience of its historical vocation," and that the party's task is to make the proletariat aware of its social position: an empirical proletariat that is aware of its historical assignment. With this view of the proletariat, Lukács has stated the problem of the relatedness of knowledge and thought to the position of society and at the same time he has denied the relativity of knowledge. Proletariat knowledge and bourgeois knowledge relate to each other (in the process of the historic-social totality) as truth to falsehood (ideology).

According to Mannheim, no single societal stratum or class carries the totality of the dynamic society. Therefore, in order to study the "societal enterprise," one may not orient himself or herself on only one level or class. Even if one class turns out to bear the dominant theme for a particular period, and attempts to do right as far as possible by all the other tendencies, it will never achieve a complete and comprehensive view of the whole. Mannheim calls the problem of social differentiation and of the social relatedness of thought and knowledge an enriching of the vision of the sociology of knowledge.

Interpretations, as for instance, that of Lewalter (1930: 63-131), which regard the core of Mannheim's philosophy as Marxist, are debatable and suspect. Mannheim's Marxist critics (among them Horkheimer, Adorno, Lukács, Fogarsi and Wittfogel), who reject him because his philosophy is not materialistic, have a more legitimate right to speak although one must reject in their interpretations that his ideas only support bourgeois society and would lead to relativism.

The Second Approach to the Sociology of Knowledge

In his report for the Sixth Conference of German Sociologists (1928), "Competition as a Cultural Phenomenon," Mannheim declares that competition is not primarily an economic phenomenon. It is primarily a social phenomenon, and for that reason appears in economic life (BK: 191, 193):

> ...competition does not operate merely at the margin, as a stimulus, an inducement, a sporadic cause of intellectual production (...), but ... it enters as a constituent element into the form and content of every cultural product or movement. (BK: 191)

Because he sees competition neither as a peripheral nor as the most central phenomenon in social processes, he characterizes it in what follows as a "co-determinant" of social life (BK: 192), one of several other relationships and processes that shape society. The role of competition in human thought and particularly in existentially-determined thought, is central in his essay. He implicates in this regard historical, political, sociological, and everyday thought. He explicitly excludes thought in the natural sciences (BK: 193, 194). He states the problem concerning competition in thought as follows:

> It appears that the various parties are all competing for the possession of the correct social diagnosis (*Sicht, Auslegung*), or at least for the prestige which goes with the possession of the correct diagnosis. (BK: 196)

This statement of the problem is carried through by the sociological perspective, that every historical, sociological and any knowing oriented to the world-view "is clearly rooted in and carried by the desire for power and recognition of particular social groups who want to make their interpretations of the world the universal one" (BK: 196, 197). This public interpretation of reality, according to Mannheim, can come into being on the following bases: 1. Consensus of opinion, of spontaneous cooperation between individuals and groups; 2. The monopoly-position of one particular group; 3. Competition between many groups, each determined to impose on others its particular interpretation of reality; and 4. Concentration around a few points of view which become more and more dominant for a number of competing groups (BK: 198).

I shall not discuss Mannheim's discussion of these four points. His argument arrives at a provisional and careful pleading for a synthesis of styles of thought, which will be discussed in Chapter XII. Ideas such as those concerning the social relatedness of thought, the social perspective of a thinker, and the truth of thought, all of which Mannheim already mentions here – all of these ideas come up for discussion in a more lengthy and more balanced essay about the sociology of knowledge in 1931.

That article from 1931 had as its title "Knowledge-sociology" (*"Wissenssoziologie"*), included as the last chapter in *Ideology and Utopia* (1936). In this book the sociology of knowledge is the topic – an academic field which Mannheim does not regard as a philosophical field, but as a branch of sociology (IU: 237). Next he defines this branch of sociology as the theory which examines the historical-sociological bonding between social reality and thought, both in the past and present.

From one point of view the sociology of knowledge is a *theory*; from another, an historical-sociological *method* of investigations. As theory it can adopt two forms: 1. Pure empirical reserarch, by means of description and structural analysis of the various ways in which the validity and relevance of thought's bondedness to social reality becomes the problem. 2. This empirical research can be transformed into an epistemological research, in which the validity and relevance of thought's bondedness to being becomes the problem. In this distinction between 1) and 2) the dualism comes to expression again which was already pointed out.

Although Mannheim does not make the distinction, I should prefer to speak of the former study as the empirical knowledge-sociology and of the latter as philosophy, a distinction which presupposes a connection.

I. *Pure empirical research*: The bondedness of thought to being can be regarded as a fact in those spheres of thought in which we can demonstrate the following:

a. That the knowing process does not simply run according to an immanent law of development, but that extra-theoretical factors *(Seinsfaktoren)* determine the existence of thought and the forms of thought in decisive ways; by *determine* he does not mean a mechanical, causal determination; the empirical investigation must demonstrate the measure of determination (IU: 239).

b. That these extra-theoretical factors of being have no peripheral importance, but determine both the form and content of thought. As examples of extra-theoretical factors he names these: various interpretations of the world are to be reduced to *conflicting* groups in the battle for power on an intellectual level; various interpretations of the world and forms of knowledge can arise between different generations, different sects, and different social classes (IU: 241; cf. BK: 196, 197).

Why do different people interpret the same data in different ways? Because they have different *perspectives* as members of one group. Perspective in this conection means the manner in which someone *as member of a group* perceives something and how he reconstructs it in his thougt. Which characteristics determine this perspective? He lists the following points (IU: 45ff):

1. The same *word* can mean something different for people in different situations. The various situations can also lead to different definitions. The absence of certain concepts indicates not only the absence of certain perspectives, but also the absence of a need to secure a grip on certain problems (for instance, the recent use of the word *social*, as in sociology).

2. Not only the concrete content of concepts, but also meanings of *basic categories* can vary from each other in correlation with social positions. Thus, the nineteenth-century and twentieth-century conservatism in Germany had the inclination ot preserve the concrete totality of everyday experience in its uniqueness. The parties to the left had the inclination to approach these totalities analytically and split them into smaller entities, which, with help of certain categories, could be bound together again as causal and functional integration. Mannheim sees it as his task, not only to declare that people in different social positions think differently, but also insightfully to determine the causes for the ordering of the material of experience, with help from various categories. This at the same time makes clear that even abstract categories, which apparently are far removed from the power play of politics, have their origin in the meta-theoretical, pragmatic nature of the human spirit.

3. There are differences between *models of thought* which implicitly function in human consciousness whenever anyone reflects on any object. For instance, organicism and personalism as counter-positions to a functional-mechanical and other models of thought in the natural sciences. And so a relationship exists between models of thought and political streams and also between models of thought and social positions. It is clear that Mannheim, speaking about groups, their worldviews, and their models of thought, does not only think about classes, but also about generations, status groups, sects, professional groups, etc. Only if one has an eye for this differentiation of groups, can one, according to Mannheim, acquire insight into the variety of ideas, categories, and models of thought. The idea of class is too undifferentiated to be able to comprehend this finer differentiation.

4. As fourth characteristic of a perspective he lists the *level of abstraction*. It is not accidental that a given theory cannot raise itself above a certain level of abstraction and will not proceed to greater concreteness. Here, too, social positon plays a part. Marxism had already long been albe to occupy itself with the relation between thinking and being; Marx's discovery of the theory of ideology implied an impulse toward the sociology of knowledge. That an elaboration lagged behind was to be attributed to the fact that Marxism only directed its critique of ideology toward opponents. At this stage one's own social position becomes a handicap for a general, theoretical formulation of a

viewpoint (IU: 248, 249). The sociology of knowledge needs continually to be refining its methods. It must not only acquiesce in the existence of a relationship between thought and being, but at the same time specify the scope and validity of an utterance. In this process it is always critical; it also occupies itself with redefining the scope and boundaries of the perspective which is present in the utterances of people.

It is noteworthy that Mannheim sees both the content and the form of knowledge as determined by extra-theoretical factors. This contradicts his viewpoint as expressed in Chapter VIII that the content is determined, but not the form of knowledge as such.

Although it is implicitly present, he makes no distinction between social conditions for knowledge and the social perspective. In other words, there are conditions which make knowledge possible, advance or inhibit it (for instance, schooling for acquiring information, owning or having access to the media of communication, etc.), and the manner of implementing these from a social perspective (cf. Plamenatz, 1970: 56).

II. *Epistemological Research*: In the last chapter of *Ideology and Utopia* Mannheim returns anew to the proposition he already defended in his dissertation, that epistemology, which is often regarded as the basis for all sciences, in fact is determined by the conditions of the basic disciplines in a given time (IU: 259). Not only the development of theories about scientific knowledge is determined by empirical data; also the revolutions in methodology and in epistemology are a result of revolutions in the empirical givens. The sociology of knowledge penetrates into the domain of epistemology by means of its very particular method. As such, the sociology of knowledge has five functions according to Mannheim:

1. It makes it necessary to revise the position that a proposition itself in all circumstances is irrelevant compared to the truth of it. The duality between facts and judgments is one of the axioms of an idealistic philosophy and at the same time an obstacle for the sociology of knowledge. The sociology can point out to epistemology how to incorporate the abundance of relationships between facts and judgments, between being and value; the various kinds of knowledge refer to various social positions each of which has its own sifnificance and character of meaning that determines the truth-value of assertions (IU: 263, 264).

2. Another consequence of the sociology of knowledge for epistemology in this: the axioms from the natural sciences are taken over by traditional epistemology; we must reformulate these axioms with reference to the "countermodel" of the kinds of knowledge which to greater or lesser degree are determined existentially (IU: 264, 265).

3. The discovery of an activistic element in knowledge it the third consequence. According to idealistic philosophy, knowledge was pure if it was clear theoretically and it was theoretical if it worked according to a methematical

170

model. The problem of knowledge needs to be reformulated, so that purposeful activity becomes involved in knowledge. This reformulation does not open the possibility for propaganda and value judgements in the fields of scholarship. With this sociology of knowledge Mannheim wants to arrive at the place where, after knowledge is freed from the elements of propaganda and value judgment, it still retains an activistic principle (IU: 265, 266).

4. Fourthly, the actual perspectival element in knowledge. The problem is not how to arrive at a non-perspectival image, but how knowledge and objectivity are still possible, given various points of view standing in oppositions to each other. How can every perspective be acknowledged and a new level of objectivity be achieved each time?

5. Finally the opposition to truth-as-such. The positing of truth as such is the creation of a perfect sphere which does not carry the traces of the original givens; measured against the perfection all happenings and processes seem finite and incomplete. The process of knowing, according ot Mannheim, only becomes understandable when we strictly limit ourselves to factual thought, and when we see this process as an act of living people. It is clear that the sociology of knowledge is not in quest of eternal verities, but after *three other factors*: a) the nature and structure of life situations, b) the historical-social make-up of the subjective self, that is, the volitional element in an actor, and c) the position of the sociologist of knowledge who studies point a above. This last point implies that the sociology of knowledge is a reflexive and evaluative discipline: it not only studies the social relatedness of knowing an thinking in other people, but it also analyzes the manner in which it itself studies and evaluates these problems. This reflexive attitude must lead to a critical self-consciousness and a clarification of one's own existence. These three factors also condition the ideal of truth which the sociologist of knowledge can construe from the products of thought (IU: 268, 43).

Or again: objectivity and truth are not abandoned (IU: 254) but established by means of detours. The sociology of knowledge sees mental products according to their nature, as bound to point of view. The result of this is not *relativism* in the sense of subjective whimsy, but *relationism:* every assertion is, according to its very nature, only to be honored as relational. One can interpret this relationism, according to the author, as *relativism* only if one connects it with the old static ideal of desubjectivized and unperspectival truth. The sociology of knowledge as a non-evaluative discipline must pursue its investigations in the field of historical-social situations; also, it must along this line elaborate "on the criteria for exactness for establishing empirical truths" (IU: 275). With this perspectival relationism Mannheim rejects two other positions already mentioned: both that concerning absolute soundness as well as that concerning absolute unsoundness of someone's statements, seen from his social position (cf. Rempel, 1965: 21, 22).

When he discusses the methods of the empirical sociology of knowledge,

Mannheim summarizes the ideas as we have seen above, and then distinguishes three kinds of imputation (*Zurechnung*):

1. *Imputation according to meaning (Sinngemässe Zurechtnung*, which reconstructs the integral styles of thought and relates various expressions of thought to the Weltanschauung, which lies at the basis of styles and expressions.

2. *Imputation according ot facticity (Faktizitätszurechnung)*, which provide hypotheses for investigation. It asks for the range of a particular style of thought in an intellectual stratum. To what extent is a style of thought actually realized in some individual's thought?

3. After these immanent analyses of the *Weltanschauung* comes the *sociological imputation*, which studies which social strata stand behind the intellectual stratum. It investigates what style of thought can be imputed to a particular group. It also wants to study the development of thought in a particular situation and the changes it undergoes on account of a changed historical-social structure (IU: 276-278; cf. SW: 187, 188).

The method of the sociology of knowledge, which takes place by way of the detour of the sociology of culture, comes about in these *three phases* of imputation. Mannheim here comes to a methodological nuancing of his first approach to the sociology of knowledge. The idea of the "ideal type" in the imputation of facticity deserves some attention. Mannheim uses this methodological idea as a part of his theory. In that direction, in his discussion of general sociology, Mannheim is clearing a place for Weber's approach to "ideal types."

Provisional Conclusions

I gave the following characterization of the development of Mannheim's thought: from the philosophical sociology of knowledge to knowledge-sociology. We saw that his first approach was chiefly philosophical-epistemological in kind and that in his second approach he makes a clear distinction between a philosophical study and the study of an academic discipline. In his philosophical study of the sociology of knowledge he declares that he recognizes no duality between being and meaning, fact and norm. All fields of reality and facts have a character of meaning which determines, with other factors, the truth value of the statements concerned. Every field of reality has its own meaning and so, variety of meaning lies in the ontic; that is, it is locked into the order of reality itself. What appears above implies that a particular view of reality in its variety and context is actually a condition in judging the truth-value of statements.

In context with the distinction between empirical-sociological and philosophical-epistemological investigation, Mannheim knows the distinction, respectively, between a *non-evaluative* and an *evaluative* sociology of knowledge. The non-evaluative approach gives no judgments about the truth, correctness, or falsehood of statements; it restricts itself to the description of the relationships between thought and life-situations, of competitive groups in their struggle for power and for recognition in their interpretation of reality (BK: 196, 197, IU:

141); it investigates carefully how it happens that in a specific social structure, thought proceeds in this way or that; it concerns only the *relational* procedure (cf. IU: 71, 253).

Concerning the social relatedness of thought, Mannheim discusses the situationally-*determined* quality *(Seinsgebundenheit)* of thought and the situationally-*conditioned* quality *(Seinsverbundenheit)* of thought (see his "Wissenssoziologie" in Alfred Vierkandt's *Handwörterbuch der Soziologie*, 1931: 674; cf. SW: 137; BK: 226). As one becomes conscious of this social relatedness to thought, one breaks through from an unconscious, situational determinism *(Seinsgebundenheit)* to a consciousness of situational conditionedness *(Seinsverbundenheit)*.

We saw, however, that relationism implies questions about the truth of knowledge, the nature of social reality, and the objectivity and relativity of knowledge. These questions arise from the non-evaluative sociology of knowledge and are handled explicitly in the evaluative approach. Hence, we cannot separate the evaluative and non-evaluative models, but we can only distinguish them from each other.

A particular epistemology lies at the basis of the evaluative sociology of knowledge. This epistemology can not be regarded apart from Mannheim's conception of historicism. Relationism, which is studied through the non-evaluative sociology of knowledge, he calls significantly a "dynamic relationism" (IU: 88); he also speaks about a "dynamic truth" (SW: 368). The results of the evaluative sociology of knowledge certainly have consequences for the validity of the knowledge studied. It does not affect this knowledge completely, but it does accentuate the particularization of that knowledge.

Although Mannheim rejects a static, desubjectivized, and eternal truth and at the same time says that statements are bound to various viewpoints according to their nature, he defends his view against the accusation that it leads to relativism. He wants to avoid this relativism by taking account of three points in connection with relationism: 1. the structure of life-situations in the whole of the historical-social constellation, 2. the functioning person in these situations, and 3. the social position of the investigator. In addition, Mannheim claims that with these factors he has provided the conditions for *reaching the ideal of truth*. *The truth of statements is achievable*; by research it can be constructed from all kinds of products of thought, but this way is not easy. The question of truth is for Mannheim, as a practising academician and primarily as in intellectual, a question of conscience. The intellectuals must answer it precisely. According to him, they are in the position for the posing and the answering of the problems in hermeneutics, scholarship, and politics, and because they are in the position, they are called to pose and answer these questions. Intellectuals are bound to no particular perspective (cf. Ricoeur, 1981: 239, 242). Who are these intellectuals and what kind of particular qualifications do they have? Are they the people to whom Max Weber ascribed an "intellectual integrity?" These questions are to be answered in Chapter XII.

The Third Approach to the Sociology of Knowledge

I characterize the first chapter of *Ideology and Utopia* as Mannheim's third kind of approach to the sociology of knowledge. At first glance it does not offer much new information, compared with the first two kinds of approach. Still, this chapter requires special attention because he wrote it for the English edition of his book. In a letter of February 15, 1936 he wrote to Louis Wirth (see Appendix 3), that most English readers would regard his *Ideologie und Utopie* (1929) as too abstract and as a document from an inaccessible world, unless it had a new and clarifying first chapter. In what follows Mannheim writes that he has introduced altertions in the English manuscript of the translators, which he judges an accurate translation, and these emendations and insertions often vary greatly from the German text. He also judges that these annotations will be of particular importance for English readers.

When we compare the German and the English text with each other, the first thing we notice is that the title of the first chapter of the German edition in which the author speaks about "false consciousness" *(falsches Bewusstsein)*, is changed in the English edition: "Objectivity and Bias." David Kettler (1976) has made a painstaking comparison of both editions, and has discovered more than a hundred significant changes between the German and the English texts. He writes that Mannheim translates the German word *Geist* with words more appropriate for the psychological vocabulary of English philosophy and of American pragmatic psychology. It is not necessary to repeat all of Kettler's discoveries; only a few examples serve as illustrations. *Geist* regularly is translated *intellect* or *mind*. *Bewusstsein* becomes *mental activity* and sometimes *evaluation*. *Falsches Bewusstsein* becomes *invalid ethical attitude*. Mannheim has not consistently followed through with these and other emendations. It remains an open question why in some contexts he changed typical German concepts to be more colloquially English and in other contexts he kept them as German as possible. Noteworthy is the title of the second chapter of the German edition, which in English reads: "Is Politics as a Science Possible?" In the English edition it is called "The Prospects of Scientific Politics." The first-mentioned title alludes clearly to the essays by Max Weber: "Politics as a Vocation" and "Science as a Vocation"; Weber's conception of the problem is formulated in Kantian terms. The problem addressed in Weber's essays is very important in Mannheim's epistemology and political sociology. With the change form "politics as a science" to "scientific politics" Mannheim suggests at least that he gives Weber's dilemma less weight than he had, although the content of the chapter concerned is largely the same, in both the German and the English editions. In any case, it is clear that he wanted to promote a greater degree of accessibility for a new reading public; a new introductory chapter also served this purpose, for in it he could delineate the chief themes of his sociology of knowledge (cf. Kettler, Meja, Stehr, 1984: Chapter III).

In the first chapter of his *Ideology and Utopia* Mannheim formulates the

174

purpose of the sociology of knowledge in a very succinct way as an investigation of the functioning of thought in public life. It is not an investigation of thought following the rules of a specific logic, but a study of thought as an instrument of collective behavior. Our everyday, pre-theoretical way of thinking cannot only be grasped by means of logical analysis. Mannheim wants to work out a method for the purpose, not only of analyzing theoretical thought by the sociology of knowledge, but also pre-theoretical thought. The method of this study has two characteristiscs:

1. The various ways of thinking in society can only be adequately understood if the socio-historical situation within which a mode of thought functions is clear. Not thought-as-such, nor "pure thought," nor *the* thought of *the* human being, but the thought of people who speak the language of their group. In various groups a particular mode of thought is developed, by which the participants can react adequately to the typical situations that characterize their social position.

2. The existing modes of thought are not separated from the context of collective activity. This activity gives access to a sociological understanding of the world. People are not seen as physically measurable entities, but as beings who can react to each other. Thought is not separaterd from collective life nor form ordinary activity (IU: 3). This investigation, according to the author, will offer a fund of data for the social sciences and also give an answer to the question about the possibility for academic leadership in political life.

Divergent opinions and modes of thought are no problems, so long as a social stability lies at the base and a *Weltanschauung* guarantees the internal unity of the society. Especially the intensification of social mobility (particularly the horizontal combined with the vertical) shocks the supposed invulnerability and soundness of one's mode of thought.

Seen from a sociological point of view, a determining social change takes place when a particular phase is reached in the historical development in which the social classes which have been isolated until then begin to comunicate with each other. So long as a society is established on the basis of authority and only those who have attained the highest class have prestige, so long there will be little motivation for this class to bring up its social position and its values for discussion. The social mobility mentioned before only becomes important when there is talk of universal democratizing. Only then does the thought of other social levels acquire soundness and prestige.

Referring to his dissertation, Mannheim says that all epistemological speculations have always been oriented on the polarity of subject and object. Either a thinker chooses his starting point in the world of objects (an ontology referring to the world order), or in the subject (either the rationalism of Descartes by way of Leibniz to Kant, or the more psychologically oriented: Hobbes, Locke, Berkeley, Hume). One hoped in the new time to be able to support the truth-value of human thought by means of the empirical method of natural science.

The psychology between the Middle Ages and our own time was strongly influenced by the religious ontology of the soul. It was a psychology in which concepts such as despair, sin, and salvation had a place. In the course of time this religious ontology began to atrophy. In a society where the meaning of words like *God, life,* and *person* are less self-evident and obvious, the agreement on the meanings of words like *sin, despair, salvation,* and *loneliness* will also certainly diminish. Those interpretations which provided meanings with a rich content are now replaced by more formal concepts: feelings of anxiety, perceptions of inner conflict, experience of alienation, libido. Psychology proceeded in imitation of a simplified scheme of the mechanics: position, motion, cause, result (IU: 15, 16):

> The interconnections of meaning which were in this procedure heuristically excluded (in the interests of scientific simplification) so that formal and easily definable entities could be arrived at, are not recaptured by a mere further perfection of formalization through the discovery of correlations and functions. (IU: 16, 17)

The mechanistic and functionalistic theory fails when it is placed in a context of life-experience:

> Just as the most exact theory of cause and function does not answer the question as the who I actually am, what I actually am, or what it means to be a human being, so there can never arise out of it that interpretation of one's self and the world demanded by even the simplest action based on some evaluative decision. (IU: 17)

Every decision, both concerning someone's opinion about someone else or concerning the organization of society, implies a judgment of good and evil related to the meaning of life.

It was the achievement of the sociological approach that, next to the individual bestowal of meaning, it placed another which arose out of "the context of group life" (IU: 25). But the danger of formalization and the ideal of exactness also threaten sociology because it enforces the strivings to de-anthropomorphize already described. And so there is nothing left for sociology than static data and the task of testing it, while the most important problems concerning the *typically social* in the realm of social reality could not be adequately understood by quantitative methods. Also epistemology is always approached from the minds of individuals who would live separated from the group. In contrast to this conception, Mannheim says,

> It is much more correct to say that knowledge is from the very beginning a cooperative process of groupslife, within the framework of a common fate, a common activity, and the overcoming of difficulties. (IU: 26)

In a differentiated society, groups, sub-groups and strata all have various experiences of the world. So every sub-group has its own concerns. That the social factor in knowledge came about so late is recognized, according to

Mannheim, through the fact that epistemology and psychology got much attention particularly in the West during a time of radical individualism and subjectivism, that is, after the disintegration of the social order of the Middle Ages and at the beginning of liberal bourgeois capitalism. What had always been an "objective" criterion all at once became something "subjective,"and in epistemology this tendency appeared just as it did everywhere: from an objective world order to an individual subject.

Mannheim, however, defends a new conception of *objectivity* based on his sociology of knowledge. This will not be achieved by someone's giving up his will for activity nor by his accepting a hesitant, uncertain attituede, but by research into the sociology of knowledge. Not only the object, but we ourselves belong to the field of research. That is, a sociological approach to our social position leads to an academic clarification of existence. This leads, moreover, to a paradox: to a relative emancipation from social determinism; it leads specifically to insight into this determinism (IU: 42, 43), without being able to transcend it.

Provisional Conclusions

This third approach to the sociology of knowledge offers little new information, compared to the first two. The sciences work ever increasingly with formalized concepts and seem to have lost the interpretations which bestowed significance by means of religious content. We encountered this complaint earlier; in his view of "Soul and Culture" Mannheim said that Western humanity has lost its religious self-awareness. Mannheim calls this apostasy. Only by the detour of cultural objectivizations is fulfillment of soul still to be achieved. Later this detour seems to peter out by way of the interpretation of the *Weltanschauung*, which he requires anew in his sociology of knowledge.

Comparing the three methods of approach, we can conclude that Mannheim comes closer and closer to working out systematically the principles of the sociology of knowledge; especially in his article "Wissenssoziologie" ("Knowledge-sociology"), the last chapter of *Ideology and Utopia*, this is the case. In the second place, an increasing concreteness is noteworthy: the detour of the sociology of culture, his analysis of the *Weltanschauung* is worked out in the study of the relationship of thought to the differentiated socio-historical situations. The cultural-sociological analysis of the *Weltanschauung* has not disappeared. In his approach to the sociology of knowledge, Mannheim has increasingly been working with the interpretive framework of the sociology of culture. The question of truth, which is asked in the evaluative sociology of knowledge, cannot be handled without the *Weltanschauung*.

Mannheim continues to look for the proper understanding of the meaning of social reality. He seeks a grip on it, because the danger of epistemological relativism is lurking everywhere. That is why it is important to strive for a new concept of objectivity. The questions already asked concerning the social relatedness and the relativity of knowing are here brought to mind again.

These conclusions still carry a provisional character; in addition, they have remained limited to summaries of some of the kernel problems, directed to the question of truth. We can only discuss these subjects more elaborately after we have seen exactly what role the intelligentsia ought to play in the sociology of knowledge. Even before we treat Mannheim's conception of the intelligentsia, we shall listen to a few of the critics of his sociology of knowledge. Only those critics will be discussed who have specifically gone into his sociology of knowledge, and who by their work have contributed to a better understanding of his work.

Mannheim and Criticism

Although Mannheim provided contributions to various fields of sociology, his sociology of knowledge is the most familiar part of his work. As far as this last-mentioned branch of science is concerned, it was a stroke of genius which enriched human insight. From a study of his work, however, it appears that he never worked out sharp distincions between thinking/knowing/philosophizing and the social structures, and hence did not always arrive at clear conclusions. He gives some methodological suggestions, but does not work these out sharply. He is more of a visionary who offers astounding insights, and not so much a rigorous philosopher of science (Neusüss, 1968a: 78ff). Mannheim has not been spared criticism, neither during his lifetime nor after his death.

Adorno: The Charge of Positivism

Soon after the appearance of Mannheim's *Ideologie und Utopie*, Max Horkheimer, the philosopher from Frankfurt, published a criticism of this book. Because Horkheimer addresses himself chiefly to Mannheim's use of the concept of ideology, we shall discuss his criticism in a later chapter. A critical discussion of Mannheim's sociology of knowledge also appeared, written by Theodor Adorno, Horkheimer's friend and intellectual brother (1981: 25-49).

Adorno establishes that especially after World War II a renewed concern for Mannheim's sociology of knowledge has arisen – an attention that arose, according to Adorno, from a benign scepticism. Although Adorno brings his criticism to expression particularly on the basis of Mannheim's *Man and Society in an Age of Reconstruction (Mensch und Gesellschaft im Zeitalter des Umbaus*, 1935), there is no reason, in view of the extent of his criticism, to conclude that Adorno's comments have no reference to earlier publications. Mannheim's orientation is called positivistic:

> ... social phenomena are taken "as such" and then classified according to general concepts. In this process social antagonisms invariably tend to be glossed over. They survive merely as subtle modifications of a conceptual apparatus whose distilled "principles" install themselves autocratically and engage in shadow battles. (1981: 37)

178

A little farther on Adorno writes that Mannheim flirts with positivism to this extent, that he depends on inarticulated facts which are then reworked into general sociological concepts. But social reality, according to Adorno, is very articulated, and the thesis of the primacy of being above consciousness, implies a *methodological imperative* to form concepts which will bring to expression tendencies toward activism in social reality. Mannheim's sociology of knowledge has eclipsed this demand (42, 43); his sociology seems like "a mockery of reality" (1981: 43).

From Adorno's neo-Marxist perspective, the reality principle is lacking in Mannheim's philosophy. Both in the second and in the third part of this study, I have pointed out that Mannheim expressed pricipial criticism of Marxism, and his own viewpoint can be called *transcendental realism*; he works out this viewpoint in a sociologically differentiated historicism. The accusation by Adorno that Mannheim's sociology of knowledge is positivistic is untrue. We discussed in Chapter VI that Mannheim affirmed a "positivism well-understood" and by careful argument rejected the positivism oriented on the natural sciences.

Quite apart from Adorno's Marxist-oriented critique, Mannheim's sociology of knowledge can indeed be called *inarticulated*. Various inconsistencies and unclear definitions of concepts have already been pointed out (cf. Grünwald, 1934: 201-217; Speier, 1937: 164 f; Shils, 1974: 86).

It can hardly be surprising that Lukács criticized Mannheim severely. Lukács sees Mannheim's distinction between relativism and relationism as the distinction which Lenin made to Gorki in a letter (14-11-1913) between a yellow and a green devil. Mannheim's discussion of the relatedness of all thought and his criticism of Marxism – that Marxist criticism of ideology should apply also to one's own thinking and particularly in the case of Marxists to the thought of the proletariat, by which many forms of false consciousness would be revealed – all of this makes Lukács conclude that Mannheim comes to "what we know as the night of thorough-going relativism, in which all cats look grey and all perceptions relative" (1980: 634). According to Lukács, Mannheim's "reasoning was the result of simply eliminating both the dialectic of the absolute and relative, historical development and its concrete facts, which always clearly illustrate how this dialectic of the absolute and the relative works out in any given case" (1980: 634). In addition to the criticisms by Adorno and Lukács, related interpretations of Mannheim can be examined in the work of Fogarasi (1930: 359-375) and Wittfogel (1931: 83-102).

Another criticism from the Marxist side, heard from Lieber (1965: 96, 97) and others, is that Mannheim regarded economic factors as outside of his sociological field of investigation, and that consequently he could arrive at his "formalization of the categories of the sociology of knowledge." We must oppose this interpretation. It is noteworthy that Lieber, to support his accusation, refers to Mannheim's essay on historicism. It is important to notice the course of development of Mannheim's thought. Already in his first and also in his second phase he had pointed out the importance of analyzing economic factors for the proper understanding of his own time. He will not, however, speak in such a way about these factors that he would use oversimplifications and clever schemes for explaining society; of this latter oversimplification he accuses Marx. Economic factors are important for understanding society, but he wants to distinguish these from social matters for the purpose of being able to comprehend the social dimension of life in its own terms (BK: 195; cf. ISI: 119, 120; SK: 66).

Popper: The Charge of Vulgar Marxism

Karl Popper regards all sociologists of knowledge as holding to one form or another of "vulgar Marxism," which means they are a group of philosophers who attempt to discover the hidden motives behind human thought. The popularity of the sociology of knowledge is, according to Popper, the result of the ease with which it can be applied. He continues:

> This pleasure would be harmless, were it not that all these ideas are liable to destroy the intellectual basis of any discussion, by establishing ... a "reinforced dogmatism." (1952, II: 215)

Popper blames the harmful pleasure on the Hegelians, who defended the fruitfulness of contradictions. He throws the following judgments against them: "If contradictions need not be avoided, then my criticism and any discussion becomes impossible since criticism always consists in pointing out contradictions either within the theory to be criticized, or between this theory and some facts of experience" (1952, II: 215). He directs his accusations against psychoanalysis as well: "the psychoanalyst can always explain away any objections by showing that they are due to the repression of the critic" (1952, I: 215). For Marxists the same holds, according to him, because they are "accustomed to explain this disagreement of an opponent by his class basis." Mannheim, according to Popper, will explain the difference of his opinions from others with the help of his "total worldview" or "total ideology." Popper is of the opinion that all these methods "clearly destroy the basis of rational discussion, and they must lead, ultimately, to anti-rationalism and mysticism" (1952, II: 216). He continues that the approaches mentioned above do not apply their methods to themselves. On the contrary, they claim seriously that they have achieved a higher level of objectivity. That is a serious mistake, according to Popper, because, as a result, the sociology of knowledge cannot comprehend its own problems: the social aspects of knowledge, or rather, of their own scientific method (1952, II: 217). Because the sociologists of knowledge regard knowledge as a process in the consciousness of the academic scholar as a participant in social groups and strata, they cannot understand what Popper calls "scientific objectivity." If this objectivity is founded on the social vision of the academic scholar, as the sociologists of knowledge state, then Popper rejects it. He claims

180

to want to be more radical than the sociology of knowledge. He acknowledges that all people have their prejudices and ideologies. According to him, also academic scholars must perceive that they are afflicted with prejudices and ideologies. Individually they are not equipped to ascend to the level of scientific objectivity:

> Objectivity is closely bound up with the *social aspect of scientific method*, with the fact that science and scientific objectivity do not (and cannot) result from the attempt of an individual scientist to be "objective," but from the cooperation of many scientists. Scientific objectivity can be described as the inter-subjectivity of scientific method. But their social aspect of science is almost entirely neglected by those who call themselves sociologists of knowledge. (1952, II: 217)

According to Popper, scientific objectivity has two characteristics: First, all scientific work must be subjected to the criticism of competent practising scientists. Second, scientists in their discussions attempt to avoid misunderstandings; they attempt to speak the same language, which assures a public and controlling factor for their perceptions and experiments. Their theories are tested by means of these controlled perceptions and experiments. These two characteristics determine "the public character of the scientific method" (1952, II: 218). These two aspects also mean that scientific work is first of all to be judged by method rather than by results. This process of competent public criticism is never completed, but is does constitute scientific objectivity. This means that the objectivity of scientific results is relative; they are the results of a particular phase in the scientific process; in the course of this process, results can be replaced by newer results. However, this does not imply that truth is relative. Popper claims explicitly to be a proponent of a theory of absolute truth, which is in agreement with the idea "*that a statement is true if*, and only if, *it agrees with the facts it describes*" (1952, I: 273; cf. 1952, II: 221). This idea of absolute truth may not be confused with concepts such as *believed, verified, highly confirmed*, etc., which are, in fact, relative. The relativity of scientific results means only that they have the character of hypotheses. At any moment they can be tested and reconsidered. According to Popper, it is meaningless to construct sociological theories about knowledge. All results of knowledge must be construed as hypotheses, which can be subjected to public testing (1952, II: 222).

Popper agrees with Mannheim that no scientist has "purely scientific" thoughts, without, for instance, political interests being involved. The sociologists of knowledge, however, make a terrible mistake when they say that the sociological study of socially prejudiced people can help them to free themselves from these prejudices. According to Popper, the sociologists of knowledge can only increase the significance of social factors in the process of knowing, instead of fighting prejudice with the help of a public and competent discussion (cf. Popper, 1970: 57, 58; cf. Carlsnaes, 1981: 220).

Popper's scientific method of trial and error has consequences for his view of the application of results of scientific investigation to the solution of social problems. He also wants to attack these problems with the help of his scientific method. For a discussion of this problem of Popper's criticism of Mannheim, whom he regards as an enemy of democratic society, as well as for my criticism of Popper, I refer to Chapter XII. Now already it can be plain that the presuppositions of Mannheim's sociology of knowledge and of Popper's rationalistic scientism are not to be reconciled.

Merton: Methodological Criticism

In an extensive discussion Robert Merton asks the question which spheres of thought are included in Mannheim's view of thought's relatedness to social existence. Sometimes Mannheim construes knowledge and thought so broadly as to include both folklore on the one hand and the most stringent methodological-scientific thought on the other. But we also saw that formal knowledge like mathematics and logic were not regarded by him as being influenced by social-historical situations (cf. BK: 194; SW: 180, 181; IU: 278).

What is the nature of thought's relatedness to social existence? We saw already that Mannheim does not characterize it as deterministic in the mechanical-causal sense. For the nature of thought's relatedness to existence he uses various descriptions: "in accord with...," "in close harmony with...," "bound up with and grow into," "causal determinants," "in harmony with...," "in close connection with," "it is no accident that...." For the nature of the relationship of thought to being, which he states in a variety of ways as recorded here, the general concept he uses is always the same: "correspondence" (Merton, 1968: 552-556).

Merton concludes that Mannheim's contribution to the sociology of knowledge has an *introductory and provisional character*; his methodology is not elaborated. This criticism is also expressed by Von Schelting (1934: 100-117), who discusses this question: What significance does the functionalization of thought and knowledge have with regard to social existence? Does Mannheim mean that thought is a function *of* being? – in the sense that changes in thought correspond to changes in the existence of social structures? Or does he mean that thought is a function *in* being? – in the sense that it has a function within social processes? Both ideas occur in Mannheim, but their underlying relationship in his work is unclear (Von Schelting, 1934: 101). Putting aside Von Schelting's negative attitude toward the sociology of knowledge as such, he observes accurately that Mannheim's observations demonstrate great deficiencies because of "their basic lack of logical and epistemological consistency and their incompatibility with empirical facts" (1936: 664, 665). This criticism is also expressed by Horowitz (1961: 41, 82), by Maquet (1973: 31, 32, 52, 56) and by Hofstra (1937: 47-51).

In this connection it is important to recall that Merton understands by the sociology of knowledge an empirical-scientific investigation of factual relation-

182

ships between ideas, concepts, knowledge, and
attention in this discussion to the question whi(
heim, the question of "existential truth," n(
problems of society and culture can be solved.
a neo-positivistic way: "The institutional go
certified knowledge. The technical methods (
the relevant definition of knowledge: empiri
sistent statements of regularities (which a
270).

In contrast to Mannheim's understandir
content, basic premises, and models of thoug
conditions, Merton (1968: 554) asserts that "... the criteria of
scientific knowledge are not matters of national taste and culture. Sooner
later, competing claims to validity are settled by the universalistic facts of nature
which are consonant with one and not another theory." Phillips (1977: 164)
concludes correctly: "Merton's view is, I believe, that held by most sociologists
and philosophers of science, 'universal facts of nature', existing out there, will
provide the ultimate source of evidence for the superiority of one theory or
another, for distinguishing between science and pseudo-science. Merton simply
takes it for granted that scientists constitute a legitimate part of the contemporary social structure."

C. Wright Mills: Pragmatic Interpretation

At first also Charles Wright Mills took the position of Merton's conception of
the sociology of knowledge. Later the question of truth, already mentioned,
came to the fore. The development in Mills' thought has been clearly described
by Verhoogt, the Dutch sociologist (1976: 107-131). That description states that
originally Mills' formulation of the problem is directed toward "a confrontation
between the pragmatically oriented social-psychological theory of Mead and
the sociology of knowledge of Mannheim, in the reduced [empirical-scientific]
meaning of the sociology of knowledge. That is how he [Mills] criticizes theories
of the sociology of knowledge, like Mannheim's in his [Mills'] 'Language,
Logic, and Culture' (1939). True, Mannheim's theories demonstrate a social-
historical determination of ideas and conceptions, but they do not indicate how
this determination is executed in the individual's life, nor indeed how it is
possible" (Verhoogt, 1976: 107).

The central question now is that of the relationship of his sociology of
knowledge to the pragmatic-behavioristic view of society and people. Mills
treats this question in his "Methodological Consequences of the Sociology of
Knowledge" (1940). In this essay he asserts that the concepts *truth* and *objectivity* have their meaning and practical significance only in a recognized model or
system of verification. He continues, thus:

183

s the irrelevance of social conditions to the truthfulness of propositions ought
conditons upon which he conceives truthfulness actually to depend. He ought
y exactly what it is in thinking that sociological factors cannot affect and upon
truth and validity do rest. (1940: 317)

s means the criteria or models of verification have no transcendent charac-
. On the contrary, the historical variety of these models, according ot Mills,
pleads for Dewey's conception, that they arise form investigations in particular
societies. He also concludes, then, that no principial difference exists between
Mannheim and Dewey on this point. Only those who operate on the basis of a
supra-temporal, a-historical truth can dispute these conceptions; they will use
the accusation of relativism. Joining the pragmatism of Peirce and Dewey, Mills
(319, 320) feels at home in the relationism defended by Mannheim.

Although one can strike a few pragmatic tendencies in Mannheim's sociology
of knowledge (Von Schelting, 1934: 118-120), an unnuanced accusation of
pragmatism is not true. In spite of the unquestionable agreements in epistemology and methodology, there are remarkable differences between Mills and
Mannheim. First, we must notice that Mannheim's concern is not simply epistemology and methodology. Not in the line of pragmatism, but in the tradition of
the thought of historicism, Mannheim wrestles above all other questions with
the question of truth, as developed in the philosophy of culture; the answer
would need to be given by the intelligentsia in a cultural synthesis.

Mills agrees with Dewey and Peirce's formulations, that one can only judge
an utterance as true or false in relationship to a verifying model. Of this model
of thought Mills says: "Granted that this model is no absolute guarantee, it
seems the most probable we have at present" (1940: 323). Over against the
supra-temporal or absolute truth, Mills posits *probability*, which always implies
moments of relativity. "Assertions can properly be stated as probabilities, as
more or less true. And only in this way can we account for the fact that scientific
inquiry is self-correcting" (1940: 323, 324). The conclusion of Krüger (1968: 91)
is correct: "The fact that truth always only settles for an expression and is not
capable of being absolutely expressed, does not now mean, according to Mills,
that the results of investigations must be false. Under the given conditions, they
are true."

Mills' assertion of the relativity of the models of thought implies at the same
time a plurality of models of thought. The sociology of knowledge must study
with tolerance these models and their criteria for truth (1940: 327f). This
position implies a relativity in Mills' sociology of knowledge. "Truth always
appears to him [Mills] as relational truth. (...) Every claim to absoluteness for a
model of thought is rejected; the social connections, which lead to the accepting
of one model of thought and the rejection of the other, are exposed by means of
the sociology of knowledge." Thus Krüger (1968: 95), who continues thus: "At
the same time, however, it grants the sociology of knowledge the opportunity ot
contribute to the completion of a better methodology of social sciences by
means of insight into the conditions of the models of thought."

It is characteristic of Wright Mills that he actually avoids the problem of relativism by taking it up in a pragmatic interpretation of science, as Verhoogt (1976: 110) remarks, who writes as follows:

> The potential relativizing by the dominant pragmatic conception of people and science out of the sociology of knowledge is avoided here by founding the sociology itself on pragmatic-positivistic grounds and this establishing it in the pragmatic conception of science.

Although Mills, just as Mannheim, asks the questions concerning truth in the sociology of knowledge, it seems as though he only asks these methodologically and not from the perspective of the sociology of culture.

In the later work Mills undergoes a development *in the direction of* a sociology of knowledge, which indeed posits the question of truth; he himself later comes to criticize Dewey's pragmatism. The society which Mills knows is primarily characterized by structural antitheses, in this case based on power. Change in this society is, according to him, only possible with help from adequate knowledge and political power. The central question is then also whether pragmatism for him has outlived any further usefulness; his question cannot be answered affirmatively. He continues to reach back to the view of humanity which is hiddenly implied in pragmatism, in which on the one hand the plasticity of human nature adapts itself and then readapts itself to the changing socio-historical situation, and in which on the other hand the creativity of the human Prometheus has its place. It is a view of humanity in which a socio-historical determinism and a psychological determinism proceed together (Verhoogt, 1976: 117, 118, 129).

We saw that Mills, in his criticism of pragmatism and in his distinguishing of the power-antitheses in society, attempts to transcend the sociology of knowledge reduced to an empirical discipline. It remains an attempt. Mannheim states in his sociology of knowledge the problem of the synthesis of culture and for that purpose calls on the intellectuals. Mills also issues a mighty call to them. According to Mills, they have lost their grip on social processes. They are imprisoned in the power structures of society. The following is an example (1963: 297):

> The United States' growing international entanglements have subtle effects upon some American intellectuals: to the young man who teaches and writes on Latin America, Asia, or Europa and who refrains from deviating from acceptable facts and policies these entanglements lead to a voluntary censorship. He hopes for opportunities of research, travel, and foundation subsidies.
> *The means of effective communication are being expropriated from the intellectual worker. The material basis of his initiative and intellectual freedom is no longer in his hand. Some intellectuals feel these processes in their work. They know more than they say and they are powerless and afraid.*

What is the reason for this lack of power? The intellectuals, according to Mills, have lost their pragmatism, which gave such power to progressive thought during the first decades of this century. Society has fallen into the hands of a small group of men in power. What intellectuals want is a politics of truth in a democratic society; in our society, however, it depends on this: that the intellectual changes his mind about the possibilities of dealing with matters in a politically effective way (1963: 304); it is a remark that is typical for a pragmatic mode of thought. In spite of his accurate characterization of the powerlessness of many intelecctuals and his appeal to them to understand their political and social task, Mills finally does not rise above an intellectual strategy within the boundaries of what is achievable. His pragmatism takes away his power and his vision to break his way through the boundaries of the existing order and to summon intellectuals and others to help bring about the new order.

Dooyeweerd: Transcendental Criticism

Herman Dooyeweerd is one of the few Dutch philosophers who has written about Mannheim and shows great admiration for this practitioner of the sociology of knowledge. As Calvinist, Dooyeweerd works out his insights in his own way.

Dooyeweerd has a rather limited conception of sociology. He defines sociology as the "total science" of human society. That is, the science which studies the typical total structures of social relationships and their subordinate concerns. So he pays elaborate attention to the analysis of the structural characteristics of marriage, family, the extended family, the church, the state, and other totalities, all of which he intends to distinguish by their own particular natures (1957: 262-264). His sociology lacks a study of such problems as interaction, processes of institutionalization, social strata, groupings, communes, horizontal and vertical social mobility, generations, and many more (cf. Woldring, Kuiper, 1980: 91-127, 163-178).

Dooyeweerd's sociology is to be characterized as a philosophical sociology of the structures of identity. He wants to characterize the structure of social entities according to their nature, with help from a certain "qualifying function" which gives guidance. Because thought for him is a typically human quality and, therefore, it also comes to expression in social contexts, we can distinguish in social relationships the aspects of *thought communities*. For instance, he speaks of the family as a community with its own mode of thought. Before children are grown up, they usually lack an independent judgment – they are dependent on parents. In line with the structural characteristics, he calls the family an ethical community, and regards it as a social form characterized by love; also as a community of thought it is characterized by love. The development which this community of thought undergoes is closely connected with the phases of the historical development of the extended family and society as a whole. According to Dooyeweerd, the family as community of thought frequently exhibits the typical prejudices with regard to class, church, and politics, which together can be imputed to the interwoven relationships of family with other social struc-

186

tures. Just as a family forms a community of thought, so it also exists in a business characterized by an economic qualification, in a church with the characterization of a community of Christian faith, in marriage and friendship relationships characterized by love and trust, and in the organization of the state characterized by the juridical quality of public justice.

With reference to the sociology of knowledge, Dooyeweerd continues thus:

> It is, however, of primordial importance for this study not to neglect the typical structural differences between the various communities of thought. It should especially guard against a confusion of the necessary structural conditions and presuppositions of communal thought with illegitimate social prejudices which impede correct judgment and are to be unmasked by sociological science. (1957: 289)

Dooyeweerd regards the qualifying characteristics of social entities mentioned above as sufficient criteria for determining the various kinds of communities of thought. In this regard we must discuss several problems critically. Are the structural differences Dooyeweerd mentions between social relationships adequate criteria for distinguishing various communities of thought? For instance, families can form very different communities of thought. Dooyeweerd acknowledges this. He asserts that the development of a community of thought is closely related to the historical development of that particular community and also with the development of society as a whole. This means that the various ways in which thought can go on in one family about political and social topics, are not only characterized by the ethical qualification of love in the family structure, but also, and in a significant degree, by the social stratum to which a family belongs. Also a church community or an ethnic minority, to which members of a family belong, can determine the thinking of that family. On the other hand, a church community consisting of immigrants or oppressed minorities has a different stance toward social and political issues, and thinks about and discusses them differently, than does a church which is attended by a priviliged elite.

On the grounds of which criteria will Dooyeweerd judge as illegitimate certain social prejudices which arise from the connection with class, generations, rural or underpriviledged sectors of society? Dooyeweerd can give two answers to this problem. First, he would say that opinions and thoughts are antinormative and, thus, illegitimate, when they break and damage the realization of the family as a fellowship characterized by ethical qualifications or hinder the realization of the church as a fellowship of Christian faith, or inhibit any other normative, properly qualified relationship. And so, within one family there can be differences of opinion about political, economic, religious, and other topics, without damaging the family as a community of love. Secondly, he writes that his transcendental critique, which studies thought radically and critically for the purpose of exposing its ultimate presuppositions, will bring to light the religious ground motives of thought. According to Dooyeweerd, this implies, that in philosophy "social prejudices of an illegitimate character can show themselves, which hang together with a limitation of vision of the social environment and consequently should be overcome – class and racial prejudices, prejudices of a limited church group, etc., etc." (1953: 164, 165; cf. 195 f, 288, 289). Which criteria would Dooyeweerd want to use for judging class prejudices and the narrow prejudices of ecclesiastical and political groupings? He says that these prejudices are bound to a restricted view of the social environment, and that they must be overcome. Sociology can unmask such narrow prejudices. That is, *his* sociology is in a position to accomplish this unmasking. But in his philosophical sociology, Dooyeweerd gives no attention to such subjects as interaction, horizontal and vertical social mobility, classes and positions, generations, or other collectivities, strata, groups, and groupings. Still, all people participate in these social forms, which to a greater or lesser degree influence their social prejudices. Were one to adopt Dooyeweerd's limited conception of sociology, it would still be difficult and risky to judge which prejudices are illegitimate. For the rest, what Dooyeweerd says is true, that the modern sociology of knowledge (Scheler, Mannheim, Jerusalem and others) "has cast a penetrating light" concerning the unmasking of those prejudices (1953: 165). Although these sociologists of knowledge and Dooyeweerd have two contrasting philosophical approaches to the discipline, they both contributed to the unmasking of prejudices. Here we must consider that both Dooyeweerd as a philosopher and the sociologist of knowledge each does this unmasking in his own way.

On the basis of his sociology of knowledge, Mannheim would need to consider Dooyeweerd a typical Calvinist thinker. At the end of the nineteenth century and in the twentieth centruy the theory of "sphere sovereignty" occupied a central place in the thought of Calvinists in the Netherlands. This theory was championed particularly by the Dutch theologian-statesman Abraham Kuyper. Against atomistic and collectivistic theories about society, Kuyper and the others wanted to present a third approach. Although Dooyeweerd had some criticism of portions of Kuyper's theory, he elaborated the idea of "sphere sovereignty" both in his cosmology and in his sociology of the social structures of identity.

Mannheim would call Dooyeweerd's philosophy a prime example of thought bound to a position. According to Mannheim, Dooyeweerd would not belong to a free-floating intelligentsia. Dooyeweerd would assent to this assessment. Given his radical-Christian starting point, he dismisses all synthetic thinking out of hand. As we still shall see, the thought of the intelligentsia is characterized by a cultural synthesis, according to Mannheim. On principle, Dooyeweerd would reject the identification of social thought by how it is bound to a social position. As mentioned, he, by means of his transcendental investigation, wants to expose the deepest roots of scientific thought. In this investigation he sets out to be essentially critical. That is why he rejects all thought of an autonomous pure reason; this proceeds, according to Dooyeweerd, from the starting point of an invincible and self-sufficient reason. Scientific thought, according to him, is an expression of the heart of a person, as are all contingent human activities; it is an expression of his "existential center of life" and, for Dooyeweerd himself, this should be his relationship by faith to Jesus the Christ.

When Mannheim says that all thought, thus also religious-transcendental thought, is always influenced by cultural and social situations, Dooyeweerd would not take exception to that position. At the same time, Dooyeweerd would supplement this position with the remark that, with the help of transcendental thought, the critical perception must and can be sharpened continually, for the purpose of discovering the deepest religious motives which give direction to thought. Dooyeweerd would then ask whether in the sociology of knowledge the deepest, that is, the religious, motives of thought are being exposed. He would remind Mannheim next of the proposition which Mannheim himself has defended, that not the academic practitioner, but the evidence of the object – that is, the nature of meaning in the particular field of reality – ultimately determines the truth-content of thought and knowledge. Questions about the meaning and the nature of the object of sociology and the nature of the ontic structure of other fields of reality presupposes a philosophical cosmology concerning the differentiation and context of reality. On the basis of which worldview or perspective on life is this cosmology to be elaborated? We saw already that Mannheim's sociological elaboration is strongly determined by his sociological historicism.

In summary, we can formulate the problems as follows: 1. Is the transcendental critique – which, according to Dooyeweerd, inescapably leads to the discovery of the religious presuppositions of thought – is this critique possible from the point of view of Mannheim's sociology of knowledge? 2. Is Mannheim's sociology of knowledge adequate for exposing the presuppositions of thought, or does it require a thinking through on the basis of a transcendental-critical investigation?

Both for Mannheim in his sociology of knowledge and for Dooyeweerd in his transcendental critique of the question of knowledge, two matters are at issue: the question of truth as it concerns human knowledge and the question of the development of Western culture. Because these matters are still at issue, we cannot answer the questions posed in the penultimate paragraph above until the end of this study.

Conclusions

The critique of the authors discussed is directed both toward Mannheim's philosophical sociology of knowledge as toward his more specialized discipline of knowledge-sociology. The critique of this disciplinary specialization came primarily from Merton and Von Schelting, who pointed out methodological deficiencies. Also the pragmatic interpretation which Mills provided was knowledge-sociological; his appeal to the intellectuals seemed powerless because of its pragmatic roots. Popper wanted to transcend the sociology of knowledge by means of his critical-rational conception of science. Mannheim and his sociology of knowledge would remain stuck in a pre-theoretical phase, according to Popper. Adorno gave attention not only to knowledge-sociology, but also to the questions which lie at the foundation of the sociology of knowledge. The inarticulated knowledge-sociology, according to Adorno, arose from an inarticulated vision of reality; the primacy of being which determines consciousness implies the methodological demand for the transformation of concepts, by which the primacy is brought to expression.

Also Von Schelting criticized Mannheim's sociology of knowledge with the charge of epistemological inconsistencies. Also Sorokin can be named in this connection, who says of Mannheim's sociology of knowledge:

> He rightly looks for the cause of the group-affiliations of a person, but he does not give any systematic theory of groups or of social mobility. His theory remains vague and in many respects incorrect. (1947: 352)

With respect for the insights into the sociology of knowledge, Dooyeweerd has questions concerning the adequacy of the sociology of knowledge. Not from a Marxist lens, but from his own religious presuppositions and from the Calvinist theory of "sphere sovereignty," Dooyeweerd came to an articulated view of reality.

The kernel problems of Mannheim's sociology, mentioned by those critics and already formulated in the "Provisional Conclusions" in this chapter, can be summarized as follows: 1. To what extent is relational knowledge relative? Not at all, or in a moderate degree? Is true knowledge possible? 2. Which qualities and tasks do intellectuals possess? 3. What meaning does Mannheim's sociological-historical view of reality have for the question of truth in the sociology of knowledge? 4. What significance, in connection with the question of truth, does it have to talk about the *nature*, the *evidence*, and the character of *meaning* of the object?

Chapter XI

Ideology and Utopia

Mannheim on Ideology

Mannheim kept on investigating the problem of ideology in his essay "Ideologische und soziologische Interpretation der geistigen Gebilde" published in the *Jahrbuch für Soziologie* in 1926 ("The Ideological and the Sociological Interpretation of Intellectual Phenomena"). It was a preparatory study for his *Ideology and Utopia* which appeared in 1929.

During the nineteenth century the word *ideology* acquired an increasingly pejorative meaning. In contemporary times, not only Marxist thinkers use this term in order to disqualify bourgeois thought, but all kinds of groups use the term as a weapon against other groups.

An idea is studied as an idea when one interprets it from the inside, when one considers its logical structure. An idea is perceived ideologically when one studies it from the outside. Mannheim then makes the distinction between phenomenological-ideological and sociological interpretation. The first he calls a prelude to the sociological interpretation. The latter deals with ideas as expressions of social strata (sw: 140, 141). The question is to what extent these two interpretations resemble each other. In Mannheim's opinion neither the phenomenological nor the functional sociological approach is entirely adequate. He chooses a combination of the two and writes, "that extrinsic interpretation, while relativizing 'immanent meaning' by functionalizing it, at the same time bestows a new sense on it, precisely by incorporating it into a higher context of meaning" (ISI: 124). He continues to distinguish between two levels of meaning, a higher and a lower.

In 1926 Mannheim began his sociology as a science of criticizing ideas. The problem of his sociology is the relevance of the values embodied in social structures of knowledge. Mannheim was interested in the question of the cognitive value of ideology. At the same time he regarded ideologies as important because they contribute to a political orientation.

Mannheim remarks that in the recent discussion of ideology the idea is used in two senses: one particular and the other, total. The particular conception of ideology applies to distrust of the specific cognitive claims of an opponent who is described as ideological; his assertions are doubted because they are thought by the observer to be more or less intentional distortions of the real situation for the advantage of the person making the assertion. In the total conception of ideology, the entire *Weltanschauung* of the opponent is interpreted as a product of a collective life in which he participates. An ideology in the total sense is a fundamental, comprehensive ordering of a time or of a group.

In the particular conception of ideology ideas are analyzed with reference to the person asserting them. The total conception directs attention not only to the content of ideas, but also to the fundamental patterns of thought, theories, and experiences of which the specific assertions are a part.

The particular interpretation of ideology makes ideas functions of interests as these are experienced by an individual; the total interpretation of ideology sees ideas as parts of a broader pattern of thought which is associated with a specific group or class.

Mannheim prefered the total interpretation, which, according to him, lies at the basis of the individual's perception and judgment (IU: 51). According to Mannheim, one cannot call the view of others ideological simply because it is erroneous. These erroneous views are not individual mistakes; they are functions of the whole social situation in which individuals find themselves. All thought can, therefore, be termed ideological in the sense of being conditioned by the situation in which it arises (IU: 239). In an earlier age an opponent, as a representative of a particular political movement, was accused of deliberate or unwilling falsification of the facts. Now his statements are regarded as a function of a social situation. Arguing from the total conception of ideology, Mannheim raises the question how it has been possible that a "false consciousness" could exist, which totally distorts or falsifies everything in its purview. Mannheim's total concept of ideology is close to that of Marx's "false consciousness."

According to Mannheim, a dispassionate investigator does not seek to answer the question as to which of the contending parties is right. He will not aim at "the discovering of truth," but at the prior circumstances, not yet discovered, which can be relevant for finding the truth. The purpose of evaluating neutral studies of ideology is to point out the relationship between the elements of knowledge to the larger framework of meanings, particularly to an historical and social context.

Although we can strive for an evaluatively neutral research, it is difficult to achieve. When we study history, it is unavoidable that we emphasize certain aspects to the neglect of others. This neglect and accentuation of certain aspects of an historical totality is the first step in evaluative and ontological judgment, according to Mannheim (IU: 83). Thus, to say that ideology is an expression of *false consciousness* is a pejorative use of that term, from a Marxist perspective. Speaking about a false consciousness is, moreover, according to Mannheim, not fruitful for an understanding of the dynamics of ideology and social reality.

According to him, a philosophy or a cognitive statement is ideological when it contains ideas in a concrete situation and these ideas to some extent hamper people when they attempt to apply them to their situation. Obsolete and not adequately applicable norms, modes of thought, and theories become ideologies, when they do more to obscure the actual motions and consequences of conduct than to clarify them (IU: 85). Knowledge becomes ideological when it fails to reckon with new situations in reality and when it obscures these changes by inadequate categories.

This concept of ideology is *evaluative*, because it has certain presuppositions about the perception of social reality and ideas as structures of consciousness; it is *dynamic* because the validity of these judgments is measured by the standard of a reality which is in perpetual change. In both the concept of ideology and in the concept of utopia every idea must be tested for its *congruence with reality*. The truth of our knowledge is measured by the degree to which correspondence exists with an actual situation. To the extent that the social perspective of participants in groups is a form of collective ego-centrism, to that extent a distortion of knowledge occurs.

This ideological distortion is, according to Gabel, often the illegitimate confusion of *is* and *ought*. People who belong to marginal groups, for instance, the intelligentsia, are in no position "to think outside the social reality. But they are sometimes able ... to disentangle the axio-cognitive admixture of ideology." In other words "the collective, ego-centric distortion of reality appears as the main target of Mannheim's critical analysis of the problem of ideology, and social marginality is considered by him as the specific remedy" (Gabel, 1983: 15, 16). For a proper understanding of Mannheim's analysis of ideology, we must perceive that his approach is not only of a political kind (although it has important political implications), but primarily of a methodological kind (cf. Carlsneas, 1981, 181, 184).

Mannheim on Utopia

The word *utopia* (Greek *ou*, "not"; *topos*, "place, location") means literally "a never-never land," or "a place which does not exist." It was first used by Thomas More (1516) as a name of an imaginary island with an ideal society. After that the word has often been used to describe a society which is free of human imperfections.

Mannheim sees More and writers of "Utopias" as "free intellectuals" who, though they are children of their time, could achieve an "objective attitude" with regard to their current social norms and institutions (U: 200). The most realistic vision of a utopia, according to Mannheim, was developed by Harrington in his *The Commonwealth of Oceana* (1656). He described a democracy on a small scale, which acknowledges private property, but only in a restricted degree; it also offers a basis for a stable and just government of the state.

In his "A Sociological Theory of Culture and its Knowability," Mannheim wrote that in conjunctive thought, as soons as that becomes dynamic, ideals and utopias arise. A utopia is, according to him, a theoretical promulgation of a striving to form a world in accordance with some fundamental evaluative intention or norm.

> Utopia contains the directon, the point of view, the perspective, and the set of questions from which the present and the past first become comprehensible at all. Investigating the structure of utopia is, therefore, one of the most essential tasks of the sociology of thought. (ST: 246)

He further distinguishes two kinds of utopias: an idea as an intention which until now has not received an historcially important degree of realization; and the *ideal*, which he calls a Kantian regulative idea, in which the idea is associated with a dynamic striving.

The concept *utopia* is applicable, according to Mannheim, to every process of thought that derives its passionate motivation from the striving to transcend the existing social order, and from the concepts, symbols, fantasies, dreams and ideas with no correspondance or counterparts in existing reality. Mannheim does not refer to a pre-scientific, naive thought, but a thought loaded with clear intentions, directed toward a reorganization of society (Neusüss, 1968b: 18, 26). Regarded sociologically, such utopian constructions, when they are shared in some collectivity inspire the members to change society in keeping with stated transcendental purposes. This is in contrast with ideologies, which support the existing social order (U: 201). As such, the utopian proposal is an integral part of the intellectual equipment of various social groups which wish to change society, and they reveal social reality by means of it. This utopian element does not only work as a progressive-liberal or revolutionary power in politics. The utopian vision also makes social phenomena intelligible to those who possess it.

In development of modern times, Mannheim sees four forms of utopian consciousness:

1. The *orgiastic chiliasm* of the Anabaptists, Thomas Münzer and others, who like anarchists, wait, but more mystically, for a complete revolution which could come at any moment and which requires no preparation. The ideas of the Anabaptists and anarchists particularly occurred in the lower strata of society, expecially among poor peasants. Their poverty called for a speedy and complete transformation; their faith made them look forward to it. This is a religious form of a utopia (IU: 190-197).
2. *The liberal-humanitarian idea*: Mannheim namens the Girondists, De Condorcet, and other "liberals," who saw history as the movement towards a rationally constructed, ideal state (IU: 197-206).
3. *The conservative idea*: The conservatives need no utopia because they are in power. At best they change their minds because of the attacks of the liberals (IU: 206-215).
4. *The socialistic-communistic utopia*: In socialism and communism the historical idea of evolution is very complicated. A sharp distinction is made between the immediate and the distant future. In contrast to the liberals, Marxian socialists gave no blueprint for a future society. History unfolds

itself according to an immanent, historical, dialectical law. Speculation on a distant future has no meaning; the necessary processes of social development will produce the socialist and communist society of the future. It is more urgent to formulate a scientific theory of the phase in which we now find ourselves and must function, directed to the realization of a later phase (IU: 215-222).

Although Mannheim says that utopian thought arises among the governed and oppressed groups which strive for emancipation, ideologies arise in groups which control the social and political means of power. Similarly, conceptions of freedom and democracy correspond with social positions of various groups. For conservatives, freedom means the right of every socially organized community, to live in accord with its own privileges and freedoms. For the liberals, freedom means that everyone has the same social and political rights and that the political order, for that reason, ought to change to accomodate these rights. (IU: 245). Not just substantive theories but also basic categories of thought are related to social groups. Thus, conservatives in nineteenth-century Germany often used amorphous categories in their political doctrine. The parties on the left, aiming at social reconstruction, used analytical ideas. Members of a marginal minority, like Jews, often give more evidence of abstract, reflective thought than do members of a majority. This arises from the fact that the marginal groups are only minimally tolerated, and must always adapt themselves to the social environment. They must thus be reflecting on their image in the world.

A state of mind is utopian, according to Mannheim, when it is not congruent with the situation in which it exists. But not every incongruent state of mind is utopian. To be utopian it is necessary that the state of mind *transcends* reality and that it be *transformed* into a behavior which seeks to change the existing order, as a whole or in part. An ideology may also transcend the existing order, but depite that, it wishes to support that order (IU: 173, 174).

All ideas which do not fit into the existing order he calls "situationally transcendent" or "non-realistic." Ideas which indeed fit into the present order are "adequate" or "situationally congruent," but this is rare. Both ideologies and utopias diverge from this congruent pattern of thought. Mannheim had several different and not wholly consistent ideas of ideology.

Next to this concept of ideology, intended to indicate the situation-conditionedness of all thought, another concept of ideology can be distinguished, which is evaluative with regard to the existing historical-social constellation and, as such, is situationally incongruent, without its being clear still whether it should be appraised as closer to ideology or utopia. There are ideologies which are based on ideas which transcend situations and which are never realized; for instance: living consistently following the Christian idea of the love of one's neighbour is impossible, according to Mannheim, in a society organized on the principle of slavery. In specific cases it is difficult to determine what is ideological and what utopian. Each of Mannheim's conceptions of ideology is reasonable, and it would be a mistake to overlook their heterogeneity. It is difficult to find any unity in all these conceptions except to say that they all refer to a comprehensive and fundamental pattern of thought. The difference between ideology and utopia is determined by the view of reality that one has and that one applies as a standard. Thus, groups which represent the existing order will call utopian all conceptions which from their viewpoint cannot be realized. Mannheim himself never uses this judgment of *absolutely utopian*. He manages a relative view of utopia which "seems to be unrealizable" *only* on the basis of a total social constellation (IU: 177). This concept of utopia does the best justice to the dynamic character of social-historical reality.

The relationship between utopia and the existing order is a dialectical one; in every period, different groups give birth to ideas and values in which are contained the unrealized and unfulfilled tendencies which reproduce the needs of that period; the existing order demonstrates the utopian, which in its turn breaks open this order, but nothing is established for the direction of development for the following social order (IU: 179). The real problem is to trace the concrete reciprocal action between the differentiated forms of social existence and the differentiations in utopias which arise out of them and which transform them. The ruling group helps to determine what is regarded as utopian in its society, while the arising group, in conflict with the established order, helps to determine what appears to be ideological.

Utopias can turn into ideologies. So, in the nineteenth century, the utopia for the rising bourgeoisie was freedom. Later, people could establish the degree to which this utopia was realized and to what extent the idea of freedom contained not only utopian elements, but ideological elements as well. Only when we look at the past, can we formulate an adequate criterion for the distinction between ideology and utopia. That is this: their capability of being realized. Ideas which are only representations of a bygone social order are ideological; ideas which have been realized are utopian (IU: 179-1984).

Mannheim was never really clear about utopia. His ideas of utopia postulated an idea of progress in accordance with which societies have "needs" which are perceived by some pioneering minds who then formulate them as ideals. It was part of the progressivistic outlook to think that there was a continuing generation of new ideals which moved to realization and then to decay – then only to be replaced by newer ideals or utopias. But the same ambiguity which attended his conception of ideology was present in his conception of utopia. Mannheim sometimes used ideology in a general, non-evaluative sense to show the situational conditionedness of thought, but this also applies to utopian thought. Then again he uses the term ideology to mean "transcending situations," or again "inadequate to situations" – he counts some utopias as the latter. Sometimes he says that ideologies and utopias can be established in a particular society; elsewhere he calls the criterion for what is an utopia its capacity when seen in retrospect to be realized. Similarly he uses the idea of utopia in various ways: sometimes as transcending situations, then again as adequate to situations (for instance, the revolutionary ideas behind certain revolutions), or as inadequate (for instance, illusions). Mannheim's multiple uses of these terms may be summarized as follows (cf. Neusüss 1968a: 134-139):

1. A general, total, and value-free concept of ideology, which concerns the situation-conditionedness of all thought. It is uncritical because it says nothing about the truth or falsehood of thought. No reference is implied in this usage to any distinction between ideology and utopia.
2. A general, total, and evaluative concept of ideology, which describes the "false consciousness" as error; it includes no distinction between ideology and utopia.
3. A state of mind which is incongruous to certain situations, is inadequate as a description or explanation of these situations and is also inadequate for effective practical action. This state of mind can refer to ideology or to utopia.
   a. A pragmatic concept of ideology which refers to propositions which veil social and political reality as a means of protecting the interests of the ruling classes.
   b. A particular concept of ideology, which refers to specific idea-content.
   c. A total and specific concept of ideology, which refers to the comprehensive outlook of a ruling class.
4. A situation-transcendent and situation-transforming consciousness.
   a. A revolutionary utopia which belongs to the oppressed classes; it is a complement to the concept of ideology in 3b and 3c.
   b. A potential utopia, which refers to ideologies which have it within them to become utopias.
   c. A dynamic concept of utopia for identifying dynamic elements in human thought.
   d. A situationally immanent and situationally adequate concept of utopia, which refers to the dynamic synthesis of utopias that are situationally adequate utopias; in fact, this concept refers to Mannheim's idea of an evaluative sociology of knowledge.

Neusüss (1968a: 136) concludes as follows:

> This review shows the many-sidedness of the problems which appear, without raising the question of the empirical-sociological usefulness of categories. In the essays of Mannheim, all these usages of ideology and utopia are introduced and defined, next to each other and mingling with each other, without terminological differentiation and without clarification about their relationship to each other.

In summary, we can say the following about the concepts of ideology and utopia: Ideologies are systems of thought or a whole *Weltanschauung*; they are also products of a collectivity. These two points imply that all thought (including utopian thought) is situationally conditioned and as such can be called ideological. This is a *non-evaluative* conception of ideology which raises no questions about the cognitive validity of the propositions asserted.

Distinghuised from this conception, he also recognizes the *evaluative* interpretation of ideology, for which we list the following characteristics:

1. Conceptions that are incongruent with the situation, without the possibility for differentiating between utopian or ideological incongruency with the situation.
2. Ideas and conceptions that hinder human beings in their adjustment to their current situation; they hinder an adequate understanding of the situation.
3. Because reality is dynamic and must be understood dynamically, the current social situations are constantly in change. Ideology means (see 2 above) that one wants to support the existing social order with specific ideas; these ideas will most likely be found among the ruling classes.

As concerns utopia, we list the following characteristics:

1. Conceptions incongruent to the situation, which belong to specific social levels, categories, and groups, and which have intentions directed to the future; they transcend existing attitudes; they tend to be transformed into activities which aim to transform existing social structures. Utopias, consequently, are differentiated qualitatively, historically, and socially (fiction, revolution, and reformation).
2. The relation of utopia to the existing order is dialectical.
3. Like ideologies, utopias emerge from the existing social order. Mannheim himself envisions a social order which consists of a synthesis of all existing utopias. His conception can indeed be termed incongruent with the situation, but not inadequate to the situation. It is intended as dynamic and transformational of the situation, and that is why it is adequate to the situation *and* transcendent to the situation. This task of achieving a transcendental synthesis is reserved for the intelligentsia.

An adequate criterion is needed in order to establish whether ideas are ideological or utopian. The criterion can lie in the society which exists at the time in which existing groups ascribe to themselves and/or to each other ideological or utopian ideas. Mannheim gives greater emphasis to the fact that the criterion never lies in the existing social situation, but can only be reformulated retrospectively. Looking back into the past, one can establish whether a utopia turns out to be capable of realization, or whether an ideology seeks to preserve the status quo.

Ideology and Utopia in Criticism

After the publication of Mannheim's *Ideologie und Utopie* various lengthy reviews appeared, among others, those of Hannah Arendt, Max Horkheimer, Herbert Marcuse, and Paul Tillich. Also in later studies by these and other authors concerning the subjects *ideology* and *utopia*, attention is often given to Mannheim, in varying degrees. As said before, discussed here are only those authors who have made an elaborate critique on Mannheim and who have at the same time contributed to the better understanding of his work. We limit ourselves in this mainly to Horkheimer, Adorno, Geiger, Tillich, and Gouldner.

Horkheimer and Adorno: the Charge of Powerlessness
Soon after the appearance of Mannheim's *Ideologie und Utopie* Horkheimer published a critical review of that book. He established that before Mannheim's study appeared the concept of ideology was usually used to disqualify the social and political views of opponents, viewed from a social position. Mannheim states that the thinking of every person is conditioned by position *(standortge-bunden)* and, thus, the concept of ideology, according to Horkheimer, becomes used as a general and evaluatively neutral concept (1930b: 15). A false consciousness, according to Mannheim, only exists when old, no longer valid ideas and norms are harked back to; that is when these patterns of thought no longer adequately explain reality. The horizon of the knowing process must extend so that "the totality" comes into view. This is the purpose of Mannheim's sociology of knowledge and in it he aims meanwhile to free human beings from outdated certainties. In Mannheim's work the meaning of history, according to Horkheimer (1930b: 17,18), is the completion of the human being. Horkheimer asks: "What does Mannheim mean by *the* human being?" He can not mean, according to Horkheimer, that the existence of humanity is the same at all times – an opinion that Dilthey held for instance. Such a view of humanity would doubtless be included in Mannheim's "concept of total ideology." Still, for him, the investigation of history should lead to knowledge of our own being, a view which, just as that of Dilthey, is called *classically idealistic* by Horkheimer; it is a view which, knowing one's self as a result of the study of history, places sufficiency in the subject on whom the "totality" is dawning. Horkheimer's criticism directs itself to the following: that, according to Mannheim's line of thought, it is not clear why the fulfillment of the human being does not fall into the category of total ideology; concepts like "becoming human," "totality," "unity," and "meaning" are not in agreement with the fundamental themes of Mannheim's philosophy (1930b: 21).

Marx attempted with his criticism of ideology to throw metaphysics away. Mannheim wants to think through the concept of ideology, deepen it, and put it to general use, and in doing so, according to Horkheimer, he has reconciled it with metaphysical thought. In this thinking through, according to Horkheimer, he has destroyed the insight we learned form Marx. Not *the person*, but the concrete collective humanity, the members all dependent on each other and from nature, is the active and leading subject of history. Given Mannheim's idealistic and metaphysical way of thought, Horkheimer concludes – as does Adorno – that his sociological concepts are totally unusable for comprehending social life.

Idealistic and *metaphysical* are the central words in Horkheimer's critique. Apart from the question as to what extent idealistic and metaphusical ideas are to be found in Horkheimer's own work, he presents himself in this review as a mighty Marxist. From this standpoint it is not difficult to charge Mannheim with idealism and metaphysics. Horkheimer, however, does not do justice to the realism in Mannheim's thought; he ignores this entirely. Granted that Mannheim's thought includes idealistic and metaphysical moments, particularly on such topics as the meaning of history, human existence and development, the totality of a particular field of culture, and of a given period of culture (*Weltanschauung*). Horkheimer should not, however, have ended with this criticism.

Horkheimer pays no attention at all, and very unfairly, to Mannheim's criticism of Marx's concept of ideology. Horkheimer's criticism of Mannheim's domesticating the concept of ideology for general use may be true to some limited extent, but at the same time, Horkheimer does not give sufficient attention to the fact that Mannheim in his sociology of knowledge and in his study of ideology asks *the question about truth in connection with the knower*. This was a problem always close to the heart of Horkheimer.

Also, Horkheimer's charge that Mannheim thought to interpret the concept of ideology as evaluatively neutral is not quite fair. The evaluative element does exist in Mannheim's conception of ideology.

Horkheimer says in an article published later that the concept of ideology has no pregnant meaning for this century (1951: 59). According to him, one understands no more by it than a certain context of thoughts, a theory, or an idea. But, he says, no matter what a generalized, domesticated meaning this concept has acquired, it still always includes an element "which stands in opposition to the testimony of the mind, to count its being or its content as autonomous" (1951: 59). Also here is a realistic interpretation as opposed to an idealistic one. Horkheimer writes that the investigation of ideology through the sociology of knowledge never has a foundation in philosophy of economics (61).

What does Horkheimer mean by ideology? He speaks of totalitarian systems which despise humanity. However, people who find themselves in dehumanizing situations may not rule out the tendencies toward revolt within themselves. Where the brutality and dehumanization in a situation are no longer even recognized, there an appeal to ideas such as the good, true and beautiful is pointless and powerless. Then the good, the true and the beautiful are only loved and held in honor when everything which threatens or inhibits the realization of these ideas is acknowledged – or otherwise these ideas indeed degenerate into ideology (1951: 66). Still, his speaking about the ideas of the good, the true, and the beautiful is not totally materialistic. He does not only discuss the economic power structures which work toward dehumanization; he directs his criticism against all brutal and enslaving social relationships (cf. Horkheimer 1937; 1951: 66).

Some idealistic and metaphysical impulses are not to be denied in Horkheimer's work. He also deals with the question of truth and concludes that ideologies are opposed to truth. Turning directly against Mannheim (without mentioning his name) and against what Mannheim calls the "socially free-floating intelligentsia," he concludes thus:

> The assigning of value, however, to the extent that it believes it is possible to free itself from the historical entanglements... is itself ideology, in the narrow and exact sense. (1951: 67)

Adorno also criticized Mannheim's concept of ideology. Just as Horkheimer, Adorno is of the opinion that Mannheim's conception of ideology is powerless. Adorno keeps on insisting "Ideology is justification" (1973: 189). Just as people commonly separate truth from falsehood, so Adorno wishes to distinguish (and separate) ideology, as the justification of a de-humanizing social order, from a protest against this justification, establishing goodness and truth over against that corrupt order (189, 190). In finding criteria for distinguishing truth from lies, Adorno simply follows the track of Marx. He points out the structural changes which Western societies have undergone in the last century and the antropological changes which occurred as a result. A change in the concept of ideology is part of this context of change:

> Ideology today is the condition of consciousness and unconsciousness of the masses, as objective spirit, not the miserable products which imitate and debate this spirit in order to reproduce it. For ideology in the proper sense, relationships of power are required which are not comprehensable to this power itself, which are mediated and therefore also less hargh. Today society, which has unjustly been blamed for its complexity, has become to transparant for this. (1973: 191)

In summary, the ideology of the mass culture of our Western world means the following: the justification of the existing power relationships with the elimination of all transcendent and critical possibilities. Since that moment when the ideology began to say little more than that the situation is as it is, its own untruth withers until it becomes this notion: the situation could not be otherwise than it, in fact, is. But, says Adorno, because we can see this untruth, we can also see through it (Adorno, 1973: 197, 198).

Marxist criticism of ideology has a direct relationship to the possibility of and the necessity for a distinctive practice of science on its own. With the idea of utopia, this is different; it has no analytical character and for that reason it can be no basic category in a Marxist theory of society (Neusüss, 1968b: 18). Utopia can indeed aim at a true and just ordering of society and can give critical impulse to a theory of the social sciences, but at that point the concept of utopia has not yet become a theoretical instrument. When in the old Marxist literature utopia was discussed, this usually happened in this meaning: a particular pre-scientific way of dealing, which is characteristic of earlier phases of thinking about society. Projected utopias from More to De Saint-Simon are, in Marxist categories of thought, impressions form a time when capitalistic powers of production were not yet strongly developed. After that, they have lost their legitimacy because of being replaced by a Marxist "scientific" analysis of society. Utopias since Marx all stand under a criticism of ideology (Neusüss, 1968b: 19-21).

Because not only in Marxism, but also in other streams of academic thought, the concept of utopia (although present in a sense) is no theoretical instrument, we shall be able to devote only restricted attention to this idea. Although we will not go into it further, to expand on, the critic Von Schelting also needs te be named here. Mannheim he says, is not clear about the terms *realization, objective realization, adequate realization, transformable, realizable*, for he uses them all mixed through each other (Von Schelting, 1934: 128). Although Mannheim interprets utopia as a theoretical reflection, it seems inarticulated in how he works it out.

Horkheimer places utopia opposite to ideology:

> If ideology provides the appearance, then opposite to it is the utopia of the dream of a "true" and just ordering of life. (1930a: 9)

Although opposite to each other, ideology and utopia form a very narrow closely-woven context between them. According to Horkheimer, utopian ideas (for him good, true and beautiful) are present in the ideological, and according to their nature, present in a *working* capacity. The extent that it is working is a question. If it is true that utopia is already present in ideology, though only the seed of it is hidden behind appearances, then one can ask to what extent utopia is to be known in its purity.

* Utopia has two sides, says Horkheimer (1930a: 64): it is a critisicm of the existing order and at the same time a demonstration of what ought to be; its meaning lies, according to him, "actually decided in the first moment"; these longings are conditioned by the social strata; when the social strata change, the idea of utopia changes; and finally these longings for utopia will bring about a completed society.

Geiger: Scientific Critique of Ideology

The philosophers at Frankfurt, Horkheimer and Adorno, disqualified Mannheim's concepts of ideology as evaluatively neutral and positivistic. A confrontation with a positivistic thinker on the subject of ideology can demonstrate how unnuanced the epithet *positivistic* can be, and how inapplicable it is for Mannheim.

The positivistically oriented sociologist Theodor Geiger gave a great deal of attention to the problem of ideology in his publications. The critisicm of ideology he sees as one of the most important tasks of scholarship, particularly of sociology; this task, according to him, is not simply a specialized sociological problem, but an epistemological one. A great problem in the sciences is that continually non-intellectual elements creep in. He wants to separate clearly the scientific and the non-scientific from each other. Real theories are "purely oriented to the object or the objective," while the charge of ideology confronts the intellectual or social scientist who mixes subjective feelings into his statements.

Scholarship is established in order to know the objective-rational truth, that is, to know the totality of all the "phenomena of time and space." Scientific knowledge of reality means, that one makes statements about phenomena, and these statements are verifiably true or false on the basis of perceptions (Geiger, 1949a: 229, 231). Of ideology Geiger says that it

> rests on the theorizing and objectivizing of primary relationships of feeling which exist between the speaker and the object he speaks about. (1949a: 231)

In a scientific sense, an ideology cannot even be characterized as false, because it cannot be rendered false with the help of the rules of ordinary logic; it is not false in a logical sense, but in an epistemological sense; it is for that reason not a true theory, but an apparent theory *(Scheintheorie)*.

Ideology for Geiger always has a negative, disqualifying significance. He simply dismisses out of hand any ideology which comes from a false consciousness. False consciousness and lies by definition have nothing to do with science, according to Geiger. He also dismisses particular conceptions of ideology, expressing themselves in certain pronouncements, which are expressed by feelings and interests. Practising scientists must emancipate themselves from ideologies, particular and general (1953: 27, 28; cf. Topitsch, 1961: 23-32; Nagel: 1961: 498-502).

That is why he dismisses Mannheim's distinction between the sociology of knowledge and the critique of ideology as untrue. People must be able to liberate themselves from their social situations and think according to strict scientific rules:

> One must make himself a boundary on the one hand of the mathematically-related, purely formal, conceptually analytical statement of theoretical possibilities; and on the other, in respect for physical material, a boundary out of the positively, empirically verifiable, established facts, by means of controlled premises. (1949a: 234)

In the genealogy of ideology we would place Geiger in the line of Destutt de Tracy, to the extent that he, too, regarded the ideas of mathematical science, logic, and grammar as fundamental for pursuing science, and thus eliminated all "other ideologies." According to positivistically oriented scientists, we live in a time in which technical-scientific development will occupy more and more the place of ideologies and this will spell the end of the epoch of ideologies (Bell, 1960: 17).

It need not amaze us that Adorno sets himself apart from Geiger in sharp language (1973: 184). Mannheim would have delivered an equally strong critique of Geiger. We think of the problems already discussed of ontic and methodological pluralism, the situational conditioning of thought, and the concept of ideology, also in terms of what follows.

Geiger states that it is impossible to answer the so-called "burning issues" concerning our existential relationship to social reality. Here, too, he differs from Mannheim, who found the most important issue to be the existential relationship concerning the development of society. True, questions remain open on this point of Geiger, because he allows that the choice of scientific problems can be stimulated by non-scientific impulses. To what extent can there still be talk of a scientific practise conditioned by societal and cultural factors? We shall not repeat in this connection the critical questions which can be addressed to the positivistic, scientific practise, which were handled by Mannheim (Chapter V).

Tillich: General and Particular Conception of Ideology
In this context we need to pay attention to the theologian Paul Tillich, who, like Geiger, also criticized Mannheim's distinction between general and particular ideology. Tillich does not comprehend the relevance of Mannheim's distinction, *unless* both conceptions of ideology are interpreted concretely and politically, which especially happens on the basis of social strata to be analyzed. Tillich, thus, interprets the *particular* concept of ideology on a social and political level.

For Tillich the concept of ideology must retain its concrete political character; a particular ideological idea may not be dissipated into a general ideology, and thus be rendered politically neutral. Every idea must be investigated for its ideological character. To the extent that an idea is free from someone's social position, and free from furthering personal concerns, to that extent it is not ideological. But to what extent is a political party, which claims to exist for the service of the community, intent on the usurpation of power? To what extent does a power elite form itself within a party? Tillich asks these embarrassing questions.

There is a great danger in ideological problems to deal with the general conception of ideology rather than with (in Tillich's words) the "concrete actual." The practising scientist must not only be rational toward the reality which stands over against him for him to analyze, but he must penetrate the problem, psychologically and sociologically: to that extent he will not wrecklessly uproot a utopia, thinking it an ideology. That is why socialism, according to Tillich, is correctly aimed at the proletariat; only this social stratum is in a position to form a unified consciousness which can accomplish adequate, concrete, and actual analyses of society. Tillich never expresses that Mannheim's psychological interpretation of the particular conception of ideology is wrong; Tillich's criticism is instead an elaboration of Mannheim's ideas: "the little life's histories" of individual people, who belong to specific groups, strata, and classes can come to expression in particular ideologies, which in turn can be interpreted socially, politically, and psychologically. However, Geiger would criticize even more Tillich's elaboration of Mannheim's particular conception of ideology as a distortion of doing true scientific work.

Horkheimer and his followers assume the position of relating science to their Marxist view of humanity and society. As such, they combine science and values. Entirely different is the position of the positivistically oriented practising scientists; they are convinced that the time for ideologies is past. Some of the people I already named are Geiger, Topitsch, and Bell; we can also mention the name of Shils, who first formulated the thesis of "the end of ideology," Aron, O. Brunner, Lipset, and Schelsky. True, according to them, ideologies were necessary in the bourgeois society of the last two centuries to take the place of theoretical and metaphysical thought; now social and political decisions must be taken on a purely scientific, rational basis. They are all adverse to totalitarian systems of ideology, both of the left and right, both fascism and Marxism, which sprang up during the course of the twentieth century. The technical-scientific thought will determine the way society must take. This thinking, thus, is directed to the future. In reaction to that point Bell says: "The end of ideology is not – should not be – the end of utopia as well." The Dutch philosopher Plattel (1970: 73) is right in adding to these words the remark that this utopia is becoming starved by an empirical-scientific prognosis and to a planning for the future on the basis of the *existing* social order.

Just as we could have discussed more authors under the concept of ideology, so we could have discussed more authors in connection with utopia. For instance, the philosopher Bloch (1959) comes to mind, the sociologist Bauman (1976), Dahrendorf (1967), and Thoenes (1976). However, they either do not go into Mannheim's work at all or only obliquely. In standard works about utopia Mannheim is named only by the bye. Typical is the following quotation:

Karl Mannheim's redifinition in his own private language of the idea of utopia and his typologizing of the whole body of political and social thought in his *Ideologie und Utopia* (1929), though it hardly won universal acceptance among sociologists and political scientists, has been hailed in its day as the outline of a discipline that promised a new and more profound understanding of social life. (Manuel and Manuel, 1979: 11; cf. Lasky, 1976: 617; Manuel, 1966: 101-104)

Gouldner: Acknowledging Ideology
Gouldner advocates a rehabilitation of the concept of ideology. In everyday colloquial language, in most sociological literature, and certainly in Marxist circles, the concept of *ideology* has a negative significance; it is interpreted as wrong, impure, irrational, and something that should be opposed (Gouldner, 1976: 3). Against this position Gouldner (19) asserts that we must realize that

sociology is substantially more ideological and far less scientific than it claims, and that ideology is often more rational and even scientific, than sociology conventionally grants.

Moreover, he also sees that there are rational grounds for the negative critique on ideology. Science, in particular sociology, and ideology, thus, do not oppose each other as Marxists say they do, or, in another sense, as positivists say. Ideology presupposes "normal" people in "normal" situations, who can think and speak: "A fundamental rule of the grammar of all modern ideology, tacit or explicitly affirmed, was the principle of the unity of theory and practise mediated by rational discourse," according to Gouldner (1976: 30). As such, ideology is distinguished from religious and mythical consciousness because it justifies its content with the help of logical rules and "evidence" on the basis of its view of society and it never falls back on faith, tradition, or revelation.

Gouldner refers to Marx, who, according to him, correctly broke through the objectivity and neutrality of ideologies; he spoke about ideologies as expressions of a false consciousness and related both to the bourgeois class. Gouldner also refers to Mannheim, who, according to him, has criticized Marxism correctly because it absolutized its own view, and, just as much as the idealism which it opposes, is guilty of "objectivism." Characteristics of ideologies are, according to Gouldner, that they form a "rational mode of discourse"; the rationality refers to the ability to reflect on something that people have already long accepted as established; one can make something into a problem. Objectivism, its opposite, also lurks in ideologies, that is the reflective ability to make something a problem is lacking (45, 49). Moreover, one may not conclude from this that Gouldner shares Mannheim's concept of ideology. He himself says explicitly that this is not the case:

> I do not at all think of the ideological as did Mannheim, i.e., as connected only with the defense of the status quo and contrasted with the utopian (1976: 87).

Ideologies, according to Gouldner, play a structuring role in society. They presuppose temporal sensitivity, which orients itself to past and future, practical realism, and the concluding of compromises. They determine how people speak, how people regard and reflect themselves and others. Ideology is, therefore, to be valued positively, to the extent that it accepts that the world is equipped for a rational diagnosis.

Ideology and utopia for Gouldner are not simply opposites, Mannheim often said that, but the relationship seems to be somewhat more complicated. Gouldner calls utopia "non-historical," because it does not see the contemporary situation in relationship to what preceded, but only in relation to the ideal. Mannheim's conception of utopia and that of Gouldner have this in common, that they have the capacity for being realized; the difference comes to expression in this, that Gouldner judges *also* the utopia according to its ideal content. Gouldner (250) regards the dominant factors in the Western societies to be *technocratic thinking and administrating,* while the *media* stimulate these factors. The great danger of this dominance is that reflection and public discussions (both proper to ideology) become impossible and, therefore, the idologies will disappear. Can we still call technology an ideology? No, it makes ideology impossible; it itself is so rigid in its "bull's-eye rationalism" that its reflective powers have disappeared (255). Because Gouldner has an eye for technocracy's threat to free communication, he cannot call technocracy an ideology.

Conclusions

In large measure people let themselves be led, even let themselves be ruled, by conceptions and ideas which they themselves have not formulated but which they have adopted from the collective community of which they form a part; this phenomenon has received attention after the Middle Ages and particularly in the nineteenth century. Especially Marx is called the pioneer in this regard, while after him, among others, Scheler and Mannheim deserve mention.

In the framework of the socially-related thought, the concept of ideology assumed an important place. We have encountered numerous implications of this concept. Some use it in particular sense to clarify certain ideas, while others use it to refer to a total view of the world, which can both be used to criticize or to justify the society. An ideology can also acquire a *neutral* significance: a whole, made up of ideas which form a context together. Still others want to use it in an exclusively *critical* meaning, particularly to point out the thought of opponents, and their thought is simply disqualified as apostate and wrong. Still others see ideology as speculation, which must emancipate people scientifically.

The Dutch philosopher Beerling (1964a: 262) correctly points out that the tendency in the doctrine of ideology was originally positive. Behind it lay the conviction that thought itself had the capacity to discover its own prejudices and free itself from them. Beerling (1965: 17), following Lenk (1961: 15), points out that the origin of the problem of ideology is closely connected with the emancipation of the early European bourgeoisie. In this regard the concept of ideology works, according to him, as a two-edged sword. Originally it was used in the name of rationality, freedom, and progress as a critical weapon against the established social order and against the politics and scientific knowledge which helped to support this order. The social unrest of the eighteenth century, arising from economic and political developments, culminated in bourgeois revolutions and at the same time found its expression in various utopian ideas (often inspired by Renaissance thinkers). Engels (1892) names authors as Babeuf, De Saint-Simon, Fourier, Cabet, and Owen "utopian socialists." They thought to change society by means of abstract ideals, instead of striving for a *scientific socialism* on the basis of an analysis of economic powers and social relationships. Later, therefore, the concept of ideology acquired a radicalized interpretation, in such a way that it made bourgeois consciousness the object of criticism, though originally it had fought for bourgeois values in the name of reason, freedom, and progress. Untrue, wrong, incomplete, distorted, and inadequate notions attach themselves to many interpretations of ideology. The one exception is the neutral and justifying conception of ideology.

Mannheim introduced a remarkable distinction between true and false consciousness. Originally Mannheim thought that the ideological consciousness was caused by the social relatedness of thought. In his evaluative conception of ideology this criterion no longer seems satisfactory; ideology also seems to mean the following: staying behind with the existing social reality, or not understanding reality as such very well. According to Beerling (1965: 21), a fundamental *ambiguity* lurks in the social relatedness of thought: it can both mean that the content of thought is in correspondence with the social reality as given, or that thought diverges from that reality. Either diverge from social reality by staying behind with what was once thought reality and be ideological, or move out ahead and be utopian. And yet Mannheim qualifies the incongruency of both ideology and utopia as "untrue."

As a cause of this ambiguity I refer to Grünwald (1934: 205, 206), who correctly points out the distinction, ignored by Mannheim, between two inadequate consciousnesses: the one situationally inadequate and the other objectively inadequate; consciousness can be inadequate as regards its object of thought, but also inadequate as regards its social position. When Mannheim speaks of "situationally congruent" thought, it implies the idea of objectively adequate thought (cf. ıu: 175).

Does situationally congruent thought then simply predicate truth? Beerling (1965: 21,22) denies this. Truth could then be established simply by the precision with which a given theory would determine and demonstrate correspondences between objectively adequate thought and social groups According to Beerling, Mannheim nowhere discusses this problem. This last statement of Beerling's is accurate. Mannheim occupied himself chiefly with the philosophical sociology of knowlege and not with a careful, empirical, knowlege-sociological investigation of situationally congruent thought. But given his argument above, Beerling ought not to answer this question negatively: does situationally-congruent thought acquire the judgment of *true* for Mannheim? Situationally conditioned thought, according to Mannheim, can lay claim *to* the truth. But more needs to be taken into account in the subject of truth. Mannheim deals with judging thoughts and ideas as ideological or utopian on the basis of their capacity for being realized; the achieved realization demonstrates the truth. We ascertain something ambiguous in Mannheim's concept of truth: both the study of the structure of the situation which reveals the truth of a time period, as well as the utopian ideal which, in becoming realized, might turn out to be true. This last element contains *still another ambiguity*: utopia, which is situationally incongruent, must be characterized as unreal and untrue, but later, in its realization, it can be true: a lie turning to truth, and unreality becoming reality.

Also an ambiguous view of reality is to be noted in Mannheim's system. The given reality, in which thought has its place, congruent or not, and which, in any case, is the truth-criterion for thought when Mannheim addresses himself to reality as a continuously transforming dynamic; this last conception of reality, with its dynamic, renders the first interpretation of realizability as incomplete and inadequate as a criterion for truth.

Who allows himself to be led by conceptions which are situationally congruent? Mannheim's answer: *only the consciousness which has been totally enlightened sociologically* (ıu: 175). In Chapter V the point was already made that Mannheim can be called a *transcendental realist*, but that the idea of *transcendental* must be interpreted not as Husserl would as a "pure consciousness" which remains after the phenomenological reduction. Mannheim discussed in his "Interpretation of Weltanschauung" the *historical consciousness*. In what followed we saw that in Mannheim's opinion, after the succession of religious, rational, and historical explanations of reality, the sociological explanation of reality is most adequate. Not that he abandoned historicism; he had worked out historicism in sociological terms, and made it more precise. The *sociological consciousness* replaces the historical consciousness. It is a consciousness which, with reference to its function in a given historical-social constellation, can arrive at insight into the self, which is free from illusions and speculations, and which guarantees the understanding of this constellation according to its own nature.

Does Mannheim mean by this sociological consciousness that a transcendental sociological subject has appeared and that sociology has replaced philosophy? I have several times pointed out that the distinction between philosophy and sociology is unclear in his views. Although in his elaboration he *de facto* grants the place of philosophy to sociology, he distinguishes *de jure* sociology's task from philosophy's, and he says so explicitly (PSD: 621), that philosphy is not replaced by sociology.

The sociologically enlightened consciousness is a characteristic of the socially free-floating intelligentsia, which, however, only seems to be relatively free-floating, socially, and consequently, neither can nor may be entirely free from the social class to which it belongs. Even that modifier *relatively* raises the question: To what extent is Mannheim's conception about truth, congruency, and faithfulness to reality itself contaminated with ideology? To the extent that thought, dynamically and rationally, is situationally conditioned and answers congruently to an adequate understanding of the internal structure of the historical-social constellation – to that extent one will emphasize the small extent of the contamination in Mannheim's conception of truth. The relatedness to a specific class, which is unavoidable, implies, however, unavoidably, an ideological or utopian element.

Mannheim's intention concerning the sociological consciousness makes one think of the familiar words of Hegel about philosophy, which "comprehends its time in thought." Is the sociological consciousness, then, not also trapped in the limitations of time? If one answers this question negatively, one can ask next: Which views of past and future together are determiners for the study of one's own time? If one answers the previous question affirmatively, then the question comes up: To what extent is Mannheim's view of the study of his own time loaded down with all of its attachments to that time? Mannheim will seriously combat this latter answer and refer to the dynamic of reality and, therefore, to the dynamic relationism of thought and truth. The question comes down to the direction of the dynamic and the inescapability of social, that is, ideological, relatedness. The crux of Mannheim's outlook is that the intelligentsia would be in a position to make clear the structure of their time, which shows its truth in that structure. This structure, however, always needs to be structure as intellectuals reconstruct it, and not the structure of the age itself. Because the intelligentsia operates by means of the characteristics which determine its identity and constitute its knowlege, "time," according to Plessner (1931: 278), has become "a new thing in itself" *(ein neues Ding an sich)* in Mannheim's work. Mannheim regards reality as knowable, and this vision implies concerning the situationally congruent thinking of the intelligentsia, that their analysis can provide reliable insights and reliable scientific knowledge of reality.

It may be clear that, according to Mannheim's evaluative and non-evaluative sociology of knowledge, most interpretations of ideology function as a cloak for the support of the existing social order; a critical vanguard is entirely lacking. Utopias and ideological conceptions which include nonfictitious utopian ideas within them do have this critical vanguard function. His vague and sometimes inconsistent descriptions of nonfictitious utopian ideas, however, are detrimental to the sharpness of this function (cf. Holzle, 1969: 138).

The following definition helps to clarify Mannheim's conception of ideology:

> a recognizable whole of cognitive conceptions and evaluative attitudes concerning social reality, held by the members of a social entity. (Kruithof, 1964: 283)

This definition contains four elements:
1. *Cognitive conceptions* concerning social reality, which do not have reference to the individual or social behavior itself, but to the beliefs (ideas and assignments of significance) which are contained in the behavior and which give it direction.
2. *Evaluative attitudes*, which do not only concern past, present, and future, but which are primarily directed to what is desired.
3. *A social entity* for whom all this is characteristic, a group, a collective organization, a social stratum or class.
4. Ideology is volitional. It arises from everyday practises and serves as a guideline for action.

Although we indeed encounter these characteristics in Mannheim's writings these characteristics do not adequately present what Mannheim in his evaluative sociology of knowledge understands by ideology (which contains no utopian elements). In line with Mannheim's evaluative sociology of knowledge, we must add five characteristics to those above:
5. Theoretically incoherent and inconsistent
6. Not defended on rational grounds by its defenders.
7. Out of data as regards content.
8. Uncritical.
9. Inhibited from understanding its own time adequately and from adequate practical application of the understanding it does have (cf. Gramsci, 1971: 320, 366, 376, 377 ff; Heeger, 1975: 44; Larrain, 1979: 80-83)

Not only Mannheim's conception of ideology is vague and unnuanced, but also his conception of utopia suffers from the same. It is freed from the concrete situation and is described as directed toward the future, and in the future directed to the more nearly true, the more just, and the generally better society. Plattel (1970: 78) writes:

> Mannheim does not see through his scientism, that two kinds of rationality and reality must be distinguished, but at the same time, must not be separated from each other: the scientific rationality and the empirical reality in the narrower sense; and the hermeneutical rationality, and the reality of life in the broader sense.

Scientific rationality needs a broader interpretation; this *raison élargie* or rationality dependent on context gives insight into the whole world of values, in which facts can be recognized as facts.

Plattel (1970: 78) is not entirely accurate when he says that Mannheim has not acknowledged the distinction between the scientific rationality and the hermeneutic rationality. However, in his interpretation of utopia he does not work with this distinction, so that the relationship remains vague.

On the one hand he calls utopia impractical; on the other, it stand in dialectical tension with the existing order. This dialectical relationship gives it a characteristic of unreality and at the same time a relationship to reality. Plattel (78) concludes thus:

> At one moment the utopia is pure distance without horizon, particularly when its proposals are foreign to reality. However, at another moment utopia is an horizon not so distant, when its proposal is transformed into reality and by that process has become congruent with reality. If Mannheim took seriously the vanguard function of utopia as a power which transforms reality, he would need to abandon the characterization of "unreal."

Plattel remarks that utopia in fact must be construed as a form of ideology, particularly as a rationalization foreign to reality, for utopia can be examined only afterwards on the basis of its capacity to be realized, a conclusion at which Neusüss (1968b: 28) also arrives. This strikes me as inaccurate. Letting a utopia be taken up into ideology does not do justice to the differences Mannheim expressed concerning the intention behind these concepts – in spite of the fact that Mannheim does not distinguish these concepts sharply enough. Mannheim bestows great value on utopian thought, because maintaining it makes the progress of human society possible. On account of its social relevance, utopia awaits its realization; utopia's desire is to break into the social order and to break it open (IU: 236).

If Mannheim had given a sharper analytical-theoretical meaning to utopia, it would have gained greater scientific relevance. In that case it could have been an instrument of the vanguard for a critical theory of society (cf. Neusüss, 1968b: 29-37).

The sociology of knowledge – as it seems – does not only have the problem of ideology for investigation, but also other ways of thinking, among them, the utopian. Situationally congruent thought also belongs to its field of study; situationally congruent thought is the mode of thought which, in its understanding of society, develops in correspondence with the developments of the social constellation in which it finds itself. Reality is dynamic; that is why congruent thinking is dynamic thinking. It does not go too far ahead of its time, nor does it lag behind; it is neither too utopian nor too ideological. To be situationally congruent we could characterize as simultaneously-dynamic. The intelligentsia is in a position to think congruently with the situation. They have a well-developed sociological consciousness. They strive for the control of their emotions and both by offering themselves as well as by being able to take distance, they will make their contribution, by means of an articulate whole of reasonable discourse – a contribution to the political form the society takes and to the new cultural synthesis. This subject will be worked out in the following chapter.

Chapter XII

The Cultural Mission of the Intelligentsia

The Socially Free-floating Intelligentsia

The intelligentsia assumes a central role in Mannheim's sociology of knowledge. Already in his sociology of culture and in his essay supporting his appointment to academia, he had spoken about the "socially free-floating intelligentsia" (ST: 269, KD: 125, 126).

Mannheim borrowed the concept "socially free-floating intelligentsia" from Alfred Weber without acknowledging his source; possibly Weber used this concept during lectures or discussions. In his *Die Not der geistigen Arbeit (The Need of Intellectual Labor*, 1923), he does not use it, though he speaks in it about the freedom of the intellectual work of the intelligentsia.

In the first chapter of *Ideology and Utopia* Mannheim speaks about the intellectual as a type of thinker not bound to any particular social stratum. The more static a society is, the more clearly circumscribed the status of that category called intelligentsia, and the clearer the monopolistic control over the forming of the *Weltanschauung* of society. As exponents of a strictly organized collective (for instance, the society of the Middle Ages), the intellectuals are scholasticists. In modern society a "free intelligentsia" came into being. The recruiting for it took place on various social strata. In their thinking they were not bound to a strictly caste-like organization. They could exchange their experiences, insights, and methods of thought with other people. Yet a form of competition began to play itself out on an intellectual level; in the more democratized societies, the intellectuals competed for the favors of the public, that is, for certain groups of the public. The "intellectual illusion," with only one way of looking at a thing (on the part of a certain caste or of the church), disappeared entirely. In its place "a sudden flowering of an unexampled intellectual richness" appeared (IU: 11; LH).

These intellectuals formed a particular sociological phenomenon. They occupied unstable social and economic positions. As "free-lance" writers they could hardly live from their publications. The "socially free-floatingness" of these intellectuals did not only have to do with their labled economic position; they combined this difficult position with a very rich and broad intellectual horizon, in which they united great sensibility and "moral uncertainty" and ethical openness; they had the inclination within them to be adventuresome. Yet, they could not remain socially "free-floating." They often offered their services to the governments, for instance of Prussia and Austria. However, they were not officials, but felt the need to influence popular opinion. Their thinking acquired the characteristics both of other-wordliness, and of an orientation to concrete reality. They were, according to Mannheim, born philosophers of history; he especially names Von Ranke, Von Treitschke, and Marx (KD: 127). He remarks in relationship to the social position of this category:

> These unattached intellectuals are the typical advocate-philosophers, *ideologues* who can find arguments in favor of any political cause they may happen to serve. Their own social position does not bind them to any cause, but they have an extraordinarily refined sense for all the political and social currents around them, and the ability to detect them and enter into their spirit. By themselves they know nothing. But let them take up and identify with someone else's interests they will know them better, really better, than those for whom these interests are laid down by the nature of things, by their social condition. (KD: 127)

According to Mannheim, these intellectuals are not rooted in a particular social stratum, because they do not think so much from a starting point as to a goal. Elsewhere Mannheim says of the "socially free-floating intelligentsia" that it is supposed to have "a certain distance, but also a certain amount of solidarity with some of the factors involved" (KD: 137). As an example he names the English historian Burke:

> Burke was not a member of the nobility himself, he was a self-made man who sought admission to the inner circle of the aristocracy; his own social status was a mobile one. For that very reason he was able to determine in an exemplary fashion – although with an apologetic intention – the social significance and peculiar character of the nobility. (KD: 138)

In an earlier publication he wrote about the two groups of intellectuals in Heidelberg: the groups around Max Weber and Stefan George. He demonstrates great admiration for Weber, who not alone was a great intellectual in economic and social fields, but also wanted to give political leadership. In contrast to them he criticizes the intellectuals in the line of George, who delved into each other's works and devoted their lives to literary interests without striving for new cultural and political insights (LH).

Although the various groups of intellectuals are discernable, there is, according to Mannheim, a sociological characteristic that these groups have in common: "education, which binds them together in a striking way. Participation in a common educational heritage progressively tends to suppress differences of

214

birth, status, profession, and wealth" (IU: 138). The intellectuals must inform themselves and raise their consciousnesses concerning the structural problems which are characteristic of a time, for the purpose of fulfilling the task to which they are called. In our time, according to him (SPI: 87191; SC: 92-94), society is demanding national control. The intellectuals have an important task in this and other regards. Through what kind of lens must they regard their tasks? From what perspective in other times have intellectuals regarded their task? In the history of humanity, he distinguishes four stages of self-awareness: 1. from God's perspective, 2. from reason's perspective, 3. from history's perspective, and 4. from sociology's perspective.

As examples of the *interpretation of the human self from God's perspective* he names two possibilities: the relationship between God and humanity, individually or collectively, can be either that of master-servant or father-son. Deity was the quarantor for social norms; that is, social norms were derived from deity. After the Middle Ages *reason* increasingly assumed the function of deity. More and more, humanity came to discover that *reason* must be seen as an expression of a historical situation. Later, particularly after the Enlightenment, reason was inserted as one category in a higher order: *history*. But history seemed too vague a concept. The answer to the new problem of self-interpretation must be provided from a position that is higher even than history: *sociology*. Very succinctly he formulates his philosophy, and declares that sociology must ask clear questions about the "concrete subject" of history and then must provide clear answers. That is why sociology is higher than history for the interpretation of life. According to Mannheim, what historians often are inclined to neglect and exactly what sociology emphasizes are these factors: 1. that life in history is the life of human beings, 2. that changes in the Spirit are changes in the spirit of people, and 3. that the issue in history is not changes among individualists, but changes among socialized people – people in their relationship to groups in their reciprocal collisions in every sort of social situation – and 4. that the development of the spirit of society is the reflection of specific social groups in their reciprocal collisions in a social totality.

In the process of consciousness-raising among the intelligentsia, various axioms of interpretation are imposed on it, for instance, the proletariat's axioms. If the intelligentsia does not see through this, then it is in the grip of a dilemma: "either the intelligentsia is a class, and thus, something, or no class, and thus, nothing." According to Mannheim, the intelligentsia must see its own significance and cultural task from the perspective of its own situation. The proletarian method of approach had made this difficult by only thinking in terms of class; this is not an adequate approach for the intelligentsia *which forms no class* and is in no position to form one. Precisely intellectuals are extremely varied in background, and he gives examples: bank directors, professors, yellow journalists, and behomians. He adds that this division is one according to classes. Indeed, according to Mannheim, who now definitively formulates the place of the intelligentsia in "community culture" and in "culti-

215

vated culture" (see Chapter VIII), the intellectual must know precisely to which class he belongs and must be part of that class, honestly and with conviction, and not to some other. *In addition*, he is also an intellectual, a cultivated person, which means that he takes part in the life of the mind and the life of culture. With reference to culture, two streams always stand opposite each other throughout history: the vulgar stream, which is directed toward practical daily work and the technique of human life, and the refined, cultivated culture developed in isolated circles. Participation in the life of the mind and the life of culture by cultivated people is not limited to a specific social stratum; it has broken open to people of all classes. A cultivated person changes significantly in his motivation through his participation, and is no longer the same as the person of his class without the advantage. The cultivated person can also acquire something from someone else's perspective. Not that always, in any circumstance, he always declares another alternative just as good as the one chosen; rather, he has the power of a broad orientation and of making a well-argued choice. With this gift he can also juggle ideas, and this is his great danger. The great crisis of our time for intellectuals, according to Mannheim, lies in the warfare against powers which intend to make an end to his intellectual and cultural development. A danger for the intellectual is, for instance, that he must display how cultivated he is by securing a diploma. At that point, however, he ceases to be genuinely intellectual. There are, of course, certified intellectuals who serve as bureaucrats and can think in no way other than for performing their functions. The lack of critical powers threatens these functional intellectuals as well as specialists in some sciences, depriving them of a general orientation and a total philosophy, on the basis of which to produce corrections in their specialized and functionally limited thought. Not that the intellectual should need to live a self-sufficient and retiring life. He must precisely be equipped for confrontations and politicized on all kinds of issues, without becoming self-encapsulated.

Mannheim's advice to the intellectuals is this: "Go to your party, but do not only think functionally, but freely!" (SPI: 90, 91).

> Join, but carry out free, living thoughts – and then you will notice how soon you are thrown out. (...) And it is the task of intellectuals, by means of a self-conscious sociological orientation, to do what is necessary at this moment: to fulfill their becoming self-aware and to live according to the newly won insights. (SPI: 91)

Mannheim concludes that our time offers great opportunities for intellectuals, but it is a struggle to make their task a reality.

Thus, Mannheim feels himself totally misunderstood when people continue to maintain that the typical intellectual formation of a person by education alone would be *sufficient* to eradicate class-relatedness. He calls the extraordinary element "of this new basis of assocation" of the intelligentsia, that it *preserves* the variety of elements in which those class categories exist. Within these categories the conflicting parties can measure their powers. Moreover,

216

the vision of the intellectuals is directed toward the *totality* of a period of time with its own problems.

So, he speaks about intelligentsia as a social stratum "which is to a large degree unattached to any social class" (IU: 57), a "relatively uncommitted intelligentsia" (SC: 106).

Although something of class influence is to be noticed among intellectuals, they have over and above it the potential energy to put them in a position to develop a social sensibility on behalf of a dynamic synthesis. That some intellectuals choose the side of a certain class to which they have never belonged arises from the fact that they can adapt themselves to any vision. Still, the particular class often responds to them with suspicion, because in their attachment to that class they are circumscribed by the psychical and social characteristics of their being intellectuals. The noticeably radical and fanatic positions which precisely these intellectual radicals adopt in the class struggle arise, after all, according to these suspicious classes, only from a psychological compensation for the lack of a more fundamental integrity among intellectuals. Other intellectuals who do not attach themselves to any one class have done much to become conscious of their own position and of their new mission. Mannheim establishes that only few intellectuals of his time in Hungary and in Weimar Germany during the first decades of this century came to their own, typically intellectual views on politics. The contradictions between the classes were too sharp and too narrowly focussed on mass activity in order to allow a personal view on politics. The meaning of Mannheim's sociological theory about the intelligentsia is precisely to direct it to its mission: it must have a view of the totality of a social and political structure. It has something to speak out about, particularly against the one-sidedness of the classes. Precisely their relatively free social position equips the intelligentsia for this function (SC: 103-106; LH).

This conception of intellectuals was succintly worded by Lederer in his advice to the faculty of Heidelberg concerning Mannheim's essay written to support his appointment to academia: "Since intellectuals are rooted nowhere, they are not single-mindedly engaged in one line of thought. But at the same time, they feel in their fingertips the collective strivings of the epoch and they form them into a system. Without intellectuals there would be only a naked conflict of interests. They, however, insert the historical-philosophical aspect into history, a viewpoint that statesmen never have. They simultaneously sublimate and conceal the various streams of interests."

Mannheim also defines in terms of the sociology of knowledge his own thought as a free intellectual thinking about free intellectuals, when he says (given the social and political situation in the Weimar Republic):

It is only today, when we have become aware of all the currents and are able to understand the whole process by which political interests and *Weltanschauung* come into being in the light of a sociologically intelligible process, that we see the possibility of politics as science. (IU: 144)

He makes a distinction between party indoctrination and political science when he continues:

> Since it is likely, in accord with the spirit of the age, that more and more party schools will arise, it is all the more desirable that an actual forum be established, whether it be in the universities or in specialized higher institutions of learning, which shall serve the pursuit of the advanced form of political science. (IU: 144)

It is clear in this connection that politics and political science, according to him, must both rely on the insights of the free intellectuals.

Provisional Conclusions

In conclusion we can provisionally say of the intelligentsia as Mannheim describes them

- that hey originally have the intention to establish themselves as socially independent;
- they are not entirely, but *relatively* independent from social strata; thus, we must speak about a "socially *relatively* free-floating intelligentsia" (on which points and to what degree relative is never made clear);
- as soon as they are hired by the government or a particular group or social stratum, they lose some of their relative independence;
- they are characterized by a broad intellectual horizon, ethical openness, great sensitivity for tracing the tendencies of the time; at the same time they have a view of and a knowledge of the *totality* of epochs and of the totality of the social and political structure;
- they can take a distance from actual social and political problems;
- they form a unity, thanks to an education and sociological consciousness directed toward transcending differences in origin, status, profession, and wealth;
- they have a cardinal function in Mannheim's sociology of knowledge: striving for new cultural and political insights which the time requires, and pointing the direction for social and political processes.

We may compare Mannheim's idea of the socially free-floating intelligentsia with Hegel's "bureaucratic officialdom" and Marx's proletariat as "universal class." Marx, as well as Mannheim, did not accept Hegel's identification of bureaucratic officialdom with the universal class, but he holds on to the idea of *a* particular "social class" as a universal class. Marx does not give to one particular class a priori the characteristics of universality. Only that social class can claim the universality, which within a particular social-historical situation represents the universal social-economic concerns. In the course of the dialectical historical development of a society various social strata can be acknowledged as the "universal class" (cf. Avineri, 1968: 57, 58). In other words, in a certain period a particular class represents the socio-economic concerns of society as a whole and in another period, with other social-economic structures, another social stratum or class is acknowledged in the same way. Concepts such as

218

ideological consciousness, alienation, truth, and falsehood are all bound to a particular historical-social phase, with the differences in classes which exist within that phase. This "layering" is not permanent; it must and can change, by which process new and different interpretations will be made about truth and falsehood than in the foregoing phase (cf. Beerling, 1965: 15; cf. H. Marcuse, 1929: 387,390 ff.). However, although criteria for truth in various societies may differ, Marx would surely defend that within every society truth or untruth can be judged according to the criterion of praxis,which is a collective, social process of transformation of the material and social structures of reality (cf. Bottomore, 1956: 52-58; F. Adler, 1957: 399-405). Although Mannheim has the opinion that proletarian thought is certainly not free from ideological elements, he transfers Marx's view of the proletariat to the intelligentsia. However, he does not discuss the idea that only in a given period the intelligentsia is a "universal class," and that in other periods another stratum might be acknowledged in the same way. Moreover, it will appear that Mannheim's view of the cultural task of the intelligentsia is totally different from Marx's vision of the revolutionary practise of the proletariat.

A critical note on the periphery of Mannheim's analysis is this: that the intellectuals do not count themselves as belonging to any particular class does not negate the fact that they grew up in well-defined milieus which, already from the start, have contributed to their cultural and literary forming. For instance, they have had opportunities for enjoying good educations. Mannheim saw the problem and posed the questions: To what extent does the socially free-floating intelligentsia form a clearly recognizable category? And if so to what extent within this category do differences in positional relatedness reveal themselves? Where do these differences come from?

Mannheim himself was a "socially free-floating intellectual." He did not let himself be "hired in" by a particular government to justify the current policy. He strove for social and political independence, which he wished to combine with a broad intellectual horizon and with the appropiate tendencies of the time. He was also independent financially because he had come from a particular social class: the very well-established bourgeoisie of Budapest.

The intelligentsia acquires the Sisyphus role for Mannheim. On the one hand it is, according to its nature, driven by free necessity to climb the mountain of collective culture, and on the other hand it has the free necessity of turning to its class. Again we meet paradox and dialectic. According to its nature, the intelligentsia knows the ontic paradox between "social free-floatingness" and orientation to a class, which by way of the dialectic must be elevated continually to a higher level; it is a way which properly leads to the continuous search for a new cultural synthesis. Mannheim's sociology of knowledge and his conception of the intelligentsia, which is implied in his sociology of knowledge, are contributions toward overcoming the crisis of Western culture, a crisis which also exists in the humanities (Lenk, 1972: 89).

Mannheim is of the opinion that with the disappearance of utopian thought, a static, business-like manner arises in society in which a person himself becomes an object. In conection with the development of the bourgeois society, Lukács had already spoken about "Making Consciousness into an Object." Max Weber had spoken about a "a mechanized petrification" in connection with the rationalization of Western culture. Just as Lukács longed for a future socialistic society, and just as Weber looked forward to prophets who would arise or that there would be a mighty regeneration of old ideas and ideals, so Mannheim looks forward to the revelation of what he calls the "socially free-floating intelligentsia" (cf. Wolff, 1978: 310).

I pass by the question of whether Mannheim's historical interpretation of the intelligentsia's relative freedom from social bondedness is correct or not. Brym (1977: 174) defends the opposite: intellectuals easily fall into elitist attitudes when they do not engage themselves to social strata or classes. He demonstrates, for example, in Russia around the turn of the century the obvious involvement of many intellectuals with the working class. Even if Brym is correct in general, and even if Mannheim's historical interpretation of the social position of the intelligentsia is highly selective, even then Mannheim intention remains clear: the issue is the tasks and positions of the intelligentsia *as they are supposed to be* and how, according to Mannheim, it is possible for the tasks to be realized.

The Socially Free-floating Intelligentsia and Cultural Synthesis

Referring back to the problem of the truth question in the sociology of knowledge, we can establish that the intelligentsia can attain the most adequate insight into the knowledge of the totality of a particular historical period, into the *Weltanschauung*, and into the internal structure of the historical-social constellation. For the rest, no knowledge of truth with the predication of absoluteness or perfection exists; the intelligentsia itself seems in its "socially free-floatingness" to possess something relative. Still, the intelligentsia strives for the *ideal* of true and objective knowledge. Precisely because it can acquire the most adequate perspective on and the knowledge about the cultural totality, and can transcend the various interpretations, often at odds with each other – because of all of this, the intelligentsia is in a position to bring about a cultural synthesis.

In Chapter VII we already discussed Troeltsch's "contemporary synthesis of culture." Troeltsch understood by this the necessity of a creative uniting of tendencies from the past with the present; his ideal was the formation of objective standards in a historical-social constellation. These standards were necessary for him to combat the charge of the relativity of knowledge. No religious authority, nor methods in the natural sciences, nor a metaphysics could be of help here. The person, the subject relevant for the philosophy of history, had the task, according to Troeltsch, to assign itself this action: to be precise, to take the social components and intellectual motives from various periods of culture, and to bring these all together with the institutions and intellectual motives in the present.

Who determines the objectivity, according to Troeltsch? And in which way? The formation of a cultural synthesis is, according to him, not only the work of an individual; it is prepared by many, both in personal contemplation and in discussions; it is brought about by people who live in a cultural community which has traditions. Do not the personal choice and decision of the investigator play an important role in this process? Are not whim and relativism unavoidable after all? Troeltsch saw these problems. The synthesis of culture was more of a necessity for him than an ideal, for the purpose of forestalling and combatting relativism. Will this succeed? Does Troeltsch himself hesitate at the objectivity of his cultural synthesis when he writes as follows?

> The most practical would be a large artistic symbol, just as once it was the *Divine Comedy* and later it became *Faust*. Except that those were lucky accidents, when an epoch is granted a symbol like that, and most often they do not occur until the end of an epoch. It must also happen without them, and still, where the world war has thrown the whole previous epoch into the crucible, we dare not even expect anything of the kind. (1922: 772)

Troeltsch would gladly have had a better grip on particular symbols, but when a particular period offers such symbols, they only assume the form of "lucky accidents." Courageously he adds that one can manage things without these symbols. Confronted by the cultural crisis caused by World War I, he sees, however, no new standards for a new form of community on the horizon. But Troeltsch keeps his courage when he closes his volume on historicism with the remark that the task of a synthesis of culture is particularly urgent:

> The idea of building is to conquer history by means of history, and to clear the platform for new creations. (1922: 772)

Both theoretically and practically, Troeltsch finds himself in a circular argument, and he does not have the ability to snap out of it.

Mannheim approaches the problem of the cultural synthesis entirely differently. He also wants to avoid cultural relativism and not take flight to religious, metaphysical or scientific explanations. He has fixed his hope on the "socially free-floating intelligentsia." Just as Troeltsch, Mannheim had experienced World War I and the processes of fermentation in Weimar Germany; these facts certainly discouraged hem, but they did not deprive him of hope.

Though before I called the cultural synthesis more of a necessity than an ideal for Troeltsch, for Mannheim it is as much one as it is the other. Though we noticed a pessimism and a vicious circle in Troeltsch, Mannheim is not to be called pessimistic, and he attempts to break through the vicious circle with his appeal to the intelligentsia and his challenges for them. But it is only relatively free-floating. Mannheim does not escape the paradox and the dialectical tension which characterizes the assignment of the intelligentsia. He, however, is convinced that he follows the right way. In spite of the tensions which are inherent in the position of the intelligentsia, tensions which cannot be overcome, and in spite of the fact that the tensions make the task particularly difficult – inspite of all that, these tensions, according to his view, do not make a break with the high calling and the great opportunities of the intelligentsia. This intention is accurately worded by Ringer (1969: 433, 434):

Mannheim clearly pictured the intelligentsia as a progressive element in society. He knew that very few of his colleagues shared his radical outlook. But he apparently hoped to convert some of them to the ideals of "active" knowledge and utopian synthesis.

The Intellectual as an Academic Problem

Criticism of Mannheim's conception of the intelligentsia has been expressed by various authors. The intellectuals whom Mannheim has in mind, all of whom satisfy all of the specified criteria, form a unity, according to him, and a special social category.

Bláha has submitted the argument on the opposite side, that there is no social category which Mannheim's word *intelligentsia* covers. It forms no specific professional group, no position, and no class; also the group is not adequately circumscribed by education, nor by economic nor political position. According to Bláha (1937: 380, 381), the intelligentsia can only be comprehended on the basis of *functions within society*; these seem to be highly differentiated. It has an intellectual-creative function in society, it creates values in society, and it assumes a position of leadership at the levels of organization and of knowledge. In no sense, however, does it form a coherent category. Also Neusüss (1968a: 190,191) concludes that Mannheim has not provided a sociology of groups of intellectuals, but that he has developed a theoretically articulated program *for* the intelligentsia (cf. Idenburg, 1953: 22; Gadourek, 1955: 30; Thoenes, 1966: 97ff).

Geiger (1949: 63-64) formulates a concise and pointed critique of Mannheim:

1. The intelligentsia is not "socially free-floating." Intellecltuals arise form various classes and traditions; these influences work their way into the intelligentsia and split this category into just as many accents as there are classes and traditions. Besides, ideologies do not simply appear in the various classes; they are produced and promoted precisely by the intellectuals of these classes.

2. Geiger grants Mannheim that intellectuals occupy a special place in society. Although they do not form a homogeneous group, according to Geiger, nor a class in the comon use of the world, they do have their importance. They defend the place and the function of academic work in society. Not infrequently, however, they are inclined to overvalue the social significance of their work. This overvaluation can be seen in this fact, that, according to Geiger, Mannheim ascribes to intellectuals their own ideology, to wit, a synthesis of the class ideologies in conflict with each other. (At this point Geiger is not totally fair in his criticism of Mannheim: a. Mannheim's pleading for a cultural synthesis is not simply a synthesis of ideologies. b. The concept *ideology* for the intelligentsia is unfair – Mannheim would rather have intended a certain form of utopia).

3. The cultural synthesis which is aimed at is, according to Geiger, less objective than Mannheim thought. Which criteria are valid for this objectivity? Geiger sees all kinds of subjective insights playing a part here. He also asks, who

must be responsible for realizing in political and social life the insights of cultural synthesis? The intellectuals have no means of power and the politicians are bound, precisely to the concerns of party and class.

4. Although Geiger does not want to disqualify Mannheim, he indicates that his conception of intelligentsia was used in a very threatening way by the national socialists; these used their false learning to justify their political and social system (1949b:65). Still, Geiger also sees an important task reserved for intellectuals: "The intelligentsia champions the creative spirit in society." It creates renewal within a given period of culture. For that reason, by definition, intellectuals are in an adversary relationship with the holders of power, who would rather support the existing order. For that reason a discrepancy exists between intellectuals on the one hand and men in power on the other. This does not mean, however, that intellectuals should keep to the periphery in politics. One of their most important tasks is exactly to pursue a continuing criticism of politicians. This implies that the intelligentsia fulfills a constant role of opposition in society. Geiger speaks of the antagonism which cannot be abolished: Spirit versus Power.

Zijderveld's conclusion (1974: 188) seems justified, that Geiger's conception of intellectuals as "the front line creativity" – although worked out differently – is not so far removed from Mannheim's conception of the "socially, relatively free-floating intelligentsia." Even though Geiger sees through certain problems in Mannheim's thought and even though he, according to Ellemers (1974: 199, 200), for convincing reasons is turning against the political leadership of intellectuals which Mannheim defends – in spite of all of this, the question remains whether Geiger in the solution of these problems has come very much further. In any case, between the two and between their views of intelectuals there is this agreement: that the questions which Mannheim asked concerning the cultural task of intellectuals and concerning truth and objectivity in science have remained open questions.

Mannheim against Max Weber

Mannheim attributed many sociological insights to Max Weber and also accepted Weber's ideal types in his own methodology; in his sociology of culture and especially in his ideas on the mission of the intelligentsia, however, Mannheim opposes Weber.

The mission of the intelligentsia may not be interpreted as a striving for a Weberian "freedom from value judgment," or for any freedom at all. Intellectuals never, after all, are perfectly free from ideology. They study the totality and structure of epochs and of political and social constellations; their studies must lead to results and also to judgments. Therein they will reveal what Mannheim calls "the absolute in process of becoming" (sw: 146) and "the truth of the age" (H: 117; see Chapter X).

Also Mannheim's conception of the "socially free-floating intelligentsia"

223

may not be equally yoked with Max Weber's *intellectual integrity* (1917:3). Weber has his eye set on a "specialized training" for specialized, qualified, practising scientists. These qualifications have reference to a "specific soundness" which makes a sharp distinction between "statements of logically deduced or empirically observed facts on the one hand and statements of practical, ethical, and *Weltanschauung-related* evaluations on the other" (1917: 2; see Chapter VI).

Weber wanted to keep the purely rational practise of science free form ethical, political, and worldview judgments. At the same time, he defended that these judgments might not be deduced from science. It is a separation which, according to Weber (1917: 9), is a difficult assignment for every practising scientist, but one which he must, nevertheless, strive to make.

Of course, it is possible to study ethical norms and political ideals scientifically. One can study the consistency between the axioms and content of ethical norms and political ideals. The question whether the practising scientist who himself accomplishes this research shall also choose these norms and ideals is a question which does not belong to the field of science. Now, for instance, there are problems of a political kind, which are not only to be solved with the help of a technical analysis of purposes and means; in these cases the conflict is often about normative standards. Weber calls these problems "questions of culture" (1904: 56). With reference to these problems the conflict is between various versions of the *Weltanschauung*. Weber adds the following:

> ... the more "general" the problem involved, i.e., in this case the broader its cultural *significance*, the less subject it is to a single unambiguous answer on the basis of the data of empirical sciences and the greater the role played by value-ideas (*Wertideen*) and the ultimate and highest personel axioms of belief. (1904: 56)

It is also clear that from norms which lie at the basis of someone's personal and subjective activity, no normative cultural content can be deduced. Complicating the matter is that the highest ideals which motivate one person or one group of people can be in conflict with the ideals and convictions of others. Weber makes the suggestion that an "optimistic syncretism" could eliminate this conflict, both theoretically and practically. But *scientific objectivity* about questions of culture and normative cultural content is not to be attained in any precise form (1904: 57). That the practising scientist, according to Weber, neither can nor may make normative statements about culture is clear from the following quotation:

> The fate of an epoch which has eaten of the tree of knowledge is that it must know that it cannot learn the *meaning* of the world form the results of its analysis, be it ever so perfect; it must recognize that general views of life and the universe can never be the products of increasing empirical knowledge, and that the highest ideals, which move us most forcefully, are always formed only in the struggle with other ideals which are just as sacred to others as ours are to us. (1904: 57)

224

With the expression "the tree of knowledge" he alludes familiarly to the Old Testament in the Bible, and particularly to the story from Genesis 2 about Adam, Eve, and "the tree of the knowledge of good and evil"; this last-mentioned expression refers to a normative knowledge, particularly, one that makes a distinction between good and evil. Weber only speaks of "a tree of knowledge" and suggests in this abbreviation: a scientific, non-normative knowledge.

Indeed, can one then still speak of the fate of a culture, if one is not able to speak about the meaning of events in the scientific investigation of culture? Mannheim characterizes Weber's position concerning evaluative neutrality and objectivity, in which there is no room for utopian thought, as "the realism of disillusionment" (CNSM). In order to conquer this disillusionment, Mannheim permist himself to speak of hope, faith, and meaning, with the result that intellectuals become an academic subject by themselves, both concerning their concept of science and concerning their task in culture.

Weber limits true and objective knowledge to the practise of the empirical sciences. In connection with the study of the problems of culture, the difference between norm and fact becomes very difficult. The danger is great that one comes to the point of making subjective pronouncements and calls them normative. But these pronouncements, then, also have no more than a subjective validity.

Weber does not know the term "socially free-floating intelligentsia" in Mannheim's sense, while Mannheim does not count all of Weber's practising scientists as intelligentsia. The task which Mannheim attributes to the intelligentsia is not only intended to achieve adequate insight into and knowledge of reality on behalf of society, as Weber advocates; the intelligentsia must also transcend the various forms of the *Weltanschauung* and be in a position to develop the cultural synthesis. In short, the intelligentsia must, by means of "objective" scientific thought, become capable of making normative statements about cultural problems and cultural values (cf. Hughes, 1958: 421, 422).

Intelligentsia and the Quest for Truth

On the instigation of what precedes, this question suggests itself: Did Mannheim actually solve the problem of the relativity of knowledge? It is a question of conscience for all intellectuals. He does not want to remain at a value-neutral sociology of knowledge, but wants to arrive at a sociology of knowledge which evaluates and judges.

He gave a number of answers to the charge of relativism. In the first place, he sought for a dynamic criterion for the soundness of knowledge. In the second place, he distinguished between correctness and truth of knowledge. In the third place, he looked for a new criterion for true knowledge without relativism.

Dynamic Truth

In the first place Mannheim looked for a *dynamic* criterion for the validity of knowledge. According to him, a theory is invalid if someone in a particular situation uses concepts and categories which belong properly in another historical phase, and which, on that account, inhibit that person from adjusting himself to his own situation (IU: 85). Knowledge is invalid if it does not give an accurate account of a new reality, "the absolute in the process of becoming." Science proclaims the truth about this reality as a dynamic truth. A person must be able to establish himself in his situation with the help of his ideas, be able to define his place, be able to fit into it and adjust to it; in this connection Mannheim uses "social adjustment" as a "normative" concept.

There is also a kind of thought which transcends the socio-historical situation and desires to change. How does he distinguish this utopian thought which aims at change form the thought which aims at adjustment? Mannheim attempted to answer this problem as follows. In the future the possibility for judging thought would lie in declaring ideas utopian or ideological. Ideas which after being tried are judged unrealizable because they stem from a period whose time has passed, such ideas are ideological ideas. Ideas which are adequately realized, and which have brought changes in society are called utopian. The dynamic criterion for truth is the process and the result of the realization of ideas and knowledge of the dynamic reality. Merton's critique (1968: 558), which implies that Mannheim proposes an *ex-post-facto* criterion for truth, is untrue. According to Mannheim, the criterion for judgment lies precisely *not* in the future, but the *criterion* lies in the process of realization of ideas, while the *judgment* of this realization takes place afterwards. Merton is right, of course, when he says that this judgment afterwards precludes the possibility of judging contemporaneous thought. Speaking about judging the truth-value of ideas afterwards implies a relativity of knowledge in the here-and-now. Mannheim acknowledges this problem, and finally he adopts another point of view for the purpose of avoiding this relativity.

Correctness and Truth

Mannheim continues to search for a dynamic truth and speaks in the second place about the *relatedness* of truth to situations which now obtain. With this point of view he effectively denies an *absolute* truth which could be ascribed to knowing. He also demolishes the point of view that the truth-value of thought is non-existent. Someone's social position indentifies the particularity of his thought and at the same time the character and the limitations of its validity. Situational thought does not simply imply ideological thought, but it does imply the probability that someone, given his position, will think in a particular way. The sociology of knowledge affords insights into the boundaries within which statements are valid; perception, thought and knowledge are not universal, but true under given conditions.

226

Mannheim uses the ideas of "validity" and "truth" interchangeably. There is a good reason to distinguish from each other the following two matters: 1. questions of validity and correctness of a statement made by someone about an objective topic in relation to the social situation of the speaker, and 2. the *existential question of truth* in the judgment of this same statement in relation to the object and to the cultural synthesis. Truth, for Mannheim, is the agreement which is established between the scientific description of a thing and the thing itself (IU: 259, 270). As a result the question arises, what can scientific knowledge teach us about reality? Before even answering this question, one must be aware of one's social perspective. To what extent does the boundness of knowledge with a definite social perspective give a distorted or limited view of reality? The identification of this problem is a *preparation* for solving the question of truth; it is not *the* solution itself (IU: 256). Does not the perspectival character of knowledge imply a relativity of knowledge, instead of a preparation for solving the question of truth?

Mannheim is of the opinion that one must not hide the various perspectives from which one can come to knowledge; one must rather investigate how – given these perspectives – a genuine knowledge combined with truth is still possible. For that reason, Mannheim does not speak about the *relativism*, but about the *relationism* of knowledge. Relationism comes down to this: that there are types of knowledge in which thinking manifests itself as an instrument of action. The validity of this knowledge is related to the social perspective concerned (cf. Maquet, 1973: 63, 64). This standpoint implies that knowledge, independent from its correctness related to the social position of the knowing subject, cannot be called *true*.

As we already have seen, the sociology of knowledge, which studies the relationship between thinking and social positions, does not only investigate the social conditions of thought and knowledge, but also the object, the thing itself to which statements refer (IU: 4). In spite of philosophical inconsistencies which I called attention to in Mannheim's line of thought, we must take this attention to the object seriously. On the basis of his directing us toward the object, one may not conclude that Mannheim's sociology of knowledge only occupies a supplementary or a marginal place in relation to philosophical epistemology. Mannheim holds that it has its own legitimate place next to other epistemological approaches, because it directs itself to its own field of research. Mannheim's attention is especially compelled toward questions concerning the social nature of knowledge, the coming about of knowledge, the reliability of knowledge, the insights into social reality, and the establishing of the ontic significance of the object of knowledge (cf. Maquet, 1973: 75-77; cf. Schaaf, 1956; cf. De Gré, 1941: 110-115; cf. A.O. Lovejoy, 1940: 17, 18).

Is the epistemological problem concerning the truth of knowledge to be answered with help from the sociology of knowledge? Mannheim does not want to replace epistemology by the sociology of knowledge, as Rempel (1965: 17) claims he does. But can he solve the epistemological problem of truth sociologically? In his concept of relationism as different from relativism defensible?

We must recognize that the empirical knowledge-sociology easily arrives at a relativizing of all the truth it studies. If the knowledge-sociology acquires the philosophical sociology of knowledge and itself as objects of its own study the relativism of knowledge is unavoidable. Mannheim was certainly interested in the question raised by knowledge-sociology about the origin of the philosophical sociology of knowledge; the relativism of knowledge mentioned above he emphatically never aimed at. On the contrary, he sought a foundation for knowledge-sociology in the evaluative sociology of knowledge, for the purpose of avoiding the relativism of knowledge.

Truth without Relativism?

In the third place Mannheim is looking for a new criterion for truth, a criterion which is both dynamic and sound. Put another way: he looks for structural guarantees for the soundness or truth which supercedes the obvious conclusions conditioned by perspectives. This investigation must be directed toward the object itself. In one statement not only the social conditionedness of the thinking subject is hidden, but also the *evidence* of the object. Mannheim says (IU 4; cf. Coser, 1971: 435) that the truth or untruth of a statement cannot be attacked by a sociological or any other kind of explanation, but that truth only can be found in the examination of the *object itself*! The character of meaning of the various objects and fields of reality determines the truth of the statements about it (IU: 263, 264). This means not only a relating of thought to the social strata by the sociology of knowledge, but also a relating *of* the sociology of knowledge itself to the field of reality concerned.

Which people adequately study the object? Mannheim will indicate sociologists; more precisely, sociologists of culture who belong to the intelligentsia. His conception of them did not seem to be a match against immanent criticism. Although the "socially free-floating intelligentsia" is supposed to arrive at a cultural synthesis and at an adequate answer for the question of truth in science, ultimately it seems, nevertheless, to be bound to all kinds of social strata, and to be only *relatively* free-floating. We may conclude that here is a paradox in Mannheim's sociology of knowledge (cf. Mandelbaum, 1938: 79, 80). In the case of the sociology of knowledge Mannheim points out that the soundness of the knowledge is limited on the one hand by the social perspective and on the other by the agreement with the object. Is the study of the object possible without being bound to a social perspective? Is socially related knowledge in agreement with the peculiarity of the object of reality being studied? In other words: is objectivity to be studied without partial subjectivity? Can a partial perspective ever do full justice to objectivity? If one answers all these questions affirmatively, one transcends sociological relationism and relativity. But this transcending does not seem entirely possible, even for the intelligentsia. If those questions are answered negatively, then one can proceed by asking whether the relativity of knowledge is not unavoidable.

On the subject of Mannheim's sociology of knowledge, I answer these questions negatively. If Mannheim maintains that all thought and knowing is socially related and, on that account, is partial knowledge, he also has an eye for the possibility of integrating various points of view. I wrote already that his sociology of knowledge contains a reflective element of self-criticism. As a result of this, Mannheim is of the opinion that people can change their social perspective. As he himself says,

> ... social groupings, which have hitherto lived more or less isolated from one another, each making itself and its own world of thought absolute, are now, in one form or another, merging into one another. (IU: 251)

One of the most important functions of the sociology of knowledge is that it "seeks to overcome the 'talking past one another' " (IU: 252). This discussion concerns all social groups and on that account also groups of sociologists who hold various worldviews and use various methodologies. The sociology of knowledge investigates the obstacles which stand in the way of a "cross-perspectival" of "cross-contextual" understanding. The procedures for interpreting various kinds of socially related thought can become topics for revision, refining, and reformulation. To speak with Simonds(1978, 164):

> What Mannheim rejects is not the norm of intersubjective transmissibility, but rather the claim to be able to dispense with the interpretative process altogether by adopting the "universal framework" of science in the monolithic, ahistorical, formalized model.

Because the sociologists of knowledge themselves have various social perspectives, objectivity is only achievable when one succeeds by means of discussions to discover the common denominator for various social, political, theoretical, and other insights. As soon as such a common denominator is found, it is possible to distinguish necessary points of conflict between differing perspectives from mistakes and arbitrary differences (IU: 270). The differences and conflicts between the various social perspectives can neither, according to him, be conquerred with a call on a non-perspectival view, nor by an appeal to the so-called "evidence of the object." Also, Mannheim himself does not want to make a choice between social perspectives, but *for the perspective which grasps the object most adequately*. He advocates "the broadest view of totality." This view is not provided immediately, nor does it have eternal value. It is the result of a "continuous process of the expansion of knowledge" which results in the "broadest possible extension of our horizon of vision" (IU: 94, 95). That is why Mannheim can declare that this sociology of knowledge "does not signify that there are no criteria of rightness or wrongness in a discussion" (IU: 254). This means that those criteria are not provided immediately by the object itself in its evidence but by means of "the broadest view of totality." It is clear that Mannheim stands in the tradition of Kant and Hegel, which makes the distinc-

229

tion between Intellect/Understanding (*Verstand*), which produces fragmentary knowledge, and Reason (*Vernunft*), which attempts to place understandable insights in a higher and broader context of the totality, and then to judge them. Mannheim also saw his sociology of knowledge as a preparaton for the intended discussion (IU: 251-256) or as "a methodology for dialogue" (Baum, 1977: 69). As such, his sociology of knowledge leads to self-criticism, for the purpose of examining one's own social perspective critically and of acquiring access to other "contexts of meaning." This view implies that he regards the existing society in relation to an utopian synthetic thought. This view, directed to the future from the present, stimulates him in his plea for a vision of totality, "the broadest possible extension of our horizon of vision" (IU: 106).

Mannheim seems optimistic about the possibility of this synthesis being realized. This certainly seems to be true from the fact that, in various regards, he calls all of the following very different streams of social and political thought as *complementary* to each other: bureaucratic, conservative, conservative-historical, liberal-democratic thought by the bourgeoisie, socialistic, communistic, and fascist (IU: 132). This conception precludes a model of confrontation and implies the possibility for a consensus. Mannheim is also realistic enough, however, when he says: "the motor impulse behind diverse interpretations of the world which, when their social background is uncovered, reveal themselves as the intellectual expressions of conflicting groups struggling for power" (IU: 241; BK: 196, 197). His optimism must certainly also hold for the social perspectives of participants in competing groups (SW: 178; cf. Abercrombie, Longhurst, 1981, 1983).

If one proceeds in the quest for a synthesis, one must consider himself as only one party among many parties, and that admission requires enormous humility. This does not mean that Mannheim abandons himself to relativism. In his own words:

This problem of relativism, as it has become the question of our life, can only be mastered if we make it into the axis, the starting point for theory, and only afterwards ask how it could be overcome at the stage at which it confronts us. Applied to our problem-setting, this means that the fact of the existence of diverse tendencies of thought, of diverse standpoints for viewing history, each of which dynamically changes itself, can be mastered only if one does not only avoid neglecting this fact, but actually if one makes it one's starting point, asking oneself only afterward: how is it now with truth about history? Does it too resolve itself into these standpoints and is truth itself dependent on standpoint? And here we must say no. (ST: 178)

In what follows he recalls what was already described in Chapter VII, that every period of culture has its own truth:

There is a truth about every epoch; the epoch did exist in some certain way; its structure of meaning actually and truly has being in some certain way. But no one comes into possession of this truth at a bound, as if inspired by revelation, because in so far as the truth can be seen by us at all, this is possible only from standpoints that have formed themselves in history and arise as a function of history. Since every tendency of thought is partial ... totality can be comprehended only in a synthesis. (ST: 178, 179)

230

This synthesis is, according to Mannheim, possible and necessary, for the purpose of bringing into existence the highest and best expression which has been vouchsaged to human consciousness, restricted by history:

> ...to see the body of history itself from within the underlying currents of time. But syntheses are relative, since they cannot transcend the limitation imposed by existence. (ST: 180)

These boundaries are, according to Mannheim, two-fold: 1. Like any thought, synthetic thought can only take into account the elements of life and the currents of thought which are visible in a particular period and which, on that account, can only be grasped with the assistence of the methods of thought, perspectives, and concepts which are considered valid in that period. 2. All streams of thought can only be studied on the basis of a particular social position, because knowing is also contained in a dynamic process, a fact which makes these boundaries variable.

The synthesis which Mannheim intends is a dynamic process. It is not only a synthesis of various kinds of "partial knowledge" for the purpose of arriving at the truth. The synthesis Mannheim aims at is more than the largest comon denominator. It is intended as a contribution to the progressive development of thought, for the purpose of achieving a "dynamic reconciliation" (IU: 152, 168, 169). The intellectual must analyze and evaluate the various insights and "thus can arrive at a nonbiased view of reality," (a situationally congruent view; see Ch. XI). Thus Sagarin and Kelly (1970: 281), who say elsewhere (283):

> Such an intellectual must be committed, because having examined, he cannot refrain from a viewpoint, but his commitment is scientific analysis must take precedence over the commitment to an ideology, whose partial and inadequate view he has brought to the surface by his won awareness. His position is correct, not because it will be useful in arriving at an end which he finds desirable; but the position will aid in arriving at an end which is desirable because it is correct.

The recognition of the social relatedness of all thought always forms a new challenge for Mannheim to further research, and no substitute for research. But how on the one hand can he defend the social relatedness of thought and on the other hand declare that thought has the capability of judging this social relatedness? Mannheim himself is conscious of this problem when he says: "... the opportunity for relative emancipation from social determination increases proportionately with insight into this determination" (IU: 43). He admits that these words contain a paradox. It is possible to solve this paradox?

For answering this question and the problem of truth of knowledge, an element from Chapter V must be recalled, specifically the position of "without presuppositions." In his dissertation Mannheim had declared that all epistemologies have in common that they look for the ultimate presuppositions for knowledge, while the epistemologies want to stand without presuppositions.

He spoke about a paradoxical situation, which we interpret as a principial epistemological paradox. This paradox becomes even more complicated by means of the nature of the social paradox related to the "socially free-floating" intellectuals.

Not only in his *Structural Analysis*, but also in his "Soul and Culture," in his "Interpretation of Weltanschauung" and in his essay on historicism; everywhere he speaks about paradoxes. The dialectic arises from these paradoxes. Here we discover the *paradox in the sociology of knowledge* between objectivity and subjectivity (the latter construed as social conditioning), between truth and relativity.

We have already seen that Mannheim calls his philosophy dynamic and that this dynamic character is interpreted dialectically: the scientific theories which follow each other, solve and resolve each other; and the most recent theory about a particular field of reality (or part of it), with a new systemizing center, takes up into itself earlier theories, which then were less formalized, less detailed, and less elaborated. The new systemizig center spoken of is determined by metalogical, ontic, original givens, which in the development of the science are taken up and concluded in concepts. In this way science pronounces the truth in a given phase of time concerning a particular field of reality; it always remains a "relational" and dynamic truth, never an absolute or ultimate truth. As such, the paradox in the sociology of knowledge is not cancelled, but it is elaborated in a dynamic conception of science.

Mannheim regards the various socially-related modes of thought synchronically, and their synthesis is a problem which continually must be formulated in new terms. An absolute and permanent synthesis would lead to a static *Weltanschauung*. In a continuum in which everything finds itself in a process of becoming, a dynamic synthesis is the only adequate theory. *The truth of knowledge which emerges from this synthesis is socially-culturally-related, dynamic truth, and the only possibility, and hence the most nearly absolute*. No person has a consciousness that can comprehend the socio-cultural totality from the beginning of human history to the present. Empowered by the sociological-historical consciousness, one can, according to Mannheim, only grasp a particular social totality in a particular period. On the one hand, Mannheim declares that the historical-sociological consciousness is in a position for a total vision, and that this reasonable insight into the totality of a socio-historical constellation reveals the truth of this totality (sc: 188-199). On the other hand, he declares that intellectuals as representatives of various social perspectives need discussion. Apparently this historical-sociological insight provides less light than one would have expected at the start. The question is whether on the basis of a dialogue between intellectuals, with various social backgrounds, the most absolute criteria for truth are likely to, and able to, arise.

Grünwald's criticism (1934: 213), "that Mannheim with his dynamic synthesis intended to create a personal criterion for establishing truth," is not fair to Mannheim's conception. Another problem is to what extent Mannheim's solu-

232

tion to the discussion is realizable and to what extent it remains stuck in a subjective-idealistic pattern. It serves us well to perceive that Mannheim is not a simple relativist, who wants to reduce the discussion of objects to social perspectives with the result that everyone has his own social-subjective truth. But no more is he a simple realist who intends to test all statements against the facts. As a transcendental realist, he strives, also in this connection, for a synthesis of these two positions: *facts* are perceived and elaborated scientifically out of a specific *social perspective*; this synthesis is combined with the one named earlier: the synthesis of social perspectives leads to the most nearly adequate vision and truth.

A Thorn in the Flesh

Several times I pointed out inconsistencies in Mannheim's line of thought. They appear again abundantly in his view of the task of the intelligentsia, in its quest for truth and its avoiding relativism, and at the same time it is not able to avoid completely the relativity of knowledge. Does this inconsistency signify a tragedy for his theories? Mannheim denies this:

> If there are contradictions and inconsistencies in my paper this is, I think, not so much due to the fact that I overlooked them, but because I make a point of developing a theme to its end even if it contradicts some other statements. I use this method because I think that in the marginal field of human knowledge we should not conceal inconsistencies, so to speak, covering up wounds, but our duty is to show the sore spots in human thinking at its present stage.
>
> In a simple empirical investigation of straightforward logical argument, contradictions are mistakes; but when the task is to show that our whole thought system in its various parts leads to inconsistencies, these inconsistencies are the thorn in the flesh from which we have to start. (BKHW)

Just as he wanted to conquer relativism by adopting it as the starting point for his theory, so he now wants to explain the inconsistencies in his theory, and possibly overcome them later, by means of the unmasking of paradoxes in society and inconsistencies in the thinking of people (cf. MS: 33). Just as he was unable to overcome the relativity of thought, so he also seems unable to overcome the inconsistencies in his theory. We saw already that the inconsistencies emerge not only from the imperfect thinking of people in general, but are also preserved in his own philosophy. The "thorn" of inconsistency, as a result of inconsistent thinking in society, remains in the "flesh" of his theory – and he werstles with it. Also the "thorn" of immanent inconsistencies remains in the "flesh" of his sociology of knowledge – but he seems to have less of a problem with it (cf. Wolff, 1959: 570-582; Wolff, 1963: 49).

Not only contradictions in society lead to inconsistencies in Mannheim's theory and to a fragmentary approach; also a new science like the sociology of knowledge, by its very nature, brings these characteristic inconsistencies along with it. It must still test its new approach. It is developed in a struggle with old modes of approach.

Conclusions

With reference to Mannheim's conception of the intelligentsia it becomes clear that this category is not absolute but *relative*: "socially free-floating." It is called to the revelation of truth in science and to the cultural synthesis, but it is seriously weakened in this by a double paradox: a principial epistemological paradox with reference to the position "without presuppositions" and a social paradox.

His conception of the intelligentsia is attacked from various sides, and virtually nowhere has it found support; yet the discussion has not fallen silent on this account. Many sociological studies describe as their main topic the actual function of intellectuals in history (for instance, as revolutionaries) and in society (for instance, in making a profile of nationalism, or in connection with political power structures); see, among others, Aron (1957), Coser (1970), Gouldner (1979), Schumpeter (1942), Shils (1961, 1972), and Znaniecki (1940). The issue for Mannheim, however, was not only revolution, nor even only the synthetic character of the intelligentsia. Right at the heart is the statement of Thoenes (1963: 137), that the interest in "social free-floatingness" had disappeared "when one no longer occupied himself with the epistemological background out of which the free-floatingness acquired its rare value." It is noteworthy, because Mannheim did not only fix his hope on intellectuals in a naive way, as Gurvitch (1971: 4) charges, but because he clearly recognized the relationship between the intelligentsia and epistemological problems. There is the crux between his cultural sociology and his sociology of knowledge.

The intellectuals need to avoid two kinds of relativism in the sociology of knowledge and bring to light the truth of the object and the structure of an era. In the first pace they need to oppose the relativism of positivistically oriented practitioners of science; these see their research as value neutral; the normative insights which come to expression in various statements in various societies and cultures leave them indifferent. We cannot in the manner of Baum (1977: 23) decide here only for an "ethical relativism" for these scientists, but for a total relativism, specifically in the areas of politics, society, religion, culture, etc. In the second place the intellectuals need to defend themselves against historistic relativism. According to historicists, in every historical constellation criteria exist for truth and falsehood, good and evil, but these are dependent on social conditioning; they are not universal. This plurality of "truths" does not lead directly to the relativity of knowledge, but does imply it.

Mannheim desires to transcend the non-evaluative sociology of knowledge. He wishes to transcend relativism by means of relationism. Relativism emerges when one confronts the truth of socially-conditioned knowledge with criteria for absolute truth; relationism emerges when the truth of culturally-conditioned

234

knowledge is related to the dynamic criteria for truth (cf. Baum, 1977: 40). Dynamic criteria for truth are established with help from the internal structure of the dynamic historical-social constellation. Knowledge seems to be conditioned in two ways: by someone's social position and by the object.

Relativism is abolished with help from a conception of truth emerging from the dynamic synthesis, as a dynamic truth, related to the structure of the historical-social constellation, which at the same time is the only possibility for truth and the most nearly absolute.

Questions which remain unanswered and open: Is this truth convincing and clearly attainable? Who can attain it in a given constellation? Who determines its internal structure and the object concerned, especially the object of the sociology of culture? These tasks are reserved for the intelligentsia, who, moreover, until now have not been able to complete them. The double paradox mentioned above culminates in the paradox of the sociology of knwledge, between truth and relativity. My conclusion, consequently, is that Mannheim's sociological relationism indeed signifies victory when compared to the "ethical relativism" of the positivists and to historicistic relativism, but that principially it has not abolished relativity. True, in the dialectial process of science relativity is always posed anew in the framework of new theories, and within these systems relativity always returns again. For my final conclusion I refer to the last sections of Chapter XXI.

Chapter XIII

Studies in Knowledge-sociology

- *Empirical Studies*
- *Sociological Interpretation of Conservative Thought*
- *Sociological Interpretation of the Generation Gap*
- *Conclusions*
- *Transition to Part IV*

Empirical Studies

In the preceding chapter I have distinguished between Mannheim's philosophical sociology of knowledge and his empirical knowledge-sociology. On the basis of his structural analysis of epistemology, I called his sociology of knowledge a chiefly philosophical discipline. In the period from 1925 to 1933 we see, however, a development in the direction of knowledge-sociology. This discipline is defined as an empirical investigation for the reciprocal influences between thinking and knowing on the one hand and on the other the influence of the social, external phenomena.

In his publications in the field of the sociology of knowledge, knowledge-sociology is materially present. In 1927 and 1928 Mannheim published two studies in knowledge-sociology: "Das konserative Denken" ("Conservative Thought," 1927) and "Das Problem der Generationen" ("The Problem of the Generations," 1928). These are empirical studies which are based chiefly on investigations of the literature and which also contain a philosophical analysis of the problems concerned. In these philosophical analyses various distinctions return, concerning the sociology of knowledge, the interpretation of the *Weltanschauung*, ideology, and utopia.

In the period from 1925 to 1933 a few other socioloogical publications of Mannheim also appeared: among others, "Zur Problematik der Soziologie in Deutschland" ("Concerning the Problematics of Sociology in Germany," 1929) and *Die Gegenwartsaufgaben der Soziologie (The Contemporary Task of Sociology*, 1932). Along with other sociological publications, these will be discussed in Part IV.

Sociological Interpretation of Conservative Thought

As the academic essay to support his candidacy for academia in Heidelberg, Mannheim had used *Das Altkonservatismus: Ein Beitrag zur Soziologie des Wissens (Old Conservatism: A Contribution to the Sociology of Knowing)*. In 1927 it appeared in a substantially reduced form: "Das konservative Denken: Soziologische Beiträge zum Werden des politisch-historischen Denkens in

Deutschland" ("Conservative Thought: Sociological Contributions to the Becoming of Political and Historical Thought in Germany"). The complete German text appeared in 1984 and an English translation in 1986 (CNSM).

Mannheim calls conservatism a style of thought. In former chapters it was already pointed out that one cannot bring a mode of thought into a *direct* relationship with the interests of a social class. It is anchored deeply in a system of *Weltanschauung*, and a *Weltanschauung* is to be divided into *Weltwollungen*, "world aspirations" or "world strivings," of which *Denkwollungen*, "thought aspirations" or "thought strivings" are sub-categories. A style of thought belongs to a particular psychological stratification, which in its "world aspiration" and in its "thought aspiration" is bound to both a particular *Weltanschauung* and to a specific social stratum.

Conservatism, with its own style of thought as a characteristic political and intellectual current is, according to Mannheim, a modern phenomeon. For a sharp sociological investigation we must distinguish it from traditionalism. Traditionalism, for Mannheim, means a pre-theoretical "formal psychological characteristic of every individual's mind," which is oriented to the time of grandparents and which is inhospitable to social renewal. Mannheim names it a common human possession, which expresses itself in holding fast to that which has already gone by (KD: 94, 95).

Conservative thought, by contrast, is "conscious, reflective thought," about an "objective, intellectual, structural context." It is not to be characterized as reactionary in a purely formal sense, but rather as oriented toward the socio-historical context. Conservatism, as a "structural context," is a whole "of spiritual and intellectual content." One acts conservatively to the extent that one acts and thinks in agreement with this typical structural context and acts and thinks within the framework of a dynamic, historical-social constellation. As such, conservative thought is oriented toward a context of meaning which changes from time to time. This all implies that traditionalism has no history, because it is by definition a reactionary attitude while conservatism can be comprehended *historically* and *sociologically*, because it refers to a particular social and historical situation (KD: 97, 98). Only after a sociological analysis of the structure of the socio-historical context which makes the phenomenon capable of being labled *conservative*, can the term be explained in its specific historical significance.

Mannheim distinguishes three phases in his analysis. The first phase concerns the sociological description of the history of ideas and concepts. He describes the central place which political ideas occupied in the intellectual life of the eighteenth and nineteenth centuries, particularly in Germany. Afterwards he describes why a worldview with conservative political ideas became so important after the French Revolution. In this phase of his research, conservatism is a manner of thinking about persons and society which are oriented to material and spiritual concerns. This manner of thought "at the same time, provides a particular orientation with a measure of effectiveness in the newly politicized and rationalized world. It thus clearly belongs to the new time, like its opponents" (Kettler, Meja, Stehr, 1983a; 1983b; 1984: Chapter II).

Mannheim names four sociological-historical factors which have led to the emergence of modern conservatism (KD: 100, 101). The first three he presented already in his description of the rise of the sociology of culture:

1. The *Western societies* have an *outspoken dynamic* character. The separate events in society have the tendency to orient themselves on central problems (the buildup of a nation's unity, participation of citizens in the government of the state, giving the state a place in the problematic concerning the world economy, solving the problem of the individual with regard to society; KD: 99).
2. The *dynamic character* of the social complex fulfills itself along the lines of *social differentiation*. That is: increasingly horizontal strata reacting to events in a more or less homogeneous way, some of which move social development forward, others hold it up, and still others defend turning back.
3. *The world of ideas splits up* and the lines of thought which come into existence thus run parallel to the social differentiation.

The fourth and new development:

4. The dissolution of the various *intellectual currents* along the line of social differentiation happened originally on the basis of *political* and later on the basis also of *economic* considerations. In summary: the basic cause for the emergence of conservative thought is the dynamic character of society which was caused by social differentiations; later the social strata involved various intellectual differentiations.

The second phase of his analysis concerns the morphological explication of the internal structure which the various and changing forms of conservatism have in common. This common element is the particular attitude which precedes the theoretical elaboration; it is an attitude which is rooted in concrete experiences of discrete events and which achieves its elaboration on a theoretical level in opposition to all rationalistically constructed norms.

One of the characteristics of conservatism Mannheim names is the clutching at "the immediate, the actual, the *concrete*" and practical (KD: 102). This implies an aversion to revolution and to the discussion of what is "possible" and "speculative." All discussion of the concrete presupposes a specific ontology. Conservatism always refers to immediate activity, to changing specific, practical matters and hardly troubles itself with the structure of the world. *Progressive* activity is *consciously oriented* on the *possible* and *transcends* the concrete givens, not to replace the concrete elements at hand with new concrete elements, but it thinks on the basis of *another systematic* beginning or another norm (KD: 109). *Conservative reformism* establishes itself with an eye on the improvement of a particular matter, but with the overriding purpose of improving the whole society of which the particular matter is only a part (KD: 103).

238

Progressive thinking is necessarily abstract.

Mannheim elucidates the difference between conservative and progressive thought by means of illustrations: the concentrations of ownership and freedom. I discuss only the differences in the conceptions of freedom, because freedom assumes such an important part in the later work of Mannheim. On the subject of freedom, Mannheim discusses revolutionary liberalism and romantic conservatism.

Revolutionary liberalism means by freedom in the field of economics the liberation of the individual from every bondage to the state or to a corporation; in the field of politics, freedom means being just to a person's desires and to what that person considers fair. This conception of freedom is only to be understood on the basis of the assumption of the political sameness of all people, and no empirical given affects this equality. This liberalism does not plead for a freedom and equality in all spheres of life any more than does romantic conservatism; it only pleads for freedom in the spheres of economics and politics.

Romantic conservatives regard the discussion of freedom and equality as a judgment about a factual situation; they need to work out their concept of freedom with greater care. They handle a qualitative concept of freedom. They attack the revolutionary concept of equality which lies behind the concept of freedom. They declare as evidence that people are not equal in talent or in other personal qualities.

The revolutionary liberal thinks from the perspective of the possible, the abstract, and places the freedom of the individual in the framework that all people ought to be given the same opportunities. The romantic conservative thinker sees freedom as limited to political freedom and speaks of the "individual law of growth," in which every person finds his own possibilities and limitatons. The qualitatively different freedoms are interpreted in such a way in conservative thought that they are imbedded in a whole which stands above them. Still, no tension exists between the qualitative freedoms and the totality. Freedom becomes subjectivized, while all external social relationships are subordinated to the principle of order and discipline. Between both, the subjectivized freedom and the disciplined social relationships, according to Mannheim (KD: 107), exists a "pre-established harmony," guaranteed either by God, or by national forces of society and the nation. In the historical school the concepts of "folk," "nation" and "the national spirit" is spoken of as a totality which protects the liberty of the individual or group from anarchistic situations. For Von Savigny and Von Ranke the qualitative or subjectivized freedom of the individual and of his position in society are brought into relationship with the nation, that is, the state; answering to their laws of growth, all individuals' freedoms should be realized.

In summary: *progressive* thought of revolutionary liberalism approached existence from the point of view of a "norm": the possible, the future, the utopia; romantic *conservative* thought, on the other hand, wants to understand the normative on the basis of the existing order. *Traditional* thought approaches the concrete present existence from a "backwards" look, on the basis of the past; it is an ideology. The conservative looks for a house out of which he can examine all that now exists; the progressive strivies for a map for the purpose of realizing intellectually connections not seen before. The conservative experiences the present as the last phase of the past, the progressive as the beginning of the future (KD: 111, 112; cf. IU: 206-215).

The third phase concerns the analysis of the historical interwoveness of the interpretations of a "text" with the socio-cultural context; in this phase Mannheim combines the results of the first two phases and describes how a conservative style of thought emerges. In this connection he pays elaborate attention to Justus Möser (1720-1794), Adam Müller (1778-1829), Gustav Hugo (1764-1844), and Friedrich von Savigny (1779-1861) who combined – in different manners – the thought of the romantics with political ideas (cf. Loader, 1985: 86-91).

It is conspicuous that Mannheim in this phase points out social characteristics in conservative thought and in the later proletarian and socialistic thought. Both modes of thought see the substratum of history existing, not in individual people, but in sociological entities. The conservatives construe historic life out of "organic collectives" (family, extended family), while proletarian thought sees the substratum of society established by such entities as production relationships and social classes (KD: 92, 112, 113). In bourgeois thought he acknowledges an atomistic conception of society.

In summary: *conservative* thought is directed toward the past, to the extent that the past functions in the present; *bourgeois* thought, as the bearer of the contemporary time, is directed toward what is now becoming new; *proletarian* thought is directed toward the future and toward the present, to the extent that it can nourish the sprouting seeds of the future forms of society, which already exist in the present.

Conclusions
This study is knowledge-sociology is based on the insights of the philosophical sociology of knowledge, which only can be acquired by means of the detour of culture-sociology, the analysis of the *Weltanschauung*. In other words: the empirical investigation of conservative thought in a society is based on the epistemological insight of the social condition of thought; this epistemological insight is elaborated with help from the basic discipline of the social field of reality: sociology. The insight of the sociology of knowledge is dependent on the analysis of the *Weltanschauung*.

Mannheim faithfully follows the way that he outlined for himself. The *Weltanschauung* in each of the various social strata and classes is not ony bound to this social entity, but also to be distinguished from it; the *Weltanschauung* is

240

a-theoretical. Particularizations of the *Weltanschauung* are *Weltwollungen*, "world strivings," which again are particularized into *Denkwollungen*, "thought strivings," and styles of thought. The grouping which is bound in a particular *Weltwollen* and which at the same time has a particular style of thought, he calls a *geistige Schicht*, "an intellectual stratum"; these intellectual strata run through all relationships within and between classes. By his method Mannheim comes to establish a correlation between particular forms of conservative thought and particular groups, but his explanation of this correlation is weak. Abercrombie and Longhurst state this correctly (1983: 11) and they continue thus: "We know that conservatism appealed to the nobility and intellectuals because it opposed the categories of bourgeois rationalism, but the further question, 'why those ideas and not some other oppositional set' is left largely unanswered."

The determination of the "world strivings" (*Weltwollen*) and the progressive or conservative style of thought of a particular stratum is totally dependent on the analysis of the structure of the historical-social constellation. By way of the cultural-sociological analysis of the *Weltanschauung*, the study of the philosophical sociology of knowledge, and the study of knowledge-sociology, Mannheim actually desires to arrive at "a morphology of styles of thought" (KD: 408). He claims to abandon the "chain of problems" of knowledge-sociology alone. In his essay on conservative thought he has brought to light "only one group of problems from such a more extensive context of investigations and exhibited it as a contribution to solving them all together" (KD: 408; German edition; tr. s.w.).

Wolff calls Mannheim, in connection with this essay on conservative thought, both acutely sensitive and *blind*. He bases this last characterization on the fact that Mannheim only speaks of "the rationalized world and the depolitization of the philosophy of life, where, after all, in five years already there was Fascism." Wolff (1964: 52) states that there is no evidence of such blindness in the work of Horkheimer and Adorno. This criticism does not seem accurate nor fair. 1. Mannheim at the time of his first draft of the essay, when he entered academia (1926), did not yet have German citizenship. His Hungarian and Jewish connections brought about great difficulty in acquiring his citizenship. Should we wonder that Mannheim expressed himself so cautiously in his publication? 2. We characterized him as belonging to the "socially free-floating intelligentsia." We already spoke about his somewhat shy personality. He was characterized by modest political statements – also out of necessity (see point 1). Do these considerations and statements mean that Mannheim was "blind" to the dangers of Fascims? He was deeply shocked and preoccupied with the crisis of Western culture; it appears in his very earliest publications! His longing for a new synthesis of culture and his academic work for that synthesis stand central *all the way through his career*. Mannheim saw Fascism as a danger for the human being and for culture – beside still other dangers! His broad intellectual horizon, his insight into social processes, and his feeling for tendencies in culture brought him in 1935 to the publication of *Mensch und Gesellschaft im Zeitalter des Umbaus (Man and Society in an Age of Reconstruction)*. It is a book which during the decades since its publication always fascinates younger generations anew because of its sharpness of insight into scientific, social, and political problems.

The analysis above is based on Mannheim's article "Das Konservative Denken," (1927) and the English translation "Conservative Thought," which in some respects deviates from the German. These articles contain approximately half of the original text of Mannheim's essay submitted to support his candidacy in academia: *Das Altkonservatismus (The Old Conservatism*, 1926), which after the death of Paul Kecskemeti in 1980 was found in his archives. After the completion of the manuscript of this book on Mannheim, I took note of the complete text of this essay on "Old Conservatism." Because I, alas, could only insert isolated supplementary notes into my manuscript, I refer to the complete text by Mannheim (CNSM). My analysis in this chapter is too restricted. Mannheim's complete text does not only contain an empirical study, but is, to a significant degree, a philosophical and cultural-sociological study. It is strongly oriented toward Hegel and builds forward on the basis of his cultural-sociological essays, which, just like Mannheim's essay on "Old Conservatism," were also published posthumously (ST). Also it seems from the complete text that Mannheim describes the political element as a "crystalization point" of ideologies, because they have a strong relationship to social and political processes. At the same time he describes the sytematic connection between a *Weltanschauung* totality and a political theory. It is not fair to regard Mannheim's essay as only an example of a study in knowledge-sociology. It also allows a view of which cultural and intellectual currents and their opposites lie at the basis of contemporary social currents and conflicts. He wants to let it be seen that the forming of concepts and methods of obtaining knowledge and strategies in the cultural and social sciences – all these are opposed to the natural sciences with their abstract logical systemization. He places on one line the thought in the natural sciences, capitalism, the modern forms of the state, and other processes of social rationalization (cf. Kettler, Meja, Stehr, 1983a; 1983b; 1984: Chapter II; cf. C. Loader, 1985: 78-94). The significance of this essay goes beyond the boundaries of the empirical knowledge-sociology. It also yields an historical-philosophical meaning. In this conection we must mention his references to Hegel, from whom he takes over the dialectical method for the purpose of defeating contrary theses by means of syntheses. At the same time he suggests that Hegel's philosophy culminates in the develolpment of conservative thought, while this philosophy is seen at the same time as a preparation for dynamic contemporary thought. His appeal to Hegel is – just as in his other writings – rather fragmentary, so that his exact relationship to this philosopher remains unclear.

Sociological Interpretation of the Generation Gap
Mannheim begins with a sketch of two approaches concerning this problem: the positivistic and the romantic-historical, a *quantitative* and a *qualitative* approach respectively. According to positivism, questions of life and death, longevity, the succession of generations, and other problems are all to be recorded in numbers; positivists strive for the formulation of a general law of the rhythm of the succession of the generations. This law would be based on the biological law of the restricted human life span. Mannheim is of the opinion that the problem of the generations is over-simplified in this way. The only problem remaining for positivists: finding the space of time in which one generation is replaced by another. Are there clear intervals in society characterized by a dynamic continuity (SIG: 278-280)?

242

The romantic-historical approach to the problem of generations is totally different. If positivists regard the problem in the framework of a linear conception of progress (with a mechanized concept of time as an objective standard), the romantic-historical way of looking, with the help of an "inward time of experience," seeks to understand the problem qualitatively. (Mannheim orients himself here on the thought of Dilthey, Heidegger, and others; SIG: 282, 283). An extreme example of this direction is W. Pinder, the art historian, who was chiefly interested in the "non-contemporaneity of the contemporary": a variety of generations are alive at the same time; because actual time should be experienced time, these various generations live in the same perid of time in qualitatively differently-experienced times. According to Pinder, every period of time has more dimensions because it always acquires its unfolding from various generations. A second point is that, according to Pinder, every generation has its own entelechy, its inborn feeling for life and for the world. This purposeful feeling and striving of a generation must, according to Pinder, replace discussion about the unity and discussion of the purposeful striving of a given period of time. According to Pinder, society is formed by an interplay of constant and temporal factors; to the first belong the cultural space, nation, race, family, individuality, and to the second, entelechies.

Mannheim finds it noteworthy that in romantic-historical philosophy no attention is granted to the socially-formed powers which lie between the two kinds of factors. It is precisely these social factors that have Mannheim's attention, by which he can approach the sociological study of the problem of the generations. In his sociological approach to the problem he poses, Mannheim calls on "formal sociology" for help. This sociology knows the difference between *statics*, which studies groups of people, and *dynamics*, which investigates the processes of change and the powers which lie at the basis of changes. On the boundary between these two lies the problem of the generations, and from that position Mannheim wants to take the step to an "applied historical sociology"; these three together form the whole field of sociological inquiry (SIG: 286-288).

According to Mannheim, a generation is not a social unit based on specific principles of group formation. Although specific groups can emerge within a generation, "it is possible in general to draw a distinction between generations as mere *collective facts* on the one hand and *concrete social groups* on the other" (SIG: 288). He compares a generation with a class, which is a particular stratum of people who feel related to each other in economic concerns and in economic and power structures of a particular society. By an individual or collective social-blimbing up or coming down, someone can leave a particular class. In general it holds, says Mannheim, that we find ourselves *in* a class and *in* a generation, quite apart from the consciousness which one *can* have of classes and generations other than one's own. Just as with a class, a generation is a social entity. As a social entity it has a negative tendency, in this sense, that it rules out a number of ways of doing and experiencing for an individual, and a positive tendency, in that it provides ways of doing and experiencing available in no other generation. These tendencies are to be worked out by sociology and to be explained in the context of the historical-social constellation. A generation is a particular "course of years" in this constellation. If the characteristics of a class are determined by socio-economic conditions, the charateristics of a generation are determined by the natural data of experiencing and thinking which arise from the change from one generation to the next, and which are conferred to its members (292).

Mannheim then names five structural characteristics of the phenomenon of generations:

1. As a result of the succession of generations, a continual starting out by new *bearers of culture* exists. Continually, new people acquire access to the cultural products already developed.
2. The continual leaving of earlier bearers of culture; this promotes the process of forgetting in a society, which is just as necessary as continually remembering.
3. *Paricipation* in a restricted part of the historical process. The previous points form a context for the rejuvenation of society. Participation in generations makes the stratification of generations visible; various generations take part in the same social totality. Not the various points in time of birth and being young, mature, and old which flow forth from the time of birth – these do not constitute the stratification of generations in society, but rather the possibility which arises from it for people of different ages to paticipate in the same social sectors, although they experience and go through this participation in very different ways.
4. The necessity of *continual transfer* of inherited cultural goods. The essence of this transfer is the new generation's "letting it grow" within them; this generation is, in fact, barely present in the participation in society when its members are seventeen; that is when they can formulate data "in questions," when they have become reflective. They come to stand closer to the actual problematics of their time as they mature, and can attach themselves to causes militantly. Because the older generations become rigid in their earlier "new" orientation, a tension exists in the transfer of culture.
5. A *continual reciprocal action* between the generations, in which the contradictions do not exist between the youngest and the oldest generations; they influence each other most. The contradictions exist primarily between the youngest and the middle generation and attitude toward life.

The stratification or "layering" of generations needs to be distinguished form both the "generational context" and the "generational unit." The stratification of generations only means that people of approximately the same age, who participate in the same events of the day, acquire the possibility for a similar direction of life. Whether this possibility becomes an actuality depends on other factors. The "generational context" is one phase further than the stratification of the generations; in the "generational context" the mentioned possibility is realized. A process of forming the generations has begun by which a "community of common fate" emerges on the basis of a conscious accepting of the problems of one's time or a conscious blocking out of them. The "generational context" can grow into a "generational unit," if this "context" is coupled with group-forming tendencies. So the young romantic conservatives and the young liberal-nationalists of the nineteenth century could belong to the same "generational context" and at the same time to different "generational units," who work through the vicissitudes of their time in totally different ways (SIG: 292-304; cf. P. Smits, 1969: 13-35)

Characteristic of a "generational unit" is the relatedness in *content of consciousness*: this is sociologically relevant, because it has a socializing function. To grow into a collective entity means not necessarily to judge the way that collective entity judges, but to be able to see things by the light with which that collective entity sees them. That is, one takes into oneself the basic intentions and principles of formation of the group and thereby binds oneself to that "striving for the collective entity." That the *basic intentions* and *organizational principles* have a power to bind people together is the result of the fact that, to a greater or lesser degree, it is an adequate expression of one generation; that is, it gives form to the typical *experiences* of the "members" of one generation. A class-ideology is such a basic intention. We could also, no doubt, speak about a generational ideology.

The most important matter in this connection, according to Mannheim (SIG: 309), is that not every generation should bring a new impulse for a new "collective" or for a new "basic intention" to expression. If this does happen, there can be talk of a "realization of potentialities" inherent in the location of the generation. The realization of these potentialities hangs together with the social dynamic; it can particularly crystalize in a period of rapid social, political, and intellectual changes. Then a new style of generation or a new striving for a goal is given form by its members, sometimes consciously, sometimes unconsciously and intuitively. In contrast to dynamic societies, in stable societies "generational units" do not arise with new strivings toward a purpose.

In his study of the problem of the generations, Mannheim wants to avoid every monistic method of explanation: economic, biological racist, folkloristic, etc. He wants to see the phenomenon of generations in the framework of the structure of an epoch, and the polarities of form-giving causes of groups/strata which emerge in this phase. Thus, in the nineteenth century the liberal and later the proletariat-socialist movements stood over against the conservative-traditional movement; a dynamic relationship of tension existed between the opposite groups, oriented on each other and in conflict with each other about the same intellectual and social problems of the time. It is to be understood from the structure of the epoch; the currents produce various "basic intentions," which, superceding the ordinary change of generations, are always present as enduring (although also transforming) intentions in an historical-social constellation; the new "generational unit" transforms these enduring intentions into its own form-giving causes. These form-giving causes of the generations, therefore, belong to specific currents in the time, and these causes can strengthen these currents and make them more precise. At the foundation of this study of the generations, naturally, lies the study of the historical-social constellation in which generations exist; according to Mannheim (319, 320), this formal sociological study can contribute much to the explanation of relevant structural elements.

In this connection I now point out an essay Mannheim published fifteen years after this study about generations, the generational-sociological essay "The Problem of Youth in Modern Society," published in his *Diagnosis of Our Time* (1942). His sociological insights have not changed significantly. He had then lived in London for ten years already, and he wrote about his outlook on youth against the background of English democracy, which, from his point of view, was threatened in its functioning. He lays particular emphasis on the life-force of the youth, which, according to him, must be utilized in English democracy. In static societies the older people enjoy great respect and the powers of the young go unused; child-rearing and education are directed toward the transfer of the traditions of the existing social order. In dynamic societies it is an art to utilize the present reserves of self-renewing life-force. Youth still has no social concerns, and it is available for new initiatives. It depends on the structure of the society, however, in which way this renewing power will be used (DT: 32-37). He sees the England of his day as an antiquated democracy. Although the time was dynamic, traditions had a very strong life and governed child-rearing and education. The danger was great that the youth would remain an unused social potential. Moreover, a positive evaluation of youth as the creative generation is not sufficent. This insight must be coupled with a conviction which knows in which direction it wants to stimulate the society. The striving for "planning for freedom" in society, and ideal which he propagates, could lead, with the help of the youth, to a higher form of democracy (ST: 37-40).

According to Wohl (1980: 80), Mannheim's approach was a considerable step forward, compared with the theories of the generations which were current at the time. Mannheim made no attempt in his essays to apply his distinctions to an analysis of the generations in constant friction with each other in the Weimar Republic. The turbulent period after World War I in Germany created a generation which was too old to participate actively in political and social events, another generation which was too young to fight but which had experienced the events both after and during the war, and still another generation which had not experienced the war and which knew the events only by word of mouth. Each of these generations had its own consciousness and its own particular characteristics. That is how Mannheim's theory can explain that the veterans of the war, returning from the front, could play no decisive role in the politics of the Weimar Republic – as many had expected. In no way can there be a discussion of "the" war generation. Although the National-Socialists ascribed the victory of Hitler to what they called "the war generation," it can only be ascribed to a part of that generation (cf. Wohl, 1980: 80; Sorokin, 1941: 514, 515, 522).

Mannheim makes a distinction here between generation and class, but he also acknowledges parallels: just as for generations, he distinguishes class stratification, "class context," and the class unit. Wohl (1980: 81) concludes correctly that an implication of Mannheim's theory of the generations is that the attachment of people to a generation is more important than any other social attachment they have. Classes have particular material concerns, but, by contrast, generations have the values of the *Zeitgeist* (the spirit of the time). That is why class-determined thinking is called ideological in Mannheim's interpretation.

In Mannheim's thought, yet again, there is a new and striking tension to notice. We saw that he strives to transcend class-determined thought by means of the thought of a "socially, relatively free-floating intelligentsia." How much the more shall we expect and demand of this thought, relatively free from social constraints, that it transcend the thought constrained by the generations, generations influencing thought even more strongly than to the classes? Mannheim in the second and third decades of this century belonged to a young generation; suffering from the problems of his time, he called the intellectuals for help for the purpose of letting them lead the way out of the crisis of culture and to work for a cultural renewal – a renewal of culture and a restructuring of society for which he, as spokesman for his *generational unit*, longed.

Conclusions

In the study about the generations as a sociological phenomenon it occurs to one that Mannheim does not begin with the analysis of the *Weltanschauung* by means of the sociology of culture, but places the problem in the framework of *formal sociology* (of which Simmel is a representative). On the boundary between statics and dynamics he places the problem of the generations. That is, between the *stratification of the generations* on the one hand and the *enduring basic intentions* of various currents which are present in every socio-historical constellation on the other hand. The generational context is determined by the bondedness of a generation's experiencing "a common fate" in a particular time. By that "common fate" we must understand the political and social events, as well as the polarity of a variety of intellectual currents. Members of generations take part in these currents and bring to expression the basic intentions, mentioned above, in their own generation's entelechy, that is, in its form-giving striving for a purpose. They work out their participation in the fate and in the intellectual currents in a variety of ways, by which differentiated "generational units" emerge.

We already declared the tendency to be present in Mannheim's thought: from a cultural-sociological analysis of the *Weltanschauung* to formal sociology. The author himself gives no explanation of this. We can only give a provisional answer, in anticipation of a closer study of Mannheim's sociological writings. The provisional answer is comparatively simple. In his essay about conservative thought the author referred to typical categories of thought, styles of thought, and intellectual strivings *(Denkwollungen)* as subdivisions of world strivings *(Weltwollungen)*, which in their turn form the various *Weltanschauungen*.

In all of this he wanted to break through the Marxists'' highly schematicized thought about society. Generations as a sociological problem concerns not only or pimarily the *kind of thought*, but a unique social reality as such. His intention is to explain sociologically a particular social stratum in a dynamic society. He strives in this for a synthesis of social psychology and social morphology, which makes it possible to understand and to explain the historical-social constellation in its differentatedness and context. The distinction between statics and dynamics from "formal sociology" is *not ony useful* for studying the problem of the generations. He establishes at the same time that *statics, dynamics*, and *applied historical sociology* form the entire field of sociological research. What significance this pronouncement has concerning the synthesis between two very different approaches – formal sociology and historical sociology – will come up again in Chapter XIV (SIG: 287, 288).

Transition to Part IV

In Part II, I described a development in Mannheim's thought from idealism to realism. His realism was characterized as transcendental. This transcendental realism receives a more careful elaboration in his essay on historicism. In historicism two lines are visible: 1. historicism conceived as a continuous stream of becoming and 2. historicism conceived as a continual becoming, in which *discrete phases* of culture are to be distinguished. The essence of historicism, according to Mannheim, is grasped if one knows how to distinguish the various periods of culture from each other and studies the internal structure of these periods separately, and also studies the structure which lies at the base of the processes of change from one period to the other.

In Part III sociological historicism received an epistemological and cultural-philosophical working out. A sociological study of an historical-social constellation serves to clarify the relationship between thinking/knowing on the one hand and social reality on the other. Questions which refer to the ideological and utopian thought and the "socially, relatively free-floating intelligentsia" flow forth from these studies and discharge into cultural-philosophical questions concerning a new cultural synthesis.

We established that Mannheim also in his second phase was still primarily philosophically involved, that is, preoccupied with epistemology. Although it does rely heavily on sociology, his elaboration of a particular epistemology, the sociology of knowledge, is central. Many questions remain unanswered in this

248

part, among others these: concerning the nature of the object of sociology and the other social sciences; concerning the direction of culture and of the new cultural synthesis; concerning the specific tasks of the intelligentsia in connection with the cultural synthesis; concerning an analysis of the structure of meaning of the historical-social constellation; concerning the necessary changes which people must bring about for the purpose of succeeding at the new synthesis of culture; and, consequently, questions concerning anthropology and ethics.

These questions were all actually locked up in the problematics which he cut into in "Soul and Culture," and they are also present in later publications, most often implicitly, but sometimes explicitly. In the answering of these questions lies the point of Mannheim's thinking about humanity, society and culture. In spite of the enriching insights which Mannheim offers in his philosophical sociology of knowledge and which have found a greater elaboration in a more empirical, more specialized knowledge-sociology – in spite of all that, his sociology of knowledge, as already was demonstrated earlier, can not be seen independently from a philosophy of culture.

Part II shows us the image of a young intellectual, shocked by the cultural crisis of the West, turned aside from its purpose by totalitarian regimes, and this young intellectual looks for a way of his own in other societies and in the world of scholarship. In sociological historicism he found this way. In Part III this way has been described but also this part looks in many respects like no more than a preparatory phase for the problems which will dominate the third phase of Mannheim's life, the period from 1933 to 1947 in London.

PART IV: Sociology, Social Ethics, and the
Reconstruction of Society

Chapter XIV

Mannheim as Orchestrator of the Social Sciences

Introduction

In this fourth part I discuss chiefly Mannheim's publications written during his residency in England, thus, after 1933. The heart of this portion of the study lies in his view of society as he worked this out in *Man and Society in an Age of Reconstruction, Diagnosis of our Time*, and in works published posthumously. An analysis of his description of the field of sociology and the various differentiations which particularly concerned him precedes the discussion of these works; this is because of the fact that the knowledge of sociology and its various differentiations forms the sub-structure for his view of society. One of these differentiations is the sociology of education. A year before his death he became professor in this branch of sociology, which already in the thirties and early forties had been his concerns. As will be evident, education occupies a fundamental place in his view of society. Had he lived longer, we would have been able to expect interesting publications in this field because his intellectual and spiritual development had not yet reached a plateau. To hear it from Ernest Manheim:

> Quite the contrary, the end came at the beginning of what was in the nature of a new period in his life, entered with the accustomed burst of mental energy which characterized his career as a sociologist. (1947: 471)

In Chapter III, I already pointed out that Mannheim was a thinker influenced by the domain of German culture. Although after 1933 he made an intensive and elaborate study of English and American sociologists and social-psychologists, and although he worked through their ideas, he had some trouble with this reorientation. To judge him by applying the English and American categories

253

of thought (in case these exist) does not do justice to his independence and the power of his thought. Shils praises this independence:

> Karl Mannheim was a good European. (...) He was even more, a prefiguration of that type of citizen of the world which mankind must produce in increasing numbers if its greatness and its dignity are not to disappear. (1947: 196)

The Intellectual Milieu in England

Compared with the practice and development of sociology in Germany, France, and the United States, this discipline led a shabby life during the first decades of the twentieth century in England. Germany had produced sociologists with international reputations: Tönnies, Simmel, Von Wiese, Max and Alfred Weber, Vierkandt, Oppenheimer, Spann, Freyer and Sombart. In France there were De Roberty, Fouillée, Durkheim, Tarde, Le Bon, Halbwachs, Bouglé, Mauss, Lévy-Bruhl, all with international reputations. In the United States this was true for Ward, Giddings, Sumner, Small, Ross and Cooley. England had produced Herbert Spencer (1820-1903) as a classical sociologist. With his *Principles of Sociology* (2 volumes) and *The Study of Sociology* he had accomplished a great work in the field of sociology, but he had formed no school.

English society, with its tradition and its relatively stable character, offered no fertile soil for sociology. The solutions for social problems were often sought in applying traditions and customs. A structural grip on the social problems which affected the foundations of social order was seldom, if ever, brought up for discussion.

Not sociology, but other social disciplines were pursued with great industry: history, economics, psychology, and ethics. The highest priority for an Englishman was to direct his attention to ad hoc problems of practical politics. As Mannheim (DT: 39) says:

> If one comes from the Continent, one of the striking facts about this country [England] is the peculiar depreciation of theory and general ideas. (...) We English dislike principles, abstract thought, and ideas. We prefer to muddle through. We dislike theory. We are inarticulate and wish to be so.

Still, in the twentieth century England did produce a few leading sociologists. One of the most important was L.T. Hobhouse, who from 1907 to 1929 was a professor at the London School of Economics and Political Science. Also the successor to Hobhouse, Morris Ginsberg, who brought Mannheim to London, was an important sociologist and, like Mannheim, was interested in the interdependence of social processes and of disciplines.

Although Mannheim as an academic, particularly as a sociologist, stood in the shadow of Simmel and Max Weber, after his arrival in England he was one of the most important sociologists in that land during the first half of the twentieth century. He developed himself into a sociologist with an international reputation. This does not mean that he found no inspiration in the works of and in conversation with all kinds of English scholars. To the contrary. He was much interested in the psychological publications of Professor Clarke, from the Institute of Education of the University of London. He also participated in discussions with colleagues, literati, and politicians. Mannheim was forty at the time of his arrival in London. He was a scholar who had undergone his apprenticeship and was already formed. The most important academic influences exerted on him in England were, with respect to philosophy, pragmatism, and with respect to his specialized science, the influence of American social psychology and sociology. According to his student W.A.C. Stewart (1957: xv-xix; 1967: 29), he was particularly influenced by James, Dewey, Watson, G.H. Mead, Cooley, and W.I. Thomas. He valued the work of these American social philosophers, psychologists, and sociologists, because they inspired him with regard to such problems as the relationship between individuals and institutions (or society) and possibilities for change in both directions. In general he was critical about American sociology, which seemed to him to lack historical orientation and thought too little in terms of structural processes, and for that reason remained stuck in an isolated empiricism and in an ad hoc sociology (Coser, 1971: 456).

I this connection I do not go into all kinds of critical questions which have already often been asked concerning the theories of the sociologists and social-psychologists mentioned above. The issue here is only mentioning those theories which Mannheim in various respects acknowledges as fruitful, which he quoted with agreement, and which he worked into his own theories.

In conclusion, Mannheim's settling in England meant no break with his past. His thought acquired new impulses, new topics drew his attention, and the perspective of his thought became more profound; topics already discussed – such as historicism, the sociology of knowledge, and the functions of the intelligentsia – remained relevant and received a new elaboration during his English period. He is sometimes said to have abandoned the sociology of knowledge (Coser, 1971: 437) and to have seen no further task reserved for the "socially, relatively free-floating intelligentsia" (Remmling, 1961: 27), but it will be shown that these are untrue interpretations.

The Field of Sociology
To describe the object of sociology, Mannheim makes a distinction between maximum and minimum definition. Under the maximum definition he counts all the problems which, in one way or another, fall under the rubric of sociology. The minimum definition determines what in the most compact sense must be regarded as sociology's object. With this distinction he wants to demonstrate a particular principle, an underlying bonding between sociologists, and at the same time a maximum freedom in research and teaching. Mannheim does not choose for one of the two; to the contrary, they belong to each other. A great

danger which threatens sociology is this, that the maximum and minimum definitions are presented as a choice. In this choice the danger is for sociology to become either a boundless study of all the world, or a crabbed dogmatism. The distinction between the maximum and minimum definition of sociology can, according to Mannheim, also be named as follows: sociology is both a "basic discipline," the foundation for all other social disciplines, and an academic discipline on its own, a "specialized discipline" (GAS: 2-6; SS: 1).

In formulating the object of sociology as a specialized discipline raises these issues: 1. *processes* (conflict, socialization, competition, social distance); 2. *relationships*, which become crystallized on the basis of the processes (antagonistic as well as solid relationships; for instance, adversary as well as friendship and neighbourly relationships), and 3. *complicated forms of society* (family, extended family, positions, classes, states, etc.).

Mannheim divides the object of sociology, as briefly described above, into two parts: *statics* and *dynamics* (PS: 206, 207). To statics belongs the *systemization of general sociology*, which studies the fundamental social factors and social mechanism which are operative in the structure of every society, which are responsible for the continuous reproduction of social processes, and for the structural balance in a society (social contacts, individualization, isolation, socialization, cooperation, division of labor and integration). It concerns the minimum concept of sociology. It abandons the historically variable formations, and distills the constant and irreducible principles, and abstracts them from the social processes. At the same time to statics belongs *comparative sociology*, which studies the historically variable formation of social forms and processes; it attempts to formulate an elaborated and comparative typology of these forms and processes (marriage, family, child-rearing, justice, forms of government, etc.). *Comparative sociology* at the same time constitutes part of *historical sociology*, to which also *dynamics* belongs and to which historical sociology forms a transition. *Dynamics,* studies the antagonistic factors which cause changes in the structure of society. For that purpose it studies the interrelations between specific social phenomena and institutions in a specific socio-cultural context; to the study of this branch of sociology belong, among other elements, what are called the *principa media* (see Chapter XVI). *Dynamics* presupposes knowledge of systematic (or general) and of comparative sociology (SS: 2; cf. SSS: 218-224). That is why Mannheim devoted so much attention to systematic sociology, for the purpose of being able to study dynamics.

Comparative sociology, which depends on elaborate empirical-sociological studies, was not studied systematically by Mannheim. It is not totally absent, but only comes to expression in citing instances. That is why, in connection with the division of labor in Western society in the twentieth century, he describes that phenomenon in terms of primitive tribes and old agrarian milieus. The conceptions above can be summarized in the following scheme:

256

statics $\left\{\begin{array}{l}\text{1. systematic or general sociology}\\\text{2. comparative sociology}\\\text{3. dynamics}\end{array}\right.$ $\left.\begin{array}{l}\\\\\end{array}\right\}$ historical sociology

In sociological studies these three groups of approach need to be recognized. Through them Mannheim wants to conquer both an historical relativism and an historically meaningless and ad hoc empiricism in sociology (GAS: 10, 11; PS: 204-206).

Speaking about the distinction between statics and dynamics, Mannheim states in what follows (GS: 15) that relationships and groups are always formed in a particular cultural context with the spiritual factors which operate in it. This context forms just as crucially the field of sociology in its maximum definition, though not exclusively. At the same time it is the field of the study of other sciences, by which a cooperation develops between these sciences and sociology. And so the sociologists of academic disciplines develop, "the multiple-word sociologies": economic sociology, the sociology of law, the sociology of religion, the sociology of literature, the sociology of art, sociolinguistics, educational sociology, the sociology of knowledge.

We saw that the maximum concept of sociology is filled in by the sociologies differentiated according to other disciplines. The minimum concept refers to the sociological statement of the problem in the most fruitful sense, so that the problem is presented to sociology as an academic discipline, with its own field of research to maintain, while the maximum concept makes sociology the basic or central science of all the other social sicences. So Mannheim calls economics "a particular concretion of sociology" (SC: 52). As the basic science sociology strives for an integration of the results of the sciences (SS: 1). The most fundamental problems which come up for discussion in the academic disciplines are studied particularly by sociology, and in the various disciplines "the multiple-word sociologies" study "all the problems which belong to ultimate questions" (GAS: 16). And elsewhere: "It is absurd to expect that there can be any organic division of labor in the field of the social sciences without general sociology as the basic social science" (PS: 203).

We can summarize this conception of sociology in the following scheme:

1. Systematic sociology, following the minimum definition as an academic discipline.
2. Differentiated or multiple-word sociologies.
3. Sociology according to the maximum definition, as a basic science for all the social sciences.

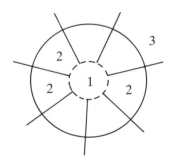

Chapter VII discussed Mannheim's distinctions between pure sociology, which studies the essence of social relationships; general sociology, which studies the existing forms of social relationships; and historical-dynamic sociology, which studies the empirical types of collectives in different socio-cultural era's. This division, though formulated in another way and with another emphasis, is not essentially different from his later division between systematic or general, comparative, and historical sociology. Elsewhere he calls historical sociology *structural* sociology (sc: 58), while still elsewhere he designates dynamic and static sociology together as structural sociology (ps: 206).

Mannheim's Nominalism: The Influence of Simmel

In Chapter XIII the observation was already made that Mannheim planned to combine the statics and the dynamics of formal sociology with applied historical sociology; together these form the whole field of sociology. In what is written above the underlying relationship between these three components may have become clear. Although other sociologists, especially Comte and Spencer, use the distinction between statics and dynamics, Mannheim does not refer to these scholars. Apparently he did not want to run the risk that his sociology would be interpreted on the evolutionary model. Even more noteworthy is Mannheim's reference to Simmel's "formal sociology" (see Chapter XIII). Probably Mannheim saw in Simmel's handling of the Kantian distinction between social forms and their content, a reason for speaking of statics and dynamics in formal sociology. Although Mannheim shared important philosophical insights made by Simmel (see Chapter IV), at the same time he criticized his conception of sociology (st: 101-110; see Chapter VIII). This criticism does not, however, take away that in his description of sociology (as mentioned, consisting in processes, relationships, and societal forms) he agrees with a basic idea of Simmel's sociology: his nominalistic approach, in which no value of reality is accorded to groups beyond the existence of their individual members. Mannheim characterizes social forms as constructions, concepts, and abstractions which are built up on the basis of interaction and communication (sc: 20; cf. E. Manheim, 1965:5).

> We accept the aim of the nominalists to comprehend the behavior and motivation of the persons, but we oppose their tendency to construct the individual as a socially detached and residual entity. We believe that the individual as such can be understood only through his participation in a multitude of groups. (sc: 110, cf. 69)

About his sociology Mannheim has this to say:

> It is still safe and feasible to outline with Simmel the scope of the field as the "forms of sociation." (sc: 18)

And elsewhere:

258

As already appeared from the description of systematic or general sociology (the minimum conception of this science), *social actions* form the basis concept in the "framework of behavior" construed by sociological theory (sc: 81).

Although Mannheim explicitly claims to look for a connection with Simmel and to have a nominalistic conception of sociology, at the same time he distances himself from nominalism. Mannheim's earlier publication "A Sociological Theory of Culture and its Knowability" treats this matter with clarity. All communications, knowledge by people, and experience arise from a "total relationship" which two or more people have together. This "total relationship" does not refer to one or more aspects of the lives of these people, but they are involved in it with the totality of their being. He characterizes this existential involvement with the concept of contagion or existential reception of "something out there" into consciousness. From this contagion what is called "conjunctive knowledge" emerges, which is not a universally valid knowledge, but which has only a conjunctive validity. They who hold this knowledge in common form a *we*. Without adopting Scheler's metaphysics, Mannheim claims to have borrowed this idea, basic to his sociology, from Scheler's *Zur Phaenomenlogie und Theorie der Sympathiegefühl und von Liebe und Hass (Concerning Phenomenology and the Theory of the Feeling of Sympathy, Love, and Hate*, 1913, st: 185-284, see Chapter IX). In what follows Mannheim makes clear that social forms which include a variety of people must be analyzed sociologically in two ways: 1. as a "framework" (Simmel), the sum of interpersonal relations, and 2. as a contextual whole, a totality. According to Mannheim, a community as a totality is not exactly the same as the sum of actions in the relationships between people. The community as a "framework" has an intellectual structure which posseses a supra-individual objectivity. As such, the community is not only a constellation of relationships, but a meaningful *spiritual totality*. This conception about societal forms as "spiritual contexts" brings Mannheim to take a critical position toward an "exaggerated theoretical nominalism." He especially criticizes Max Weber, who desires to construct the social form in such a way that it coincides with the "common subjective meaning" of individual people. In Mannheim's own words:

> Nominalism proceeds from the unjustifiable assumption that only the individual subject exists and that meaningful contextures and formations have being only to the extent that individual subjects think them or are somehow oriented toward them in a conscious manner. But this is just as much a prejudice determined by philosophical-systematic factors as is the opposite assertion that significancies are to be thought of as ontological realities, which is to say, that they are to be hypostasized in the manner of the doctrine of conceptual realism. (st: 224)

He marks out his own position clearly with regard to extreme nominalism and conceptual realism when he says this:

It is not to be doubted ... that ... all other more than subjective formations only exist in the form and to the degree that they are actualized by individuals. Nevertheless – and this opposes nominalism – the contexture of meaning (dynamic as such) is something which ranges above the individual consciousnesses taking part in it and which holds them together. Therefore, when the historian and the sociologist asks (with Ranke) "how it actually occurred," he is concerned with these supra-individual contextures and not with conceptions about them. (ST: 224)

What is of interest is the spiritual-systematic contexture ranging beyond the conceptions of the separate individuals, which resulted from the meaningful interplay of individual acts of consciousness at the time at which the ceremony took place. (ST: 225)

In other words: Mannheim does not want a reductionistic nominalism, which acknowledges the existence of societal forms only in ideas. He acknowledges the existence of communities as spiritual realities. A person cannot simply create knowledge about these realities out of himself, nor on the basis of a supra-temporal system of concepts, but on the basis of conjunctive experiences of the community concerned and the interaction based on it. This implies that the idea of a community does not determine the identity of the community concerned. Social forms as spiritual realities can undergo changes as the perceptions which concern the individual participants change; with the changes in perceptions which concern the individual participants, and with the changes in the spiritual realities themselves, the concepts concerned also change. Hence, the fact that Mannheim's nominalism changes from that of Weber and connects with that of Simmel.

From an historical point of view Mannheim says "that not the isolated individual but the community with its conjunctive experimental space and its language arose first" (ST: 206). With a reference to Durkheim, he continues thus: "The world is covered by collective representations, as Durkheim calls them, which exercise a compelling force over the members of the group" (ST: 206, cf. 207). The collective assumptions mentioned before are, according to Mannheim, not only contexts of experience, but, as spiritual realities, supra-individual objectivizations. That Durkheim, as a positivistic sociologist, regards these collective assumptions as things does not do justice, according to Mannheim, to their changeability; they are bound to the existence of concrete groups in a particular historical phase (ST: 208-213).

From the above, does there seem to be a contradiction in Mannheim's argument? On the one hand his societal forms and experimental contextures are based on contagion and conjunctive knowledge; on the other hand he calls societal forms supra-individual collectives. We must distinguish that the first approach concerns a genetic explanation of the process of obtaining knowledge form collectives, while the second approach concerns an historic analysis of the values of this genetic explanation. The historical approach does not imply a rejection of his nominalism; the supra-individual collectives are changeable constructions by members of the group. Sociologically his argument means that an interpretation of the actions based on the function of the group (in opposition to that based on the individual alone) is the only adequate one (SC: 47).

Although various interpreters (Floud, 1969; Shils, 1974) emphasize Marxist influences are definitely present (see Part III), it seems to me that the influence of Simmel is stronger. Also in what follows the influence of Simmel will be perceived as stronger.

Just as Durkheim, Mannheim occupied himself with the sociology of knowledge, of religion, and education. The conclusion of Floud (1959: 40ff; 1979: 72), that Durkheim and Mannheim, although they have very different approaches, nevertheless are in fundamental agreement, is untrue. Although agreement between them exists concerning the functions of collective assumptions, their sociological elaboration of this concept is fundamentally at odds. Mannheim, who in the basis of his historicism sees collectives as spiritual realities, rejects both Durkheim's view of these realities as things and also his positivistic orientation.

Functional and Causal Explanation

Mannheim can be seen as a poineer in the field of structural-functionalism (E. Manheim 1956; Stark, 1958: 261-263). Germinal ideas in his sociology are *structure* and *function*. Already in his sociology of knowledge he speaks about "the social structure as a whole, that is, the web of interacting social forces from which have arisen the various modes of observing and thinking" (IU: 45). The catch words in his sociological publications are these: *structural account, structural perspective, structural view, structural interpretation*, etc. (SC: 73-79). His structural method of interpreting social phenomena is not causal but functional. In a causal explanation, according to Mannheim, we look for the following:

> ...to *construe* an event through as many of its determinants as we are able to isolate. The final construct is largely an approximation of the actual event, and when the approximation is close enough for a given purpose we say the event is *explained*. (SC: 76)

According to him, a causal explanation says *why* something happens, but it gives no insight into the functioning of a system as a whole. He takes as an example the capitalistic system, which consists of interlocking operations, such as production, distribution, the price mechanism, the credit system, the competitive stimulation of demand, the recruitment of the labor force, and so forth (SC: 74). And he continues:

> The *causal* perspective ... makes it clear to us *why* the investor performs his role, but it is the functional scheme which shows us *how* he may perform successfully and *what* his scope of action is. The sum total of causal motivations does not explain the complete structure: in fact, not all actions for which inducements exist are necessary for the functioning of the capitalistic system. (SC: 73, 74)

He summarizes his view germinally as follows:

> ...the causal method reconstructs events in their temporal sequence, while the structural interest focuses on the patterns which operate in a functional system. The latter is the aim of sociology. (SC: 79)

This does not mean that he simply dismisses causal explanations. He regards these as important *within* the functional system. As such we must also understand his acknowledgement of Max Weber's method of interpretive understanding and explaining (SC: 75-77); he interprets the latter in the framework of the former.

Also in his view of planning, he speaks of structure, functions, interdependences, balance, etc. Mannheim does not call his sociology functionalistic and he does not speak about a functionalistic method. This is to be explained, because in his time the concept of *function* constituted part of the jargon of biology and other natural sciences. The source of his speaking about function and functional system lies in historicism and not in the biology which is regarded as one of the sources of American structural-functionalism (Lavine, 1965: 560-571). Although his sociology cannot be called structural-functional, because he did not offer an elaborated theory as such, his sociology does contain elements of such an approach.

Sociological Differentiations

Sociology has the central place in Mannheim's third period. He is not exclusively engaged in sociology, but explicitly engaged there just the same. That is, he does not study exclusively sociological material but is open to the help from other disciplines for the purpose of acquiring adequate insight into the social aspect of reality and into the development of sociology as an independent discipline. Above we already mentioned "the multiple-word sociologies," or the sociologies oriented toward other aspects of reality and toward other academic disciplines. Mannheim himself was occupied with several of those sociological differentiations. In Part III I devoted attention to his cultural-sociology and his sociology of knowledge. No I shall give a sketch of his social-psychology (which he conceived as a sociological differentiation), political and economic sociology, educational sociology, and social ethics. In the following chapters these various differentiations come up for discussion again in an integrated way, when his views on democracy, freedom, and the possibilities for human change are discussed.

Social Psychology

It is noteworthy that Mannheim counts psychic factors with the minimum concept of sociology. In a lecture delivered in September 1933 in Amersfoort, he introduced the concept *socio-analysis* and says (according to the account, ANTW: 39):

> This should be viewed as a complement to psychoanalysis. While the latter breaks the whole terrain of phenomena down into factors which it then studies, socio-analysis, in contrast, attempts to uncover the connection between phenomena and their context, the structure of the situation. Its objective is education as well as therapy, especially with regard to social pathologies. It seeks to achieve this by analysis and illumination of the situation. While psychoanalysis penetrates to the un- and sub-conscious, socio-analysis is concerned with the semi-conscious, where there are also processes under way which have great effect on the persons affected. (translation of Kettler, Meja, Stehr, 1984: 80, 81)

In what follows it will be shown that he describes socialization processes with the help of psychoanalytic concepts (as also Boris, 1971: 48-53, demonstrates), while in what follows also his socio-analysis will be evident. Erös and Stewart (1957: xiv) maintain that Mannheim's analysis is restricted to its time and, therefore, antiquated. It is antiquated in this sense, that he was no longer able to work through the studies of later authors. At the same time they take note of the fact that his social psychology must not only be studied for historical interest; it forms a chapter, a link in his enduring significant thought.

In speaking about the psychical equipment of a person, Mannheim does not record purely biological or purely psychological views. He uses these sciences only to the extent that they can clarify the facts of the formation of the person through society. He calls this flexibility a fundamental quality of a person (ss: 7). After 1920 a number of social psychologists let themselves be heard: Dewey, Znaniecki, and G.M. Williams, who made their scientific program on the basis of the following words of Dewey: "The instincts do not make the institutions; the institutions make the instincts" (quoted from ss: 11). Mannheim concludes that there are tendencies in social spychology "which come to be fixed by specific tasks presented by the changing situations" (ss: 12). "Institutions are nothing but forms of adjustments" (ss: 10). That is why he can follow up this statement by maintaining that in fundamentally changing situations, nothing is less advantageous than a rigid way of acting which does not adjust itself to the changing process. Because rapid change is a characteristic of our society, it is necessary to study the mechanism of changing behavior. One such mechanism is education. Tarde has described the social role of imitation: imitation as a conditioned reflex. It is a method which carries the cultural content of a society from generation to generation. Mannheim distinguishes this imitation as effectively conditioned stimuli from the imitation which is realized by people themselves and undertaken voluntarily, an imitation Mannheim himself approves (ss: 14).

In studying the relationship of the individual to society and particularly the capability for change in the individual, he seeks support from behaviorism, pragmatism, Marxism, and psychoanalysis. Although behaviorism, pragmatism, and Marxism can provide fruitful contributions to the study of adjustment

263

mechanisms, his own social-psychological approach to contemporary problems (like the situation in Nazi Germany, in Mussoloni's Italy, and in inadequately functioning democracies) is chiefly psychoanalytic.

According to Mannheim, a clear correlation exists between the disorganization of society (as a result of the process of rapid transformation) and the disorganization of the personality. In this connection it is noteworthy that Mannheim does not refer to Durkheim's study of loss of identity and suicide, a reference which would have been very plausible. Perhaps he was of the opinion that Durkheim's studies were too descriptive and analytical, while he at the same time wants to be occupied with therapy in his analysis. Hence he formulates as his central question the following:

> What is the contribution psychology can make to the solution of the problem of war of peaceful change? Is there anything in human nature which necessarily makes for war? If not, what is the process whereby a highly industrialized society becomes a martial state with a wholly different psychology? (...) Under what circumstances do people who were formerly striving for economic gains, for the raising of their standard of life, invert their scale of values in a relatively short time, and now seem to rank the honour, prestige, and glory of their country far higher than before? In short, why do people sometimes prefer guns and sometimes butter? And, finally, if such fundamental psychological changes do occur are they the ultimate causes of war or are they rather the effect of institutional maladjustments in society? (MS: 120)

One can also ask the question whether war is to be attributed to the agressiveness which is inherent in human nature. On the basis of specialized studies done by others, Mannheim concludes that there is nothing in human nature which makes war inevitable. People simply seem to be very pliable in relation to the social structures in which they find themselves. When the national or international social structures bring people into particular situations, then in some circumstances they counter agression with aggression, but in other circumstances they do not. Mannheim answers the questions about the attitudes and behavior of people always on the basis of the social structures. Hence, the fact that he advances the thesis that social psychology needs the help of sociology (MS: 123). Because, according to him, psychology leaves the question unanswered whether – and if so, when – a person is warlike and people-loving, and this question can be answered sociologically. He asks two sociological questions in this connection: 1. Have there been societies in history which produced peace-loving attitudes? and 2. Which reasons and which social mechanisms could change a peace-loving society into a warlike one? The first question he answers affirmatively. He names as examples "primitive" tribes and in the Western world the Netherlands as an example for him of the fact that a person and a society can live without war. (Apparently he intended the neutrality of the Netherlands at the time of World War I). But a warlike attitude within the whole pupulation can emerge as an example of "collective regression." What causes this "collective regression"? This can occur, according to him, on the basis of "a collective uncertainty or danger," which can lead to either a total or a partial disintegration of society (MS: 125). According to him, it is too simple to assert, however, that social insecurity can change human behavior. There are various forms of uncertainty and just as many ways of changing behavior. The uncertainty of nomadic peoples during times of drought or epidemics, by which they are forced to migrate, differs from uncertainty in modern Western societies. A symptom of social uncertainty which to a greater or lesser degree can lead to social dislocation, is, for instance, unemployment. The horror of increasing unemployment does not restrict itself only to a certain number of people who are without work; it means as well that these people lose their emotional balance, and this has results for the interaction and integration of every institution in which they associate. Although the manner of working through social uncertainty can be extermely varied at different social levels (the independently wealthy, entrepreneurs, unskilled workers, laborers, artists, students), still everywhere there is a loss of self-respect. Mannheim refers to the study by Lasswell, *World Politics and Personal Insecurity* (1935), which demonstrates that as self-respect is lost and previous wishes and impulses remain unfulfilled, the greater the probability that human energies seek release in aggression and move toward externalization of that aggression. People look for scapegoats, for example, Jews, and the agression expands to the frustrated people present in all social classes and strata (MS: 129).

A phase of social uncertainty is unorganized at the start, unaccountable, and coupled with a growing doubt concerning the soundness of institutions and traditional values; also, ideologies are exposed. If it expands massively, this situation becomes dangerous for a society. This means that the original expectations of thousands of people are disappointed and that no authority is acknowledged. A phase of general scepticism sets in, in which people have lost their orientation; that is, they have lost their symbols, assumptions, and ideals as fundamental and unifying means for communicating. The central question for this period, according to Mannheim: Which substitutes can be found for the purpose of metamorphosing uncertainty, which cannot be kept up, into certainties?

This process of transformation from an unorganized social uncertainty into an organized uncertainty occurs, according to Mannheim, in three phases. With the lack of purposes worthy of striving for, certain new symbols are used as substitute purposes. They must dispel the social uncertainty and anxiety and give people something visible that makes for unity: hammer and sickle, swastika, brown or black shirts, red flags, the outstretched arm, the balled fist, specific cries. As soon as these substitute purposes are integrated, one reaches the second phase, specifically, the utopian: the symbols become new driving forces for new forms of integration of groups. A person deliberately and openly opposes the relationships of the existing society. The symbols in this phase do not only serve as substitutes; they continue to work into society in this sense, that they bring along with them changes in personality and group-context. This phase passes into the third: the symbols become characteristics of the group which always continues to organize itself more strongly. The utopian phase passes over into a period in which this reorganized group can exert power in society and can attempt to realize its ideas. The unorganized uncertainty has made a place for an organized uncertainty; the causes of the uncertainty have not been taken away; the economic problems and the structural enemployment still exist. Examples of social and economic *substitute* purposes in national projects are these: unnecessary highways, work camps, rearmament, and others; at the same time people find scapegoats, who are pointed out as threatening to the realization of the designated projects. And thus a new, collective, substitute enthusiasm emerges.

In this society with an organized uncertainty, which suggests certainty, citizens lose their individuality and the leaders in the top of the organization assume a position of rulers of all. Their rational decisions are led and overruled by pure irrationality. If the tensions in the new social, economic, and political system threaten to assume domestically dangerous forms, the leaders can turn for refuge to a war. This can be waged in the most extremely rational way, but, just as the domestic search for scapegoats, this proceeds from irrational motives (ss: 23-28).

Mannheim is fully aware that he does not give a comprehensive analysis of the causes of war. He only sets out to give a sociological, social-psychological, and psychoanalytical interpretation. Sociologists must realize the importance of psychoanalysis and especially the process of the ego ideal. This ideal is indeed more important for the functioning of personality than are other patterns of behavior. "It offers a key to the way in which society, apart from the conditioning or encouragement of habits, can influence people" (ss: 25).

In this interpretation war is partially an unjust working out of psychical tendencies by means of particular institutions and partially a despairing flight of people into collective aggression when existing expectations fall away and feelings of general uncertainty arise. The great problem for sociologists is to find ways which can lead to the use of energies in a way that is constructive for the society. The manner of the use of human energies does not only depend on someone's individual character, but more on the processes which are operative in the society. These processes are studied by sociologists and can be influenced by means of social techniques. Nobody desires a war, and still everyone at some time expects a war, but war can be forestalled, says Mannheim, if we can summon the courage for a new way of thought which adequately applies to the situation in which we live; it must be a situationally-congruent manner of thought (ms: 129-143). Although the psychic factors figure in the minimum concept of sociology, and although by means of psychic factors such subjects as ideals, sublimations, projections, day dreams, rationalizations, and symbols are systematically treated, still, at the same time, the elaboration of these elements in social psychology belong to social dynamics.

Political and Economic Sociology

Already in the third chapter of *Ideology and Utopia* Mannheim had spoken of the political sociology which studies political behavior. He uses his broad background in sociology of knowledge to study the various forms of political-historical thought of the various political currents (for example, bureaucratic conservatism, conservative historicism, liberal-democratic bourgeois thought, socialistic-communistic thought, and fascist thought; IU: 104-130). He deems it unattainable to separate *Weltanschauung*, evaluations, concerns, and results of thought form each other; the task of political sociology is precisely to make clear the relationships between these factors. Because political sociology always remains bound to the dynamic practice of politics and, hence, establishes the problem of theory and practice as central, it is always involved in a process of becoming (IU: 102, 152, 153). As a sociologist of knowledge Mannheim is conscious that all political knowledge is fragmentary and that politics as a discipline and political sociology cannot be based on this partial knowledge. Also, political studies may not be construed as a "party science" (IU: 132). As a science it can only be realized if it can give a comprehensive view of the whole political sphere. that is why he pleads for a synthesis of the differing political viewpoints (IU: 134, 135). This synthetic thought was already, discussed in Chapter XII. There it seemed that this thought is necessary in order to realize a cultural synthesis and for answering the question about truth. Now Mannheim seems to elaborate this thinking about political sociology; this elaboration means that he "clarifies his attempt to place a 'science of politics' at the top of a hierarchy of all fields of knowledge" (Wagner, 1952: 306). Because political sociology strives for a dynamic synthesis, it belongs, according to Mannheim, to the social dynamics. Also in Mannheim's statics the state occupies an important place, because he regards this institution as "the frame-group in our epoch" (ss: 118), and he continues thus:

> The framework is the power organization which acquires the greatest control among existing groupings within a territory and is able to regulate the interrelations between all other fighting, competing or co-operating groups. The modern state has the power and claims the right to interfere more or less decisively in many of the relationships binding together all the other groups. (ss: 118)

The representatives of the state claim the right of intervention on the basis of the idea of legitimacy. This idea of legitimacy leads the activities of the members of the state, so long as they recognize the state. In a period of revolution the state does not exist as a frame-group with a foundational idea of legitimacy. The basis of the legitimacy can vary from state to state. It can be based on tradition, on existing laws, on popular votes, and usually on a combination of these factors. The state is the most comprehensive social group, in this sense, that, compared to other groups, it includes the most people and at the same time in the sense that it can interfere most generally and most intensively in the life of society. The state is an organization based on power which can and must establish order in the affairs of society – that is, in the totality of whatever is found within the boundaries of the state's jurisdiction: classes, strata, groups, social powers, and social processes. One of the processes of social change is the "reconstruction of society" along the lines of "planning for freedom." In the realization of this reconstruction the state and especially the planners of the official policy have an important function. We may conclude that the state forms, as a sociological category, a hinge between social statics and dynamics (ss: 103-122).

In his *Freedom, Power, and Democratic Planning*, Mannheim describes political sociology as that branch of science which describes

> ...the forms of co-ordination between all political groups prevailing in a given social structure, and the sociological problem, the relations between groups and their regulation, which can be hierarchical, federative, or co-ordinating in a democratic sense. (FPDP: 42)

This definition, he says, has two advantages: 1. political sociology can also grant attention to social powers; it does not direct itself narrowly in a traditional sense toward the state and the bureaucracy, and 2. the distinction between state and society, which he considers antiquated, is abandoned. He considers the distinction antiquated for the following reasons:
1. In the private sector, bureaucracies have developed which have just as much power as federal bureaucracies;
2. The distinction between chosen, appointed, and independent management personnel becomes more and more vague;
3. The distinction between the directors of private management and chosen or appointed leaders becomes more vague;
4. Many undertakings and organizations other than the state have public significance and are not strictly private matters;
5. The state increasingly becomes a partner in particular undertakings; this underscores the increasing vagueness between private and public concerns;
6. In bureaucracies, in government, and elsewhere a new personality type has emerged: a mixture of freedom for initiative and behavior by the rules for the purpose of thinking in terms of general concern.

In summary: "...in our modern world everything is political, the state is everywhere, and public responsibility is interwoven in the whole fabric of society" (FPDP: 43). In the framework of political sociology, he discusses the phenomenon of power in society, the structure of communistic and capitalistic societies, and the modern Western state as welfare state. That is why Mannheim's conception of political sociology comes up again for an expanded treatment in the following chapters, in which the topic of "planning for freedom" is treated, and that topic is nothing other than a political-sociological problem. Now already I point out that Mannheim speaks of the state as a sociological category; that means that the state is a social form which not only has structural characteristics, but which *ought to have* them. The institution is based on the principle of legitimacy and is more narrowly characterized as an organization of power in the service of the common good. This means that Mannheim places justice at the basis of the power of the government, as a means within the perspective of the common good.

Because political and economic power are very closely intertwined, economic sociology also occupies an important place in Mannheim's work (WE). Also economic sociology, according to Mannheim, belongs to social dynamics, which he does not discuss in a systematic way, but does bring up in a fragmentary elaboration in *Man and Society in an Age of Reconstruction*. Concerning economic sociology, he agrees with Marx; Mannheim, too, regards economic structures as ultimately important for the social (dis-)order and for the processes of change. Because Marxist theories of social change, according to Mannheim, are the most consistent and the most discussed, he takes it as his starting point for discussing social dynamics. By Marxist theories he means only the theories of Marx himself, who sharply analyzed the economic and technical factors in an industrial society, though, on the other hand, these Marxist theories exaggerate these factors, according to Mannheim. Following Marxist theory, he sees the production-factors as the cause for social change. In the area of these factors, changes and new inventions take place, which do not only alter the machinery, but especially the social, legal, and political relationships in society, to which specific forms of consciousness correspond. In this regard Mannheim warns against a deterministic interpretation of the superstructure by an economic-technical substructure. Instead of speaking of a dialectical relationship between substructure and superstructure, he speaks of a continuous relationship between the two. In his own words:

> It cannot be denied for instance that the legal organization – the property system for instance – varies with the changing economic structure, or that the political and other ideas people hold are somehow connected with the social context in which they live. (ss: 137)

The structure of the production-forces carries with it a specific social structure, which gives rise to tensions and sometimes to revolutionary outbursts. According to Marxist theories, only the proletariat, which has no concern for keeping the existing social order in its position, can cause the consciousness and insight to be awakened for the necessity of changes in the economic conditions of society. Mannheim is of the opinion that the analysis of technical and economic factors is important for the study of social change. But he wants to go further than Marx. Not only economic techniques, but military techniques also carry social changes along with them. He also points out the influence of social techniques, for instance, techniques for influencing human behavior: propaganda organizations, bureaucracies, management. Although in his opinion technological factors are important in the processes of social change, he at the same time establishes that technological factors can only be used in conformity with the human purposes concerning which agreement exists in the particular

269

cultural context. That is why it is necessary to acquire insight into the factors which must be used for the reconstruction of institutions which bring about injury and pain for people, and for strenthening those tendencies which favorably influence the quality of life. Sociale reconstruction means, for that reason, not the building of a totally new society, but the *strategic bending* of the existing social order in a desired direction (ss: 139).

Another point that Mannheim values in Marx's theory is this: that Marx construes society as a coherent structure. Just as Marx, Mannheim wants to replace the "piecemeal interpretation" of society with a reconstruction of the society as a whole. The serious deficiency of Marxist theory of social change and class conflict, however, is that it does not present its analysis as an hypothesis, but as a dogmatic proposition. Mannheim regards Marxists" approach inadequate first because its division of society into two classes is too simple; and second, Mannheim regards it unjust to declare that the social classes always stand in an antagonistic relationship to each other. Mannheim admits that originally Marx had an eye for middle classes which were crushed between the owners of the capital and the proletariat. In fact, these middle classes, according to Mannheim, have grown larger and larger. Marx was right in his opinion that the small entrepeneurs and small businessmen would have an increasingly difficult time, but new middle classes also were constituted, for instance technicians and "white-collar" groups. A theory which does not take account of these middle classes is misleading in its analysis of society. Although Mannheim acknowledges that tensions and conflicts exist between the classes, chiefly latent but here and there overt, he totally rejects Marx's pronouncement about a generalized class struggle and the inevitability of a revolution of the proletariat. He sees a peaceful and patient reconstruction as the only possible way, which in principle should lead to the solution of the most important problems in our society (ss: 136-146).

The Sociology of Education and Social Ethics
Mannheim wants in the first place to create "the scope for reflection" and in the second place to establish a contextual whole of facts and principles which make it possible to carry on education, both in school and elsewhere on as scientific a basis as possible. He is of the opinion that philosophical reflection on these two points is more necessary in our time than ever (ISE: 3).

The processes of change, which in the course of the twentieth century in Western societies have gone on with increasing complexity, make necessary a reflection on the nature, purpose, and methods of education. In our time we cannot be content with an education based on tradition. Education is a dynamic process, based on the adjustability of the human being to a changing society. That is why educational sociology belongs to social dynamics. That is why Mannheim states a central thought:

> ...we must bear in mind that education has to prepare members of a society to conform on the one hand and, if it is a democratic society, to have the opportunity and scope for individuality on the other. (ISE: 10)

In communist and fascist countries one knows exactly what to expect of education; in Western countries one only knows that one does not want to indoctrinate, but which ideals do we aim for? That is Mannheim's chief question (ISE: 8; FPDP: 1-6).

He distinguishes education from training, instruction, and learning. He regards *training* as drilling for purpose of becoming capable of greater achievements. He describes *instruction* as the passing on of information; the emphasis is on the content of the communication. *Learning* refers to the relationship between teacher and student. At the same time there is a continuum in learning: the material taught is understood and learned for the purpose of being able to work through new material. Also, the interest of the student in learning is presupposed. *Education*, according to Mannheim, has reference to the physical and mental bringing up of children; in two senses of the word it is a dynamic activity: 1. it is directed toward the development of a person in such a way that he adjusts to society and 2. it is directed toward the processes of change in a society (ISE: 12-15). The most important powers which play a role in education are the society and groups in which the children live. These collectives impose demands on the people who constitute them. That is why Clarke speaks about "an educative society." Because Mannheim directs himself particularly to the *sociology* of education, that is, because he invites attention to the relationship between education and the changing society, he sees that education in our time needs greater scope and greater profundity in three areas: 1. the *democratizing* which brings with it a spreading of responsibilities to greater numbers of people; 2. the *greater control of our environment*, which comes to expression in these ways among others: in the expansion of social services, in the media of mass communication, and in other social techniques with the help of which people can exert more firm control on society; 3. *the concern of the community*; education is not only provided by the school, but by the whole community. The school has a unique task in society, because it teaches children along the lines of play, to participate in social processes. Given the enormous differentiation in society in various groups and processes, and given the enormous variety among people in physical and psychical respects, in social background, in life-history, in talents – given all of these differences, great demands are placed upon education in the family, in the school, and elsewhere. That is why a great variety of educational and instructional possibilities is necessary. Experiments in the field of education and instruction are for that reason unavoidable. It is not surprising that Mannheim speaks about "education as groundwork." Knowledge of the processes of fundamental democratizing and gaining insight into those processes; the increasing interdependence of social, political, and technical processes; and the need for a Third Way characterized by "planning for freedom" – these elements belong at the very center of education. The issue is not to propagate an ideal of equality in education, which can only lead to a lowering of requirements, but an education which furthers creativity and which gives adequate form to *social maturity* (FPDP: 296-265).

Although liberals may think that the individual is the driving force of history and the source of all norms, others are of the opinion that society is the only important entity and that its controlling social powers are to be studied scientifically. The latter view characterizes Hegelianism and Marxism. Following Clarke, Mannheim calls the former approach "society-blind" (ISE: 47-48). With reference to education, liberals see it as a process of interaction between individuals which can easily be regarded as ends in themselves. The collectivist, with regard to education, directs his attention to the place of the individual and his function in society.

Mannheim rejects both approaches, which he sketches only in broad strokes, and pleads for "a third way" which integrates the valuable elements in both schemes (ISE: 48). Determining his position over against liberalism, he asserts that a person is not an abstract personality, but develops himself as "a social self in the society." Against collectivism he declares that the society is not a mechanism which only models the individual. For education, his third way, which he calls the *sociological approach*, means that "a progressive society" is dependent on a variety of personalities which acknowledge their responsibility with regard to society. It is clear that Mannheim means by a *progressive society* a society which demonstrates *moving forward* in realizing the planning for freedom.

Once more Mannheim repeats that the more we realize the educative power of society, to that extent we shall be compelled to revise and reconsider our conceptions of humanity. Not only is a great deal of our behavior open to social influence, but even our individuality, our personality, develops itself on the basis of this interaction (ISE: 49, 50). This conception presupposes the opinion that human nature is flexible. That is why it is of great importance that people in the West become conscious of the need to acquire clarity about ideas and "long-term aims" which lie at the basis of education. This clarity is dependent on the view which one has of human personality. Many of our conceptions of personality are, according to Mannheim, based on Plato's philosophy. According to this thinking, a person lives on two levels at once: 1. having access to the ideas, the philosophical person can, through the propelling power of eros, come to behold the Ideas, the "true reality." Compared to this world of the Ideas, the everyday experiences of a person are no more than "bubbles on the surface of a flowing stream," the stream being the everyday course of life; 2. the daily experiences form the second level of the existence of a person. Although there are important differences which exist between Christian and Platonic views of humanity, according to Mannheim, they are in agreement the following on this point: both views contain the ideas of the unity of the person and the supra-temporal character of the soul; Mannheim also says that in Christian doctrine one proceeds on the basis of a person's being a stranger on earth and heaven as his true home. In spite of his intellectual sophistication, Mannheim's presentation of Christianity remains a Platonized caricature (see Chapter XVIII).

Without devoting a further word to Plato's view on the society of his time or to the relationship of the Christian religion to manifestations of it in various views of society, Mannheim makes a transition to a sociological elaboration of everyday social life; he refers to the theories of G.H. Mead, Linton, Kardiner, and Dewey. They are representatives of theories about personality in which they merely give attention to the interaction between people and social environment. Especially G.H. Mead receives a great deal of attention. Mannheim analyzes Mead's theory about *self*, *I* and *me*, but not critically. He describes this theory only briefly and then concludes thus:

> The value of Mead's approach is that he underlines for us that the self is not given but emerges out of our social experience. Responsibility is not a quality with which we are born but emerges out of the chances we have had to learn, according to our degree of maturity, how to act responsibly, so that as time has passed we have been able to develop a concept of what it means. (ISE: 94)

Already earlier he had written (LSE: 92):

> Social maturity and responsibility depend on being able to take part in a number of human relationships while at the same time distilling out from these a certain generalized consistency and continuity of the kind of part which we want to play, the kind of person we want to be.

In any case, according to Mannheim, it is clear that the *self* for Mead is no metaphysical entity; it is not innate, but acquired progressively, built out of experiences of social processes in which it finds itself.

In this connection Mannheim poses a critical question. According to him, a person is conscious of himself not only as someone who has performed actions and has gained specific experiences, but also conscious of the fact that he will continue his actions in a way that cannot be predicted now. This consciousness of acting in the past, present and future, which concentrates itself in the self-identification, is, according to him, a worthy notion in Platonic, Christian, and other "idealistic" philosophies. For the "idealistic" thinker, the growth of the moral personality exists in the *individual* development of each person, in the improvement of the self-consciousness, and in the sharpening of his possibilities for reasoning. The idealist concentrates, according to Mannheim, on the individual person, but he says little about the method to achieve the improvement he demands. He does not occupy himself enough, or perhaps not at all, with the social-psychological theory on which Mead is so intent (ISE: 96, 97).

Mannheim says nothing negative about the Christian religion. He establishes that the sociologists cited by him, that is, the social psychologists, have a naturalistic approach to humanity and do not regard a supra-natural approach of either the Platonic or Christian sort necessary. Mannheim himself does not want to negate his relationship with idealistic philosophies and the Christian religion on the one hand, nor the theories of social psychology and sociology on the other. In the preceding passage we saw that, in connection with self-consciousness, he points out the value of idealistic philosophies and of the Christian religion. Representatives of these directions have not, however, worked out their points in terms of social science. I think that Mannheim regrets this fact, because he would like to expect a constructive contribution from that quarter. This problem is all the more fascinating when one remembers that he, from the end of the thirties on, had regular discussions with Christian thinkers in *The Moot*, and in his *Diagnosis of Our Time* calls for a more extensive contribution from Christians to make a further development of his social philosophy possible.

With the anaysis of Mannheim's vision on the minimum and maximum concept of sociology and with the elaboration of this last concept in sociological differentiations, the basis is laid for discussing his chief theme: *man and society in a period of reconstruction directed toward the planning for freedom*. Before the transition to this subject, I shall discuss in a digression his critique of American sociology.

Digression: Mannheim's Critique of American Sociology

In his discussion of *Methods in Social Science* (edited by Stuart A. Rice) Mannheim attempted a comparison between the German and the American style of practicing sociology in his time. He establishes that the issue here is about two types of sociology and about "different mental habits" (AM: 1985). Typical of American sociology, he says, is the direct involvement with the problems of daily life: criminality, social adjustment, the problems of immigrants, ethnic minorities, ghettoes, etc. The practice of the science is seen as a task of helping to solve these problems. He judges these "elements" as positive, just as he does the clear and exact defining of concepts and of the relationships between them. His criticism of this way of practicing sociology is that American sociologists in their investigations address themselves too much to discrete problems, isolate them from the context of the society as a whole, and in doing so they oversimplify the problem. He is of the opinion that, if a "comprehensive view of social reality" is lacking, people can gain no view of the context of the problem. In spite of the attraction of sociology for everyday life, American research seems to go on in a "social vacuum." He also speaks of an "isolating empiricism" (GS: 225). That is why he does not consider it surprising that American sociologists take a very reserved stance toward problems concerning social and political policy. A political and social "background," on the basis of which questions of practice can be asked, is lacking. How can science help to solve the problems if it does not serve "the purpose of reforming or reorganization of society" (AM: 191)?

274

Although Mannheim criticizes this pragmatic and positivistic practice of science as fragmentary, he states that being occupied theoretically without empirical investigation leads to a meaningless and sterile sociology. The Americans are rightly afraid of this. Mannheim is in total agreement with them when they, with Comte, declare that the theological phase and the metaphysical-philosophical phase are past, but this does not mean, according to Mannheim, that the time has now arrived for an ad hoc empiricism "without a comprehensive social view." To the contrary:

> In order to know social reality one must have imagination, a particular brand of imagination which I should like to call "realistic" because it does not create fiction but exerts itself in binding together apparently unrelated facts by means of a vision of structural correlations which alone enable us to see the framework into which every fact, even the most casual one, is fitted. Like other qualities required for science, such as self-criticism, control of methods, etc., this realistic imagination must be cultivated through generations. (AM: 190)

That, holding this view, the charge of politicizing might be levelled against him, he regards as unjust and unjustified. The lack of a consciousness shaped by the sociology of knowledge increases the possibility for this politicizing. The sociology of knowledge has the task specifically of stimulating self-criticism and "critical self-control" in the sociologist (AM: 192). The sociology of knowledge is one of the two most important developments in German sociology. The second is psychoanalysis. Knowledge-sociology makes understandable why American sociologists do the work as they do, but they must at the same time allow the following insights to ripen: 1. that every isolated social fact is part of a changing social totality, and 2. that every intellectual phenomenon and idea stands in a specific relationship to the whole. Psychoanalysis directs attention to a person's mental posture and makes clear that every form of human behavior is an adaptation to new situations from out of the subconscious.

Speaking about German sociology, he says that this is never understood well without taking the philosophy of Hegel into account. In German sociology the dynamic conception from Hegel's philosophy has remained intact. In the second place Marxism plays an important role in German sociology; it remains enormously indebted to Hegel concerning the conception of history as the development of opposing social forces. Marx and Lorenz von Stein have given this conception of history a more realistic quality by assenting to the economic aspect and the class struggle. In the third place German sociology is thoroughly influenced by Dilthey, who makes a distinction between natural sciences (with their method of interpretive explanation which strives for mathematical exactness) and the cultural sciences (with their method of understanding directed toward discrete objects; EEZ). Referring to Max Weber's carrying forward of the method of interpretative understanding, Mannheim describes the difference between these methods in German sociology and behaviorism, which exerts itself strongly in English and particularly in American sociology. In the fourth place he names Simmel, "one of the most important precursors of recent German sociology." He combined the insight into structural powers in social life with a refined analysis of social details (GS: 213-217). In the fifth place he names the philosophically oriented sociology of Scheler and Troeltsch. It strives for unification of faithfulness to empiricism on the one hand and on the other to statements of the problems directed toward knowledge concerning the peculiar character of the sociological object and the laws which hold for it (PSD: 615, 616).

In these tendencies of German sociological thought (the dynamic-dialectical thought of Hegel, the political realism of Marx and Von Stein, the philosophical approach of Scheler and Troeltsch, the interpretative understanding of Dilthey and Max Weber, and the coming together of micro- and macro approaches in the sociology of Simmel) – in these tendencies Mannheim sees the intellectual equipment for a modern sociologist, equipping him for analyzing the disintegration of Western society and culture (GS: 217). He is clearly directed toward synthesizing these tendencies and regards the materialistic approach to social problems just as wrong as the idealistic approach. According to him, it is impossible to separate the economic and social changes on the one hand and mental developments on the other.

Comparing German sociology with American and English sociology, he sees as the dominant characteristic of American sociology the already mentioned "isolating empiricism." Although Germany and England were enclosed in the same history of Western Europe, he sees the history of the English people determined by an evolutionary and reforming development, while the history of the German people underwent a turbulent development. Various groups and social-political currents strove after radical transformations of society as a whole; indeed, they strive for unity among their very different and mutually exclusive insights. Just as the German sociologies reflect the turbulent and confrontational currents in social/political life, so English sociology reflects the development of its society. The first consequence of this for English sociology is that it formulates the problems in isolation and it works these out in very precise detail within the framework of existing theories. The best sociological studies also found a place then in the field of anthropology, social and economic history, social psychology, and political science. This had a disadvantage: that the comprehensive view of its own field of sociology was never acquired. The integration of sociological principles which were worked out in separate sciences lagged behind. Mannheim calls it noteworthy that in German sociology the social classes, the class struggle, and other social conflicts occupy a central place, while in England this is not the situation (GS: 226-228).

Although the two previous centuries were characterized by revolutionary changes in the area of technical sciences and natural sciences, the centuries to come will be characterized by moral and social changes (PS: 195; DP). For a scientific, sociological understanding of these changes, not only historical and psychological studies are important, because "they themselves do not contain those points of view by which the principles of the changes in human life can be found, the latter being mostly based upon interaction and the laws of living together" (PS: 200).

Mannheim is no opponent to empirical research, nor to the use of and the refining of quantitative methods in the social sciences. The danger is that practitioners of these sciences only study problems to the extent that they are quantifiable; according to him, it is easier (and for the development of the society in turn, more dangerous) to measure factors which are not "significant," than to make a start at the study of "significant" factors (F: xii, xiii).

Chapter XV

Diagnosis of Society in a Time of Reconstruction

- *Introduction*
- *"Laissez-faire" versus Regulation: A Structural Approach*
- *Rational and Irrational Elements in Society*
- *Substantial and Functional Rationality*
- *Substantial and Functional Morality*
- *Conclusions*

Introduction
In 1935 Mannheim's *Mensch und Gesellschaft im Zeitalter des Umbaus* (MG) appeared, brought out by the Dutch publisher A.E. Sijthoff (Leiden). This study contained three chapters after the foreword: I. "Rational and Irrational Elements in our Society," II. "The Sociological Causes for the Contemporary Crisis in Culture," and III. "Thought at the Level of Planning." In 1940 the English edition of this book appeared: *Man and Society in an Age of Reconstruction* (MS). In addition to a totally new introduction, Mannheim added three new chapters to the book: Chapters I and II were preserved from the German edition. Chapter III was new: "Crisis, Dictatorship, War." Chapter III from the German edition became Chapter IV in the English edition, followed by a new Chapter V, "Planning for Freedom" and a new Chapter VI, "Freedom at the Level of Planning." At the same time the English edition was provided with an expanded bibliography. With *Ideology and Utopia, Man and Society* belongs to the most frequently read and most frequently quoted works of Mannheim.

"Laissez-faire" versus Regulation: A Structural Approach
Mannheim strove "to make the experiences of the recent years accesible to a sociological analysis." He speaks about the "contemporary concerns of research" which arise from the need of the time. The practising scientist may not isolate himself from political, economic, and social events and processes; even a distanced objectivity is irresponsible. He thinks that "science's hour of conscience" has arrived. Although he makes social and political processes the themes of his scientific research, he warns against a politization of science (MG: vii).

The totality of actual changes in Western culture which have taken place in the twentieth century can be understood properly only if we see those changes as the disappearance of older forms of society and the construction of new forms. Social changes, however, never have the character of something

278

radically new. In the process of social changes old and new elements always go together; when we speak about new social forms, we know that the old is always present in the new (MG: 1).

The deepest root of cultural tensions in the West is, according to Mannheim (MG: 2), to be grasped as follows: down the line of culture and at virtually every level the issue is an unreconciled constradiction between the principle of *laissez-faire* on the one hand and the principle of *regulation* on the other. *Laissez-faire* stands for an unplanned and free promotion of self-interest (by individuals, groups, and other parts of society) characterized by competition and conflict. Opposite to this, *regulation* stands for an unplanned but routinized, institutionalized, and totalitarian-controlled conduct. That these two principles exist side by side without "planning," creates enormous tensions in economic and political life. So Western production is geared to world trade, and, at the same time, we create economic autarchies with the help of a very refined protectionism. In spite of progress in the area of the natural sciences, technology, and economy, the problems of poverty and of economic crises have grown much greater. People strive for supra-national organizations, but this process of integration often founders because of the claims of small and large power states. Mannheim wants to make clear that in Western culture – in relationships with society, in relationships between people, and within the person himself – tensions exist with devastating consequences.

The manifestations of crisis which emerge in many kinds of fields are not only of an incidental kind: both practising scientists and non-scientific workers (called "lay workers" by Mannheim) regard these crises as manifestations of a *structural* collapse of Western culture. That is why he wants to transform (translate, really) economic, political, anthropological, social-psychological, and social problems into sociological problems: that is, he wants to interpret these partial problems in the context of the totality of the social reconstruction.

> What Newton did when he regarded an apple falling from a tree not as an apple, but as an expression of the law of gravity, has not yet happened for psychological and cultural phenomena. (MG: 7)

To this great task in the field of sociology Mannheim desires to make a contribution. He does not deny the right to exist to the discrete sciences (law, economics, aesthetics, psychology, etc.). He does not regard these sciences either as subdivisions of sociology, but he regards sociology as the basic science for all of these sciences (see the previous chapter). That is why he is of the opinion that these disciplines must undergo "a labor of sociological translation" – if one of the most important aspects of their research is not to escape them. The transformation of problems of various disciplines, mentioned above, shows that he strives for a more comprehensive and more profound theory.

In his "Newtonian approach" to the problems, he does not present a sociological system. He strives rather for this: to analyze various problems in their "original interwoveness of reality" and then to *synthesize them sociologically*. This synthesizing of and gaining insight into the interdependence may not be allowed to lead to the results of disciplinary studies next to each other ("the bookbinder's synthesis"; F: x), but it must lead to finding a method to bring the problems within the sociologist's grasp by sociological methods; the synthesizing of the problems must lead to the insight that the method of planning for the advantage of all is unavoidable(MG: 3, 9; F: viii, x; PP). Later he speaks of sociology as "The New Science of Human Behavior," which must coordinate and integrate the results of anthropological, psychological, economic, and differentiated sociological research (NSHB: 1; cf. SSS: 216-218). A widespread misunderstanding is that people should wait with this integrating research until "all relevant givens" are known and that the intended integration will take place spontaneously when the time is ripe. Mannheim regards this point of view as a misconception of the responsibility of the sociologist in this century (F: xi). Certainly for sociology he regards the words of Max Weber (1904) as applicable (GAS: 62):

> There are sciences whose eternal youthfulness is established, and those are the sciences ... to which the eternally forward flowing stream of culture continuously conducts new problems to be formulated and solved.

That Mannheim was also optimistic about the synthesizing and therapeutic power of sociology can be seen from the fact that in January 1933 he was still of the opinion that with help from sociology a scientific politics could become sufficiently skillful to expel the phantom of Nazism in no more than two months (H. Maus, 1959: 72). Boris (1971: 130-153) concludes correctly that Mannheim was not only optimistic for his conception of sociology, but that he particularly fell short in his sociological analysis of Fascism. As we already have seen in Chapter XIV, he speaks chiefly in social-psychological terms about fascism. He does not discuss the economic conceptions in fascism: the criticism of a free market, the protection of the concerns of industry, and the criticism of international organizations, both economic and political. The Fascist conceptions of law and property, its vitalistic background, its anti-parliamentarianism and anti-corporationism are only mentioned in passing. Also lacking is an analysis of the Fascist use of ideas such as tribal identity, unity and harmony.

In summary, we can say that Mannheim's sociology is not a disciplinary science as is economics, or law, or natural science. It studies not only one aspect, but, according to the Dutch sociologist De Valk (1963: 119), "a series of concrete problems, of which as many aspects as possible are investigated and brought into connection with each other." Sociology is, therefore, a total science: it studies reality in its multiformity and in its contextuality. In this way it hardly distinguishes itself from philosophy. It does not, however, concern itself with abstract philosophical problems as such; but as a social philosophy it studies epistemological, anthropological, and ethical problems, so that it can make a contribution to the formation of policy (cf. Remmling, 1957a: 384, 388).

The introduction to *Man and Society* is not only more elaborate than that of

Mensch und Gesellschaft (1935), but it has a different tone. In Germany Mannheim had seen what the economic malaise, the political and social chaos, and the rise of National Socialism meant. From painful first-hand experience he knew what it means to live in an age of reconstruction. In the edition of 1940 he states as his purpose the description of this reconstruction in its causes and consequences for people who only know about these changes on the basis of word of mouth and who still live with the illusion of a traditional stability in their society; this illusion came to expression among those who were of the opinion that the collapse of liberalism, the collapse of various Western democracies, and the emergence of totalitarian states would be passing phenomena: symptoms of a crisis which would remain restricted to a few countries. Mannheim judges these changes, not as incidental, but as structural for all Western democracies. He wants to warn the English and American democracies; *laissez-faire* policies lead to chaos, to the lack of planning, and finally to anarchy. No description of utopia is his aim, but a realistic description and a theoretical analysis of the crisis of Western democracies. Although in the England of his time, and in other Western countries, democracy through the strenght of its traditions was still functioning, he had the impression that the people in these countries were living on a volcano (MS: 3, 5; FPDP: xix). It was clear to him that this awareness was present in only a few people as yet. The Dutch philosopher and sociologist Bierens de Haan relativizes the universal significance of Mannheim's diagnosis when he writes: "The experiences in Germany, so bitter for the writer, which form the substance of this book, are thought through from a sociological perspective. The situation in our country is different in many respects. Our historical situation is a different one, our culture and mind-set is a different one." Still, it is evident that Bierens de Haan does not deny the relevance of Mannheim's diagnoses: "Much of what is stated as fact here is only (still?) hypothetical. But the sociological concept of the situation which is dominated entirely by several tendencies which also work among us in another context is illuminating for the understanding of our own situation" (1935: 312). Unambiguous agreement with Mannheim came from the Dutch sociologist Bouman, who wrote, "I read until now no view of the current world situation which can stand in the shadow of Mannheim's penetrating analysis of the apparently chaotic phenomena around us" (1936: 285).

The principle of *laissez-faire* is not interpreted by Mannheim only as an economic principle of eighteenth-century economists. Neither does he see liberalism as a social, political, and economic movement in the second half of the eighteenth and the nineteenth century only. He uses any of these terms as "ideal types." The concepts of *laissez-faire* and *liberalism* do not refer to reality as this is or was, but they put the emphasis on certain characteristics which are of concern for the manner in which the subject concerned ought to be studied (DT: 166). For the interpretations of Mannheim's ideal types I can refer to chapters VI and VIII where the subject is "interpretive understanding in context," that is, seeing by means of understanding the richly varied factors in functional relatedness. Hence, Mannheim sometimes speaks about liberalism to clarify particular characteristics of the development of Western culture since the Middle Ages. Regarded from a historical viewpoint, Mannheim's interpretation of liberalism is vulnerable. His description of liberalism as an ideal type only corresponds to the liberal ideology which proceeds in its social view from the private property of "small-time citizens" and from individual and horizontal trade relationships. The liberal-capitalistic society, however, is not described adequately by these characteristics of a pre-industrial phase. Mannheim's ideal types applied to liberalism do not do full justice to the important, but desperate relationships between entrepeneurs and laborers. Neither does his description do justice to modern capitalism. Are Mannheim's characterizations of liberalism as an ideal type totally inadequate? His ideal type is constituted one-sidedly, because he directs himself in his characterizing to a society based on skilled trades and agriculture. As such, his characterizing apparently has the function to fulfill of designating as sharply as possible the differences between the liberal *laissez-faire* society and the social order which he advocates of "planning for freedom" (Boris, 1971: 95-102). And so he does not interpret *laissez-faire* only as an economic principle but more broadly; according to him, during many centuries and in all sectors of society a lack of planning existed, a lack which would be catastrophic for the twentieth century.

Regulated thought came to view in the dictatorships, and Mannheim warns that planning can lead to dictatorship. But we must not allow this danger to blind our eyes to the possibilities which planning can and must provide. With no less emphasis he points out that a malfunctioning democracy will also without doubt lead to dictatorship (sc: 174; cf. dz).

Speaking about the diagnosis of Western society, Mannheim says that not only the growth of populations confronts us with great problems, but also new technology, telephone, radio, television, rapid means of transportation, and modern techniques of organization which adopt centralizing characteristics; these tendencies advance concentrations of power in society. The competition between small enterprises has to a great extent been replaced by competition between world-scaled businesses. Traditional patterns of behavior disintegrate and religious convictions, moral norms, values, and virtues become debased and collapse. All of this brings a disorganization of personality along with it, while an adequate coordination of the various large-scaled organizations is lacking (FPDP: 3-21). The choice, according to him, is not *laissez-faire* or planning, but good or bad planning. At the same time, he perceives that a theoretical thinking through of planning is an advantage for its application for the purpose of guaranteeing maximum freedom for people. Hence his famous expressions "planning for freedom" and "planning for democracy."

This new direction of society will not emerge automatically. Not only the economic order, but thought, the conception of humanity, education, and morality must all be thoroughly transformed, that is, they must be brought to a higher and more comprehensive level (FPDP: 119, 120). This means that historians, psychologists, anthropologists, moral philosophers, theologians, and other practitioners of the sciences must learn to think in a new way. Most often they think as specialists; they are intent on the compass of their own disciplines and in many instances only on a single subdivision of a field. These scientific practitioners are quickly inclined to develop "defense mechanisms" when another form of thought is expected of them for the purpose of contributing to an adequate knowledge of society. Mannheim's purpose is "an attempt to diagnose the changes in the social structure from the symptoms of this critical period" (MS: 32). This diagnosis encompasses not only an analysis, but also a synthesis which must lead to thinking on the level of interdependence. This implies a therapy.

In realizing his planning for freedom, Mannheim does not want to impose an ideology on society, nor apply abstract principles in a universal way. Only a sociological analysis can lead to a sociological clarification of existence and to an adequate knowledge of the changed and changing situation. They who say that planning and freedom are irreconcilable, foster traditional and thus, according to him, outdated interpretations. They must learn to think at a higher level, in contemporary terms, directed toward the future and toward opening the future. Every society formulates and reformulates in its own way its ideas about such matters as the state, authority, justice, etc.; that is why people ought also to "fine-tune" such ideas as planning and freedom (MS: 6-14).

Rational and Irrational Elements in Society

Mannheim is of the opinon that a therapy leads to utopia unless there is diagnosis. The diagnosis is important because we must learn from the crisis of the West. This crisis had brought two accepted presuppositions into great discredit: 1. the idea of the permanence of the national character of states and 2. the belief in the orderly progress of reason throughout history. The falling away of the second presupposition is the more important in Mannheim's opinion. The progress of reason in history had been accepted so long as true, and for that reason the phenomena of crises were long regarded as mere incidents. The progress of reason had been accepted because of the harmony which could still prevail for a long time in "the social strucure" (MS: 39) between the psychological development of society and the technical development.

Mannheim notices that particular groups that had believed in the progress of reason and that had given the tone to society, began to doubt their mission; more and more they were inspired by latent irrational impulses. It is clear that the issue for Mannheim is not only rational or irratinal elements in epistemology. He deems necessary a careful analysis of rational and irrational forces in society. In this analysis he judges neither rational nor irrational forces as totally negative. The content of *rationale*, according to him, must be sought in the basic questions of the Renaissance, Enlightenment, and various worldviews. However, he does not give a clear definition of the word *rationality*. Because the word *rationality* does not have a clear meaning for Mannheim, its distinction from *irrationality* is not totally clear. This lack of clarity will play a part for us in understanding the continuation of Mannheim's argument.

In *Man and Society* three theses stand central. Humanity has achieved much with the help of reason in the areas of the natural sciences, technology, knowledge of social order and processes, but in the area of morality this development has lagged behind. And so a *disproportionality* arose in the development of human possibilities. That is why Mannheim's first thesis reads as follows:

> ...the contemporary social order must collapse if rational social control and the individual's mastery over his own impulses do not keep step with technological development. (MS: 43)

This thesis has reference to the general *disproportionality* of human possibilities. Mannheim also recognizes a *social disproportionality*; in no single dynamic and complicated society are the good forms of order and of morality, which are necessary for the control of social and economic problems, "divided" equally between all groups and classes (MS: 43).

The second thesis is related to this disproportionality, both general and social: the blossoming of reason, the ordering of irrational elements, and the giving of form to morality do not happen by accident; but neither are these matters totally dependent on the character of individual people. To the contrary: they are dependent on the structure of the existing social order (MS: 43).

Mannheim's third thesis makes a judgment of the situation which is described in the second thesis: though in earlier societies a certain disproportionality could exist because these societies were based on a certain disproportionality between rational and irrational elements, democractic societies cannot endure such disproportionality. In earlier societies despots claimed a maximum of rational insight and governing power, while underlings could not develop any initiative. Not that there was less irrationality than there is now, but its action and reaction played itself out in "narrower circles, and in private life"; in modern society, through the influence of the media of mass communications, mass-psychosis plays an important role (MS: 44, 45).

Mannheim regards the general and social disproportionality as incapable of reconciliation with modern society. That is why he wishes to activate two factors to combat this evil: 1. *the fundamental democratizing of society* and 2. *the process of growing interdependence*.

1. The principle of *fundamental democratizing of society* proceeds from the fact that it has become impossible for the elite to keep the masses ignorant. The process of democratizing has become common. A growing number of groups justify their causes and want to have them justified generally; they want to have an effective influence on social and political decision-making. Mannheim's sociological vision of life forms a context with the insight into the democratizing

process (GAS: 36); this process has as its most fundamental principle "the essential equality of all human beings." Not that there are no differences between people in qualities and talents, but all "embody the same ontological principle of humanness." This conception about the essential equality of all people has, according to Mannheim, an ideological and a sociological basis. The ideological basis is this: "the belief in the essential equality of all men derives from the Christian conception of all men as children of God." The sociological origin is the changing of the political and social structure in Western countries, which, to a greater or lesser extent, makes possible the applications of this religious idea (sc: 176).

The only way to achieve a dictatorship successfully now would be the centralization of the control of individual wills. But every step in this direction signifies a threat to the dynamic principle of fundamental democratization. Mannheim names three forms of the monopolization of social forces, which he considers in fundamental conflict with democratization. 1. Specialized experts who have knowledge in one tiny, little area of society (certain lawyers, bureaucrats, economists, and politicians). 2. Along with what is described in point 1 goes the concentration of administrative activities in bureaucracies. 3. The concentration of the instruments of military power in connection with political conflict (MS: 44-49). May we conclude that Mannheim in the interests of the advancement of fundamental democratization advocates the counterparts of these three points? That is, decentralization, or the spreading out of knowledge and of power: administrative, economic, and political? I shall return to this problem. It may now already be clear that Mannheim speaks aoubt *the principle* of fundamental democratizing. That is: a point of departure, which needs elaboration, both theoretically and practically, both in society and in politics. Elsewhere he says:

> A democratizing trend is our predestined fate, not only in politics, but also in intellectual and cultural life as a whole. Whether we like it or not, the trend is irreversible, and hence it is the supreme duty of the political thinker to explore its potentialities and implications. Only in this way will it be possible to influence the trend of democratization in a desirable sense. (sc: 171)

2. The principle of *growing interdependence* fails in a society in which a disproportionality exists between intellectual and moral possibilities. In Western society an interdependence exists among all sectors. Mannheim compares this society with a railroad network; one accident now has far-reaching consequences. A dynamic and interdependent society which is characterized by a general disproportionality will be able to endure irrational and emotional shocks (and mass-psychotic shocks) less well. This problem is not only of a national, but of an international dimension. An unhealthy economic and political situation in one land has consequences for other lands. An outburst of emotion, whether or not it turns into a guerilla war or a revolution, seldom remains isolated to the country concerned (MS: 49-51).

The increasing interdependence can not be accompanied with a general and social disproportionality, if the society is not to collapse. Not only the complexity of industrial society, but the tensions in this society are of sociological importance, because they are the causes of crises. This view, for that reason, requires a sociological investigation of society, to which Mannheim feels called.

Even before investigating the relationship between rationality and irrationality, he intends to clarify the significance of these ideas. Already in the lecture which he had given in the Netherlands (1933), he had said that rationality and irrationality stand in a correlative relationship to each other. The next question is the nature of this correlation; for instance, this correlation can be of a positive, a negative, or of a more nuanced nature. He names as an example of the first the purposeful rationality, with a playful handling of opposites as complements. As a second he lists the "self-organization" of ascetics, who either seek to curb their passions or to indulge them with moderation, with the life of passionate self-expression its opposite. For the third he speaks about "careful reflection" which increases the life force, while barbarism and meaninglessness are named the opposites (ANTW). In *Man and Society* he brings these forms of rationality and irrationality into connection with each other.

Substantial and Functional Rationality

Mannheim distinguishes, both in rationality and in irrationality, two kinds of each: *substantial* and *functional*. By *substantial rationality* he designates "an act of thought which reveals intelligent insight into the inter-relations of events in a given situation" (MS: 53). *Substantial irrationality* is everything else which either is false or not an act of thought at all (for example, passions, emotions).

Functional rationality: "a series of actions is organized in such a way that it leads to a previously defined goal, every element in this series of actions receiving a functional position and rôle" (MS: 53). All actions and thoughts, also intellectual achievements which break through and split-up a functional order, are *functionally irrational*. This means that substantial rationality and substantial irrationality can both fall under this one rubric.

It is noteworthy that Mannheim's descriptions of substantial and functional rationality and irrationality are not definitions but "characterizations." The distinctions between these concepts are not sharp intellectually. Also, he gives a somewhat unsatisfactory criterion for the use of these ideas and thus makes his division a little less than clear. Naturally, we can imagine something for ourselves about the distinctions he mentions. Certainly when Mannheim in this connection formulates the following thesis, we understand: the more a society is industrialized and the more progress has been made in the division of labor and the organization of a society, the greater is the number of fields of human activities which are organized functionally-rationally. This functional rationality inhibits substantial-rational insight, which must critically illuminate the established categories of thought and established social structures. With help from this insight, contributions can be made for the reconstruction of society (MS: 51-57).

In an earlier publication Mannheim had simply judged positively the processes of rationalizing in society:

> ...the greater the growth of social interdependence accompanying the economic develop-ment of capitalism, and the stronger the tendency for economic facts to predominate in society, the more certain it is that gaps in the structure of predictable conduct formerly subject only to indirect control through the cultivation of traditionalized ideological responses will become more or less determinable and calculable in the sense at least that the optimum behaviour serving the rational self-interest of individuals in any given situation becomes predictable.
>
> In a society the structure of which is essentially rational and integrated, behaviour will become increasingly predictable even in its "irrational" aspects, since even conduct which is determined, say, by panic or irrational motives inherited from former times, will be capable of being understood, at least as regards its direction, but more especially as regards the most likely point in the otherwise rational social structure at which it may develop. The greater the extent to which irrationalism tends to be reduced to an enclave within an increasingly rational social structure, the more calculable and controllable do these irra-tional elements become. (WE: 245)

> To the degree, therefore, that economic rationality permeates social life as a whole, we can observe the relaxation of ideological regimentation, documented by the fact that con-sciences are no longer controlled. This is the social source of the modern idea of tolerance. (WE: 246)

> This means, however, in rather more lax terminology, that the modern economic system (just because economic necessities are penetrating to an increasing extent into the very fabric of our daily lives) can "afford" to give the "ideologists" more freedom than has hitherto been possible. (WE: 246)

Boris (1971: 34) correctly judges Mannheim's conception of rationality, pre-sented above, as of particular significance. Boris summarizes it in four points: 1. Mannheim judges positively the increase of social rationality; 2. likewise, he judges positively the predictability of irrational residues which are disappear-ing; 3. these two points together bring along with them an increasing absence of ideology; 4. these points, however, are in conflict with his later conception defended in *Man and Society*. In MS he says that industrialization and bureaucratizing are founded on and promote the furtherance of functional rationality, and this is in conflict with substantial rationality. Later, speaking about planning for freedom, he attempts to harmonize functional and substan-tial rationality.

In the general sense the question arises in which respects and to what degree the substantial and the functional rationality influence each other. In the social sense this problem arises: that in a society permeated with science, with techno-

287

logy, and with heavy industrialization, a small group of people occupying key positions think through the complex of activities and the direction of development (which is often identified with progress); the mass of people moves within a social framework of functional rationality, without being able to comprehend the framework in its interdependency; the elite which assumes leadership and makes decisions acquires more and more responsibility, with the result that a cleft develops between the elite and the masses. It is a potentially dangerous situation.

Mannheim has not elaborated on the tension between functional and substantial rationality in the general sense. This tension had his attention only as a social and sociological problem. My preliminary interpretation of Mannheim is that substantial rationality, in clearing its way for "planning for freedom," takes up into itself the "consequent calculability" of functional rationality. A question, however, is whether the social tensions mentioned above can also be sublimated and "taken up" in this manner.

Substantial and Functional Morality

Parallel to the distinction already made, Mannheim also recognizes *substantial* and *functional moralities*. By a *functional morality* he means "those standards which, when realized in conduct, guarantee the smooth working of society." *Substantial morality* exists on the basis of "certain concrete values, such as dictates of faith and different kinds of feeling, standards which may be completely irrational in quality" (MS: 67).

Concerning this division, the same kind of lack of clarity exists which I pointed out also in connection with the distinction between substantial and functional rationality. Here, too, there is a tension between the functional and substantial: the more strongly a functional morality works, the more a substantial morality becomes neutralized or is relegated to private lives.

In old, stable societies, defined by traditions, a mechanical or horde-solidarity was dominant, according to Mannheim. There was no individual who arrived at consciousness of his own position and responsibility. The individual was one part of the totality; he stood or fell with it. Durkheim had spoken already about the mechanical solidarity of the horde mentality. In the phase of individual competition a person is no longer limited by the immovable and indisputable customs of the collective entity. As an individual he now has his *own responsibility*. This conception is stimulated by the ownership and the increase of personal possessions. The principle of *laissez-faire* also gives this kind of thought a powerful push forward. In Mannheim's opinion, the time is ripe now, even though many people do not yet perceive it, for *a new, contemporary group-solidarity*. Our time is made up of groups in which individuals are forced to turn away from their own concerns; private concerns are subordinated to the concerns of larger entities; entrepeneurs join together; laborers organize themselves into huge labor unions. Not antagonistic relationships between people, but insight into a new solidarity will help people. Insight into the facts of general and social disproportionality, striving for fundamental democratization, and the ongoing process of interdependence will cause the consciousness of the new solidarity to ripen. The substantial rationality and substantial morality awaken within a person, according to Mannheim, the consciousness of the need for planning.

It is noteworthy in this regard that Mannheim does not refer to Durkheim, who had already written about "organic solidarity" and "moral density" in society. Durkheim placed himself against egoistical individualism and was a proponent of moral individualism. In an industrial society with its division of labor, individuals came to stand in isolation, while in the relationships among themselves they found that their functions in the labor process were complementary. According to Durkheim, a person can only realize his true humanity as a member of the group. Mannheim, with some qualificatons, additions, and elaborations, could have agreed with these ideas. Although in earlier publications (ST: 208ff) he had referred to Durkheim's conception of the "collective consciousness" with agreement, he later quoted Durkheim only rarely. As I already noted before, this arises apparently from his critical attitude toward positivism, increasing by the year; apparently he did not want to run the risk of being interpreted positivistically.

It is clear that Mannheim does not see a person as only a rational being; irrational elements also pay a role. He evaluates the irrational positively:

> ...the irrational... is among the most valuable powers in man's possession when it acts as a driving force towards rational and objective ends or when it creates cultural values through sublimation, or when, as pure élan, it heightens the joy of living without breaking up the social order by lack of planning. (MS: 62, 63)

Also in a rationally organized society these irrational elements are utilized. Such a society has certain safety values for the purpose of offering people the possibilities for working away their irrationality, for instance, in sport and celebrations. In societies in which the masses dominate and the irrational is either not at all or inadequately integrated into the societal structure, it can find an outlet in politics, which is, according to Mannheim, an existentially dangerous development, because then irrationality arrives at the very place where rational decisions are demanded. In such a situation we see, according to him, that in a democracy of a strictly rational orientation, irrational processes can gain ground and lead toward a "negative democracy" (MS: 63). From earliest times a "social mechanism" works in the structure of society, which regulates the growth of the repression upon both rational and irrational elements. The operation of this mechanism in an industrial society must be studied, according to him, in interdisciplinary research, because in the shadow of the most rational and predictable behavior, the possibilities of war and revolution thrive. Hence Mannheim's conclusion:

There is a complete parallel between the factors making for the growth and collapse of rationality in the intellectual sphere and those making for the growth and collapse of morality. (MS: 66)

Precisely in a society organized functionally and rationally, dangers concerning the collapse of rationality and morality exist in a particular way. A democracy is a means for expressing all kinds of opinions and for radiating all kinds of social influences. With the help of modern mass-communications, these influences can be used constructively or destructively with respect to morality. The negative influences can prove disastrous: the democratic process functions then as an "elevator," because it brings up into view the uncontrollable outbursts of mass psychosis.

Mannheim summarizes his opinion about the social mechanism in modern democratic society, organized in the functional-rational manner, as follows:

...on the one hand we see that human reason and moral discipline are able to attain the level of planning and self-responsibility; on the other hand, we see how with the same dynamic drive the will to destruction becomes a public force. (MS: 73)

In this quotation Mannheim speaks in terms of on-the-one-hand, on-the-other-hand. From the preceding it may have become clear that on-the-other-hand arises from the on-the-one-hand – and eliminates it. In this conection we can speak of a negative dialectic: irrationality emerges from rationality as its counter-balance and eliminates the rational; that is, it does not raise up the rational in the sense that it appears in a new form at a higher level socially. Rationality is eliminated, chaos and barbarism dominate, without anything constructive being albe to develop from it.

Mannheim is convinced totally of the necessity of planning. In the first place because it is the only remaining alternative. In the second place because in the modern Western democracies the possibilities for a successful realization are already present in the principles of rationality and morality, and the crisis of Western culture can be avoided. The crucial question which consequently suggests itself to him with some urgency is this: Which ideas and ideals stimulate and direct those who have the responsibility for planning? "Who plans those who are to do the planning?" (MS: 74) In this question he distinguishes two sides: a *religious-resigned* side and a *realistic-political* side.

In the first place it often seems that we ourselves are acting according to existing rules which are imposed on us and which stand above us. Very often we can control the rational and irrational forces in the various sectors of our lives, but often we also notice that on a specific matter these forces lie outside of our control, for instance, impulsus from the society at large, which permeate the sectors of our individual lives. That is why Mannheim asks this question from the religious-resigned perspective: "Who plans the planner?" The answer to this question, according to him, lies in the theory of planning or, as is often said these days, in political science. In the second case the point of issue is the realistic-political question: "Which of the existing groups shall plan us?"

Mannheim has not presented these two sides of the question regarding the background of planning as a choice. According to my view these two "sides" do not only form a context together as different aspects of the same matter. They spill over into each other. The *religious-resigned* and open question "Who plans the planner?" makes the other question come up: "Which groups shall carry out the plans?" But also for the planning group, the first question still counts: "Which ideas and ideals give direction to our planning?"

Mannheim attempts to develop a theory of planning for the purpose of guiding social, economic, and political processes and irrational powers. The purposes of the planning are conceived on the basis of the substantial rationality in the framework of a total vision of society. On the basis of the functional rationality the attention directs itself on devising the most appropriate means. The functional rationality ought to be in a position to serve the substantial rationality, although in the still existing practicality, the functional rationality, which functions within the existing organizations with their short-term vision, still contrasts with the substantial rationality. Mannheim is not only conscious of this problem, but also of the fact that the devised substantial-rational plan with its purposes and the functional-rational means must lead to certain planning actions, which in their turn must aim at specific effects. In other words, the plans of thought lead to the actions of thought, and consequently, to intended (and some not intended) effects. In this connection the question also arises about the tension between the social freedoms envisioned by Mannheim's planning at a macro-level and the individual freedom of choice at a micro-level. For the rest, I discuss only specific aspects of Mannheim's theory of planning in the following chapters, especially the social-philosophical aspects. Many subjects, among others those concerning political science, are either not discussed or only mentioned in passing. For instance, problems concerning "incrementalism" (Braybrooke and Lindblom, 1963), classical theories of planning, the development of politics as a "mixes scanning" (A. Etzioni), and other modern ideas either do not come up at all or are briefly discussed.

Conclusions

In this chapter I have described the most important points of Mannheim's diagnosis of society in a time of reconstruction. His maximum conception of sociology (see Chapter XIV) received its applications in this diagnosis. His diagnosis touched chiefly the inadequacy of *laissez-faire* thought in this century and the need for the transitional phase into "planning for freedom." As far as this last-mentioned subject is concerned, he states clearly that there is no choice between planning and no planning; stating the problem in these terms is irrelevant. In the twentieth century the Western democracies have arrived at a position where planning is unavoidable. The only relevant question is this: good or bad planning?

In the diagnosis as described the concepts of rationality and irrationality stand central. The processes which he regards as threatening for the Western democracies are on the one hand "outbursts" of irrationality (for instance, fascism) and on the other hand the functional-rational structures of organizations which threaten to overwhelm democracies. As for the rest, conceptual lack of clarity seemed to exist in his distinction between rationality and irrationality, substantial and functional rationality, and substantial and functional morality.

In the following chapter I shall continue the analysis of his diagnosis and therapy. In that analysis his conceptions concerning the elite and the masses, the *principia media*, and "planning for freedom" occupy the central place.

Chapter XVI

Thought at the Level of Planning

- *The Function of the Governing Elite in Society*
- *A Closer Look at Mannheim's Theory of the Elite*
- *"Principia Media"*
- *A Closer Look at "Principia Media"*
- *Planning without Utopia?*
- *Education for a New Mode of Thought*
- *Conclusions*

The Function of the Governing Elite in Society

In his analysis Mannheim makes a distinction concerning society, specifically between the unregulated part of society on the one hand, which gives form to intellectual and cultural life by its freedom and spontaneity, and on the other hand the social organizations (universities, churches, radio, the press, and others), which give form to intellectual life in an organized way. In the liberal mass culture, according to Mannheim, an unregulated social and economic order exists; thus there are also unregulated and uncontrolled effects on culture.

His sociological analysis begins with the study of those who make culture possible: the intelligentsia. It has the opportunity to inspire cultural life and give it form. Is not a basically democratized society characterized by the absence of an elite class? According to Mannheim, such a society is characterized by the emergence of the new elite, who have new criteria of selection and a new interpretation of their social role; these are entirely different from the aristocratic elite determined by traditions. Not only do these new elite have new criteria for being selected and other interpretations of their social position and of their relationship to other social groupings, but they also have a different internal structure (sc: 201; cf. 200-203). Mannheim distinguishes the following elite among the intelligentsia: the political, the organizational, the intellectual, the artistic, the students of theoretical ethics, and the religious. The political and organization elite desire to integrate people; they strive for ordered forms of society. The other elite, called the "normative elites" by Fisher (1954: 17), work in the "free" or unorganized sectors of society and are directed toward the sublimation of the psychic energy which is insufficiently used up in the society. The tasks of these elite are not exclusive. While the political and organizational elite work according to rational patterns, the normative elite are called to a reinterpretation of these patterns. The way in which these elite accomplish their task is dependent on social circumstances: the manner in which people use their leisure time and the way in which intellectuals are recruited. If in a society all human energy is consumed by functional-rational organizations, then there is little room for reflection and creativity; analogous to this, the danger always threatens that in a society in which the political and organizational elite are dominant, there is little room left for the other elite. In such a society, the capability to inspire and renew the culture will decline. Only in that culture in which "the average person has enough leisure to sublimate his surplus energies, and where ...there is a dominant cultural group, do there arise mutually adapted classes which create and assimilate culture" (MS: 83, 84). Just as previously in Sparta the political and military elite overwhelmed the whole society, so in the United States of the twentieth century, the organizational elite dominate society. These phenomena are disastrous. That is why Mannheim pleads for cultural sublimation in a mass democracy: small groups of judges and connoisseurs in the areas of art and fashion and in other areas occupied creatively in making forms, can *slowly on radiate their influence* through society. In all sectors of culture these elite can bring their cultural and psychological powers to expression and provide leadership in a collective assimilation of that expression. These elite are responsible both for the cultural tradition and for the cultural initiatives. If these elite were all struck dumb and if their selection and educations were halted, the social conditons for the continuation and progress of culture would disappear.

Mannheim names four factors which further the crisis of Wetern culture:

1. The number of the elite grows and at the same time the number of those who aspire to be elite grows. Because of the large number of elite in society who wish to play a role of leadership, their influence declines. The effect of one group of elite is diminished by that of another.

2. The destruction of the exclusivity of the elite arises from a lack of talent, initiative, and creativity; the mediocre dominates, by which the elite lose their leadership. Indecisiveness and confusion in society are the result, while groups with extreme positions arise as reactions, such as dictatorial and fascist organizations, and other totalitarian expressions.

3. Important criteria for selecting the elite are often "blood," wealth, and achievement. In aristocratic societies the elite chose its members on the basis of "the principle of blood." In a bourgeois society wealth serves as the criterion. Both criteria have often been accompanied by the characteristic of achievement. This third element Mannheim calls "the dynamic element." In Nazi Germany he saw this criterion degeneratively coupled with a theory of race, blood, and land. In a mass democracy the characteristic of achievement can only be handled if it is coupled with the principle of an equal chance for everyone.

4. In the course of time a change has appeared in terms of the composition of the elite. In previous ages the elite in Western culture were not bound to specific territories. They were strongly international in inclination. This inclination had its cause in education, which operated under the leadership of the church, and the clergy was a typical international class. With democratization a tendency

began toward regionalization. According to Mannheim, Western culture did not develop itself from a regional, national, and ultimately to an international level, but rather from an international integration into local and regional integration, and consequently into national patterns of culture. In spite of the desire for and need for international contacts in various cultural fields (among others, on the economic field), self-sufficient movements seem to keep arising. If the old criterion for selecting the elite placed these purveyors of cultural values at the top, Mannheim sees that in his time the standards of the old criterion would be found too light to gain the supremacy (MS: 86-96).

A subsequent problem concerns the relationship between the "new elite" and the mass democracy: how do they function in the modern society? In previous ages the elite and the masses of the population had no direct contact with each other. Specific social structures existed which played an intermediary role between the two. In a mass democracy these intermediary structures have disappeared. In earlier times authors in literature and in theater addressed themselves to a particular and stable public, while in a mass democracy writing and acting are addressed to a broader, more flexible audience. In the relationship between the new elite of authors and the mass public, the factors of mass psychology play a role which must not be overlooked, and the authors thoroughly take them into account, "play up to them," and are often intent on achieving a short-term effect. One produces a play, for instance for labor unions, youth organizations, and other groups. These examples do not only indicate that the public has become more uniform; they also indicate that the public has become much more differentiated. There is a development in the composition of the public: from an organic elite-public in an earlier time by way of a disintegrated mass-public, to a differentiated organized-public.

Also in politics there formerly existed an intermediate group between the politically elite and the masses, which intermediate group consisted of rather constant groups of the electorate and of political parties. With the introduction of universal suffrage and lowering of the legal voting age, other groups and categories, like women, laborers, and youth, came to be important. Politicians now concentrate their attention on the masses of our time, and in that, the emotional and irrational motives play a role. However, as soon as this irrationality leads to chaotic situations, the chance for a dictatorship increases, which, according to Mannheim, will transform the unorganized masses into organized masses and which will impose a mass discipline by means of a strongly organized party (MS: 96-98).

Given the increase in the number of the elite mentioned by Mannheim, the destruction of their exclusivity, and the change in their criteria for selection and their terms of organization, as well as the changed relationship to the public – given all of these changes, the social position and the role of the elite has changed. This change has as its first negative consequence, according to him, "the proletarization of the intelligentsia" (MS: 99). There are, according to him, more intellectuals than there is intellectual work; this decreases the "social value" of intellectuals and of "intellectual culture." According to Mannheim, this is not to be judged entirely negatively. The intellectuals, who formerly were recruited chiefly from high society, in general held a view of culture which corresponded with the conceptions of that social stratum. In this century more intellectuals have been recruited from other classes, something which has brought along with it "a wonderful flowering of a free intellectual and cultural life" and "the great plasticity of mind and the deep sense of moral responsibility ... free to a very great extent from class prejudices" of a sort demonstrated, for instance, by the intellectuals of Czarist Russia. In this connection Mannheim must have thought about the intellectuals in Budapest and in the Weimar Republic, situations he himself had known (MS: 101; cf. Chapters I and II). In this positive evaluation of intellectuals we see the characteristics which he designated as "the socially, relatively free-floating intelligentsia" (Chapter XII).

For the purpose of finding a way out of the problems of an unorganized social and economic development and the social and moral disintegration as its consequences, Mannheim does not assume an elitist position, which would exclusively assign a cultural task to the intellectuals and which would snobbishly curse the masses and keep them ignorant. Although he highly esteems the task of the intelligentsia and other elite, he calls on *all people* for whom *freedom* and *justice* are the highest values. He wants to direct them to guard the means for realizing these values, under changing social and technical circumstances. Liberalism does not offer this means, according to him, and cannot supply them. He characterizes the time in which he lives as a period of rapid transformation (MS: 106, 107). Liberalism is not capable of solving the problems; repeatedly it demonstrates its lack of ability. Not that a dictatorship is the only alternative. That is why he wants to state the problems in sharp sociological terms; the problems do not lie in liberalism itself, nor in dictatorship as a reaction against liberalism, but in an *extraordinarily rapid transformation* from a "minority democracy" or an elite democracy to a mass democracy, now in the processes of learning interdependency, achieving fundamental democratizing, and adjusting to the tension between functional and substantial rationality.

A Closer Look at Mannheim's Theory of the Elite

Mannheim quotes the following theoreticians about the elite: Mosca, Pareto, and Michels. All of them study, to be precise, the existence and the nature of a particular elite which has a great influence on social and political events. They have in common in the germ of their conceptions that in every society a minority exists which takes the most important social and political decisions, while the majority is ruled by these decisions. This minority has usually acquired its position in a manner independent of democratic elections; often it distances itself from the control of the majority (Parry, 1969: 30, 31).

Those who criticize democracies for the purpose of defending a theory of the elite often begin with establishing that in practise only a minority can take effective measures (Mosca, 1939: 53, 54-69; Pareto, 1935, III: 1423-24; Michels, 1958: 418). The difference between the functioning of the elite in a democratic and a non-democratic society is this, that in the former society the elite can function freely according to democratic rules, can compete with each other, and that the population, following certain rules, can exert its own influence; in a non-democratic society the elite in positions of leadership determine their own rules. Karl Mannheim fervently advocates the first alternative. Particularly he finds common ground with Mosca (1939: 159), who, as a remedy for over-centralization, rejected the self-rule of the people and who pleaded for a parliamentary democracy wherein creative forces and the integration of forces would be fostered (FPDP: 250, 258, 336, 337). Mannheim wants to elaborate Mosca's conceptions and places a challenge on all those who acknowledge freedom and justice as their highest values, to make their creative contributions. A pluriformity of the elite, constituted from people who can provide constructive cultural achievements, is his aim. Although sometimes he quotes Pareto affirmatively by way of exception, in the main Mannheim has a critical position over against him. He particularly disposes of the consequences which can easily be derived from Pareto's work; this is very clear when Mannheim names Mussolini as one of Pareto's students (SC: 152). Elsewhere Mannheim rejects the unconditional subjection to a leading elite, defended by Mussolini, because it is built on total irrationality (IU: 119, 120). He clearly expresses in words his own ideal concerning the functioning of the elite in a democracy:

> ...the actual shaping of policy is in the hands of *élites*; but this does not mean to say that the society is not democratic. For it is sufficient for democracy that the individual citizens, though prevented from taking a direct part in government all the time, have at least the *possibility* of making their aspirations felt at certain intervals. (...) Pareto is right in stressing that political power is always exercised by minorities (élites) and we may also accept Robert Michels' law of the trend toward oligarchic rule in party organizations. Nevertheless, it would be wrong to over-estimate the stability of such élites in democratic societies, or their ability to wield power in arbitrary ways. In a democracy, the governed can always act to remove their leaders or to force them to take decisions in the interests of the many. (SC: 179)

> What changes most of all in the course of democratization is the distance between the élite and the rank-and-file. The democratic élite has a mass background; this is why it can mean something for the mass. (SC: 200)

In contrast to these classical theoreticians whom Mannheim quotes, this study now discusses some authors who criticize Mannheim. Mannheim's conception of democracy above has, according to Bottomore (1964: 106), helped him gain ground in the twentieth century, particularly owing to the favorable circumstances influencing its reception. Bottomore gives the following three reasons: 1. The enlargement of the scale of things, international economic competition, and the decolonized countries demonstrated the importance of an efficient and enterprising elite.

2. The evident opposition between the governing elite in a society with a one-party system and the competing parties in a democratic multiparty system.

3. The capitalistic system of competition advanced the competition also between political parties.

Aron (1950: 10) has especially elaborated on the motive of competition. He writes that the most important difference between the Soviet Union and Western democracies is that in the former country only a party elite exists and the Western democracies are pluriform societies with a variety of elite (politicians, entrepeneurs, labor-union leaders, and others). Still, Aron's conception of the pluriform elite as characterizing Western democracies is one-sided. Mannheim does not only speak about the quantity of people among the elite, but above all about the participation of a growing number of people in the elite. Just as Mannheim, Aron is of the opinion that in a large and complicated society only a system of proportional representation can work; the elite have great power, but from time to time can be criticized by direct elections.

Concerning Mannheim, Bottomore (1964: 121) says that he has not presented us with a theory of the elite which has complete equilibrium; sometimes he points out the competition between the elite as a safeguard for democracy and elsewhere he suggests that no elite, group or class can guarantee a political stability unless it adopts the characteristics of a ruling class. The only thing that is consistent in Mannheim's theory, according to Bottomore, is that it rules out a society without an elite. This observation is correct. Already earlier I pointed out the inconsistencies which keep coming up in Mannheim' view and I pointed out his fragmentary approach (see Chapter VIII and XII; cf. Thoenes, 1966: 91).

Although Bottomore criticizes Mannheim's "representative democracy" and defends an effective direct democracy, he agrees with Mannheim, without referring to him, when he says that a democracy can function only when democratizing is being realized in all sectors of the society and when differences in income and in economic positions of power are diminishing. Just as Mannheim, Bottomore pleads for equal opportunities of instruction for everyone. Bottomore points out that in practise little circulation occurs in leadership positions; he also points out the accumulation of leadership functions by a few. Speaking about the stratification of classes in society, Bottomore says that the elite usually belong to the class of those wealthy in economic, poitical, and social influence. In conclusion, Bottomore pleads for a lessening of the distance between the elite and the masses and for the creation of conditions which put all citizens in a position to participate in decisions concerning the issues which directly affect their lives. Although Bottomore rejects Mannheim's conception about a representative democracy and about the elite, it is remarkable that his pleading for a greater circulation of leadership positions for lessening the distance between the elite and the masses, and for the participation of citizens in decision-making processes which directly affect them is shared by

Adorno rejects even more of Mannheim than Bottomore does. states that, for Mannheim, the problem of the cultural crisis has changed problem of the elite; Mannheim's analysis veils the facts. The falsehood Mannheim's description exists in this according to Adorno: that the privileged position of these groups is interpreted technologically as the result of an objective process of selection. According to Adorno, such an objective selection process does not exist. The elite are formed through their own selection (1981: 38f). In his description of the elite, Mannheim abandons the social relationships of power; he uses the concept *elite* in a formal-sociological and descriptive manner (1981: 39f). When he alleges that the mass democracies make it easier for everyone to acquire access to the social processes and to exercise influence and that the elite gradually must give up their exclusiveness, then, according to Adorno, he is in conflict with everyday experience. Mannheim's conception about the elite is a fiction; the elite are still always strongly homogeneous and exclusive. According to Adorno, Mannheim estimates the cultural crisis superficially. He masks the suffering in this time and rather fosters the social barbarism than that he opposes it. He complains, according to Adorno, only sentimentally about the cultural crisis (1981: 39f). According to Adorno, Mannheim's criteria for selection of the elite are these: blood, possessions, and achievement; one step farther, and Mannheim, according to Adorno, would be in the track of Hitler's conception of blood and land.

This criticism by Adorno is unjustified. First, because Mannheim points out the decay of the old and aristocratic elite, often constituted on the criterion of blood, as one of the causes for modern social and cultural instability. He does not want to institute the criteria of blood and money again, but sees them replaced by culturally relevant achievements, so that it would be possible for a contemporary stability to exist again. In the second place, Adorno's reference to Hitler's "blood and land" conception is hostile to Mannheim, who because of his Jewish descent, regarded it as necessary to flee nationalist-socialist Germany. In the third place, Adorno speaks about the actual functioning of the elite while Mannheim describes how the elite *ought* to function. Did Mannheim have too little awareness of reality in this regard? I answer this question negatively, because he clearly describes that in his time the elite were constituted chiefly on the criteria of family and money, and deplores that it is difficult to change this (MS: 89-91). Moreover, I doubt whether Mannheim had a sufficient sense of reality concerning the possibilities for change in a strictly, functionally, and rationally organized government of bureaucracies. If rulers from the planning elite are to form the policy and see it implemented adequately, then something must change in the functional-rational bureaucracies: a problem Mannheim does not discuss. Was he optimistic about the possibilities for change? In my view, it is a difficult question to answer. In any case, he was convinced of the need for change and of his mission to make that point clear. To talk with Thoenes (1966: 91): "Whatever difficulties may have been Mann-

ieory of the elite shows no malice. No doubt it
ul thinking, but the general design has a greatness of
ar above personal prejudice.''

ejects the managerial elite described by Burnham
: described by Wright Mills (1956) as dangerous
: that a society dominated by a functional rationality
: creativity. A society in which the political and
organizational elite are dominant will reserve little room, according to him, for
bringing in the other elite and for democractic control; politicians and
bureaucractics are characterized by a declining power to inspire the culture (cf.
Shils, 1941: 148).

Mannheim's social image concerning the elite is constituted as follows: 1. The
population which does not belong to an elite, which from time to time, following
democratic procedures, can exercise its influence on the conditions of association with and on the policy of the elite. 2. The pluriformity of the elite, who are
constituted according to this principle, "equal opportunities for everyone," and
according to the criterion of "merits," which refers to creative and constructive
contributions to the culture. 3. The planning elite, which is recruited form the
elite which were mentioned before. Characteristic for the members of all the
elite must be that they have already demonstrated their achievements (in the
business world, in politics, in administration, or in science), that their thought is
not restrictively bound to classes or groups, that they have "open minds," that
they are prepared to change their minds, that they perceive their reponsibility
for society as a whole, and that they, as participants of an elite, demonstrate
unity among themselves (FPDP: 100, 102; Hoyle, 1962: 67, 68, 74-78).

Although Mannheim gives no definition of an elite, he says that it is no class
or party (sc: 104). Apparently we must think in a sociological sense about
groups and groupings; we can reckon among "the normative elite" also the
discussion groups in which he himself participated.

The relationships of the elite among themselves, and especially those between the political and organizational elite, on the one hand, and the political
parties and governmental bureaucracies, on the other, is left unclear. It is clear
that the rulers must be counted among the planners. To what extent adminstra-
tive functionaries and advisors to the government belong to the elite is not clear.
To claim that Mannheim took an elitist position (Hoyle, 1962: 212) is unfair. He
was too democratic by conviction for that. Or, as Hoyle says elsewhere (28):
"His heart was in the ethic of democracy." On the other hand, he did not defend
egalitarianism (Floud, 1959: 57). He pleads for an effective democratic interaction between the elite and the masses. In this position, to be sure, a problem
lurks, correctly called a paradox by Hoyle (1962: 64, 65, 91, 93): the control
exerted on the elite by means of the majority approval demands that the

majority be able to think substantially, while they most often think functionally-rationally. Mannheim, as far as this is concerned, could answer that we live in a process of reconstruction, in which education must be conceived of as directed to substantial thinking as the "groundwork" (Nyberg, 1957: 159; cf. Eliot, 1948: 36-42).

To understand Mannheim's theory of the elite, two ideas are important, according to Thoenes (1963: 134): 1. His historical vision: society is an historical entity with a past, present, and future. 2. Sociology must draw essentials from the past and present, which make it possible to strengthen the grip on the future. Mannheim's analysis of the socially elite is directed to this: to study what must be done to guarantee a constructive functioning of the elite in a changed society. To what extent this functioning is, indeed, constructive is a political problem. As a socially and politically engaged thinker and strategist, Mannheim knows that he shares the responsibility for the solution of this problem. The constructive functioning is, according to him, providing leadership from the vantage point of "key positions" in a democratic society. Thoenes observes correctly (1963: 135) that there is no reason to doubt Mannheim's opinion that the "socially, relatively free-floating intelligentsia" must be recruited form the existing elite and that they will constitute the planning elite (the same also found by Hoyle, 1962: 166).

In Chapter XII this study noted that in modern sociological literature about intellectuals (and about the other elite) there is no more discussion in the framework of the sociology of knowledge as a subdivision of the sociology of culture. "The dynamic element which can proceed from this conception is to be recognized in virtually none of the modern conceptions. One studies the status quo of a group recognized on positional grounds as elite and at the very most one is prepared to express what one thinks about the factual ideas of such a group in some kind of evaluative innuendo or in an evaluative footnote" (Thoenes, 1963: 137). That is, it often seems that the sociologists concerned cannot agree with the stated purposes and ways of acting of the elite, and particularly of the political elite. Thoenes states further that in the modern sociological literature about the elite, the theory of "free-floatingness" in sociology has received no continuation and is no longer taken seriously.

Standing open to the challenges of the future means for Mannheim that the new elite must also function constructively; new situations demand a new elite. That is Thoenes' conclusion (1963: 139), who adds: "No matter how lovely his well-functioning elite are to him, they never acquire the role of disseminators of God's decrees; always they are assumed to be the servants of a public opinion as well-informed as possible. Although concessions in practical matters might be forced upon him, in actuality his concept of the elite would always be diametrically opposed to the ideology of the Third Reich" (Thoenes, 1963: 139; cf. A. Salomon, 1947: 359).

"Principia Media"

Repeatedly Mannheim pleads that planning is indispensable; he wishes to clarify and deepen insight into this indispensability. Just as often he pleads for a *new way of thinking*. It is unfair to judge planning on the basis of antique categories of thought or even currently existing categories. Pointing out the advantages or disadvantages of liberal or totalitarian society is not without value – he himself also does it – but judging planning with the help of liberal or totalitarian categories of thought is inadequate from the point of view of ideology and the sociology of knowledge. The society characterized by planning for freedom concerns the society of the future and must, therefore, be studied and judged with ideas that are adequate or congruent with that new reality. That society of the future is not a dream image; it is no utopia. A transformation of the will and of human thought is a condition *sine qua non* and, according to Mannheim, the most important problem (MS: 147). He takes up the central thesis from his sociology of knowledge, namely, that thinking is not an independent, self-sufficient, or abstractly intelligible matter; it is directly connected with the life situation of a person. Thought does not create the world, but in a given society with its given structures, specific forms and contents of thought arise as "instruments" of change, which people desire and strive for. He speaks not only about the attachment of thought to human behavior and actions, but also declares that thinking is really a part of behavior and actions (MS: 149).

In this connection Mannheim makes a distinction between *a radius of action* and *a radius of foresight*. By a radius of action he means the causal results which arise directly out of activities and which we can more or less continue to dominate. The radius of foresight is a series or chain of succession, which, on the basis of our activities, can be foretold in greater or lesser degree. The greater the technical and institutional mastery in a society, the greater the radius of action and the radius of foresight. Thinking at the level of planning means not only thinking directed toward a purpose, but also, and especially, a rational regulation and control of the relationships between the various purposes. In other words, not one-dimensional, but multi-dimensional thinking is necessary, for the purpose of thinking of economic politics and other fields, not as we did formerly, as fields that are separate and independent from each other, but as interacting spheres: changes in one sector are only to be interpreted adequately in context with others. This implies the possibility of being able to plan the whole from key positions, with the aim on purposes in the long perspective. In which direction can and must the planning occur and in which not? This question demands study of the *principles* or *generally accepted laws* which are characteristic of a definite socio-historical situation; that is, a study is necessary of what is called the *principia media*.

Mannheim adopted the concept of *principia media* from John Stuart Mill, who in turn had it from Francis Bacon. Mannheim defines *principa media* as "a kind of regularly recurring special laws, special relationships of a certain historical phase in a particular social setting" (MS: 177). According to him, historians have often attempted to understand a specific epoch with help of a "special historical logic"; they wanted to understand the unity of each period by means of an immediate intuition (as in Romanticism) or to reduce it to a specific historical dialectic (as in historicism, Hegelianism, and Marxism). It is remarkable that Mannheim only mentions these approaches and shoves them to the side as scientifically inadequate.

In Chapter VII I described Mannheim's own conception of historicism and his sociological elaboration of it. With help of the *principia media* he now gives a methodological deepening to this elaboration. It concerns an analysis of universal powers which are actively engaged in the integration within a specific socio-cultural constellation, and can be distilled form it. On the one hand, they are general "principles" or "laws," and on the other hand they must be seen in their specific "setting," because they confront us with a specific phase of the development of these principles (MS: 177, 178).

Every person has an unconscious knowledge of the *principia media*, which present themselves in everyday life. We are prepared for all kinds of experiences which we more or less expect and find normal. We get the paper and read there about all kinds of facts and events, while the framework, the system of coordination in which these facts and events are situated, remains more or less constant. The waiting pattern of someone who moves in a society of continuous and profound change is totally different. Such a person is prepared for possible changes in what have been his *guiding principles*. He does not take account only of the fluctuations in buying power and in the opportunities for employment, but also of an economic and monetary collapse. Not only the crisis in the cabinet, but also the *coup d'état* belongs to the possibilities. If one can understand the changes in the *principia media*, then one can also understand changed facts which no longer fit into an old structure of society and which indicate a new organizational principle.

Principia media are historically conditioned groupings of general factors closely interwoven with each other, each of which factors operates as "a single causal factor" (MS: 182). The uncertainty and danger which many people experience in our time does not arise from the many unexpected events, but from the fact that they cannot adjust the principles of their horizon of expectation quickly enough to the *principia media* of their time. This failure can bring disappointment, lack of comprehension, and despair along with it. It is the task of sociologists to understand the *principia media* of socio-cultural periods and to make them yield insights for others.

To discover the *principia media* one must first study the structure of the society; this means that "the organizing principle of social reality itself" must be studied. Analysis of this structure must begin with the study of facts of relationships between facts which are structurally relevant. This demands special training in sociological observation. One must specifically have an eye for the possibility of some events having a particular significance because they represent a new *principium medium*. Not all facts are important, but only those which represent "key positions" in social processes. Since reality is dynamic, since facts change rapidly, since *principia media* are modified, and since social structures are flexible, we must regard the formulations of the *principia media*, not as dogmatic theses, but as flexible hypotheses (ms: 230, 231).

The more Mannheim lays the emphasis on the integrated study of the society as a whole, and on the general laws operating within it, the more urgently he feels the need of an analysis of the structure of society. A socio-cultural relationship is not controlled only by a *principium medium* but by many *principia media*, which together form a context and structure. It is not sufficient to distinguish one or two *principia media* and to analyze them; the danger of interpreting all kinds of phenomena from the point of view of one or two principles easily leads to dogmatism and one-sidedness. Without naming Marxism in this regard, Mannheim addresses himself clearly against this apporach when he says that one *can* interpret all kinds of social and political phenomena on the basis of economic structures. Then one has too little eye, however, for the uniqueness of psychological and political factors and one makes himself guilty at the same time of dogmatism. In a multi-dimensional study of society as a totality one can, according to Mannheim, problably discover a hierarchy of *principia media*. Quantitative precision in this investigation will be available only seldom, if at all. That is why a qualitative analysis of *principia media* is necessary. That is why, according to Mannheim, one must never establish quantification as a demand, because one then no longer asks concerning what is worth knowing, but only deems the measurable elements worthy of knowing (ms: 186, 187).

The most central question which comes up in this regard is this: In which way can we get into the track of the *principia media*? Mannheim regards as unfruitful the viewpoint that the present cannot be studied scientifically because it still operates in a process of becoming and we ourselves are involved in this process without being able to take a distance on it. Neither does he see as desirable the "prophetic" standpoint of those who, although they have an eye for the *principia media* in the contemporary time, also, however, seem to know already ahead of time what will emerge from the development. Mannheim pleads for a rational observation of the present time in a nascent state, which observes the horizon of expectations as an open horizon. In this regard we can think of a distincion which he already made in his dissertation: the *systemization* of phenomena as an open activity, without already including this systemization in a *rounded-out system* which was formulated before.

Mannheim's conception of planning is a continuation of his idea of *principia media*. Planning is not the formulation, establishing, and realizing of an elaborated scheme or blueprint; it means not the projection of a new society. Planning is oriented toward reconstruction; it begins with what exists, with what is immediately available:

The ends, means, and foundations of planning exist on the same plane of histrocial reality: the crowding together of men and things in society is the foundation of planning. This provides the means, and only on this basis can we attain our next goal, and undertake the moulding of society in the right way. (MS: 192)

As a sociologist of knowledge, Mannheim strives to make attractive the necessity of thinking with the help of *principia media*. As he himself says: "As soon as a new type of conduct emerges in history a corresponding type of thought necessarily follows to accompany it" (MS: 149). It is an absolute statement which, however, is in contradiction to the factual situation in the social sciences; of that situation Mannheim says this: "...the social sciences are still at the stage of partial thinking, whereas in the practical adjustments which are bound up with the real conflicts of social life people are forced more and more to attack their problems in terms of interdependent thinking" (MS: 164). This problem concerning the relation of thinking and being was already discussed in Part III. The conclusion of De Valk (1963: 120) is then also justified: changed circumstances form the stimulus for another mode of thought, while new and adequate modes of thought must be judged for the purpose of being able to understand the modified social situation.

Mannheim attempts in what follows to make the changed manner of thought open to the cultural-sociological insights in an interdependent and fundamentally democratic society. He distinguishes three phases of development in a society, each with a manner of thought characteristic for it. 1. The phase of primitive thinking or of *chance discovery (Finden)*; one strives for the solution of problems by means of trying out various possibilities until the solution is found, more or less by accident (MS: 150). 2. The phase of *inventing (Erfinden)*, in which one goes to work more conscious of purpose; with the help of present knowledge, one attempts to solve a particular problem (MS: 151). 3. The phase of *planned thinking (Planen)*, in which one not only attempts to realize specific goals, but, taking account of the interdependence of social phenomena and of the gaps which still exist in the relationships between these phenomena, one wants to realize the possibilities for and what is desired of a socially and politically integrated policy, directed toward an interdependency which functions well (MS: 153, 154).

A Closer Look at "Principia Media"
During his stay in England Mannheim kept himself occupied chiefly with practical-methodological problems. During this period he developed increasingly from a critical perceiver into a social and political strategist (cf. Remmling, 1957a; 1957b: 282). The demand which Mannheim states for sociology is this: that it must study specific, concrete, and actual problems. According to De Valk (1963: 115), Mannheim was striving "to make sociology see as much of the concrete as possible instead of the abstract, as much of the unique in place

of the general, without limiting itself, nevertheless, to simple description and without giving up the claim of making statements of more or less general validity." According to De Valk, Mannheim understood well that he attempted to realize two statements of purpose which mutually exclude each other: on the one hand, the formulation of generally valid statements and on the other hand the understanding of the specific social situation (1963: 115, 116). In a creative way, Mannheim has attempted to build a bridge between the nomothetic and idiographic method: he introduced the intermediate category *principium medium*, a law with a restricted validity. Mannheim did perceive that it is not easy to learn to know the *principia media*; hence, the various formulations which he gives of it.

He speaks in *Man and Society* about *principia media* which were not necessarily contained in general laws (174), "a kind of regularly recurring special laws" (177), "universal forces in a concrete setting as they become integrated out of the various factors at work in a given place at a given time – a particular combination of circumstances which may never be repeated" (178), "in a certain sense nothing but temporary groups of general factors so closely intertwined that they operate as a single causal factor" (182). One may not combine various factors at whim; a stipulation is that they will be "those social forces which mould the age" (202). De Valk (1963: 117) observes correctly that this demand makes the quest for the *principia media* particularly difficult. It is difficult to establish which "particular general laws" are valid in a definite social situation, and even more difficult to choose the forces from it which have a formative influence in a particular period. De Valk concludes that much will depend on the insight, choices, and judgments of the investigator. Mannheim himself was conscious of this danger. He opposes subjective and intuitive approaches (170) and defends a rational and scientific grasp (236). Still, a little later (185), he admits that he cannot operate without a qualitative analysis, and elsewhere he says he accepts the risk "that a certain amount of intuition will be involved" (232). Mannheim's methodology concerning *principia media* is not only difficult to follow; most of all it is vague and not consistent in establishing concepts.

Adorno is even of the opinion that Mannheim in general uses concepts without specific content; this shows particularly in the concept of *principia media*, to which he demotes the dialectical processes of reality. Adorno (1981: 45ff) is of the opinion that Mannheim reasons in a totally irresponsible way. Historical phenomena are partially determined by Mannheim on the basis of general and partially on the basis of particular causes; he packages causes one way or another arbitrarily. According to Adorno, Mannheim keeps exchanging abstract and concrete causes. In his discourses about "general powers" Mannheim sees the weakness of dialectical thought. Adorno replies correctly that general powers may not be placed over against particular entities, as though the specific entities were brought about by "causality" in particular historical situations. The particular cannot be caused by the general powers, which are academic abstractions. "Causality" is not a cause, but a general concept under which particular phenomena can be subsumed.

A philosophical weakness is also described by Laan (1963: 147, 148). No philosopher could improve on Mannheim when he writes: "*principia media* are in the last analysis universal forces in a concrete setting" (MS: 178); a philosopher, however, would never predict the previous sentence from the parallel formulation made by Mannheim: "*principia media* ... are ... a particular combination of circumstances which may never be repeated." How, Laan asks, can someone combine "regularly special laws" (MS: 177) with "will never be repeated" (MS: 178). According to this critic, Mannheim negates totally in this regard the distinction between the orders of being and knowing.

It already becomes clear that Mannheim tries to open up the changing manner of thought concerning *principia media* and planning to the insights of the sociology of knowledge and culture, with the help of the three phases: chance discovery, invention, and planning. The division is artificially made, and Mannheim discusses it too briefly and with very little historical documentation. Already antiquity and the Middle Ages were characterized by planning rather than by invention. Mannheim grants this point and discusses invention as characteristic for the liberal *laissez-faire* society, which lies midway between the Middle Ages and modern society (MS: 159, 160). De Valk (1963: 122) concludes correctly that there is little occasion to speak of "three fundamental stages in the history of thought" as Mannheim does. The issue for Mannheim actually only concerns the types of societies characterized respectively by *laissez-faire*, totalitarianism, and planning for freedom, and particularly the transitions from the first to the third. Had he limited himself as a sociologist of knowledge and culture to the modes of thought which correspond to these types of society, his discussion of the "fundamental stages of thought" would have been more convincing.

According to Adorno (1981: 41f), the three phases of thought listed above mean no more than a dialectical scheme for epochs. The three changing modes of behavior and thought are represented in such a way by Mannheim that the social oppositions disappear. Mannheim sees the boundaries between these modes of thought as fluid crossings. They are represented, according to Adorno, as transitions between modes of thought, without precise stimulations for the power structures which conditon them, a lack which Adorno criticizes.

Conclusions

The conclusions concerning Mannheim's view of the *principia media* are very limited because such conclusions can hardly be drawn. The vagueness and the inconsistencies in his reasoning hinder a clear understanding of this subject. Apparently the vagueness and inconsistencies together arise from the fact that the *principia media* themselves are so difficult to comprehend. Mannheim wishes to bring up a fundamental problem for discussion, a phenomenon that indeed is so fundamental that it can be defined only with difficulty, just as the questions, "What is love, justice, beauty, time?" The issue is general tendencies which function as "realities" in a particular socio-cultural constellation. He wants to make clear that these realities are not to be denied, that the reconstruction of society implies comprehending what exists for the purpose of consequently bending around what exists into the desired direction.

Planning without Utopia?

To give form to society in the right way, proceeding in the process from existing reality, means that we must comprehend it with the *principia media*. That is why thinking at the level of planning needs a specific strategy.

For a good understanding of planning, Mannheim wants to distinguish it from "administration," which can arise when the phase of planning is past and the transition is made into the phase of a completely organized state; then a complete control of all social forces will exist. It is possible that the phase of planning will be followed by the phase of administration, but administration falls outside of Mannheim's argument, because it is a form of social thought which lies outside of "the framework of history," while he means by planning

> ... the reconstruction of an historically developed society into a unity which is regulated more and more perfectly by mankind from certain central positions. It is possible, of course, that the age of planning will be followed by one of mere administration. It is also possible that at a later stage all that we now call history, namely the unforeseeable, fateful dominance of uncontrolled social forces, will come to an end. As contrasted with administration, planning is thus a form of conduct still operating within the framework of history. (MS: 193)

Planning is a deliberate looking ahead, applied to society, so that the social processes are no longer only the product of conflict and competition. Whether the Western world will be completely successful in this is not a point Mannheim considers worth discussing; the question of whether the phase of administration will follow that of planning he regards as utopian and, thus, totally irrelevant.

It is not responsible simply to call Mannheim a utopian thinker. He strives for a society which will be characterized by the "planning for freedom"; this striving bears witness to a reality-congruent thinking, which his impulses do not simply receive from the existing social order, but also from not yet realized, abstract concepts. To this extent he is a utopian thinker, that he – stimulated by a guiding principle – strives for a new order of society, seeking continuity in it with the *principia media* which exist now. This striving, moreover, does not arise from a compulsion for social and political perfection (FPDP: 3-5); Mannheim is too realistic for that. By this striving he seeks to overcome the problems of Western culture. His philosophy of planning is the course of necessity; although not a path of perfection, there is, according to him, no other way. The discussion of a perfect society, an ideal society in the future, is a utopia

308

in the sense of a dream, a fantasy, which has no criteria for discussing its capacity for realization, starting with the present. This utopia is subjective and incapable of being discussed scientifically, and, exactly for that reason Mannheim finds it unacceptable. In Chapter XI I already indicated that, for Mannheim, utopia transcends the existing situation and at the same time stimulates activities which will transform the situation. Another problem is that Mannheim has named the capability of being realized as the characteristic of utopia, which can only be recognized after the fact. Measured by this criterion, his philosophy of planning may be called utopian to the extent that in various countries it has been realized.

In Chapter XI I also pointed out the social differentiation within utopian thinking; this thinking arises from dominated and oppressed groups, intent on emancipation. We can say with respect to "planning for freedom" that the intelligentsia is always burdened by the challenge of the crisis of Western culture. They can see through that crisis and they alone have the capability to transcend it; they can help to overcome the crisis. Precisely the intelligentsia, on the basis of their qualities, are in a position to think interdependently and comprehensively about the totality.

The "will to plan" must not remain restricted to an individual, but it also is not necessary that a majority take the initiative for it. Minorities can take the initiative for planning (MS: 194). Although the planning philosophy and the insight that this thinking is unavoidable can begin with a minority, this does not take away that it must take root in society as a whole; in the course of time, and rather soon, it must be carried out by the majority of people. They must not be frightened by their dislike of planning as dictatorial governing. They must acquire insight into the new phase of Western culture which has been set into motion during our century. The "fundamental democratizing," mentioned before, undoubtedly contributes to this insight.

How can this new attitude, which is necessary as a drawing board for planning, awaken within people? A new society, which presupposes another manner of thought, also presupposes at the same time that people change. That is why one of the most important chapters in this regard to be found in *Man and Society* bears the title: "The Problem of Transforming Man" (MS: 199).

Education for a New Mode of Thought

Analogous to his opposition to speaking about general, independent, and pure thought, Mannheim also manifests protest against the static psychology which discusses "the person in general" and "eternal human nature." Also, he does not want to speak about the unlimited plasticity of the person. He claims not to know enough about the nature of the fundamental human instincts, but is certain of a high degree of shaping that can take place in a person (cf. NSHB: 2). It comes down to seeing the Western person in the socio-cultural context of the twentieth century with the *principia media* functioning within that person. A society structured another way needs, as a condition, a vast range of people who learn to think in another way. Not only the education at home and at school, but also radio programs, newspapers, magazines, films, student organizations, adult education, and other means must make their contributions to advance this process of change (CRCE). These media may not only be directed toward the improvement of technical skills, but especially toward the planning of the *principia media*, which together determine the formation of character and which can transform the principles on which the social structures rest. In Mannheim's own words,

> ...contemporary education is slowly but consciously beginning to plan not only the communication of skill, knowledge and technique, but also those *principia media* of character formation which have hitherto been left to themselves and through which even the principles on which the social structure rests are to be transformed. In other words, through these efforts, the entire person is to be remoulded so that by using these new types of personality, it will be possible to transform the social structure in its psychological dimensions. (MS: 203)

Mannheim regards as futile the old social-philosophical dilemma: do institutions make the person, or does the person make the institutions? Also the question: do we first change the person for the purpose of being able to change the institutions, or do we change institutions for the sake of changing people? The truth, according to him, in these processes – as we already saw in Chapter XIV – especially pragmatism, behaviorism, and psychoanalysis have a progressive significance. Pragmatism, according to him, has made a contribution toward interdependent thought, because it acknowledges a direct relationship between thought and action. Behaviorism gives insight into the functioning of a person in a mass society and into the transformation of the personality. With the study of the unconscious and of the "hidden mechanism," psychoanalysis also has given insight into the possibilities for the transformation of the personality. Although Mannheim is critical of the concepts of humanity and of society in the pragmatism, behaviorism, and psychoanalysis of his day, one must call his partial esteem for these approaches eclectit (cf. Aron, 1955: 75-96; Remmling, 1968: 108).

Conclusions

Because "planning for freedom" does not fall ready-made out of the sky, and a society cannot be transformed by tomorrow, Mannheim advocates involvement with the existing social reality here and now and with the "handles" which various philosophies and academic disciplines offer him, for thinking at the level of planning means thinking according to a specific strategy. That Mannheim was no radical revolutionary may be clear. To see his ideas as "rooted in a deep conservatism" (Floud, 1959: 42), because he pleads for integration and balance among the social forces, strikes me as unfair. He wants to establish a connection between the existing social order and the *principia media*; integration and balance of social forces is high on his priorities for avoiding the dangers of social disorganization and demoralization. The characterization *conservative* is unfair, to the extent that this means that he wishes to maintain existing traditions, existing patterns of behavior, and existing patterns of thought. The opposite is true: thoroughgoing changes in the social order are his aim. We can call him a reforming sociologist, who strives for thoroughgoing changes along a progressive path (Bramstedt and Gerth, 1951: xiii, xiv).

Chapter XVII

Therapy: Planning Toward Realizing Freedom, Freedom Toward Realizing Plan

Characteristics of Planning for Freedom

In connection with planning, Mannheim's intention is not to discuss the "enforced equality" *(Gleichschaltung)* or "the goose-stepping coordination of the dictators," but about another form of *coordination* altogether, by which he means "the intelligent correlation of all the resources at one's disposal, the harmonizing of the various instruments of an orchestra" (MS: 262; DT: 4, 5). This coordination, naturally, can still come about in a variety of ways. Mannheim does not wish to interpret this coordination in a "monotome" manner, but to realize the "polyphony" in it, as differentiated as possible; not a monopolistic manner of planning, which eliminates creativity and spontaneity and brings about bondage. Planning must offer room precisely for freedom, which leads to creativity and spontaneity; yes, it can be put even more strongly: good planning can only occur if there is this kind of latitude in the society. Free discussion is necessary for planning. Good planning is carried out in "citadels" of freedom. In short:

> Planning in this sense means planning for freedom; mastering those spheres of social progress on which the smooth working of society depends, but at the same time making no attempt to regulate the fields which offer the greatest opportunities for creative evolution and individuality. (...) It is the freedom of a society which, since it has the whole coordinated system of social techniques within its grasp, can safeguard itself of its own accord against dictatorial encroachment on certain spheres of life, and can incorporate the charters of these citadels within its structure and its constitution.
>
> Anyone who plans for freedom, that is, provides for citadels of self-determination in a regulated social order, has of course to plan for necessary conformity as well. (...) Planning for freedom does not mean prescribing a definite form which individuality must take, but having both the knowledge and experience to decide what kind of educaton, what kind of social groups and what kind of situations afford the best chance of kindling initiative, the desire to form one's own character and decide one's own destiny.(MS: 264, 265)

Elsewhere he writes:

> ... a dynamic society must not merely encourage its members to work for reward, it must also develop fresh initiative and spontaneity, especially in the ruling elite. (MS: 284)

To put it succinctly, Mannheim does not only speak about "planning for freedom," but also about "democratic planning"; he names the following characteristics:

1. *Planning for freedom*, which is subject to democratic control;
2. *Planning for plenty*, which grants the advantage neither to great corporations nor to labor unions, but which strives for full employment and for advancing the common welfare;
3. *Planning for social justice*, which has an eye for the differentiation in status and prestige and which advocates neither an ideal of egalitarian uniformity or an ideal of the privileged few;
4. *Planning not for a classless society*, but for eliminating the enormous discrepancies between rich and poor;
5. *Planning for cultural standards*, which strives for progress in the coordination mentioned above, without the elimination of cultural values;
6. *Planning that counteracts the dangers of a mass society* and which interferes according to collective criteria, only in cases of institutional and moral decay;
7. *Planning for balance* between centralizaton and distribution of power; and
8. *Planning in order to encourage the growth of personality*, for the purpose of transforming the society by this means (FPDP: 29).

Democracy in a time of planning is, according to Mannheim, confronted by an "almost paradoxical task." On the one hand the critical powers of political parties are stimulated and strenthened; on the other hand the parties must be conscious of their collective responsibility and of the rights of opposing parties within the plan for social reconstruction. Speaking about the starting points of the politics of planning, Mannheim lists other characteristics concerning centralization:

1. *Only a strongly centralized governmental power* can carry out planning. In the hands of a weak government, planning is not an efficient means. A strong, centralized governmental power which is directed toward the common good is not in conflict with social freedoms. These freedoms are threatened by oligarchies which know no responsibility for the common good.
2. *Centralization is necessary* because coordination of various measures is essential for planning.
3. *Centralization* in a planned society is only necessary for basic political issues. For other political issues a functional decentralizaton in favor of lower authorities is encouraged.
4. In a planned society, *governmental authority and the unity of the people are*

not separate entities. The operation of the government occurs for the purpose of social freedom.

5. *The constitutional state intervenes* in economic life by means of regulation for the purpose of protecting full production of controlling monopolies (FPDP: 112-116).

However clearly these characteristics may accent the competencies of the central government, Mannheim reiterates that they are subject to democratic control. For the purpose of protecting social freedoms in a modern democracy, Mannheim names ten "virtues" which the democratic government ought to fulfill:

1. *Integration of all social powers*; this implies that the government can depend on a majority of the population.

2. The government must encourage *competition between ideas*. That is, discussions between people of contrasting opinions is necessary, for the purpose of testing the strong components of various social and political views and for discovering the points of agreement and of difference.

3. *Judging the parliamentary system as more worthy than the corporation system*, because corporations are less able to realize in society the necessary integration than is apparent in parliamentary representation. The dangers of disintegration and conflicts between groups and the domination of one department are all greater in corporational life.

4. *Emotional identification* of the individual citizen *with* the community and *responsibility for* the community.

5. *Public defense of the execution of actions*: full accountability.

6. *Clear demarcation of responsibilities of the rulers*, so that the voters can judge who is responsible for which parts of which policies.

7. *Flexible politics*, by which he means a regular and controlled circulation of people in administrative functions.

8. *Constructive alignment of the opposition.*

9. *Democratic discussions must not inhibit the ability to make decisions*, but rather stimulate that ability.

10. The *progress* in the direction which Mannheim desires and characterizes is dependent on creative personalities "who have the mental power to break the crust of convention in every sphere of life by penetrating into new possibilities of the mind and of social living" (MP: 7). This creative influx may not only come about at the highest level, in small groups (of planners), but also at many other levels of the society (MP, 8; DP, 79-82).

Planning for Freedom: Tension without Paradox

In what precedes, it was written that Mannheim confronts democracy in an epoch of planning with an "almost paradoxical task"; thus, it is not a real paradox compared with his use of the word in other contexts (see Chapter VII);

314

here, the word is used in a general, non-restrictive sense. In the elaboration no sign of a genuine paradox is to be found, but rather signs of tensions between freedom to criticize and conformity to collective responsibility; between the macrocosmic options for social freedom and the freedom of the individual to choose. This tension, no doubt, will always continue to exist, but will be endurable and humane if two conditions of planning, which he mentions, are satisfied: 1. consistency and 2. acceptability to the majority. The proper functioning of a modern democracy requires "political mass education" for the citizens, for the purpose of their being able to understand the sources and techniques of anti-democratic dangers. The dangerous enemies of democracy are, according to him, not the concervatives who want to hang on to as much power as possible, but those who want to give the democratic government as much legal pwer as possible and by this means to prepare the way for tyranny (FPDP: 149).

The greatest challenge for thinking in terms of planning is to control the irrationality in a rational manner. This means that people, on the basis of interdisciplinary studies, must know which social techniques they must use with reference to specific problematical situations. It also means knowing *how* and *where* these techniques must be used; that is, knowing how the strategy of planning must be carried out from "the key positions of social control."

Freedom and discipline, according to Mannheim, do not exist as abstractions, but they always acquire form in a particular social context; they are functions of a group or a society and hence they acquire a different form in a soccer club than they do in a military organization. The discipline which exists in both examples limits the freedoms for initiatives and choices in very different ways. His "third way"

> will try to combine the two techniques by allowing for rigid organization where efficiency demands it, and by pleading for the flexible pattern wherever feasible. Progress toward freedom consists in a steady advance toward flexibility. (FPDP: 276)

In his conception about planning, freedom and discipline are "defined by the nature of groups, sub-groups, and their purposes." In this social order people should strive for great flexibility and maximum freedom of choice and for self-expression, both on the part of groups and individuals. This striving must be defended by the planners, who, however must combat the egoism of both groups and individuals. The squelching of the opposition by a specific group or combination of groups – for instance, the tyranny by business and by governmental bureaucracies – must be opposed. The planners shall, however, not only strive at the macro-level for the furthering and justifying of the individual's freedom of choice, but shall also give direction at a micro-level for the freedom of choice of the consumer. The planners shall exert leaderhsip for the welfare and happiness of the population by means of a public policy of prizes, of subsidies, of credit, of housing, and of education.

315

Mannheim is opposed to anarchistic, liberal, totalitarian, and plutocratic interpretations of freedom. In a planned society the citizens must be able to distinguish sharply and adequately that there are areas where planning and discipline must be dominant and areas (especially small groups and personal relationships) where freedoms and experiments are possible and are required. Where planning in one way or another is valued too highly, or where it is absolutized, where the social freedoms which planning must advance are, in fact, crushed (or where the opposite happens, where planning and discipline is impossible because of chaotic freedom): there a paradoxical situation exists. Mannheim is aware of these dangers (hence his phrase "almost paradox"), and he opposes them.

Just as *laissez-faire* thinking did not remain restricted to one economic sector, but characterized all sectors, so Mannheim is conscious that planning does not only affect the economy, but all spheres of social life. A defect in the democracies which existed in his time was not that they were characterized by too much democracy, but by too little. The "planning for freedom" is meant to further these processes of democratization, for the purpose of completing them. That is why Mannheim very often speaks about "democratic planning" (DP: 80, 82).

Mannheim's Concept of Planning: A Closer Look

There are interpreters of Mannheim who accuse him of assigning the greatest weight in his argument to planning, that this conception implies a form of political totalitarianism, and that very little is left of his social and political freedom once planning is implemented. I shall discuss only a few critics.

Popper: Criticism of a Holistic Perfectionism

A sharp criticism against Mannheim's theory of planning was brought out by Karl Popper (1957: 64-104). This begins with a distinction between "piecemeal engineering" and "utopian engineering." Piecemeal engineering is a form of social reconstruction which, with help of the appropriate technological knowledge, directs itself toward concrete purposes and occupies itself with stating those very purposes; this lies outside of the domain of technology. It works step by step, does not aim at solving many problems, and attempts to establish as clearly as possible the relationships between causes and results in the studied social phenomena and processes. That is why it is theoretically possible and practically realizable.

Activists, according to Popper, will not be satisfied with this fragmentary approach. Popper counts Mannheim among these "stormers of the social establishment." These "stormers" hold to a "utopian" or "holistic engineering." On grounds of a blueprint for society, they intend to reconstruct it as a totality. Because they want to attack a large number of complex problems, their

316

approach is theoretically too global to be clear. In addition, the plan is impractical to implement. In practise, utopian engineering directs itself toward concrete purposes, just as the piecemeal engineering does.

Popper acknowledges that purposes, regarded microscopically, contain ideas which do not relate to a total reconstruction of society, but which are only directed toward "small adjustments and readjustments." The purposes as Popper proposes to formulate them are first of all intended to solve existing problems, rather than to strive for the realization of ideals in the future. Popper's words (1952, Vol I: 158) are familiar: "The piecemeal engineer will ... adopt the method of searching for, and fighting against, the greatest and most urgent evils of society, rather than searching for, and fighting for its ultimate good. (...) In favour of this method, the piecemeal engineer can claim that a systematic fight against suffering and injustice and war is more likely to be supported by the approval and agreement of a great number of people than the fight for the establishment of some ideal." The actual difference between piecemeal and utopian engineering is that the latter always holds a blueprint for the whole society, while the piecemeal engineer does not regard this as necessary. "I think that a fairly concrete and realizable end may justify temporary measures which a more distant ideal never could" (1952, Vol I: 161; cf. 157-161).

I pass by the fact that Popper includes organic holism and historicism under one rubric (1957: 73). He is of the opinion that Mannheim and other utopian social critics want to think at "the level of large-scale planning" and by their planning, intend, in key positions, to increase the power of the state indefinitely; according to Popper, this is a totalitarian idea (1957: 91, 92).

Should someone object that each instance of planning in a particular sector of society nevertheless presupposes a view of society as a totality (if planning is not to become too framentary and if it is not to come into conflict with planning in other sectors of society), then Popper would answer that he is against a macroscopic vision of society, unless one strives after macroscopic purposes by means of short little steps, the only kind available. Or, as Braybooke and Lindblom (1963: 46) say: "Above all, he [Popper] insists that a decision-making system must be adapted to the experimental nature of social reforms, in which ends are as much adjusted to means, through reappraisal of objectives in the light of success or failure with policies, as means are to ends."

Popper also criticizes the three phases of Mannheim: 1. "chance discovery" or "trial and error," 2. "imitation," and 3. "planning." According to Popper, "trial and error" is not a primitive mode of thought which belongs to the past; to the contrary, it approaches the method of the modern sciences more closely than do the other two modes of thought. He goes a step further: the holistic mode of thought in the social sciences, on which Mannheim's ideas of planning are based, is, in Popper's regard, a pre-scientific mode of thought, because it still contains the primitive idea of perfectionism. Popper states, arguing against utopian and holistic interpretations of society, that we cannot realize a heaven on earth and we can only strive for improvement by bits and pieces (1957: 75, 87, 96).

Popper's critique of Mannheim strikes me as not tenable. In the first place Popper grants that also piecemeal engineers have specific ideas about society as a framework within which they place their concrete purposes (1957: 66, 68ff). Although the task of piecemeal engineers is unobtrusive and theoretically sound, they do not seem to limit themselves to this task in the strict sense. He cites as an example that piecemeal engineers can have a vision of greater uniformity of income. He, however, passes by the fact that the inequality of income is a part of a context of constellations of power and of concerns which are dominant in a society, and these constellations doe not only affect income, but also other social phenomena (for instance, the influence of heavy industry on politics, on communication media, and on the military). Popper's statement that piecemeal engineers also have ideas about improving society implies the strong probability they secretly harbor views of society as a totality.

In the second place, Popper passes by the many passages in Mannheim's work from which it is evident that Mannheim has no intention of imposing his planning on society; Mannheim wants to see planning carried out through democratic procedures. Although Mannheim is explicitly opposed to piecemeal engineering because of its fragmentary grasp, its lack of a clear view of society, and its lack of an interdependent style of thought, still planning must take place cautiously and gradually. At the start, according to him, planning can have application only to concrete economic and political problems. In its applicaton, Mannheim's position approaches Popper's piecemeal engineering.

Thirdly, Popper's interpretation of Mannheim concerning the state is unfair – that it would acquire as much power as possible and become totalitarian. Popper cites *Man and Society* (337) to support Mannheim's supposed totalitarian view of the state, while Mannheim on that very page describes the totalitarianism of dictators and *opposes* it.

In the fourth place, Popper seems actually to reverse Mannheim's three phases of thought. While Mannheim saw a progression in the sequence of these phases, Popper regards the thought involved in planning as a reversion to a pre-scientific mode of thought; precisely because of its perfectionism, it must have something primitive about it. Popper's criticism of the perfectionism implied in holism has more to do with a mechanistic interpretation of holism than with Mannheim's view of society. I already pointed out that Mannheim warns against perfectonistic thought at the level of planning, because this perfec-tionism is peculiar to totalitarian planning.

Boris (1971: 201) asks pointedly whether Popper's criticism actually strikes Mannheim's position as sharply as Popper intended. Concerning piecemeal engineering, astonishingly many agreements exist between Popper and Mann-heim. Concerning the perfectionism of holism, Popper interprets Mannheim unfarily. Concerning the totalitarianism in Mannheim's conception of the state, Popper did not read Mannheim correctly.

Van Riessen: Criticism of Scientific Planning

The Netherlandic engineer and philosopher of culture Van Riessen discusses extensively Mannheim's theory of planning. I discuss Van Riessen – whose ideas about planning demonstrate a great deal of agreement with F.A Hayek's *The Road to Serfdom* (1944) – because also he is one of the best examples of a negative interpretation of Mannheim. For Van Riessen the central queston is *how* Mannheim and other thinkers about planning take humanity into account: "Man's value, especially his beliefs, are ultimately decisive for the future of our civilization" (1952: 183). According to Van Riessen, planning means a conscious choice for the advancement of social processes in a particualr direction. With help from planning, leaders want ot lead; an ideal in the future beckons the promoters of planning. "Their weather vane is not the unavoidability of the present and the future, but *faith* in an ideal: *the forming of the community*" (1952: 175-177). Van Riessen is of the opinion that planning "deals with the essence of cooperative activity" (1952: 180). He comes to this interpretation of planning (also of Mannheim's conception concerning it) because it is of a scientific nature; it aims not only at scientific research, "but its aim is application. It does not simply give advice, but offers a plan by means of which *to control and organize* the *activity* of *man* in an essential sense" (1952: 180). People want to leave nothing to chance, individuality, or whim. A scientifically-based planning, according to Van Riessen, comes to be characterized because of its very nature by domination, centralization, and petrification (1952: 176-191). He grants that Mannheim envisions a dynamic planning, which adjusts itself to circumstances; this conception can mitigate the petrifying influence of planning, but, according to Van Riessen, does not stop it. Although he also grants that Mannheim's thinking about planning is nuanced and does not intend a dictatorship, he does not attribute much importance to this nuancing: "...planning prospers only in a society of new, collectivistic, centralized structure" (1952: 197). Summarizing Mannheim's plea for a militant democracy, Van Riessen writes as follows (1952: 201, 202):

> Democracy must become militant. A unifying scheme, a spiritual integration, is required in a planned social structure. If our civilization is to escape the grasp of a dictatorial planning, spiritual adaption must be sought through planning. This adaption of the whole man is the real meaning of "planning for freedom": the triumph over chaos within our society.
>
> It is useless to speak of planning unless all of society is included. And such planning needs an *ideology*, the longing for a better world. It has to supply the religious and moral recommendations in order "not ony to lay down some principles, but also a set of concrete patterns of behavior, the image of satisfactory social institutions and a whole world view as a connecting link between them."

Van Riessen continues that Mannheim regards values as necessary in order to realize his plan, and concludes: "The discovery of such values is a matter of a rational adaption to the social structure" (1952: 202).

Van Riessen's markedly one-sided approach to Mannheim makes him come to a number of unfair interpretations on a number of points. Although he mentions Mannheim's nuanced thinking, he does not take sufficient account of it.

1. Mannheim indeed intends to give direction to social processes, with the help of planning. Perhaps he has an ideal in mind, but he does not speak of it. Not the belief in the ideally-formed community compells him, but his search for an escape from the disintegraton and the increasing chaos in the Western democracies.

2. Joining with the *principia media* and social circumstances, Mannheim wants to point the way for the "planning for freedom," which would be different for various societies. Not a fixed ideal of planning, and certainly no totalitarian implementation of the plan, is ever envisioned by him.

3. By means of "key positions in society" Mannheim wants to direct the planning, and not in an "essential sense" dominate and organize human activities. Van Riessen's insistence that Mannheim wishes to plan society in an "essential sense," eliminating personal creativity, is simply wrong. Mannheim regards creativity as a necessary *condition* for planning.

4. The militant democracy is interpreted by Van Riessen as a spiritual integration by planning, while Mannheim describes it as a *condition* for planning.

5. Interpreting planning as based on the ideology of the existing society is only partially true, particularly true for that part of planning which, according to Mannheim, must connect with the *principia media* and social circumstances. No less important is the condition that planning must be based on values, either new ones or ones that have been lost. Finding these values is not only a matter of functional-rational adjustment to the existing social order, but it transcends this by a substantial rationality.

6. Speaking about the nature of scientific planning, Van Riessen comes to conclusions which Mannheim does not draw – and which he could not draw. Van Riessen's conclusion that "comprehensive planning in practise is a silent process toward totalitarian planning" (1952: 202), would be rejected out of hand by Mannheim. He would reproach Van Riessen as the representative of an antiquated philosophical style of thought and, because that style of thought inadequately represents reality, of an ideological style of thought as well. Mannheim does not aim at a "planning for freedom" which would simply be based on the existing social constellation. Child-rearing and education will provide in a democratic way for the insight into the need for new values and must then advance the realization of those values. *On condition* that a new style of thought emerges, the way of the "planning for freedom" can safely be taken. Put another way: feedom, democracy, and personal responsibility are not simply ruled out of the thinking about planning, but planning can only be realized when at the same time the conditions for realizing freedom, democracy and personal responsibility are being fulfilled. With Randall (1941: 343), I

conclude that for Mannheim "freedom and personal responsibility have always been the highest values"; or as Remmling (1957c: 391) says: "The pedagogical goal of our society is the democratic personality." Mannheim emphasizes countless times that a bad planning, of the sort that exists in communistic and fascist countries, is evil; he advocates only a wholesome planning. It is evidence of almost hostile reading that someone, nevertheless, connects Mannheim's "good planning" with the totalitarian and evil planning in communistic Russia, as Van Riessen does (1952: 195, 205).

To make thinking at the level of planning possible, according to Mannheim (following his own criteria), demands a dynamic manner of thought adequate for comprehending reality. If one concludes on the basis of an ideological manner of thought, inadequate for comprehending reality, that "planning for freedom" is a contradiction in terms (cf. Van Riessen, 1952: 212; cf. Hayek, 1944: 23-31), then on the basis of his own manner of thought as adequate for comprehending that reality, Mannheim would dismiss the criticism.

In Part III I discussed this question: What is thinking which is adequate for comprehending reality? With the argument that his critics do not think in terms which he would judge adequate for comprehending reality, Mannheim disengages himself easily from their criticism. The conclusion of S.U. Zuidema is then also correct:

> Scientific planning has the right to prove itself true and may not be disturbed in the execution of this: its right and calling. This right belongs to scientific planning simply because it is the most social and brotherly activity thinkable, for it will always permit mankind to share in the benefit of progress in the most efficient manner or at any rate in a "better" way. Any opposition to this planning must be branded as reactionary. (1961: 155)

Continually it has been my concern to describe and judge Mannheim according to his own intention. Critical questions were not omitted. That is why two closely connected questions still deserve our attention. In the first place the question of Van Riessen: Is Mannheim right in placing so much confidence in mankind? Or, is mankind by nature good so that with the help of a sociological consciousness he can come to clarifaction about existence and to a correct, normative insight into the processes of society? Or, where does the normative content come from for the values which Mannheim deems necessary? A second question, which is the extension of the first, concerns the planning elite. Does not the study of history teach that the concentration of power in individuals and in small groups, also in democracies, always leads to the abuse of power? In Van Riessen's judgment, Mannheim underestimates the selfishness of mankind and how deeply the results of original sin cut into human lives.

However, these questions do not arise only from Van Riessen's Christian view of society. Also the socialist Thomassen asks on what grounds Mannheim's optimism might be placed; he, too, fears that freedom and democracy will be lost in the implementation of Mannheim's ideas of planning (1936: 132, 134). Mannheim's regular discussion partner, Lord Lindsay, calls attention to this problem as well. He is of the opinion that Mannheim makes the idea of "democratic planning" insufficiently clear. The abuse of power by the planning elite and tendencies toward totalitarianism are seen by Lindsay as real dangers in the implementation of Mannheim's ideas. He adds that Mannheim usually dismissed all criticism absolutely: "Mannheim always resisted very strongly any suggestion that there was a limit to sociological knowledge, any suggestion that legislation, like moral action, was partly a leap in the dark. One always felt that he had a sociological faith that all these blanks of ignorance about society could be overcome" (Lindsay, 1952: 86). While Lindsay speaks of a sociological faith, Busch (1959) formulates that faith as follows: "Mannheim believed in an Archemedian point in sociology." I shall return to the "sociological faith" ascribed to Mannheim and to his relationship to the Christian faith. First the problem of "planning in the crisis" invites our attention.

Planning in the Crisis

Various conceptions of planning in the modern state are considered valid currently. Van Gunsteren (1976; 1980) mentions the rational or orthodox planning, the system-rational, the communicative planning, and planning as a learning process.

The *orthodox* planners plead for a rational formation of policy. What happens rationally, according to them, cannot fail; only non-rational influences lead to failures. The expansion of this idea of planning, according to Van Gunsteren (1976; 3-7), goes accompanied by four problems.

1. At the start rational planning is limited to the technical operations and coordinations of an engineer. He makes a plan for the construction of a machine. The rational planning which is used in a technological context is also applied in another context, the context of social structures and interaction. The question is whether technical-rational planning can be applied also on a social level (cf. Peper, 1974: 10).

2. Orthodox planning needs, as a condition for its success, a consensus concerning purposes, values, norms, and coordinating institutions. The existing purposes, values, and norms were developed in a pre-planning phase of society, which, as such, forms an entirely different context from that which is required for the rational planning.

3. The increased volume of research in the social sciences into the interdependence of the social structures and processes has led to this phenomenon: that planning began to function as a technique for controlling social processes. This interdependence continues to increase and confronts the planning authorities with great problems. Also here the problem of the alteration of context arises: can one carry over scientific theories and methods into the context of state interference? Scientific knowledge differs from knowledge directed at application.

4. The orthodox planning which is applied to enterprises acquires application

322

also in the sphere of government. Thus, a new alteration of context: can one apply planning techniques for business enterprises (with a fairly reliable budgetary, administrative, and executive structure) to the field of government (with an entirely different administrative structure)?

These four factors of rational-scientific planning developed into rational-orthodox planning by the government, "which can be characterized as comprehensive coordination and control of complex networks of interdependencies on the basis of scientific knowledge by way of big formal organizations" (Van Gunsteren, 1976: 6, 7).

From these four points it seems that defenders of scientific-technical or orthodox planning are of the opinion that their conceptions of planning are not bound to a particular context. Their presupposition is that this planning is rational and, as such, universal. Van Gunsteren observes correctly (1976: 7, 45; 1980: 16, 17) that rationality never appears in a pure form, but always in a social and cultural context; it is a social-cultural product. These rational planners tend toward conceptions of rationality which are currently held as valid in society and particularly in the universities. They base their scientific investigation, then, on a cultural situation. Moreover, it appears that adequately rational knowledge and information about planning is provided by various sciences and, indeed, in a variety of ways, which correspond to the various fields in which these sciences operate and which correspond to the various views of society held by the social scientists.

Orthodox planners proceed from three premises: adequate knowledge and information; a reliable base of power and cooperation; and a static and submissive field in which to apply their theories (Van Gunsteren, 1980: 19). The ideal of this conception of planning, however, collides sharply with the political reality, in which cooperative relations, contradictory concerns, compromises, and conflicts exist. People and organizations simply do not work in a mechanistic way. In addition, the government and other administrative centers do not have the power or the means to let people function "obediently" as such. People, both implementers as well as others connected with the decisions of planning, and organizations are much less pliable than rational planners wish. This orthodox planning (in Van Riessen's words, scientific planning) is no danger for a democratic society; a vital democracy is a danger for orthodox planning, In my opinion, orthodox planning is doomed to failure and cannot solve the crisis of the welfare state.

The *system-rational* planners, especially E. Jantsch and H. Ozbekhan, are of the opinion that orthodox planning fails because it is too fragmentary, is directed toward partial problems, and is too unsystematic in practise; one must take into account the comprehensive systems which includes the partial systems. The practise of system-rational planning brings throughgoing structural and organizational reforms along with it. According to Van Gunsteren (1976: 38-40; 1980: 22), this thinking, along with other deficiencies, takes too little account of the reality of political accretions and sensitivies. In addition, the system-rational planners have various political preferences, obstacles to clear methods of application.

Communicative planning is based on the creation of democratic structures of deliberation for the purpose of arriving at the formation of political decisions. Communicative planners (especially J. Habermas) desire all those concerned to discuss the necessary knowledge and information. These planners direct their invitation to all those concerned, to participate in the planning processes. They do not regard scientific techniques of planning as superfluous, but they are of the opinion that these techniques are doomed to fail, because the stable basis for communication and cooperation necessary for success are lacking. They have no operational, or distinctive or elaborated theory of planning. Whether the discussion structures will lead to an efffective planning is still an unanswered question in the opinion of Van Gunsteren (1976: 42, 43).

For the conceptions of planning mentioned above, the greatest obstacle is the organizational reformations which are a condition for the success of the particular form of planning. Although Van Gunsteren calls this organizational aspect the greatest problem (1980: 25), the root of the organizational problem, along the line of his own argument and in the line of Mannheim's thought, is "the problem of transforming man."

According to Van Gunsteren, planning in the welfare state has been too incidental, fragmentary, and devoted to sub-topics. A strategic planning is required as an alternate, one which is directed toward the interdependence of the most important sectors of social life; this strategic planning is also sometimes called corporative planning, in which politicians, business people, and other citizens together attempt to formulate an adequate policy. One can say this method of planning is based on a business model. However many objections one can bring against this manner of planning and however pessimistic one may be about its capability for being realized, the choice, according to Van Gunsteren, is apparently nothing other than this: "Either a welfare state without oppressive planning, or oppresive planning but no welfare state" (1980: 30). Van Gunsteren chooses for the first alternative because the values of the welfare state are precious, and cautious planning is still possible within it; people will need to attempt to minimize the failures of planning, but at the same time people must have a great enough simplicity and sense of reality to expect some degree of failure as a consequence of the fact that planning is always a part of the social context.

The conclusion of Van Gunsteren (1976: 150-154) is that we still must actually *learn* how to plan. This *we* does not only refer to the "enlightened few." "What is needed is responsible and semi-autonomous adaptations at many levels of the policy. This is so because the context – changing local circumstances – is an essential component of any viable complex system of interaction" (152). This

324

conception about planning as a process of "public learning" is time-consuming and related to the existing forms, traditions, and processes of society. Elsewhere he says (1980: 31): "Planning is then no longer the purifier of everything and the solution to everything, but an historically variable activity which can serve to remedy some forms of failures, but which, in case it is used on too broad a scale, brings its own forms of failures along with it." This standpoint implies that planning is conceived as a democratic process and as a *learning process* and that it is a continual subject for discussion at all strata of the society; every stratum by means of democractic structures will be able to contribute. Not only scientific academicians, politicians, or businessmen, but all of these together and in cooperation assume the burden of a strategic, modest, and flexible planning, which is conceived as an "open-ended" learning process to be borne by democratic structures of communication (cf. Popper, 1952, Vol. I: 162ff; 1957: 91, 92). This form of planning demands a specific attitude, a consciousness of responsibility, and, indeed, sound ethics. This is the opinion of Atteslander (1969: 477), who concludes concerning the strategic planning mentioned above:

> Sociology will not be judged for this first of all, whether it has found satisfactory means for its task in achieving of its plans, but rather according to the weightier matter, whether it was in a position to perceive clearly the demand of the time and to ask clear questions. It is useless only to point out that greater social conflicts are to be expected; we must find the ways today to diminish them in the future. In that attitude is implied that we abandon the concept of wanting to plan *for* people; we must increasingly plan *with* them. In this program for greater participation, according to my evaluation, lies the basic democratic mental attitude, determined on future planning. Planning conceived in either a purely economic or technological manner must gradually and slowly shatter.

The way of strategic planning is not easy. It is to be expected that planners regularly become frustrated through the participation of citizens in democratic structures of communications, while the citizens will have the same experience because of the decisions already taken by the planners. The question is whether there is now an alternative way. In every instance it may be clear that this conception of strategic planning corresponds exactly with Mannheim's interpretation of "planning for freedom."

Conclusions

The critique of Popper, Van Riessen, and others that Mannheim absolutizes planning at the expense of freedom is untenable. Also the interpretation that practically the power of planners is unlimited (Floud, 1959: 51) is not fair to Mannheim's intention. He appears to be an opponent of technocratic planning. Mannheim could have met this criticism and made his argument stronger if he had formulated his ideas more precisely. On several essential points he remains vague, for instance, the control of bureaucratic excesses, the guarantees of

325

social freedoms, and the functioning of parliamentary control (Shils, 1941: 152). It is obvious that Mannheim's neglecting to make a choice between existing economic-political systems somewhat blurs what he means by "planning for freedom." However, he does not want his critics to stigmatize him by means of identification with an existing economic-political system.

From the foregoing description of the modern state, from various conceptions about planning, and from the plea for a strategic planning (which is as democratic as it is educational), the social and scientific relevance of Mannheim's thought about the welfare state is clear. One can level elaborate criticisms at his lack of a clear definition of planning and at inconsistencies in his view (Boris, 1971: 228). Not to be denied, however, is that the post-war discussion on planning at particular points coincides with his conception exactly, no matter that these other interpretations proceed from other starting points and no matter how little these positions refer to Mannheim. Many elements of social planning which are currently in the discussion already appeared in Mannheim's work (Argenti, 1974; Boris, 1971; Bruton, 1974; Fromm, 1955; Jaspers, 1953). His interpretation of "planning for freedom" includes the following elements as part of his strategy: 1. a circumscrption of purposes by the planners; this statement of purposes concerns an integral approach to the society and not a fragmentary one; 2. an effective implementation of policy; 3. investigation into the results of planning, both the predicted and unpredicted results, for the purpose of evaluating planning; 4. the education of citizens so that they can follow and evaluate the planning process as well as possible; 5. the creation of democratic structures for the purpose of making the intended participation possible; and 6. in all of this planning he aims at opposing and forestalling the crises and to keep society in control, that is, to create a social balance.

It is clear that planning occupies a central place in Mannheim's thought; he distinguishes it sharply from dictatorship. It also is clear that freedom for convictions about life, for creativity, and for democratic decision-making is no less important than planning. It seems responsible on my part to compare his thought about this subject to an ellipse, of which freedom and planning form the two focal points. I defend this interpretation no only on grounds of the preceding, but also with help from the manner in which Mannheim speaks about social techniques for realizing the "planning for freedom."

Social Techniques
A mass democracy can, according to Mannheim, only be systematically ruled by means of finding out and improving social techniques; they form "the sum of those methods which aim at influencing human behavior and which, when in the hands of the Government, act as an especially powerful means of social control" (DT: 1; cf. FPDP: 608). Mannheim distinguishes direct and indirect methods of influencing human behavior. The direct methods are always based on personal

influence at close range; they are identified with those who exert the influence, and the layman does not notice that he is an exponent of the claims of the society. Thus, the influence of parents, teachers, and pastors can be called direct, although sociological insight makes clear that society speaks "through" them and that they have a reflective influence. Indirect influence of behavior works at a distance by means of impersonal, natural, and cultural environment (MS: 274, 275). But in the final analysis, the indirect influence works by means of the direct. This means in the first place that direct and indirect influence are interwoven with each other, and in the second place, that we never can speak in the abstract about social techniques, but we must see them in the social context in which they are used.

The influence of behavior, according to Mannheim's sociological analysis, takes place in the following five ways:

1. *In unorganized masses*. Particularly in revolutionary periods, but also in other phases of social disintegration, the masses can influence the behavior of people and lead them to irrational outbursts, for which a person as individual does not wish to be held responsible (MS: 288).

2. *In specific groups*, which as social entities in time and space can be clearly identified: a. communities such as state, tribe, family, village; they comprehend every aspect of the life of the members, because one "is born into" these structures, and b. rationally organized relationships (for instance, bureaucracies), which do not contain the whole lives of the members, who can freely join and be separated from them. While the former groups is characterized by traditional patterns of behavior, the latter form relationships by statutes, rules, and administrators (MS: 289ff).

3. In *"field structures,"* which are formed through the interdependence of human activities, without being centured in specific communities or organizations. They lie between the communities and the large organizations and can emerge from contacts of a regional or an international sort. The "field-structural influences" exist, for instance in one's field of work or profession. They do not express themselves usually in specific groups, but cut diametrically across these; they form a "magnetic field" of a social kind. These field structures do not contain the whole personality, but they have a specific partial influence (MS: 296).

4. In *situations* as "a unique configuration formed in the process of interaction between certain people" (MS: 299). The situation does not coincide with a group or context; it has its place within groups. Mannheim distinguishes situations of conflict, rebellion, harmony, and adjustment.

5. By means of *social mechanisms* such as competition, division of labor, division of power, social hierarchy, and social distance. Although these mechanisms work in the four previous points, it is good to list these separately, because they do not only work within groups but between groups, and situations. These mechanisms are particularly important because they must be controlled in the planning phase by means of social techniques (MS: 307).

327

In his view of the necessary processes of influencing behavior, the question always looms up for Mannheim again, whether the state itself can be sufficiently controlled, as a centralized, coordinated, and controlling organism; that is, whether the principle of planning can be compatible with democracy and freedom. In his scientific analysis he answers these questions affirmatively, while at the same time he asserts that they concern *very complicated political problems*. For the purpose, also in politics, of making the chance for success of "planning for freedom" as great as possible, he lists the following social techniques for the functioning of parliamentary democracy: 1. the establishment and upholding of the sovereignty of national states, 2. the upholding of the division between the legislative, executive, and judicial powers of government, 3. the prevention of a *coup d'état*, by means of the upholding of a balance of power between the groups represented in parliament and the prevention of a usurpation of power by a specific political party or groups outside of parliament, 4. the maintenance of a dynamic balance in the parliamentary system by using the parliament as a new technique for reconciling conflicts – growing of consensus by compromises is always better than a rational manipulation, 5. the banishment of egoism of the group, from wavering and conflicting motives in the parliamentary system, which aims at achieving consensus (see point 4), 6. the regular changing of elite leaders, and 7. the prevention of unpredictable outbursts of mass-psychosis, especially in times of stress (MS: 331-335).

Precisely in a planned society these parliamentary-democratic techniques are necessary and possible to forestall a dictatorship (MS: 335):

> Contrary to the theory current in England, that democracy and planning are mutually exclusive, we believe that democratic control is possible. (...) There is nothing in the nature of planning or of democratic machinery which makes them inconsistent with each other. (MS: 338, 339)

From the whole of Mannheim's later work it is clear that he *believes* in "planning for freedom"; as he says in the quotation above: *we believe*. Moreover, it appears to be not only a belief, but just as much a sociological-scientific, elaborated vision of society and a political view which he regards as realizable. The greatest dangers which threaten this striving are, according to him, the class struggle and an international war. Again he renews his distance from Marxism as a current which regards its extreme position as the only correct one. It has some elements of truth within it, but because it is extreme, the heart of social and cultural problems ceases to be a concern. An international war would be a total war, in which a state which does not make use of the social techniques of planning will collapse; at the same time the risk of a *coup d'état* is very great in such a situation (MS: 338, 341). When, with the help of sociological knowledge, people can realize planning, then at least people will also realize, along with and at the same time as planning, the growth of democracy and freedom. "Planning...ultimately leads to the spread of democracy in the sense of a fundamental equality" (MS: 363, 364). Planning will oppose the dangers which critics see in it.

As far as this is concerned, Mannheim is optimistic; at any rate, he sees the *chance* for success; he has a hope which is based on his "belief in the power of reason" (MS: 365).

Speaking about freedom, Mannheim means "that the forms of freedom can only be formulated in reference to a given society and to the social techniques existing in it" (MS: 370). He calls an abstract method of approach vague, which in general terms speaks about feedom without referring to specific socio-historical situations; it speaks often about freedom as a human initiative and as the will to influence social circumstances. As is known, Mannheim rejects this individualistic *laissez-faire*. It is vague, because it does not give an answer to the question of the relationship of freedom to the nature of the social structures in which it is to be realized. In the answer to this question lies the very heart of his speaking about freedom, which he interprets as social-structural freedom. The experience of giving a form to freedom is different in friendship than in an organization, a political party, nursery, religious group, family, etc. (FPDP: 15). He speaks of freedom as social freedom, which as such is always related to the differentiated social reality. Reality-congruent thought means adequate insight into the problems of this time and into the unavoidability of planning. Thinking at the level of planning means, that old interpretations of social and political freedom are inadequate and not congruent with reality. Thinking at the level of planning brings along with it a new kind of thinking about freedom.

In the foregoing sections I quoted a few critics of Mannheim's ideas of planning. I myself used the image of the ellipse to interpret Mannheim's thinking about "planning for freedom." For the purpose of being able to refute the unfair criticism of his ideas of planning and in order to clarify the interpretation about *social techniques* which can be used in the strategy of planning, this study proceeds to a discussion of the phenomenon called *technique*.

The word *technique* is etymologically derived from *technè*, which in Greek has many meanings. All human ability and particularly human skills are referred to by that word; *technè* can also be interpreted as method. The word is used in connection with all kinds of human activities: the art of argument, the art of music, the art of painting, and others. This interpretation of *technè* is different from that of technique in our time. Still, there is a relationship. Skills and methods are conditions for modern technique.

Humanity has never been at a loss for technique. From the beginning of the history of humanity, tools were used for work; tools still always determine the heart of modern technique, and only they can give us insight into the central questions concerning the nature, the meaning, and the purpose of technique. The use of tools is the heart of technique, which, according to its nature, is characterized by *giving form*. Modern technique, particularly during the last two centuries, has developed into *a power of giving form which extends over the whole of reality*. Technique as the capability for giving form is a *particular* mode of human existence; that is why technique is not neutral; it is an expression of a particular way of living and of relating to nature and to society. It does not exist for itself; but *in* technique and, consequently, with its help, mankind gives form to nature and to society.

In Mannheim's discussion of social techniques we find this same discussion of technique all over again. Social techniques are not independent powers which dominate society by autonomous laws. They are means for realizing the goals which people set for themselves. In Mannheim's own words:

> I call them techniques because, like all techniques, they are neither good nor bad in themselves. Everything depends on the use that is made of them by the human will. (DT: 2)

Mannheim sees the *nature* of social techniques as human instruments. The *meaning* of social techniques is restricted to something which lies outside techniques themselves, namely, in "planning for freedom" within society. Still it is noteworthy that he is not satisfied with this instrumental view of the nature of social techniques. According to their *nature* they are, says Mannheim, characterized by *efficiency* and as such

> they limit the direction in which modern society can develop at all. The nature of these social techniques is even more fundamental to society than the economic structure or the social stratification of a given order. By their aid one can hamper or remould the working of the economic system, destroy social classes, and set others in their pace. (DT: 2).

Although he says that social techniques by themselves are neither good nor bad and that they are dependent on the use which a person makes of them, he immediately adds the following: "The most important thing about these modern techniques is that they tend to foster centralization and, therefore, minority rule and dictatorship" (DT: 2, 3; cf. ASP). He distinguishes various social techniques of exercising power: army, politics, economic organizations, churches, schools, and many more. He speaks of a "transmutation of power," which corresponds with the various techniques which are used in the processes of changing behavior (ASP).

According to Mannheim, democracy cannot function without power relationships, but these must not be glorified. "Democracy's main aim is to define the functions of power in society and to elaborate its controls" (ASP). That is why he describes the already mentioned principles which must be applied in a democracy, both of them characterized as essential for "planning for freedom": control of arbitrariness and of centralization of power. These principles must be balanced with the following: division of power in the form of total democratic elections and independent institutions which control it, strengthening of local administrative organizations, democratizing the army, greater economic equality between citizens, democratizing the leadership by which possibilities are offered for people from less privileged groups and classes, and rotation in executive and leadership positions.

Consequently, Mannheim makes an important distinction between the humanization and the spiritualization of power. The issue is not only replacing the brute exercise of power by a more subtle and humane form. He pleads for the spiritualizing:

> Power is spiritualized if the rulers do not use it for its own sake but for the sake of a "higher" spiritual purpose, which has its place in a spiritual cosmos. Spiritualized power may be brutal and very fanatic, but, at some point, it sets itself a limit. Spiritualized power is rooted in the idea of legitimacy. The modern deterioration in the use of power follows not so much from a new outburst of barbarism as from the gradual extinction of the belief in the possibility of justifying the legitimate use of power. Thus the use of power, especially of state power, becomes increasingly a matter of expediency and this is bound to lead to limitless destruction (ASP)

Conclusions

In the above I made clear that social techniques, according to Mannheim, are by nature neither good nor bad, but by *nature* they are characterized by efficiency. As such, they are not neutral instruments, because their significance is revealed in their use. But its nature, the use of social techniques, involves centralization, which can become dangerous for the society. If technique is primarily connected with the work of the engineer, speaking about *social techniques* brings the changing of the social context into Mannheim's consideration. This means that he rejects a technocracy of planners; a technocracy, in which administrative techniques are made independent and by their immanent regulation of society give the leadership to such a technocracy, according to him, is one of the primary dangers for a democracy. Although he wants, with help from social techniques, to direct social attitudes and especially power attitudes in a direction he desires, this technocratic touch does not make him a technocratic wolf in democratic sheep's clothes. His elaborate exposition of democratic procedures, which the planning process must promote, are evidence of this (Boris, 1971: 170-180).

In the above I have attempted to explain the ellipse as an interpretation of his "planning for freedom," "planning for democracy" or "democratic planning"; that in his conception, and certainly in the realizing of "planning for freedom" a *dynamic tension* exists between freedom and planning was also described. To conclude in *static paradox* does justice neither to his publications nor to his intention.

Criteria for Freedom

In the American and English liberal tradition freedom is usually attached to individuals. In the countries mentioned this connection is so self-evident that many people would be surprised to hear that freedom can have another wellspring or foundation than the individual. In Europe, however, freedom, is often brought into relationship with rationality; those who allow themselves to be controlled by reason would be genuinely free. Thus Dewey's brief characterizations of the two conceptions of freedom (1939: 24).

It is not astounding that Mannheim attempts to combine these two as his inheritance from continental and Anglo-Saxon culture. In the first place he recognizes an *integral freedom*, which has its basis in a substantial-rational insight or in "sociological reason." In the second place he recognizes *individual freedom*, for creativity and protest against every form of totalitarianism; this freedom must be tested for its fruitfulness by means of "sociological reason." In the third place he recognizes *institutional freedom*, which is the freedom which is realized within social relationships and institutions and between institutions. These institutions are, among others, families, schools, businesses, churches, professional organizations, labor unions, universities, and media of communication. Mannheim acknowledges, as was already mentioned, the peculiar nature of each. In this connection we must also pay some attention to "social structure," a concept he uses but does not clearly define. Sometimes he means the structure of a society as a totality, that is, the "social order" or the manner in which relationships, institutions, groups, groupings, strata, and other social phenomena form contexts together. Sometimes he means the institutions themselves. He also regularly uses the term *situation*. Kanning (1953: 31) gives the following description of the concept of structure:

> For Mannheim *structure* means the concrete situation of a particular whole, made up of combinations of various kinds of relationships. By concrete situations is to be understood the real original givens of an empirical whole of various styles of relationships belonging to the range of reality. Structures, one can also say, are *creations, in which concrete, working contexts are integrated with each other multi-dimensionally.*

This realistic definition of the concept can be applied as well to the structure of a social order as to that of institutions and situations. The analysis of social structures shows itself to be important for discovering the *principia media* and the key positions on the basis of which planning must take place (cf. Remmling, 1957c: 1963). What is remarkable is that, according to Mannheim, differentiated-qualified social freedoms do not exist simply in correspondence to the variety of concrete situations and institutions. He does not deny these separately differentiated social freedoms; to the contrary, and in line with all of his thought, we can say that the integral freedom of "sociological reason" *(Vernunft)* and individual freedom "encounter" each other in concrete situations and institutions. "Sociological reason" must provide clarification of existence and provide inspiration for taking the Third Way; in its light a good relationship between planning and freedom can be realized. Mannheim recognizes the *peculiar nature* and independence of relationships, institutions, situations, etc. He regards this independence, however, as a relative one, or better, as a related one; the *significance* of institutions becomes clear in their functioning in relation to the realization of the "planning for freedom." In this realization lies the criterion for judging the freedom within and between institutions.

332

In the Twilight of the Sociological Reason

As was already described, social techniques by their very nature are directed toward efficiency and centralization. That their use strengthens the chance for minority rule does not mean that this necessarily will happen. That is why the crucial matter is to come to the position of understanding that in our time "planning for freedom" is recommended as the only course, and to achieve this insight in time to forestall undesirable developments. However, we must be careful with the interpretation of the meaning of social techniques. The meaning of something is always understood as that which has a close relationship to someone's vision of reality or worldview. Mannheim's worldview is not determined by "planning for freedom." According to him, "planning for freedom" is not blueprint for a future society. It is a strategy, a way which must be taken. The possibility and need for this way can be grasped by everyone *who believes in reason*. Mannheim's worldview is an historicism, sociologically elaborated. In Chapter XI I wrote that historical consciousness, according to Mannheim, had made room for sociological consciousness. That is, that "sociological reason" can and must offer an adequate insight into the interdependence of reality. Especially the intellectuals, those who must provide for the planning, are in a position to acquire this insight. The question about the *meaning* of social techniques must also then be combined with "sociological reason."

Whether we can conclude that Mannheim has a sociolog*istic* vision of things ia a question which must be handled with the necessary circumspection. In his dissertation he had already argued that every field of reality has its own structure, which is of an ontic kind. Also, he never returned to the thesis, that the various social sciences such as psychology, economics, jurisprudence, and others, each has its own object and statement of the problems. True, sociology is the basic science of the social sciences, which must study the interdependence of societal phenomena. When we examine his sociological argument critically, then we see that he distinguishes the various metalogical original givens according to their own structure. This thinking stands opposite to reality, which itself is not thought, and analyzes this reality. Consequently, we saw that this thought can enter into a synthesis with a specific field of reality as it develops itself into a scientific thought of the *disciplinary*, academic sort, to be taught. On the basis of an ontic pluralism, a methodological pluralism emerges. Finally, we see in the third phase of his work, that sociology is a synthetic science in a particular sense. It is not only to be interpreted as an academic discipline to be taught, which strives to attain a synthesis between logic-analytical thought and the social field of reality (the minimum definition). It also aims at synthesizing the facts and processes of other fields of reality and at studying the results of the academic disciplines in these fields; this is its particular aim (in the maximum definition) though broad in scope. He intends that sociology as a comprehensive and integrating "synthesizing science" should study the development of culture and, given the tragic need of Western culture, must go to work not only diagnostically, but therapeutically as well. Sociology must direct culture on its way to the future.

What difference is there then between sociology and philosophy, each having its own distinctive way of thinking? Both study reality in total context and in its differentiations; both ask the questions concerning the meaning of existence. Mannheim writes: "It is an incorrect grasp of sociology when one accepts that it wants to occupy entirely the place of philosophy" (GAS: 53, 54). This sentence, written in 1932, fits into the context of a discussion justifying sociology as an academic discipline. In his later work sociology is seen also as a cultural philosophy. It then transcends even its maximum definition and becomes a sociological view of the totality: "My task is to draw together key facts and to elaborate, with a specific type of scientific imagination, the kind of interdependence which is likely to prevail," says Mannheim (BEAS).

According to my interpretation, no principial distinction exists in Mannheim's work after 1935 between philosophy and sociology. The philosopher must be equipped with a sociological consciousness. He must have sociological knowledge and insight, for the purpose of being able to think synthetically and with a vision of the whole. At this moment the interpretation of Mannheim revolves in a vicious circle: from academic discipline to philosophy and then back to academic discipline again. And here precisely lurks the tension in Mannheim's thinking as well: if sociology is an academic discipline which is helped by certain theories and methods, and which studies the social field of reality, then it is not philosophy; if it is a philosophical science of totality, then it is not a specialized academic discipline. In addition, the academic discipline wants to conduct empirical research and test its hypotheses; as such, on principle, it cannot be a science which studies the totality of culture, because that cannot be studied empirically. Mannheim, however, expects the one no less than the other of his sociological philosophy. This causes his works sometimes to be restricted to sociology as an academic discipline and sometimes to sociology as a cultural philosophy.

It is clear that "sociological reason" must bring to light the meaning of reality, and also point out where that meaning gets derailed. Those who bear the burden of this sociological reason, the intelligentsia, must show the path ahead; they must plan with the help of all kinds of social techniques. Apart from the question of the direction of the planning, the question first arises whether they *are able* to carry out this task. They are, after all, "socially, *relatively* free-floating." Mannheim has argued at great length that in Western culture a "gap" has emerged between the development of the natural sciences and their application in technique on the one hand, and on the other hand the moral development, which lags behind, Will the intellectuals in their relative freedom from constraint be able to manage the task? Is the sociological reason a guarantee that the task can be achieved? This sociological reason is not an abstract or pure logic which is granted to the intelligentsia as a revelation from God. It must be seen on the basis of the sociology of knowledge as a mode of rationality bound to time and culture. It arises from a torn and disproportionately developed culture. How can a clear sociological rationality arise from such a culture? Also in Chapter XI I pointed out already the problems involved in the relativity of the social "free-floatingness" of the intelligentsia. Mannheim has not only recognized this problem, but criticized it as a shortcoming in his view of "sociological reason." Particularly in his *Diagnosis of Our Time* he devoted attention to it. "Sociological reason" which generates insufficient light from within itself seems to require help from outside. The following chapter treats this problem.

Chapter XVIII
Conditions for Therapy

- *Sociological Analysis of Changing Values*
- *The Need for a New Social Philosophy*
- *Mannheim on Kant's Ethics of Conscience*
- *Mannheim on Max Weber's Ethics of Responsibility*
- *A New Social Ethics as Basis for "Planning for Freedom"*
- *The Necessary Cooperation between Sociologists and Christian Thinkers*
- *Social and Moral Maturity*
- *Mannheim's Ethics*
- *Conclusions*

Introduction
In this chapter I discuss Mannheim's view of ethics, in which his philosophy and his sociology arrive at the crux of their development. Here all the lines of his understanding merge: historicism, cultural sociology, sociology of knowledge, planning, freedom, and education.

Sociological Analysis of Changing Values
When Mannheim speaks about the crisis in Western culture, then he means not only politics, social, and economic evidences of crisis, but also a crisis of values and norms. He saw this crisis of spiritual values and norms coming to expression in "contradictory philosophies of life": 1. *the religion of love* and of universal brotherhood, chiefly inspired by the Christian tradition, 2. *the philosophy of Enlightenment and liberalism* with its emphasis on freedom, personality, wealth, work, success, tolerance, and charity, 3. *the socialistic movement*, with its pleading for equality, social justice, self-confidence, and its planned social order, and 4. *demonic philosophies*, which place the emphasis on fertility, race, power, military conquest, discipline, and blind obedience (particularly fascism). It is noteworthy that Mannheim does not speak here about complementary philosophies (IU: 132), but about contradictory ones. This means that reaching a synthesis will demand conflict; hence, he speaks about the need for a "militant democracy," which he contrasts to "compromise." He advocates a "creative tolerance" and a "muscular mentality"; easy compromise for him was a form of relativism (FPDP: 199-206).

What is lacking in the societies of Western Europe, also in England with its functioning democracy, are the established conceptions about the correct forms of human conduct relative to freedom and social order. The heart of this lack is the weakness of fundamental convictions in education and in child-rearing. And

336

we know that it is not good to live in a society without established norms and values, certainly not in a time when society is threatened internally and externally (DT:12-14).

About the causes for the crisis in spiritual values, especially idealists and Marxists, according to Mannheim, are in bitter conflict. Religious and idealistic thinkers see in the crisis itself the cause of the cultural crisis, while Marxists on the contrary see the cause in the transition from one economic system to the other. According to them, the value of the Marxist approach is that it has a dependence of spiritual values placed on economic factors; the reorganization of the economic order would make the spiritual crisis vanish. Mannheim does not disagree with this view, but finds it incomplete. In his view it is meaningless to study spiritual values in the abstract. This study must occur in context with the social processes. In a static society established values and "subjective" judgments of values will not be debatable. In a period of social change the conceptions about values will change. A new social order cannot exist without new values, which must inspire a person to a new mode of operation. The process of the forming of values , according to Mannheim, does not only flow forth from economic changes, but changing values are one aspect of modifications in the social order and actually function in every field where a changed behavior is necessary.

An important question for Mannheim in this connection is this: Which social processes lie at the basis of the changing values and norms and of the subjective judging of them? Then he names eight factors:

1. Disturbing factors in the functioning of spiritual values develop through a rapid and uncontrolled "growth" of the society. Without naming Tönnies in this connection, Mannheim means the transition here from community *(Gemeinschaft)* to society *(Gesellschaft)*. He refers to Cooley who wrote that in our time life is lived less in primary groups (family and neighborhood) and more in larger contexts. According to Cooley, for that reason, we must apply "primary" and personally-directed virtues, actions, and ideals (love, mutual help, brotherhood) in the larger contexts, and, in the process, adjust these virtues to the larger context when necessary. The comand "Love your neighbor" can not hold anymore only for the members of a family or for a village community, but must be reinterpreted and made applicable to the great undustrial complex and for all humanity.

2. Even though *some values* are easy to fit into the new social order, others must be drastically *reconsidered*. For instance, the right to property. In an earlier time this right was intended for the protection of the equipment of small farmers and craftsmen. In the world of heavy industry this right received an interpretation which laid the basis for the exploitation of paupers by "owners." The revalidation of such concepts as right to property and social justice, according to Mannheim, is necessary in every age.

3. The transition from a pre-industrial to an undustrial society brought along with it changes in judgment concerning the relationship between *labor and*

leisure. A thoroughgoing mechanization of the production process has arisen, but all the while problems still exist concerning the human and social attitudes in the business world, which stand in the way of the forming of personality and the quality of social relationships. And although the possibilities for using leisure time are of generous and democratic stamp, it is a problem for many people how to use this time meaningfully in personal and social activities.

4. In the sphere of values and norms, confusion arose because of the *increasing contacts* between different social groups via modern media of communication and social mobility, both horizontal and vertical. The confrontation with the variety of norms makes uncertainty increase, but at the same time increases the necessity for judging and choosing independently.

5. *New forms of behavior and new sanctions* have arisen. In an earlier time social norms were explained on the basis of the tradition, or on the basis of the will of God, or on the basis of a combination of these two. Since then, the number of churches and sects have become numerous and extremely divergent from each other in content, with the differences and controversies concerning their judgment of values.

6. In a society which is founded on traditions, values are accepted as self-evident; in these latter days a *conscious and rational judging of values* has emerged. By itself this is progress, provided that this conscious rationalization is carried through into all areas of society. In case this process is carried out only in fragments and not through the whole society, the balance between rational and irrational, between conscious and unconscious powers in the structure are disturbed.

7. An increasingly conscious and rational judgment of values brings along with it a *reeducation* of the human being. This has implications for education in the home and in the school; no rational definition of values can take place if specific taboos remain in place in the educational system and if those taboos oppose the rational developments.

8. An *aggressively progressive rationality*, that is, a substantial rational insight and judgment of values, which Mannheim applauds. He does, however, attach this question to it: Which generally accepted values does our contemporary society need in order to give its social order the necessary spiritual stability?

Although values first come to expression in the choices of individuals, they are not only subjective choices but also "objective norms"; they function as social "traffic lights" (DT: 16). Mannheim adds that he is conscious of the one-sidedness which is present in his sociological analysis of values. His sociological approach does not exclude other approaches, but makes room for them. In his discussion of values, however, he wants to begin with the "simplest aspects." A discussion at the highest level means judging the qualitative content of values. He states, moreover, that "any real appreciation of values is primarily concerned with their qualitative aspects" (DT.: 166). When he states elsewhere that the sociological analysis of the moral crisis is not *only* the result of the corruption of modern humanity, but also to be blamed to *a considerable degree* on social problems (DT: 104), then in these words he announces clearly that a sociological analysis only signifies one "aspect of approach"; he allows room for others, among which is judgment based on a worldview.

The judgment of values thus has two kinds of origins: 1. partially it is the expression of subjective desires and longings and 2. partially it is the expression of the manner in which a society allows people to behave in a way that will allow them to adjust to the existing order. I shall return to the subjective judgment of values and the establishing of new values. Now I can mention that Mannheim calls attention to the fact that in this century values are no longer accepted because they are transferred by tradition or because they are seen as the will of God. *A conscious substantial-rational judgment* and acceptance of values has emerged. This change he calls a "Copernicus-like change on the social plane and in man's history" (DT: 22). According to him, this is a very important and positive turn of events. People who only accept values on the basis of tradition, imitation, or blind obedience will not be in a position to understand values which are based on reason. Because of the "Copernican turn of events" an entirely new strategy of education is necessary, namely an education for rational insight (DT: 23).

Although he postpones the conceptual elaboration of this rational insight until his handling of ethics, he states, discussing the objective social function of values, that in democracies no indifference concerning values may be allowed to exist. The war against fascims, once the War was over, needed to be continued on a spiritual plane. It is an imperative demand to look for the elements which make for unity in a democracy and work with those elements for the "progressive evolution of the social implication of democracy" (DT: 26, 27). This consensus does not happen automatically; looking for it is necessary and then there is a *chance* for its realization.

Sociology has the task of studying the social circumstances under which disunity and conflicts develop. But just as urgent is its task to study those circumstances and social techniques which can lead to consensus. Cleaning up differences alone is not sufficient. A sense of community must develop. Also, a new, rational child-rearing, education, adult education, developmental education, etc., are not enough by themselves if they do not follow through to "a more conscious philosophy of their meaning, a more deliberate co-ordination of their policy, and a focussing of their efforts on the strategically important points" (DT: 29). With this last comment he again is pointing out the task of the intelligentsia in the strategy of planning and with a "more conscious philosophy" nothing other can be intended than his sociological philosophy, as was already described.

The Need for a New Social Philosophy
In the last chapter of *Diagnosis of Our Time* Mannheim provides a way for those

who must lead us to a new social philosophy, a social philosophy which finds its purpose in *a new social ethics*. To elaborate this social philosophy and ethics, he makes a "Challenge to Christian Thinkers," as the title of that chapter reads.

After the Renaissance, Christendom has seemed less and less able to maintain its grip on society. Where the church still held its grip on people who continued to think in traditional terms, its influence was great. Where it lost touch with actual social problems, it concentrated often on a "formal service" and lowered religion to a matter of attending church services on Sundays. In most countries of Western Europe, the church lost its supremacy and a new society developed: socially differentiated and pluriform in views of life and ethics with competitive systems of values. Where the church maintained its influence, more or less, this development usually accompanied the readiness to cooperate with the ruling political and social classes, and it defended the established social and political order as though given by God. Thus for many this choice existed: religious and thus conservative, or progressive and thus atheistic.

Mannheim makes an exception for England, because in this land, already at a very early stage, when religion still permeated the whole society, the rise of capitalism was coupled with social revolutions, and both conservative and progressive powers came into prominence in English philosophies. In England it seemed to be possible to be progressive and religious. (In this context I pass by the question whether Mannheim's distinction between England and the continent is entirely sound.)

In a liberal society, according to Mannheim "neutral values" could function fairly well. By *neutral values* he means values which are not directed toward integration of society and which demand no foundation on any deeper grounds than individual and subjective concerns. This founding and integrating directedness of values becomes necessary when a society is threatened, either from the inside out (a collapse inside the society of *laissez-faire* thought, a collapse which leads to chaos) or from the outside in (war, false ideologies). In the Western world both threats are present, according to Mannheim: the political and economic crises on the one hand and the rise of communistic and fascist totalitarian ideologies and dictatorships on the other. The latter suggest an alternative, for the purpose of conquering chaos. Communism and fascism strive for a pseudo-religious integration of society, for the purpose of creating a psychological and sociologcial background for planning. These spiritual streams are poisonous, and Mannheim is deeply convinced of their falseness, but also convinced that in the conflict of ideologies people with false ideals will prevail over people with no ideals. Both the threat of false ideals and the lack of ideals characterize, according to him, the extremely unstable and dangerous situation of the Western democracies. One of the most important branches of sociology is to point out to the society of the future, characterized by "planning for freedom," the functions and activities which can bring about a social integration. One of these functions is the revalidation and reformulation of the germinal thoughts of religion. This revalidation cannot happen partially, in the sense that it is meaningful for only some specific groups; it must be functional within the new world-picture. He regards the religions as integrating forces in society (cf. HIJM). A social order can only continue to exist on the basis of "a sound statement of belief." In case there is only one Truth, citizens of a democracy must perceive that not only one group may identify its conceptions with this Truth and exclude all others. People will need to listen to other people and to other groups, because it is never clear by means of which person or group "the voice of God" may speak. This is the only way to arrive at a religious unity and integration which is reconcilable with a dynamic, planned society, based on the ideal of a planned freedom. The individual person and the society, according to Mannheim, have a need for certainty, for foundation. In short, they need "a transcendental religious foundation" (FPDP: 286-289). Mannheim is of the opinion that a need exists and there is room within modern society for, this revalidation, reformulation, and re-experience of religion. This means: Go back to the wellsprings of religious experience. Then a new democratic order can emerge which will be Christian; so says Mannheim (DT: 106). He does not mean by this comment a *totalitarian* Christian society. If a Hitler or a Goebbels would be replaced by clergymen of comparable persuasion, we would be just as far from home. Although "planning for freedom" requires a process of integration in society, it desires just as urgently to offer the opportunity for a deeper experience on the part of individuals; "planning for freedom" implies and presupposes creating room for experiment and growth. Accepting "planning for freedom," which depends on integration, is not based on existing customs and explicit agreements of opinion. Discussion, persuasion, imitation are necessary. The crystalization of the necessary spiritual values can occur best in the spaces in which experiment and growth of agreement in matters of opinion flourish. In short: we must *learn* a number of fundamental, elementary things: manners, mutual help, honesty, and social justice. Education and social influence are the most preferred means to learn these. These primary virtues give stability and solidarity to the social order. The basic virtues mentioned do not differ from those which the ethics of Christianity and the ethics of other world religions regard as vital. Then "higher forms" of thought, art, and literature can also remain free, just as they also are free under liberalism (MS: 352; E, I: 3; E: IV; 5). In a conversation with Lord Lindsay, Mannheim formulated his thoughts about this matter succinctly and fruitfully; it would be, he said, better to emphasize the need

not of planning, but of awareness. Only as the whole community becomes increasingly aware of the problems facing it, and each group in its own sphere is thinking out its jobs and doing its work from the same background and the same assumptions, can you get democratic planning, for democratic planning will in various degrees be done by everyone, and by all the seperate organs of social life. (Scott, 1971: 267)

It is a non-negotiable certainty for Mannheim that democracy never will be able to exist if all institutions within it are not democratized (FPDP: 173).

Mannheim on Kant's Ethics of Conscience

The primary virtues mentioned above are designated by Mannheim as moral or ethical virtues. According to him (DT: 111), this means that there is no room any longer for a formal ethic. That is, an ethic which deliberately separates itself from concrete recommendations of what may or may not be done in specific instances and restricts itself to abstract formulations of good and evil, such an ethic has no place in the modern world. He cites Kant in this connection, who did not formulate concrete imperatives, but a *categorical imperative*, namely: "Act as though the principle of your action might become the principle of action in general" (DT: 111; Kant, 1785: 421). Mannheim analyzes and explains Kant's formal viewpoint from the perspective of the sociology of knowledge. This philosopher lived in a phase of history in which society was based on expansion and dynamism; pioneer work and research were carried out in all kinds of fields. The phase of the early capitalism and liberalism, of free competition and individualistic development, provided the space for adjustment of actions to situations. Although Kant himself was not aware of the sociological basis of his ethics, this explanation is illuminating, according to Mannheim, for understanding Kant's position.

In conclusion, comparison with Kant needs mention. For Kant, epistemology and ethics are not to be imagined as separate from each other; the critical quest for "pure reason" is a necessary preparation for the study of "practical reason." Mannheim's concern as well is not only for an accurate analysis of epistemology, but (as we have already noted) his concern is to strive for a new culture and for the new ethic which this new culture requires.

It is noteworthy that Mannheim does not pay attention to another formulation of Kant's categorical imperative: "Act so that you always treat humanity, both in your own person and in the person of everyone else, as a purpose, and never as a means" (Kant, 1785: 429). This imperative implies that Kant intended to promote social community. Mannheim could have used this argument for strengthening his discussion of a new morality.

Mannheim on Max Weber's Ethics of Responsibility

Mannheim refers next to Weber's *ethics of responsibility* which has constantly become more important in our century. Weber's ethics expects of an individual that he foresees the immediate consequences of his actions and that he is reponsible for them. That Mannheim rejects Kant's "ethics of conscience" arises solely from the considereation that the acting person may not be "blind to society." That he chooses for Weber's "ethics of responsibility" arises from the necessity for a society based on "planning for freedom" to strive for specific

342

social goals; the "planning for freedom" presupposes the cultivation of primary ethical virtues, which inspire one to act in the light of the consequences.

The relationship of Mannheim to Weber also invites our attention for another reason. The presentation he gives of Weber's "ethics of responsibility" is from one point of view simplistic. In fact, Mannheim does damage to himself with his interpretation of Weber's ethics.

In his famous essay "Politics as a Vocation" (*"Politik als Beruf"*), Weber discusses several differences between the "ethics of conscience" and the "ethics of responsibility." In the former, according to Weber's interpretation, one acts on the basis of his own conviction, without bearing the responsibility for the consequences; one feels responsible only for the purity of the conviction and the inclination to do it. In the latter instance, the responsibility is accepted for the consequences of action, to the extent that these can be determined. Consequently, Weber indicates that in every ethical theory the problem is familiar, that people, to reach good purposes, sometimes use morally disreputable means. Often reaching a specific goal is accompanied by a more or less different ancillary purpose, often less desired. According to Weber, there is no ethical theory which can explain conclusively to what extent a good purpose can justify morally questionable means and questionable ancillary purposes. He describes how in revolutionary theories an enormous tension exists between ends and means. There are revolutionaries who, when they stand before the choice whether a few years of war resulting in a revolution is better than peace without the revolution, choose for the revolution. According to Weber, an upright socialist, however, would answer that the opportunity for a socialistic revolution is very slight; he will acknowledge that perhaps a society might be able to emerge which would be a little less capitalistic than the existing one. Weber calls the "ethics of conscience" of the revolutionary socialists laughable. They are blind to reality, because they justify an "ethics of conscience" by means of which "the purpose hallows the means," when the purpose cannot even be achieved (Weber, 1919: 120, 121, 128).

Weber himself takes the position that in the "ethics of responsibility" the "ethics of conscience" is always present. One cannot separate these two. Every person who justifies an "ethics of responsibility" has also a certain conviction. An upright person, who is consious of his responsibility for his actions and who also knows that he is being compelled by his conviction, will sometimes come to the conclusion: "Here I stand; I can do no other." Although Weber distinguishes the "ethics of conscience" from the "ethics of responsibility" he regards these two not as opposites. The "ethics of responsibility" must be complemented by the "ethics of conscience" (1919: 126ff).

It is noteworthy that Mannheim does not mention this complementary relationship. He presents Weber simply as a defender of the "ethics of responsibility." This may make us wonder even more, because Mannheim himself in his ethics also does not simply choose for an "ethics of responsibility." Although he calls himself an advocate of an "ethics of responsibility," his work gives evidence that the "ethics of conscience" is also present in his theory. He speaks about realizing "planning for freedom," the burden of which must be borne by specific moral virtues. He also speaks about judging moral values, which are partially an expression of conviction. He demonstrates in the elaboration of his ehtics to be a better disciple of Weber than he allows us to suspect in his discussion of Weber.

A New Social Ethics as Basic for "Planning for Freedom"

In what is written above it becomes clear that Mannheim, on grounds of his sociological analysis, comes to a discussion of moral values and virtues, about an ethic as a human life-style, and about ethics as a science. Consequently, we saw that his conceptions about ethics lie at the basis of, and are conditons for, realizing his "planning for freedom." If this latter will have a chance for success, then in the area of morals, something fundamental will need to change within people themselves. His thinking is to be characterized as a "moral-philosophical enterprise" (Kettler, 1967: 402-407; 1975: 69). We see this same order of events in other classical sociologists who occupied themselves with ethics: Comte (1851: 73ff, 564ff), Spencer (1879: par. 7), Durkheim (1957), and others.

Mannheim discusses the relationship between sociology and ethics in his own way. Western people no longer live in collective groups which are characterized by mechanical solidarity and a horde morality. With the rise of individulism people were confronted with the assignment of creating a new morality, based on individual self-orientation. The "ethics of conscience" which arose from this state of affairs is no longer adequate now in the twentieth century; it must, according to Mannheim, acquire a new elaboration in a sociologically differentiated "ethics of responsiblity."

Although theologians are often occupied with social ethics, they can only practise this branch of science with the help of an adequate sociological knowledge. By the lack of this insight they not only neglect to serve the field, but they damage the image of social ethics. Besides, they aggravate their lack of sociological knowledge most of all by a theological dogmatism and moralism.

The germ of Mannheim's view is that ethical norms must be formulated in a way that is adequate for modern society. People who speak about the declining awareness of norms in the twentieth century can expect the question from Mannheim whether thy themselves have an accurate perception of norms. Do they, perhaps, handle norms of a bygone era as their criteria? He is of the opinion that many people speak about

> ethical norms, which, inherited from earlier times, correspond less and less to man's life and actons in the contemporary social structure. Here, and not in a general decadence, lies the cause why the mass is losing its belief in norms generally. (DZ: 354; cf. KLS)

The Necessary Cooperation Between Sociologists and Christian Thinkers

Mannheim states that norms become concrete only when one refers them to the surroundings in which they function. Without this social framework a norm lacks all significance. Mannheim is of the opinion that reformulation of norms must happen *in consultation with* sociologists; they can say something about the working out of rules in practise. And he adds this: "The final recasting of norms will still be left to the theologian and philosopher" (DT: 115). They must return to the wellsprings of religious experience and to the origin of the content of norms.

In this connection the relationship between Christians, particularly theologians, and sociologists invites our attention. To the extent that theologians proceed on the assumption that their formulations of Christian truth have eternal value, to that extent their opportunity for cooperating with sociologists is narrow. If there is room for the concept that values acquire form in a social context, undergo modifications in the framework of social change, and thus make room for experiment, then the possibility for cooperation between sociologists and theologians is real. According to Mannheim, a danger which threatens churches after World War II is that, in one way or another, they take a distant attitude toward world politics and social tumult; also the believers themselves concentrate then on their personal faith. In this way they aim too short, however, in their social responsibility and in their contribution to a militant democracy (TM). The sociologist has an important mission in promoting this insight, because democracy must prepare itself for an enormous conflict. As an illustration of the importance of clarity in sociological analysis, he quotes the Apostle Paul, who, however, was speaking about the proclamation of the gospel (I Corinthians 14:8): "If the trumpet give an uncertain sound, who shall prepare himself to the battle?" (MSMD)

We saw already that in the sociological interpretation of values Mannheim gave an approach to the social functioning of values. Also in the discussion with Christians he presents a sociological approach "in its most radical form" (DT: 116). He intends by this characterization to say that sociology is the most secular approach to human life. He also calls this radical approach "immanent" as well. His immanent approach does not mean ony his avoidance of theological presuppositions, but also of metaphysical ultimates. As a sociologist he does not want to do more than study the functioning of values within historical-social processes.

One must not be afraid of sociology, according to Mannheim, as if its analysis would be able to lead to the abandoning of religious institutions. Let sociology develop its ideas, hypotheses, and methods as fully as possible. If this science can convey its insights as much as possible, it will, according to him, also automatically reveal its limitations; that is, it will never set foot on the field of religious presuppositons. Then it will be possible to discern clearly to what extent human behaviors and values fit into functional categories. Without sociological analysis, theologians and philosophers have an image of life which is cut loose from the most characteristic problems and processes in the society of our time (DT: 119).

I have already mentioned a fruitful cooperation between sociologists and theologians is prohibited by barricades if one thinks that Christian values and ideas are established in unchangeable formulations. Then no religious reawakening will be able to happen at all. Mannheim pleads for Christian concepts to be given in *concrete paradigms*, which only provide the direction in which the good may be looked for; then the freedom will emerge again which is necessary for a creative contribution to a changing society in our time (DT: 117). By these paradigms he understands "those decisive, basic experiences which are felt to reveal the meaning of life as whole. Their pattern is so deeply impressed upon our mind that they provide a mould into which further experiences flow. Thus once formed they lend shape to later experiences" (DT: 172). Mannheim then also calls it characteristic of these "basic experiences" or "archetypes of Christian attitude" that they were not originally formulated in abstract commandments, but in the form of parables which Jesus told: not abstract principles of exemplary behavior, but specific examples in an historical-social context. That is why a Christian is compelled to adjust the examples and intentions of Jesus to changed circumstances. To understand the latter point, a sociological analysis is necessary, which as such is helpful for the fresh interpretation of the norm-principles or normative starting-points which are "packaged" in the parables of Jesus. Here Mannheim calls a halt to rational formulation. Rational formulatons of a paradigmatic experience are misleading; it is as though the logical consistency is the criterion for truth. A "paradigmatic" or an "archetypical" experience can give us an image of concrete outward behavior and inner motives, in concrete circumstances that are personal and social. These experiences must not be worked through by sociological analysis into abstract formulations. He imposes a specific limitation on sociological analysis: it must use its equipment for analysis in order to arrive at a higher consciousness of these experiences. Otherwise it is an analysis which leads to nothing. He also calls a halt to specific modes of religious and idealistic thought, which very often occupy themselves only with the justification of norms. They seek to answer the question why commandments must be obeyed, without giving attention to the question of how they must be obeyed when social situations change.

Mannheim's interpretation of Christian truths as "paradigms" has two sociological consequences: 1. these truths are fundamental experiences, which regulate human behavior and which offer *latitude for adjustment*, to different social situations; 2. this interpretation opposes rigidity and dogmatic formulatons which make changes in behavior difficult and which will lead to disintegration of personality and society(DT: 118, 119, 132, 133). He wants to make a clear distinction between fundamental Christian experiences and the Christian behavior and practises of faith which arise from these fundamental experiences in a particular epoch and situation (DT: 139, 140). A problem for

346

Christians not to be underestimated, however, in his opinion, is that they simply do not want to adjust to the world. They desire only such adjustment as agrees with their fundamental experience of life and of faith. Mannheim does not mean "compromise" when he says "adjust," for in compromise one mixes the water of the world with the religious wine. What criterion for adjustment is then valid? His answer is this: that the Christian religion, just as other views of life, is not only a moral experience or a strict regimentation of behavior, but a way of analyzing life and society on the basis of a center of paradigmatic experiences. The sociologist will purify these paradigms form social-cultural forms which attached to the paradigm in a previous epoch. According to Mannheim, we can debate whether the fundamental Christian experiences are formed through concepts like original sin, redemption, the redeeming and creating power of love, the cross and the deeper meaning of suffering; but we cannot debate that on the basis of these "foci of experience" the forms of adjustment which constitute good behavior must always be reconsidered. When these paradigmatic experiences vanish, then the adjustment of human behavior becomes only a matter of goal-orientaton, without our being able to answer the question: what is the purpose of this goal-orientation? On the other hand, when the meaning of paradigmatic experiences has become clear, then it seems to provide the key to the "despiritualizaton" of modern life. We can think iin this connection about what Weber called "the disenchantment of the world" (*Entzauberung der Welt*). Mannheim also warns against this "disenchantment," because the very oldest images or achetypes have determined the experiences of living for people for centuries. These archetypes must not be allowed to go the route of dead orthodoxy, simply because they are old.

As examples of these archetypes he names these: the hero, the wise man, the virgin, the saint, the penitent; other images which dominate the Christian imagination: baptism, absolution, the love feast or the eucharist, the Good Shepherd, the cross, the liberation. One understands these images imperfectly if they are only seen as survivals of a pre-scientific age. If nothing takes their place before their disappearance, the disintegraton of personality and of society will come about. Mannheim is convincd that without paradigmatic experiences, no consistent behavior, no formation of character, no society, and no cooperation are possible; without these fundamental experiences which give direction to life, life loses its contextuality and the adjustment to changing circumstances becomes fragmentary.

Although Mannheim reveals his intention cautiously, he deems it probable that the religious indifference in most Western societies is, at least in part, caused by the disappearance of paradigmatic experiences and also, perhaps, by the replacement of extremely old images which formerly gave direction and meaning to human affairs. Not only for Christians, but also for humanists, socialists, and others it holds, that they must return to the wellsprings of their convictions. Although he says of Christians that they are obliged on the one hand to be conservative with reference toward the core of their religious experiences, on the other hand they must be striving forward in their understanding of social change. This statement is valid for people of other philosophies of life as well (DT: 149). These conceptions connect with the already-mentioned process of fundamental democratization and his plea for an internally-militant democracy.

When the paradigmatic experiences are no longer learned in schools and churches, then other institutions will assume this task, namely, movies and other commercial interests, but they will deliver very different models and archetypes (DT: 148, 149).

Christian values were first realized in small agrarian communities; Christian values belonged to the virtues of the "primary group," "the nursery of human nature"; this is not only because they form our personalities and our basic virtues, but because they first entrust us with the basic processes of social life and, as such, they contain such "standards of morality" as cooperation, mutual help, sympathy, friendliness, love, tolerance, etc. Primary groups are the simplest forms of social life. In all cultures they are directed toward satisfying the elementary needs and in most societies they lead, according to Mannheim, to the acquisition of the identical virtues. This acquisition is not based on logical insight or deliberation; it does not happen on grounds of the acceptance of a specific social or ethical theory. To the contrary: the acquisition happens on grounds of an unconscious imitation of the parents (E, IV: 3, 4). Not only do we learn the basic virtues in these primary groups; in these small communities based on personal contact, the commandment to "love your neighbor" is not lacking in opportunity for applicaton. In our large, impersonal society, this commandment is harder to practise. Christendom operates in a paradoxical situation: the spreading of virtues from small agrarian communities into great industrial societies, and finally at the level of the world community itself. The solution of this paradox can not only happen by applying the principle of love to everybody. The solution can only be found by interpreting the world on the basis of this paradigm of love or by projecting that paradigm of love on a contemporary social level. In a world of large organizations, the paradigm of love means that only such institutions will be allowed that in their basic structure make possible or incarnate the principles of these primary virtues. So he sees democracy as a projection of the principle of brotherhood in a modern, organized society (DT: 150, 151; E, IV: 5, 6).

This new sociological position-finding of Christianity becomes possible when a new generation abandons its old religious interpretations and emotional attachments and when it creates new religious and emotional attachments which fit adequately into a new social order, still to be formed. (cf. ss: 33).

Conclusions

Mannheim distinguishes the separate fields of theologians and sociologists, while at the same time he stresses their mutual context and the necessity for cooperation between them. Also, we saw as well that his sociological analysis

and diagnosis of Western democracies and his sociological therapy called "planning for freedom" leads to a usefulness for religion, and particularly the Christian religion, for this therapy. The sociologists sketch out in rough outline the
way to the society of the future, and they grant religions, theologies, and
churches a place inside that framework. The following conclusion, which is
unavoidable on the basis of *Diagnosis of Our Time*, is drawn by Mannheim
himself in a work which appeared posthumously:

> In periods of change in the past it was the function of religion and of the Church to interpret
> the transition: to let the members of the community know man's fate, his place in the
> world, and what man should live by. Today, such collective guidance will have to embody
> the sociological approach, in order that we may understand social change and its causes.
> (FPDP: 312)

He then says again that religion occupies a central and integrating place in
society, and he lists three social functions of religion (quite apart from its
"internal significance," which he acknowledges but does not evaluate): 1. the
diagnosis of a society in change, 2. the attention it bestows on important issues
in this process, and 3. the integration of human behavior at various levels of
social thought. These functions he attributes to progressive religions (FPDP:
313); sociologists, in his opinion, are to assign and evaluate the functions of
religion.

Mannheim does not relate his view of history and of society to faith in God:
"...as a sociologist he could not speak as a disciple" (Stewart, 1953: 110). That is
why he does not evaluate religions on the basis of content, but only on the basis
of social functions. He acknowledges that the religious life is multi-faceted; it
affects both the personal relationship to God as well as social activities. He
acknowledges that in planning, all aspects of life must be given their due and
that there must be room for prophecy and mysticism (Banning, 1955: 77, 78;
1936: 212). That is why Mannheim challenges Christian thinkers to think along
with him about the problems of the "reconstruction of man and society." The
Christian religion has the unique possession of the concrete paradigms. He
regards the help of Christian thinkers as necessary, because they, by means of
these paradigms, can provide constructive contributions to the thinking about
and the realization of the new social order. Sociologists who practise their
"secularized discipline" and philosphers equipped with sociological reason are
not in a position, apparently, to bring about this new social order in their own
strength. In Chapter XVII I already wrote that the light of sociological reason is
less bright than Mannheim originally had supposed. The "twilight of sociological reason" must be turned to dawn with the help of religious paradigms. The
discourse here is of the nature-grace scheme: on the wordly, sociological
substructure a religious superstructure arises. Thus, religion has its social place
assigned to it by sociology; sociology, preparing the way for "planning for
freedom" is complemented by religion.

Concerning paradigms and religious archetypes, it seems that Mannheim makes a distinction between these two. Paradigms are the normative principles packed into the parables of Jesus; archetypes are the religious images which Christians have created during the course of their history. On the other hand, he sometimes uses these terms interchangeably and calls "the cross" and "liberation" pradigms as well as archetypes. In addition, he mentions orginal sin, love, suffering, the hero, the wiseman, the virgin, the penitent, baptism, absolution, the eucharist, and the Good Shepherd. Curtis, the English pedagogue, comments(1958: 208) correctly on this list:

> This list appears to be rather a strange mixture to a Christian. Mannheim regretted that they had lost their inspirational force in modern times, and that nothing had taken their place. To the Christian this would appear as an overhasty generalization. One has the impression that Mannheim regarded them as means to an end, as useful patterns of thought rather than essential truths of Christianity.

Curtis continues:

> Influenced by the maxim that all thought is socially determined Mannheim concluded that religion can and ought to be planned.

This conclusion seems to me to be largely, but not completely, true about Mannheim. The purpose which Mannheim has in mind is "planning for freedom." This panning can only be realized if "fundamental virtues" are being learned in education and in child-rearing. Without arguing on the basis of religion, he names manners, mutual help, honesty, and social justice, which he as sociologist finds present in all philosophies of life. When he says that he reserves the ultimate reformation of norms and values for theologians and philosophers, then this means no more than that their task is to distill the paradigms from diverse philosophies of life and to work them out in contemporary terms – that is, to provide the support for the basic virtues formulated by sociologists in order to realize "planning for freedom." With the education in families and schools, religions and their institutions are means for achieving his purpose. That Mannheim wants to use religion as a means of achieving his purpose is sharply formulated by Gremmels (1952)

> Theologically Mannheim can and must be confronted, for in his morality he forces faith to the side by the purely human power of reason, even if not directly, then indirectly, and always persistently; and he must be confronted, because in doing this he is stealing by craft what is God's gift of grace.

Curtis wants to see the paradigms named by Mannheim placed in a context. The basis of the Christian religion is "the conviction that through sin man has become estranged from God. The function of the church is to offer a means of redemption to fallen man, who is unable to raise himself by his own efforts. (...) It makes an authoritative claim to bring salvation to those who accept Christ as

350

their Lord and Saviour and try to carry out his teaching in their own lives" (Curtis, 1958: 209, 210).

The last sentence of this quotation demonstrates the social relevance of the Christian religion, in which ideas such as the love of one's neighbors, help, honesty, social justice, and also solidarity, loyalty, and responsibility occupy an important place. Above, I wrote that the conclusion of Curtis is in large part true; not totally. He takes too little account of the distinction Mannheim makes between the functions of church and religion in a society on its way toward "planning for freedom" and religious paradigms. Mannheim correctly made a distinction between the paradigms, or norm-principles which are present in the parables of Jesus (and in other Bible stories), and opposite to them, the form which they help to create in society and culture. Church teaches the meaning of the parables, but religion applies them in society. He also understood that the criterion for judgment does not lie in theoretical views of these paradigms, but in their practical application. It is a fundamentally Biblical notion that Truth must not only be professed, but must be *done*. Not that problems cease to exist once this is clear; there are a variety of ways of bringing the norm-principles into practise. The germ of Mannheim's view and of the Christian religion: truth in action; this takes the discussion out of the atmosphere of theoretical abstraction and prods it toward concrete actions and specific policy. That Mannheim saw this provocation toward practise in the framework of "planning for freedom" does not necessarily need to be in conflict with the elaboration of Christian principial norms. The judgment of this problem is dependent on the fact of *how* the planning for freedom and the norm-principles of Christianity are to be realized. In this *how* a dreadful problem lurks. On grounds of the sociology of knowledge we know that people with differing social positions think and act in different ways. Their adequate action is demanded and only possible in the light of sociological reason; this sociological reason, however, appears to possess too limited a capability to achieve adequate action and needs the supplement of religion. And so church and religion have had their functions assigned again by sociologists. Mannheim's view places us before a tangled skein of problems which he was not able to bring to a satisfactory conclusion.

One can also ask the question whether Mannheim's acceptance of paradigmatic experiences is not in conflict with the basic idea of his sociology of knowledge. He denies in this branch of science that universally valid values can exist, while he now defends them. Also a knowledge-sociological elaboration of these values raises questions. Mannheim considers a minimum of conformity concerning values a necessity. What must we understand by *minimum*? Will not various groups and classes interpret differently first of all what the values concerned are? And then disagree some more about what constitutes *minimum conformity*?

Thinking in the line of his argument, it is unjust to conclude that "planning for freedom" in practise will mean an elimination of the religious principles. The challenge to guard and cherish these principles brings this difficulty along with it, that this guarding may also influence the "planning for freedom." Like Mannheim, so Christians will admit that the truth of these principles is a related or a relational truth; that is, that in various socio-historical periods and situations these truths are understood and practised in various ways. This does not mean that the meaning and uniqueness of these norm-principles is dependent on subjective-human views and actions. This meaning, uniqueness, and evidence are to be combined directly with the Biblical perspective of fall, cross, and the message of liberaton. Although Mannheim speaks about a number of paradigms as free from this Biblical perspective and speaks about paradigms as subjective experiences, he acknowledges – placing himself in the position of Christians – paradigms as supra-personal in their meaning and evidence and as "a superior force." They have authority and persuasiveness; they have a meaning which energizes and gives direction. Although they can be "locked up" in static formulations, they must be "unlocked" in thinking and action which is adequate for the situation.

With a variant of a statement of Immanuel Kant one could say: "Sociology without religion is empty and religion without sociology is blind" (cf. Bramstedt, Gerth, 1951: xi; Wagner, 1953: 106). Although religion without sociology, according to Mannheim, is indeed blind, his sociology is less empty than the statement suggests, because it must direct society the way to the future. Mannheim says that he finds thinking and acting based on paradigms to be important. They concern fundamental truths which, according to him, do not belong in the field of sociology. They must be elaborated by Christians, who in this regard supplement sociology. Mannheim's discussion of paradigms, however, is so fragmentary, so little integrated with the Biblical perspective, and so little integrated with his own sociology and ethics, that paradigms function neither as dynamic principles nor as a necessary supplement in his theory. In the following paragraph this will become even more clear.

Social and Moral Maturity
In society we need not only physical and mental maturity, but also social and moral maturity. According to Mannheim, this maturity is:

> The capacity for effective and satisfactory participation in grown-up life, the ability to play the roles in society which life has in store for us. Social maturity is acquired through social experiences – experienced in society – and not only must you have the right social situation from which to learn what is needed for adult life - you also have to learn how to learn from these situations. (ws, I: 3)

By nature a person is neither competitive nor cooperative. Both attitudes are acquired in a learning process which is dependent on the society in which one lives and the education one has received. There is no society characterized entirely by total cooperation or entirely by total competition. Western society, however, is particularly characterized by competition; in some sectors of society cooperation is expected of people (family, work context, sport, etc.), while in sport and elsewhere competition also appears. Cooperation and competition run their courses for the most part in our society following determined "patterns" (ws, II: 2, 3; FPDP: 191-197).

Mannheim nowhere says that personality is totally determined by the society. He does go rather far when he states that "there is hardly anything in the individual man which is not somehow influenced by the society in which he lives" (ws, X: 1). This problem, according to him, is of great importance for Western societies. No society will be able to continue existence if it is indifferent about the question of what kind of people it needs. He rejects fascistic and communistic methods of education, but the question remains: "Is there a type of behavior which might be called 'democratic behavior'?" and "Is there a type of personality which could rightly be called 'a democratic personality'?" (ws, X: 2). He answers these questions affirmatively. There is in Western societies a decline to be noticed from extreme competition in favor of cooperation. Also, leadership in the Western world differs fundamentally from that in a dictatorship.

Following H.H. Anderson, Mannheim distinguishes *dominative behavior* from *integrative behavior*. *Dominative* behavior means the control of others, which we see clearly in dictators. *Integrative* behavior is more difficult to describe. It is more than cooperative behavior, which helps and supports others and which often depends on friendliness. It rests also on a deep interest in the various ways in which things are done and in the various motives which characterize someone's striving and ultimate purposes. While in dominative behavior someone imposes his ultimate purposes on others and limits them in their alternative styles of behavior, integrating behavior comes to expression in a deep concern for others and in the desire to help them realize their goals and to enlarge their alternatives in behavior and in their possibilities for development; at the samen time, integrative behavior desires to arrive at an integration of one's own ultimate purposes with those of other people. Someone who strives for this integrating behavior does not choose to function with people who agree with him; he does not judge, but demonstrates himself to be open, dynamic, creative, and alert. Mannheim continues:

> This is exactly the kind of behaviour for which we have consciously to train our next generation if democracy is to survive. ... a dynamic democracy cannot be satisfied merely with helpful and cooperative people – people who can only cooperate with their fellows along traditional lines. What is wanted is that all the members should be able to learn from new experience. They have a new challenge to meet – they must try to cooperate with people whose purposes are different, continually looking ahead for opportunities for enlarging the scope and aims of cooperation. (ws, X: 5; cf. FPDP: 16, 17, 197)

In bringing up children and in educating them, this behavior can and must be taught and learned, and the society, according to Mannheim, must do all it can to support this learning process. He is convinced that this learning process does not only refer to the acquisition of a new pattern of behavior, but at the deepest level is connected with a change in the personality, "a change of heart."

Dominating behavior belongs to a personality which is fearful of change and of throwing one's self into the balance; such a person is unsure of himself. This is contradiction to the integrating behavior, which is an expression of an open and creative personality, which is characterized by stability and certainty, and which does not soon feel threatened. That is why child-rearing and education must be directed toward the nurture of "integrating personalities." And the social sciences will need to study under which conditions this integrating type can emerge, live, and survive. While the "dominating personality" only attaches value to force, the "integrating personality" will speak about freedom with responsibility, and freedom as a necessity; this limitation arises from respect for the other person.

Democratic personalities are not born; people can become democratic personalities. Just as a democracy is not only a question of some particular new way of voting, but of a "new way of life," so also the democratic personality is a new kind of person. Social and moral maturity is a condition for arriving at a society at the democratic level. It is a condition for and the basis of the "integrating type" of person. This condition, however, is only to be realized if one has faith in the latent possibilities which are present in people. In this connection he cites Bergson: "The essence of man lies in his powers of creation, both material and moral. Materially he is the maker of things, morally he is a maker of himself" (ws, X: 10; cf. FPDP: 199-207).

The above means for Mannheim that on the way to a society planned for freedom both cooperation and competition (in the sense of creativity and inventiveness) are necessary. In society one can further and justify initiatives for the purposes of arriving at the new social order (FPDP: 196).

As far as the democractic type of person is concerned, one must not have too ideal an image, as though in this type of person all contradictions are abolished, all tensions eliminated, and all powers functioning in an harmonious balance. Mannheim perceives that the authoritarian and the liberal images of humanity are dangerous and unusable for the social order which he desires. The democratic type of person restores, in the anthropological sense, an approach to the way which must be taken to achieve social order. He does not hide himself from the fact that the democratic type of person contains a duality within himself; on the one hand it is characterized by the process of socialization or by learning to be a player of roles, which never may go so far that it smothers individuality; and on the other hand it is characterized by the process of the emancipation of the ego, which may never go so far that social chaos emerges (FPDP: 244). In Mannheim's own words'

The moral question is ever the conflict between the need for cooperation and the wish for self-aggrandizement. The conflict has to be solved. And it is a moral problem. (E, VIII: 3)

Although Mannheim had experienced Fascism at first hand, was well-informed about the societal life in the Soviet Union, and recognized the dangers which

354

still threatened the existing Western democracies, he had an optimistic image of the future. He saw that is was possible to check group-egoism and that the concern for and the insight into national and international problems was growing. This process, according to him, must be intensified. However critical people may be, when one examines several centuries at once, it is not to be denied, according to him, "that there has been quite a considerable progress in history" (E, VII: 6). Concentrating on Nazi Germany, Mannheim perceives how deep the human being can fall and can degenerate into a barbarous being. But he has fixed his hope on the capability of the individual to change. By means of modern media of communication, such as radio, newspapers, books, and films, a social bringing-up and a social education can acquire form, which should contribute to the social and moral maturity of people (E, VIII: 5, 6; NSHB: 3). In this context he does not speak at all about religious paradigms.

Mannheim's Ethics
Mannheim distinguishes three kinds of ethics: 1. a general ethics, 2. an ethics of personal relationships, and 3. an ethics of organized relationships.

1. In his *general ethics* he describes the principles which regulate behavior in general and which are independent from special social relationships and organizations. For instance, he analyzes "survival values," by which he means "those values which characterize all activities with the purpose of guaranteeing and safeguarding the survival of the individual or the group" (DT: 153). In the philosophy of National Socialism no other values existed than those which advanced the principles of race, blood and land. The Nazis sacrificed millions of people for the sake of this ideology. Naturally, Mannheim casts off this ideology, but translates this problem into another: a conflict can emerge between the demands of the individual's surviving and the group's. A conflict can also arise between efficiency and democratic planning. Dictatorial planning will lead to solutions more rapidly than democratic planning. The important questions in this connection are these: "What is the good of democracy if we cannot survive?" and "What is the good of surviving if we must lose our freedom in the process?"

In a society organized on the functional-rational model, these questions are urgent. In modern societies one takes elaborate and comprehensive measures which have far-reaching effects. If people, for instance, do not take the necessary measures in time during a period of war, they run the risk of losing the war. During a period of war and in other borderline situations, an absolute choice emerges between efficient functioning and democracy. The relationship between these two will change according to the nature of the various tasks; so in transportation the efficiency, figured in time and costs, will be absolutely dominant, while in child-rearing and in education efficiency will be subordinate. According to Mannheim, life to an important degree is a "struggle for survival." He describes three ethical answers to this problem: 1. the philosophy of National Socialism, which leads to barbarism; 2. its oposite is the denial of the moral right of self-defense, which leads to altruism and pacifism, and often ends in hypocrisy; 3. Mannheim himself regards self-defense, sticking up for one's self, as unavoidable; according to him, the problem is how to be able to control this egoism; he wants to permit this egoism to the extent that it is necessary for the survival of the individual and the group. This control is dependent on the sociological study of society and its tendencies and on society's developing in the direction of "planning for freedom" (DT: 153-157).

2. In the sphere of the *ethics of personal relationships* Mannheim explains, as one of the changed attitudes, the gradual diminishing of the meaning of seclusion; in its place a process of mass-satisfactions and mass-ecstacies arise. According to him, it is to be very much lamented that there are fewer possibilities in society to retreat and to exchange ideas and reflect in small groups. Privacy and contemplation are to be desired as means toward individualizing the personality and helping it to grow. Precisely in a dynamic and in some respects an explosive society, such opportunities are necessary now more than ever (DT: 157-161).

3. In the sphere of *ethics of organized relationships* we can hardly expect anything positive without moral consciousness. The moral crisis of our time is chiefly to be attributed to the rapidity of the technical, scientific, and industrial revolution and its new social organization. There was insufficient time to realize the moral implicatoins of these changes. In Mannheim's sociology it is clear that there is a collision between the rational principles of organizations, and the psychic and moral needs of the individual. When institutions do not succeed in winning a following, then they grow bitter and one can expect irrational explosions. Our fundamental needs have a two-fold nature: 1. they need an efficiently working social order and 2. they must be satisfied psychically and morally. Mannheim names a few conditions which every ethics of organized relationships must fulfill: sanctions, discipline, rules of behavior, bearing responsibility, labor incentives, fair wages, insight into the purpose for work, the social prestige of work, and the social hierarchy (DT: 161, 162).

Conclusions

In the description of these three kinds of ethics, the general ethics, the ethics of personal relationships, and the ethics of organized relationships, Mannheim does not speak of what he calls "the basic virtues." I think he does not do this because he regards them as the basic "values" which lie at the foundation of his whole ethics.

It is clear that in his description of the three kinds of ethics, he names only a few examples; his description, too, is framentary. Moreover, the boundaries between the three ethics are fluid. It is self-evident that the principles of general ethics return in the other two kinds of ethics; these latter two constitute the field of social ethics. What he describes as issues of the ethics of personal relationships (privacy and contemplation) also have significance for the ethics of organized relationships. However, these issues of the ethics of personal relationships are, in my mind, questions which primarily concern the individual person and concern social relationships less (though they have something to do with that subject). That is why I should like to characterize his second kind of ethics (and as a consequence also the third kind of ethics) "a personalistic ethics." He looks for a new group solidarity and for a new social ethics. When he speaks about general ethics and about the ethics of personal relationships, then he always means that these kinds of ethics must strive for a new education, a new formation of personality for the purpose of being able to achieve the "planning for freedom." Still, I characterize his "social" ethics as *personalistic*. This personalistic social ethics is not individualistic. The personalism comes into view when a tension develops between the calling of an individual person and the still unregulated social reality, that is, between the subjective person who judges the social order and who has the calling to bring about a new social order on the one hand, and on the other hand the society of "planning for freedom," which must order the behavior of people to a large extent. I speak of a tension in his personalism, but not of an opposition or paradox. This last would mean, in Mannheim's terms, that we are not prepared to think at a higher level, the level of planning. This tension was also already explained between subjective and the social origins of values, between theological and sociological thought, between ethics of conscience and of responsibility, between cooperation and competition. This tension also comes to expression in the distinction he makes between "general morality" and "contextual morality." This distinction emerges from the fact that we live on two levels in society. On the one hand we use general arguments which are directed toward concerns of the community, and on the other had we weaken these arguments when we take our own doing and abstaining into account, and place our own concerns and experiences into a specific social context (FPDP: 303-305). Precisely because social ethics is a building block in bringing-up children, in their education at school, and in the new sociology which must prepare to cooperate on the way to "planning for freedom," the tension of a personalistic ethics in Mannheim's work is not surprising. It simply repeats that we live in a society of conflicts and tensions and that the society characterized by "planning for freedom" is not a streamlined one. It is a path of conflicts – a learning process with progress and failures. Not that Mannheim simply accepts these tensions mentioned above. He would want to overcome them, but he can live with them because the need for his alternative, "planning for freedom," is so clear for him. Hence, the words of De Montaigne, which he submitted as the epigraph for *Diagnosis of Our Time*: "No wind makes for him that hath no intended port to sail into."

For me, as for Van Riessen (see Chapter XVII), it is rather a question whether Mannheim had fathomed deeply enough the problems of the possibility for the transformation of human beings, of society, of morality, and of the crisis of culture. Although we can philosophize long about this "deep enough," I answer this question negatively. Speaking about fascism, he acknowledges that a person can decline into barbarism. How is it possible that people can sometimes have a barbaric and sometimes even demonic behavior? On the other hand, he speaks of progress in the history of humanity. He has an optimistic image of humanity, based on the sociological reason. We saw that this basis is not totally adequate, and that it needs the help of religious paradigms. This breaks down somewhat the reliability and persuasiveness of his belief in the sociological reason. At the same time we saw that the paradigms do not entirely fulfill either a foundational or a complementary function. Moreover, it seems that his discussion of Christian paradigms is fragmentary and oddly detached from the Biblical perspective of the fall into sin, the cross, and the liberation. Where does his optimism come from? Mannheim touches on all kinds of fundamental anthropological, ethical, and religious problems, but these are not given an adequate solution in his philosophy. The germ of these problems escapes him, according ot Gremmels (1952), who goes on to say this:

> Mannheim's moral tendency is disillusioning because of only superficial observations. Indeed, through education, the virtues, which are the means, can restore and preserve that philosophy of order to a certain extent, and without that philosophy every economic plan must fail. On the other side, however, these virtues bring individuals necessarily to an experience of failure, since human nature, now, as at all times, is incapable of enjoying the demands of virtue. In moral failure, however, that consciousness of sin is awakened, which fervently yearns for genuine faith, and then brings that faith about.

Already in his student days he was gripped by Dostoevsky; also in *Diagnosis of Our Time* he refers to this Russian Orthodox author, who wanted to connect primal religious experiences or paradigms with the psychological, social and cultural problems of his time. The depth of these religious experiences, especially the tension between original sin and grace, in which human thought and activity occur, were felt by Mannheim, but never experienced. I conclude with the correct and well-formulated conclusion of Gremmels (1952):

> This final theological questionability about thought and activity contained in Mannheim's theory does not, however, make the effort of this theory pointless, because all of our activity is theologically questionable, and still it must be done. Yes, it is simply true that the consciousness of the theological questionability of human action is the actual element of order in our decadent existence in the occident. The "going under" of this consciousness led to the gradual decline of order in life, which we complain about as an acute disease of the times, as our cultural crisis.

Chapter XIX

Mannheim's Significance

That the influence of Mannheim declined after his death is, according to Ernest Manheim (1947: 473) and Shils (1980: 188), primarily to be attributed to the fact that he established no school. The significance of the institutionalizing of a theory may become clear if we compare Mannheim and Horkheimer in this regard.

According to Shils, Mannheim was more original and more multifaceted than Horkheimer; he also had a more differentiated approach to society and a more lucid perspective on details. Mannheim's knowledge of empirical investigation was greater, and also various ideas of his could be applied more easily in concrete empirical research. Mannheim, for instance, brought up these matters for discussion: the conditions for political action, intellectuals as partisans and as non-partisans, the value of the presuppositions of faith in society, various kinds of political action, problems concerning the generations, and consensus between the generations. Still, the influence of Horkheimer in the intellectual world is greater than that of Mannheim (Shils, 1980: 189).

Although Mannheim was a sparkling and stimulating lecturer, his professorship in Frankfurt was too brief for him to form a school. Few graduate students attended the London School of Economics, and the economic depression blocked the financial means which he needed for research. The series of books which he began, *The Library of Sociology and Social Reconstruction*, bore the mark of his thought in only the most limited way; only after his death did this series become a significant publication in sociology.

In Horkheimer's philosophy and sociology, a theme, or a cluster of themes which form a single context, is to be more clearly discerned than in Mannheim's work. Horkheimer's theme: all thinking is embedded in a socio-cultural context; the modern society which forms this context is impersonal and destructive for the individual; the individual is manipulated and has little or no opportunity for organizing his life by "reasonable insight"; the task of "critical theory" is to bring reason to realization in the world, to bring people to consciousness, and to help them free themselves from enslaving social relationships. From the beginning of his professorship in Frankfurt (1930) Horkheimer inspired and was inspired by the Institute of Social Research *(Institut für Sozialforschung)* and the *Journal for Social Research (Zeitschrift für Sozialforschung)*. From the beginning he had a number of assistants around him. In 1933 Horkheimer and his assistants left Germany. The Institute was allied to Columbia University in New York. The publication of their journal was continued, just as their scientific research was, which resulted in the lengthy book, *The Authoritarian Personality* (Adorno and others, 1950) and in other publications. The Institute already had built up contacts with various other universities; it achieved fame and influence in intellectual circles. Various assistants form the Institute became professors in American universities: Leo Löwenthal, Herbert Marcuse, and others. After the war, after the return of the exiles to Germany, the Institute began to bring out a series of monographs. Jürgen Habermas, a student of Horkheimer, became an exponent of his critical philosophy during the 1960's. Another student of Horkheimer, Ludwig van Friedenburg, became the Minister of Education in the state of Hesse. Conditioned by foreseen and unforeseen circumstances, stimulated by Horkheimer as an organizer, and particularly carried forward by the conviction by Horkheimer's followers of the correctness of his critical philosophy, the Institute for Social Research has been able to develop itself, and its influence has been tremendous (cf. Shils, 1980: 190-192).

Institutionalizing of a theory, according to Shils, says nothing about the truth-value of that theory. It promotes a possible consolidation, elaboration, and expansion of a theory. As such it can promote a more permanent influence and continuity in the development of a theory. This process of institutionalizing was lacking for Mannheim's theory, a lack which explains to a great extent his narrower influence.

Another reason for Mannheim's more restricted influence (see Shils, 1941: 153) is that most of his publications display serious defects: unclear descriptions of ideas, the use of certain ideas with differing meanings without these differing meanings being made precise, vague formulations, and contradictions. Critics like Grünwald (1934), Von Schelting (1934), later Merton (1968), have pointed out these defects. Sometimes they are studied in an intensive way (Neusüss, 1968a). It is not unlikely that criticism acquired an echo effect, so that those of Mannheim's ideas which continue to be discussed are overwhelmed by criticism. That in contemporary studies of conservatism, generations, culture-sociology, sociology of knowledge, ideology, and planning, Mannheim continues to be quoted against such odds shows all the more that he may be counted among the classical sociologists.

Mannheim was a sociologist with a great influence, particularly in ecclesiastical circles, in educational circles, and in adult education, as well as in sociology. He exerted a thoroughgoing influence on his students. Indirectly, he had influence on the coming into existence of the Education Act (1944) of Minister Butler. After the war his influence on the Ministry of Education could still be felt.

His influence in the English university world and among English sociologists was narrow and has remained narrow. As reasons for this could be listed the already-mentioned factors which are typical for English society: strongly determined by tradition; feeling little for the German method of practising sociology (which, in spite of his orientation in American social sciences, continued to characterize Mannheim); the social, emotional, and moral distancing of science from life (while Mannheim, both orally and in writing, was a more and more *involved* thinker).

The shock of the economic crisis of the 1930's, the total mobilization of 1939, the threat of World War II, the refusal to state priorities in official policy when stating priorities is a condition for being able to survive: all of these demonstrated the impossibility of the liberal society to survive, and at the same time demonstrated the need for changing the social and political order – on which change Mannheim earnestly insisted and for which change the English society and many of its sociologists had too little concern, as well as for Mannheim's sociological insight.

Mannheim reached many people with his publications, both in the university world and outside of it. Therefore, one can say in a general sense he was an influential sociologist. Still, it is difficult to determine on whom, with which ideas, and to what extent he has had influence, and perhaps still has. His students who have written about sociology are, among others, J. Floud, Professor-emeritus of Sociology at Cambridge; W.A.C. Stewart, Professor-emeritus of Education at Keele; and K.H. Wolff, one of Mannheim's students in Frankfurt and Professor-emeritus of Sociology at Brandeis University at Boston (Waltham). Gradually his influence declines as those who have known him leave active life. This holds not only for England, but also for his influence in other European countries. In the countries of Western Europe, Mannheim continues to belong to the classical sociologists, with Durkheim, Weber, Simmel, Tönnies, Spencer, and others. He was rooted in the intellectual history of Western Europe. Although he is counted among the classical sociologists in England and the United States, his significance and influence there is estimated less highly.

English sociology in Mannheim's day was under the influence particularly of the great sociologists named earlier: Durkheim, Weber, Spencer, and Pareto. Later came the influence of American empirical sociology. After World War II the Marxist influence among English sociologists also became strong. In the United States the practise of sociology was dominated by pragmatism, social behaviorism, instrumental research, and an empiricism lacking in theory. These factors formed a barrier for the proper understanding of Mannheim's work; these factors led to lack of comprehension and mistaken interpretation of his sociology (Krüger, 1968: 18, 19). After the discussion of the sociology of knowledge by L. Wirth, E. Hartung, V.G. Hinshaw, R.K. Merton, C. Wright Mills, T. Lavine, A. Child, and K.H. Wolff, Krüger (1968: 209) concludes as follows:

...that the striking of most American knowledge-sociologists aims in the direction of a "scientizing" *(Verwissenschaftlichung)* of their discipline, the consequences of which are a renunciation of epistemological-philosophical reflections on the reciprocal dependence of subject and object on the one hand, and, on the other, a renunciation of political engagement in the specific society.

From this conclusion it appears that many American sociologists who explicitly have occupied themselves with Mannheim have missed the epistemological, cultural-philosophical and political significance of his views (cf. Dittberner, 1979: 21-42). However, I must acknowledge the competent books about Mannheim by North American scholars like A.P. Simonds (1978), D. Kettler, V. Meja, and N. Stehr (1984) and C. Loader (1985).

In addition we must consider that various sociologists who have totally gone their own way own a debt of gratitude to Mannheim. The ethno-sociologist Harold Garfinkel (1967: 77-79) claims to have been inspired by Mannheim in this way. This inspiration was also experienced by the Dutch sociologists Bouman (1974), Thoenes (1966), Zijderveld (1970), and many others.

It is difficult to establish definitively Mannheim's significance and influence in the field on the sociology of education, but the students who attended his lectures at the Institute of Education from 1941 to 1947, who also attended other lectures he delivered, and who read his publications were enthusiastic; they were inspired by him. With reference to his influence in the sociology of education, Lauwerys wrote me (17-9-1980): "I do not think Karl Mannheim ever had nor has any influence in the science of education. (...) his name does not appear in elementary books on sociology of education. (...) I suppose one might say that Karl Mannheim is largely concerned with problems that do not seem very relevant to British educationists or teachers." Lauwerys is right only to the extent that he means publications of the last two decaded; in these the name of Mannheim appears only sporadically or not at all. In older handbooks and textbooks in the field of the sociology of education one will find his name and discussions of his work (for instance, A.K.C. Ottaway, 1953; Curtis, 1958). Mannheim's sociological-pedagogical publications awakened concern about the relationship which he described between pedagogical problems and changing social processes. This problem, however, was examined not only by Mannheim, but also by others, for example, by Clarke. Mannheim's study in this field still had an introductory character. Still, this work contained promise, as Lauwerys, who wrote me that Mannheim had no influence in the sociology of education, attests in that same letter: "I very much regret his early death. Had he lived for another twenty years, he would have adapted his work, research, teaching, and writing to the British. And *then* he would have had immense influence. In his lectures he certainly did adapt to his young but intelligent audience and discussed their problems." Mannheim's premature death was according to Lauwerys "a great personal loss and a terrible professional loss to me and many others." I close with a quotation by Leopold von Wiese (1948: 99):

...he not only occupied a prominent place in the history of science; he was not only a scholar, but a spiritual revolutionary; he had many characteristics of an Old testament prophet, and with his whole being belonged in the ranks of great Jews: Marx, Gumplowicz, Durkheim, and Trotsy. Just as these Jews combined a strongly rational thought with a glowing passion to change the practical world, so did Mannheim, transforming human nature as well as the social order.

PART V: Summary and Evaluation

Summary of the Development of Mannheim's Thought Within the Framework of his Sociology of Knowledge

- *Worldview Analysis*
- *The Development of Mannheim's Thought*
- *Characterization of Mannheim's Thought within the Framework of his Sociology of Knowledge*

Worldview Analysis

Applying Karl Mannheim's sociology of knowledge to his own philosophy means that we need to use the ingredients of his interpretation of worldview *(Weltanschauungs-Interpretation)*. First, this interpretation contains a three-"dimensional" analysis; he distinguishes between the objective, the expressive, and the documentary meaning. The "objective" concentrates on the product "as such"; the "expressive," on the subjective intent of the creator; and the "documentary," on the structure as a "manifestation" of the worldview of an historical period (wi: 43ff; see Chapter VI).

Later on, in his study of the evaluative sociology of knowledge, Mannheim elaborates the worldview-analysis. In an historical way he considers Western societies as dynamic totalities. One cannot begin by studying thoughts in relation to societal strata, he insists. They must first be considered as parts of the "process of totality," i.e., the fundamental outlook or worldview *(Weltanschauung)* of an era; this non-theoretical totality is a functional constellation of the differentiated connections of human experiences.

Further, Mannheim analyzes the structure of the worldview of a given era that contains *particular worldviews*, for instance, Roman Catholic, Calvinistic, humanistic, and Marxist, and embodied in these worldviews are certain *general intentions* or *aspirations*, for instance the intention to Christianize, to secularize, or to humanize the society. Mannheim subdivides the general intentions into *special strivings*: economic and political strivings, strivings of art, thought-strivings, etc. Thought-strivings are, for instance, rationalism, irrationalism, idealism, or organic ways of thinking. Within a thought-striving Mannheim further distinguishes *styles of thought* such as traditionalist, conservative, ideological, utopian, reformist, and revolutionary. Those groups of people which combine their world postulates and a given style of thought he mentions as *intellectual strata (geistige Schichten)* (sw: 184; see Chapter X).

Mannheim wants to analyze worldviews, because in his evaluative sociology of knowledge he wants to judge the quality of truth in the different kinds of thought. Does this mean that the complex concept "worldview" might be a criterion of truth? According to Mannheim, the socially unattached or free-floating intelligentsia has true insight and knowledge necessary to evaluate thought within the bounds of the dynamic societal order. This does not include all intellectuals, but only those whose intellectual training has resulted in an independent social position, a broad spiritual horizon, an open mind on ethical issues, a feeling for tendencies of a given period, and an overall view of economic, societal, and political questions. These intellectuals will be able to make the judgments necessary for forming a new synthesis of culture. They will point the direction of Western societies and Western culture and overcome the crisis of this culture. Mannheim acknowledges that intellectuals also have their relation to the societal groups from which they descend and that those groups will influence their outlook. Therefore he speaks of the "relatively" socially unattached or free-floating intelligentsia (IU: 138ff; SC: 103-105; see Chapter XII).

The Development of Mannheim's Thought

We can distinguish Mannheim's life and thought into three stages: 1. the Hungarian stage (1893-1919), in which he wrote his philosophical publications, 2. the German stage (1920-1933), in which he developed the principles of his sociology, and mainly of his sociology of knowledge, and 3. the English periods (1933-1947), in which he elaborated his political sociology concerning problems of democracy, freedom, planning and education.

The *objective* meaning of his philosophical publications can be shortly characterized by the analysis of the crisis of Western culture, in which he defends an historistic approach. He also presents an analysis of epistemological theories, in order to make clear the presuppositions of studying a discipline. The objective meaning of his sociology of knowledge can be shortly characterized by his analysis of the social rootedness of all human thought and knowledge. The objective meaning of his political sociology can be shortly characterized by his elaboration of "planning for freedom," and by his criticism and rejection of *laissez-faire* thought and totalitarian ideologies (communism and fascism).

The *expressive* meaning of his whole work may be summarized as an attempt to overcome the crisis of Western culture. Based upon his philosophical insights, especially upon his historicism, he elaborates his sociology of knowledge. In this elaboration the socially free-floating intelligentsia plays an important part. It alone would be able to transcend the social rootedness of thought, and, therefore, the partial outlooks. It could attain the broadest view of a certain socio-cultural totality, in order to reveal a "cultural synthesis." Although Mannheim speaks of the "relatively" socially unattached or free-floating intelligentsia, the adverb *relatively* does not diminish the cultural calling of the intelligentsia to show the way to the future. In his political sociology he describes that from this intelligentsia, the planners for freedom will be chosen.

The *documentary* meaning of Mannheim's work needs to be judged from a total view or the worldview of a period. It is difficult to characterize the general worldview of Central Europe during Mannheim's life in Hungary. It was mainly dominated by a spiritual and cultural crisis. There was an alienation between the human "soul" or existence and the objective culture. People could not identify themselves with nor recognize themselves in economic, societal, and political structures. During Mannheim's stay in Germany, this cultural crisis exploded into an economic collapse, into the rise of fascism, and into the decay of democracy. During his stay in Great Britain, the dominant worldview might be characterized by a traditionally founded superiority of the cohesive British culture and its force to survive. English people were not aware of the fact that the decay of democracy and other cultural crises were also a danger to their own society.

In sum, we may say that Mannheim attempts to present adequate analyses of the Central European, and of the threatening English, cultural crisis. Although one questions whether his "socially free-floating intelligentsia" is a solution, his analyses are largely accurate, instructive, and stimulating. His therapy of planning for freedom is instructive too, and has been proved to be fruitful and promising, especially in Sweden and in the Netherlands, in which an extensive system of social security and much planning of economic and social life have been implemented. But this philosophy is even to be noted in other Western countries. Representatives of this thought in the United States were, for example, the Kennedy's; in France, Francois Mitterrand; in Great Britain, Harold Wilson; and in West Germany, Willy Brandt and Helmut Schmidt.

Characterization of Mannheim's Thought within the Framework of his Sociology of Knowledge

This sociological characterization of Mannheim's thought, I attempt to clarify with the help of his analysis of the worldview. As I wrote already, in this analysis he distinguishes a general worldview, particular worldviews, worldstrivings or aspirations embodied in worldviews, special strivings (for example, economic and thought strivings), and styles of thought. The general *worldview* of the Central European culture of the second and third decades of this century was characterized by a cultural and spiritual crisis which exploded into an economic collapse, a decay of democracy, and the rise of fascism.

Several *particular worldviews* can be distinguished. In his Hungary, for example, there were socialist, communist, bourgeois, Jewish, Roman Catholic, and fascist worldviews. Mannheim participated in circles of Jews, socialists and communists. He dissociated himself from the Jewish religion, and sympathized with the socialist worldview. The world strivings or general intentions embodied in the socialist worldview was characterized by humanizing and democratizing of the society. Within this socialist world striving, *particular strivings* can be distinguished: the *economic striving* of the distribution of large landownership, the improvement of the economic situation of the employees, and the *political striving* of universal suffrage. Of course, these particular strivings were borne by a thought striving that was elaborated in political programs. However, in the intellectual circles of the socialist movement – as in other movements – different philosophical influences can be distinguished: Dostoevsky's and Kierkegaard's religious philosophies, Nietzsche's criticism of reason, Marx's criticism of bourgeois thought, Dilthey's and Simmel's philosophies of life *(Lebensphilosophieen)*, Rickert's and Windelband's philosophies of science, Troeltsch's historicism, and other philosophies. During his Hungarian and German stage Mannheim switched from idealism to realism: from a Hegelian manner of thought – influenced by Dilthey's and Simmel's philosophies of life, by the artistic idealism of Lukács, and by neo-Kantian, phenomenological, and positivist philosophies – to a sociologically elaborated historicism, influenced by Dilthey, the Marxist Lukács, Simmel, and Troeltsch. This sociological historicism impeded his identification with any political party. As I said, he sympathized with the socialist movement, but he dissociated himself somewhat from this movement as well. He considered himself belonging to the "socially free-floating intelligentsia" which was able to synthesize particular worldviews in order to attain the broadest view of the totality of a social-cultural period. Therefore his *style* of thought is a *synthetic* one.

Recall that the dominant general worldview in Great Britain during Mannheim's stay in this country was the traditionally founded superiority of the cohesive British culture. Here also it is possible to distinguish different particular worldviews, and the world strivings embodied in them. Further, we can distinguish economic, political and other particular strivings.

Sympathetic to Labor, and its thought striving, Mannheim had been influenced by pragmatism, behaviorism, psychoanalytic, and theological studies. Belonging to the "socially free-floating intelligentsia," which had the calling of a cultural synthesis, he elaborated his political sociology of "planning for freedom." Advocating this cause, he was not a revolutionary. He wanted to realize his ideals gradually. Therefore, I characterize his style of thought as a *reforming* one. As in his German stage, he was aware of the fact that the intelligentsia is *relatively*, socially free-floating. It cannot dissociate itself completely from its societal and political background and engagement. Mannheim himself combined his reforming style of thought with a socialist worldview. Therefore he might be located within the intellectual stratum *(geistigen Schicht)* of the socialist movement.

At last, although we could describe it more extensively, the framework of Mannheim's sociology of knowledge described above clarifies the many issues Mannheim discussed, his most important decisions, and the main lines of this thought; all these stand in relationship to his social position. However, this framework does not explain completely his nuanced manner of thinking and feeling, his detailed arguments, nor the vexing crossroads he walked. Those come from his subjective and creative intellectual capacity, which cannot be explained sociologically and which documents the restrictedness of the competence of the sociologist of knowledge.

Chapter XXI

Evaluation of Mannheim's Sociology of Knowledge in Relation to Some Contemporary Philosophers of Science*

- *Introduction*
- *Sociology of Knowledge as a Meta-theory*
- *The Discussion between Karl Mannheim and Michael Polanyi*
- *Sociology of Knowledge as a Reflexive Discipline*
- *An Imaginary Discussion between Karl Mannheim and Herman Dooyeweerd*
- *A Proposed Solution: Praxis-oriented Truth*

Introduction

In chapter XX I briefly attempted to locate Mannheim's thought with the help of his analysis of worldview. Rightly, Shils (1968: 560) says: "The sociology of knowledge as practiced by Mannheim has found no succession. (...) Much work has been done since World War II which may be said to fall within the jurisdiction of the sociology of knowledge broadly conceived, yet very little of it bears the impress of Mannheim's thought." Shils continues:

> More recent works like Thomas S. Kuhn's *Structure of Scientific Revolutions* (1962) and Michael Polanyi's *Personal Knowledge* (1958), which have carried very far the systematic analysis of patterns of thought and their modes of change, owe nothing to Mannheim's analysis of *Weltanschauungen.*

Although Shils is right, historically speaking, from a systematic point of view the following question remains: What relevance does Mannheim's sociology of knowledge have for those philosophers of science? Discussing this question in the following sections, I shall pay special attention to Thomas Kuhn and Michael Polanyi, *and* to Mannheim's contemporary, the Dutch philosopher Herman Dooyeweerd (who is important in discussing the presuppositions and consequences of Mannheim's sociology of knowledge, as we already noticed in Chapter X), and focus attention on the problem of knowledge and truth.

Sociology of Knowledge as a Meta-theory

Until the sixth decade of this century, most theories of science were characterized by positivist philosophers with an emphasis on empiricism, on formal

---

* This chapter in a shorter version appeared in an article: "Karl Mannheim's Search of Truth: Sociology of knowledge in relation to the contemporary philosophy of science," *Sociale Wetenschappen* 27 (1984): 137-165.

analysis, and on the unified nature of science. However, this old and non-socially oriented image of science is being replaced slowly by a new image: scientific theories are considered as having a social basis. Thomas Kuhn and Michael Polanyi are representatives of this new image of science.

Thomas Kuhn, a critic of positivism, argues that in all respects science is a human and social activity. Science is governed by what he terms "paradigms," that is, "universally recognized scientific achievements that for a time provide model problems and solutions to a community of practitioners" (1962: x). As expressed by Kuhn in his early publication, scientists do not often study the validity of their methods, theories, and epistemological questions. Laws, theories, methods, and techniques which are adopted by individual scientists are taken for granted. A student already is socialized into the scientific community with its shared paradigm of the rules of scientific practice. In this way the student learns what is a "normal science," for the taught and learned paradigm presents the standards of a theory – methods and techniques together – as a coherent "vision" determining his view of the world and of the practice of his work (Kuhn, 1962: 102, 108). This means, according to Kuhn, there are no "pure" or "neutral facts," but all facts are facts-as-interpreted. Kuhn argues thus:

> Some of the principles deployed in my explanation of science are irreducibly sociological, at least at this time. In particular, confronted with the problem of theory-choice, the structure of my response runs roughly as folows: take a group of the ablest available people with the most appropriate motivation; train them in some science and in the specialities relevant to the choice at hand; imbue them with the value system, the ideology, current in the discipline (...); and, finally, let them make the choice. If that technique does not account for scientific development as we know it, then no other will. (1970: 237, 238)

If a paradigm changes, people get another way of looking at the world (1962: 17, 18, 110). This clarifies why Aristotle, Galileo, Newton, and Einstein considered and explained natural phenomena in different ways. Derek Phillips (1977: 67), Professor of Sociology at the University of Amsterdam, concudes rightly:

> In fact, Kuhn's investigations are very much in keeping with the aims of sociological inquiry. (...) The "new image" of science, as represented by Kuhn, conceives of science as a social enterpirse, with an organized consensus of scientists determining what is and what is not to be considered scientific, what is and what is not to be warranted as knowledge. Since scientists belong to communities, traditions and paradigms, what they can think, see and say are all dependent on the game as played at a particular time and place.

Is it possible to judge a paradigm as a good or bad one? According to Kuhn, a criterion for judging this does not exist; there is no super-paradigmatic point of view. Scientists working within one paradigm, using its concepts and rules, do not share the concepts and rules of colleagues who are working in other paradigms, and vice versa. The consequence of Kuhn's view is that scientists sharing different paradigms will disagree about what a problem is and what its solution should be; they will inevitably talk past each other (1962: 108; cf. Harvey, 1982:85-88). According to Kuhn, absolute truth and scientific objectivism cannot exist. We can only speak of a paradigm-bound truth and objectivity (cf. Suppe, 1977: 137). In a later work Kuhn revises his conception of paradigms, and argues that the objectivity of *theory choice* can be analyzed in terms of criteria like accuracy, consistency, scope, simplicity, and fruitfulness (1977: 320-339). Even personal preferences, he says, play a part. However, the justification of the theory choice as a matter of public scientific discussion is always paradigm-bound. Although he gives thoroughgoing discussion about these items, Kuhn's option of paradigms implies the relativity of scientific truth.

There are striking similarities between Kuhn's philosophy of science and the sociology of knowledge. I especially refer to Mannheim, who says:

> Every epoch has its own fundamentally new approach and its own characteristic point of view, and consequently sees the "same" object from a new perspective. (IU: 243)

Elsewhere he says that not only some perceptions and thought but all human perceptions, thoughts, and ideas are organized into categories.

> The extent, however, to which we can organize and express our experience in such conceptual forms is ... dependent upon the frames of reference which happen to be available at a given historical moment. (IU: 77)

According to Mannheim, the social-historical context penetrates both the forms and the content of human thought. The approach to a problem, the basic concepts, the models of thought, the levels of abstraction and concreteness are all bound up with social circumstances (IU: 241-250, 273-276). However, three differences between Kuhn and Mannheim need to be mentioned. First, Kuhn discusses paradigms of scientific communities; Mannheim discusses the fundamental approach or frame of reference of an epoch (and consequently of scientific communities). Second, Kuhn only acknowledges a few paradigm – switches in the history of science; Mannheim holds this of every epoch (without mentioning its limits). Third, in opposition to Kuhn, Mannheim, like Marx, excludes the natural sciences from the influences of social perspectives (Marx, 1859: 12; Mannheim, SW: 135; IU: 151, 243).

Both Kuhn and Mannheim reject the idea of an unchanging and timeless "truth" or "a sphere of truth itself." According to Mannheim, only a socially related truth exists (IU: 261, 262), but also says that his view of the social relationism of human thought and knowledge does not mean an epistemological relativism. "Relationism does not signify that there are no criteria of rightness and wrongness in a discussion" (IU: 254). However, those criteria only exist within the bounds of a certain social context of a given period. We have to consider seriously that both Kuhn's theory of paradigms and Mannheim's sociology of knowledge lead to the conclusion that scientific knowledge and criteria of truth are the products of consensus within scientific communities (see chapter XII). Therefore Phillips (1977: 91) concludes:

> Since there are different scientific communities with different standards for warranting truth, it follows that truth is completely relativized.

Is this conclusion right? Does this conclusion imply that every rejection of scientific "objectivity" or "neutrality" must lead to scientific relativism? Both Michael Polanyi and Herman Dooyeweerd reject scientific "objectivity" and at the same time reject relativism. I shall discuss Polanyi's argument first.

Polanyi agrees with Mannheim that "neutral" thought and knowledge do not exist, and that these are subject-conditioned. In this context Polanyi's theory is also relevant, because he wrote about these problems in a correspondence with Mannheim, and he rejected Mannheim's interpretation of that subject-conditionedness.

The Discussion between Karl Mannheim and Michael Polanyi
In a letter of April 19, 1944 to Karl Mannheim, Michael Polanyi wrote:

> As regards the social analysis of the development of ideas, suffice to say that I reject all social analysis of history which makes social conditions anything more than *opportunities* for a development of thought. You seem inclined to consider moral judgements on history as ludicrous, believing apparently that thought is not merely conditioned, but determined by a social or technical situation. I cannot tell you how strongly I reject such a view.

Mannheim answered Polanyi (26-4-1944):

> I could be very much in agreement with somebody who would say either that there is not yet enough factual or logical evidence for a theory which makes social conditions anything more than opportunities. But I cannot understand a scientific attitude which a-limine rejects such a view obviously on moral grounds only. Again, I can understand somebody who says that such a view would have detrimental moral effects on man which is a factual statement, but I cannot agree to an attitude which, for such reasons, would not face facts if they are facts, or arguments if they are well argued. What would happen in science if one were still to go on to do what one did with Galileo, to reject factual statements because they were in contradiction with some religious or moral axiom one happened to hold? I certainly do not object to you because I think that your views are freak. I can see quite clearly how seriously you have considered them. My feeling is only that on certain issues you made emotional decisions, where still a further confrontation of evidence and argument is feasible.

In his letter of May 2, 1944 Polanyi clarified his opinion:

> Scientists usually conduct their experiments on the assumption that natural events can be analyzed in terms of causal sequences. Yet, believe me, the most frequently observed course of events in our laboratories gives little encouragement to such an assumption.

374

(…) I suggest, as moral beings we are dedicated to an interpretation of human actions in terms of right and wrong. This latter form is a more complicated pattern than that of causality which had its application of course ot an entirely different field. Moreover, I suggest, that as Christians, and Westerners, we are dedicated to seek and uphold human interpretations more especially in the terms of our own moral tradition. That is what we are here for, as I understand our purpose in life. We can of course find ourselves discouraged and regard history … with Marx as the manifestation of economic necessities conditioned by technical programs. I have tried to explain …that such alternative interpretations cannot ever be disproved. I have also mentioned … that those who have become accustomed to regard material forces as the ultimate reality in human affairs will not find it easy to entrust their minds over again to a more intangible aspect of these affairs.

(…)Evidence, in short, can neither kill nor create fundamental beliefs. What we accept or reject in these matters is life itself. To some extent we can choose our forms of existence, to some extent we are born to them, to another part again we may be battered by experience to abandon one form for another. The Russian trials dislodged many people from one kind of faith (though I would prefer to call it a creed) while the battle of Britain caused many to re-discover another, temporarily forgotten, faith. But even in the midst of such enormous tides of rising and falling convictions there remains fixed a deeper secret pivot of faith round which we keep revolving; we follow throughout a code of duty of which we are so unconscious that we could not formulate one single syllable of it.

No life can be without some conviction and the necessity to embrace one is irresistible to the normal intelligence as it is to our normal moral instincts. So there is no way out. We must choose – and usually we have chosen already by implication. That is, we must choose in such a fashion that what we instinctively love in life, what we spontaneously admire, what we irresistibly aspire to, should make sense in the light of our convictions. When the prospect of such a solution opens up before our eyes, we undergo a conversion. Henceforth we do not doubt the faith to which we have been converted, but rather reject such evidence as may seem to contradict it. By exposing the fallaciousness of such evidence we fulfill our daily task and find ever renewed confirmation for our fundamental beliefs.

In my *Autonomy of Science* I have tried to demonstrate very briefly this whole apparatus for the case of a professional life dedicated to the convictions of science. In doing so I was constantly bearing in mind the generalizations arising from this scheme in the wider field touched upon by your questions. Perhaps this letter conveys a hint of the programme of such a generalization.

(The correspondence between Karl Mannheim and Michael Polanyi is in The Joseph Regenstein Library of The University of Chicago; Papers of Michael Polanyi, box 4. These parts are published by the kind permission of the Regenstein Library.)

From their correspondence, it appears that Mannheim and Polanyi have a fundamental difference of opinion, particularly about the human capability of theoretically disengaging oneself from the social environment which one has appropriated. Mannheim holds that social conditions noticeably and actually influence human thought and knowledge. Polanyi rejects Mannheim's opinion; he rejects all social analysis which makes social conditions anything more than opportunities for a development of thought. Moreover, Polanyi acknowledges all human interpretations as based upon our fundamental beliefs or moral convictions. Therefore, there also is agreement: both see thought and knowledge as subject-conditioned.

In his correspondence with Karl Mannheim, Polanyi traces the basic features of his own worldview. He presupposes the existence of a "hidden reality" to which a person is directed in order to discover truth. A scientist's mission is to recognize and to elucidate cohesion and a sense of the "hidden reality." His scientific work is guided by what he calls a search for the "universal tendency." Polanyi speaks of the "universal intent" of personal knowledge, but does not claim that his scientific work has a timeless character. It is relative inasmuch as it, like all scientific theories, may be rejected or revised as a whole or in part. Nevertheless, the scientist formulates the results of his work from the conviction of the truth and the universality of his theses.

> The assumption that the truth we seek to discover exists by itself, hidden to us only by our misguided approach to it, represents correctly the feeling of an investigator pursuing a discovery which keeps eluding him. It may also express the ineradicable tension between our conviction that we know something and the realization that we may conceivalby be mistaken. But in neither case can an outside observer of this relation compare another person's knowledge of the truth itself. He can only compare the observed person's knowledge of the truth with his own knowledge of it. ...*truth is something that can be thought of only by believing it.* (1958: 305)

From a personal frame of reference, according to Polanyi, a human being can unfold himself as a thinking and acting being. Thought is not an independent mental activity, but an utterance of one's socio-historical existence. In order to clarify the roots of human thought, Polanyi analyzes the "tacit dimension" of human existence. He attempts to present a harmonious vision of the relationship between existence and thought, rooted in the universe (1966: 4). Although thought can be objectified into language and writings, and into many other actions, most utterances of thought cannot be specified readily (1958: 56, 59, 60).

The logically unspecifiable and inarticulable dimension of thought Polanyi calls the "tacit dimension." This implies that perception, thought, and actions can never be separated from the frame of reference out of which a person *gives meaning* to the reality. If one tries to separate perception, thought, and action, a separation between existence and knowledge arises, and an harmonious view between these two will be impossible. Polanyi is concerned with the problem that our perception and thought, from our personal frame of reference, is to be a true perception and true thought.

This personal frame of reference is a preconscious and unexamined one, and it opens "opportunties" for a development of thought and knowledge. This personal frame of reference is in a great extent socio-culturally conditioned. At the same time it is to some extent characterized by the capability to transcend the forms of existence and by the capacity to change the forms of existence. So,

376

the personal frame of reference may be characterized by a "bound transcendence." As such it offers the opportunities for interpreting and changing society.

> I must admit that I can fulfill my obligaton to serve the truth only to the extent of my natural abilities as developed by my education. No one can transcend his formative milieu very far, and beyond this area he must rely on it uncritically. I consider that this matrix of my thought determines my personal calling. It both offers me my opportunity for seeking the truth, and limits my responsibility for arriving at my own conclusions. (1969: 133)

Shortly summarized: "We believe before we know" (1969: 62); and "Our believing is conditioned as its source by our belonging" (1958: 322).

This mysterious "tacit dimension" that finds its place in a personal frame of reference makes it impossible to discover adequately and completely all presuppositions of scientific work (Polanyi, 1966: 60-62). One is always involved in the situation of belonging to a socio-cultural situation and must accept it in the sense of a "calling" (1958: 322). The horizon of the social-cultural situation "determines" human vision. Those socio-cultural horizons are sensed by various thinkers and characterized in different ways; for example as a worldview (*Weltanschauung*, Karl Mannheim), a paradigm (T.S. Kuhn), or a hermeneutic situation (M. Heidegger, H.G. Gadamer). Notwithstanding their mutual differences, all these philosophers have in common a view that as "a critique of knowledge, all epistemology, must already know more than it can know according to its own premises" (Echeverria, 1981: 55).

It is understandable that Polanyi pays attention to what Heidegger and Gadamar call "the hermeneutic circle of understanding." For him the circular structure of knowledge is a characteristic of the nature of knowledge; whenever something is interpreted, the interpretation is always based upon the implicit, tacit dimension of knowledge. The American philosopher Echeverria (1981: 57, 58) observes correctly that Polanyi's "tacit knowledge" includes, but definitely goes beyond, the thesis that all facts are theory-laden and that theories are underdetermined by facts. Moreover, the tacit dimension is a totality of preconditions that determine one's identity. It opens up many new questions; it brings us to a consideration what is important or relevant; and finally it brings us to certain anticipatory hypotheses which can be verified or falsified.

Polanyi speaks both of the personal frame of reference and of the universal intent of personal knowledge. How do personal knowledge and the universality of science fit together? Polanyi asserts that the personal frame of reference does not release the scientist from the responsibility to discover the universality which is present in reality. Science is characterized by accumulative, precise, systematic, and communicable knowledge, as well as by certain insights, values, and methods. In these the scientific tradition is presented, and it is transmitted from the one generation of scientists to the other (Polanyi, 1964: 60, 61). It is an unconditioned requirement that scientists uphold and obey the scientific tradi-

377

tion. Within the framework of the scientific tradition innovations and creativity can be realized.

Is there a tension in Polanyi's work between "personal knowledge" and creativity on the one hand, and the scientific tradition on the other? Polanyi answers that scientists will internalize the scientific tradition. That tradition will then belong to the personal frame of reference (1966: 74, 75). This implies that not the scientific tradition but the personal perspective ultimately determines what is truth.

Polanyi and Mannheim hold that thought and knowledge are subject-conditioned. That is, the pre-scientific, i.e., social and cultural factors, influence thought and knowledge; neutral thought and knowledge do not exist. However, the important difference between them is that Polanyi speaks of "personal knowledge" based upon the mysterious "tacit dimension" of one's "frame of reference." This frame of reference offers opportunities for interpreting and changing the world. Mannheim, as a sociologist of knowledge, attempts to elaborate such a "tacit dimension" by analyzing its cultural and social factors. He acknowledges that, if there is "not yet enough factual or ligical evidence" for explaining existing social conditions, which determine thought and knowledge, then one should speak only of "opportunities" for the development of thought. However, Mannheim's main argument is that the social conditioning of thought and knowledge is a given, a fact. Polanyi's concept of truth means: truth within the bounds of a personal frame of reference. Mannheim wishes to transcend these personal bounds of truth, as we will see in the next sections.

Although Mannheim elaborates fruitful ideas, we need to acknowledge that he – as a consequence of his approach – claims, by his sociology of knowledge, to be capable of explaining what Polanyi considers the "hidden dimension." However, Speier says (1937: 161; see Chapter IX), no thought can be interpreted with total adequacy by the sociological method. In the next sections I shall also discuss Herman Dooyeweerd, because he sharply criticizes the claim of Mannheim's sociology of knowledge.

Sociology of Knowledge as a Reflexive Discipline
In the previous sections I discussed the intellectual community's perspective. Many contemporary philosophers of science who defend a "new image of science" reject the neo-positivist or traditional philosophy of science. Notwithstanding their mutual differences, they emphasize that specialized intellectual communities are governed by paradigms (Kuhn), personal frames of reference (Polanyi), or by social perspectives (Mannheim). I add to them Edward Shils (1981: 63-161), who writes that all men of ideas are governed by complex traditions, and that scientific traditions and their vicissitudes must be studied sociologically in reference to intellectual communities and *their* vicissitudes, of which the scientific traditions are a part.

The philosophers and sociologists just mentioned deny that scientific knowledge is neutral or purely objective. I have already pointed out that Kuhn and Polanyi acknowledge that theories are under-determined by data or objects. That is, objects do not determine completely the scientist's theory (cf. M. Hesse, 1977:1). A foundational commitment affects all of a person's consciousness and activities; it enriches his understanding, guides his theorizing and judgments, and reinforces his discussion. This commitment is existential, as Mannheim also argues. The background-questions are these: What perspective, strategy, or policy directs a person's thought and scientific work? What worldview must he integrate to disclose the coherence of the reality experienced?

These questions imply a weakening of the "strong progam" of science, that is the *causal* explanation required of the emergence and acceptance of any thought, being "impartial with respect to truth and falsity, rationality or irrationality, success or failure" (Bloor, 1976: 5). As Joseph Ben-David says (1981: 47): "...the strong thesis has to be considerably weakened, and the principle that the same causal explanation has to be given to all beliefs, irrespective of rationality or irrationality, cannot be consistently maintained."

Those questions mentioned above require reflection and self-criticism, which imply a transcendental criticism of human thought and knowledge. In Dooyeweerd's words, what is needed is

a critical inquiry (respecting no single so-called theoretical axiom) into the universally valid conditions which alone make theoretical thought possible, and which are required by the imanent structure of this thought itself. (Dooyeweerd, 1953: 37)

Dooyeweerd's uncompromising self-criticism and Mannheim's sociology of knowledge overlap somewhat. Mannheim holds reflexivity and self-criticism as important elements of his sociology of knowledge, which studies three items: 1. the nature and structure of life-situations, 2. the subject's own "make-up" (that means the volitive and creative element of the subject who participates in this situation), and 3. the position of the sociologist of knowledge who studies these two points (IU: 268; see Chapter X). This last point implies that the sociology of knowledge is also a reflexive discipline. It not only studies the relation of thought/knowledge and societal factors in the philosophies of others, but it also examines the perspective of the investigator, and his manner of studying points 1 and 2. Reflection on itself must lead to critical scientific self-awareness and "existence illumination" (IU: 42, 43). As Mannheim writes elsewhere: "The first and most important factor which makes it possible to ask sociological questions about thinking is what may be called the *self-transcendence and self-relativization* of thought" (SW: 137). "...the multiplicity of the ways of thinking will become noticeable and emerge as a theme for reflection" (IU: 6). He strives for an "intellectual transcendence" reflecting the situation of thought and action itself (IU: 42, 96; cf. D. and M.A. Weinstein, 1981). However, his "intellectual transcendence" implies an important difference with Dooyeweerd. Mannheim's reflexive and critical inquiry is an intellectual and theoretical activity; Dooyeweerd's refexive and critical inquiry is an activity which does not overlook a single intellectual or theoretical axiom, in order to uncover the ground motives of thought. I shall examine what this difference means.

In his sociology of knowledge Mannheim is concerned with the so-called "hermeneutic circle." He acknowledges that human perception and thought of a given phenomenon is socially bounded. At the same time he attempt to overcome the limitation of partial perspectives of society, and to achieve an adequate view of that phenomenon. Elaborating the intellectual transcendence in order to break the "hermeneutic circle," Mannheim speaks of the *historical-social consciousness*. If this is the final characterization of persons, Herman Dooyeweerd would say that Mannheim's sociology of knowledge does not contain an uncompromising critical inquiry; because Mannheim holds a theoretical axiom that is elaborated in a *scientistic* view of his historicistic-sociologism.

Scientism is a theoretical view of reality that exaggerates the place of scientific knowledge in life. Scientism is not the same as science. Scientism concerns a view about the place of science in our lives. It holds that scientific knowledge has the last word, and that this knowledge is sure, good, and true. Scientific knowledge, that is, knowledge tested and gained by scientific methods, has often been acclaimed in Western society as the only and adequate way to truth. We speak of our scientized society. So people talk about "scientific" sex education, "scientific" war-equipment, "scientifically" tested household goods. If in these examples *scientific* means a contribution to enrich our daily knowledge, there would be no objections. However, those examples suggest much more. They suggest that everyday thought is pre-scientific, and as such unscientific, and that it should be reformed according to the requirements of the scientific point of view. Clearly Louis Wirth (1936: xii) in his Preface to Karl Mannheim's *Ideologie and Utopia* writes: "...the voice of science was heard with a respect approximating the sanctity which formerly accorded only to authoritarian, religious pronouncements." These words show that scientism is the way people *consider* science as a *religion*.

There are many scientistic approaches. Physicists, historians, lawyers, economists, logicists, and sociologists develop them. But they all have in common that they reduce human experience to one mode or aspect (the physical, the historical, the economical, the social, etc.) of those experiences. This scientific reduction is the core of *scientism*. However, this variety of scientisms presents an unresolved problem. One universally valid   scientistic approach does not exist. The scientist is not limited to any one area of scientific knowledge. What scientific area will the scientist choose? Many scientisms are wellknown: physicism, historicism, economism, sociologism, logicism, etc. The main question is: **Do we do justice to ethical, juridical, aesthetic, social and any kind of** phenomena by an absolutized and one-sided physistic, sociologistic, or any other scientistic investigation? Rightly, the great variety of scientisms shows the diversity of areas of reality. Therefore, the only conclusion can be that every kind of scientism does not do justice to the pluriformity of the reality. The question of truth cannot be answered in a scientistic manner, but only by genuine insight into the cohesion and diversity of the pluriform reality.

At the end of my discussion of Dooyeweerd's sociology (Chapter X) I formulated two questions which need to be examined and answered in the following sections. These two questions are: 1. Is the transcendental critique – which according to Dooyeweerd inescapably leads to the discovery of the religious presuppositions of thought - is this critique possible from the point of view of Mannheim's sociology of knowledge? 2. Is Mannheim's sociology of knowledge adequate for exposing the presuppositions of thought, or does it require a thinking through on basis of a transcendental-critical investigation? These questions imply that there is a possibility of an open discussion between Mannheim and Dooyeweerd. Does this discussion open the way to truth?

An Imaginary Discussion between Karl Mannheim and Herman Dooyeweerd
In avoiding relativism, Mannheim argues that the evidence of the object must determine our assertions. He holds that there are many perspectives on the same object. The conflict that arises because of these perspectives cannot be overcome by an appeal to a non-perspectival view. He advocates the choice of the perspective that comprehends the object most adequately. According to him, accepting the possibility of inter-subjective communications implies affirming the existence of truth. In debate, differences of perspective have one thing in common: the object of discussion. In other words, it is not only a problem that participants do not understand each other, but they also do not understand the object adequately due to their different perspectives. Objectivity is attainable by discovering through discourse *the common denominator* of their different (not only theoretical) insights. Once the common denominator is found, it is possible to separate necessary differences between them from arbitrary ones (IU: 270). Objectivity is only possible by establishing a comprehensive and adequate outlook on the framework of understanding. Mannheim expresses the need for a total view that integrates partial and incompatible views. He and other "socially free-floating intellectuals" would be able to achieve this total view. This view of reality is neither immediately given nor eternally valid. It is "the continuous process of the expansion of knowledge" that has "the broadest possible extension of our horizon of vision" (IU: 94, 95; cf. Stehr and Meja, 1982a: 914-932). Mannheim does not say that all different ways of thinking are false. Speaking about the perspectives of thinkers, he argues that their thoughts represent a *partial* view (IU: 252-256).

With the help of his analysis of the worldview *(Weltanschauung)*, he tries to present his own contribution to the discussion and to advocate what he believes is the broadest view of totality. Recognition of the social relation of all thought is always treated by Mannheim as the occasion of further inquiry and not as a substitute for it. But how does one affirm the social "rootedness" of thought and at the same time affirm the power of thought to judge and to transform this thought? First of all we must consider that a given social perspective is not a statically fixed one. People can change their minds and broaden their perspectives.

We need to acknowledge that Mannheim considers the sociology of knowledge as a preparation for discussion (IU: 251-256). The sociology of knowledge contains a "methodology for dialogue" (Baum, 1977: 69) that leads to a self-reflective process. The process of self-criticism for the purpose of gaining access to the other contexts of meaning, makes possible a critical and "transcendent" approach of the existing societal order, and also a break of the "hermeneutic circle." Simonds (1978: 184) concludes correctly that Mannheim's "standard from which the world as it appears to us can be rejected as 'untrue' is a standard that can only be determined in the discursive process of inquiry itself: it is in this sense... a pragmatic standard of truth." However, this does not mean that Mannheim takes for granted the existing society. Certainly truth is tied to reality, but he believes that reality is dynamic-historical. It includes not only what is "given" but also what stands to be realized in relation to "utopian" and normative thought. This process of looking for the desirable reality will promote, in our view of totality, "the broadest possible extension of our horizon of vision (IU: 95). Mannheim's consideration of the synthesis of different views is a dynamic one which concerns not the content of ideas, but the social perspective and the conceptual contexts (cf. Baum, 1977: 38-41; Simonds, 1978: 106). This dynamic synthesis is the only adequate one. The truth that arises out of this synthesis is *the socio-culturally related and dynamic truth, and the only possible and therefore the most nearly absolute truth.* No single consciousness can comprehend the socio-cultural totality from the beginning of the history of mankind to its end. By virtue of the *historical-sociological consciousness*, Mannheim claims to grasp a given social totality in a certain period (see Chapter XII).

Dooyeweerd would have serious objections to Mannheim's approach. Dooyeweerd places value on discussion: we "must be willing to learn from our opponents, since we are responsible both for ourselves and for them." He also says that a serious dialogue is not possible, "if we are not willing to penetrate to the deepest drives that determine the various points of view. (...) Perhaps some are not aware of their deepest motives in life; if so, then we must help bring these motives our into the open" (1979: 15).

If Dooyeweerd and Mannheim were available for a discussion, Dooyeweerd would make clear to Mannheim that his characterization of human beings by an historical-sociological consiousness is based on the absolutizing of the historcial and social aspects of reality which are investigated by the science of history and sociology (or in combination by the sociology of culture). This absolutizing has, as we already was earlier in this chapter, a particular scientist view of reality as its core. Dooyeweerd regards the historical and social aspects in their irreducible nature and, at the same time, in their unbreakable coherence with other aspects of reality (like the aspect of organic life, the aspect of emotional feelings, the logical-analytic aspect, the linguistic, the economic, the aesthetic, the jural, the moral, etc.). Mannheim studies phenomenologically the particular character of different fields of reality. The object has the function of a norm; it is the ideal of adequate knowledge (see chapter VI and IX). In his later publications he singles out the historical-sociological consicousness, and declares that it most adequately reveals human awareness of reality in its differentiation. In my opinion (as already discussed in chapter XIII and IX) and also in Dooyeweerd's view, this argument of Mannheim implies a dualistic position or, at least, a serious tension. Mannheim wishes to maintain that every field or aspect of reality has its own character and norms; however, his historicistic view implies that those characteristics arise from (and as such are products of) the historical processes of societal developments. Therefore, Mannheim's view undermines the right understanding of the irreducible character and meaning of those aspects (Dooyeweerd, 1960: 106; 1979: 64).

Dooyeweerd's alternative is a philosophical cosmology, based on the dynamic "cosmic order." He holds that the different fields of reality are governed by various norms which are given in the cosmic order as *principles* for human behavior. In the historical aspect, as in all other aspects of reality, these principles require formation by human beings. He seems to have an affinity with Mannheim's view when he acknowledges that the process of giving form to those normative principles must always take into consideration the level of cultural development of a people, for all subsequent aspects of human life are interwoven with that historical level of development. Accordingly, lingual principles require the forms of language; social principles of decency, respect, etc. require formation in social manners; legal principles require the juridical forms of laws, decrees, regulations, etc. "All... [these] aspects thus display an inseparable coherence with the historical aspect" (Dooyeweerd, 1979: 69). That distinction between normative principles and the cultural or historical formation or elaboration by human beings keeps him from, what he names, the "historicistic error," and sharpens his ability to discern the particular and irreducible character of those principles. The normative principles of the various aspects of reality cannot be reduced to the historical aspect: "giving form to material in free control over the material. It consists in giving form according to a free design" (Dooyeweerd, 1979: 64). All historical formation, Dooyeweerd says, requires power, and this never takes place without struggle against tradition and social conflicts. He continues, that progressive historical activity ought to move in the direction of increasing differentiation. That is, the differentiation of culture into spheres which possess their own unique nature; cultural differentiation calls for the disclosure or unfolding of everything in accordance with its inner nature. This differentiation occurs by means of a "branching out" of culture into the intrinsically different spheres of science, art, the state, the church, industry, trade, the school, and voluntary organisations

(1979: 74, 79). The ultimate ground of Dooyeweerd's conviction that the cultural activity of differentiation is good is the conviction that such activity brings about the realizations of the potentialities stored in all aspects of reality, especially humanity.

The difference between Mannheim and Dooyeweerd is this: Mannheim acknowledges the particular character of different fields of reality, based upon an historical-social order that is the *product* of historical and social processes. Dooyeweerd acknowledges the particular, irreducible character of different fields of reality based upon a cosmic order of irreducible aspects (and their normative principles), and the development of the historical aspect *conditions* the human formation of the principles of the other aspects.

In this context Dooyeweerd would speak of a dialectical tension within Mannheim's starting-point, the historical-sociological consiousness. Mannheim may speak about the particular character of the social field of reality, but at the same time he acknowledges that determining its particular character depends on historical processes. On the other hand, Mannheim may speak of the particular character of the historical processes of becoming, but he also acknowledges that we can only understand those processes adequately by sociological investigation. How and how far may these two positions be bound together in a higher unity or synthesis?

Answering this question brings another problem to our attention: the historistic way of thinking opposed the Enlightenment, especially its science-ideal, based on the method of the natural sciences. This new historical way of thinking contains the idea that the historical tradition is not identical for every nation; it presents individual variants in accordance with the particular character of a people. Therefore, Mannheim elaborates the historicism sociologically. Opposed to the "natural necessity" of the science-ideal, creative freedom is defended by the historical-sociological way of thinking; culture and society will be the free, autonomous products of particular social collectives. However, Dooyeweerd argues, a "hidden law" is at work in this new way of thinking; a new universalistic claim is presented; lingual, economic, jural, aesthetic, moral and any phenomena could only be interpreted adequately from the historical-sociological point of view. A serious dialectical tension appears: from the original freedom motive of the historical-sociological way of thinking a new science-ideal arises: a sociological scientism (cf. Dooyeweerd, 1979: 183, 184).

Mannheim would correctly answer to Dooyeweerd's criticism that his sociology does not intend to repress creative freedom; we saw that his argument is very nuanced and sophisticated. However, he could not deny that Dooyeweerd's critical analysis confronts him with philosophical implications of his theory. The dialectic tension in his theory cannot be overcome with the help of a new synthesis. In fact it is solved by an immanent position choice: a sociological sceintism. This scientistic approach conditions one's possibility for changing one's mind and for broadening one's perspective. It also conditions

Mannheim's plea for a total view of reality and the possibility to integrate the various partial views. He wishes to overcome theoretically (i.e. sociologically) the divergence of particular views which contain not just theoretical elements. Does Mannheim acknowledge adequately the moral presuppositions or other basic options participants have, which they bring into the debate? Does he do justice to the particular and irreducible character of those presuppositions by his synthetic attempt based upon his scientistic view? Dooyeweerd would argue that no intellectual can defend the validity of an argument without an ultimate, pre-theoretical (i.e. religious) basis for appeal. Although Mannheim intends to promote a true discussion, a real listening to each other, and, consequently, a sound determination to practise self-criticism, we may ask the question whether Mannheim's presuppositions for that discourse do not imply the "hidden law" of a totalitarian idea: not a consensus as a result of the discourse, but a sociologically prepared consensus as the basis of the discourse.

Mannheim might answer that he appreciates Dooyeweerd's contribution in the debate, inasmuch as he presents his cosmology as to total view. However, he would stress the particularity of Dooyeweerd's thought as a Calvinistic one. In answer to Dooyeweerd's conviction that the Bible has significance for all cultural periods, Mannheim would argue that *in* different periods and out of different perspectives the Bible has been interpreted in different ways. Concerning the essence of the Biblical message or the Biblical ground motive – *creation, fall, and redemption by Jesus Christ* – he would ask if it makes sense to speak of it in relation to the different social perspectives of concrete societal, political, and economic problems. Mannheim agrees that the Bible contains fundamental and universal values (love, justice, honesty, mutual help, politeness, etc.), but they need an elaboration in relation to concrete social problems. He desires to elaborate those values in order to realize a society that is characterized by planning for freedom. Mannheim himself does not integrate those values into his own sociology (see Chapter XVIII).

Mannheim acknowledges that the Biblical ground motive and basic values are principles of orientation and interpretation of social phenomena, but he would also say these do not imply a clear perception of and solutions for concrete societal problems. In short, speaking about Truth with religious conviction is neither the same as the true vision of societal problems nor as doing truth in society.

A Proposed Solution: Praxis-oriented Truth
From the discussion of Kuhn's theory, earlier in this chapter, I concluded that for Kuhn relativizing of scientific truth is unavoidable. From the discussion of Polanyi's theory I concluded that he both holds a personal frame of reference and, at the same time, rejects relativism of scientific truth. Moreover, the discussion of the theories of both philosophers occured on a theoretical level. Mannheim would ultimately force the discussion with any philosopher into the

direction of applying "basic values" to concrete social situations and problems and ultimately to praxis-oriented knowledge. I continue the imaginary discussion, between Mannheim and Dooyeweerd, which now settles on a praxis-oriented knowledge and concept of truth.

Gaining true knowledge is socially dependent, and therefore, it stands continually in need of correction. Dynamically understood, it retains an openness to other socially related viewpoints, especially to what Mannheim calls the "total view." The sociology of knowledge not only studies the nature of one's social situation, but also, the volitional element of the actor. Opennes to other views and to a total view implies a social and political élan that fosters social changes. Thought and knowledge are grounded in action and lead to action; they are parts of world building (cf. Baum, 1977: 24).

In elaborating on his total view of society as well as on societal and political changes, Mannheim listens especially to the voices of the minorities and oppressed people (IU: 77, 78); not only to the proletariat, but to humanity itself, which is suffering the cultural crisis, in the West and in the East. Although influenced by Marx, Mannheim does not agree with Marx's thesis of the cognitive superiority of the proletariat. According to him, the society cannot be divided only into socio-economic classes. Society and the proletariat itself are differentiated; poor and oppressed people are in different social strata and groups. He especially listens to the cries of all people who are suffering from the status quo, and in some ways the status quo itself suffers. In the struggle for realizing a more humane society, Mannheim brings out the relationship between knowledge and socio-political commitment; he advocates praxis-oriented concepts of knowledge and truth for the healing of society as a whole (cf. Baum, 1971: 276, 277).

In this context, I think, Dooyeweerd would ask: What do praxis-oriented concepts of knowledge and truth mean? If one answers that those concepts ought to serve to disclose societal structures, to open the future to oppressed people, to realize more solidarity and justice, Dooyeweerd would ask in what direction one wants to open the future. First, he would argue that we need a theoretical context of understanding to study a given societal or political problem; the proper goal of scholarly endeavor would be to develop a body of theory: a body of general, abstract, and integrated "laws." Second, this theory must contain normative principles; otherwise we cannot determine how to interpret and to realize solidarity and justice concretely.

Mannheim would criticize Dooyeweerd's opinion. He would stress that we need ot listen to the cries of the wretched and oppressed people, and he would criticize that in Dooyeweerd's opinion. He would criticize that in Dooyeweerd's philosophy the cries of the wretched of the earth are not really given voice. Although Dooyeweerd does speak of oppressed people (1957: 596; 1979: 196-199), there is little talk of liberation from oppression. The talk is more of the normative principles of various aspects and social "authority structures." There is indeed talk of social conflict, but it is mainly the religious conflict: "The turbulent spirit of darkness which wages war in the most revolting forms against the spirit of Christ." This antithetical struggle is not a dividing line between Christians and non-Christians; it cuts right through the individual Christian's life itself (Dooyeweerd, 1979: 3). However, we have to keep in mind that this religious struggle motivated the activism of original Calvinism as a "world-formative Christianity"; activism also characterized the neo-Calvinist movement in the Netherlands that began at the end of the nineteenth century and that was represented by the activist statesman Abraham Kuyper (Dutch prime minister, 1901-1905). Characterized as a "world-formative Christianity," it listened to the cries of oppressed people; it arose out of commitment to the cause of these people. It was a struggle for their social, economic, and political liberation (cf. Wolterstorff, 1983: 54). However, Dooyeweerd's philosophy is different from this "world-formative Christianity"; his philosophy is not primary a praxis-oriented theory.

Mannheim would argue that Christian philosophers should not think of religious principles or starting-points only; neither should they formulate nomoligical theories only. They should integrate theorizing and social commitment. Of course, theoretical thought attempts the theoretical articulation of certain moments of reality and of the realization of life. However, according to Mannheim, studying reality in a Christian perspective implies a certain vision of reality and its problems. For instance, Mannheim as a sociologist would find Dooyeweerd's philosophy seriously lacking in the historical aspect, any serious analysis of the cuases of the increase in differentiation and its cognates in the Western world. Mannheim would surely point out the social processes of (national and international) "social interdependence," "fundamental democratization," the rise of capitalist economy, uncontrolled consequences of the *laissez-faire* principle, and the lack of a good planning. Mannheim would suggest that also a philosopher cannot pass by the analysis of those causes of the increase of differentiation in the West.

According to Mannheim, all scholars, Christian scholars too, need to formulate those problems as clearly as possible, *in order to* contribute to their solution. In other words, there can be no understanding of the nature of theorizing without concrete situations to act on; theorizing needs to serve action. In this context I repeat that Mannheim rightly insists that Christians must transform the basic values of their convictions into values which can adapt to changing environments (DT: Ch. 7; see Chapter XVIII). They must help to disclose structures, and they must help to open the future so that concrete problems may be solved and specific goals reached. Therefore, Christian philosophy must not only be characterized by principle-oriented thought and nomological theories, but also by praxis-oriented thought.

Although Mannheim does not discuss the problem, we need to be aware of the foundational relationship between theory and praxis. In my opinion, however, Mannheim would rightly stress that Christian scholars ought to be praxis-oriented theorists who acknowledge that social commitment is the governing interest of their theorizing. Mannheim, though not a committed Christian, would call back Dooyeweerd from pure theory to a more profound awareness of his own Calvinistic tradition.

A praxis-oriented philosophy neither implies politicizing nor ideologizing of scholarship, in which philosophy is made dependent of a political party or ideology. Neither does it mean that representatives of a praxis-oriented philosophy hold dogmatic political visions. Truth always stands in need of the dialogue, both with participants of given societal problems and with others who are investigating this from other religious and social points of view.

In this connection Dooyeweerd would correctly point out that the distinction between *principle-oriented* and *praxis-oriented* thought is not entirely adequate. Jewish and Christian thought implies specifically the fundamental idea that the world is a created reality, and, therefore, it is a dynamic reality: the principle of the various fields of reality, are "principles of temporal *potentiality* or *possibility*. In their realization in individual things or events they have time-duration and *actuality* as transitory factual structures. Everything that has real existence, has many more potentialities than are actualized" (1953: 105). This means that the person as a created being, or on the basis of his creatureliness, has a mandate and a calling; he is a person on a mission. This calling implies that a person must accept nature and society as gifts, must carefully tend his relationship to nature and society, and must strive to develop nature and society according to their genuine principles. That is why this calling implies a program in which purposes can be formulated. Mannheim cannot say that in those religious philosophies there is found no place for no attention given to social and political problems to be solved. On the other hand, he could criticize that in Jewish and Christian philosophies, the relationship is often unclear or completely lacking between these fundamental ideas on the one hand and the programs for solving specific societal problems on the other. Mannheim is correct in stating that the truth of principles must be demonstrated in actions. Therefore, he would have an affinity with Dooyeweerd's sympathizer Nicholas Wolterstorff who writes:

> One has to say that one human being is being wronged by another, and to say that is to take sides with the former. It is to declare solidarity with him or her in opposition to the oppressor. It is to take sides on a struggle... And if one's declaration of solidarity is serious, the actions of liberation will flow forth. (1983: 67)

In my opinion Dooyeweerd would rightly criticize the scientistic onesidedness and the dialectic tension within Mannheim's starting-point, the historical-sociological consciousness; on the other hand Mannheim would rightly criticize the underdeveloped notion in Dooyeweerd's philosophy of praxis-oriented thinking. Therefore, I think Dooyeweerd and other Christian philosophers should accept Mannheim's invitation for the discourse (not agreeing with Mannheim's scientistic view) in order to acquire a broader and praxis-oriented horizon.

Now let us return to the two questions posed before (see chapter X), which still remain to be answered: 1. According to Dooyeweerd, the radical transcendental critique ultimately leads to the discovery of the religious presuppositions of thought: "Is this critique possible form the point of view of Mannheim's sociology of knowledge?" I think that within the framework of his sociology of knowledge we can say that Dooyeweerd's transcendental critique and the discovery of religious presuppositions is possible. However, Mannheim as a sociologist of knowledge would investigate the social relatedness of such a Christian philosophy, and regard its partial view of society as a result of its social perspective. Mannheim would stress that Christian philosophers must not only speak of their religious convictions and formulate their bodies of theory. They should also elaborate their philosophies as praxis-oriented thought and test the truth of their theories solving practical problems. Without praxis orientation they do not contribute to problem solving. It makes no sense to speak of a Christian philosophy if there is a missing link between the confessed truth according to one's conviction and doing truth in praxis.

2. "Is Mannheim's sociology of knowledge adequate for exposing the presuppositions of thought, or does it require a thinking through on the basis of a transcendental-critical investigation?" I can answer the second part of this question affirmatively. In the previous section I made clear that there is a serious tension in Mannheim's starting-point: the historical-sociological consciousness, and that he is operating with a very disputable and even dangerous sociologism. I cannot answer the first part altogether affirmatively. If I were to answer the first part affirmatively, I would be falling into a scientism of sociology. Religious convictions belong to the most existential presuppositions of thought. I believe that we need a leading, orienting, or "normative" view of reality. Otherwise we cannot determine how to interpret and how to realize human thought in actions of solidarity and justice. On the other hand, Mannheim's sociology of knowledge must challenge the transcendental critique as a continuous process of critical investigation. On the basis of his sociology of knowledge, we must acknowledge that the following matters are always conditioned by a specific socio-cutural context: the manner in which the transcendental critique is practised, the reformulation of the religious presuppositions, and the elaborated interpretation of the basic concepts. In this last remark I do not make the social and cultural aspects of reality autonomous, nor do I make a socio-historical consciousness autonomous, but I do arrive at a recognition that the transcendental critique does not possess a universal validity. The transcendental critique will never be studied within a social vacuum. This conditioning does not need to result in a paradox. Between the transcendental critique and the analysis of the sociology of knowledge, I see a fruitful tension, the possibility of reciprocal and critical exchange. I conclude my study with these words: they imply an on-going program of closer cooperative investigation.

Appendix 1: *Mannheim's doctoral diploma.*

ALMAE AC CELEBERRIMAE REGIAE SCIENTIARUM UNIVERSITATIS HUNGARICAE BUDAPESTINENSIS

Facultas Philosophica.

Magnifice Domine Rector!

Dominus *Carolus Mannheim*

oriundus *ex Budapest* .

annorum *25.* religionis *mosaicae*

superatis examinibus rigidioribus in honores Doctoris Philosophiae promoveri

petit.

Cum autem Ordo Philosophorum supplicantem

ex *Philosophia*

ceu principali

item ex *Paedagogia et*

ex Historia Literarae Germanicae

tamquam subsicivis studiis ~~rite~~ ~~cum laude~~ summa cum

laude approbaverit, promovendi causa eundem, pro incumbente mihi

munere, ea qua par est observantia, hisce propono et actus huius academici

terminum praefigi oro.

Magnificentiae Vestrae

Budapestini, die *8. November* 1918

humillimus servus

Promovebitur die *9ᵃ Nov.*

Dr David Angyal
Ordinis Philosophorum h. t. Decanus.

hora *12.*

h. t. Rector.

Appendix 2: *A play written by students and performed for Mannheim on the occasion of his departure from Heidelberg: "The Clouds" or "Politics as Science"**

"DIE WOLKE" oder "Politik als Wissenschaft"

frei nach Aristophanes verfasst vom "SOZIOLOGISCHEN KOLLEKTIV 1930"

Personen:
Frau Strepsiades, eine Witwe aus dem absteigenden Kleinbürgertum
Pheidippides, ein Aufstiegs- und Umbruchsproblem
Zwei Musterschüler des Sokrates
SOKRATES
Chor der entwurzelten Intelligenzen
Chor der verwurzelten Existenzen
Willmanios, Schaffner der Denkanstalt
Hexä, sein Hund

Szenische Anmerkung
Die Besitzer des "einzig richtigen Bewusstseins" d.h. Sokrates, seine Schüler und der Chor der Intelligenz, treten auf der oberen Bühne, im Hause des Sokrates, auf.

Die Personen, deren "Umbruch" noch nicht vollzogen its, d.h. Frau Strepsiades, Pheidippides, der Chor der Verwurzelten, Willmanios und Hexä, spielen auf der unteren Bühne, auf der Strasse vor dem Hause des Sokrates.

> Der Historismus hat uns zwar gelehrt,
> Daß nichts in gleicher Weise wiederkehrt,
> Die Griechen aber waren so begabt,
> Daß sie selbst dieses Weltgesetz durchbrochen
> Und zwei Jahrtausende vorher gerochen,
> Was wir und ihr heut' für Probleme habt.
> Wer denkt an Aristophanes nicht gern?
> Ihr kennt die "Wolken" des berühmten Herrn.

* Probably two students, Löwenthal and Goldenborg, were the main authors of this play. They adapted their play with great freedom and creativity from the Athenian poet Aristophanes (448-380 B.C.) who in 423 wrote the comedy "The Clouds" in which an important role is played by Socrates and his "thinkery," a school propounding the new thinking of the Sophists in opposition to traditionalism current in Athen. Without annotating this comedy on Mannheim, we may say that, compared with Aristophanes' text, the authors made significant changes. For example Aristophanes wrote about Strepsiadès as a farmer, the authors present Strepsiadès as a widow. Aristophanes used one chorus, the authors use two choruses: the chorus of the socially "uprooted" and critical intelligentsia, and the chorus of the status quo and traditionalistic intellectuals, referring to the dispute in Aristophanes' play between the *adikos logos* (the unjust logos of the new thinkers) and the *dikaios logos* (the just logos of traditionalist).

Er sprach von Sokrates, doch meint' er einen,
Den ihr und wir an diesem Abend meinen.
Ihr alle wißt, wie's Sokrates erging,
Der stets freischwebend in dem Korbe hing.
Von dort aus übersah er Sein und Leben,
Sah Ideologien Wolken gleich
Ueber der Welt realen Händeln schweben,
Und hingegeben diesem Wolkenreich
Hat es den großen Weisen nie gestört,
Wie sehr die braven Bürger er empört.
Auch ihn verdammte man einst wutentbrannt
Weil er, der nichts Unfragbares gekannt,
Und nicht mehr an die alten Götter glaubte,
Der Jugend ihre Ideale raubte. –
So hat es Aristophanes bedichtet,
Drum, wenn euch heute unser Stück nicht paßt,
Beklagt euch nur bei dem, der es verfaßt!
Wir kommentieren nur, was er berichtet.

Strepsiad.: O je, O je.
O Vater Zeus, was schlägst du mich mit Unglück schwer!
Zehn fette Hennen würd' ich opfern dir,
Wenn diese Lauserationalisierung,
im Bankgewerbe von Athen
Nicht meinen lieben Sohn Pheidippides getroffen.
Wie glücklich war ich, daß er endlich mal
'ne feste Stellung hatte, wo er früher nur
Mit schwarzer Reichswehr gegen die Spartaner
Mit Pfeil und Bogen durch Gebirg' und Tal
Herumgezogen und mit den Hetären
Des Vaters schwer erworb'nes Geld verprasst.

Gab ich dem Priester nicht Talente zehn,
Daß er in uns'rer Depositenkasse,
Meinem Pheidippides 'ne Stellung schafft,
Die jetzt die Götter, o! in ihrem Zorn geraubt!
Jetzt will er in der Politik sein Glück versuchen,
O, gebe Zeus, daß ihm sein neu' Bemüh'n gelingt
Und er aus der politischen Versammlung
Lorbeerbekränzt zu seiner Mutter kehrt! –
  Doch still, unruhig pochend Mutterherz,
  Dort kommt er.

Pheidipp.: O je, O je.
O Vater Zeus, was schlägst du mich mit Unglück schwer!
mit frohem Hoffen zog ich in den tempel,
Der hehren Göttin Harmonie,
Dem Volk zu sagen, was es wissen muß.

392

"Athene" sprach ich, "folget nicht
Der neuen Weise roher Oligarchen.
Denn", wollt' ich sagen: "Freiheit, Brüder, Friede!"
Eh' ich's gesagt, saust schon der erste Dreifuß
Durch die Luft, Furcht fährt mir in die Glieder,
Und Hiebe prasseln ganz furchtbar auf mich ein;
Ich aber rannte angstgepeitscht davon.

Strepsiad.: O je, O je,
O Vater Zeus, was schlägst du mich mit Unglück schwer!
Erst flogst du aus der Bank heraus,
Jetzt fliegst du aus dem Tempel!

Pheidipp.: Was fang ich nur an?
Strepsiad.: Was soll er nur tun?
Pheidipp.: Wo kann ich nur hin?
Strepsiad.: Soll er stempeln geh'n?
Chor: Was jammert ihr laut, daß die Straße erschallt?
Unbärtiger Knabe, als Erzdilletant bestiegst du die Bühne
nicht meisternd der Rede wildfließenden Strom.
Als künder der Rettung kommen wir dir,
Die Intelligenz, die oft verleumdete,
Fürchte uns nicht! Uns, die wir frei
Zwischen Göttern und Menschen – Synthesis beider, –
Schweben dahin; Vertraue dich uns, wir können dir raten.
Sieh dort die Erleuchtung, des Sokrates' Haus!
 Er lehrt dich das Denken,
 Er lehrt dich zersägen die feinsten Begriffe,
 Er lehrt dich zerspalten das spärtlichste Haar.

Chorführer: Das ist die Denkanstalt der wisen Geister, Sohn,
Brutofen pflaumenweicher Küken so wie du.
Du komsst herein ganz ohne Fragen,
Haus ist dir Haus und Baum ist Baum, sonst nichts.
Problemlos ist die Welt, problemlos.
Stammtisch wie Staat, doch bist du einmal drin,
 Dann schwillt dein Kopf,
Das Selbstverständliche/wird fraglich, jedes kleine
Ding/leuchtet dir auf in einem neuen Sinn.
Wir nennen das den Umbruch von Ideen
Erbrodelt dein Gehirn, dein Mund/füllt sich
mit Worten neu und unbekannt.

Pheidipp.: Und lernt man davon Politik zu machen.
Und ohne Stottern reden auf dem Markt?

1. Chorf.: Ganz wunderbar! Die andern werden stottern,
Wenn ihren Standort plötzlich du enthüllst,

Wenn du sie langsam ausziehst, alle Hüllen
Der Ideologien – nach und nach –
Von ihrem Leibe ziehst, als Maske abtust,
Was sie für ihre Heiligtümer hielten,
Sodaß sie frieren, ohne große Worte
Im Kalten Lufthauch stehn der Wirklichkeit.

Pheidipp.:   Und wenn man ihnen so die Kleider nimmt,
Dann kriegt man keine Prügel mehr?

2. Chorf.:   ...und wie!
Wenn freventlich du das Heilige anrührst,
Die Gottheit lästerst, unmündiger Knabe,
Zerstören willst, was die Väter verehrten,
Dann zürnst der Olymp: er sendet als Räch er
Uns Schützer des Alten, uns Wahrer des Hehren
Mit Stöcken bewaffnet. Die Würde zu lehren!
Der eherne Phalanx der Tradition.

Pheidipp.:   Whe mir, zu Hilfe, wer seid ihr, wer droht mir?

2. Chorf.:   Persönlichkeiten sind wir, Existenzen.
Ja, Existenzen nur und nichts als das.
Der ekelhaften Masse Funktionär
Seid ihr, Barbaren, die dem Individuum
Abnehmen die verantwortliche Tat.
Entwurzeln wollt ihr alles, was gewachsen.
Die Formel setzen für lebendges Blut
In uns siehst du die Blüte der Nation,
In jenen den

Löw.u.Gold.:   Wir sind des Sokrates Produkte,
Die Erben seiner Geisteskraft.
Wohl keinen gabs, der lieber schluckte
Die Politik als Wissenschaft.

Refrain:
1. Chor: Seht sie an, seht sie an,
Unter euch gibts keinen Mann,
der so wie dieser reden kann.
2. Chor: Seht sie an, seht sie an,
Unter uns gibts keinen Mann,
Der wie dieser schwindeln kann.

Löw.u.Gold.:   Daß Dialektik er uns lehre,
Die über Massen gibt Gewalt,
Gaben wir Sokrates die Ehre,
Besuchten seine Denkanstalt.
    (refrain wie oben)

Damit in der Debatte Ringen,
Wir ins Gedränge kämen nie,
Lehrte er uns vor allen Dingen
Die neuste Terminologie.
(Refrain wie oben)

Dann lehrte er uns aufzuzeigen
Die Sicht des Gegners als Beschränkt,
Beschämt muß jeder Laie schweigen,
Erfährt von uns er, wie er denkt.
(Refrain wie oben)

Ist alles aufgelöst so weise,
Ob Wissenschaft, ob Religion,
Löst selbst sich auf zum Schluss ganz leise,
Des Meisters eigne Konzeption.
(Refrain wie oben)

2. Chorf.:   Hör nicht auf sie und laß dich nicht verführen,
Wir wissen besser, was sich ziemt.

(2. Lied: "Als ich noch Prinz von Arkadien", Orpheus i.d.U.).

Chorf.:   Als wir regierten noch in Attika,
Da war die gute alte Zeit,
Da warn noch nicht so viele Fremde da,
Und unter uns war Einigkeit.
Da waren wir allein die Seligen,
Lebten in Reichtum, Gut und Geld,
Da konnten wir allein befehligen,
Ein Gutshof war die ganze Welt.

Chor: Als wir regierten noch in Attika, da war die gute alte Zeit.

2. Chorf.:   Als wir regierten noch in Attika
Da herrschte Sitte noch und Zucht. } sprechen
Nie widersprach die Frau dem Manne da,
Den man ihr einmal ausgesucht.
Da ließ sie sich noch nicht verführen,
Lebt nur für Kinder, Haus und Herd,
Da durfte sie auch nicht studieren.
Da war'n die Frauen noch was wert.

Chor: Als wir regierten noch in Attika,
Da herrschte Sitte noch und Zucht.

2. Chorf: Als wir regierten noch in Attika
Da galt noch Kraft und Männermut,

Ein halber Gott war jeder Krieger da,
Die Uniform stand uns so gut!
Und konnt' man keinen Feind erkundigen,
Wir schlossen doch kein Kompromiss:
Wir schlugen selber uns die Wundigen,
Und zeigten stolz dann unsern Schmiss!

Chor: Als wir regierten noch in Attika
Da galt noch Kraft und Mannesmut.

2. Chorf.: Als wir regierten noch in Attika,
Da gabs noch keinen Literat.
Denn ins Gefängnis kam ein jeder da,
Der unterwühlte seinen Staat.
Nur das Bestehende durfte heiligen
Der Wissenschaftler und Poet.
Mocht' sich das Publikum langweiligen,
Da gab es noch Autorität.

Chor: Als wir regierten noch in Attika,
da gabs noch keinen literat.

2. Chorf.: Als wir regierten noch in Attika,
Da hatt' die Jugend noch Respekt.
Die Kinder glauben ihren Eltern da
Und waren sittlich nicht defekt.
Bis in den Inhalt ihrer Spiele.
Bestimmte Tradition sie nur
Und aus der Einheit der Familie
Erwuchs die Einheit der Kultur.

Chor: Als wir regierten noch in Attika,
Da hatt' die Jugend noch Respekt.

Pheidipp.: Entscheidung ist so schwer. Ein jeder scheint
von seinem Standpunkt aus mir Recht zu haben.
Doch hilft mir alles das für meinen Beutel
Und meine Laufbahn in der Politik?

1. Chor: Folge nur uns!
2. Chor: – O, höre nicht auf sie!

Pheidipp.: Was bietet ihr? Ich brauche Geld und Ruhm
Die süße Chloe schielt schon längst nach mir.
Ich brauche geld und etwas Charisma,
Daß sie mit mir sich sehen lassen kann.
Was könnt Ihr geben?

396

1. Chorf.	Aufstieg durch Erkenntnis!
Pheidipp:	Das dauert mir zu lang! – Was bietet Ihr?
2. Chorf.:	Wir haben Konnexionen zu vergeben.
Pheidipp.:	Das geht mir schnell genut, ich bin der Eure!
Loew.u. Gold.:	Entflieh' nicht, eh' den Meister du geseh'n, Vielleicht, daß er dich überzeugen kann. (Sokrates wird in einer Hängematte schwebend sichtbar.)
1. Chor:	Willkommen, o, Gries, ehrwürdiges Haupt, Du Weidmann kundiger Rede/du Priester Erhabenster Spitzfindeleien, Hör' an, was unsres Begehrs ist! Denn keinen so gern befragten wir sonst Von den Ideologen des Tages. Ja dir, der die Straßen entlang du stolzierst, Und prüfend die Augen umherwirfst, Erforschend der Kinoplakate Gehalt in soziologischer Hinsicht. Stets barfuß, nicht der Bequemlichkeit fröhnst, Und auf uns stolz, höher den Kopf trägst.
Loew.:	O, Sokrates, diesen Niedergeschlagenen Bringen wir dir aus der Harmonie. O lehre ihm gütigst, du Weister der Weisen Wie eint man wohl Wissenschaft mit Politik?
Sokrates:	Fürwahr, Löwenthales, mit schwierigen Fragen bedenkst du mich heute, Wie soll ich erwidern? Du glaubst, ich sei weise, – ich weise, Daß ich nichts weiß/das ist mein Geheimnis. Zuerst aber sage:/Gibt es denn Wissenschaft Frei von Bewertung? Was ist denn Wissenschaft? – – nun? – Ihr schweigt? Soll ich denn gleich in die Wolken entschweben? So redet doch endlich! Ihr wißt doch die Antwort. Ich gehe jetzt fort, ich mach' nicht mehr mit! Sag an, Goldenborgias, herrlicher Redner, Warum fehlt Wissenschaft drüben in Sparta?
Goldenbor.:	In Sparta herrscht seit je die Diktatur Sie rekrutiert sich aus der beßren Bürgerschicht.

397

Daneben findet man die Periöken,
Und diese sind noch nicht erwacht,
Zu klaren Überschauen ihrer Lage.
Die beiden Gruppen sind organisiert/in
Straffem Zentralismus durch den König
Und knechten die Heloten in gemeiner Weise.
Daher betrachten sie die Wissenschaft als Feind,
Weil sie am End' den Periöken Klarheit brächte,
Und sie als afgeklärte Mittelschicht
Sich auf die Seite der Heloten schlügen.
Es zeigt sich diese

Pheidipp.:   O könnt' ich auch so phrasenreiche Rede
In überzeugtem Tone leiern her,
Ohne zu stocken, daß es andre mitreißt!
Dann braucht ich keine Prügel mehr zu fürchten,
Könnt' ohne Scheu aufsteigen zum Erfolg.

Sokrates: Da haben wir's. Erfolg! Soeben hab' ich
Darüber erst gesprochen, wie ein jeder,
der danach strebt, zu ihm gelangen kann,
Durch Hellas größte Städte führte mich
die Vortragsreise; ja, ich weiß Bescheid,
Wie man Erfolg an seine Fersen heftet.
Ich bring' dir's bei, komm nur herauf zu mir.

Pheidipp.:   Das glaub'ich nicht. Erfolg durch Wissenschaft?

Sokrates: Kleinbürgerliche Skepsis durch und durch,
Du bist nicht reich, noch adlig von Geburt.
Wie willst du anders zum Erfolg gelangen
Als durch den Intellekt, durch Wissenschaft?
Am Boden gilt Geburtsschein nur und Beutel;
Doch hier im Luftreich der Intelligenz,
Hier bist du, was du selber aus dir machst.
Hier schwebend, hebst die Welt du aus den Angeln.
Dir fehlt'bisher der richt'ge Ansatz nur.
Hehrer Willmanion, bringt ihn herbei!

Beide Chöre: O sehet, es nahet der Wahrer des Hauses,
dem ehrfurchtgebietenden Corbemus gleich!
Der Karten abnehmende, Mappen durchprüfende,
Rauchen verbietende, Herr über Mensch und Getier.

Pheidipp.:   (auf die Leiter steigend):
Wohlan, ich nahe dir erwartungsvoll.

2. Chor:	O frevelnder Knabe – welch Idiotopie!
	Wurzellos schwebst du als bleiche Iemure –
	Blutlos, haltlos, schwankend dahin.
	O bleib' im Konkreten, o hafte am Boden!
	O schreite nicht weiter, verankre dich rück!
Pheidipp.:	Weicht von mir, abgelebte Illusionen,
	Ich will von nun an in den Wolken wohnen.
	(Lied: Melodie aus dem Orpheus)
2. Chor:	Ach, wir haben ihn verloren,
	Und sein Glück ist nun dahin.
Pheidipp.:	Ach ich fühl mich so verworren
	Und die Luft wird mir zu dünn.
1. Chor:	Nein, er ist jetzt neugeboren
	Aufgelockert ist sein
	Halleluja! der Umbruch ist vollzogen!
Pheidipp.:	(Die Brüstung übersteigend):
	Verändert schau ich schon die ganze Welt!
Sokrates:	Willkommen, Sohn, im hehren Wolkenreich!
	Hier herrscht das einzig richtige Bewußtsein.
Pheidipp.:	Noch kann ich nicht ganz richtig atmen hier,
	Ich fühl' mich leichter, aber ohne Halt.
Sokrates:	Das gibt sich, Freund, wenn du dich orientierst.
	Von hier nur hast du den Totalaspekt,
	was siehst da unten Du?
Pheidipp.:	...Ich seh' Parteien,
	die alle glauben, nicht Partei zu sein,
	Die eigne sache halten für gerecht,
	Die fremde Meinung immer nur für schlecht.
Sokrates:	Sehr wahr, mein junger Freund! Wie klärt dein Geist,
	Sofort sich hier in des Abstrakten Reich.
	Du sprichtst schon völlig repräsentativ
	Für meine Schule der Intelligenz
	Parteien dort, hier die Totalität.
	Ideologen dort und hier Synthese.
Chor:	Verdammter Greis, ich habe jetzt voll die Nase
	Von deiner unverbindlichen Synthese!!

1. Chorf.:	Was schiltst da den Meister, altfränkischer Flaps?! Ich schlage dich krumm wenn du weiter ihn störst!
2. Chorf.:	Du krummschlagen mich? Totreden, das kannst du! Ganz Schnauze bist du ja und weiter nichts!
Sokrates:	Du siehst, schon liegen sie sich in den Haaren, Der Logos adikos und dikaios.
2. Chorf.:	Ihr Zungendrescher, die mit leeren Worten, abstraktem Zeug die arme Jugend ködert, Sie schwankend macht und haltlos ganz und gar!
1. Chorf.:	Gespenster Ihr, aus längst vergangner Zeit! Ins Grab, ins Grab mit Euch, Ihr seid vorbei. Man kann nicht leben mehr, man kann nicht, hört Ihr's, Wie früher leben heut, da das Problem von Ideologie und Utopie so wie von diesem radikal gestellt ist!
2. Chorf.:	Man kann nicht leben, Wehe, wehe! sagt: Wie kann man leben, wenn man niederreißt, Wie ihr den alten Glauben und zersetzt Wie ihr die alten Werte, die schon gaben Den Vätern und der Väter Väter Halt? Ich wende mich an Euch, das Publikum Und frage Euch! Müßte man diesen nicht Anklagen, weil die Jugend er verführt, Ihn ins Gefängnis werfen und ihm reichen Den Schierlingsbecher für die böse Tat.
1. Chorf.:	Ihr Memmen, habt Ihr Angst um Eure Jugend? Packt sie in Watte ein, versteckt sie freundlichst In einen festen Schrein, dann spürt sie nichts Von dem gefährlich Neuen dieser Zeit. Ihr sprecht von Heldentum und schreit, weil er Die falsche Sicherheit der Jugend raubt, Das nutzlose Korsett der Tradition Und sie statt dessen in den Kampf hinausschickt. Ich wende mich an Euch, das Publikum Und frage Euch: Müßte man diesem nicht Von Staates wegen längst ein Lehramt geben Und ihn im Prytaneion täglich speisen?
2. Chorf.:	Das fehlte noch, Ihr Erzsophistennarren! Daß unser Staat den eigenen Totengräber Den Geisterzerfresser selbst ernährt.

Sokrates:	Da siehst du Freund, wie sie mich mißverstehen,
	Sie sind wie Männer, die in Ketten träumen,
	Sie seien frei, und so besessen sind
	Von dieser falschen Wohltat ihres Traums,
	Daß sie den einen, der sie weckt und ruft:
	"Ihr seid nicht frei, Ihr müßt Euch erst befreien"!
	Als Mörder ihres schönen Traums beschimpfen.
	Als Narr'n, der von erdachten Ketten faselt,
	Obwohl ihr Geist doch frei ins Weite schweift.
	Ich bin der Narr nicht, Freunde, und ich trage
	Im Herzen ganz den gleichen Traum wie Ihr.
	Von einem Dasein voll von Menschlichkeit,
	Darin sich die Gesichter nicht wie heute
	Durch Kampf, durch Haß, durch Krampf, durch Not und Gier,
	Umformen zu erbärmlichen Grimassen,
	Von einem Leben, das der Geist beherrscht,
	Und jedem frei läßt, was er ist, zu sein,
	Und nur das eine unterscheidet mich
	Bei alledem von Euch: ich mache nicht
	Aus meinem Wunsche eine Wirklichkeit;
	Ich kann mich nicht betrügen: Heute hält
	Das Leben uns gefangen, heute ist
	Freiheit ein schöner Traum. Dort oben mag
	Es kampflos eingebor'ne Freiheit geben,
	Hier unten müssen wir uns selber erst
	Die Welt der Freiheit schaffen. Darum lehr' ich
	Euch die Gefangenschaft des Geistes seh'n,
	Darum die Seinsgebundenheit. Wir müssen
	Die Ketten spüren, um uns zu befrei'n,
	Dann wird – wenn Ihr es wollt – der Traum von heute
	Die Wirklichkeit von morgen sein.

Pheidipp.:	Erhab'ner Meister, das war fabelhaft.
	Ich möchte reden können so wie du,
	So bilderreich voll Tiefsinn, denn was tut's
	Wenn man es auch nicht immer gleich versteht.
	Ich bin jetzt umgebrochen ganz und gar.
	Klar seh' den Weg ich zum Erfolg: Bisher
	Schlugen die andern mich, jetzt schlag' ich sie!
	Doch dreifußschleudernd nicht, wie's jene taten.
	Du legst mir bess're Waffen in den Mund.
	Drum will ich gründlich jetzt bei dir studieren.
	Nimmst du mich in die Denkanstalt auch auf?

Sokrates:	Ja gerne
	(Das Telefon klingelt)
	– deus ex machina – das Telefon!

401

Hallo, wer spricht? Jawohl, hier Sokrates.
Wie bitte, wer ist dort? Ah, sehr erfreut.
So, so. Hm. Ja. Gewiß, hm, warten Sie,
Da müßt ich aber meine Frau erst fragen.
(wendet sich zum Hintergrund)
So eilig, ein'n Moment.
– Sag', woll'n wir's tun?

Stimme der Frau Sokrates:

Ganz wie du willst/doch
Wenn du mich fragst – Ja!

Sokrates: (ins Telefon)
Sie sind noch da? Jawohl, ich nehme an.
Sehr gerne, höchst erfreut. Ich danke Ihnen.
(ins Publikum)
Denkt Euch, ich bin nicht mehr Privatsophist,
Man ruft mich auf den großen Lehrstuhl in –

Pheidipp.:   O, Zeus, was wird aus uns, die du verläßt?

Sokrates: Ja, das ist traurig, von hier wegzugehen,
Von dieser Stadt, die ich so sehr geliebt;
Von diesem Haus, dem ich so sehr verbunden;
Von meinen Schülern, die mir nah' gestanden;
Von meinen Freunden, die mit mir gewirkt.

Pheidipp.:   O Meister, welcher Schmerz, kaum hab' ich dich gewonnen
Verläßt du uns und nichts bleibt mehr zu tun,
Als dir nach altem Brauch das Abschieslied zu singen.

1. Chorf.:   Wohlan, stimmt ein!
In dieser schweren Stunde tritt jeder Streit zurück,

2. Chorf.:   Gewiß, er geht,
Und wenn der Gegner scheidet, so feiert man ihn gern.

2. Chor: (stellt sich feierlich in Positur. Alle räuspern sicht, Chorführer taktiert;
langsam und getragen)
Nun zuguterletzt! – geben wir dir jetzt
Auf die Wand'rung ...

1. Chorf.:   (unterbricht)
Falsches Bewusstsein! Falsches Bewusstsein!

SCHLUßLIED

1. Chor: Stimmt an, Seinen Ruhm zu künden
Er wird nun entschwinden
Aus der Stadt, die er so lang belehret hat.

402

Nicht leicht werden wir's verwinden,
Keinen Bess'ren finden
Wir an seiner statt.

2. Chor: Fiel er uns auch auf die Nerven
Ist er doch ein großer Mann
Der des Geistes Kampfes Schärfen
Oft beträchtlich mildern kann.

Lag er uns auch schwer im Magen
Hat er Richt'ges doch geseh'n
Darum woll'n wir's heute sagen,
Seine Zeit, sie war doch schön.

1. Chor: Ach, ach, ach, ach: Seine Zeit, sie war doch schön!
Ja, ja, ja, ja, Seine Zeit, sie war doch schön!
Wenn er lehrt jetzt in der Ferne
Hören wir es gerne,
Daß sein Wort hinausdringt über unsern Ort.

Drum soll niemand darob trauern
Weil aus unsern Mauern
Ihn sein Weg führt fort.

2. Chor: Alles was wir lang bestritten,
Hat sich dennoch durchgesetzt.
Hat er oft durch uns gelitten,
Avanciert er doch zuletzt.
Ueber uns'rer Heimat Fluren
Braust der neue Gest dahin.
Folge ruhig seinen Spuren,
Wiederstand hat keinen Sinn!

1. Chor: Ach, ach, ach, ach Widerstand hat keinen Sinn!
Ja, ja, ja, ja, Widerstand hat keinen Sinn!

Heil dir Jubel soll dich grüßen!
Knieend dir zu Füßen
Liegt des Gegners Schar,
Ist das nicht wunderbar?

Daß dir Glück und Ruhm hält Treue,
Immer sich erneue,
Wünscht der Jünger Schar.

FINIS

Appendix 3: *Letter from Mannheim to Louis Wirth in Chicago*. This letter is published by the kind permission of the Joseph Regenstein Library of The University of Chicago (Louis Wirth papers; translated from German by S.M.W.).

Russell Square W.C.1.
15 February 1936

Dear Friend Wirth,

Thank you again and again for your letter of 2 February and for the great effort and seriousness with which you and Mr. Shils centered your discussion on the content of the manuscript I sent you. Although I feel with your argument at most points, there is a fact which persuades me to build that manuscript into the book after all. That fact is, as I have already explained to you in my telegram, the situation here in England. If I were bringing out the book only in America, then I would publish it in the old form, exactly as you advise me. Your preface, which penetrates so deeply into the matter, would have smoothed the way sufficiently. The difference in England strikes me as being a double one. The great security which reigns in this land has not revealed the problem of the sociological backgrounds of consciousness to even the clearest heads of the intelligentsia living here. For most of them the old book would simply appear as a document out of a time inaccessible to them. I attempted to make these difficulties more accessible by means of analogies with the sophists and Socrates by establishing the origin of this method of thought. The second difficulty which one encounters in this country is that there is, as it were, absolutely no tradition of sociology in existence, and by the term one either means "social surveys" or "descriptions of social situations." People have no clear conception here of an empiricism which could also be something more than simply tallies, statistics, and inventories. Something introductory must be said about these matters, to make the path of the reader generally secure. If the book had begun so that the reader would immediately fall into the definitions of total and particular ideologies, then practically every Englishman after a few pages of reading would have put down the book as "too abstract." So I believe that both your introduction and the new opening of the book involves the reader in a context of problems in a concrete form, so that, when once the reader is interested in these matters, he then comes to enjoy a great deal of what his tradition did not provide him adequately.

As a further motive for moving to the very beginning of the English edition, those ideas of the last pages of the manuscript which you received after composing your letter to me – as yet a further motive for presenting those ideas early, I could bring up that this is an absolute and emphatic need if I want to spare myself many misunderstandings, which I have noticed on the part of some German critics. Although I had already said it in the German edition, I needed to say it even more clearly here: that these investigations must be regarded as essays, as a search, and not as uncontested final formulations. By that I shall perhaps spare myself that a critic like Von Schelting, for instance (who otherwise has performed very good work indeed), who takes his task to be the gathering of contradictory evidence, although I myself emphasized that I allow contradictions to undergo the test openly, because they lie situated in our thought and one cannot construe them away immediately, before the testing process, but rather, one must make them transparent. And so, as things stand now, I no longer have the feeling that your introduction and my rewriting of a part of the manuscript work against each other, but rather, that, without the author himself saying anything to that effect in the text, many of your arguments could be taken as an apology rather than a genuine interpretation of the text. You can believe it or not, that I, during the first and second terms, which in the educational establishment here are the very heaviest, would not have undertaken this work of revision if I had not had the personal conviction that I needed to build a bridge to the reader in England.

I myself did not hit on the idea in an idiosyncratic way, that your introduction and my new text would clash. My friend Löwe supports me in this opinion, to whose judgment I have submitted both manuscripts. Löwe found your introduction a full-fledged work of art, which nothing can damage. (This objectivity and distance is, naturally, impossible for you to bring to the evaluation of your own achievement.) He did, however, make a few criticisms of me: that I had forgotten to strike out the word *Introduction* from the title of the new part and to print the new manuscript as the first part of the book, thus as a substantial part of the book itself. The second part would then be that one which until now was the first part, except that a few sentences have been deleted because they had until now fulfilled an introductory frunction – among others, the first seven pages of the German edition. Thus the book has only one unique introduction, which you have written, and the book acquires the character of a collection of essays, related contextually, but still independent essays which center on the same problem. It will then be experienced, not as if after many introductions one still is not coming to the point, but rather, as if from various points of view, one strives in various ways to achieve the same center. I hope that these arguments will convince you and be very thoroughly understood, for I must take account of my English public.

It is so dreadfully difficult to come to mutual decisions across this great distance, and we must try very hard to avoid misunderstandings. I ask for your full best wishes when you read this letter, and I remind you that in a personal conversation so much can be set right by the wave of the hand, for which one needs a long and weighty analysis in a letter.

In this connection I could also point out now that I have allowed myself the very special privilege, in the essays about utopia and sociology of knowledge, to reconstruct a rather large number of sentences. You will be surprised, not because I found them in too strong a contrast to the original text, but rather because the translation was too literal in my perception. This brought about a certain difficulty in reading, which one can avoid by a reformulation. Please do not misunderstand this either: the author can allow quite a few reformulations and departures from the original text, which the translator cannot assume as his responsibility. For that reason it is also valuable for me to know in connection with the further translation work by Mr. Shils, that to begin with he should translate exactly wherever possible and then give me the opportunity later to reformulate some parts. I cannot admire enough the labors of translation on the part of the two of you. There is probably no more difficult task in this field of translation than this one. Perhaps I should still send you, though, the final text before the typesetting, although you have declined the opportunity. I am afraid particularly that if one changes too much in the corrected version, the publisher might charge our account with these fees. Of course, the opportunity is open for you in your preamble to shift the responsibility for the changes from you to me. So let me know whether I should send the text.

I have read with great interest about your plan concerning a later publication in the field of the sociology of knowledge, and it would make me happy if our further cooperation would continue. I have abundant material at my disposal for writing a chapter in such a book. Likewise, I hope that this field of work shall be very wide open for development and that our common task will only deepen our connection.

Do greet Mr. Shils on my behalf, most heartily. With friendly regards,

Yours,
K. Mannheim

405

Appendix 4: *Schematic overview of Mannheim's analysis of the "Weltan-schauung" in relation to his sociology of knowledge.*

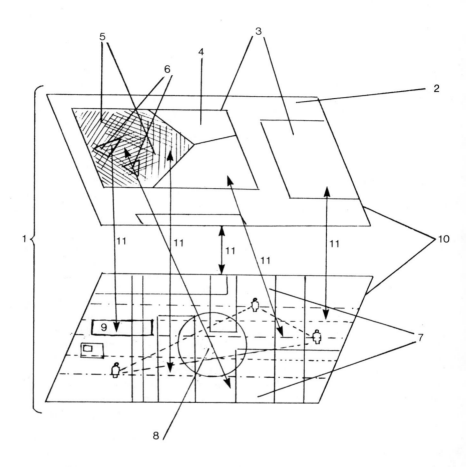

1. A period as a dynamic totality.
2. The worldview of a socio-cultural period.
3. Particular worldviews.
4. World strivings or world postulates.
5. Strivings of thought, art, economic ones, etc.
6. Styles of thought.
7. A society consisting of differentiated social relationships, groups, strata and other collectivities.
8. The relatively free-floating intelligentsia.
9. An intellectual stratum.
10. The structure of a period.
11. Commitments.

Appendix 5: *List of illustrations* (published by the kind permission of the proprietors or archivists).

1. Opposite the title page: photo of Karl Mannheim (plm. 1935).
   From the archives of Dr. J. Baracs (London).
2. Photo with A. Hauser (1916).
   From the archives of Professor G. Révész, more recently from those of his daughter, Mrs. J. Révész Laqueur (Malcesine Sul Garda).
3. Photo of Karl Mannheim.
   From the archives of the Magyar Tudománya Académia Könyvtára (The Hungarian Academy of Sciences) at Budapest.
4. Photo of the Lukács Group.
   From the archives of the Petöfi Irodalmi Museum (Petöfi Museum of Literature) at Budapest.
5. Caricature by G. Tibor (1918).
6. Photo of Juliska Lang (plm. 1918).
   Both from the archives of Professor G. Révész.
7. Photo of Karl Mannheim (plm. 1930).
   From the archives of Mrs. J. Molnear Piliszanska (London).
8. Photo of Karl and Julia Mannheim (plm. 1935).
   From the archives of the Petöfi Museum.
9. Photo of Karl and Julia Mannheim (plm. 1940).
10. Photo of Mannheim's study in London.
11. Photo of the crematorium at Golders Green (London).
    From the archives of H.E.S. Woldring (Amstelveen).
12. Photo of Julia Lang Mannheim (plm. 1945).
    9, 10 and 12 from the archives of Mrs. J. Molnear Piliszanska (London).

Appendix 6: *Sources*: Archives, correspondence, and interviews.

Biographical givens were drawn from the following:

A. The Archives of the following institutions and/or persons:

Szabó Ervin Library at Budapest
Eötvös Loránd University at Budapest
Magyar Tudománya Akadémia Kézirattára at Budapest
Petöfi Irodalmi Muzeum at Budapest
Minicipal Archives at Freiburg (in Breisgau)
Albert Ludwigs University at Freiburg i.B.
Badische Generallandesarchiv at Karlsruhe
Rupert Karls University at Heidelberg
Johann Wolfgang Goethe university at Frankfurt a.M.
Publ. Comp. J.C.B. Mohr (Paul Siebeck) at Tübingen
Sozialwissenschaftliches Archiv, University of Constance
London School of Economics and Political Science at London
Institute of Education at London
BBC at Reading, England
Routledge and Kegan Paul at London (in the archives of the University College Library)
K. Mannheim Papers, Library University of Keele (Staffordshire)
A.D. Lindsay Papers, Library University of Keele (Staffordshire)
M. Polanyi Papers, Joseph Regenstein Library, University of Chicago
L. Wirth Papers, Joseph Regenstein Library, University of Chicago
Rockefeller Archive Center, North Tarrytown, New York
Archives of L.C. Cooper, Champaign, Illinois
Archives of D. Kettler, Peterborough, Ontario
Archives of G. Révész, property of Mrs. J. Révész Laqueur at Malcesine Sul Garda (Italy)
Archives of E.A. Shils, Chicago
Archives of N. Stehr, Edmonton, Alberta.

B. Interviews with:

J. Baracs (London), S. Baracs (Doesburg), J. Ben-David (Chicago/Jerusalem), L.C. Cooper (Champaign, Illinois), P.J. Bouman (Groningen), N. Elias (Amsterdam), Mrs. J. Floud (Cambridge), Mrs. E. Gábor (Budapest), J. Hajnal (London), D. Kettler (Peterborough, Ontario), M.J. Langeveld (Utrecht), Mrs. J. Révész Laqueur (Malcesine Sul Garda), D. Levine (Chicago), D. Macrae (London), E. Manheim (Kansas City, Mississippi), K. Martin (The Hague), G. Nador (Northwood), Mrs. J. Molnear Piliszanska (London), Mrs. M. Alexander Révész (Amsterdam, transcript of an interview (6-3-1970) prepared by P.J. de Jong), H.G. Schenk (Oxford), E.A. Shils (Chicago), N. Stehr (Edmonton, Alberta), W.A.C. Stewart (Brighton), P. Thoenes (Utrecht), A.J. Vidich (New York), and K.H. Wolff (Waltham, Boston).

C. Correspondence with:

R.C.F. Aron (Paris), L.C. Cooper (Champaign, Illinois), Mrs. E. Gábor (Budapest), D. Kettler (Peterborough), J. Lauwerys (Blackheath, England), A Löwe (Bronx, New York), A. Megill (Iowa City), H. Plessner (Erlenbach, Switzerland), E.A. Shils (Chicago), H. Speier (Hartsdale, New York), N. Stehr (Edmonton, Alberta), K.H. Wolff (Waltham, Boston).

Bibliography

I. *Works by Karl Mannheim*

Written in Hungarian, French, German, English and Dutch (with the abbreviations used in this book). Translations into French, Spanish, Italian, Chinese, and other languages are not mentioned.

A. *Unpublished and hitherto unretrieved manuscripts*

Die Lehre vom Urteil in der logischen Literatur der Zweiten Hälfte des XIX. Jhrt's. The entry.

Erkenntnistheoretische und logische Probleme.
Lectures during the first semester, for the "Free School for Social Sciences" at Budapest (1917), loaned to E. Fekete and E. Karádi, 1981: 71.

Wilhelm v. Humboldt als Kritiker.
Louise Labé et la Renaissance francaise.
Two academic exercises written for the state examination in the French and German literatures, 1918.

Die Liebe in Ungarn.
On a postcard (7-1-1930) to Mrs. F. Gundolf, Mannheim refers to this piece. This card is preserved in the Gundolf Archives at London. Loaned to L.C. Cooper, M.d.: 2.

Ist Politik als Wissenschaft möglich? Das Problem der Theorie und Praxis.
According to a letter from Mannheim to Dr. S. Kracauer (26-6-1928), this is a typed manuscript of 90 pages. Loaned to L.C. Cooper, M.d.: Appendix N.

Max Weber (1929).
A manuscript of 300 to 350 pages, according to a letter to the publisher J.C.B. Mohr (Paul Siebeck), Tübingen (2-10-1929).

B. *Unpublished but Preserved Works*
Photocopies of these works are in the possession of the author of this book.

410

Dairy notes (1911-'14)
Parts of these dairy notes in: M. Sárközi, "The Influence of Georg Lukács on the Young Karl Mannheim in the Light of a Newly Discovered Diary." *The Slavonic and East European Review* LXIV, 3 (July 1986): 432-439.

LSI   *Leibniz as a Source of Inspiration* (1918).
Notes in longhand; collection projected by George and Eva Nador, Northwood, Middlesex.

DDB   *Die Dame aus Biarritz: Ein Spiel in vier Szenen.*
Typescript 1920. Magyar Tudományos Akadémia Kézirattára, Budapest.

VWM   *Transcript A. Weber-Mannheim Seminar at Heidelberg*, 21-2-1929.
In L.C. Cooper, M.d.: App. R.

SCCE   *The Sociological Causes of the Cultural Crisis in the Era of Mass-Democracies and Autarchies.*
Typescript 1933, 24 pp. Rockefeller Archive Center, North Tarrytown, New York

EGG   *Die Entstehung der intellektuellen Gruppen aus der sich wandelnden Gesellschaftsstruktur.* Part II (1934-35).
In archives of E.A. Shils, Chicago.

HIJM   *Some remarks on "Humanism Intégral" by Jacques Maritain.*
Paper written for "the Moot" on the occasion of a dinner with Maritain (11-5-1939). L.C. Cooper, M.d.: App. W.

MSMD   *The Place of the Study of Modern Society in a Militant Democracy: Some Practical Suggestions.*
Notes addressed to Lord A.D. Lindsay (Spring 1940), L.C. Cooper, M.d.: App. U.

TM   *Topics for the next meeting of the Moot.*
Paper of 9 pp. in preparation for a meeting of "The Moot" on 10-1-1941. L.C. Cooper, M.d.: App. Z.

CW   *Calling the World "inside the Nazi-Mind."*
Lecture for the BBC, broadcast on 31-5/1-6-1941.

ASP   *A Syllabus on Power.*
Paper in preparation for a meeting of "The Moot" in January, 1942. L.C. Cooper, M.d.: App. CC.

CRCE   *Cultural Reconstruction in Central Europe. Planning for the Eradication of Fascist Mentality in Europe.*
Paper in preparation for a meeting of a discussion group of professors and officials, 1942 (archives of the Institute of Education).

E   *Ethics.*
Nine lectures for the BBC, broadcast weekly from 24-9-1943 to 26-11-1943.

WS   *What is Sociology?*
Ten lectures for the BBC, broadcast weekly from 19-1-1945 to 23-3-1945.

NMNS   *New Man in a New Society.*
Lecture broadcast by the BBC on 17-4-1945.

CM   *The Condition of Man.*
Lecture broadcast by the BBC on 14-8-1945.

411

NSHB *The New Science of Human Behavior.*
Lecture broadcast by the BBC on 20-6-1946. The texts of Mannheim's BBC lectures are preserved in the *BBC Written Archives Centre,* Reading.

A *Notes* on lectures and seminars in Germany and England. In Keele University Library.
ZE *Die Zukunft der Erwachsenenbildung* (6 pp).
PN *Das Problem der Neuerziehung* (8 pp).
WN *Wie ist Neuerziehung möglich* (10 pp).
Manuscripts of three articles in Keele University Library.

C. *Published Works*
1911
FK "A Filozofiai kritika lenyegéröl altalában és Kulonosen a filozofia mai állapotához valo viszonyáról."
KA "Ki gondolkodik absztrakte?"
"Über das Wesen der philosophischen Kritik überhaupt und ihr Verhältnis zum gegen-wärtigen Zustand der Philosophie inshesondere" (1802) and "Wer denkt abstrakt?" Two texts by Hegel translated into Hungarian by Mannheim. Mannheim does not mention when the latter article appeared. There is a difference of opinion on this matter. J. Hoffmeister (1956: xiii) places it in 1807-1808; H. Glockner (1930: xvi), K. Rosenkranz (1844: 355), and W. Kaufmann (1965: 113) place it in Hegel's Berlin period. The Hungarian texts appeared in *Szellem* I, 2 (1911): 187-197.

1916
AL Arthur Liebert, *Das Problem der Geltung.* Berlin: Reuter v. Reichard 1914. Review in *Athenaeum* II, 6: 489-493.

1917
ALB "A Láboru bölcseletetéhez" (Georg Simmel, *Der Krieg und die geistigen Entscheidungen: Reden und Aufsätze.* München und Leipzig: Duncker und Humblot 1917. Review in *Huszadik Század* XXXVI: 416-418.

C Ernst Cassirer, *Freiheit und Formstudien zur deutschen Geistesgeschichte.* Berlin: Bruno Cassirer 1917. *Athenaeum* III: 409-413.

1918
GSF "Georg Simmel, mint filozófus." *Haszadik Század* XXXVIII: 194-196.

EB Ernst Bloch, *Geist und Utopie.* München, Leipzig: Duncker und Humblot. *Athenaeum* IV-V: 207-211.

SK "Lélek és Kultura." German translation: "Seele und Kultur," K. Mannheim, *Wissenssoziologie* (1964): 66-84.

"Az Ismeretelmét Szerkezetá Elemzése" *Athenaem* IV (1918): 233-247, 315-330. German translation "Die Strukturanalyse der Erkenntnistheorie," *Kant-Studien* Ergänzungsheft nr. 57. Berlin: Reuther und Reichard 1922.
SE English translation "Structural Analysis of Epistemology", K. Mannheim, *Essays on Sociology and Social Psychology* (1953): 15-73.

1920
Georg Lukács, *Die Theorie des Romans: Ein geschichtsphilosophischen Versuch über die Formen der grossen Epik.* Berlin: Cassirer 1920. Review in *Logos* IX, 2: 289-302.

412

K. Mannheim *Wissenssoziologie* (1964): 85-90.

English translation: "A Review of Georg Lukács Theory of the Novel," K.H. Wolff, *From Karl Mannheim*, New York: Oxford University Press, 1971: 3-7.

1921-22

"Heidelbergi Levelek." *Tüz* 1921 (November/December): 46-50; 1922 (April): 91-93.
English translation: "Letters from Heidelberg I, II" L.C. Cooper, M.d.: App. J.

"Beiträge zur Theorie der Weltanschauungs-Interpretation." *Jahrbuch für Kunstgeschichte* I, 4: 226-274.
K. Mannheim, *Wissenssoziologie* (1964): 91-154.
English translation: "On the Interpretation of 'Weltanschauung,' " *Essays on the Sociology of Knowledge* (1952): 33-83; also in K.H. Wolff, *From Karl Mannheim*: 8-58.

"Zum Problem einer Klassifikation der Wissenschaften." *Archiv für Sozialwissenschaft und Sozialpolitik* L, 1: 230-237;
K. Mannheim, *Wissenssoziologie* (1964): 155-165.

"Wissenschaft und Jugend." *Frankfurter Zeitung*, 30-11-1922.

1924

"Historismus." *Archiv für Sozialwissenschaft und Sozialpolitik* LII, 1: 1-60.
K. Mannheim, *Wissenssoziologie* (1964): 246-307.
English translation: "Historicism," K. Mannheim, *Essays on the Sociology of Knowledge* (1952): 33-83.

"Levelek az imigrációbol." *Diogenes*, 1924, 1: 13-25; 1924, 2: 20-23.
English translation: "Letters from Exile, I, II." L.C. Cooper, M.d.: App. M.

1925

"Das Problem einer Soziologie des Wissens." *Archiv für Sozialwissenschaft und Sozialpolitik* LIII, 3: 577-652;
K. Mannheim, *Wissenssoziologie* (1964): 308-387.
English translation: "The Problem of a Sociology of Knowledge." K. Mannheim, *Essays on the Sociology of Knowledge* (1952): 134-190; also in K.H. Wolff, *From Karl Mannheim*: 59-115.

1926

"Ideologische und soziologische Interpretation der geistigen Gebilde." *Jahrbuch für Soziologie* II: 424-440.
K. Mannheim, *Wissenssoziologie* (1964): 388-407.
English translation: "The Ideological and the Sociological Interpretation of Intellectual Phenomena." K.H. Wolff, *From Karl Mannheim*: 116-131.

1927

"Das konservative Denken: Soziologische Beiträge zum Werden des Politisch-historischen Denkens in Deutschland." *Archiv für Sozialwissenschaft und Sozialpolitik* LVII, 1: 68-142; LVII 2: 470-495.
K. Mannheim, *Wissenssoziologie* (1964): 408-508.
English translation: "Conservative Thought." K. Mannheim; *Essays on Sociology and Social Psychology* (1953): 76-164; also in K.H. Wolff, *From Karl Mannheim*: 132-222.

1928-1929

"Das Problem der Generationen." *Kölner Vierteljahreshefte für Soziologie* VII, 2: 157-185; 3: 309-330.

K. Mannheim, *Wissenssoziologie* (1964): 509-565.

SIG   English translation: "The Problem of Generation," K. Mannheim, *Essays on the Sociology of Knowledge* (1952): 276-322.

"Die Bedeutung der Konkurrenz im Gebiete des Geistigen." *Verhandlungen des sechsten deutschen Soziologentages vom 17. bis 19. September 1928 in Zürich*. Tübingen: J.C.B. Mohr (Paul Siebeck) 1929: 35-83.

K. Mannheim, *Wissenssoziologie* (1964): 566-613. V. Meja/N. Stehr, 1982: 325-370.

BK   English translation: "Competition as a Cultural Phenomenon," K. Mannheim, *Essays on the Sociology of Knowledge* (1952): 191-229; also in K.H. Wolff, *From Karl Mannheim*: 223-261.

S   "Schlusswort von Dr. Mannheim: Diskussion über die Konkurrenz." *Verhandlungen des sechsten deutschen Soziologentages vom 17. bis 19. September 1928 in Zürich*. Tübingen: J.C.B. Mohr 1929: 119-124. V. Meja/N. Stehr, 1982: 395-401.

"Diskussion über das Verstehen." *Verhandlungen des sechsten deutschen Soziologentages vom 17. bis 19. September 1928 in Zürich*. Tübingen: J.C.B. Mohr 1929: 238-243. V. Meja/N. Stehr, 1982: 371-395.

SV   "Der Sechste deutsche Soziologentag in Zürich." *Frankfurter Zeitung*, 5-10-1928: 1-2.

Ideologie und Utopie. Bonn: F. Cohen 1929, 250 pp.

IU   Expanded English edition: *Ideology and Utopia: An Introduction to the Sociology of Knowledge*, introd. L. Wirth. London: Routledge and Kegan Paul, New York: Harcourt, Brace a. World 1936, 318 pp.

Expanded German edition: *Ideologie und Utopie*, Frankfurt a.M.: Schulte-Bulmke 1952.

EEZ   "Über die Eingliederung der Erforschung des Zeitungswesen in die Universitätswissenschaft." *Zeitungs Verlag und Zeitschriften Verlag* XXX, 22: 20-21.

"Zur Problematik der Soziologie in Deutschland." *Neue Scheizer Rundschau* 22 (November 1929): 820-829.

K. Mannheim, *Wissenssoziologie* (1964): 614-624. V. Meja/N. Stehr, 1982: 427-437.

PSD   English translation: "Problems of Sociology in Germany," K.H. Wolff, *From Karl Mannheim*: 262-270.

1930

"Über das Wesen und die Bedeutung des Wirtschatlichen Erfolgsstrebens: Ein Beitrag zur Wirtschaftssoziologie." *Archiv für Sozialwissenschaft und Sozialpolitik* LXIII, 3: 449-512.

K. Mannheim, *Wissenssoziologie* (1964): 625-687.

WE   English translation: "On the Nature of Economic Ambition and its Significance for the Social Education of Man," K. Mannheim, *Essays on the Sociology of Knowledge* (1952): 230-275.

1931

"Wissenssoziologie." A. Vierkandt, ed., *Handwörterbuch der Soziologie*. Stuttgart: F. Enke 1931: 659-680.

W   English translation: "The Sociology of Knowledge." K. Mannheim, *Ideology and Utopia*, Ch. V.: 264-311.

"Grundlegung einer Socioanalyse (Probleme aus der Grenzgebieten der Soziologie, Psychologie und Pädagogik)."
Paper given at a conference of the International School of Philosophy, Amersfoort, 12-27 September 1933. Report published in *Alg. Nederlandsch Tijdschrift van Wijsbegeerte en Psychologie* XXVII (1933-1934): 39.

"American Sociology." Review of Stuart A. Rice, ed., *Methods in Social Research*. Chicago: University of Chicago Press, 1931.
American Journal of Sociology XVII (1932): 273-282; also in Karl Mannheim, *Essays on Sociology and Social Psychology* (1953): 185-194.

1932-1933
Die Gegenwartsaufgaben der Soziologie: Ihre Lehrgestalt. Tübingen: J.C.B. Mohr (Paul Siebeck) 1932, 65 pp.

"Die Soziale und Politische Bedeutung der Intelligenz" (translated under the title "De Sociologie der Intellektuelen"). Amsterdam Student Weekly, *Propria Cures* XLIX, 7 (29-10-1932).

"Die geistige Krise im Lichte der Soziologie." *Stuttgart Neues Tageblatt*, 31-12-1932. Somewhat edited form: "Geistige Krise der Gegenwart in Licht der Soziologie," *Koningsberger Hartungsche Zeitung*, 1-1-1933, and under the title, "Die Wurzeln der Geistigen Krise," *Hamburger Fremdenblatt*, 7-1-1933.

1933-1934
"German Sociology (1918-1933)." *Politica* I (1934): 12-33.
Also in K. Mannheim, *Essay on Sociology and Social Psychology* (1953): 209-228.

Rational and Irrational Elements in Contemporary Society. Hobhouse Memorial Lecture (7-3-1934). London: Oxford University Press, 1934, 36 pp.
Under the title "Rationele en Irrationale Elementen in de Maatschappij" this lecture was also given at a congress of the International School of Philosophy, Amersfoort (12-27 September 1933). The proceedings are published in *Algemeen Nederlandsch Tijdschrift voor Wijsbegeerte en Psychologie*, XXVII (1933-1934): 37-38.
A more elaborate version appeared in K. Mannheim, *Mensch und Gesellschaft im Zeitalter des Umbaus* (1935: 11-36), and in *Man and Society* (1940): 39-75.

"Franz Oppenheimer: Glückwunschschreiben von Karl Mannheim (24-3-1934)." Frans Oppenheimer, *Lebenserinnerungen*, Düsseldorf: Jozeph Melzer, 1964: 327-328.

"The Crisis of Culture in the Era of Mass-democracies and Autarchies." *Sociological Review* XXVI, 2 (1934): 105-129.
Expanded version in K. Mannheim *Mensch und Gesellschaft* (1935): 57-92, and in *Man and Society* (1940): 79-114.

1935
"Ernst Troeltsch." *Encyclopaedia of the Social Sciences*, eds. E.R.A Seligman, A. Johnson, vol. XV. New York: Macmillan: 106-107.

"Utopia." *Encyclopaedia of the Social Sciences,* eds. E.R.A. Seligman, A. Johnson, vol. XV. New York: Macmillan: 200-203.

'W

MG   *Mensch und Gesellschaft im Zeitalter des Umbaus.* Leiden: A.W. Sijthoff, 208 pp.
MS   Expanded English edition: *Man and Society in an Age of Reconstruction: Studies in Modern Social Structure.* London: Routledge and Kegan Paul, New York: Harcourt Brace, 1940, 469 pp.

1936

"The Place of Sociology." *The Social Sciences: Their Relations to Theory and in Teaching.* London: LePlay House Press: 164-189.
PS   K. Mannheim, *Essays on Sociology and Social Psychology* (1953): 195-208.

IU   *Ideology and Utopia: An Introduction to the Sociology of Knowledge,* introd. L. Wirth (based on *Ideologie und Utopie,* 1929). London: Routledge and Kegan Paul, New York: Harcourt, Brace and World, 1936, 318 pp.

FT   "Ferdinand Tönnies." *Sociological Review* XXVIII, 3 (1936): 313-314.

1937

"A Few Concrete Examples Concerning the Sociological Nature of Human Valuations: The Psychical and Sociological Approach." J.E. Dugdale, *Their Relations in Theory and Teaching.* London: LePlay House Press: 171-193.
FCEC   K. Mannheim, *Essays on Sociology and Social Psychology* (1953): 231-242.

PP   (Untitled). *Prager Presse,* 28-3-1937.
English translation in K.H. Wolff, *From Karl Mannheim:* cv-cvi.

"A tarsadalmi technika." *Szép Szó* (Budapest), July-August, 1937.
MS   Expanded English translation, "Social Techniques," in K. Mannheim, *Man and Society,* 1940: 239-265.

"Zur Diagnose unserer Zeit." *Mass und Wert* I, 1: 101-121.
DZ   English translation in K.H. Wolff, *From Karl Mannheim:* 350-366.

"A modern haboruk keletkezesenek pszichologiajahoz." *Szép Szó* V, 2: 193-202.
English translation: "The Psychological Aspect," in C.A.W. Manning, ed., *Peaceful Change: An International Problem.* London, New York: Macmillan & Co., 1937: 101-132.
MS   Expanded version: K. Mannheim, *Man and Society* (1940): 117-143.

"Present Trends in the Building of Society" R.B. Catell, J.I. Cohen, R.M.W Travers, eds., *Human Affairs.* London: Macmillan and Co: 278-300.
MS   Based on: K. Mannheim, *Mensch und Gesellschaft* (1935); expanded version: K. Mannheim, *Man and Society* (1940): 311-369.

SSS   "Les sciences sociales et la sociologie." *Les convergences des sciences sociales et l'esprit in Sernational.* Travaux de la conférence internationale des sciences sociales. Paris: Centre d'études de politique étrangère; P. Hartmann (éditeur): 208-224.

1939

AE   "Adult Education and the Social Sciences." *Tutors' Bulletin of Adult Education.* 2nd series, No. 20: 27-34.

"The History of the Concept of the State as an Organism: A Sociological Analysis." Lecture given at the University of Cambridge, 20-1-1939.
ESSP   K. Mannheim, *Essays on Sociology and Social Psychology* (1953): 165-182.

"Mass Education and Group Analysis." J.I. Cohen, R.M.W. Travers, eds., *Education for Democracy*. London: Macmillan and Co: 329-364.

K. Mannheim, *Diagnosis of Our Time* (1943): 73-94.

1940

"Planned Society and the Problem of New Personality: A Sociological Analysis." Four lectures at Manchester College, Oxford (January-March, 1940).

K. Mannheim, *Essays on Sociology and Social Psychology* (1953): 255-310.

Man and Society in an Age of Reconstruction: Studies in Modern Social Structure (Based on *Mensch und Gesellschaft im Zeitalter des Umbaus*, 1935). London: Routledge and Kegan Paul/ New York: Harcourt, Brace, 1940, 469 pp.

"Über die durch den Krieg verursachten Änderungen in unserer psychischen Okonomie." *Internationale Zeitschrift fur Psychoanalyse und Image* XXV, 3, 4 (1940): 346-355.

English translation: "On War-conditioned changes in our Psychic Economy." K. Mannheim, *Essays on Sociology and Social Psychology* (1953): 243-251.

1941

"Letter to E.A. Shils" (3-3-1941). *The Journal of Liberal Religion* III, 1: 55, 56.

1942

"Planning for Freedom" Part I: "Social Techniques in a Mass Society," Part II: "The Necessity if Social Justice." *Times Educational Supplement* (5-9-1942): 433; (12-9-1942): 443.

K. Mannheim, *Diagnosis of Our Time*: 1-11.

1943

Diagnosis of Our Time: Wartime Essays of a Sociologist. London: Routledge and Kegan Paul/ New York: Oxford University Press, 1943, 180 pp.

Dutch translation by L. van Kranendonk under the title *Diagnose van onze tijd*. Leiden: A.W. Sijthoff, 1947, 213 pp.

1944

"Sociology for the Educator and the Sociology of Education." D.E. Dymes, ed., *Sociology and Education*. London: LePlay House Press: 4-9.

"Democratic Planning and the New Science of Society." J.R.M. Brunwell, ed., *This Changing World*. London: Georg Routledge and Sons: 71-82.

1945-1946

"The Meaning of Popularisaton in a Mass Society." *The Christian News-Letter*. Supplement to No. 27 (7-2-1945): 7-12.

"The Function of the Refugee: A Rejoinder." *The New English Weekly* XXVII, 1 (1945): 5-6.

"Die Rolle der Universitäten." *Neue Auslese: aus dem Schriften der Gegenwart*, ed. The Allied Information Service, I, 4 (1945-46): 49-53.

"Foreword." V. Klein, *The Feminine Character: History of an Ideology*. London: Kegan Paul, Trench, Trubner & Co., 1946: vii-xiv.

1947

P   "Preface to the English Edition." W.F. Ogburn, M.F. Nimkoff, *Handbook of Sociology*. London: Routledge and Kegan Paul, 1947.

1951

FPDP   *Freedom, Power and Democratic Planning*, edited by E.K. Bramstedt, H. Gerth; introduction by Adolph Löwe. New York: Oxford University Press, 1950; London: Routledge and Kegan Paul, 1951, 384 pp.

1952

ESK   *Essays on the Sociology of Knowledge*, edited by Paul Kecskemeti, editorial note by Adolph Löwe, introduction by Paul Kecskemeti. London: Routledge and Kegan Paul; New York: Oxford University Press, 1952, 327 pp.

KM   "Karl Mannheim" (written by himself, 1946). *Who was Who*, 1941-1951, IV. London: Adam and Charles Black, 1952: 759.

1953

ESSP   *Essays on Sociology and Social Psychology,* edited by Paul Kecskemeti, editorial note by Adolph Löwe, introduction by Paul Kecskemeti. London: Routledge and Kegan Paul; New York: Oxford University Press, 1953, 310 pp.

1956

SC   *Essays on the Sociology of Culture*, edited by Ernest Manheim in cooperation with Paul Kecskemeti, editorial note by Adolph Löwe, introduction by E. Mannheim. London: Routledge and Kegan Paul; New York: Oxford University Press, 1956, 253 pp.

1957

SS   *Systematic Sociology: An Introduction to the Study of Society*, edited by J.S. Erös, W.A.C. Stewart. London: Routledge and Kegan Paul; New York: Oxford University Press, 1957, 169 pp.

MW   "Max Weber" (1946). *Encyclopaedia Brittanica*. London: William Benton (in various editions between 1957 and 1969). Vol. XXIII.

1959

BKHW   "Letter to K.H. Wolff" (15-4-1946). K.H. Wolff, "Sociology of Knowledge and Theory," L. Gross, ed., *Symposium on Sociological Theory*. New York: Harper and Row, 1959: 571-572. Also in K.H. Wolff, *Versuch zu einer Wissenssoziologie*. Berlin, Neuwied: Luchterhand, 1968: 133-135.

1962

ISE   *An Introduction to the Sociology of Education* (with W.A.C. Stewart), Introduction by W.A.C. Stewart. London: Routledge and Kegan Paul; New York: Humanities Press, 187 pp.

1964

W   *Wissenssoziologie. Auswahl aus dem Werk*, introd. and ed. by K.H. Wolff. Berlin, Neuwied: H. Luchterhand, 750 pp.

1971

FKM   *From Karl Mannheim*, edited and introduced by K.H. Wolff. New York: Oxford University Press, 386 pp.

1975

"Karl Mannheim's Letters to Lukács 1910-1916," edited by E. Gábor. *The Hungarian Quarterly* XVI: 93-105.

1980-1982

Strukturen des Denkens (Containing "Über die Eigenart kultursoziologischer Erkenntnis" and "Eine soziologische Theorie der Kultur und ihrer Erkennbarkeit (Konjunktives und Kommunikatives Denken), eds. D. Kettler, V. Meja, N. Stehr. Frankfurt a.M.: Suhrkamp Tachenbuch Wissenschaft 298, 1980, 322 pp.

English translation: *Structures of Thinking*, edited and introduced by D. Kettler, V. Meja, N. Stehr. London: Routledge and Kegan Paul, 1982, 292 pp.

1984-1986

Konservatismus: Ein Beitrag zur Soziologie des Wissens . (Complete edition of Mannheim's *Habilitationsschrift*, which originally had as its title, *Alkonservatismus: Ein Beitrag zur Soziologie des Wissens.*) Eds. D. Kettler, V. Meja, N. Stehr. Frankfurt a.M.: Suhrkamp, 1984, 288 pp.

English translation: *Conservatism: A Contribution to the Sociology of Knowledge,* editors D. Kettler, V. Meja, N. Stehr. London: Routledge and Kegan Paul, 1986, 256 pp.

II. *Articles in Memory of Karl Mannheim*

Anonymous, "In Memoriam Karl Mannheim." *Amerikanische Rundschau: Zeitschrift für Politik und Kultur* III, 12 (March 1947): 125, 126.

Anonymous, "Zum Tode Karl Mannheim." *Kurier* (15-1-1947).

Anonymous, "Karl Mannheim." *Neue Züricher Zeitung* (15-1-1947).

Anonymous, "Professor Karl Mannheim." *International Bureau of Education* XXI, 82 (February 1947): 14.

Anonymous, "Professor Karl Mannheim: Education and the Planned Society." *London Times* (11-1-1947).

Anonymous, "Prof. Karl Mannheim." *Manchester Guardian* (11-1-1947).

Anonymous, "Dr. Karl Mannheim, Leading Sociologist." *New York Times* (10-1-1947): 22.

Anonymous, "Karl Mannheim." *Times Educational Supplement* 18-1-1947 (nr. 1655): 29.

Anonymous, "Professor Karl Mannheim: An Irreparable loss." *Times Educational Supplement* 18-2-1947 (nr. 1655): 36.

Anonymous, "Karl Mannheim." *Umschau: International Revue* II (1947): 241-243.

Banning, W. (1947) "In Memoriam Karl Mannheim" *Socialisme en Democratie* IV: 44-47.

Barth, H. (1947) "Karl Mannheim: In Memoriam." *Neue Züricher Zeitung* (15-1-1947). Reprinted in *Neue Auslese* II, 5 (Mai 1947): 121-122.

Bogardus, E. (1947) "Mannheim and Social Reconstruction." *Sociology and Social Research* XXXII: 540-557.

Clarke, F. (1947a) "Karl Mannheim-Obituary." *Nature*, vol. 159, 4034 (22-2-1947): 255-256.

Clarke, F. (1947b) "Karl Mannheim." *The Londonian: Magazine of The Institute of Education*, 54: 4-5.

Clarke, F. (1947c) "Karl Mannheim at the Institute of Education: The Beginning." (typed memorandum) Published in F.W Mitchell, 1967.

Doderlein, J.L. (1957) "Historismus, Perspektivismus, Relativismus: Zum 10. Todestag von Karl Mannheim am 10. Januar." *Die Deutsche Woche* VII, 3: 14ff.

Eliot, T.S. (1947) "Professor Karl Mannheim." *London Times* (25-1-1947).

Holz, H.H. (1953) "Wissen in Zweifel und Sicherheit." *Frankfurter Allgemeine Zeitung* (17-3-1953).

Kollar, K.G. (1947) "In memoriam: Karl Mannheim'. *Erasmus* I 15-2-1947: 196.

Lieber, H.J. (1949) "Sein und Erkennen: Zur philosophischen Problematik der Wissenssoziologie bei Karl Mannheim: Aus Anlass seines Todes." *Zeitschrift für Philosophische Forschung* III, 2: 249-264.

Manheim, E. (1947) "Karl Mannheim, 1893-1947." *American Journal of Sociology* III, 6: 471-474.

Remmling, G.W. (1957a) "Karl Mannheim 1893 bis 1947." *Archiv für Rechts- und Sozialphilosophie* XLIII, 2: 271-285.

Remmling, G.W. (1957b) "Kann Freiheit geplant werden? Zum zehnten Todestag von Karl Mannheim." *Frankfurter Neue Presse* (9-1-1957).

Révész, G. (1947) "Karl Mannheim." *Nederlandsch Tijdschrift voor de Psychologie* II, 1: 79-80.

Salomon, A. (1947) "Karl Mannheim 1893-1947." *Social Research* XIV: 350-364.

Shils, E.A. (1947) "In Memoriam: Karl Mannheim 1893-1947." *Erasmus* I (15-2-1947): 193-196.

Treurniet, A. (1947) "Karl Mannheim: een groot socioloog ging heen" *De Vlam. Socialistisch Weekblad voor vrijheid en cultuur* III, 3 (25-1-1947): 6.

Vago, M. (1947) "Mannheim Károly 1893-1947." *Huszadik Század* XXXV: 68-70.

Vidler, A.R. (1947) "Editorial." *Theology* L (nr. 321, March 1947): 81-82.

Wiese, L. von (1948-49) "Karl Mannheim 1893-1947." *Kölner Zeitschrift für Soziologie* I, 1: 98-100.

Wirth, L. (1947) "Karl Mannheim, 1893-1947." *American Sociological Review* XII, 3: 356-357.

III. *Reviews of Mannheim's Works*

a. *Soul and Culture* (1918)

Lang, J. (1918) "Mannheim Károly: Lélek és Kultura." *Athenaeum* IV, V (1918-'19): 159-160.

Jászi, O. (1918) "Mannheim Károly: Lélek és Kultura." *Huszadik Század* XXXVII: 192.

b. *Ideologie und Utopie* (1929)

Anonymous, *Berliner Tageblatt*, 9-6-1930.

Anonymous, *Freie Volksbindung* (Frankfurt) VI: 137.

Anonymous, *Zeitschrift für Politik*, vol. XIX: Beiblatt: Berichte der Deutschen Hochschule für Politik: 67.

Arendt, H. (1930) "Philosophie und Soziologie: Anlässlich Karl Mannheim, Ideologie und Utopie." *Die Gesellschaft* VII, 2: 163-176. Also H.J. Lieber, 1974: 530-547; V.Meja/N Stehr, 1982: 515-531.

Burckhardt, G. (1929) *Kölnische Zeitung* (27-10-1929).

Curtius, E.R. (1929) "Soziologie und ihre Grenzen." *Neue Schweizer Rundschau* XXII (Oktober 1929): 727-736. Also Meja and Stehr, 1982: 417-426.

Dunkmann, K. (1929) *Archiv für angewandte Soziologie* II: 71-83.

Eisermann, G. (1953) "Ideologie und Utopie: Aus Anlass der dritten Auflage von Karl Mannheim's Buch." *Kölner Zeitschrift für Soziologie* V, 4: 528-534.

Fogarasi, A (1930) "Die Soziologie der Intelligenz und die Intelligenz der Soziologie." *Under dem Banner des Marxismus* IV: 359-375. Also H.J. Lieber, 1974: 483-504.

Freund, M. (1930) *Deutsche Literaturzeitung* (Heft 45, Nr. 445; 8-11-1930): 2148-2156.

Günther (1931) *Die Internationale: Zeitschrift für Praxis und Theorie des Marxismus* (Berlin) XIV: 93-96.

Gurian, W. (1929) "Grenzen und Bedeutungen der Soziologie" *Germania* (15-6-1929/22-6-1929).

Heiss, R. (1929) *Kölner Vierteljahreshefte für Soziologie* VIII (1929-'30): 240-243.

Horkheimer, M. (1930b) "Ein neuer Ideologiebegriff." *Archiv für die Geschichte des Sozialismus und der Arbeiterbewegung* XV: 33-56. Also M. Horkheimer, *Sozialphilosophische Studien*. Frankfurt a.M.: Fischer 1972: 13-32. Also K. Lenk, 1961: 283-303, H.J. Lieber, 1974: 505-529; V. Meja/N. Stehr, 1982:474-496.

Kracauer, S. (1929) *Frankfurter Zeitung* (28-4-1929).

Kraft, J. (1929) "Soziologie oder Soziologismus: zu Mannheim's Ideologie und Utopie." *Zeitschrift für Völkerpsychologie und Soziologie* V: 406-417.

Lewalter, E. (1930) "Wissensoziologie und Marxismus: Eine Auseinandersetzung mit Karl Mannheims Ideologie und Utopie von marxistitscher Position aus." *Archiv für Sozialwissenschaft und Sozial Politik* LXIV: 63-121. Also H.J. Lieber, 1974: 404-482; Meja/Stehr, 1982: 551-583.

Marck, S. (1929): "Zur Problem der Seinsverbundenheit des Wissens." *Archiv für systematische Philosophie und Soziologie* XXXIII: 238-252. Also V. Meja/N. Stehr, 1982: 438-450.

Marcuse, H. (1929) "Zur Wahrheitsproblematik der Soziologischen Methode. Karl Mannheim: Ideologie und Utopie." *Die Gesellschaft* VI, 10: 356-369. ALso H.J. Lieber 1974: 379-394; V. Meja/N. Stehr, 1982: 459-473.

Menzel, A. (1931) *Zeitschrift fur Nationalökonomie* II: 408-17.

Meyer, G. (1930) *Hamburger Fremdenblatt* (2-1-1930).

Neurath, O. (1930) "Burgerlicher Marxismus." *Der Kamp: Sozial-Demokratischer Monatsschrift* XXIII: 227-232. Meja/Stehr, 1982: 584-593.

Plaut, P. (1930) *Zeitschrift für angewandte Psychologie und Characterkunde* XXXVIII: 334-336.

Plessner, H. (1931) "Abwandlungen des Ideologiegedankens." *Kölner Vierteljahreshefte für Soziologie* X, 3: 147-170. Also K. Lenk, 1961: 265-282. Also H.J. Lieber, 1974: 589-616; Meja/Stehr, 1982: 637-662.

Speier, H. (1930) *Vossische Zeitung* (Berlin) (13-2-1930).

Speier, H. (1930) "Soziologie oder Ideologie." *Die Gesellschaft* VII: 357-372. Also H.J. Lieber, 1974: 568-588.

Stern, G. (1930) "Über die sogenannte 'Seinsverbundenheit' des Bewusstseins: Anlässlich Karl Mannheim 'Ideologie und Utopie' ." *Archiv für Sozialwissenschaft und Sozialpolitik* LXIV: 492-509. Also H.J. Lieber, 1974: 548-567; V. Meja/N. Stehr, 1982: 497-514.

Stoltenberg, H.L.G. (1930) *Schmoller Jahrbuch* LIV, 1: 169-173.

Tillich, P. (1929) "Ideologie und Utopie." *Die Gesellschaft* VI (Oktober 1929): 348-355. Also H.J. Lieber, 1974: 395-403; V. Meja/N. Stehr, 1982: 451-458.

c. *Ideology and Utopia* (English edition 1936; German translation 1952)

Abel, Th. (1936) *Political Science Quarterly* LI: 447-478.
Anonymous, *Revue de Metaphysique et de Morale* XLIV (Supplement): 18.
Anonymous, *The Economist* (London) CXXV (14-11-1936): 311.
Anonymous "Das Politische Buch: Karl Mannheims Wissenssoziologie." *Neue Zeitung* (28-3-1953).
Ascoli, M. (1938) "On Mannheim's Ideology and Utopia." *Social Research* VI, 1: 101-106.
Bagger, E. (1936) *Discovery* XVII, 204 (December 1936): 393.
Becker, C. (1937) *New Republic* LXXXIX (27-1-1937): 388.
Becker, H. (1938) "Mannheim's Ideology and Utopia." *American Sociological Review* III, 2: 260-262.
Bowen, I. (1936) *Spectator* (London) CLVII (11-12-1936): 1050.
Brightman, R. (1937) *Nature* (18-9-1937): 481-483.
Bruke, K. (1937) *Nation* CXLIV: 131 (10-1-1937). Also in Kenneth Burke's "The Contraints of Social Reality" in *The Philosophy of Literary Form*. Louisianna State University 1941.
Bruns, D. (1936) "Beyond Karl Marx." *The Observer* (24-11-1936).
Catlin, G. (1938) *Political Science Quarterly* LIII: 307.
Demant, V.A. (1937) *The Criterion* (London) XVI (1936-37): 537-540.
Duprat, G.L. (1937) *Revue internationale de sociologie* (Paris) XLV, 1: 56-58.
Eisermann, G. (1953) "Ideologie und Utopie: aus Anlass der dritten Auflage von Karl Mannheims Buch." *Kölner Zeitschrift für Soziologie und Sozialpsychologie* V, 4: 526-534.
Homans, G.C. (1937) *Saterday Review of Literature* (9-1-1937).
Hook, S. (1937) "The Sociology of Knowledge." *Marxist Quarterly* I, 1: 450-454.
Hutton, G. (1936) "Politics Psycho-analysed." *Time and Tide* XVII, 45 (7-11-1936): 1558-1560.
Kaye, M. (1937) *Philosophy* (London) XII: 363-364.
Larrabee, H.A. (1937) *Journal of Philosophy* XXXIV, 6: 162-163.
Laski, H.J. (1936) *New Statesman and Nation* (London) XII: 778-780.
MacIver, R.M. (1938) *American Historical Review* XLIII, 4: 814-816.
Oakeshott, M. (1936-37) *Cambridge Review* LVIII: 257.
Pickford, R.W. (1937) *British Journal of Psychology* (Cambridge) XXVII (1936-37), 438-439.
Rowse, A.L. (1937) *Political Quarterly* VIII: 610-613.
Schelting, A. von (1936) *American Sociological Review* I, 4: 664-674.
Shillinglaw, A.T. (1937) *Mind* XLVI: 535-537.
Shils, E.A. (1974) *Daedalus*, CIII, 1: 83-89.
Smith, T.V. (1937) *International Journal of Ethics* XLVIII, 1: 120-128.
Speier, H. (1937) *American Journal of Sociology* XLIII (1937-38): 155-166.
Thomsen, A. (1937) *The Social Frontier* IV, 28: 31.
Wilson, C.H. (1937) *Sociological Review* XXIX: 414.
Wolff, K.H. (1953) "Wissenssoziologie." *Aufklärung* II, 4-6: 361-362.

d. *Über das Wesen und die Bedeutung des wirtschaftlichen Erfolgsstrebens* (1930)

Becker, H. (1930) *Social Science Abstracts* II, Nr. 16055: 1888.
Feld, (1930) *Zeitschrift für Handelsschulpaedagogik*(Langensalza) II: 294.

e. *Die Gegenwartsaufgaben der Soziologie* (1932)

Anonymous, *Neue Züricher Zeitung* (20-12-1932).
Becker, H. *Annals of the American Academy of Political and Social Science*, vol. 171: 300.
Bernard, L.L. and J.S. (1931) *Social Forces* XII, 2: 288-289.
D., L.W. (1934) *Sociology and Social Research*, XVIII: 89.
Halbwachs, M. (1936-37) *La Revue critique d'histoire et de litterature* (Paris) C: 364-365.
Heberle, R. (1937) *Weltwirtschaftliches Archiv* (ed. Harms) XXXVIII: 130.
Klocke (1936-37) *Blätter für deutsche Philosophie* (Berlin) VII: 203.
Lorke, M. (1932-33) *Zeitschrift für Sozialforschung* (Frankfurt) II: 116.
North, C.C. (1934) *Philosophical Review* XLIII: 638.
Salomon, M. (1932) *Kantstudien* XXXVII: 200-201.

f. *Mensch und Gesellschaft im Zeitalter des Umbaus* (1935)

Anonymous, *Juristische Blätter* (Wien) LXVI: 195.
Anonymous, *The Journal of Philosophy* (New York) XXXII: 165.
Bierens de Haan, J. (1935) *Mensch en Maatschappij* (Groningen) LI: 312.
Bollnow, O.F. (1937) *Die Literatur* XXXVII: 567.
Bouman, P.J. (1936) *Tijdschrift voor Geschiedenis* (Groningen) LI, 1: 284-286.
Brinkmann, C. (1935) *Archiv für Rechtsphilosophie* XXVIII: 582-583.
Busch, G. (1959) "Mannheims Gesellschaftstheorie." *Süddeutsche Zeitung* (30-5-1959).
Friedmann, *Internationale Zeitschrift für Individualpsychologie* (Wien) XIV: 244.
Hennig, J. (1937) *Kantstudien* XLII: 55-56.
Jászi, O. (1936) *American Political Science Review* XXX: 168-170.
Kraus, F. (1935) *Frankfurter Zeitung* (1-12-1935).
Littauer, H.A. (1938) *Philosophia* (ed. A. Liebert) III: 593-595.
Marcuse, H. (1935) *Zeitschrift für Sozialforschung* IV: 269-271.
Neumann, J. (1937) *Theologische Literatur-Zeitung* (Leipzig) LXII, 1: 39.
Rosenthal, E. (1935) *Der Morgen* (Berlin) XI, 6-7: 326-328.
Salomon, A. (1936) *Social Research* III: 113ff.
Stark, J. (1935) *Wirtschafts-Jahrbuch* (Berlin) XI, 438.
Thomassen, J. (1936) *De Socialistische Gids* (Amsterdam) XXI: 130-134.
Wiese, L. von (1935) *Zeitschrift für Nationalökonomie* (Berlin) VI: 565-571.

g. *Man and Society in an Age of Reconstruction* (1940)

Anonymous, *Times Literary Supplement* (London) (1-6-1940): 270.
Burns, C.D. (1940) *Manchester Guardian*, 27-5-1940: 7.
Compton, A.H., et al. (1940) *Scientific Book Club Review* XI: 1.
Dewey, J. (1940) *Saterday Review of Literature* XXII (31-8-1940): 10.
Eliot, T.S. (1940) *Spectator* 164 (7-6-1940): 782.
Flugel, J.C. (1940) *International Journal of Psychoanalysis* XXI: 485-490.
Hook, S. (1940) *Nation* 151 (26-10-40): 398.
Huxley, J. (1940) *Nature* 146, 3688 (6-7-1940): 3-4.
Jászi, O. (1941) *American Political Science Review* XXXV: 550-553.
Mills, C.W. (1940) *American Sociological Review* V: 965-969.
Norton, J.D. (1940) *New York Times* (17-11-1940): 16.

Randall, J.H. (1941) *Journal of the History of Ideas* II: 372-381.

Rowse, A.L. (1940) *Political Quarterly* XI: 303-305; also Rowse's *The End of an Epoch.* London: Macmillan 1947: 305-309.

Rowse, A.L. (1940) *World Review* (August): 80-83.

Woolf, L. (1940) *New Statesman and Nation* XIX (29-6-1940): 807.

h. *Über die durch den Krieg verursachten Änderungen in unseren psychischen Okonomie* (1940)

Geroe, G. (1942) *The Psychoanalytic Quarterly* XI: 598.

i. *Diagnosis of Our Time* (1943)

Anonymous, *Commonwealth* Xl (26-5-1944): 136.

Anonymous, *Times Literary Supplement* (London) (17-4-1943): 189.

Anonymous, *The Times Educational Supplement* (20-2-1943).

Barnett, J.H. (1944) *Annals of the American Academy of Science.* Vol. 235: 142.

Catlin, G. (1943) *Nature* (11-9-1943): 287.

Ehrmann, H.W. (1944) *New Republic* CXI (3-7-1944): 139.

Eliot, T.S. (1943) "Planning and Religion." *Theology* (May 1943): 102-106.

Gremmels, H. (1952) "Politischer Moralismus." *Frankfurter Allgemeine Zeitung* (2-8-1952).

Hook, S. (1944) *Nation* CLIX (11-11-1944): 596.

Hufner, A. (1943) *Darmstädter Echo: Die unabhängige politische Tageszeitung Südhessens* (3-1-1943).

Joad, C.E.M. (1943) *New Statesman and Nation* XXV (19-6-1943): 405.

Kean, C.D. (1944) *Springfield Statesman* (11-6-1944): 4d.

Lynch, W.S. (1944) *Saturday Review of Literature* XXVII, 10 (27-5-1944).

Mumford, L. (1944) *American Sociological Review* IX: 592.

Oldham, J.H. (1943-44) *Christian News-Letter Supplement*, nr. 104, nr. 174.

Weintraub, P. (1944) *Social Forces* XXIII: 98-100.

j. *Freedom, Power and Democratic Planning* (1951)

Anonymous, *Times Literary Supplement* (London) (13-4-1951): 223.

Anonymous, *Kirkus Review* XVIII: 540.

B., I. *San Francisco Chronicle* (26-11-1950): 20.

Bogardus, E.S. (1951) *Sociology and Social Research* XXXVI: 110-115.

Borome, J. (1950) *Library Journal* LXXV, 1402 (1-9-1950).

Brown, B.E. (1951) *Political Science Quarterly* LXVI: 463.

Dahl, R.A. (1950) *American Sociological Review* XV, 6: 807-810.

Heindel, R.H. (1951) *Annals of the American Academy of Science,* vol. 273: 272.

Hightower, R.L. (1951) *Crozer Quarterly* XXVIII: 66.

Irving, J.A. (1951) *Canadian Forum* XXX: 275.

Joughin, G.L. (1950) *Nation*, vol. 171 (11-11-1950): 443.

Kleeck, M. van (1950) *Survey* LXXXVI: 515.

Lindsay, A.D. (1952) *British Journal of Sociology* III, 1: 85-85.

Marvich, D. and E.W. (1953) *The American Journal of Sociology* LVIII (1952-53): 432-433.

Plamenatz, J. (1951) *Hibbert Journal* IXL: 417.

Polanyi, M. (1951) *Manchester Guardian* (3-7-1951): 4.
Spitz, D. (1951) *American Political Science Review,* XLV: 224.
Wagner, H.R. (1953) "The scope of Mannheim's Thinking." *Social Research* XX, 2: 100-109.
White, M. (1951) *New Republic* 124, 20 (22-1-1951): 800.
Wolff, K.H. (1951) *Commentary* XII, 4: 402-404.
Wright, B.F. (1951) *Yale Review* XI, 40: 345.
Wright, D.M. (1951) *Journal of Political Economy* LIX: 175.

k. *Essays on the Sociology of Knowledge* (1952)

Anonymous, *Times Literary Supplement* (London) (9-1-1953): 17-18.
B., I. *San Francisco Chronicle* (12-2-1953): 14.
Bernard, B. (1943) *American Sociological Review* XVIII, 4: 444-445.
Bottomore, T.B. (1956) *Brittish Journal of Sociology* VII: 54-55.
Brunner, E. de S. (1953) *Annals of the American Academy of Science,* Vol. 287: 204.
Jensen, H.E. (1953) *Social Forces* XXXII: 196.
Osborn, A.D. (1953) *Library Journal* LXXVIII (1-2-1953): 220.
Polanyi, M. (1952) *Manchester Guardian* (9-12-1952): 4.
Sorokin, P.A. (1953) *Kyklos* VI: 178.
Touraine, A. (1952) *Anée Sociologique* (3e Series): 251-256.
Wagner, H.R. (1953) "The Scope of Mannheim's Thinking." *Social Research* XX, 2: 100-109.

l. *Essays on Sociology and Psychology* (1953)

Anonymous, *Times Literary Supplement* (London) (11-6-1954): 381.
B., R. *Saturday Review* XXXVII (16-9-1954): 44.
Davis, A.K. (1954) *American Sociological Review* XIX, 5: 628-629.
Hughes, E.C. (1955) *American Journal of Sociology* LX, 6: 599-600.
Schwartz, B. (1955) *World Politics* VIII: 134.

m. *Essays in the Sociology of Culture* (1956)

Abel, Th. (1956) *American Sociological Review* XXI, 5: 630.
Adler, F. (1957) *American Journal of Sociology* LXII, 5: 523-524.
Anonymous, *Times Literary Supplement* (London) (31-8-1956): 512.
Bogardus, E.S. (1956) *Sociology and Social Research* XLI, 2: 127-132.
Edel, A. (1956) *Nation.* Vol 183 (4-8-1956): 105.
Timasheff, N.S. (1956) *Annals of the American Academy of Science.* Vol. 308: 202.
Watkins, J.W.N. (1956) *Spectator.* Vol. 197 (14-8-1956): 258-259.

n. *Systematic Sociology* (1958)

Adler, F. (1959) *Social Forces* XXXVII: 273.
Bogardus, E.S (1959) *Sociology and Social Research* XLIII, 3: 213-317.
Neely, W.C. (1959) *Social Studies* L: 116.
Schreiber, L. (1958) *Library Journal,* vol. 83: 1442.
Spencer R.F. (1959) *American Anthropologist,* vol. 61: 126.

o. *Strukturen des Denkens* (1980)/*Structures of Thinking* (1982)

Gordon, J. (1983) "On Structures of Thinking." *Newsletter.* International Society for the Sociology of Knowledge IX, 1, 2: 19-22.

Longhurst, B. (1982) *Network: Newsletter of the British Sociological Association*, Nr. 23 (May 1982): 19.

Woldring, H.E.S. (1983) "Nieuw posthuum werk van Karl Mannheim." *Mens en Maatschappij* LVIII, 3: 285-289.

IV. *Other Studies about Mannheim's Works*

Abercrombie, N. (1980) "Mannheim." N. Abercrombie, *Class, Structure and Knowledge: Problems in the Sociology of Knowledge*. Oxford: Basil Blackwell 1980: 32-53.

Abercrombie, N. and B. Longhurst (1981) "Mannheim's Soul: A Comment on Vallas." *Sociology* XV, 3 (August 1981): 424-427.

Abercrombie, N.and B. Longhurst (1983) "Interpreting Mannheim." *Theory, Culture and Society* II, 1: 5-15.

Adams, J.L. (1941) "Freud, Mannheim and the Liberal Doctrine of Man." *The Journal of Liberal Religion* II, 3: 107-111.

Adler, F. (1957) "The Range of Sociology of Knowledge." H. Becker, A. Boskoff, eds., *Modern Sociological Theory in Continuity and Change*. New York etc.: Holt, Rinehart and Winston 1957: 396-423.

Adorno, Th. W. (1981) "The Sociology of Knowledge and its Consiousness." Th. W. Adorno, *Prismen*. Cambridge, Mass.: The MIT Press: 35-49. Original "Über Mannheims Wissenssoziologie." *Afklärung* II (1953): 224-236. Also Th. W. Adorno, *Prismen. Kulturkritik und Gesellschaft*. Berlin, Frankfurt a.M.: Suhrkamp 1955: 32-55. Also K. Lenk, 1961: 314-326.

Adorno Th.W. (1973) "Ideology." In: *Aspects of Sociology* by The Frankfurt Institute for Social Research. With a Preface by M. Horkheimer and Th. W. Adorno. London, etc.: Heinemann 1973: 182-205. Original "Beitrag zur Ideologienlehre." *Kölner Zeitschrift für Soziologie* VI (1953-54): 360-375. Also M. Horkheimer, Th. W. Adorno, *Soziologische Exkurse*. Frankfurt a.M.: Europäische Verlaganstalt 1956: 162-181.

Albini, J.L. (1970) "Crisis or reconstruction: Mannheim's alternatives for the Western democracies." *Sociological Focus* III, 3.

Anonymous, "Mannheim's influence." Bookreview of G.W. Remmling's *The Sociology of Karl Mannheim. The Economist* (London) (15-3-1975).

Anonymous, "Die Moderne Soziologie in England: Der Anteil Karl Mannheims." *Englische Rundschau:* Eine Auslese aus der Britischen Presse III, 6 (1953): 66-67.

Aron, R. (1935) *La Sociologie Allemande Contemporaine*. Paris: Libraire Félix Alcan: 75-96.

Ashcraft, R. (1981) "Political Theory and Political Action in Karl Mannheim's Thought: Reflection upon 'Ideology and Utopie' and its Critics." *Comparative Studies in Society and History* XXIII, 1: 23-50.

Bailey, R.B. (1958) "Rationality reconsidered." R.B. Bailey, *Sociology Faces Pessimism*. The Hague: Martinus Nijhoff.

Bantock, G.H. (1947) "A Study of Mannheim's the Meaning of Popularization in a Mass Society." *Scrutiny* (Spring 1947): 171-184.

Barak, J.A. (1972) "Karl Mannheim: The Quest for Objectivity." *Kinesis* IV: 79-87.

Bash, H.H., (1964) "Determinism and avoidability in socio-historical analysis." *Ethics*, vol. 74, 3: 186-200.

Baum, G. (1974) "The Pluralism of Truth in Scheler and Mannheim." I. Beaubien, C. Davis and others, eds., *La pluralisme*. Symposium Interdisciplinaire Pluralism: Its Meaning Today. Montreal: Fides: 251-271.

Baum, G. (1977) *Truth beyond Relativism: Karl Mannheim's Sociology of Knowledge*. Milwaukee: Marquette University Press.

Bauman, Z. (1978) "Understanding as the Work of History: Karl Mannheim." Z. Bauman, *Hermenentics and Social Science*, London: Hutchinson: 89-110.

Beerling, R.F. (1964) "Mannheim en de Ideology." *Mens en Maatschappij* XXXIX, 4: 255-269.

Beerling, R.F. (1965) "Ideologie." R.F. Beerling, *Wijsgerige sociologische verkenningen* II. Arnhem: W. de Haan, Van Loghum Slaterus: 7-63.

Belgion, M. (1945) "Views and Reviews: The Germanization of Britain." *The New English weekly* XXVI, 18: 137-138.

Bloor, D. (1973) "Wittgenstein and Mannheim on the Sociology of Mathematics." *Studies in the History of Philosophy of Science* IV, 2: 173-191.

Bobilin, R.Th. (1961) *Values and Social Change: A Study in the Thought of Karl Mannheim* (diss.). University of Southern California.

Boris, D. (1971) *Krise und Planung: Die Politische Soziologie im Spätwerk Karl Mannheims*. Stuttgart: J.B. Metzler.

Borries, A.v. (1968) "Demokratie und Planung – Hinweis auf Karl Mannheim." *Blätter für deutsche und internationale Politik* (Köln): 300-305.

Borries, A.v. (1970) "Sociologie-Defizits." *Frankfurter Allgemeine Zeitung* (22-7-1978).

Boskoff, A. (1969) "Karl Mannheim: Theories of Social Manipulation in Transitional Society." A. Boskoff, *Theory in American Sociology: Major Sources and Applications*. New York: Thomas Y. Crowell Co.: 159-181.

Bouman, P.J. (1974) "Karl Mannheim." L. Rademakers, E. Petersma, eds., *Hoofdfiguren uit de sociologie*, vol.I. Utrecht, Antwerpen: Het Spectrum: 174-186.

Bramstedt, E.K. (1957) "Vital Problems of Democratic Culture: Review of Mannheim's works on Sociology." *Australian Outlook* (March 1957): 45-48.

Bramstedt, E.K., and H. Gerth (1950) "A Note on the Work of Karl Mannheim." K. Mannheim, *Freedom, Power and Democratic Panning*. London: Routledge and Kegan Paul, New York: Oxford University Press: vii-xv.

Brym, R.J. (1977) "Democracy and the Intellectuals: A Test of Karl Mannheim's Thesis." *Scottish Journal of Sociology* I, 2: 173-182.

Busch, G. (1959) "Mannheims Gesellschaftstheorie." *Süddeutsche Zeitung* (30-5-59).

Campbell, H. (1958) "Tension in the Planners: Karl Mannheim." *Australian Journal of Education* II, 2: 114-120.

Carlsnaes, W. (1981) *The Concept of Ideology and Political Analyses: A Critical Examination of Its Usage by Marx, Lenin and Mannheim*. Westport (Conneticut), London: Greenwood Press.

Child, A. (1941) "The Problem of Imputation in the Sociology of Knowledge." *Ethics* LI, 2: 200-219.

Child, A. (1941) "The Theoretical Possibility of the Sociology of Knowledge." *Ethics* LI, 4: 392-418.

Child, a (1942) "The Existential Determinism of Thought." *Ethics* LII, 2: 153-185.

Child, A. (1943) "The Problem of Imputation Resolved." *Ethics* LIV, 1: 96-109.

Cild, A. (1946) "On the Theory of the Categories." *Philosophy and Phenomenological Research*, VII: 316-335.

427

Child, A. (1947) "The Problem of Truth in the Sociology of Knowledge." *Ethics* LVIII. 1: 18-34.

Child, A. (1970) "The Concep tof Class Interest." *Ethics* LXXX, 1: 279-295.

Congdon, L. (1977) "Karl Mannheim as Philosopher." *Journal of European Studies*, vol. VII, Pt. I, 25: 1-18.

Coombs, R.H. (1966) "Karl Mannheim: Epistemology and Sociology of Knowledge." *Sociological Quarterly* VII: 229-233.

Cooper, L.C. (M.d.) *The Hindu Prince: A Sociological Biography of Karl Mannheim.* Vol. II: Appendices (unpublished typescript).

Coser, L.A. (1971) "Karl Mannheim." L.A. Coser, *Masters of Sociological Thought: Ideas in historical and social context.* New York, Chicago, etc.: Harcourt Brace Jovanovich: 429-463.

Corradini, D. (1967) *Karl Mannheim.* Milano: Giuffré 1976².

Cox, R.H. (1969) "A Critique of Mannheim's Concept of Ideology." R.H. Cox, ed., *Ideology, Politics, and Political Theory.* Belmont, California: Wadsworth Publishing Co.: 79-89.

Cressler, D.L. (1951) *Karl Mannheim: An Interpretation* (diss.). Cambridge, Mass.: Harvard University.

Crittenden, B.S. (1964) *Sociology of Knowledge in Durkheim and Mannheim and its Bearing on Educational Theory* (diss.). University of Illinois.

Curtius, E.R. (1932) *Deutscher Geist in Gefahr.* Stuttgart, Berlin: Deutsche Verlag-Anstalt.

Dahlke, H.O. (1940) "The Sociology of Knowledge." H.E. Barnes, H. Becker, F.B. Becker, *Contemporary Social Theory.* New York: Appleten-Century Co.: 64-89.

Dittberner, J.L. (1979²) *The End of Ideology and American Social Thought: 1930-1960.* UMI Research Press (1976).

Eppstein, P. (1928) "Mannheim: Die Fragestellung nach der Wirklichkeit im historischen Materialismus." *Archiv für Sozialwissenschaft und Sozialpolitik* LX: 449-469. Also V. Meja and N. Stehr, 1982: 251-324.

Erös, J.S., Stewart, W.A.C (1957) "Editorial Preface." K. Mannheim, *Systematic Sociology: An Introduction to the Study of Society.* London: Routledge and Kegan Paul, New York: Oxford University Press 1957: xi-xxx.

Farberman, H.A. (1970) "Mannheim, Cooley and Mead: Toward a Social Theory of Mentality." *Sociological Quarterly* 11, 1: 3-13. Also G.W. Remmling, e.d., 1973: 261-272.

Floud, J. (1959) "Karl Mannheim." A.V. Judges (ed.), *The Function of Teaching: Seven Approaches to Purpose Tradition and Environment.* London: Faber and Faber: 40-66.

Floud, J. (1963): "Karl Mannheim and the Sociology of Education." *Sociologische Gids* X, 3: 123-131.

Floud, J. (1966) "Karl Mannheim." *New Society,* no. 222 (29-12-1966): 969-971.

Floud, J. (1969) "Karl Mannheim." T. Raison (ed.), *The Founding Fathers of Social Sciences,* Harmondsworth, Middlesex: Penquin Books 1963: 204-213.

Floud, J. (1976) "Review of G.W. Remmling: The Sociology of Karl Mannheim" *The Time Literary Supplement* (30-1-1976): 116.

Fisher, M. (1954) *Leadership and Intelligence.* New York: Teachers College Columbia University.

Frisby, D. (1983) *The Alienated Mind. The Sociology of Knowledge in Germany 1918-33.* London: Heinemann; New Jersey: Humanities Press.

Gabel, J., *Karl Mannheim et la "Sociologie" de la classe intellectuelle.* Rabat (Maroc): No. 1 des Cahiers de Sociologie de l'Institute de Sociologie de l'Université Mohammed V.

Gabel, J. (1966) "Mannheim et le marxisme hongrois." *L'Homme et la Société* (Paris) I: 127-145.

Gabel, J. (1969³) *La fausse conscience: Essay sur la réification*. Paris: Editions de Minuit (1962): 127-145.

Gabel, J. (1970a) "Conscience et connaissance dans l'oeuvre de Karl Mannheim." *Annales de Sociologie* (Rabat: Institute de Sociologie) 1970: 55-66.

Gabel, J. (1970b) *Sociologie de l'aliénation*. Paris: Presses Universitaires de France.

Gabel, J. (1974) *Ideologies*. Paris: Editions Anthropos.

Gabel, J. (1979) "Karl Mannheim et la sociologie marxiste." *Recherche Sociale*, nr. 72: 33-48.

Gabel, J. (1981) "Lucien Goldmann als Leser Karl Mannheims." N. Stehr, V. Meja, 1981: 384-392.

Gabel, J. (1982) *Acutalidad de Karl Mannheim*. Unpublished paper for the 10th Worldcongress of Sociology in Mexico-City.

Gabel, J. (1983) "The 'Mannheim Problem' in France." *Newsletter. International Society for the Sociology of Knowledge* IX, 1, 2: 15-18.

Gábor, E. (1977) "Adalékok a fiatal Mannheim Károly portréjához." ("Contributions to the portrait of the young Karl Mannheim.") *A Magyar Filozofai Goudolkodás*: 440-471.

Gábor, E. (1983) "Mannheim in Hungary and in Weimar Germany." *Newletter: International Society for the Sociology of Knowledge* IX, 1, 2: 7-14.

Gluck, S.E. (1954) "The Epistemology of Mannheim's Sociology of Knowledge." *Methodos* VI, 23: 225-234.

Grisso, O.L. (1971) *Applications of Karl Mannheim's Sociology to Education in a Multi-group Society* (diss.). George Peabody College for Teachers.

Grüneberg, H. (1951) "Der Griff nach der Geschichte: Der Weg des Sociologen Karl Mannheim." *Bayerrische Schule* (München) IV: 258-260.

Gurvitch, G. (1957-59) "Le problème a la sociologie de la connaissance." *Revue philosophique* LXXXII (1957): 492-502; LXXXIII (1958): 438-451; LXXXIV (1959): 145-168.

Hamilton, P. (1974) "Karl Mannheim." *Knowledge and Social Structure." An introduction to the classical argument in the sociology of knowledge*. London, Boston: Routledge and Kegan Paul: 120-134.

Harms, J.B. (1982) "Mannheim's Sociology of Knowledge and the Interpretation of Weltanschauungen" (unpublished paper). The University of Kansas: Department of Sociology.

Hartung, F.G. (1952) "Problems of the Sociology of Knowledge." *Philosophy of Science* XIX: 17-32.

Heeren, J. (1971) "Karl Mannheim and the Intellectual Elite." *British Journal of Sociology* XX, 1: 1-15.

Hill, B.V. (1973) "Karl Mannheim." B.V. Hill, *Education and the Endangered Individual*. New York: Teachers College Press: 97-124.

Hinshaw, V.G. (1943) "The Epistemological Relevance of Mannheim's Sociology of Knowledge." *Journal of Philosophy* XL: 57-72. Also G.W. Remmling (ed.) 1973: 229-244.

Horkheimer, M. (1951) "Ideologie und Wetgebung." *Soziologische Forschung in unserer Zeit*. Ein Sammelwerk. Leopold van Wiese zum 75. Geburtstag, ed. K.G. Specht. Köln, Opladen: Westdeutsche Verlag 1951: 220-227. Also H.J. Lieber, 1976: 259-269. Under the title "Ideologie und Handeln" in M. Horkheimer, *Sozialphilosophische Studien*. Frankfurt a.M.: Athenäum Fischer Taschenbuch Verlag 1972: 59-67. Also M. Horkheimer, Th. W. Adorno, *Sociologica II*. Frankfurt a.M.: 1962, 1973³: 30-47. Also K. Lenk, 1961: 304-313.

Horowitz, I. L. (1981) "Mannheims Wissenssoziologie und C.W. Mills' soziologisches Wissen." N. Stehr, V. Meja, 1981: 360-383.

Hosoya, T. (1959) "Historismus und Karl Mannheim's Wissenssoziologie." *Japanese Sociological Review* IX, 4.

Hossfeld, P. (1965) "Historismus und Wissenssoziologie bei K. Mannheim." *Sociologia Internationalis* (Berlin) III, 2: 230-238.

Hoyle, E. (1962) *Karl Mannheim and the Education of an Elite* (diss.). London: University of London.

Hoyle, E. (1964) "Elite Concept in Karl Mannheim's Sociology of Education." *Social Research* XII: 55-71.

Hubscher, A. (1949) "Karl Mannheim." A. Hubscher, *Philosophen der Gegenwart*. München: 98-100, 162-163.

Hughes, E.C. (1955) "Essays on Sociology and Social Psychology by Karl Mannheim." *American Journal of Sociology* LX, 6: 599-600.

Hughes, H.S. (1958) "The role of the intellectuals: Mann, Benda, Mannheim." H.S. Hughes, *Consciousness and Society: The Reorientation of European Social Thought* 1890-1930. New York: Alfred A. Knopf & Random House: 404-431.

Jay, M. (1974a) "The Frankfurt School's Critique of Karl Mannheim." *Telos* XX: 72-89.

Jacobs, R.H. (1972) "Karl Mannheim's Search for a Philosophy of Education Consistent with Relativism." *Studies in Philosophy and Education* VII, 3: 190-209.

Kahn, P. (1950) "Idéologie et sociologie de la connaissance dans l'oeuvre de K. Mannheim." *Cahiers Internationaux de Sociologie* VIII, 1-2: 147-168.

Kecskemeti, P. (1952) "Introduction." K. Mannheim, *Essays on the Sociology of Knowledge*. London: Routledge & Kegan Paul 1968: 1-32.

Kecskemeti, P. (1953). "Introduction." K. Mannheim, *Essays on Sociology and Social Psychology*. London: Routledge and Kegan Paul: 1-11.

Kettler, D. (1967) *Marxismus und Kultur: Mannheim und Lukács in den ungarischen Revolutionen 1918/19*. Neuwied, Berlin: Luchterhand.

Kettler, D. (1967a) "Sociology of Knowledge and Moral Philosophy: The Place of Traditional Problems in the Formation of Mannheim's Thought." *Political Science Quarterly* LXXXII, 3: 399-426.

Kettler, D. (1971) "Culture and Revolution: Lukács in the Hungarian Revolutions of 1918/19." (Revision of D. Kettler, 1967). *Telos* X: 35-92.

Kettler, D. (1975) "Political theory, ideology, sociology: the queston of Karl Mannheim." *Cultural Hermeneuties* III: 69-80.

Kettler, D. (1976) *Rhetoric and Social Science: Karl Mannheim Adjusts to the English-Speaking World*. Unpublished paper for the conference of the *American Sociological Association* 1976.

Kettler, D., V. Meja, N. Stehr (1980) "Karl Mannheims frühe kultursoziologischen Arbeiten." K. Mannheim, *Strukturen des Denkens*, 1980: 9-31. English transl.: "Karl Mannheim's early writings on cultural sociology." K. Mannheim, *Structures of Thinking* 1982: 11-29.

Kettler, D., V. Meja, N. Stehr (1983a) "Arguing for Democracy." *The Times Higher Education Supplement* (15-7-1983): 11.

Kettler, D., V. Meja and N. Stehr (1983b) "Karl Mannheim and Conservatism" *Newsletter. International Society for the Sociology of Knowledge* IX, 1, 2: 3-6.

Kettler, D., V. Meja, N. Stehr (1984a) "Mannheim und der Konservatismus: Über die Ursprünge des Historismus." K. Mannheim, *Konservatismus* (1984): 11-40. A somewhat revised version: "Karl Mannheim and Conservatism: The Ancestry of Historical

Thinking." *American Sociological Review* 49: 71-85. Also in Karl Mannheim, *Conservatism* (1986): 1-26.

Kettler, D., V. Meja, N. Stehr (1984b) *Karl Mannheim*. Chichester: Ellis Horwood; London, New York: Tavistock.

Krüger, M. (1968) *Wissenssoziologie zwischen Ideologie und Wissenshaft: Zur Rezeption der Wissenssoziologie Karl Mannheims in Amerika. Eine Kritik amerikanischer Wissenssoziologische Theorien* (diss.). Berlin: Freie Universität.

Krüger, M. (1969) "Sociology of Knowledge and Social Theory." *Berkeley Journal of Sociology* XIV: 152-163.

Kurucz, J. (1963) "Mannheims Werk in sozialphilosopher Sicht." *Archiv für Rechts- und Sozialphilosophie*, XLIX 1: 85-95.

Laan, H. (1963) "De Denktrant van Karl Mannheim naar analyse van zijn werk Man and Society." *Sociologische Gids* X, 3: 140-155.

Lakshmanna, C. (1975) *Democratic Planning: Problems and Process*. Calcutta: T.K. Mukherjee, Minerva Associates.

Lamberts, T.A. (1972) "The Development of Karl Mannheim's Sociology: An Alternative View." *Sociological Analysis* II: 69-73.

Laslett, P. (1979) "Karl Mannheim in 1939: A Student's Recollection." *Revue européenne des sciences sociales* XLVI: 223-226.

Lavine, T.Z. (1965) "Karl Mannheim and Contemporary Functionalism." *Philosophy and Phenomenological Research* XXV,4: 560-571. Also G.W. Remmling (ed.) 1973: 245-257.

Lenk, K. (1960) "Karl Mannheim." *Handwörterbuch der Sozialwissenschaften* (E. von Beckerath et al.) vol. 7. Stuttgart, Tübingen, Göttingen: G. Fischer, Mohr, Vandenhoeck & Ruprecht.

Lenk, K. (1961) "Soziologie und Ideologienlehre: Bemerkungen zur Marxismusdiskussion in der deutschen Soziologie von Simmel bis Mannheim." *Kölner Zeitschrift für Soziologie und Socialpsychologie* XV, 2: 323-337.

Lieber, H.J. (1948) "Sein und Erkennen: Zur Philosophischen Problematik der Wissenssoziologie bei Karl Mannheim." *Zeitschrift für philosophische Forschung* III, 2: 249-264.

Lieber, H.J. (1959) "Karl Mannheim." W. Bernsdorf, ed., *Internationales Soziologie Lexicon*. Stuttgart: J.B. Metzler.

Loader, C. (1985) *The Intellectual Development of Karl Mannheim: Culture, Politics, and Planning*. Cambridge, etc.: Cambridge University Press.

Ludz, P. (1956) *Der Ideologiebegriff des jungen Marx und seine Weiterentwicklung durch Karl Mannheim und Georg Lukács* (diss.). Berlin.

Makoto, T. (1958) "Karl Mannheim und die Probleme des Historismus: Ein Gedankengeschichtliches Momorial." *Japanese Sociological Review* IX, 1: 17-31.

Manheim, E. (1956) "Introduction." K. Mannheim, *Essays on the Sociology of Culture*. London: Routledge and Kegan Paul; New York: Oxford University Press: 1-13.

Maquet, J.J. (1973) *The Sociology of Knowledge. Its structure and its relation to the philosophy of knowledge. A critical analysis of the systems of Karl Mannheim and Pitirim A. Sorokin*, translation J.F. Locke, preface F.S.C. Northrop. Westport, Connecticut: Greenwood Press (translation of the French edition, 1951).

Martin, A. von (1930) "Soziologie als Resignation und Mission." *Neue Schweizer Rundschau* I.

Martindale, D. (1960) "Karl Mannheim." D. Martindale, *The Nature and Types of Sociological Theory*. Boston: Houghton Mifflin: 414-418.

Meja, V., N. Stehr, eds. (1982) *Der Streit um die Wissenssoziologie.* 2 vols. Frankfurt a.M.: Suhrkamp.

Merton, R.K. (1968) "Karl Mannheim and the Sociology of Knowledge." R.K. Merton, *Social Theory and Social Structure.* Glencoe, Illinois: The Free Press: 543-562. Earlier in *The Journal of Liberal Religion* II (Winter 1941): 125-147.

Middleton Murry, J. (1949) "Karl Mannheim." J.M. Murry, *Katherine Mansfield and other Literary Portraits.* London, Peter Nevill: 152-163.

Mullins, W.A. (1979) "Truth and Ideology: Reflections on Mannheim's Paradox." *History and Theory* XVIII: 141-154.

Neale, R.N. (1981) "Mannheim, the Sociology of Knowledge, and Social History." R.S. Neale, *Class in English History 1680-1850.* Oxford: Blackwell 1981 (Ch. II): 47-67.

Neusüss, A. (1968a) *Utopisches Bewusstsein und Freischwebende Intelligenz: Zur Wissenssoziologie Karl Mannheims.* Meisenheim am Glan: Verlag Anton Hain.

Nyberg, P. (1957) *The Educational Implications of Karl Mannheim's Sociology* (diss.). Cambridge, Mass.: Harvard University.

O'Neill, D.P. (1970) *Sociology of Knowledge and the Development of the Ethic of Property in the Social Encyclicals: A Testing of Theory in Mannheim and Buckley* (Diss.). Boston University.

Phillips, D.L. (1974) "Epistemology and the Sociology of Knowledge: The Contributions of Mannheim, Mills and Merton." *Theory and Society* I, 1: 59-88.

Remmling, G.W. (1956) *Wandlungen der Sociologie Karl Mannheims unter dem Einfluss Angelsächsischer Philosophie und Sozial Wissenschaft* (diss.). Berlin: Freie Universität.

Remmling, G.W. (1957a) "Karl Mannheim 1893 bis 1947." *Archiv für Rechtswissenschaft und Sozialphilosophie* XLIII, 2:271-285.

Remmling, G.W. (1957b) "Menschenformung im Zeitalter der zweiten industriellen Revolution: Karl Mannheims Beitrag zur modernen Strukturpädagogik," *Kölner Zeitschrift für Soziologie und Sozialpsychologie* IX, 3: 371-396.

Remmling, G.W. (1957c) "Kommt die Kultur noch mit? Die Soziologen und die technische Vorherrschaft." *Deutsche Stimmen* XXXIII: 10.

Remmling, G.W. (1960) "Zur Soziologie der Macht: Der Beitrag Karl Mannheims zur politischen Soziologie." *Kölner Zeitschrift für Soziologie und Sozialpsychologie* XII, 1: 53-64.

Remmling, G.W. (1961a) "Religion und Politik: Eine Untersuchung am Schnittpunkt von Religionssoziologie und politischer Soziologie." *Zeitschrift für die Gesamte Staatswissenschaft* CXVII, 1: 166-174.

Remmling, G.W. (1961b) "Karl Mannheim: Revision of an Intellectual Portrait." *Social Forces* XL, 1: 23-30.

Remmling, G.W. (1963) "Das Unbehagen an der Gesellschaft." *Soziale Welt* XIV, 3, 4: 241-263.

Remmling, G.W. (1968) *Wissenssoziologie und Gesellschaftsplanung: Das Werk Karl Mannheims.* Dortmund: F.W. Ruhfus.

Remmling, G.W. (1970) "Karl Mannheim." G.W. Remmling and R.B. Campbell, *Basic Sociology: An Introduction to the Study of Society.* Totowa, New Jersey: Littlefield, Adams: 333-334.

Remmling, G.W. (1971) "Philosophical Parameters of Karl Mannheim's Sociology of Knowledge." *Sociological Quarterly* XII: 531-547.

Remmling, G.W. (1973) "Karl Mannheim and Historicist Sociology of Knowledge." G.W. Remmling, ed., 1973: 217-228.

Remmling, G.W. (1975) *The Sociology of Karl Mannheim: With a bibliographical guide to the sociology of knowledge, ideological analysis, and social planning.* London: Routledge & Kegan Paul.

Rempel, F.W. (1965) *The Role of Value in Karl Mannheim's Sociology of Knowledge.* London, etc.: Mouton & Co.

Robinson, D.S. (1948) "Karl Mannheim's Sociological Philosophy." *The Personalist* XXIX: 137-148.

Rosenmayer, L. (1964) "Max Scheler, Karl Mannheim und die Zukunft der Wissenssoziologie." A. Silbermann, ed., *Militanter Humanismus: Von den Aufgaben der modernen Soziologie.* Frankfurt a.M.: S. Fischer: 200-223.

Rüschemeyer, D. (1950) *Probleme der Wissenssoziologie: Eine Kritik der Arbeiten K. Mannheims und M. Scheler und eine Erweiterung der wissenssoziologischen Fragestellung durchgeführt am Beispiel der Kleingruppenforschung* (diss.). Köln.

Rüschemeyer, D. (1981) "Die Nichtrezeption von Karl Mannheims Wissenssoziologie in der Amerikanischen Soziologie." R. Lepsius, *Soziologie in Deutschland und Österreich 1918-1945: Materialien zur Entwicklung Emigration und Wirkungsgeschichte.* Opladen: Westdeutsche Verlag 1981: 414-426.

Sagarin, E. and J. Kelley (1970) "Karl Mannheim and the Sociology of Knowledge." *Salmagundi,* no's 10, 11 (Fall 1969-Winter 1970): 273-283. Also R. Boyers, ed., *The Legacy of the German Refugee Intellectuals.* New York: Schocken Books 1972: 273-283.

Schoeck, H. (1948) *Karl Mannheim als Wissenssoziologe* (diss.). Universität Tübingen.

Schoeck, H. (1949) "Der Weg der Soziologie: Die Geistigen Phasen Karl Mannheim's." *Rheinische Merkur: Wochenzeitung für Politik, Kultur und Wirtschaft* (Koblenz) IV, 17: 5-6.

Schoeck, H. (1949-50) "Die Zeitlichkeit bei Karl Mannheim." *Archiv für Rechts- und Sozialphilosophie* XXXVIII: 371-382.

Schoeck, H. (1950) "Der sozialökonomische Aspect in der Wissenssoziologie Karl Mannheims." *Zeitschrift für die gesammte Staatswissenschaft* CVI: 34-45.

Schrader, W. (1970) "Die Begruendungszirkel in Karl Mannheim's Theorie der Seinsverbundenheit." *Philosophische Perspektieven: Ein Jahrbuch* (Frankfurt a.m.) II: 252-296.

Shils, E.A. (1974) "Ideology and Utopia by Karl Mannheim." *Daedalus: Journal of the American Academie of Arts and Sciences* CIII, 1: 83-89.

Shils, E.A. (1941) "Irrationality and Planning: A note on Mannhem's Man and Society in an Age of Transformation." *The Journal of Liberal Religion* II: 148-153.

Shils, E.A. (1968) "Karl Mannheim." *International Encyclopedia of Social Sciences,* D.L. Shils (ed.), vol. IX. London, New York: Macmillan Comp.; The Free Press: 557-562.

Siefer, G. (1971) "Karl Mannheims vergessene Erbe." *Soziologenkorrespondenz* II: 253-270.

Simirenko, A. (1966) "Mannheim's Generational Analysis and Acculturation." *British Journal of Sociology* XVII, 3: 292-299. Also G.W. Remmling, ed., 1973: 331-338.

Simonds, A.P. (1975) "Mannheim's Sociology of Knowledge as a hermeneutic Method." *Cultural Hermeneutics* III: 81-104.

Simonds, A.P. (1978) *Karl Mannheim's Sociology of Knowledge.* Oxford: Clarendon Press.

Sinha, A.K. and K. Klostermaier (1966) "Karl Mannheim." Sinha and Klostermaier, *Masters of Social Thought.* Agra, India: Lakshmi Narain Agarwal: 248-263.

Stanley, W.O. and R.H. Holtzmann (1969) "Perspectives and Unity: Karl Mannheim." *Educational Theory* XIX: 271-287.

433

Stewart, W.A.C. (1967) *Karl Mannheim on Education and Social Thought*. London: G.G. Harrap and Co.

Takashi, H. (1959) "Historismus und Karl Mannheim's Wissenssoziologie." *Japanese Sociological Review* IX, 4: 21-32.

Thoenes, P. (1963) "Actualiteit van Mannheims elitetheorie." *Sociologische Gids* X, 3: 132-140.

Tokunaga, M. (1958) "Karl Mannheim und die Probleme des Historismus: ein gedankengeschischtliches Memorial." *Japanese Sociological Review* IX, 1.

Vallas, S.P. (1979) "The Lesson of Mannheim's Historicism." *Sociology: The Journal of the British Sociological Association* XIII, 3: 459-474.

Valk, J.M.M. de (1963) "Mannheims Wetenschapsleer." *Sociologische Gids* X, 3: 114-123.

Wagner, H.R. (1952) "Mannheim's Historism." *Social Research* XIX, 3: 300-321.

Weinstein, D. and M.A. Weinstein (1981) "Intellectual Transcendence: Karl Mannheim's Defense of the Sociological Attitude." *History of European Ideas* II, 2: 97-114.

Wirth, L. (1936) "Preface." K. Mannheim, *Ideology and Utopia* 1936: x-xxx.

Woldring, H.E.S. (1980) "Sociologie der kennis: Een hoofdstuk uit de filosofie van Karl Mannheim (1893-1947)." *Algemeen Nederlands Tijdschrift voor Wijsbegeerte* LXXII, 4: 227-241.

Woldring, H.E.S.(1984) "Karl Mannheim's Search of Truth. Sociology of knowledge in relation to the contemporary philosophy of science." *Sociale Wetenschappen* XXVII, 2: 137-165.

Wolff, K.H. (1959) "The Sociology of Knowledge and Sociological Theory." L. Gross, ed., *Symposium on Sociological Theory*. New York: Harper and Row: 567-602.

Wolff, K.H. (1963) "Karl Mannheim Interpretation: Introductory Notes." *Studies on the Left* III, 3: 45-59.

Wolff, K.H. (1964) "Karl Mannheim in seinen Abhandlungen bis 1933." K. Mannheim, *Wissenssoziologie: Auswahl aus dem Werk*, ed., K.H. Wolff. Berlin, Neuwied: Luchterhand: 11-65.

Wolff, K.H. (1968) *Versuch zu einer Wissenssoziologie*. Berlin und Niewied: Luchterhand.

Wolff, K.H. (1971) "Introduction: A Reading of Karl Mannheim." K.H. Wolff (editor), *From Karl Mannheim*. New York: Oxford University Press: xi-cxxiii.

Wolff, K.H. (1978) "Karl Mannheim." D. Käsler, ed., *Klassiker des Soziologischen Denkens*, vol II: *Von Weber bis Mannheim*. München: C.H. Beck: 286-387.

Wylie, J.F. (1956) *Karl Mannheim's Social Theory and Concept of Education* (diss.). University of Illinois.

Wylie, J.F. (1957) "Education and Planning for Freedom: A Discussion of the Views of Karl Mannheim." *Australian Journal of Education* I, 1: 21-26 .

Zeitlin, I.M. (1968) "Karl Mannheim." I.M. Zeitlin, *Ideology and the Development of Sociological Theory*. Englewood Cliffs, N.J.: Prentice Hall: 281-319.

V. *Other Quoted Literature.*

Achterberg, G. (1967) *Verzamelde Gedichten*. Amsterdam: Querido.

Adorno, Th.W. (1966) *Negative Dialektik*. Frankfurt a.M.: Suhrkamp. Engl. transl.: *Negative Dialectics*. New York: The Seaburry Press 1973.

Albrecht, R. and R. Trautmann, eds. (1983) "Das Frankfurter Gespräch." *Paul Tillich: Briefwechsel und Streitschriften*. Frankfurt a.M.: Evangelisches Verlagswerk 1983: 314-369.

Antoni, C. *Vom Historismus zur Soziologie*. Stuttgart: Koeher. Engl. Transl.: *From History to Sociology*. London 1962.

Argenti, J. (1974) *Systematic Corporative Planning*. New York: John Wiley and Sons (A Halsted Press Book).

Aron, R.C.F. (1950) "Social Structure and the Ruling Class." *British Journal of Sociology* I, 1: 1-16; I, 2: 126-143.

Aron, R.C.F. (1957) *The Opium of the Intellectuals*. Garden City, New York: Doubleday and Comp.

Atkinson, D. (1971) *Orthodox Consensus and Radical Alternative: Study on Social Theory*. London: Heinemann.

Atteslander, P. (1969) "Soziologie und Plannung." *Mens en Maatschappij* XLIV: 469-478.

Avineri, S. (1968) *The Social and Political Thought of Karl Marx*. Cambridge: The University Press.

Banning, W. (1955) "De probleemstelling van kerkelijk-sociologische arbeid." *Sociologisch Bulletin* IX, 1, 2: 74-82.

Banning, W. (1936) *Theologie en Sociologie: Een terreinverkenning en inleiding*. Assen: Van Gorcum.

Barth, H. (1974) *Wahrheit und Ideologie*. Frankfurt a.M.: Suhrkamp.

Baum, G. (1971) "Science and Commitment: Historical Truth According to Ernst Troeltsch." *Philosophy of Social Sciences* I: 259-277.

Bauman, Z. (1976) *Socialism: The Active Utopia*. London: George Allen and Unwin.

Becher, E. (1921) *Geisteswissenschaften und Naturwissenschaften. Untersuchungen zur Theorie und Einteilung der Realwissenschaften*. München, Leipzig: Duncker und Humblot.

Beerling, R.F. (1964a) "Ideologie." *Wijsgerig Perspectief op Maatschappij en Wetenschap* IV (1963-64): 261-265.

Beerling, R.F. (1964b) *Wijsgerig-sociologische verkenningen* I. Arnhem: W. de Haan, Van Lochum Slaterus.

Beerling, R.F. (1965) *Wijsgerig-sociologische verkenningen* II. Arnhem: W. de Haan, Van Lochum Slaterus.

Bell, D. (1960) *The End of Ideology*. Glencoe, Ill.: The Free Press.

Ben-David, J. (1981) "Sociology of Scientific Knowledge." J.F. Short Jr., ed., *The state of Sociology: Problems and Prospects*. London: Sage Publication 1981: 40-59.

Bentwich, N. (1953) *The Rescue and Achievement of Refugee Scholars*. The Hague: Martinus Nijhoff.

Beveridge, W. (1960) *The London School of Economics and its Problems 1919-1937*. London: George Allen and Unwin.

Bláha, I.A. (1937) *Sociologie Intelligence* (Summary: "The Sociology of Intelligentsia"). Praag: 377-386.

Bleuel, H.P. (1968) *Deutschlands Bekenner: Professoren zwischen Kaiserreich und Diktatur*. Bern, München, Wien: Scherz.

Bloch, E. (1959) *Das Prinzip Hoffnung,* 3 vols. Frankfurt a.M.: Suhrkamp 1973.

Bloor, D. (1976) *Knowledge and Social Imagery*. London: Routledge and Kegan Paul.

Bollnow, O.F. (1939) *Dilthey: Eine Einführung in seine Philosophie*. Stuttgart, Berlin, etc.: W. Kohlhammer 1967.

Bottomore, T.B. (1956) "Some Reflections on the Sociology of Knowledge." *The British Journal of Sociology* VII, 1: 52-58.

Bottomore, T.B. (1964) *Elites and Society*. London: C.A. Watts.

435

Bouman, P.J. (1955) "Rathenau." P.J. Bouman, *Roep en Roeping*. Amsterdam: H.J. Paris: 133-197.

Bouman, P.J. (1958) *Sociologie, begrippen en problemen*. Antwerpen, Amsterdam: Standaard.

Bouman, P.J. (1960) *In de laagvlakten der cultuur*. Groningen: J.B. Wolters. Also in P.J. Bouman, *Wetenschap en Werkelijkheid*. Assen: Van Gorcum 1967: 276-286.

Bouman, P.J. (1966) *Fundamentele sociologie*. Antwerpen, Utrecht: Standaard, Het Karveel.

Bouman, P.J. (1969) *Een handvol mensen: Uit de tijd der beide oorlogen*. Assen: Van Gorcum.

Braybrooke, D. and C.E. Lindblom (1963) *A Strategy of Decision: Policy Evaluation as a Social Process*. New York: The Free Press; London: Collier-Macmillan.

Brent, A. (1975) "The Sociology of Knowledge and Epistemology." *British Journal of Educational Studies* XXIII, 2: 209-224.

Bruton, M.J., ed. (1974) *The Spirit and Purpose of Planning*. London: Hutchinson.

Burnham, J. (1942) *The Managerial Revolution*. New York, London: Putman.

Collini, S. (1979) *Liberalism and Sociology: L.T. Hobhouse and Political Argument in England 1880-1914*. Cambridge, etc.: Cambridge University Press.

Comte, A. (1851-54) *Système de politique positive ou traité de sociologie instituant la religion de l'humanité*, IV vols. Paris: Le siège de la société positiviste 1929.

Comte, A. (1844) *Discours sur l'Esprit Positif* (and the German tr.) *Rede über den Geist des Positivismus*, ed. I. Fetscher. Hamburg: Felix Meiner 1956.

Congdon, L. (1973) "The Making of a Hungarian Revolutionary: Bela Balazs." *Journal of Contemporary History* VIII, 3: 57-74.

Coser. L.A. (1970⁸) *Men of Ideas: A Sociologist's View*. New York: Free Press; London: Collier MacMillan.

Cumming, R.D. (1970) *Human Nature and History*, vol. I. Chicago: The University of Chicago Press.

Curtis, S.J. (1958) *An Introduction to the Philosophy of Education*. London: University Tutorial Press 1965².

Dewey, J. (1939) *Freedom and Culture*. New York: G.P. Putnam's Sons.

Dilthey W. (1883) *Einleitung in die Geisteswissenschaften*, Col. Wks, I. Leipzig, Berlin: B.G. Teubner 1923.

Dilthey, W. (1911a) "Die Typen der Weltanschauung und ihre Ausbildung in den Metaphysischen Systemen." W. Dilthey, B. Groethuysen, *Weltanschauung – Philosophie und Religion*, M. Frischeisen-Köhler, ed. Berlin: Reichl und Co.

Dilthey, W. (1911b) *Die Geistige Welt: Einleitung in die Philosophie des Lebens*. Col. Wks. V. Leipzig, München: B.G. Teubner 1924.

Dilthey W. (1927) *Die Aufbau der geschichtlichen Welt in den Geisteswissenschaften*, Col. Wks. VII. Stuttgart: Treubner; Göttingen: Van den Hoek & Rupert 1973.

Dooyeweerd, H. (1953, 1957) *A New Critique of Theoretical Thought*, vol. I, II. Amsterdam: H.J. Paris; Philadelphia: The Presbyterian and Reformed Publ. Comp.

Dooyeweerd, H. (1960) *In the Twilight of Western Thought: Studies in the Pretended Autonomy of Philosophical Thought*. Philadelphia: The Presbyterian and Reformed Publ. Comp.

Dooyeweerd, H. (1979) *Roots of Western Culture: Pagan, Secular and Christian Options*. Toronto: Wedge.

Durkheim, E. (1957) *Professional Ethics and Civic Morals*, Preface by H. Nail Kuball, introd. by G. Davy. London: Routledge and Kegan Paul.

Echeverria, E.J. (1981) *Criticism and Commitment: Major Themes in Contemporary "Post-critical" Philosophy.* Amsterdam: Rodopi.

Elias, N. (1984) "Notizen zum Lebenslauf." P. Sleichmann, J. Goudsblom, H. Korte, *Macht und Zivilisation: Materialien zu Norbert Elias' Zivilisationstheorie 2.* Frankfurt a.M.: Suhrkamp: 9-48.

Eliot, T.S. (1948) *Notes toward the Definition of Culture.* London: Faber.

Ellemers, J.E. (1974) "Theodor Geiger." *Hoofdfiguren uit de sociologie,* vol. I, eds. L. Rademaker, E. Petersma, Utrecht, Antwerpen: Het Spectrum, Intermediair: 187-201.

Engels, F. (1890) "Letter to C. Schmidt." and "Letter to E. Bloch." K. Marx and F. Engels, *Selected Works,* vol. II. Moscow: Foreign Languages Publishing House 1958.

Engels,F. (1892) *De Ontwikkeling van het socialisme van utopie tot wetenschap,* Nijmegen: Socialistische Uitg. 1971, 1974⁴.

Fekete, E. and Karádi, E. (1981) *Georg Lukács. Sein Leben in Bildern: Selbstzeugnissen und Dokumenten.* Stuttgart: J.B. Metzler.

Forgarasi, B. (1930) "Die Soziologie der Intelligenz und die Intelligenz der Soziologie (Beiträge zur Theorie der Ideologie)." *Unter dem Banner des Marxismus* IV: 359-375.

Freund, G. (1977) "Norbert Elias als Lehrer." In: *Human Figurations: Essays for/Aufsätze für Norbert Elias.* Amsterdam: Amsterdams Sociologisch Tijdschrift: 12-14.

Fromm, E. (1955) *The Sane Society.* New York, Toronto: Rinehart and Comp.

Gabel, J. (1975) "Hungarian Marxism," *Telos* XXV: 185-191.

Gadourek, I. (1955) *Kennissociologie: Een korte inleiding.* Den Haag: Servire.

Garfinkel, H. (1967) *Studies in Ethnomethodology.* Englewood Cliffs, N.J.: Prentice Hall: 76-103.

Geiger, Th. (1949a) "Ideologie und Werturteil." (In "Kritische Bemerkungen zum Begriffe der Ideologie.") G. Eiserman, ed., *Gegenwartsprobleme der Soziologie.* Potsdam 1949: 141-155. Also K. Lenk, 1961: 228-234.

Geiger, Th. (1946b) *Aufgaben und Stellung der Intelligenz in der Gesellschaft.* Stuttgart: Ferdinand Enke Verlag.

Geiger, Th. (1953) *Ideologie und Wahrheit: Eine Soziologische Kritik des Denkens.* Stuttgart, Wien: Humboldt Verlag.

Ginsberg, M. (1948) *Reason and Unreason in Society.* Cambridge, Mass.: Harvard University Press.

Glaeser, B. (1972) *Kritik der Erkenntnissoziologie.* Frankfurt a.M.: Vittorio Klostermann.

Goethe, J.W. (1949) *Gedenkausgabe der Werke, Briefe und Gespräche,* E. Beutler, ed. Zürich: Artemis Verlag.

Goudlner, A.W. (1976) *The Dialectic of Ideology and Technology: The Origins, Grammar and Future of Ideology.* London, etc.: Macmillan.

Gouldner, A.W. (1979) *The Future of Intellectuals and the Rise of the New Class: A Frame of References, Theses, Conjectures, Arguments and a Historical Perspective on theRole of Intellectuals and Intelligensia in the International Class of the Modern Era.* New York: Continuum.

Gramsci, A. (1971) *Selections from the Prison Notebooks.* London: Lawrence and Wishart.

Gré, G. de (1941) "The Sociology of Knowledge and the Problem of Truth." *Journal of the History of Ideas* II: 110-115.

Greffrath, M. (1979) *Die Zerstörung einer Zukunft: Gespräche mit emigrierten Sozialwissenschaftlern G. Anders, H. Gerth, M. Jahoda, L. Löwenthal, A. Löwe, T. Oelsner, A. Sohn-Rethal, K.A. Wittfogel.* Interviews by M. Greffrath. Reinbeck/Hamburg: Rowohlt.

Grünwald, E. (1934) *Das Problem der Soziologie des Wissens: Versuch einer kritischen Darstellung der Wissenssoziologischen Theorien.* Wien, Leipzig: Braumüller.

Gunsteren, H.R. van (1976) *The Quest of Control: A critique of the rational-central-rule approach in public affairs.* London, etc.: John Wiley and Sons.

Gunsteren, H.R. van (1980) "Planning in de verzorgingsstaat. Van chaotisch naar systematisch falen." J.K.M. Gevers and R.J. in 't Veld, eds., *Planning als maatschappelijke vormgeving.* Deventer: Van Loghum Slaterus: 15-32.

Gurvitch, G. (1971) *The Social Framework of Knowledge.* With an Introduction Essay by K.A. Thompson. Oxford: Basil Blackwell; New York: Harper and Row.

Harvey, L. (11982) "The Use and Abuse of Kuhnian Paradigms in the Sociology of Knowledge." *Sociology: The Journal of the British Sociological Association*: 85-101.

Hayek, F.A. (1944) *TheRoad to Serfdom.* London: George Routledge and Sons 1946.

Heeger, R. (1975) *Ideologie und Macht: Eine Analyse von Antonio Gramscis Quaderni.* Upsala: Almqvist and Wiksell.

Hegel, G.W.F. (1807) *Phenomenology of Spirit*, transl. by A. v. Miller, Foreword by J.N. Findley. Oxford: Clarendon Press 1977.

Hegel, G.W.F. (1817) *Encyclopädie der Philosophischen Wissenschaften im Grundrisse.* Berlin: Duncker und Humblot 1845⁴.

Hegel, G.W.F. (1821) *Grundlinien der Philosophie des Rechts*, Col. Wks. vol. VII. Frankfurt a.M.: Suhrkamp 1970.

Hegel, G.W.F. (1908) *Vorlesungen über die Geschichte der Philosophie*, ed. G.J.P.J. Bolland. Leiden: A.H. Adriani.

Heidegger, M. (1962) *Being and Time*, transl. by J. Macquarrie and E. Robinson (of *Sein und Zeit*, 7th ed.) London: SCM Press.

Hempel, C.G. (1966) *Philosophy of Natural Science.* Englewood Cliffs, New Jersey: Prentice Hall.

Hesse, M. (1977) "Theory and Value in the Social Sciences." C. Hookway and Ph. Pettitt, eds., *Action and Interpretation: Studies in the Philosophy of Social Sciences.* Cambridge University Press.

Hinshaw, V.G. (1948) "Epistemological Relativism and the Sociology of Knowledge." *Philosophy of Science* XV, 1: 4-19.

Hodges, H.A. (1970) "Lukács on Irritation.' G.H.R. Parkinson, ed., *Georg Lukács: The man, his work and his ideas.* New York: Random House.

Hofstra, Sj. (1937) *De sociale aspekten van kennis en wetenschap.* Amsterdam: Scheltema en Holkema.

Holzle, E. (1969) *Idee und Ideologie: Eine Zeitkritik aus Universalhistorischer Sicht.* Bern, München: Francke Verlag.

Honigsheim, P. (1926) "Der Max Weber-Kreis in Heidelberg." *Kölner Vierteljahreshefte für Soziologie* V, 3 (1925/26): 270-287.

Horkheimer, M. (1930a) *Anfänge der bürgerlichen Geschichtsphilosophie*, Introd. by A. Schmidt. Frankfurt a.M.: Fischer 1971.

Horkheimer, M. (1937) "Traditionelle und Kritische Theorie" *Kritische Theorie*, vol. II, ed. A. Schmidt. Frankfurt a.M.: S. Fischer 1968: 137-191.

Horowitz, I.L. (1961) *Philosophy, Science and the Sociology of Knowledge.* Springfield, Illinois: C.C. Thomas.

Horváth, Z. (1963) "The Rise of Nationalism and of the Nationality Problem in Hungary in the Last Decades of Dualism." *Acta Historica* (Budapest) IX, 1-2: 1-38.

Horváth, Z. (1966) *Die Jahrhundertwende in Ungarn: Geschichte der zweiten Reform-Generation*. Neuwied: Luchterhand.

Hughes, H.S. (1958) *Consciousness and Society: The Reorientation of European Social thought 1890-1930*. New York: A.A. Knopf.

Husserl, E. (1913) *Ideen zu einer reinen Phänomenologie und Phänomenologischen Philsophie I*, ed. W. Biemel. Den Haag: Martinus Nijhoff 1950.

Idenburg, Ph. J. (1953²) "De maatschappelijke positie der intellektuelen." Th. Keulemans, Ph. J. Idenburg, J. Pen, *De intellektueel in de samenleving*. Assen: Van Gorcum: 19-83.

Jaspers, K. (1953) *The Origin and Goal of History*. London: Routledge and Kegan Paul.

Jászi, O. (1924) *Revolution and Counter-Revolution in Hungary*, introd. by R.W. Seton-Watson. London: P.S. King and Son.

Jay, M. (1973) *The Dialectical Imagination: A History of the Frankfurt School and the Institute of Social Research 1923-1950*. Boston, Toronto: Little, Brown and Company.

Jay, M. (1974b) "Crutches vs. Stilts: An Answer to James Schmidt on the Frankfurt School." *Telos* XII: 106-117.

Jerusalem, W. (1909) "Soziologie des Erkennens." *Die Zukunft*, Mai 1909: 236-246. Also *Kölner Vierteljahreshefte für Soziologie*, 1921, 28. Also W. Jerusalem, *Gedanken und Denken*. Wien 1925: 140-153.

Kanning, F. (1953) *Sozialwissenschaftliche Pädagogik: Untersuchungen zur Wandlung der pädagogischen Denkform in der deutschen Theorie und Praxis*. Heidelberg: Quelle und Meyer.

Kant, I. (1785) *Grundlegung der Metaphysik der Sitten*. K. Vorländer, ed. Hamburg: Felix Meiner 1965.

Klapwijk, J. (1970) *Tussen historisme en relativisme: Een studie over de dynamiek van het historisme en de wijsgerige ontwikkelingsgang van Ernst Troeltsch*. Assen: Van Gorcum.

Kluke, P. (1972) *Die Stiftungsuniversität Frankfurt am Main 1914-1932*. Frankfurt a.M.: Waldemar Kramer.

Kojecki, R. (1972) *T.S. Eliot's Social Criticism*. New York: Farrar, Strauss and Giroux.

Kraft, J. (1929) "Soziologie der Soziologismus." *Zeitschrift für Völkerpsychologie und Soziologie* V, 4.

Kruithof, J. (1964) "Ideologie en ideologische wetenschap." *Wijsgerig Perspectief op maatschappij en wetenschap* IV, (1963/64): 283-293.

Kuhn, T.S. (1962) *The Structure of Scientific Revolutions*. Chicago: The University of Chicago Press.

Kuhn, T.S. (1970) "Reflections on my Critics." I. Lakatos, A. Musgrave (eds.), *Criticism and the Growth of Knowledge*. Cambridge: Cambridge University Press: 231-278.

Kuhn, T.S. (1977) *The Essential Tension: Selected Studies in Scientific Tradition and Change*. Chicago, London: The University of Chicago Press.

Larrain, J. (1979) *The Concept of Ideology*. London: Hutchinson.

Lasky, M.J. (1976) *Utopia and Revolution: On the Origins of a Metaphor, or Some Illustrations of the Problem of Political Temperament and Intellectual Climate and how Ideas, Ideals and Ideologies have been Historically Related*. Chicago, London: University Press.

Lay, R. (1973) *Grundzüge einer komplexen Wissenschaftstheorie*, vol. II: *Wissenschaftsmethodik und spezielle Wissenschaftstheorie*. Frankfurt a.M.: Josef Knecht.

Lenk, K., ed. (1961) *Ideologie, Ideologiekritik und Wissenssoziologie*. Neuwied, Berlin: Luchterhand.

439

Lenk, K. (1972) *Marx in der Wissenssoziologie: Studien zur Rezeption der Marxschen Ideologiekritik.* Neuwied, Berlin: Luchterhand.

Lichtheim, G. (1973) *Georg Lukács*, Amsterdam: Meulenhof.

Lichtheim, G. (1967) *The Concept of Ideology and Other Essays.* New York: Random House.

Lieber, H.J. (1965) *Philosophie – Soziologie – Gesellschaft: Gesammelte Studien zum Ideologieproblem.* Berlin: W. de Gruyter u.Co.

Lieber, H.J., ed. (1974) *Ideologienlehre und Wissenssoziologie: Die Diskussion um das Ideologieproblem in den zwanziger Jahren.* Darmstadt: Wissenschaftliche Buchgesellschaft.

Lieber, H.J., ed. (1976) *Ideologie – Wissenschaft – Gesellschaft: Neuere Beiträge zur Diskussion.* Darmstadt: Wissenschaftliche Buchgesellschaft.

Lovejoy, A.O. (1940) "Reflections on the History of Ideas." *Journal of the History of Ideas* II: 3-23.

Lukács, G. (1911) *Die Seele und die Formen.* Berlin: Egon Fleischel.

Lukács, G. (1919) "Tactics and Ethics." G. Lukács, *Political Writings 1919-1929: The Question of Parliamentarianism and Other Essays*, ed. by R. Livingstone. London: NLB 1972: 3-11.

Lukács, G. (1920) *The Theory of the Novel*, transl. by A. Bostock (of *Die Theorie des Romans.* Berlin: P. Cassirer 1920; Luchterhand 1963) London : Merlin Press 1971.

Lukács, G. (1923) *History and Class Consciousness: Studies in Marxist Dialectics*, transl. by R. Livingstone. London: Merlin Press 1971.

Lukács, G. (1923) "Mein Weg zu Marx." *Internationale Literatur* III, 2. G. Lukács, *Schriften zur Idologie und Politik.* Neuwied, Berlin: Luchterhand 1967: 323-329.

Lukács, G. (1980) *The Destruction of Reason*, trans. by P. Palmer (of *Die Zerstörung der Vernunft*, 1962). London: The Merlin Press.

Mandelbaum, M. (1938) *The Problem of Historical Knowledge: An Answer to Relativism.* New York: Liveright Publishing Corporation.

Manuel, F.E. and Manuel, F.P. (1979) *Utopian Though in the Western World.* Cambridge (Mass.): Harvard University Press 1980².

Manuel, F.E. (1966) *Utopias and Utopian Thought.* Boston: Haughton Mifflin Comp.; Cambridge: Riverside Press.

Marx, K. (1845, 1846) "Die Deutsche Ideologie." *Die Frühschriften,* ed. by S. Landshut. Stuttgart: A. Kröner 1971: 339-485.

Marx, K. (1847) "The Poverty of Philosophy." K. Marx and F. Engels, *Collected Works*, vol. II. New York: International Publishers 1976.

Marx, K. (1848) "The Communist Manifesto." K. Marx, *Selected Writings*, ed. by D. Mclellan. Oxford: Oxford University Press 1977: 222-247.

Marx, K. (1859) *A Contribution to the Critique of Political Economy.* Chicago: C.H. Kerr and Comp. 1918.

Marx, K. (1857) *Capital: A Critique of Political Economy*, vol. I: *The Process of Capitalist Production.* Chicago: C.H. Kerr and Comp. 1919.

Maus, H. (1959) "Bericht über die Soziologie in Deutschland 1933 bis 1945." *Kölner Zeitschrift für Soziologie und Sozialpsychologie* XI: 72-99.

Mead, G.H. (1934) *Mind, Self and Society.* Chicago: University of Chicago Press.

Meinecke, F. (1936) *Die Entstehung des Historismus*, Col. Wks. III. München: R. Oldenbourg 1959.

Meja, V. (1975) "The Sociology of Knowledge and the Critique of Ideology." *Cultural Hermeneutics* III, 1: 57-68.

Meja, V. and N. Stehr, eds. (1982) *Der Streit um die Wissenssoziologie,* 2 vols. Frankfurt a.M.: Suhrkamp.

Meja, V. and N. Stehr (1982a) "Zur gegenwärtigen Lage wissenssoziologischer Konzeptionen." Meja/Stehr, 1982: 893-946.

Merton, R.K. (1968) *Social Theory and Social Structure* (enlarged edition). New York: The Free Press.

Merton, R.K. (1973) *The Sociology of Science: Theoretical and Empirical Investigations* (editor N.W. Storer). Chicago, London: The University of Chicago Press.

Michels, R. (1958) *Political Parties.* Glence, Illinois: The Free Press.

Mills, C. Wright (1940) "Methodological Consequences of the Sociology of Knowledge." *American Journal of Sociology* XLVI: 316-330.

Mills, C. Wright (1956) *The Power Elite.* New York: Oxford University Press.

Mitchell, F.W. (1967) *Sir Fred Clarke: Master Teacher 1880-1952.* London: Longmans.

Mitzman, A, (1970) *The Iron Cage: An Historical Interpretation of Max Weber.* New York: Alfred A. Knopf.

Mommsen, W.J. (1959) *Max Weber und die Deutsche Politik 1890-1920.* Tübingen: J.C.B. Mohr 1974².

Mosca, G. (1939) *The Ruling Class (Elementi di Scienze Politica),* ed. by A. Livingston. New York, London: Mc Graw-Hill Book Comp.

Nagel, E. (1961) *The Structure of Science: Problems in the Logic of Scientific Explanation.* London: Routledge and Kegan Paul 1974⁴.

Neisser, H. (1965) *On the Sociology of Knowledge - An Essay.* New York: J.A. Heineman.

Neusüss, A. (1968b) "Einführung." *Utopie: Begriff und Phänomen des Utopischen,* ed. by A. Neusüss. Neuwied, Berlin: Luchterhand.

Ottaway, A.K.C. (1953) *Education and Society: An Introduction to the Sociology of Education* (intr. W.O. Leister Smith). London: Routledge and Kegan Paul.

Palmer, R.R. (1956) *A History of the Modern World.* New York: A.A. Knopf (1950).

Pareto, V. (1935) *The Mind and Society* (Trattato di Sociologia generale). Vol. I-IV, ed. by A. Livingston. New York: Hartcourt, Brace and Comp.

Parry, G. (1969) *Political Elites.* New York, Washington: F.A. Praeger.

Peper, B. (1974) *Bij stukjes en beetjes? Over het zogenaamde realisme van het incrementele beleidsmodel.* Meppel: Boom.

Phillips, D.L. (1977) *Wittgenstein and Scientific Knowledge: A Sociological Perspective.* Totowa, New Jersey: Rowman and Littlefield.

Plamenatz, J. (1970) *Ideology.* New York, etc.: Praeger Publishers.

Plattel, M. (1970) *Utopie en kritisch denken.* Bilthoven: Ambo.

Polanyi, M. (1958) *Personal Knowledge: Toward a Post-Critical Philosophy* London: Routledge and Kegan Paul.

Polanyi, M. (1964) *Science, Faith and Society.* Chicago: Phoenix Books.

Polanyi, M. (1966) *The Tacit Dimension.* Garden City, New York: Doubleday and Comp. (Anchor Books).

Polanyi, M. (1969) *Knowing and Being.* London: Routledge and Kegan Paul.

Popper, K.R. (1952) *The Open Society and its Enemies,* 2 vols. London: Routledge and Kegan Paul.

Popper, K.R. (1957) *The Poverty of Historicism.* London: Routledge and Kegan Paul.

Popper, K.R. (1970) "Normal Science and its Dangers." I. Lakatos, A. Musgrave, eds., *Criticism and the Growth of Knowledge.* Cambridge: Cambridge University Press: 51-58.

Raddatz, F.J. (1976) *Lukács*. Baarn: Wereldvenster.

Remmling, G.W. (1967) *Road to Suspicion: A Study of Modern Mentality and the Sociology of Knowledge*. New York: Meredith Publishing Company.

Remmling, G.W., ed. (1973) *Toward the Sociology of Knowledge: Origin and Development of a Sociological Thought Style*. London: Routledge and Kegan Paul.

Rickert, H. (1921) *System der Philosophie*. Vol. I: *Algemeine Grundlegung der Philosophie*. Tübingen: J.C.B. Mohr (Paul Siebeck).

Ricoeur, P. (1981) *Hermeneutics and the Human Sciences*. Cambridge: University Press.

Riessen, H. van (1952) *The Society of the Future* (transl. of *De Maatschappij der toekomst*. Franeker: Wever 1951). Philadelphia: The Presbyterian and Reformed Publ. Comp.

Ringer, F.K. (1969) *The Decline of the German Mandarins: The German Academic Community, 1890-1933*. Cambridge, Mass.: Harvard University Press.

Schaaf, J. (1956) *Grundprinzipien der Wissenssoziologie*. Hamburg: Felix Meiner.

Scheler, M. (1923) *Wesen und Formen der Sympathie: Phänomenologie der Sympathiegefühle*, Col. Wks. VII. Bern, München: Francke Verlag 1913, 1923[2].

Scheler, M. (1926) *Die Wissensformen und die Gesellschaft*. Col. Wks. VIII. Bern, München: Francke Verlag 1960[2].

Schelting, A. von (1934) *Max Webers Wissenschaftslehre: Das logische Problem der historischen Kulturerkenntnis. Die Grenzen der Soziologie des Wissens*. Tübingen: J.C.B. Mohr (Paul Siebeck).

Schenk, H.G. (1966) *The Mind of the European Romantics: An Essay on Cultural History*, Preface by I. Berlin. London: Constable.

Schmidt, J. (1974) "Critical Theory and the Sociology of Knowledge: A Response to Martin Jay." *Telos* XXI: 168-180.

Schneider, E.V. (1949) *Ideology and Social Action* (diss.). Cambridge, Mass.: Harvard University.

Schumpeter, J.A. (1942) *Capitalism, Socialism and Democracy*. New York: Harper and Row.

Scott, D. (1971) *A.D. Lindsay: A Biography*. Oxford: Basil Blackwell.

Seglow, I. (1977) "Work at a research programme." *Human Figurations: Essays for, Aufsätze für Norbert Elias*. Amsterdam: Amsterdams Sociologisch Tijdschrift 1977: 16-22.

Seghers, A. (1968) *Die Gefährten*. Neuwied: Luchterhand (1932).

Shils, E.A. (1961) *The Intellectual between Tradition and Modernity*. The Hague: Mouton.

Shils, E.A. (1970) "Tradition, Ecology and Institutionalization in the History of Sociology." *Deadalus* 99,4: 760-825.

Shils, E.A. (1972) *The Intellectuals and the Powers and other Essays*. Collected Papers II. Chicago, London: The University of Chicago Press.

Shils, E.A. (1980) *The Calling of Sociology and Other Essays on the Pursuit of Learning*. Selected Papers of Edward Shils, Volume III. Chicago, London: The University of Chicago Press.

Shils, E.A. (1981) *Tradition*. Chicago: The University of Chicago Press.

Simmel, G. (1905) *Die Probleme der Geschichtsphilosophie*. München, Leipzig: Von Duncker & Humblot 1923[3].

Simmel, G. (1910) *Hauptprobleme der Philosophie*. Berlin: Walter de Gruyter & Co. 1964[8].

Simmel, G. (1911) *Philosophische Kultur: Gesammelte Essais*. Potsdam: Gustav Kiepenheuer 1923[3].

Simmel, G. (1950) *The Sociology of Georg Simmel*, translated, edited and with an introduction by K.H. Wolff. New York: The Free Press; London: Collier-Macmillan.

Smits, P. (1969) *De generatiestrijd in onze westerse maatschappij*. Assen: Van Gorcum.

Sorokin, P.A. (1947) *Society, Culture and Personality: Their Structure and Dynamics*. New York, London: Harper and Row.

Sorokin, P.A. (1941) *Social and Cultural Dynamics*, vol. IV: *Basic Problems, Principles and Methods*. New York, etc.: American Book Company.

Spencer, H. (1862) *First Principles*. London, etc.: Williams and Norgate 1900[5].

Stark, W. (1958) *The Sociology of Knowledge: An Essay in aid of a deeper understanding of the history of ideas*. London: Routledge and Kegan Paul 1967.

Stehr, N. und Meja, V. (1980) "Wissen und Gesellschaft." N. Stehr, V. Meja, eds., *Wissenssoziologie (Kölner Zeitschrift für Soziologie und Sozialpsychologie)*. Opladen: Westdeutscher Verlag: 7-19.

Stehr, N. and V. Meja (1981) *The Classical Sociology of Knowledge and Critical Theory* (unpublished paper).

Störig, H.J. (1967) *Geschiedenis van de wetenschap in de negentiende eeuw*. Utrecht/Antwerpen: Het Spectrum; (Dutch transl. of Chapter XII of Störig's *Kleine Weltgeschichte der Wissenschaft*. Stuttgart 1965).

Suppe, F., ed. (1977) *The Structure of Scientific Theories*. Urbana, etc.: University of Illinois Press.

Tacitus, P.C. (1967) *Agricola*, transl. and intr. by H.W. Benerio. Indianapolis: Bobbs-Merrill.

Thoenes, P. (1966) *The Elite in the Welfare State*, ed. by J.A. Banks (transl. of *De Elite in de Verzorgingsstaat*. Leiden: Stenfert Kroese 1962). New York: The Free Press; London: Faber and Faber.

Thoenes, P. (1976) *Van wetenschap tot utopie: Opstellen voor overmorgen*. Meppel, Amsterdam: Boom.

Tillich, H. (1973) *From Time to Time*. New York: Stein and Day.

Topitsch, E. (1961) *Sozialphilosophie zwischen Ideologie und Wissenschaft*. Neuwied, Berlin: Luchterhand 1971[3].

Topitsch, E., K. Salamun (1972) *Ideologie: Herrschaft des Vor-Urteils*. München, Wien: Albert Langen, Georg Müller Verlag.

Troeltsch, E. (1913) *Zur religiösen Lage, Geschichtsphilosophie und Ethik* (1922[2]), Col. Wks. vol. II. Aalen: Scientia 1962.

Troeltsch, E. (1922) *Der Historismus und seine Probleme*. Vol. I: *Das logische Problem der Geschichtsphilosophie*. J.C.B. Mohr (Paul Siebeck), Col. Wks.vol. III. Aalen: Scientia 1961.

Verhoogt, J.P. (1976) *Moderne maatschappijkritiek: C. Wright Mills als criticus: tussen probleem en totaliteit*. Meppel: Boom.

Walter, B. (1967) "The Sociology of Knowledge and the Problem of Objectivity." L. Gross, ed., *Sociological Theory: Inquiries and Paradigms*. New York: Harper and Row: 335-357.

Walzel, O. (1912[3]) *Deutsche Romantik*. Leipzig: B.G. Teubner.

Weber, A. (1912). "De soziologische Kulturbegriff." *Verhandlungen des II. Deutschen Soziologentags* (1912). Also A. Weber, *Ideen zur Staats- und Kultursoziologie*. Karlsruhe: G. Braun 1927.

Weber, A. (1920) "Prinzipielles zur Kultursoziologie. (Gesellschaftsprozess, Zivilisationsprozess und Kulturbewegung)." *Archiv für Sozialwissenschaft und Sozialpolitik* XLVII: 1-49.

Weber, A. (1923a) *Die Not der geistigen Arbeit*. München, Leipzig: Duncker und Humblot.

Weber, A. (1923b) "Kultursoziologie." *Der Neue Merkur* 7, vol. I. Stuttgart, Berlin. Also published under the title "Kultursoziologie und Sinndeutung der Geschichte." A.

Weber, *Ideen zur Staats- und Kultursoziologie*. Karlsruhe: G. Braun 1927: 1-54.

Weber, Marianne (1950) *Max Weber: Ein Lebensbild*. Heidelberg: Lambert Schneider.

Weber, M. (1904) " 'Objectivity' in social science and social policy." M. Weber, *The Methodology of the Social Sciences*, transl. and ed. by E.A. Shils and H.A. Finch. Glencoe, Ill.: The Free Press 1949: 50-112.

Weber, M. (1904-05) *The Protestant Ethics and the Spirit of Capitalism*, transl. T. Parsons, intr. R.H. Tawney. London: Allen and Unwin 1930, 1971[11].

Weber, M. (1917) "The Meaning of 'Ethical Neutrality' in Sociology and Economics." M. Weber, *The Methodology of the Social Sciences*. Chicago: The Free Press 1949: 1-47.

Weber, M. (1919) "Politics as a Vocation." H.H. Gerth and C. Wright Mills, eds., *From Max Weber: Essays in Sociology*. London: Routledge and Kegan Paul 1948 (1970): 77-128.

Weber, M. (1921) "The Fundamental Concepts of Sociology." M. Weber, *The Theory of Social and Economic Organization,* transl. by A.M. Henderson and T. Parsons. New York: The Free Press; London: Colliar-Macmillan (1947) 1968[5]: 87-157.

Wittfogel, K.A. (1931) "Wissen und Gesellschaft: Neuere deutsche Literatur zur Wissenssoziologie." *Unter dem Banner des Marxismus* V: 83-102. Also V. Meja/N. Stehr, 1982: 594-616.

Woldring, H.E.S., Kuiper, D. Th. (1980) *Reformatorische maatschappijkritiek: Ontwikkelingen op het gebied van sociale filosofie en sociologie in de kring van het Nederlandse protestantisme van de19e eeuw tot heden*. Kampen: J.H. Kok.

Wohl, R. (1980) *The Generation of 1914*. London: Weidenfeld and Nicolson.

Wolff, K.H. (1943) "The Sociology of Knowledge: Emphasis on an Empirical Attitude." *Philosophy of Science* XV, 3: 192-210.

Wolff, K.H. (1974) *Trying Sociology*. New York, etc.: John Wiley and Sons.

Wolff, K.H. (1981) "Wie ich zur Soziologie kam und wo ich bin: ein Gespräch mit Kurt H. Wolff," interview by N. Stehr. M.R. Lepsius, ed., *Soziologie in Deutschland und Österreich 1918-1945. (Kölner Zeitschrift für Soziologie und Sozialpsychologie*, Sonderheft 23/1981): 324-346.

Wolterstorff, N. (1983) *Until Justice and Peace Embrace*. Grand Rapids, Mich.: W.B. Eerdmans; Kampen: J.H. Kok.

Ziegler, H.L. (1927) "Ideologienlehre." *Archiv für Sozialwissenschaft und Sozialpolitik* LVII, 3: 657-700. Also H.J. Lieber, 1974: 314-360; V. Meja/N. Stehr, 1982: 232-250.

Zijderveld, A.C. (1970) *The Abstract Society*. New York: Doubleday.

Zijderveld, A.C. (1974) *De relativiteit van kenns en werkelijkheid*. Meppel: Boom.

Znaniecki, F. (1940) *The Social Role of the Man of Knowledge*. New York: Columbia University Press.

Zuidema, S.U. (1961) "Pragmatism." *Christian Perspectives* (Association of Reformed Scientific Studies). Hamilton: Guardian Publishing Comp.: 133-157.

Index

449